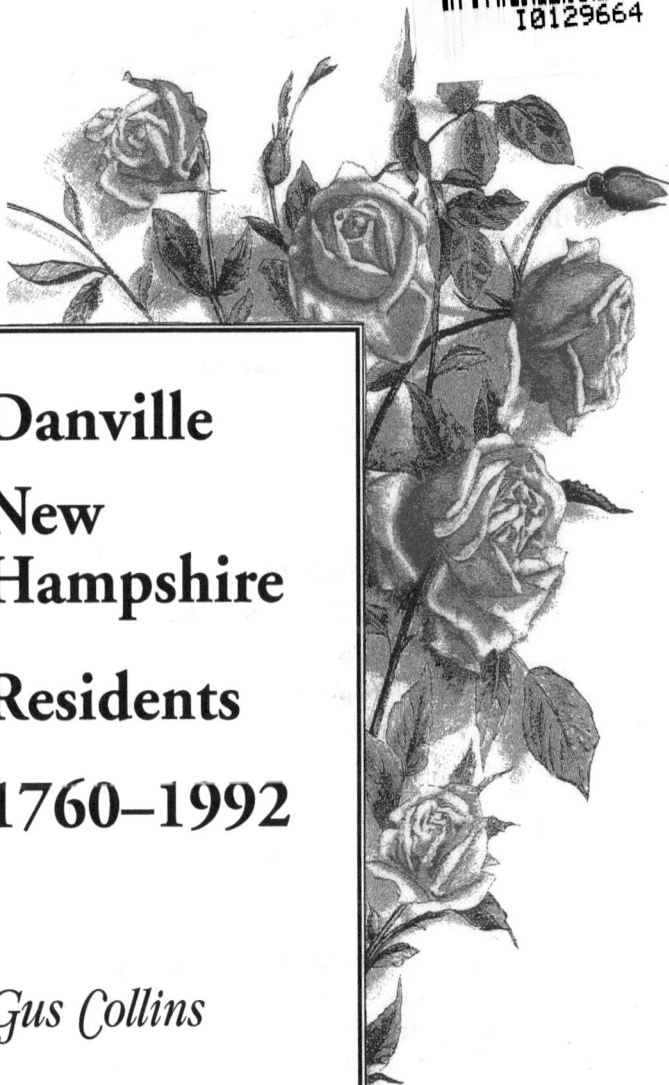

Danville
New
Hampshire
Residents
1760–1992

Gus Collins

HERITAGE BOOKS
2016

HERITAGE BOOKS

AN IMPRINT OF HERITAGE BOOKS, INC.

Books, CDs, and more—Worldwide

For our listing of thousands of titles see our website
at
www.HeritageBooks.com

Published 2016 by
HERITAGE BOOKS, INC.
Publishing Division
5810 Ruatan Street
Berwyn Heights, Md. 20740

International Standard Book Numbers
Paperbound: 978-1-55613-837-9
Clothbound: 978-0-7884-6348-8

DANVILLE RESIDENTS

This book is dedicated to all the Town Clerks of Danville who have all kept an excellent record of inhabitants of the Town of Danville, New Hampshire.

TABLE OF CONTENTS

INTRODUCTION

This book contains Birth, Marriage and Death data on people of Danville, NH (Formerly Hawke until 18 June 1836). This is not a legal record. This information is compiled from various sources. The largest amount of data was from the Town Reports of Danville, NH from 1887 - 1991 inclusive from the book *Vital Records of Danville, NH 1760-1886* published 1979 by THE HAWKE HISTORICAL SOCIETY DANVILLE, NEW HAMPSHIRE. Permission by Deborah Meigs of the Society to include their data to this book is appreciated. Some information is from residents of Danville who are relatives of mine, now deceased. Some cemetery data was obtained by my visiting the cemeteries in the years past. Often the data of each individual record is compiled from multiple sources. A few individuals were not b, m, or d (born, married, or died, "bu" = buried) in Danville, but are parents or children of those who were. The compiler took the liberty to add Jr. & Sr. to some records so as to distinguish between child & parent and so the database would sort correctly. Also in situations where a b record showed the spelling of a name like Dotty, the m record showed Dority and the d record showed Dorothy the name was all entered as Dorothy so the data base would sort and link to the spouse & parents correctly.

It would be most appeciated if any one has data that can be added or correction to this book to send this information to the compiler of this record.

Gus Collins
19384 Occidental Ave S
Seattle WA 98148-2155

vii

1790 US CENSUS OF DANVILLE, NH

NAME of Head of the House	Males Free White ae 16y+ Older	Males Free White Under ae 16y	Females Free White Inc. Family Heads	All Other Free Persons
BAECHELLER, Elisha	3		3	
BARNARD, Stephen	1		3	
BARTLETT, George	3	3	5	
BATCHELDER, David	1	1	1	
BEAN, Elisha	2	4	5	
BEAN, Jeremiah	1	3	5	
BLAKE, Hezekiah	1	2	5	
BLAKE, Jonathan	1		2	
BLAKE, Lucy		1	2	
BRADLEY, Joseph	1	1	2	
BROWN, Nathaniel	1	4	5	
BURWELL, William	3		5	
CAMPBELL, Annis	1	2	4	
CHASE, Caleb	1		5	
CHASE, Simon	1		5	
CLOUGH, Zaccheus	1		2	
COLBY, Enos	2	1	4	
COLLINS, Benjamin	1	3	1	
COLLINS, Joseph	1	1	5	
COLLINS, Richard	2	1	6	
DARLING, Elizabeth			1	
DEARBORN, Henry	3	2	3	
DIMOND, Israel	1		2	
DIMOND, Israel Jr.	1	2	5	
EASTMAN, Benjamin	1	2	2	
EASTMAN, Edward	3		3	
EASTMAN, Samuel	1	1	3	
EATON, Jabez	1		1	
EATON, Joseph T.	1		2	
FELLOWS, Joseph	1	2	1	
FELLOWS, Molly		1	3	
FRENCH, Joanna			2	
FRENCH, Jonathan	2	1	2	
FRENCH, Jonathan 3rd	1	4	2	
FRENCH, Jonathan Jr.	2	1	2	
GEORGE, William	2	4	1	
HILLS, Reuben	2	5	2	
HOOK, Humphrey	2	1	3	
HOOK, Israel	2	3	3	
JONES, Nathan	1		1	
JONES, Jonathan	1	2	5	

NAME of Head of the House	Males Free White ae 16y+ Older	Males Free White Under ae 16y	Females Free White Inc. Family Heads	All Other Free Persons
MERRILL, Samuel	1	1	2	
MORRILL, Henry	2		1	
MORRILL, Nathaniel	1	1	3	
PAGE, Anna			2	
PAGE, Benjamin	1	2	1	
PAGE, Simon	1		2	
PAGE, Thomas	3	1	4	
PHILBRICK, Mary	1	1	6	
PLUMMER, Samuel	3	2	3	
QUIMBY, Aaron	2	1	4	
QUIMBY, David	2		3	
QUIMBY, Paul	1		1	
QUIMBY, Samuel	2		3	
SANBORN, Jethro	1		2	
SANBORN, John	1	2	3	
SANBORN, Jonathan	1	1	3	
SANBORN, Joseph C.	1	3	4	
SANBORN, Josiah	1	1	1	
SANBORN, Obidiah	1	1	1	
SARGENT, Samuel	1	1	1	
SAWYER, Gideon	1		2	
SAWYER, James	1		1	
SLEEPER, Martha	1		2	
SLEEPER, Nehemiah	3	2	5	
SPAFFORD, Benjamin	1	1	5	
TEWKSBURY, Josiah	1	4	6	
THORN, James	1	1	4	
TOWLE, Caleb	2		2	
TOWLE, James	1	3	3	
TOWLE, Jeremy	1	1	6	
TRUE, Jabez	1	3	4	
WILLIAMS, Joseph	3	2	8	
WOODMAN, Moses	1	2	2	
WOODWARD, William	1		1	

Danville, New Hampshire

Residents 1760 - 1992

ABBOTT, Douglas W. b Beverley, MA; md WATSON, Judith L.

ABBOTT, Eliz b of Kingston, NH; md 23 Nov 1779 Hawk, NH GREGG, Wm; md by Rev John Page

ABBOTT, Isaac D. b Rochester, NH; md 10 Mar 1880 Danville, NH TOBYNE, Nellie B.

ABBOTT, Joshua md 11 Sep 1766 Hawke, NH FULLER, Joanna; md by Rev John Page

ABBOTT, Keith Douglas b 27 Jan 1964 Danville, NH s/o ABBOTT, Douglas W. & WATSON, Judith L.

ABBOTT, Lynne Kathleen b 18 Dec 1967 Danville, NH d/o ABBOTT, Douglas W. & WATSON, Judith L.

ABDO, Joann b 1950 Boston, MA; md 21 Aug 1965 Danville, NH BENNETT Rob't W. md by Rev Ivan Smith Jr

ADAMS, Cheryll Ann b 1949 Exeter, NH; md 17 Jun 1966 Danville, NH WEST, Errol F.; md by Rev Hugh MacLean

ADAMS, Christine C. md 22 Nov 1991 Danville, NH SMREKAR, Larry E.; md by Richard J. Rondeau (JP)

Al-EGAILY, Sadik Howard b 20 Feb 1969 Danville, NH s/o Al-EGAILY, Salah Salman & KIMBALL, Carolyn Rosalie

AKIYMA, Barbara E. md 02 Feb 1986 Danville, NH CARVELLO, Alan J.; md by Renee Houle Carkin (JP)

ALBRECHT, Alan Peter md 14 Jun 1975 Danville, NH DOWLING, Norma Anne; md by Robert S. Dejadon (JP)

ALBRECHT, Christine Kathleen b 31 Oct 1975 Exeter, NH d/o ALBRECHT, Wm J. & MOSS, Susan L.

ALBRECHT, Wm Arthur b 30 Nov 1973 s/o ALBRECHT, Wm J. & MOSS, Susan L.

ALEXANDER, Melissa J. b 24 May 1970 Haverhill, MA d/o ALEXANDER, Jarnes F. & HUNSBERGER, Dorothy J.

ALLARD, Ada J. b 05 Sep 1902 Danville, NH d/o ALLARD, Jos & ALLISON, Julia; md 01 Dec 1923 Westville, NH BUSHWAY, Alfred A.; md by M. J. Moher (P)

ALLARD, Christine Mae b 23 Mar 1925 Danville, NH d/o ALLARD, Frank A. & CRAINE, Glenna; md 21 Mar 1953 Danville, NH MONTGOMERY, Richard Lovern

ALLARD, Corinne b 23 Mar 1925 Danville, NH d /o ALLARD, Frank A. & CRAINE, Glenna; d 26 Mar 1925 Danville, NH

ALLARD, Frank Alonzo b 29 Apr 1901 Danville, NH s/o ALLARD, Jos & ALLISON, Julienne; md 27 Dec 1924 Westville, NH CRAINE, Glenna M.; d 24 Aug 1967 Danville, NH; md by Rev M. J. Mosher; 2nd child in family

ALLARD, Fred b Canada; md SHAW, Hattie M.

ALLARD, Jos b Nicolet, Canada s/o ALLARD, Ferdinand & MARCOTTE, Odile; md ALLISON, Julian; d 10 Jul 1928; d ae 62y 10d

ALLARD, Lena Florence b 25 Apr 1896 Danville, NH d/o ALLARD, Jos & ALLISON, Julia; md 27 Sep 1920 Plaistow, NH MOREAU, Ovide S.; md by M. J. Moher (P)m

ALLARD, Mary b Danville, NH d/o ALLARD, Jos & ALLISON, Julia; d 18 Dec 1891 Danville, NH

ALLARD, Phillip F. b 03 Feb 1894 Danville, NH s/o ALLARD, Fred & SHAW, Hattie M.; d 04 Feb 1894 Danville, NH; d ae 1m

ALLARD, ---- b 07 Oct 1930 Danville, NH ?/o ALLARD, Frank A. & CRAINE, Glenna; d 07 Oct 1930 Danville, NH

ALLEN, Harland G. b 11 Dec 1844 Danville, NH s/o ALLEN, Jos H. Sr. & GRIFFIN, Hannah D.

ALLEN, Jos H. Jr. b c1858 s/o ALLEN, Jos H. Sr. & GRIFFIN, Hannah

ALLEN (Cont.) D.; d 26 Dec 1862 Danville, NH; d ae 14y - Diptheria

ALLEN, Jos H. Sr. b c1818; md 22 Dec 1841 GRIFFIN, Hannah D.; d 26 Jan 1865 Danville, NH; d ae 47y - Civil War Rcds

ALLEN, Mary Ann b 24 Dec 1825 Deerfield, NH d/o ALLEN, Jos Hill & BATCHELDER, Mary; md 15 Nov 1849 Epson, NH COLLINS, Alva Blake; d 30 Mar 1907 Danville, NH; bu Danville.NH; bu Old Mtg Hse Cem.

ALLEN, Nancy b md PAGE, Aaron; d 1848 Danville, NH

ALLEN, Sarah F. b c1856 d/o ALLEN, Jos H. Sr. & GRIFFIN, Hannah D.; d 17 Dec 1862 Danville, NH; d ae 6y - Diptheria

ALLEN, Valeria Keay b 1812 Rumney, NH; md 1848 Danville, NH PAGE, Aaron; 2nd wife of Aaron PAGE

ALLEN, Annie A. b Cornish, VT d/o ALLEN, Enoch W. & GUPTILL, Martha S.; md WELCH, ---- ; d 09 Dec 1908 Danville, NH

ALLICON, Rosemary A. md 13 Jul 1985 Danville, NH JOHNSON, Steven R.; md by Rev James C. Blough

AMATO, David R. md 07 Jan 1989 Danville, NH COLLINS, Tammi; md by Wm Beane (JP)

AMAZEEN, Judith A. b md 05 Feb 1983 Danville, NH LEGERE, Wm R.; md by Rev Wendell J. Irvine

AMORELLI, Mitchel Chas of Danville, NH md MANGERI, Michelle Marie md by Richard W. Connors, Priest

ANALETTO, Benjamin Jr. md 24 Apr 1987 Danville, NH SHEA, Jeanne M.; md by Rich J. Rondeau (JP)

ANDERSON, Arthur Leslie b 25 Aug 1945 Danville, NH s/o ANDERSON, Hollis M. & CAMPBELL, Gertrude K.

ANDERSON, Beatrice L. b 24 Oct 1909 Danville, NH d/o ANDERSON, Marcus M. & DIMOND, Grace; md METEVIER, Urban

ANDERSON, Charlotte b Fremont, NH; md GEORGE, Allen P.

ANDERSON, Clara b Danville, NH d/o ---- & VINCENT, Abigail; md Allen, ---- ; d 18 May 1900 Danville, NH

ANDERSON, George M. b 31 Oct

ANDERSON (Cont.) 1843 Hawke, NH s/o ANDERSON, Moses & CHALLIS, Hannah D.; md SHERBURNE, Helen C.; d 04 Aug 1924 Danville, NH

ANDERSON, Gertrude K. b 1915 Fremont, NH; md 11 Jan 1964 Danville, NH PHILLIPS, Jos Dewey; md by Rev Theodore B. Hadley

ANDERSON, Harold Curtis b 15 Jul 1940 Danville, NH s/o ANDERSON, Hollis M. & CAMPBELL, Gertrude K.; md 20 Mar 1959 Danville, NH JEANS, Kath. Ann; md by Rev John Wood Jr.

ANDERSON, Hollis Morton b 30 Jan 1909 Danville, NH s/o ANDERSON, Marcus M. & DIMOND, Grace; md 30 Jan 1932 Danville, NH CAMPBELL, Gertrude K.; d 01 Oct 1957 Danville, NH; md by Rev Samnuel B. Enman

ANDERSON, Horace M. b 1852 Danville, NH s/o ANDERSON, Moses & CHALLIS, Hannah D.

ANDERSON, Judith Lee b 27 Aug 1961 Danville, NH d/o ANDERSON, Howard Curtis & JEANS, Kathleen Ann

ANDERSON, Laura Jean b 26 Nov 1963 Danville, NH d/o ANDERSON, Horold Curtis & JEANS, Kathleen Ann

ANDERSON, Leonora M. b 14 May 1873 Danville, NH d/o ANDERSON, George M. & SHERBURNE, Helen C.; md 22 Jan 1892 Danville, NH WEBSTER, George E.; d 05 Feb 1906 Danville, NH; md by Rev J. A. Lowell

ANDERSON, Marcia b 18 Sep 1879 Danville, NH d/o ANDERSON, Geo M. & SHERBURNE, Nellie B.; md 30 Nov 1901 Danville, NH JACKSON, Raymond W.; d 16 Dec 1938 Danville, NH; Twin

ANDERSON, Marcus b 18 Sep 1879 Danville, NH d/o ANDERSON, George M. & SHERBURNE, Nellie B.; md 06 Apr 1906 Danville, NH DIMOND, Grace M.; d 27 Jul 1961 Danville, NH; md by Rev A. B. Hyde; (Twin)

ANDERSON, Marlene Grace b 05 Oct 1932 Danville, NH d/o ANDERSON, Hollis & CAMPBELL, Gertrude; md EATON, Alfred W.

ANDERSON, Michelle b d/o ANDERSON, Arthur Leslie & MEANEY, Karen Sue; d 02 Oct 1970 Danville, NH ae 1m

ANDERSON, Moses b Hampstead, NH; md 08 Oct 1809 Hawke, NH HUNT, Betsey

ANDERSON, Moses b Hawke, NH; md 01 Dec 1841 Raymond, NH CHALLIS, Hannah D.

ANDERSON, Moses b c1821 Sandown, NH; d 23 Nov 1890 Danville, NH of apoplexy; Occupation Carpenter

ANDERSON, Pearl E. b 21 Jan 1912 Danville, NH d/o ANDERSON, Marcus M. & DIMOND, Grace; md 17 Apr 1929 Newton, NH BEAULIEU, Emedie; md by Henry L. Burbeck (JP)

ANDERSON, Ralph W. b 12 Apr 1875 Danville, NH s/o ANDERSON, George M. & SHERBURNE, Helen C.; d 01 Mar 1938 Danville, NH

ANDERSON, Rhoda J. b 02 Feb 1842 Danville, NH d/o ANDERSON, Moses & CHALLIS, Hannah D.; md 04 Feb 1860 Danville, NH COLLINS, Perley S.

ANDERSON, Romanzo C. b Feb 1867 Danville, NH s/o ANDERSON, Moses & CHALLIS, Hannah D.

ANDERSON, Romanzo C. b Feb 1846 Danville, NH s/o ANDERSON, Moses & CHALLIS, Hannah D.; d 21 Dec 1868 Danville, NH

ANDERSON, Sarah b 1850 Danville, NH d/o ANDERSON, Moses & CHALLIS, Hannah D.; d 07 Apr 1862 Danville, NH

ANDERSON, Wilbur Moses b 1848 Danville, NH s/o ANDERSON, Moses & CHALLIS, Hannah D.; d 09 Apr 1866 Danville, NH

ANDREWS, Luella Gray b 1869 Essex, MA d/o ANDREWS, Monsieur & BRIDGES, Sarah L. md 23 Jun 1894 Danville, NH DOLE, Chas Edward; d 03 Dec 1939 Danville, NH; md by Rev John A Wiggin; d ae 82y 4m 5d

ANTHONY, Rowene Maria of Danville, NH md 17 Oct 1992 OAK, Richard Dixon by Janet H. Beaulieu, JP

ARCHAMBAULT, Abraham Adam D. b 03 Feb 1983 Manchester, NH s/o ARCHAMBAULT, Jos & DRAGON, Lauren

ARCHAMBAULT, Mary Emily b 07 Feb 1975 Haverhill, MA d/o ARCHAMAULT, Leo W. & MAYER, Marie L.

ARCHIBALD, Emma Pauline b c1874 Georgetown, MA d/o ARCHIBALD, Moses Guy & ATWOOD, Eliz; d 16 Nov 1968 Danville, NH

ARCHIBALD, Moses Guy b s/o ARCHIBALD, Reuben & BAILEY, Emma; md ATWOOD, Eliz; d 30 Oct 1953 Danville, NH; d ae 74y

ARCHIBALD, Viola Pauline b 1899 Haverhill, MA d/o ARCHIBALD, M. Guy & DOLE, Pauline; md 27 Oct 1936 Danville, NH DEMING, George; d 09 Jun 1966 Danville, NH; md by Rev W. C. Chappell

AREL, Courtney Dora b 09 Sep 1991 Derry, NH d/o AREL, Peter J. & NORWOOD, Linda L.

AREL, Peter John md 19 May 1990 Danville, NH MUSSO, Linda Lee; md by Phillippe A. Arel (JP)

ARENNIE, Mark M. md 19 May 1990 Danville, NH O'NIEL, Julie A.; md by Rev Robert F. Dobson

ARMSTRONG, Carol. Ellissa md 24 Jun 1989 Danville, NH GANSENBERG, Jon Jos; md by Rich J. Rondeau (JP)

ARNOLD, Anne Eliz b 24 Mar 1902 Danville, NH d/o ARNOLD, Warren H. & LADD, Olla May; md ROSS, ---- ; d 04 Aug 1978 Danville, NH

ARNOLD, Beatrice Helen b 26 Sep 1920 Danville, NH d/o ARNOLD, Clinton John & Ryan, Helen Edna; md HUNT, John Hallowell

ARNOLD, Belen B. md 29 Sep 1979 Danville, NH DeMARCO, Jos G.; md by Rev Wm Ryans

ARNOLD, Carrie P. b 29 Mar 1894 Danville, NH d/o ARNOLD, John M. & JAMES, Anna A.

ARNOLD, Charlene Ann b 05 Mar 1946 Danville, NH d/o ARNOLD, Chas R. & ROMATELLI, Carola L.

ARNOLD, Chas Richard b 02 Feb 1910 Danville, NH s/o ARNOLD, Warren H. & LADD, Olla May

ARNOLD, Christie M. b 02 Jan 1897 Danville, NH d/o ARNOLD, WARREN M. & LADD, Olla May; d 25 May 1897 Danville, NH; d 4m 23d

ARNOLD, Clarence J. b 23 Dec 1881 Danville, NH s/o ARNOLD, John M. & JAMES, Anna A.

ARNOLD, Clifton J. Jr. b Danville, NH s/o ARNOLD, Clifton J. Sr. & TAYLOR, Carol E.

ARNOLD, Clifton Warren b Danville, NH s/o ARNOLD, Warren H. & LADD, Olla May; d 28 Mar 1967 Danville, NH; ae 67y

ARNOLD, Clinton John Jr. b 27 Aug 1931 Danville, NH s/o ARNOLD, Clinton John Sr. & RYAN, Helen Edna

ARNOLD, Clinton John Sr. b 29 Mar 1899 Danville, NH s/o ARNOLD, Warren H. & LADD, Olla May; md 18 Oct 1919 Danville, NH RYAN, Helen Edna.; d 15 Jun 1974 Danville, NH; md by Rev L.M. Bleakney

ARNOLD, Clistie May b 08 Nov 1919 Danville, NH d/o ARNOLD, Clifton W. & FEENEY, Stella

ARNOLD, Dana O. b 13 Jul 1916 Danville, NH s/o ARNOLD, Warren H. & LADD, Olla May; d 09 Dec 1933 Danville, NH

ARNOLD, Edward Stanley b 27 Sep 1937 Danville, NH s/o ARNOLD, Clinton John & RYAN, Helen Edna; md 16 Mar 1957 Danville, NH CROZIER, Mary Eliz

ARNOLD, Fred R. b 22 Dec 1891 Danville, NH s/o ARNOLD, John & COLLINS, Cora Mabel; 8th Child in Family

ARNOLD, Gary Wayne b 07 Jun 1948 Danville, NH s/o ARNOLD, Gayle Philip & GOLDTHWAITE, Evelyn Frances; md 27 Dec 1967 Danville, NH DOYLE, Maureen Denise

ARNOLD, Gayle Phillip b Haverhill, MA s/o ARNOLD, Everet Moses; md 26 Dec 1945 Danville, NH GOLDTH-WAITE, Evelyn Francis; md by W. C. Chappell

ARNOLD, Gertrude B. b 11 Jun 1880 Danville, NH d/o ARNOLD, John M. & JAMES, Anna A.; md GEORGE, Dan G.

ARNOLD, Grace b 02 Feb 1886 d/o ARNOLD, John H. & JAMES, Ann Augusta

ARNOLD, Harold W. b 1888 Danville, NH s/o ARNOLD, John M. & JAMES, Anna A.; d 12 May 1889 Danville, NH ae 16m 22d

ARNOLD, Harry A. b Danville, NH s/o ARNOLD, Warren H. & LADD, Olla

ARNOLD (Cont.) M.; d 31 Jan 1917 Danville, NH ae 16y 1m 24d

ARNOLD, Joan Shirley b 07 Feb 1940 Danville, NH d/o ARNOLD, Theodore F. & HUNT, Hilda M.

ARNOLD, John M. b Hampstead, NH; md JAMES, Annie A.; d 15 Nov 1941 Danville, NH d ae 91y 6m 14d; Occupation Grocer

ARNOLD, Judith Gay b 26 Aug 1956 Danville, NH d/o ARNOLD, Clinton J. Jr. & TAYLOR, Carol E.

ARNOLD, Karl James b 14 Jul 1909 Danville, NH s/o ARNOLD, Warren H. & LADD, Olla May md 1st 01 Apr 1939 Danville, NH STARKEY, Mary Alice by Rev Earl F. Nauss, 2nd; md 16 Jun 1951 Exeter, NH PAIGE, Alberta Ellen by Rev Paul T. Martin

ARNOLD, Marjorie b 19 Mar 1925 Danville, NH d/o ARNOLD, Clinton J. & RYAN, Helen

ARNOLD, Mary Beatrice b 11 Apr 1913 Danville, NH d/o ARNOLD, Warren H. & LADD, Olla May; d 18 May 1914 Danville, NH ae 1y 1m 6d

ARNOLD, Melvin Leonard b 21 Jun 1918 Danville, NH s/o ARNOLD, Warren H. & LADD, Olla May

ARNOLD, Mildred b 05 Feb 1906 Danville, NH d/o ARNOLD, Warren H. & LADD, Olla May; md 21 Oct 1922 Kingston, NH ORDWAY, Linwood C.; md by Rev A.M. Morrison

ARNOLD, Nellie Beatrice b 20 Oct 1913 Danville, NH d/o ARNOLD, Warren H. & LADD, Olla M.

ARNOLD, Nelson Bruce b 07 Jul 1942 Danville, NH s/o ARNOLD, Clinton John & RYAN, Helen Edna; md 18 Feb 1962 Danville, NH KERSHAW, Barbara Ann; md by Arthur M. Comeau

ARNOLD, Paul Steven b 11 Nov 1956 Danville, NH s/o ARNOLD, Edward S. & CROZIER, Mary E.

ARNOLD, Russell Wayne b 29 Sep 1958 Danville, NH s/o ARNOLD, Edward S. & CROZIER, Mary E.; md 04 Sep 1982 Danville, NH GAGNON, Audrey A.; md by Michael J. Griffin (P)

ARNOLD, Ruth b Danville, NH d/o ARNOLD, John M. & JAMES, Anna A.; d 11 Aug 1893 Danville, NH ae 8m

ARNOLD, Sharon Joy b 14 Jan 1962 Danville, NH d/o ARNOLD, Clifton J. Jr. & TAYLOR, Carol E.; md 02 Aug 1981 Danville, NH TURNER, Peter M.; md by Rev Roberet E Aspenwall

ARNOLD, Susan Elaine b 17 Apr 1963 Danville, NH d/o ARNOLD, Edward S. & CRAZIER, Mary E.; md 20 Oct 1984 Danville, NH FITTON, David A.; md by Richard J. Rondeau (JP)

ARNOLD, Susie Blanche b 1935 Haverhill, MA d/o ARNOLD, Everett M.; md 10 Jan 1953 Danville, NH KIM-BALL, Leonard Harris

ARNOLD, Theodore Frank b 08 May 1911 Danville, NH s/o ARNOLD, Warren H. & LADD, Olla May; md HUNT, Hilda M.; d 24 Nov 1961 Danville, NH

ARNOLD, Thos Brian b 14 Sep 1958 Danville, NH s/o ARNOLD, Clinton J. Jr. & TAYLOR, Carol E.

ARNOLD, Thos H. b s/o ARNOLD, Warren & LADD, Olla; d 31 Dec 1978 Danville, NH ae 73y

ARNOLD, Vida M. b 20 May 1903 Danville, NH d/o ARNOLD, Warren H. & LADD, Olla May; md FITTS, Norris Leon; d 09 Apr 1948 Danville, NH

ARNOLD, Warren H. b 20 Nov 1876 Danville, NH s/o ARNOLD, John M. & JAMES, Anna A. md; LADD, Olla May; d 10 Sep 1963 Danville, NH

ARNOLD, Wayne Paul b 01 Feb 1984 Manchester, NH s/o ARNOLD, Russell W. & GAGNON, Audrey A.

ARNOLD, Wm M. md 28 May 1983 Danville, NH MACKIE, Victoria L.; md by Florent R. Bilodeau (P)

ARNOLD, ---- b 07 Dec 1900 Danville, NH s/o ARNOLD, Warren H. & LADD, Olla May

ARSENAULT, Fred Russell b 14 Aug 1958 Danville, NH s/o ARSENAULT, Carol V. & DUCHEMIN, Brenda

ARSENAULT, Jeanne M. md 05 Aug 1980 Danville MOSES, Brett E.; md by Edward C. Garvey (JP)

ARSENAULT, Marilyn Ann md 07 Jul 1974 Danville FUSCHETTI, Carmen Genn

ARSENAULT, Sarah Eliz b 03 Jan 1984 Lawrence, MA d/o ARSENAULT, Raymond J. & JENNINGS, Janice A.

ARTHUR, Wm J. d 24 Oct 1884 Danville, NH ae 26y Mill Accident

ASHLEY, Lucy E. b Amherst, MA d/o ASHLEY, Frank & BARNARD, Lillie; md FIELD, ----; d 25 Sep 1943 Danville, NH

ASSELIN, Rich. Chas b s/o ASSELIN, Gerard & MARCOUS, Jeanette L.; d 14 Dec 1991 Danville, NH ae 41y

ATKINSON, Gary Albert of Danville, NH md 06 Nov 1992 BROWN, Michelle B. md by Richard J. Rondeau, JP

ATWOOD, Bruce D. md 23 Jan 1988 Danville, NH MILLER, Doreen R.; md by Richard J. Rondeau (JP)

ATWOOD, Frank W. Jr. md 26 Sep 1987 Danville, NH DOW, Diane; md by Rich J. Rondeau (JP)

ATWOOD, James E. md 09 Apr 1988 Danville, NH CHAMBERLIN, Lisa L.; md by Richard J. Rondeau (JP)

ATWOOD, Sandra Lea b 02 Aug 1960 Danville, NH d/o ATWOOD, Hebert & TOSHACH, Dorothy

AUFIERO, Heather Alice b 02 Oct 1971 Lawrence, MA d/o AUFIERO, Angelo A. & CAMPBELL, Lorraine A.

AUGUSTA, Jos L. V. b 1941 Martinez, CA; md 09 Jul 1967 Danville, NH WHITE, Barbara Ruth; md by Edward R. Lamb (JP)

AUSTIN, Inez S. b c1863 Kensington, NH; md 03 Apr 1881 Danville, NH KEEZER, Wm J.

AUSTIN, Isabelle b c1633 d/o AUSTIN, Francis; md TOWLE, Philip; d 1641 Hampton, NH; md 2nd LEAVITT, Thos

AUSTIN, Luther J. b 1839 Haverhill, MA; md 08 Jan 1863 Danville, NH COLLINS, Sarah P.

AVERILL, Katherine M. md 18 May 1991 Danville, NH SMITH, Perry Cloudman; md by Rev Wendell J. Irvine

AVERILL, Lauren E. md 07 Sep 1985 Danville, NH SIMMONDS, Darrin J.; md by Rev Fay L. Gemmell

AVERILL, Robert E. b s/o AVERILL, Stephen & MILLER, Doris; d 03 Feb 1984 Danville, NH ae 44y

AVERY, Alfred J. b 1850 E Kingston, NH s/o AVERY, Jos & SMITH, Eliz; d 30 Sep 1925 Danville, NH

AVERY, Annie Eliz b 10 May 1880 Danville, NH d/o AVERY, Wm P. & BRIDGES, Sarah L.; d 19 Jun 1965 Danville, NH

AVERY, Archie S. b Danville, NH; md ELKINS, Lizzie E.

AVERY, Beryl E. b 24 Sep 1916 Danville, NH s/o AVERY, Lewis F. & SMITH, Charlotte H.; md 04 Jul 1955 Danville, NH BELLACOME, Gerlando; md by Rev W. C. Chappell

AVERY, Carrie b 28 Jul 1864 Danville, NH d/o AVERY, Jos & SMITH, Eliz; d 06 Feb 1869 Danville, NH

AVERY, Carrie Josephine b c1873 Danville, NH d/o AVERY, Chas H. & EASTMAN, Ella; md 06 Aug 1892 Kingston, NH SARGENT, Walter E.; d 26 Mar 1945 Danville, NH; md by Rev J. H. Knott; d ae 81y

AVERY, Chas H. b 1848 s/o AVERY, Jos & SMITH, Eliz ; d 09 Nov 1926 Danville, NH

AVERY, Christie A. b 07 Jan 1894 Danville, NH d/o AVERY, Chas H. & EASTMAN, Mary E.; md 01 Jan 1912 Danville, NH WOODBURY, Wm H.; md by Rev A. C. Keith

AVERY, Ernest C. b 25 Mar 1886 Danville, NH s/o AVERY, Orrin S. & DARBE, Sarah V.; md 10 Jul 1915 Dover, NH CLARK, Jesse M.; md by Rev Earle B. Cross

AVERY, Frank b c1856 Beverly, MA; md 02 Dec 1875 Danville, NH DAVIS, Addie M.

AVERY, Freeman b 17 Dec 1884 Danville, NH s/o AVERY, Orin S. & DARBE, Sarah V.; d 28 Feb 1885 Danville, NH ae 2m

AVERY, Freeman b 28 Jul 1864 Danville, NH s/o AVERY, Jos & SMITH, Eliz; d 03 Mar 1869 Danville, NH

AVERY, Jos b Epsom, NH; md SMITH, Eliz d 07 Jun 1898 Danville, NH

AVERY, Lewis Freeman b 12 Nov 1883 Danville, NH s/o AVERY, Wm P. & BRIDGES, Sarah L.; md 08 Mar 1913 Plaistow, NH SMITH, Charlotte H.; d 02 Nov 1965 Danville, NH; md by Rev Charle A Towne

AVERY, Lucius O. b 02 Jan 1893 Danville, NH s/o AVERY, Orin S. & DARBE, Sarah V md PENTON, Anna M.

AVERY, Manford Elwood b 30 Jan 1914 Danville, NH s /o AVERY, Lewis F. & SMITH, Charlotte H.

AVERY, Oren S. b c1858 Beverly MA s/o AVERY, Jos & SMITH, Eliz; md 27 Sep 1883 Danville, NH DARBE, Sarah V.; d 26 Jan 1939 Danville, NH ae 81y 5d

AVERY, Phyllis S. b 26 Mar 1922 Danville, NH d/o AVERY, Lucius & PENTON, Anna M.

AVERY, Sadie E. b 26 Sep 1876 Danville, NH s/o AVERY, Jos & STANYAN, Anna L.; md 10 May 1899 Danville, NH QUIMBY, Fred C.

AVERY, Viola A. b 10 Mar 1887 Danville, NH d/o AVERY, Oren & DARBE, Sarah V.; Child #3

AVERY, Wm F. d 26 Feb 1932 Danville, NH ae 56y 8m 4d

AVERY, Wm P. Jr. b 12 Jun 1877 Danville, NH s/o AVERY, Wm P. Sr. & BRIDGES, Sarah L.; md; 30 Dec 1899 Danville, NH COLLINS, Edna B.; d 05 May 1959 Danville, NH; md by Rev A. B. Howard

AVERY, Wm P. Sr. b Candia, NH s/o AVERY, Jos; md BRIDGES, Sarah L.; d 07 Jul 1929 Danville, NH; also md SMITH, Harriet ?

AVERY, Virginia Margaret b 10 Nov 1920 d/o AVERY, Lucius O. & Penton, Anna; 3 child in family

AYERS, Chester Wm 4th b 08 Oct 1984 Manchester, NH s/o AYERS, Chester Wm 3rd & COLLINS, Carlene M

AYOTTE, Mark md 21 Feb 1981 Danville, NH SKIDMORE, Bonne E.; md by Phyllis A. Raynowski (JP) BABBITT, Howard Tod of Concord, MO md 05 Apr 1992 Bryson, Michelle Marie md by Rev Phillip Hicks

BABINE, Clarence W. b 1896 Wilmington, DE s/o BABINE, John; md 23 Jul 1919 Westville, NH DAY, Etta Blanche; md by M. J. Moher (P)

BACHELDOR, Lydia b Hampton Falls, NH; md 30 Jun 1802 Hampton Falls, NH BATCHELDOR, Nathan

BACHELDOR, Nathan md 30 Jun 1802 Hampton Falls, NH ----, Lydia

BACHELOR, Anne b 04 Mar 1762 Hawke, NH d/o BACHELOR, Reuben & FIFIELD, Miriam; md 05 Dec 1784 Hawke, NH SANBORN, Jonathan Lt.; d 18 Sep 1853 Danville, NH

BACHELOR, Daniel b 05 Dec 1807 Hawke, NH s/o BACHELOR, David & BACHELOR, Dorothy

BACHELOR, David b 24 Nov 1760 Hawke, NH s/o BACHELOR, Reuben & FIFIELD, Miriam

BACHELOR, Elisha b 22 May 1773 Hawke, NH s/o BACHELOR, Elisha Dea. & SMITH, Theodate

BACHELOR, Elisha b 14 Jul 1796 Hawke, NH s/o BACHELOR, Nathan & WILLIAMS, Sarah; d 22 Feb 1799 Hawke, NH ae 3y

BACHELOR, Elisha Dea. b 1727 md SMITH, Theodate; d 24 Feb 1813 Hawke, NH ae 86 yr

BACHELOR, Eliz b 05 Aug 1770 Hawke, NH d/o BACHELOR, Elisha Dea. & SMITH, Theodate

BACHELOR, Harriet b 06 Jul 1827 Hawke, NH d/o BACHELOR, Elisha & PRESCOTT, Ruth

BACHELOR, Huldah b 04 Nov 1767 Hawke, NH; d/o BACHELOR, Elisha Dea. & SMITH, Theodate, md 29 Dec 1794 Kingston, NH SCRIBNER, John

BACHELOR, Jonathan b 26 Apr 1773 Hawke, NH s/o BACHELOR, Reuben & FIFIELD, Miriam; d 07 Jun 1786 Hawke, NH ae 13y - Mill Accident

BACHELOR, Lydia md BACHELOR, Nathan; 2nd mar

BACHELOR, Mary b 1760; md FRENCH, Jonathan; d 06 Oct 1843 Danville, NH ae 83 yr

BACHELOR, Mary md HOOK, Jacob Jr.; d 1813 Hawke, NH

BACHELOR, Mary b 1715 Hampton Falls, NH; md SANBORN, Jonathan; d 18 May 1790 Hawke, NH ae 75 yr

BACHELOR, Miriam b 21 Dec 1766 Hawke, NH d/o BACHELOR, Reuben & FIFIELD, Miriam; md 24 Dec 1788 Hawke, NH SANBORN, Obadiah; d 31 Aug 1858 Danville, NH ae 91 yr

BACHELOR, Moses b 03 Sep 1800 Hawke, NH s/o BACHELOR, David & ----, Dorothy

BACHELOR, Nabby b 17 Nov 1762 Hawke, NH d/o BACHELOR, Elisha Dea. & SMITH, Theodate

BACHELOR, Nathan b Nov 1799 Hawke, NH s/o BACHELOR, Nathan & WILLIAMS, Sarah; d 21 May 1826 Hawke, NH ae 26y

BACHELOR, Nathan b 16 May 1765 Hawke, NH s/o BACHELOR, Elisha Dea. & SMITH, Theodate; md 05 Mar 1795 Kingston, NH WILLIAMS, Sally

BACHELOR, Nathan md 30 Dec 1807 Kingston, NH FRENCH, Abigail; 3rd marr of Nathan

BACHELOR, Nathn'l b s/o BACHELOR, David & BACHELOR, Dorothy; d 20 Aug 1794 Hawke, NH ae 2 yr

BACHELOR, Phineas b 01 Dec 1763 Hawke, NH s/o BACHELOR, Reuben & FIFIELD, Miriam

BACHELOR, Reuben b 16 Jun 1776 Hawke, NH s/o BACHELOR, Josiah

BACHELOR, Reuben b 17 Mar 1797 Hawke, NH s/o BACHELOR, David & BACHELOR, Dorothy; d 17 Mar 1799 Hawke, NH 2nd birthday

BACHELOR, Reuben b 1787 Hawke, NH s/o BACHELOR, David & BACHELOR, Dorothy; d 12 Sep 1794 Hawke, NH ae 7y

BACHELOR, Reuben b 1733 Hampton Falls, NH; md FIFIELD, Miriam; d 05 Feb 1776 Hawke, NH

BACHELOR, Rob't F. b 28 Jan 1821 Hawke, NH s/o BACHELOR, Elisha & PRESCOTT, Ruth

BACHELOR, Sarah b 28 Feb 1794 Hawke, NH d/o BACHELOR, David & BACHELOR, Dorothy

BACHELOR, Sarah b 20 Feb 1780 Hawke, NH d/o BACHELOR, Josiah; Baptized date.

BACHELOR, Sarah b 06 Jan 1823 Hawke, NH d/o BACHELOR, Elisha & PRESCOTT, Ruth

BACHELOR, Sarah b 1806 d/o BACHELOR, Lydia; d 31 Aug 1806 Hawke, NH infant

BACHELOR, Sarah b 21 Dec 1787

BACHELOR (Cont.) Hawke, NH d/o BACHELOR, Reuben & BACHELOR, Dorothy

BACHOVZEFF, Olga H. b Danville, NH; md 14 Nov 1970 Danville, NH DesCHATELETS, Jean R.

BACK, Wm T. d 22 Jan 1975 Danville, NH ae 77y

BADGER, Enoch md 12 Jul 1770 Hawke, NH SHAW, Mary; md by Rev John Page

BADGER, Hannah b Kingston, NH; md 16 Aug 1794 Kingston, NH QUIMBY, Elisha; d 29 Jan 1843 Danville, NH ae 72y

BADGER, Steven md 05 Apr 1770 Hawke, NH WEBSTER, Dolly; md by Rev John Page

BAGLEY, Andrew J. b 1829 Hawke, NH s/o BAGLEY, Wm & MERRILL, Sarah; d 27 Feb 1914 Danville, NH ae 85y 0m 3d

BAGLEY, Ann md FRENCH, Jonathan Jr.; d 06 May 1770 Hawke, NH ae 40y about

BAGLEY, Blanche b 1875 Danville, NH d/o BAGLEY, John H. & STEVENS, Ellen F. d 1881 Danville, NH ae 6y

BAGLEY, Eliza b 1839 Danville, NH d/o BAGLEY, Wm & MERRILL, Sarah; d 27 Oct 1863 Danville, NH

BAGLEY, Ellen b 03 Sep 1836 Danville, NH d/o BAGLEY, Wm & MERRILL, Sarah

BAGLEY, Emmeline b 1821 Hawke, NH d/o BAGLEY, Wm & MERRILL, Sarah; md 12 Sep 1839 Raymond, NH ROWE, George W.

BAGLEY, Eunice b c1784 d/o BAGLEY, Wm & WOODMAN, Hannah; d 04 Jun 1862 Danville, NH ae 78y

BAGLEY, Eva M. b 24 Feb 1875 Danville, NH d/o BAGLEY, John H. & STEVENS, Ellen F.

BAGLEY, George W. b Canada; md CARTER, Mary C.

BAGLEY, Hannah b 1831 Hawke, NH d/o BAGLEY, Willaim & MERRILL, Sarah

BAGLEY, Harold b 27 Mar 1883 Danville, NH s/o BAGLEY, John H. & STEVENS, Ellen F.

BAGLEY, Harriet b 16 Jan 1822 Hawke, NH d/o BAGLEY, Wm & MERRILL, Sarah; md MERRICK, Stephen; d 1905 Danville, NH d ae 83y

BAGLEY, Irene b 1812 Hawke, NH d/o BAGLEY, Wm & MERRILL, Sarah

BAGLEY, Isaiah b 03 Sep 1836 Danville, NH s/o BAGLEY, Wm & MERRILL, Sarah

BAGLEY, Iva M. b 27 Jun 1886 Danville, NH d/o BAGLEY, John H. & STEVENS, Ellen F.

BAGLEY, John H. b 08 Feb 1833 Hawke, NH s/o BAGLEY, Wm & MERRILL, Sarah; d 06 Feb 1909 ae 75y 11m 29d

BAGLEY, Julia A. b 25 Jan 1825 Hawke, NH; d/o BAGLEY, Wm & MERRILL, Sarah

BAGLEY, Julia A. b Danville, NH d/o BAGLEY, David & McCLURE, ---- ; d 18 Aug 1911 Danville, NH ae 86y 7m 25d

BAGLEY, Lewis M. b 20 Jan 1888 Danville, NH s/o BAGLEY, Samuel E. & GEORGE, Alice M.; d 21 Jan 1988 Danville, NH

BAGLEY, Mary A. b 27 Mar 1827 Hawke, NH d/o BAGLEY, Wm & MERRILL, Sarah

BAGLEY, Samuel E. b c1867 Boscowan, ME s/o BAGLEY, George W. & CARTER, Mary C.; md 24 Mar 1887 Danville, NH GEORGE, Alice M.; md by Rev J. Eastwood

BAGLEY, Sarah b 15 May 1743 Amesbury, MA d/o BAGLEY, Davis & HUNTINGTON, Mary; md 17 Jan 1760 Kingston, NH COLLINS, Jos; d 11 Feb 1854 Danville, NH; bu Danville, NH Old Mtg Hse Cem

BAGLEY, Sarah b 1825 Danville, NH d/o BAGLEY, Wm & MERRILL, Sarah

BAGLEY, Sarah B. b 15 May 1882 Danville, NH d/o BAGLEY, John H. & STEVENS, Ellen F.; d 20 Sep 1882 Danville, NH

BAGLEY, Wm b Amesbury, MA; md 16 Mar 1820 Hawke, NH MERRILL, Sarah; d 23 Jun 1868 Danville, NH ae abt 74y

BAGLEY, Wm md WOODMAN, Hannah; d 1808 Hawke, NH ae 67y

BAGLEY, Wm Merrill b 1823 Hawke, NH s/o BAGLEY, Wm & MERRILL, Sarah; d 1852 Danville, NH

BAILEY, Anna S. b 1872 d/o BAILEY, Jos G. & GRIFFIN, Susan; d 24 Jul 1880 Danville, NH ae 8y

BAILEY, Jos G. b Industry, ME s/o BAILEY, James & FLETCHER, Rebecca; md GRIFFIN, Susan; d 12 Jan 1905 Danville, NH ae 82y 9m 8d

BAILEY, Jos P. md 28 May 1989 Danville, NH DONAHUE, Susan L.; md by Richard J. Rondeau (JP)

BAILEY, Louie Glenn b 16 Oct 1862 Danville, NH s/o BAILEY, Jos G. & GRIFFIN, Susan; md 23 Jul 1885 Danville, NH SEAVER, Augustus F.; d 07 Apr 1956 Danville, NH

BAILEY, Mary E. b 25 Dec 1881 Danville, NH d/o BAILEY, Rob't H. & CHALLIS, Ella I.

BAILEY, Nicholas Jos b 08 Nov 1989 Exeter, NH s/o BAILEY, Jos P. & DONAHUE, Susan L.

BAILEY, Rob't H. b 29 Aug 1879 Danville, NH s/o BAILEY, Rob't H. & CHALLIS, Ella I.

BAIRD, James Harold 3rd b 28 Jun 1976 Exeter, NH s/o BAIRD, James Harold 2nd

BAIRD, Kathleen Virginia b 16 Jan 1975 Exeter, NH d/o BAIRD, Harold J. & RALLI, Virginia M.

BAKER, James Roy md 22 May 1988 Danville, NH DOWNING, Allison; md by Richard J. Rondeau (JP)

BAKER, Jos F. b 1875; d 09 May 1936 Danville, NH ae 61y 3m 3d

BAKER, Manda b Newcastle, NH; md RUEE, John H.

BAKER, Wille A. b c1865 Canada s/o BAKER, Jos & ----, Mary; md 12 Mar 1887 Danville, NH MORRILL, Maude L.; md by Rev John A. Lowell

BAKER, MALE b 28 Jul 1887 Danville, NH s/o BAKER, Willie

BAKER (Cont.) A. & ----, Maude L. 1st Child in Family

BALL, Wm H. b MA; md 30 Dec 1969 Danville, NH BURNS, Ann Marie; md by Leona A. Sciaudone (JP)

BALUKUS, Rob't Arthur b 1936 Kingston, NH s/o BALUKUS, Michael A.; md 09 Oct 1954 Danville, NH YOUNG, Eliz Mae; md by Rev W. C. Chappell

BANKS, Jos Lewis b s/o BANKS, Oran L. & CHAFFEY, Elsie; d 31 Oct 1989 Danville, NH ae 74y

BANKS, Wm J. b s/o BANKS, Wm R. & CARTER, Caroline; d 19 Jun 1977 Danville, NH ae 36y

BANKS, Wm Richard b s/o BANKS, Bruce & SMITH, Josephine; d 19 Nov 1991 Danville, NH ae 73y

BANTIS, ---- b 29 Oct 1960 Danville, NH ?/o BANTIS, Aristides & ULAHOS, Evanthia

BARBEAU, Betty Jane b Danville, NH; md 05 Dec 1970 Danville, NH HERRICK, Richard Wesley

BARCH, David Brian b 24 Jan 1962 Danville, NH s/o BARCH, Jos Henry & MURPHY, Margaret M.

BARCH, James Andrew b 12 Jul 1965 Danville, NH s/o BARCH, Jos Henry & MURPHY, Margaret M.

BARCH, Jos Henry b Woburn, MA; md MURPHY, Margaret M.

BARCH, Mary Katherine b 27 Oct 1960 Danville, NH d/o BARCH, Jos Henry & MURPHY, Margaret M.

BARCH, Sheila Ann b 28 Jan 1963 Danville, NH d/o BARCH, Jos Henry & MURPHY, Margaret M.

BARCLAY, Geo Ingram md 14 Feb 1991 Danville, NH LASATER, Donna Marie; md by Rich E. Rondeau (JP)

BARHANYS, Jeannie M. md 22 Jun 1980 Danville, NH RANDALL, Wm P.; md by Rev Steven Kucharski (P)

BARLOW, Gail Frances b 1941 Fremont, NH d/o BARLOW, Edward; md 24 Oct 1948 Danville, NH MITCHELL, Rob't Carlton; md by Rev Wendall J. Irvine

BARNABY, Henry E. b 15 Jul 1919 Danville, NH s/o BARNABY, John & ROCELL, Candida

BARNARD, Abigail md 06 Dec 1770 Hawke, NH JONES, John; md by Rev John Page

BARNARD, Alice md 13 Nov 1785 Kingston FIFIELD, Sherborn

BARNARD, Alice M. b c1893 Amesbury, MA d /o BARNARD, George E. & JOHNSON, Carrie E.; md 28 Jun 1919 Amesbury, MA COLLINS, Chas P.; d 29 Jul 1978 Danville, NH; md by Rev F. G. Merrill

BARNARD, Esther b Hawke, NH; md 14 Jul 1768 Hawke, NH Ring, Issachar; md by Rev John Page

BARNARD, Mary b 17 Apr 1753 Kingston, NH d/o BARNARD, Stephen & COLLINS, Mary; md 09 Nov 1780 Hawke, NH JUDKINS, Henry; d 12 Mar 1839 Kingston, NH; md by Rev John Page

BARNARD, Pearl b Winhall, ?; md LANDMAN, Elbert Augustus DR.

BARNARD, Sarah b Hawke, NH; md 07 Nov 1794 Kingston, NH RANDALL, Daniel

BARSTOW, Almira md COLLINS, Levi B.

BARTLETT, Anne b 21 Sep 1763 Hawke, NH d/o BARTLETT, Sr. Geo & TUXBURY, Priscilla

BARTLETT, Clarissa b c1812; md 29 Dec 1832 Hawke, NH CLIFFORD, Daniel; d 16 Jan 1853 Danville, NH ae 41y

BARTLETT, David b 12 Dec 1775 Hawke, NH s/o BARTLETT, Geo Sr. & TUXBURY, Priscilla

BARTLETT, Debra Marie md 26 Jun 1988 Danville, NH ROMABO, Athony Paul Jr.; md by Carol A. McEachern (JP)

BARTLETT, Dorothy b 12 Dec 1777 Hawke, NH d/o BARTLETT, Geo Sr. & TUXBURY, Priscilla; md 12 Jun 1798 Kingston, NH FELLOWS, Simon

BARTLETT, Ellen Marir md 19 Oct 1991 Danville, NH LAVERY, Michael James; md by Richard J. Rondeau (JP)

BARTLETT, George Jr. b 12 May 1771 Hawke, NH s/o BARTLETT, Geo Sr. & TUXBURY, Priscilla

BARTLETT, Geo Sr. md 01 Jan 1762 Amesbury, MA TUXBURY, Priscilla

BARTLETT, Hannah b 07 Sep 1773 Hawke, NH d/o BARTLETT, Geo Sr. & TUXBURY, Priscilla

BARTLETT, Hosea B. b Kingston, NH; md 1848 Danville, NH HOOK, Permelia A.

BARTLETT, Isaac b 17 Mar 1767 Hawke, NH s/o BARTLETT, Geo Sr. & TUXBURY, Priscilla; md YOUNG, Joanna

BARTLETT, Josiah Gov. d 19 May 1795 Kingston, NH; bu Kingston, NH - Plains Cem.

BARTLETT, Lydia md SARGENT, Peter

BARTLETT, Mary b Brentwood, NH; md TEWKSBURY, Enos F.; d 13 Dec 1851 Danville, NH d ae 57y 2d

BARTLETT, Mary b d/o BARTLETT, Jos; md BARTLETT, Josiah Dr.; d 14 Jul 1789 Hawke, NH

BARTLETT, Moses b 18 Oct 1780 Hawke, NH s/o BARTLETT, Geo Sr. & TUXBURY, Priscilla

BARTLETT, Nancy b c1800; md FULLER, Chase; d 24 Feb 1871 Danville, NH ae 71y

BARTLETT, Palowna md SARGENT, Wm

BARTLETT, Priscilla b 10 Mar 1765 Hawke, NH d/o BARTLETT, Geo Sr. & TUXBURY, Priscilla; md 12 Jan 1804 Kingston, NH FLANDERS, Daniel

BARTLETT, Sally b c1805 Kingston, NH d/o BARTLETT, Isaac & YOUNG, Joanna; d 25 Apr 1898 Danville, NH ae 92y 10m

BARTLETT, Sam b Gilmanton, NH; md 20 Feb 1803 Kingston, NH CLEMENTS, Dorothy

BARTLETT, Sarah b 01 Apr 1786 Hawke, NH d/o BARTLETT, Geo Sr. & TUXBURY, Priscilla

BARTLETT, Sarah b c1724; md SAWYER, Gideon; d 03 Mar 1797 Hawke, NH ae 73y; bu Hawke, NH - Old Mtg Hse Cem.

BARTLETT, Susanna b c1798 Brentwood, NH; md 15 Jul 1819 Hawke, NH PHILBRICK, Jedediah; d 01 Aug 1875 Danville, NH ae 75y

BARTLETT, Susannah b 29 Apr 1769 Hawke, NH d/o BARTLETT, Geo Sr. & TUXBURY, Priscilla

BASFORD, Betsey b of Hawke, NH; md 07 Sep 1802 Hawke, NH HOYT, Wm Jr.

BASILE, David S. md 21 Jul 1990 Danville, NH PALMER, Muriel D.; md

BASILE (Cont.) by Rich J. Rondeau (JP)

BASSETT, Amos b Atkinson, NH; md c1855 Danville NH HUNT, Nancy W.

BASSETT, Fred K. md 26 Jan 1982 Danville, NH GORTON, Lori A.; md by Rev Everett E. Palmer

BASSETT, Jos P. b c1867 Fremont, NH s/o BASSETT, Geo W. & BEEDE, Sarah J.; md 11 Sep 1894 Manchester, NH KIMBALL, Eva M. md by Rev W. H. Morrison

BATCHELDER, Elisha md 15 Oct 1820 Kingston, NH PRESCOTT, Ruth

BATCHELDER, Elisha md ----, Theodate; d 25 Feb 1825 ae 88y; bu Danville, NH Old Mtg Hse Cem.

BATCHELDER, Hannah W. b c1816 Raymond, NH; md 1861 Danville, NH HUNT, Eben W.

BATCHELDER, Mary md 27 Feb 1783 Kingston, NH FRENCH, Jonathan

BATCHELDER, Mary E. b 1866 Warren, NH d/o BATCHELDER, Reuben; md 13 Dec 1909 Danville, NH BRADLEY, Arthur W.; md by Rev W. C. Chappell; 3rd mar

BATCHELDER, Susan Jane md 18 Sep 1971 Danville, NH EMILO, Gary V.; md by Rev Peter Noel Knost

BATTEN, Rob't B. b 1905 Meriden, CT s/o BATTEN, Thos; md 16 May 1937 Danville, NH HOGAN, Edna D.; md by Clarence M. Collins (JP)

BATTIS, Albert W. b s/o BATTIS, Geo & ----, Sarah; d 30 Nov 1990 Danville, NH ae 80y

BATTIS, Albert Wm b Amesbury, MA md DAY, Mildred Estelle

BATTIS, Brian Paul b 12 Sep 1960 Danville, NH s/o BATTIS, Edward Theodore & JEANS, Marilyn Sandra; d 12 Mar 1978 Danville, NH ae 17y

BATTIS, Edward Theodore b 07 Feb 1934 Danville, NH s/o BATTIS, Albert Wm & DAY, Mildred Estelle.; md 22 Nov 1957 Danville, NH JEANS, Marilyn Sandra

BATTIS, Joan Caroline b 1936 NH d/o BATTIS, Albert Wm & DAY, Mildred Estelle; md 18 Mar 1955 Danville, NH BURLEIGH, Rob't Donald; md by Rev Karl J. Hislop

BATTIS, Linda Jean b 19 Apr 1970 Haverhill, MA d/o BATTIS, Edward Theodore & JEANS, Marilyn Sandra

BATTIS, Mildred b d /o BATTIS, Theodore Day & WEST, Mary A.; d 08 Aug 1991 Danville, NH; ae 77y

BATTIS, Norma Jane b 1938 MA; md 03 Feb 1968 Danville, NH; BROUSSEAU, Wm A. md by Rev Douglas Abbott

BATTIS, Paul Wm b 1939 Amesbury, MA; md 01 May 1964 Danville, NH PITMAN, Bonnie Elaine; md by Rev Wm Sleamaker

BATTIS, Richard Day b 05 Apr 1940 Brentwood, NH s /o BATTIS, Albert Wm & DAY, Mildred Estelle.; md 27 Nov 1966 Danville, NH SALO, Theresa I.; md by Rev Douglas W. Abbott

BATTIS, Ronald Jon b 24 Oct 1954 Danville, NH s/o BATTIS, Albert Wm & DAY, Mildred Estelle; md 24 Oct 1986 Danville, NH ENDES, Ereka Veronica; md by Rev Everett E. Palmer

BATTIS, Sandra Jean b 09 Aug 1947 Exeter, NH d o BATTIS, Albert Wm & DAY, Mildred Estella; md 02 Aug 1963 Danville, NH BUZZELL, Chas E.; md by Rev F. B. Hadley

BATTIS, Wm Edward b 21 Mar 1959 Danville, NH s/o BATTIS, Edward Theodore & JEANS, Marilyn Sandra;

BATTLES, Elva Jeannette b 1909 Newton, NH d/o BATTLES, Wm G.; md 01 Aug 1931 Danville, NH KIMBALL, Merle Donald; md by Rev Sam B. Enman

BATTLES, James H. b 1914 Newton, NH s/o BATTLES, James H.; md 12 Aug 1937 Danville, NH GILES, Shirley C.; md by Rev W. C. Chappell

BATTON, Rob't B.b 1905 Mariden, NH s/o BATTON, Thos W.; md 16 May 1937 Danville NH DROUIN, Edna D.

BAYLISS, Michael Frances b 15 Feb 1988 Exeter, NH s/o BAYLISS, Frank B. & DOLE, Lori A.

BAYLISS, Sean Butzer b 06 Aug 1990 Exeter, NH s/o BAYLESS, Frank B. & DOYLE, Lori A.

BEALKO, Partricia Louise md 28 Sep 1977 Danville, NH WHITNEY, Chas Stephen Jr.; md by Bernard J. Raynowska (JP)

BEAM, Juanita Audrey md 01 Dec 1990 Danville, NH MARCHAND, Gerard Emile; md by Richard J. Rondeau (JP)

BEAN, Abigail S. (Nabby b 25 Jul 1782 Hawke, NH d/o BEAN, Jeremiah Jr. & SANBORN, Lydia; md 04 Jan 1808 Kingston, NH TOWLE, Nehemiah; d 13 Jan 1864 Danville, NH ae 81y

BEAN, Benjamin md 29 Sep 1779 Hawke, NH SLEEPER, Mary; md by Rev John Page

BEAN, Christopher David b 07 Apr 1977 Stoneham, MA s/o BEAN, David C. & BOYSON, Brenda Lee

BEAN, Clarissa -d 18 Aug 1863 Danville, NH ae 37y

BEAN, David Wm md 17 Aug 1991 Danville, NH HINCLIFFE, Patricia H.; md by Richard J. Rondeau (JP)

BEAN, Eliz b 31 Oct 1789 Hawke, NH d/o BEAN, Israel & SANBORN, Lydia

BEAN, Ezra Sanborn b 16 Oct 1801 Hawke, NH s/o BEAN, Jeremiah Jr. & SANBORN, Lydia

BEAN, Gilman b 14 Sep 1794 Hawke, NH s/o BEAN, Jeremiah Jr. & SANBORN, Lydia; md 09 Nov 1820 Hamnpton, NH FLANDERS, Jane E.; d 06 Nov 1840 Danville, NH ae 47y

BEAN, Hepzibah b c1764 Laconia, NH; md EASTMAN, Edward Jr.; d 26 Feb 1857 Danville, NH ae 83y

BEAN, Huldah b 19 Jun 1778 Brentwood, NH d/o BEAN, Jeremiah Jr. & SANBORN, Lydia; md 06 Apr 1796 Kingston, NH TUCKER, Benjamin

BEAN, James b 03 May 1798 Hawke, NH s/o BEAN, Jeremiah Jr. & SANBORN, Lydia

BEAN, James H. b 07 Dec 1864 Danville, NH s/o BEAN, Amos & ----, Druscilla J.

BEAN, Jeremiah b c1825 s/o BEAN, Gilman; d 09 Sep 1847 Danville, NH

BEAN, Jeremiah b 02 Mar 1785 Hawke, NH s/o BEAN, Jeremiah Jr. & SANBORN, Lydia

BEAN, Jeremiah Jr. b s/o BEAN, Jeremiah; md 18 Mar 1778 Hawke, NH SANBORN, Lydia

BEAN, John E. b c1838 Eaton, ?; md 22 Jun 1867 Danville, NH CRAM, Mary

BEAN, Justus b 28 Jan 1830 Hawke, NH s/o BEAN, Ezra S. & HOYT, Betsey K.

BEAN, Kezia b Hawke, NH; md 25 Sep 1794 Kingston, NH Sleeper, Henry

BEAN, Levi b Candia, NH; md 09 Aug 1781 Hawke, NH BUSWELL, Eliz; md by Rev John Page

BEAN, Lydia b 10 Sep 1780 Brentwood, NH d/o BEAN, Jeremiah Jr. & SANBORN, Lydia; md Apr 1799 Hawke, NH SANBORN, Ebenezer

BEAN, Mehitable b Hawke, NH; md 08 Nov 1764 JONES, Ezra; md by Rev John Page

BEAN, Nathan b Candia, NH; md 09 Nov 1779 Hawke, NH BUSWELL, Hannah; md by Rev John Page

BEAN, Nathaniel b 10 Jun 1787 Hawke, NH s/o BEAN, Jeremiah Jr & SANBORN, Lydia; md 17 May 1781 Hawke, NH SLEEPER, Benjamin; md by Rev John Page

BEAN, Samuel md 12 Dec 1769 Hawke, NH WELLS, Dorothy; md by Rev John Page

BEAN, Sarah b of Poplin, NH; md 28 Jun 1781 Hawke, NH BROWN, Nathan; md by Rev John Page

BEAN, Soloman d 1823 Hawke, NH ae 27y

BEATON, Patricia I. md 23 Nov 1984 Danville, NH McKAY, Daniel W.; md by Richard J. Rondeau (JP)

BEATTIE, Mary b E. Dunham, Canada d/o BEATTIE. Wm; md 28 Jun 1864 Danville NH SARGENT, John H.; d 20 Feb 1908 Danville NH ae 62y 8m 19d

BEAUCHESNE, Emile Jos b s/o BEAUCHESNE, Wilfred & BANCOURT, Maria; d 11 Oct 1986 Danville, NH; d ae 61y

BEAUDOIN, Jos Andrew b s/o BEAUDOIN, Andrew & OBEY, Mildred; d 24 Nov 1980 Danville, NH; d ae 70y

BEAULIEN, Emedie b 1908 Fremont, NH ?/o BEAULIEN, Aime; md 17 Apr 1929 Newton, NH ANDERSON, Pearl; md by Henry L. Burbeck (JP)

BEAULIEU, Omer Ernest b s/o BEAULIEU, Cyprien J. & VALLIERE, Mary; d 22 Sep 1982 Danville, NH; d ae 88Y

BEAULIEU, Paul R. md 12 May 1984 Danville, NH CARIGNAN, Lorraine M.; md by Rob't J. Kemmery (P)

BECHWITH, Yvette M. md 20 Dec 1991 Danville, NH FEOLE, Richard E.; md by Richard J. Rondeau (JP)

BECKWITH, Lisa Renee b 07 Aug 1987 Derry, NH d/o BECKWITH, Leslie F. & DOBIJA, Kathleen

BEDDE, Susan L. b c1837 Fremont, NH d/o BEEDE, Daniel & FOLSOM, Ann E.; md PHILBRICK, ---- ; d 15 Feb 1919 Danville, NH ae 82y 8m 3d

BEDEL, Francine H. b France; md BYRON, Wm H.

BEECH, Marjorie Ann b 1927 MA d/o BEECH, Thos H.; md 24 Dec 1950 Danville, NH MANGANARO, Jos James; md by Agnes H. Collins (JP)

BEEDE, Arnold H. b 1910 Hampstead, NH s/o BEEDE, Henry N.; md 23 Nov 1935 Danville, NH NEWELL, Alice E. M. md by Rev Frank Dunn

BEEDE, Christine Elaine b 1935 Epping, NH d/o BEEDE, Nelson W. md 29 Jan 1954 Danville, NH GOLDTHWAITE, Richard E.; md by Rev Rob't S. Walker

BELALKO, Patricia Louis md 28 Sep 1977 Danville, NH WHITNEY, Chas Stephen Jr.

BELL, Cora A. b c1867 Amesbury, MA; md 31 Oct 1885 Danville, NH WELCH, David B.

BELL, Jane b d/o BELL, Henry & ----, Charlotte; md HARRIS, ----; d 08 Apr 1985 Danville, NH; d ae 84y

BELLACOME, Gerlando b Italy; s/o BELLACOME, Clemmente; md 04 Jul 1955 Danville, NH AVERY, Beryl; md by Rev W. C. Chappell

BELLIVEAU, David James b 01 Sep 1988 Haverhill, MA s/o BELLIVEAU, Dennis G. & MEEK, Linda J.

BELLIVEAU, Valerie Ellen b 23 Sep 1986 Malden, MA d/o BELLIVEAU, Dennis G. & MEEK, Linda J.

BELMONT, Dorothy A. d 18 May 1977 Danville, NH ae 76y

BELYES, Wm Francis b 1919 MA s/o BELYES, John H.; md 14 Oct 1950 Plaistow, NH LYMAN, Patricia Frances; md by Rev W. C. Chappell

BENNETT, Eliz Dawn md 31 Mar 1988 Danville, NH BIGGER, Mark Daniel; md by Burgess A. Robinson (JP)

BENNETT, Irene M. md 15 Sep 1984 Danville, NH SANDERS, Rob't J. Jr.; md by Rev James C. Pirie

BENNETT, Rob't Clay IV md 20 Aug 1988 Danville, NH OUELLETTE, Dawn Marie; md by Rev Everett E. Palmer

BENNETT, Rob't W. b 1944 Exeter, NH; md 21 Aug 1965 Danville, NH ABDO, Joann; md by Rev Ivan Smith Jr.

BERBINE, Veknea CHristine b 04 Sep 1920 Danville, NH d/o BERBINE, Clarence & DAY, Etta; 3rd child in family

BERGERON, Paul Richard md 12 May 1990 Danville, NH WEST, Chervl A.; md by Arthur P. Fortin (JP)

BERNABLE, ---- b 24 Aug 1916 Danville, NH s/o BERNABLE, John & ROSELLI, Carden

BERNABY, Bruce Henry b 15 Jul 1953 Danville, NH s/o BERNEBY, Frank Alfred Sr. & FROTTEN, Mareta Hardy

BERNABY, Carl Ann b 24 Jan 1946 Danville, NH s/o BERNABY, Frank Alfred Sr & FROTTEN, Mareta Hardy; md 18 Oct 1969 Danville, NH JOHNSON, John A. md by Carleton Eldridge (JP)

BERNABY, Frank Alfred Jr. b 17 Mar 1941 Danville, NH s/o BERNABY, Frank Alfred Sr. & FROTTEN, Mareta Hardy

BERNABY, Frank Alfred Sr. b Long Island, NY s/o BERNABY, John & ROSSELLI, Julienne; md FROTTEN, Mareta Hardy; d 08 Nov 1967 Danville, NH

BERNABY, Henry b 1919 Danville, NH s/o BERNABY, John & ROSSELL, Candida; d 08 Oct 1925 Danville, NH

BERNABY, John b ITALY; d 03 Jun 1958 Danville, NH ae 87y

BERNABY, John Leo b s/o BERNABY, John H. & CRUCIANI, Mary; d 12 Dec 1987 Danville, NH d ae 47y

BERNABY, Judith Marie b 12 Apr 1942 Danville, NH d/o BERNABY, Frank Alfred Sr. & FRITTEN, Mareta Hardy; md 10 Jun 1971 Danville, NH SELPH,

BERNABY (Cont.) Batrow B.; md by Leo R. Dupuis (JP)

BERNABY, Kathleen b 09 Jun 1947 Exeter, NH d/o BERNABY, Frank Alfred Sr. & FROTTEN, Mareta Hardy; md 16 Sep 1967 Danville, NH TRIJILLO, Philip J.; md by Edward J. Massa (P)

BERNABY, Peter Michael b 07 Dec 1943 Danville, NH s/o BERNABY, Frank Alfred Sr. & FROTTEN, Mareta Hardy

BERNABY, Richard John b 02 Dec 1944 Danville, NH s/o BERNABY, Frank Alfred Sr. & FROTTEN, Mareta Hardy

BERNABY, Rob't Jos b 05 Jun 1952 Danville, NH s/o BERNABY, Frank Alfred Sr. & FROTTEN, Mareta Hardy

BERNABY, Wm L. b s/o BERNABY, John & ROSELLI, Cadida; d 28 Sep 1980 Danville, NH ae 69y

BERRY, Debra Jean md 22 Feb 1990 Danville, NH OLCOTT, Wm Thos Jr.; md by Rev Everett E. Palmer

BERUBE, Michael A. md 24 Mar 1985 Danville, NH MOORE, Lorraine M.; md by Rev Dennis G. Campbell

BEUCLER, Alyssa Faith b 26 Apr 1990 Newburyport, MA d/o BEUCLER, Philip J. & MACDONALD, Ellen

BEZANSON, Daniel S. md 12 Jun 1971 Danville, NH MERRICK, Leona M.; md by Rev Cathleen R. Narowitz

BICKFORD, Eileen Eliz b 1927 MA d/o BICKFORD, Harry D.; md 07 Nov 1952 Danville, NH RIFE, Neal Dwayne; md by Rev W. C. Chappell

BICKFORD, Eliza b Kingston, NH; md 15 Oct 1832 Hawke, NH PAGE, Thos

BICKFORD, Ellen W. b Boston, MA d/o WILEY, Frank & CRYER, Eliz; d 07 Aug 1959 Danville, NH

BICKFORD, Helen Delores b 1934 MA d/o BICKFORD, Harry D.; md 26 Feb 1955 Danville, NH LOVLIEN, Lyman Wm; md by Rev J. T. Sullivan

BIELECKI, Kimberly Rose b 08 Mar 1979 Stoneham, MA d/o BIELECKI, Paul M. & AMOROSO, Phyliss A.

BIEZHERTZ, Florentine B b 1879 d/o BIEZHERTZ, Karl & ALBRIGHT, ----; d 24 Mar 1956 Danville, NH

BIGGER, Mark Daniel md 31 Mar 1988 Danville, NH BENNETT, Eliz Dawn; md by Burgess A. Robinson (JP)

BIGGER, Michelle Leigh b 24 May 1988 Haverhill, MA d/o BIGGER, Mark D. & BENNETT, Eliz D.

BILLBROUGH, Thos Floyd b 29 Oct 1987 Exeter, NH s/o BILLBROUGH, Thos & COTE, Dorothy A.

BILLBROUGH, Thos Floyd md 10 Dec 1988 Danville, NH WILSON, Dorothy Ann; md by L. Paul Blais Jr. (JP)

BILO, Jos A. 3rd md 09 Apr 1983 Danville, NH SENTER, Deborah J.; md by Rev Everett E. Palmer

BILO, Laureen A. md 14 Jul 1979 Danville, NH BLANEY, Alan R.; md by Rev Wm Ryans

BILO, Vickie L. md 21 Sep 1985 Danville, NH BUTLER, Daniel B.; md by Rev Florent R. Bilodeau

BILODEAU, Carole A. md 17 Oct 1983 Danville, NH FERRIERO, Louis C.; md by Humbert M. Oliviera (P)

BILOTTA, Anne M. md 10 Jun 1983 Danville, NH BRUNER, Thos H.; md by Rev Thos Bresnahan

BLACKWELL, Wm b England; d 12 Sep 1891 Danville, NH; Occ Farmer

BLAIR, Thos Leo md 31 Dec 1991 Danville, NH CONNERS, June Ann; md by Richard J. Rondeau (JP)

BLAIS, Wm Guy md 30 Sep 1989 Danville, NH DAVEY, Heidi Lee; md by Rich J. Rondeau (JP)

BLAISDELL, Almira b 28 Oct 1821 Hawke, NH d/o BLAISDELL, John Jr. & DOW, Lydia

BLAISDELL, Eliz b c1811 E Kingston, NH; md HUNTINGTON, Wm; d 29 Aug 1880 Danville, NH ae 69y

BLAISDELL, Henry b Kingston, NH; md 04 Mar 1772 Hawke, NH DOLLIFFE, Sarah; md by Rev John Page

BLAISDELL, Jennifer Lee b 16 Jan 1979 Haverhill, MA d/o BLAISDELL, Stephen M. & RICHARDSON, Linda J.

BLAISDELL, John Jr. b s/o BLAISDELL, John Sr.; md 09 Apr 1816 Hampton, NH DOW, Lydia

BLAISDELL, John L. b 11 Feb 1834 Hawke, NH s/o BLAISDELL, John Jr. & DOW, Lydia

BLAISDELL, Josiah T. b 18 May 1827 Hawke, NH s/o BLAISDELL, John Jr. & DOW, Lydia; md 1853 Danville,

BLAISDELL (Cont.) NH KELLEY, Mary C.

BLAISDELL, Laura C. b 1866 d/o BLAISDELL, Samuel & GEORGE, Annette; d 21 Feb 1868 Danville, NH age 2 yr & 1 mo

BLAISDELL, Lydia Mrs b c1716; md BLAISDELL, Thos; d 12 Oct 1843 Danville, NH age 27 yr

BLAISDELL, Samuel A. b 1825 Hawke, NH s/o BLAISDELL, John Jr. & DOW, Lydia; md 1859 Danville, NH GEORGE, Laura Annette

BLAISDELL, Sarah Mae b c1857 d/o BLAISDELL, Josiah T. & KELLEY, Mary C.; d 09 Oct 1857 Danville, NH ae 10 mo

BLAISDELL, Willard H. b c1864 s/o BLAISDELL, Samuel & GEORGE, Annette; d 11 Jan 1868 Danville, NH ae 3y 5m

BLAKE, Carrie A. b 11 Dec 1866 Danville, NH d/o BLAKE, Edmund R. & PEARSON, Hannah A.

BLAKE, Deborah b c1708 Hampton, NH; md TUCKER, Ebenezer; d 26 Jan 1782 Hawke, NH ae 74y of smallpox

BLAKE, Dorothy b 10 Oct 1793 Hawke, NH d/o BLAKE, Hezekiah & DIMOND, Hannah md 10 Dec 1812 Hawke; NH CHALLIS, Jos; d 08 Apr 1882 Danville, NH

BLAKE, Edmund R. b 17 Jun 1838 Danville, NH s/o BLAKE, Jos W. & GOULD, Eliz; md 1861 Danville, NH FLETCHER, Caroline B.; d 26 Jan 1920 ae 81y 7m 9d

BLAKE, Elijah b 09 Oct 1755 Danville, NH s/o BLAKE, Jonathan Sr. & SANBORN, Mary; md ----, Sarah

BLAKE, Eliz b 17 Apr 1789 Hawke, NH d/o BLAKE, Hezekiah & DIMOND, Hannah; md 06 Sep 1808 Kingston, NH WILLIAMS, Jos Jr.

BLAKE, Hannah b 02 Jan 1787 Hawke, NH d/o BLAKE, Hezekiah & DIMOND, Hannah; DURGIN, Clark

BLAKE, Hannah R. b 01 Mar 1845 Danville, NH d/o BLAKE, Jos W. & GOULD, Eliz; md 09 Feb 1866 Danville, NH HUNKINS, E. L.

BLAKE, Henry Morrill b 13 Mar 1768 Danville, NH s/o BLAKE, Jonathan

BLAKE (Cont.) Sr. & SANBORN, Mary; md 10 Apr 1794 Danville, NH CHELLIS, Hannah

BLAKE, Hezekiah b 09 May 1751 Hawke, NH s/o BLAKE, Jonathan Sr. & SANBORN, Mary; md 31 Oct 1776 Hampstead, NH DIMOND, Hannah; d 19 May 1821 Hawke, NH ae 70y

BLAKE, Hezekiah b 1746 Kingston, NH s/o BLAKE, Jonathan Sr. & SANBORN, Mary; d young

BLAKE, Irene b 27 Jan 1802 Hawke, NH d/o BLAKE, Stevens & GEORGE, Hannah; md 10 Mar 1827 Hawke, NH CURRIER, Thomnas Jr.

BLAKE, Israel b 19 Apr 1782 Hawke, NH s/o BLAKE, Hezekiah & DIMOND, Hannah; md May 1809 Kingston, NH HUNT, Miriam; d 1845

BLAKE, Jonathan Sr. b 10 Apr 1715 Hampton, NH s/o BLAKE, Moses Sr. & SMITH, Abigail md 02 Jun 1736 Hawke, NH SANBORN, Mary; d 15 Mar 1794 Hawke, NH ae 78y

BLAKE, Jonathan Jr. b 16 Oct 1753 Hawke, NH s/o BLAKE, Jonathan Sr. & SANBORN, Mary; md 18 Feb 1777 Kingston, NH ROBINSON, Lucy

BLAKE, Jos Wm b 10 Jan 1808 Hawke, NH s/o BLAKE, Stevens & GEORGE, Hannah; md GOULD, Eliz C.; d 25 Aug 1885 Danville, NH

BLAKE, Mary b 16 Jul 1744 Hawke, NH d/o BLAKE, Jonathan Sr. & SANBORN, Mary; md 23 Nov 1765 Hawke, NH EASTMAN, Samuel; md by Rev John Page

BLAKE, Mary (Polly) b 02 Jan 1779 Hawke, NH d/o BLAKE, Hezekiah & DIMOND, Hannah; md 24 Dec 1795 Kingston, NH COLLINS, Samuel; d 28 Jun 1851 Danville, NH; bu Danville, NH Center Cem.

BLAKE, Mary E. b Sep 1871 Danville, NH d/o BLAKE, Edmund R. & PEARSON, Hannah A.; d 25 Jun 1872 Danville, NH

BLAKE, Mary S. b 17 Jan 1811 Hawke, NH d/o BLAKE, Stevens & GEORGE, Hannah; md 26 Feb 1833 Hawke, NH QUIMBY, Aaron Col; d 03 Jul 1878 Danville, NH ae 67y

BLAKE, Mehitable b 06 Oct 1785

BLAKE (Cont.) Hawke, NH d/o BLAKE, Hezekiah & DIMOND, Hannah; md 01 May 1806 Kingston, NH MARTIN, Jonathan

BLAKE, Sanborn b 11 Mar 1764 Hawke, NH s/o BLAKE, Jonathan & SANBORN, Mary

BLAKE, Sarah b 05 May 1761 Hawke, NH d/o BLAKE, Jonathan & SANBORN, Mary; md Apr 1804 Kingston, NH Williams, Jos (Capt)

BLAKE, Sarah b 26 Jun 1791 Hawke, NH d/o BLAKE, Hezekiah & DIMOND, Hannah; md 24 Sep 1808 Hawke, NH GRIFFIN, Daniel; d 14 Apr 1875 Kingston, NH ae 83y

BLAKE, Sarah md ELKINS, Ephraim

BLAKE, Sarah b 1748 Kingston, NH; d/o BLAKE, Jonathan & SANBORN, Mary; d young

BLAKE, Sarah E. b 29 Apr 1842 Danville, NH d/o BLAKE, Jos W. & GOULD, Eliz; md 26 Mar 1864 Danville, NH GRIFFIN, Chas W.

BLAKE, Sophia b 31 Jul 1804 Hawke, NH d/o BLAKE, Stevens & GEORGE, Hannah; md 24 Nov 1825 Hawke, NH DIMOND, Obadiah (Capt); d 29 Mar 1883 Danville, NH

BLAKE, Sophia b 13 Oct 1802 Hawke, NH d/o BLAKE, Hezekiah & DIMOND, Hannah; md DIMOND. Obidiah; d 29 Mar 1883 Danville, NH

BLAKE, Stevens b 12 May 1777 Hawke, NH s/o BLAKE, Hezekiah & DIMOND, Hannah; md 21 Apr 1800 Kingston, NH GEORGE, Hannah; d 02 Jul 1851 Danville, NH ae 74y

BLAKE, Timothy Sr. b 14 Jul 1741 Hawke, NH s/o BLAKE, Jonathan & SANBORN, Mary; md 22 Dec 1763 Hawke, NH MORRILL, Susanna; d 25 Jul 1821 Strafford, NH

BLAKE, Tristram Sanborn b 11 Mar 1764 Hawke, NH s/o BLAKE, Jonathan & SANBORN, Mary; md HOBB, Marion

BLAND, Jared Adam b 17 Apr 1984 Lawrence, MA s/o BLAND, Craig D. & KOPRIVA, Maureen E.

BLANEY, Alan R. md 14 Jul 1979 Danville, NH BILO, Laureen A.; md by Rev Wm Ryans

BLANEY, Charlotte Victoria md 07 Dec 1974 Danville, NH RILEY, Michael Jos; md by Michael L. Griffin (P)

BLANEY, Michael Alan b 05 Mar 1990 Exeter, NH s/o BLANEY, Alan R. & BILO, Laureen A. (Twin)

BLANEY, Wm Tucker b 05 Mar 1990 Exeter, NH s/o BLANEY, Alan R. & BILO, Laureen A.(Twin)

BLEAKNEY, Luke Monroe b 1881 New Brunswick, CN; md 20 Aug 1961 Danville, NH COLLINS, Mildred Gertrude; md by Rev John Wood Jr.

BLECH, Emily Bouchelle b 12 Aug 1991 Exeter, NH d/o BLECH, Brandon M. & HUBERS, Lynne A.

BOGANNAN, Alison Lee b 27 Mar 1986 Exeter, NH d/o BOGANNAN, David S. & PEVERLEY, Susanne L.

BOHNE, Michael b 19 Jan 1978 Lawrence, MA s/o BOHNE, Geo H. Jr. & POSPICHAL, JoAnn; d 19 Jan 1978 Lawrence, MA ae 3 hours

BOHNE, Zachery John b 17 Mar 1988 Exeter, NH s/o BOHNE, Geo H. Jr. & POSPICHAL, JoAnn

BOLDUC, Bruce md 09 Sep 1991 Danville, NH PROCTOR, Linda K.; md by John H. Lampray (JP)

BOLIS, Vincent b 1915 Lawrence, MA s/o BOLIS, Michael; md 15 May 1936 Danville, NH MASCHETTO, Nellie; md by Clarence M. Collins (JP)

BONAH, Blanche b Nashua, NH; md DUSTON, Oscar

BONCZKIEW, Ronald S. md 25 Oct 1975 Danville, NH GRANA, Pilar; md by Rev Ronald E. Fortin

BONCZLIEWICZ, Ron S. md 25 May 1991 Danville, NH DIMOND, Lori Ann; md by Rev Rob't F. Dobson

BOND, Hannah C. b W.Newfield, ?; d/o BOND, Thos & SUPTINE, Peavy; md STRAFFORD, ---- ; d 28 Sep 1913 Danville, NH ae 90y 11m 26d

BONNING, Gertrude F. b MA; d/o BONNING, Jos N. & DOLAN, Margaret; d Danville, NH 18 Mar 1957 ae 80y

BOOKER, Eliz B. b 1909 N Hampton, NH d/o BOOKER, Asa A. & BROWN, Emma md 22 Oct 1937 Danville, NH Collins, Arthur A. d 13 Mar 1974 Danville, NH md by Rev W. C.

BOOKER (Cont.) Chappell

BOOTHBY, Rob't C. b 1921 Westbrook, ME s/o BOOTHBY, Everett C.; md 07 Nov 1942 Danville, NH HEWEY, Cora M.; md by Rev W. C. Chappell

BORDEN, Phyllis b 1913 Dorchester, MA d/o BORDEN, Wm C.; md 12 Dec 1934 Danville, NH CATALFAMO, Philip; md by Clarence M. Collins (JP)

BORGES, Frank Michael md 21 Jun 1975 Danville, NH HILDRETH, Teri Lynn; md by Joan M. Pichowicz (JP)

BORGES, Michael F. md 10 Mar 1973 Danville, NH MILLS, Jeanette M.; md by John H. Roby (P)

BORGES, Sidney Francis md 28 Sep 1974 Danville, NH OAK, Catherine Marie; md by Rev Cathleen N. Narowitz

BOSSHARDT, Kyle Paul b 02 Jan 1988 Derry, NH s/o BOSSHARDT, Richard A. & MARTELL, Therese C.;

BOSSHARDT, Tyler Martel b 21 Aug 1990 Derry, NH s/o BOSSHARDT, Richard A. & MARTEL, Therese C.

BOSSIO, Donald md 12 Feb 1991 Danville, NH PHILLIPS, Eliz Ann; md by Richard E. Rondeau (JP)

BOTHWICK, Harold Martin b 1924 Manchester, NH s/o BOTHWICK, Wm Henry; md 18 Feb 1947 Plaistow, NH KIRWIN, Helen Ann; md by Rev James W. Gilrain

BOTHWICK, Jos Philip b 27 Apr 1950 Danville, NH s/o BOTHWICK, Harold Martin & KIRWIN, Helen Ann

BOTHWICK, Joyce Ann b 24 Mar 1947 Danville, NH d/o BOTHWICK, Harold Martin & KIRWIN, Lelen Ann

BOTTAI, Allan Michael md 27 Aug 1988 Danville, NH ROMANO, Carolanne; md by Richard J. Rondeau (JP)

BOTTAI, Patti A. md 14 Dec 1985 Danville, NH WEINHOLD, Byron W.; md by Richard Rondeau (JP)

BOTTINO, James md 04 Apr 1987 Danville, NH TABELING, Mary Ann; md by Richard J. Rondeau (JP)

BOUCHARD, Curtis b 1934 Haverhill, Ma; md 08 Jun 1964 Danville, NH St. PIERRE, Leslye G.; md by Edward R. Lamb (JP)

BOUCHARD, Pamela b 08 Sep 1954 Danville, NH d/o BOUCHARD, Jos

BOUCHARD (Cont.) E. & SMITH, Beverly May

BOUCHARD, Pearl b 1932 Brentwood, NH d/o BOUCHARD, Hector Jos; md 27 Apr 1947 Danville, NH ROBINSON, Morris R.; md by Rev W. C. Chappell

BOUCHER, Remi Jos b 26 Feb 1980 Manchester, NH s/o BOUCHER, Remi L. & AUGER, Pierrette M.

BOUCHER, ---- b 02 Jul 1908 Danville, NH s/o BOUCHER, Ernest & MIXEN, Maggie; d 02 Jul 1908 Danville NH

BOULANGER, Laurie Ann md 03 Nov 1978 Danville, NH MITCHELL, Rob't Dean; md by Rev Wm Ryans

BOWLEY, Annie E. b Brentwood, NH; md CHICKERING, Wm H.

BOWLEY, Daniel Oscar b 03 Feb 1986 Exeter, NH s/o BOWLEY, Donald F. Jr. & TETREAULT, Deborah L.

BOWLEY, Donald F. md 05 Oct 1980 Danville, NH TETREAULT, Deborah L.; md by Retenah V. Pietrowski (JP)

BOWLEY, Donna F. md 10 Feb 1980 Danville, NH BURLEIGH, Kenneth D.; md by Rev Wm Ryans

BOWLEY, Juanita Gladys b 1940 Merrimac, MA d/o BOWLEY, Eben A.; md 27 Jul 1958 Danville, NH DUTTON, Albert Jr.; md by Agnes H. Collins (JP)

BOWLEY, Leonard Paul b 1941 NH; md 12 Aug 1961 Danville, NH HARPER, Diane Marie; md by Rev Wendall J. Irvine

BOWLEY, Lottie M. b Plaistow, NH; md LIBBY, Thos J.

BOWLEY, Oscar b 05 Oct 1963 Danville, NH s/o BOWLEY, Donald F. & SMART, Joanne E.

BOWLEY, Shelia M. md 29 Jan 1972 Danville, NH PURINGTON, Gregory W.; md by Rev Rob't W. Lewis

BOWMAN, Cathreen Anne b d/o BOWMAN, Chas E. & GRIMES, Anne C.; d 13 Oct 1973 Danville, NH

BOYLE, Ann Eliz md 26 Jun 1976 Danville, NH HOLDER, Jason Daniels; md by Rob't J. Boyle (P)

BOYNTON, Margaret A. b c1902 d/o BOYNTON, Wm A. & SOUTHWORTH, Sophie; md SALTMASRSH, ---- ;d 07 Apr

BOYNTON (Cont.) 1970 Danville, NH ae 68y

BRACKETT, Abby b Hawke , NH; md 03 Jan 1881 Danville, NH GRIFFIN, David; 2nd mar

BRACKETT, Abigail b Hawke, NH; md 02 Jul 1832 Kingston, NH GEORGE, Darius; d 26 Oct 1882 Danville, NH; m 2nd to GRIFFIN

BRACKETT, David Bruce md 11 Oct 1978 Danville, NH CONWAY, Debra Jean; md by Clara B. Shaw (JP)

BRACKETT, Hanover D. b c1787; md GOODWIN, Dorothy; d 11 Mar 1871 Danville, NH; ae 84y

BRACKETT, Mabel b 10 Aug 1873 Danville, NH d/o BRACKETT, Darius G. & EATON, Eliz H.

BRACKETT, Milan W. b Feb 1875 Danville, NH s/o BRACKETT, Darius G. & EATON, Eliz H.

BRACKETT, Zipporah b d/o BRACKETT, Anthony; md 19 Apr 1698 TOWLE, Caleb

BRADEEN, Estelle May b d/o BRADEEN, Wm & MORSE, Mabel; md DURGIN, ---- ; d 04 Jun 1977 Danville ae 82y

BRADLEY, A. E. b 16 Apr 1848 Danville, NH ?/o BRADLEY, John C. & EMERSON, Mary

BRADLEY, Arthur W. b 1879 Great Falls, NH s/o BRADLEY, Nathan'l; md 13 Dec 1909 Danville, NH PEARSONS, Mary E. md by Rev W. C. Chappell; 2nd mar

BRADLEY, Bertha E. b c1870 Tuftonborough, NH d/o BRADLEY, Nathaniel & HIGGINS, Annie; md 11 Apr 1909 Danville, NH SMITH, Harry; d 01 Dec 1933 Danville, NH; md by Rev W. C. Chappell; 3rd mar

BRADLEY, Chas b 1863 Danville, NH s/o BRADLEY, John C. & EMERSON, Mary

BRADLEY, Eliz b 19 Jul 1852 Danville, NH d/o BRADLEY, John C. & EMERSON, Mary; d 21 Feb 1855 Danville, NH age 3

BRADLEY, Isaac b 01 Mar 1809 Hawke, NH s/o BRADLEY, Jos & ----, Patty

BRADLEY, Issac b 06 Feb 1789 Hawke, NH s/o BRADLEY, Jos & ----, Mehitable

BRADLEY, Issac b Haverhill, MA; md 20 Nov 1838 Danville, NH CURRIER, Caroline

BRADLEY, John C. b 07 Jun 1820 Hawke, NH s/o BRADLEY, Nathaniel & CARTER, Eunice P.; d 10 Nov 1892 Danville, NH; Occupatiom Merchant

BRADLEY, Jos b 31 Oct 1806 Hawke, NH s/o BRADLEY, Jos & ----, Patty

BRADLEY, Luther d 16 May 1898 Danville, NH

BRADLEY, Mary b 19 Jul 1852 Danville, NH d/o BRADLEY, John C. & EMERSON, Mary; md HUNT, Page A.

BRADLEY, Mehitable F. b 14 Jan 1819 Hawke, NH d/o BRADLEY, Nathaniel & CARTER, Eunice P.; md 06 Dec 1837 Raymond, NH DIMOND, Oren; d 08 Jul 1900 Danville, NH

BRADLEY, Nanny b of Chester, NH; md 21 Sep 1779 Hawke, NH COLBY, Jethro; md by Rev John Page

BRADLEY, Nathaniel b 01 Jun 1794 Hawke, NH s/o BRADLEY, Jos & ----, Patty; md CARTER, Eunice P. d 17 Dec 1853 Danville, NH

BRADLEY, Nathaniel Jr. b c1833 Wakefield, ? s/o BRADLEY, Nathaniel Sr. & SEWARD, Joanna; d 13 Jul 1913 Danville, NH ae 80y 8m 16d

BRADLEY, Polly b 10 Jul 1803 Hawke, NH d/o BRADLEY, Jos & ---- , Patty

BRADLEY, Polly b 04 Aug 1792 Hawke, NH d/o BRADLEY, Jos & ---- , Mehitable

BRADY, Jacqueline A. md 06 Sep 1986 Danville, NH SKIDMORE, Francis A.; md by David T. Ingerson (JP)

BRAGG, Martha A. b c1846 Hampstead, NH; md 18 Mar 1870 Danville, NH GOODWIN, Henry K.

BRAGG, Shawn Matthew b 13 Dec 1979 Haverhill, MA s/o BRAGG, Walter E. & BIRD, Susanne N.

BRAINARD, Ruth Ellen b 1933 Walpole, MA d/o BRAINARD, Benj R.; md 26 Jun 1945 Danville, NH LES-

BRAINARD (Cont.) SARD, Oliver Wendell; md by Rev Norman R. Farnum Jr.

BRAULT, Rex J. md 14 Feb 1984 Danville, NH GERMAN, Priscilla S.; md by Richard J. Rondeau (JP)

BRAZEAL, Eliz b of Raymond, NH; md 30 Oct 1766 Hawke, NH GORDON, Daniel; md by Rev John Page

BREEN, Deborah Kay b 28 Aug 1954 Danville, NH d/o BREEN, Rob't Morris & THIBEAULT, Norma Irene

BREEN, Norma Irene b 1939 NH d/o THEAULT, Wilfred; md 22 Aug 1959 Danville, NH KEZER, James Chamberlin; md by Rev Albert Cornwall

BREEN, Rob't Morris b 1938 MA s/o BREEN, Arthur T.; md 23 Jan 1954 Danville, NH THIBEAULT, Norma Irene; md by Agnes H. Collins (JP)

BRENNAN, Theodore b 1911 Manchester, NH s/o BRENNAN, James; md 14 Nov 1931 Danville, NH ELLIOTT, Edna; md by Rev Harold C. Ross

BRESNAHAN, Kathleen A. md 01 Aug 1987 Danville, NH STEELE, Wm V.; md by Rev John M. Grace (P)

BRESNAHAN, Maria Theresa b 23 Dec 1989 Exeter, NH d/o BRESNAHAN, Michael F. & DUNN, Leslie M.

BREWER, David Thos md 17 Dec 1988 Danville, NH McBRIDE, Carol Sue; md by Everett J. Rondeau (JP)

BREWSTER, Jonathan M. b c1836 Alton. ?; md 06 Oct 1863 Danville, NH TOWLE, Marilla M.

BRICKELL, Florence md 08 Dec 1888 Danville, NH CURRIER, Freeman D.

BRIDGES, Sarah L. b Ipswich, MA d/o BRIDGES, Richard & LOVEJOY, Sarah; md AVERY, ---- ; d 27 Jun 1915 Danville, NH ae 63y 1m 19d

BRIGGS, Walter H. md 13 Oct 1985 Danville, NH JACKSON, Barbara L.; md by Bette C. Ouellette (JP)

BRINK, Heide L. md 13 Sep 1980 Danville, NH ROGERS, Frederick F. J.; md by Rev Peter W. Lovejoy

BROCKELBANK, Richard L. md 09 Jun 1991 Danville, NH HOEFFLIN, Debra A.; md by Richard J. Rondeau (JP)

BRODIE, Edward C. md 28 Nov 1985 Danville, NH O'BRIEN, Janet D.; md by Richard J. Rondeau (JP)

BRONK, Eben Kyle b 11 Mar 1986 Exeter, NH s/o BRONK, Kerry S. & COLLINS, Pamela L.

BRONK, Jael Whitney b 30 Jul 1988 Exeter, NH s/o BRONK, Kerry S. & COLLINS, Pamela L.

BRONK, Kerry S. md 19 Mar 1983 Danville, NH COLLINS, Pamela L.; md by Rev Everett E. Palmer

BROUSSEAU, Wm A. b 1926 MA; md 03 Feb 1968 Danville, NH BATTIS, Norma Jane; md by Rev Douglas Abbott

BROWN, Abigail b Raymond, NH; md TOWLE, Reuben; d 25 Dec 1851 Danville, NH

BROWN, Alexander Sr. b s/o BROWN, Alexander & HARDY, Minnie; d 17 Mar 1980 Danville, NH ae 75y

BROWN, Ann md ELKINS, Thos (Capt.); d 01 Mar 1797 Hawke, NH

BROWN, Arthur P. b c1882 Salisbury, MA s/o BROWN, Chas A.; md 15 Jun 1904 Danville, NH COLLINS, Olla M.; md by Rev A. B. Howard

BROWN, Barbara J. md 24 Oct 1985 Danville, NH RICHARDSON, Lyle H.; md by David T. Ingerson (JP)

BROWN, Benj b Corinth, VT; md 14 Feb 1790 Kingston, NH QUIMBY, Mary

BROWN, Blanche b Nashua, NH; md DUSTON, Oscar

BROWN, Branden Michael b 12 Jan 1987 Haverhill, MA s/o BROWN, Rob't A. & DANFORTH, Belinda M.

BROWN, Carol A. b 1946 Haverhill, MA; md 21 May 1966 Danville, NH SWEET, Earl D.; md by Rev Douglas Abbott

BROWN, Chas H. b 15 Oct 1850 Danville, NH s/o BROWN, Nathan & SANBORN, Mary; md 1867 Danville, NH Sargent, Bessie J.

BROWN, Clifton Earle b 1917 E Kingston, NH s/o BROWN, Chas Ernest; md 13 Jun 1941 Danville, NH YOUNG, Gertrude Madelene; md by Rev W. C. Chappell

BROWN, Cynthia Lee b 04 Mar 1963 Danville, NH d/o BROWN, Clifton Earle

BROWN (Cont.) & YOUNG, Gertrude M.; md 13 Dec 1981 Danville, NH

BROWN, Michael M.

BROWN, Dennis C. b 1948 MA; md 01 Jun 1968 Danville, NH MELKONIAN, Lana Joyce; md by Rev Douglas Abbott

BROWN, Dennis Harvey b 30 AOR 1948 Danville, NH s/o BROWN, Clifton Earle & YOUNG, Gertrude Madeline

BROWN, Doris Eliz b 1930 Windham, NH d/o BROWN, Leonard Francis; md 03 Jul 1949 Danville, NH HEATH, David James; md by Rev Harry L. Lesure

BROWN, Effie L. b d/o BROWN, Chas & JOHNSON, Lena; d 15 Dec 1970 Danville, NH ae 60y

BROWN, Elijah md 06 Nov 1810 Kingston, NH QUIMBY, Miriam

BROWN, Eliphalet b 08 Jan 1779 Hawke, NH s/o BROWN, Jos & PHILBRICK, Sarah

BROWN, Francellus b d/o BROWN, Tilman E. & WOODWARD, Sarah; d 04 Aug 1961 Danville, NH ae 75y

BROWN, Frank d 19 Jun 1863 Danville, NH ae 3y

BROWN, Franklin b 1846 s/o BROWN, Nathan & SANBORN, Mary; d 08 Apr 1868 Danville, NH ae 22y

BROWN, Gregory Clifford b 18 May 1951 Danville, NH s/o BROWN, Clifton Earle & YOUNG, Gertrude Madeline

BROWN, Hannah b 12 Dec 1772 Hawke, NH d/o BROWN, Nathaniel & CLIFFORD, Sarah; md 07 Jan 1808 Hawke, NH TEWKSBURY, Isaac;

BROWN, Hannah b 1722 Hawke, NH; md 11 Jan 1776 HOOK, Dyer; d 20 Sep 1800 Hawke, NH; bu Hawke, NH Old Mtg Hse Cem.

BROWN, Harriet A. b Newton, NH; md 03 Oct 1865 Danville, NH BUSWELL, Lendon

BROWN, Harry B.b 09 Jun 1862 Danville, NH s/o BROWN, Jos B. & WEBSTER, Sarah Ann.; md 17 Jun 1884 Danville, NH Hill, Ella F.; d 16 Nov 1920 ae 58y 5m 7d

BROWN, Isaac b Poplin, NH; md 28 Sep 1843 Danville, NH ----, Mary

BROWN, Isaac B. b 24 May 1761 Hawke, NH s/o BROWN, Jos & SAWYER, Eliz; md WEBSTER, Sarah Ann; d 17 Aug 1882 Danville, NH ae 49y

BROWN, Jacob b 22 Jun 1781 Hawke, NH s/o BROWN, Nathaniel & CLIFFORD, Mary; md 31 Aug 1802 Hawke, NH COLLINS, Tabitha

BROWN, Jeremiah b 30 Jan 1775 Hawke, NH s/o BROWN, Nathaniel & CLIFFORD, Mary; md Aug 1807 Kingston, NH HOOK, Mary

BROWN, John d 21 Jan 1783 Hawke, NH

BROWN, Jos b 04 Apr 1777 Hawke, NH s/o BROWN, Nathaniel & CLIFFORD, Mary

BROWN, Jos B. b c1840 Fremont, NH s/o BROWN, Issac B.; md 22 Nov 1861 Danville, NH WEBSTER, Sarah Ann; d 09 Mar 1886 Danville, NH

BROWN, Jos Jr. b s/o BROWN, Jos Sr.; md 05 Sep 1780 S Hampton, NH TOWLE, Abigail

BROWN, Kevin Edward b 24 May 1955 Danville, NH s/o BROWN, Clifton Earle & YOUNG, Gertrude Madeline

BROWN, Lavina F. b c1853 Newton, NH; md 26 Nov 1869 Danville, NH WEBSTER, John P.

BROWN, Lewis A. b Sanbornton, NH; s/o BROWN, Chase & BROWN, Celestia; md d 26 Oct 1923 Danville, NH; ae 57y 3m 11d

BROWN, Lisa G. md 28 May 1983 Danville, NH SMITH, James Wm; md by Rev Wendall J. Irvine

BROWN, Lori A. md 22 Jun 1985 Danville, NH HEALEY, Brian K.; md by Rev Everett E. Palmer

BROWN, Lowell Norris b Fremont, NH; md SAWYER, Roseann; d 24 Oct 1871 Danville, NH; Occupation Gunsmith

BROWN, Lucy S. md DAVIS, John O.

BROWN, Mary b 06 Aug 1779 Hawke, NH d/o BROWN, Nathaniel & CLIFFORD, Mary

BROWN, Mary Etta b 09 Dec 1863 Danville, NH d/o BROWN, Isaac B. & WEBSTER, Sarah Ann

BROWN, Mary N. b c1830 Raymond, NH; md 1861 Danville, NH COPP, Wm

BROWN, Mehitable md 18 Jan 1781 SEVERENCE, Jonathan; md by Rev John Page

BROWN, Michael M. md 13 Dec 1981 Danville, NH BROWN, Cynthia L.

BROWN, Nancy md CLIFFORD, Samuel

BROWN, Nathan b c1823 Danville, NH; md SANBORN, Mary; d 29 Jul 1889 Danville, NH

BROWN, Nathan md 28 Jun 1781 Hawke, NH BEAN, Sarah; md by Rev John Page

BROWN, Nathaniel Sr. md 17 Nov 1771 Hawke, NH CLIFFORD, Mary; d 09 Apr 1801 Hawke, NH

BROWN, Nathaniel Jr. b 18 May 1789 Hawke, NH s/o BROWN, Nathaniel & CLIFFORD, Mary

BROWN, Nathaniel b c1835 Kingston, NH; md 13 Feb 1864 Danville, NH CHASE, Annie F.

BROWN, Peter Daniel b 16 Aug 1988 Exeter, NH s/o BROWN, Delos B. Jr. & BURKE, Allyson M.

BROWN, Rob't Arthur Jr. b 07 Nov 1984 Haverhill, MA s/o BROWN, Rob't Arthur Sr. & DANFORTH, Belinda M.

BROWN, Roger Warren b 1898 Franklin, NH s/o BROWN, Walter R.; md 10 Jan 1947 Laconia, NH WALLACE, Geraldine Estella; md by Rev Frank J. Colman

BROWN, Ronald A. md 18 May 1985 Danville, NH WICKER, Holly Gale; md by Rev Everett E. Palmer

BROWN, Ronald Adam b 01 Feb 1987 Exeter, NH s/o BROWN, Ronald A. & WICKER, Holly Gale

BROWN, Ronald Clifton b 24 Aug 1945 Danville, NH s/o BROWN, Clifton Earle & YOUNG, Gertrude Madelene

BROWN, Sally md 14 Nov 1805 Hawke, NH CLEMENT, Ebenezer

BROWN, Sarah b Poplin, NH; md 08 Jun 1774 Hawke, NH ELKINS, Abel; md by Rev John Page

BROWN, Sarah b Poplin, NH; md 02 Feb 1843 Danville, NH PERKINS, Moses

BROWN, Sarah b 28 Jan 1784 Hawke, NH d/o BROWN, Nathaniel &

BROWN (Cont.) CLIFFORD, Mary

BROWN, Violet Lucrecia b 1898 Malden, MA; d/o BROWN, Hammond & DYMENT, Jesse; md 25 Dec 1918 Danville, NH MACE, Carlton Alva; d 21 Dec 1957 Haverhill, MA; md by Rev Luke M. Bleakney

BROWN, MALE b 06 Mar 1867 Danville, NH s/o BROWN, Lowell N. & SAWYER, Roseann; d 23 Mar 1867 Danville, NH

BROWNLEE, Kenneth David md; 17 Jun 1988 Danville, NH SHATTUCK, Lissa; md by Richard J. Rondeau (JP)

BROWNSEY, Bruce D. b 1913 Albany Co, NY s/o BROWNSEY, Herman; md 01 Jan 1935 Danville, NH TREMLAY, Mildred J.; md by Rev Overt L. Brownsey

BROWNSEY, Overt L. b 1875 England s/o BROWNSEY, Frederick & PRIDDLE, Emily; d 12 Jul 1956 Danville, NH

BRUCE, Annie B. b W Newton, MA d/o BRUCE, Harry L.; md 03 Oct 1920 Hampstead, NH McGRATH, Rodney James

BRUNER, Thos H. md 10 Jun 1983 Danville, NH BILOTTA, Anne M.; md by Rev Thos Bresnahan

BRUNS, Alton Rob't b s/o BRUNS, Alfred & AMAZEEN, Alice Forest; d 18 Feb 1974 Danville, NH ae 65y

BRYANT, Marcia b Cohan, NB d/o BRYANT, Wm & COCHRAN, Ellen; d 05 May 1917 Danville, NH

BRYSON, Andrea Jane b 29 Mar 1976 Exeter, NH d/o BRYSON, John W. & KROM, Barbara L.

BRYSON, Julie Ann b 29 Mar 1976 Exeter, NH d/o BRYSON, John W. & KROM, Barbara L.

BUCHANAN, Leslie L. md 05 Sep 1980 Danville, NH SNYDER, Danald G.; md by Rev Janet H. Bowering

BUCHARD, Curtis C. b 1916 Haverhill, MA; md 08 Jun 1964 Danville, NH St PIERRE, Leslye G.

BUCHIKOS, Louis A. md 11 Nov 1972 Danville, NH CHAMBERS, Mary A.; md by Leona A. Sciaudone (JP)

BUCKNAM, Dorisc Geraldi b c1929 d /o BUCKNAM, Wm W.; md 20 Dec

BUCKNAM (Cont.) 1952 Danville, NH POTTER, Conway Lincoln

BUDKA, Harriet G. b d/o BUDKA, Frank & KARBOWSKA, Josephine; md BURNETT, ---- ; d 21 May 1988 Danville, NH ae 75y

BULLARD, Henry N. b c1840 Swanton, VT; md 05 May 1861 Danville, NH GEORGE, Helen F.

BULLERWELL, Harry A. b 1944 Lynn, MA; md 25 Mar 1966 Danville, NH QUIGLEY, Grace M.; md by Leona A. Sciaudone (JP)

BULLOCK, Ethyl b 1896 Sandown, NH d/o BULLOCK, Leslie K.; md 02 May 1918 E. Hampstead, NH WELCH, Walter M. md by Rev J. W. Farrell

BUMPS, Fred b Craftbury, VT; md ALDRICH, Pearl G.

BUMPS, Henry Leslie b 07 Dec 1940 Danville, NH s/o BUMPS, Fred & ALDRICH, Pearl G.

BUNDY, Marian b 26 Mar 1922 Danville, NH d/o BUNDY, Theodore R. & TURPIN, Elsie

BUNDY, Theodore R. b Troy, NY; md TURPIN, Elsie

BURBANK, Emma J. b 1890 Saco, ME d/o BURBANK, Wm; md 15 Jun 1912 Danville, NH LADD, Harry W.; md by Rev A. C. Keith

BURBANK, Fannie b c1840 Danville, NH; md 13 May 1867 Danville, NH WHARTON, Henry G.

BURKE, Kevin Michael md 10 Oct 1991 Danville, NH COLEMAN, Carolyn Marie; md by Rev Gordon S. Bates

BURLEIGH, Ada M. b 28 Sep 1877 Danville, NH, d/o BURLEIGH, Jerry & ----, Clara F.

BURLEIGH, Alice C. b 27 Jan 1875 Danville, NH d/o BURLEIGH, David & BROWN, Lizzie A.

BURLEIGH, Dolores Lorrai b 26 Nov 1933 Danville, NH d/o BURLEIGH, Gerald W. & RHODES, Hazel

BURLEIGH, Donald Framcis b 1912 NH s/o BURLEIGH, Winfield S.; md 11 Nov 1952 Danville, NH RAND, Shirley Frances; md by Rev James W. Giltrain

BURLEIGH, Herman K. b 16 Nov 1875 Danville, NH s/o BURLEIGH, Jerry & ----, Clara F.

BURLEIGH, Kenneth D. md 10 Feb 1980 Danville, NH BOWLEY, Donna F.; md by Rev Wm Ryans

BURLEIGH, Kieth Alan Jr. b 29 Nov 1991 Exeter, NH s/o BURLEIGH, Kieth Alan Sr. & ELLISON, Linda M.

BURLEIGH, Rob't Donald b 1932 NH; s/o BURLEIGH, Jesse Allan; md 18 Mar 1945 Danville, NH BATTIS, Joan Caroline; md by Rev Karl J. Hislop

BURLEIGH, Sherri Lee b 19 Sep 1957 Danville, NH d/o BURLEIGH, Rob't Donald & BATTIS, Joan Caroline; md 22 Dec 1957 Danville, NH

BURLEIGH, Wm Allen b 1928 Fremont, NH s/o BURLEIGH, Jesse Allan; md 12 Apr 1953 Danville, NH SEAVER, Barbara Ann

BURLIEGH, Rob't Donald b s/o BURLEIGH, Jesse Allan; md 18 Mar 1867 Danville, NH BATTIS, Joan Caroline

BURNETT, James Francis b 10 Mar 1943 Danville, NH s/o BURNETT, John Alfred & BUDKA, Harriet Genevieve

BURNETT, John Alfred b s/o BURNETTE, John F. & HADDOCK, Eva; md BUDKA, Harriet Genevieve; d 24 Oct 1969 Danville, NH

BURNETT, Ruth Eleanor b 30 May 1948 S Danville, NH d/o BURNETT, John Alfred & BUDKA, Harriet Genevieve md 29 Apr 1967 Danville, NH THERRIEN, Wm J.; md by Roger A. Vachon (P)

BURNETT, ---- b 21 Mar 1942 Danville, NH ?/o BURNETTE, John Alfred & BUDKA, Harriet Genevieve; d 21 Mar 1942 Danville, NH

BURNS, Ann Marie b MA; md 30 Dec 1969 Danville, NH BALL, Wm H.; md by Leona A. Sciaudone (JP)

BURNS, Grace b 1912 Boston, MA d/o BURNS, Frank; md 29 Aug 1936 Danville, NH FANDREY, Leo; md by Clarence M. Collins (JP)

BURRILL, C. Herman b c1889 Danville, NH s/o BURRILL, Romanzo C. & RUSBY, Martha; d 23 May 1910 Danville, NH ae 20y 10m 12d

BURRILL, Harry E. b c1837 Danville, NH s/o BURRILL, Romanzo C. & RUSBY, Martha; md 24 Jun 1911 King-

BURRILL (Cont.) ston, NH SEAVER, Nellie G.; d 11 Sep 1961 Danville, NH; md by Rev Fred V. Stanley; d ae 74y

BURRILL, Karl E. b c1893 Danville, NH s/o BURRILL, Romanzo C. & RUSBY, Martha; md 10 Apr 1915 Georgetown, MA MURCH, Vera O.; md by Rev Arthur S. Burrill

BURRILL, Romanzo C. b s/o BURRILL, Wm & CHALLIS, Ella; md RUSBY, Martha; d 12 Oct 1960 Danville, NH

BURRILL, Wm H. b Plaistow, NH s/o BURRILL, James; d 21 Apr 1912 Danville, NH ae 71y 23d

BURROUGHS, John H. b Manchester, NH s/o BURROUGHS, Sherman E. & PHILLIPS, Helen S.; d 04 Apr 1929 Danville, NH ae 27y 8m 11d

BURT, Herschel Bacon b Waltham, MA; md KETCHEN, Thelma Merle

BURT, Holly Louise b 27 Feb 1955 Danville, NH d/o BURT, Herschel Bacon & KETCHEN, Thelma Merle

BURTON, Glenn Scott md 30 Dec 1989 Danville, NH MILONE, Rosemarie Joy; md by Barbara A. LaPointe (JP)

BUSCH, Karl Lovine b 14 Apr 1978 Exeter, NH s/o BUSCH, Edward K. & FRIEND, Yvonne M.

BUSHWAY, Alfred A. b 1896 Portland, ME s/o BUSHWAY, Jos; md 01 Dec 1923 Westville, NH ALLARD, Ada J.; md by M. J. Moher (P)

BUSWELL, Albee C. b c1841 Manchester, NH; md Mar 1865 Danville, NH MORSE, Florence A.; d 12 Oct 1982 Danville, NH ae 31y - Injured in war

BUSWELL, David b Kingston, NH; md 11 Apr 1823 Hawke, NH PAGE, Betty

BUSWELL, Edwin A. b 05 Oct 1866 Danville, NH s/o BUSWELL, Albee C & MORSE, Florence A. md 06 May 1886 Danville, NH MANN, Florence E.

BUSWELL, Eliz b of Hawke, NH; md 09 Aug 1781 Hawke, NH BEAN, Levi; md by Rev John Page

BUSWELL, Esther V. b 1870 Danville, NH d/o BUSWELL, Lendon & BROWN, Harriet A.; d 17 Sep 1873 Danville, NH ae 3y

BUSWELL, Frances S. b 11 Jun 1869 Danville, NH d/o BUSWELL, Albee C. & MORSE, Florence A.

BUSWELL, Frank P. b Danville, NH s/o BUZZELL, Edwin A. & MANN, Florence A.; d 07 Mar 1930 Danville, NH ae 40y 20d

BUSWELL, Hannah b Hawke, NH d/o BUSWELL, Caleb; md 09 Nov 1779 Hawke, NH BEAN, Nathan; md by Rev John Page

BUSWELL, Huldah md 11 Jun 1767 Hawke, NH ELKINS, Peter; md by Rev John Page

BUSWELL, Jos b 30 Aug 1770 Hawke, NH s/o BUSWELL, Wm & WINSLOW, Eliz

BUSWELL, Jos b md QUIMBY, Lucy

BUSWELL, Jos b 25 Apr 1795 Hawke, NH s/o BUSWELL, Jos & QUIMBY, Lucy; md 09 May 1794 Kingston, NH

BUSWELL, Judith b c1755 d/o BUSWELL, Wm & WINSLOW, Eliz; d 17 Mar 1795 Hawke, NH ae 40y

BUSWELL, Lendon C. b c1845 Danville, NH; md 03 Oct 1865 Danville, NH BROWN, Harriet A.

BUSWELL, Moses b 07 Sep 1800 Hawke, NH s/o BUSWELL, Jos & QUIMBY, Lucy; d 18 Apr 1801 Hawke, NH ae 7mo

BUSWELL, Moses b 19 Jun 1802 Hawke, NH s/o BUSWELL, Jos & QUIMBY, Lucy

BUSWELL, Moses b 1768 Danville, NH s/o BUSWELL, Wm & WINSLOW, Eliz

BUSWELL, Rhoda b c1789; md CURRIER, Barnard Jr.; d 26 Nov 1861 Danville, NH ae 72y

BUSWELL, Sarah b 06 Mar 1766 Hawke, NH d/o BUSWELL, Wm & WINSLOW, Eliz

BUSWELL, Sarah b 25 Nov 1755 Hawke, NH d/o BUSWELL, Samuel & WINSLOW, Mary; md 25 Jul 1776 Hawke, NH COLLINS, Richard; md by Rev John Page

BUSWELL, Sarah L. b 31 Jul 1866 Danville, NH s/o BUSWELL, Lendon & BROWN, Harriet A.

BUSWELL, Wm b c1720 Kingston, NH; md WINSLOW, Eliz; d 09 Apr 1792 Hawke, NH; ae 72y

BUSWELL, Wm b c1692 Salisbury, MA; md DAVIS, Judith; d 21 Mar 1779 Hawke, NH ae 87y

BUTEAU, Dennis E. md 20 Apr 1974 Danville, NH SANBORN, Catherine May; md by Rev Cathleen R. Narowitz

BUTLER, Daniel B. md 21 Sep 1985 Danville, NH BILO, Vickie L.; md by Rev Florent R. Bilodeau

BUTREOCCIO, Carol Anne b NH; md 05 Apr 1969 Danville, NH COLLINS, Howard Jos md by Leona A. Sciaudone (JP)

BUTTERS, Roland Worthle b Greenfield, NH s/o BUTTERS, Geo & WORTLEY, Margaret; d 09 Apr 1967 Danville, NH

BUTTRICK, Ronald H. b 1933 MA s/o BUTTRICK, Chas L.; md 13 Sep 1952 Danville, NH CARBONE, Lois J.; md by Rev James W. Gilrain

BUTTRICK, Sheryl Ann b 05 Feb 1957 Danville, NH d/o BUTTRICK, Ronald H. & CARBONE, Lois J.

BUZZELL, Chas E. b 1943 E Derry, NH; md 02 Aug 1963 Danville, NH BATTIS, Sandra J. md by Rev F. B. Hadley

BUZZELL, Edgar A. b 21 Apr 1887 Danville, NH s/o BUZZELL, Edwin E. & MANN, Florence E.

BUZZELL, Edwin A. b Danville, NH; md MANN, Florence E.; d 03 Jun 1899 ae 32y 8m

BUZZELL, Lucy b c1804 Gilford, NH d/o BUZZELL, Isaac & BICKFORD, M.; md MUNSEY, ---- ; d 17 Mar 1889 Danville, NH ae 85y Pneumonia

BUZZELL, Mary Alice b Hampstead, NH d/o BUZZELL, Wm & MEADER, Elvie; md ARNOLD, ---- ; d 20 Nov 1939 Danville, NH ae 49y

BUZZELL, ---- b 01 Feb 1890 Danville, NH s/o BUZZELL, Edwin A. & MANN, Florence E.; 3rd Child in Family

BYBEE, Max Leroy d 06 Jan 1971 Danville, NH ae 75y

BYRNE, Norman James b 1935 MA s/o BYRNE, Jos; md 13 Jul 1959 Dan-

BYRNE (Cont.) ville, NH SANBORN, Barbara; md by Rev Guy Judkins

BYRON, Marie Yvonne b 21 Nov 1965 Danville, NH d/o BYRON, Wm Henry & BEDEL, Francine H.; md 04 Aug 1984 Danville, NH JENNINGS, John C. md by Rev Everett E. Palmer

BYRON, Nancy Ellen b 27 Mar 1967 Danville, NH d/o BYRON, Wm Henry & BEDEL, Francine H.

BYRON, Wm H. b Woburn, MA; md BEDEL, Francine H.

CABRAL, Jos D. md 29 Aug 1987 Danville, NH MURTAGH, Susan M.; md by Deborah R. McCaffery (JP)

CAILLOUETTE, Bruce E. md 27 Feb 1982 Danville, NH GOLDTHWAITE, Beth Lee; md by Rev Everett E. Palmer

CAILLOUETTE, David Bruce b 29 Jul 1984 Exeter, NH s/o CAILLOU-ETTE, Bruce E. & GOLDTHWAITE, Beth L.

CAILLOUETTE, Jeffery Michael b 16 Feb 1988 Exeter, NH s/o CALIL-LOURTTE, Bruce E. & GOLDTH-WAITE, Beth L.

CAILLOUETTE, Jos J. b Plaistow, NH; md MITCHELL, Judith Ann

CAILLOUETTE, Rich Al b 05 May 1962 Danville, NH s /o CAILLOUETTE, Jos J. & MITCHELL, Judith Ann

CAILLOUETTE, Sharon A. b 13 Jan 1965 Danville, NH d/o CAILLOUTTE, Jos J. & MITCHELL, Judith Ann

CALABRIA, Nicole A. md 10 May 1987 Danville, NH COLLINS, Jeffery S.; md by Rich J. Rondeau (JP)

CALANTONIO, Eliz L md 23 Sep 1978 Danville, NH CROWELL, George E. Jr.; md by Rev Wm Ryans

CALDWELL, James Rowe Jr. b 22 Jun 1985 Manchester, NH s/o CALD-WELL, James Rowe Sr. & NIKOLAUS, Christina A.

CALDWELL, James Rowe Sr. md 12 Jan 1985 Danville, NH NIKOLAUS, Christina A.; md by Rev Everett E. Palmer

CALDWELL, John R. b s/o CALD-WELL, James & BLAKE, Helen; d 26 Mar 1987 Danville, NH ae 56y

CALF, Hannah b of Kingston, NH;

CALF (Cont.) md 28 Dec 1780 THAYER, Elihu Rev.; md by Rev John Page

CALF, Martha b of Poplin, NH; md 22 Nov 1764 Hawke, NH RING, Jonathan; md by Rev John Page

CALHOUN, Bradley J. md 20 Dec 1986 Danville, NH CHASE, Jane E.; md by Rev Everett E. Palmer

CAMERON, Charlotte A. b 1906 Nashua, NH s/o CAMERON, Wilbert H. md 22 Nov 1926 Derry, NH McGRATH, Cedrick; md by Rev Arthur D. Woodworth

CAMMARATO, John W. of Haverhill, MA md 18 Apr 1992 ROOT, Judy A.

CAMET, Silas b of Candia, NH; md 17 Jun 1779 Hawke, NH SMITH, Martha; md by Rev John Page

CAMPBELL, Abigail b 06 Sep 1771 Hawke, NH d/o CAMPBELL, Annas Jr. & WEBSTER, Eliz

CAMPBELL, Alexander md 07 Jan 1778 Hampstead, NH JOHNSON, Ruth

CAMPBELL, Annas b 13 Nov 1775 Hawke, NH d/o CAMPBELL, Annas Jr. & WEBSTER, Eliz

CAMPBELL, Annas b IRELAND; md PIKE, Abigail; d 28 Jan 1772 Hawke, NH ae 56y

CAMPBELL, Annis Jr. b c1744 s/o CAMPBELL, Annis Sr.; md 12 Dec 1765 Hawke, NH WEBSTER, Eliz; d 11 Mar 1808 Hawke, NH ae 64y; md by Rev John Page

CAMPBELL, Betty b 07 Jul 1766 Hawke, NH d/o CAMPBELL, Annas Jr. & WEBSTER, Eliz; md 30 Oct 1787 Kingston, NH WHITAKER, Moses

CAMPBELL, Dorothy b 16 Dec 1785 Hawke, NH d/o CAMPBELL, Annas Jr. & WEBSTER, Eliz; md 04 Jul 1804 Kingston, NH PEASLEE, Wm

CAMPBELL, Gertrude A. b d/o CAMPBELL, Theodore & BEAN, Ada; md PHILLIPS, ---- ; d 21 Jul 1991 Danville, NH ae 76y

CAMPBELL, Gertrude K. b 1915 Fremont, NH d/o CAMPBELL, Theodore; md 30 Jan 1932 Danville, NH ANDERSON, Hollis; md by Rev Samnuel B. Enman

CAMPBELL, Hannah b 20 Jun 1778 Hawke, NH d/o CAMPBELL, Annas Jr. & WEBSTER, Eliz; md 16 Nov 1797 Kingston, NH EASTMAN, Jacob

CAMPBELL, Molly b 05 Dec 1773 Hawke, NH d/o CAMPBELL, Annas Jr. & WEBSTER, Eliz

CAMPBELL, Phineas b 28 Sep 1761 Hawke, NH s/o CAMPBELL, Annas & PIKE, Abigail

CAMPBELL, Polly b 17 Mar 1799 Hawke, NH d/o CAMPBELL, Annas 3rd & ---- , Rhoda

CAMPBELL, Polly b Hawke, NH; md 17 Nov 1796 Kingston, NH QUIMBY, David

CAMPBELL, Robert b 10 Jul 1797 Hawke, NH s/o CAMPBELL, Annas 3rd & ---- , Rhoda

CAMPBELL, Ruth b 27 May 1763 Hawke, NH d/o CAMPBELL, Annas & PIKE, Abigail

CAMPBELL, Samuel b 29 Mar 1781 Hawke, NH s/o CAMPBELL, Annas Jr. & WEBSTER, Eliz

CAMPBELL, Sarah b 14 May 1769 Hawke, NH d/o CAMPBELL, Annas Jr. & WEBSTER, Eliz

CAMPBELL, Theresa R. b 1913 Fremont, NH d/o CAMPBELL, Theo M.; md 19 May 1932 Danville, NH GARDELLA, Gerald R.; md by Geo A. Gilmore (JP)

CANNEY, Angeline b c1833 Sandown, NH; md 1848 Danville, NH JOHNSON, James

CANUEL, Marguerite b 28 Oct 1925; md COLLINS, Cecil Spaulding

CANUEL, Robert L. b s/o CANUEL, Phillip & COTE, Marie; d 10 Apr 1985 Danville, NH ae 60y

CAPPADONA, Jodi Anne b 07 Jan 1978 Newton, NH d/o CAPPADONA, John S. Jr. & REARDON, Anne Marie

CARBONE, Lois J. b 1933 MA d/o CARBONE, Francis G.; md 13 Sep 1952 Danville, NH BUTTRICK, Ronald H.; md by Rev James W. Gilrain

CARBONE, Shirley Elaine b 1935 MA d/o CARBONE, Francis G.; md 14 Aug 1954 Danville, NH MASKELL, Albert Alton; md by Rev Stan Dahlman

CARBONNEAU, Paul George b 27 Jun 1990 Derry, NH s/o CARBONNEAU, Paul E. & WOUNDY, Carol D.

CARIGNAN, Lorraine M. md 12 May 1984 Danville, NH BEAULIEU, Paul R.; md by Robert J. Kemmery (P)

CARLSON, Carl Emanuel b Cambridge, MA s/o CARLSON, Carl A. & JOHNSON, Armanda; md DEMAINE, Marion C.; d 06 Feb 1961 Danville, NH ae 56y

CARLSON, Chas Carlson b 20 Aug 1942 Danville, NH s/o CARLSON, Carl Emanuel & CHIVERS, Mary Olivia

CARLSON, Glendon Victor b 30 Aug 1932 Danville, NH s/o CARLSON, Helmer V. & HOPKINS, Eva Maranda

CARLSON, Ida T. b c1899 Kendal Grenn, MA d/o CARLSON, Victor; md 06 Jul 1919 Danville, NH DIMOND, James T.; md by Rev L. M. Bleakney

CARLSON, Jay Scott md 12 Aug 1980 Danville, NH DuBOIS, Marilyn Jean; md by Rev Paul W. Daneault (P)

CARLSON, Jeffery Sheldo b 09 Oct 1961 Danville, NH s/o CARLSON, Winston S. & DEVEAU, Jacqueline S.

CARLSON, Louise Frances d 04 Jul 1941 Danville, NH ae 74y 11m

CARLSON, Mary O. b 1908 Boston, MA; md 03 Jul 1965 Danville, NH PEARSON, Karl M.; md by Rev F. Kieths

CARLSON, Victor d 26 Jul 1941 Danville, NH ae 82y 5m 13d

CARLSON, Wandy Sue b 11 Jun 1963 Danville, NH d/o CARLSON, Winston S. & DEVEAU, Jacqueline S.

CARLTON, Josiah b Plaistow, NH; md FOSS, Mary Ann

CARLTON, Orrin b c1826 s/o CARLTON, Josiah & FOSS, Mary Ann; d 12 May 1892 ae 66y 3m 3d; Occ Shoecutter

CARLTON, Phyliss Ann b 1925 MA d/o CARLTON, Edward J.; md 16 May 1952 Danville, NH WATERS, Ralph Elmond; md by Agnes H. Collins (JP); prev md HODGES, ----

CARLTON, Thos b c1825 Newton, NH; md Dec 1865 Danville, NH CARTER, Rebecca; md by Wm Hoyt J.P.

CARON, Diane P. md 10 Jun 1983 Danville, NH GOLDTHWAITE, Rich E.; md by Rev Florent R. Bilodeau (P)

CARON, Nathan Roland b 16 Jun 1987 Exeter, NH s/o CARON, Roland G. & LAMSON, Gloria

CARON, Tammy A. md 09 Mar 1985 Danville, NH COLLINS, Joel M.; md by Francis J. McKone (P)

CARPENTER, Brian Keith md 01 Jul 1990 Danville, NH DUNN, Lisa Ann; md by Linda S. Jette (JP)

CARR, Ann b c1813 Fremont, NH md 1857 Danville NH SANBORN, Moses

CARR, Christoph Edward b 29 Jul 1972 Methuen, MA s/o CARR, John E. & WILLIAMS, Carolyn F.

CARR, Jennifer Caroline b 12 Jun 1971 Methuen, MA d/o CARR, John E. & WILLIAMA, Carolyn F.

CARR, John E. md WILLIAMS, Carolyn F.

CARR, Rich E. b 1936 NH; md 13 Apr 1968 Danville, NH MEESE, Lillian E.; md by Edward R. Lamb (JP)

CARRINGTON, David Louis b 1946 Haverhill, MA; md 11 Jun 1966 Danville, NH STEWART, Phyllis; md by Rev John Wood Jr.

CARROLL, Chas E. b 1945 Exeter, NH; md 10 Jul 1965 Danville, NH HANSON, Patricia Maureen.; md by Roger A. Vachon (P)

CARROLL, Craig Erie b 20 Jul 1968 Danville, NH s/o CARROLL, Chas Everett & HANSON, Patricia Maureen

CARROLL, Dorothy Lida b 1916 Haverhill, MA d/o MARSHALL, Roland; md 01 Sep 1935 Danville, NH REYNOLDS, Cary Abbott; md by Clarence M. Collins (JP)

CARSON, Christie b Ireland; md CLEMENT, Jos D.

CARTER, Abigail b Newton, NH; md DIMOND, John

CARTER, Austin Robert b 1939 MA; md 02 Jul 1960 Danville, NH DWYER, Mary Blanche; md by Rev Thos J. Hannigar

CARTER, Debra A. md 23 Jun 1990 Danville, NH COLLINS, Michael Roy; md by Rev Everett E. Palmer

CARTER, Eunice P. md BRADLEY, Nathaniel; d 09 Dec 1859 Danville, NH ae 63y

CARTER, Lorenzo b Boston, MA; d 03 Apr 1918 Danville, NH ae 52y

CARTER, Luella b Newton, NH; md 12 Oct 1843 Danville, NH DIMOND, Reuben Jr.

CARTER, Mary C. b Canterbury; md BAGLEY, George W.;

CARTER, Rebecca b c1830 Kingston, NH; md Dec 1865 Danville, NH CARLTON, Thos

CARTER, Sadie A. b 04 Jan 1892 Danville, NH d/o CARTER, Walter P. & DIMOND, Cora Bell; md 30 May 1908 Danville, NH KEEZER, George Burton; md by Rev W. C. Chappell

CARTER, Walter P. b Newton, NH; md DIMOND, Cora Bell; Occupation - Shoemaker

CARUSO, Paige Alexandria b 25 May 1992 Exeter, NH d/o CARUSO, Paul J. & DAVIS, Jennifer M.

CARVEllo, Alan J. md 02 Feb 1986 Danville, NH AKIYMA, Barbara E.; md by Renne Houle Carkin (JP)

CARVER, Wendy Jane md 28 Oct 1990 Danville, NH GARON, Stephen Robert; md by Rich J. Rondeau (JP)

CARY, Catherine b W. Medway, ?; md CRAGGY, Byron

CASS, David d May 1896 Danville, NH ae 84y 5m

CASS, David Jr. b s/o CASS, David Sr.; md SARGENT, Mary

CASS, Jos md 30 Oct 1765 FLANDERS, Miriam; md by Rev John Page

CASS, Lewis b c1837 s/o CASS, David Jr. & SARGENT, Mary; d 1873 Danville, NH ae 36y

CASS, Sarah b 22 Jun 1845 Danville, NH d/o CASS, David Jr. & SARGENT, Mary md RICHARDSON, Newton; d 22 Oct 1900 Danville, NH

CASS, Warren b 1839 Danville, NH s/o CASS, David Jr. & SARGENT, Mary; md 1859 Danville, NH GORDON, Emily Frances; d 31 Oct 1860 Danville, NH ae 21y

CASSELL, Deborah A. md 28 Jul 1990 Danville, NH TILLY, Brian K.; md by Rich J. Rondeau (JP)

CASTANHEIRA, Lydia S. md 02 Dec 1983 Danville, NH MORROW, Albert R.; md by Rich J. Rindeau (JP)

CATALFAMO, Philip b 1914 Boston, MA s/o CATALFAMO, Anthony; md 13 Dec 1934 Danville, NH BORDEN, Phyllis; md by Clarence M. Collins (JP)

CATE, Mary G. b c1889 Danville, NH d/o CATE, Jos & TOUGARY, M.; d 01 Apr 1889 Danville, NH ae 10d

CATTO, Nancy J. md 21 Jun 1987 Danville, NH OLSON, Roy E.; md by Rev Everett E. Palmer

CAVERLY, Polly md PARSHLEY, ---- ; d 24 Nov 1880 Danville, NH ae 87y

CAVICCHI, David James md 16 Jun 1990 Danville, NH RICHARDSON, Cheri; md by Rich J. Rondeau (JP)

CAVISS, Arlett b Gloucester, MA; md DARBE, Elmer C.

CERASUOLO, Elaine b 1935 MA d/o CERASUOLO, Alfred L.; md 07 Sep 1956 Danville, NH MORROW, Wm C. Jr.; md by Agnes H. Collins (JP)

CHADWICK, Rose M. b Newport, MA d/o AARONIAN, James & MANION, Rose; d 25 Jan 1959 Danville, NH

CHALLIS, Augusta D. b c1834 Danville, NH d/o CHALLIS, Jos & BLAKE, Dorothy; md DARBE, James; d 04 Apr 1907 Danville, NH ae 73y 8m 4d

CHALLIS, Clark D. b 08 Dec 1824 Hawke, NH s/o CHALLIS, Jos & BLAKE, Dorothy; md 1ST LADD, Tammary, 2nd Jul 18885 Danville, NH WHITTIER, Mary, 3rd CLARK, ---- ; d 23 Jan 1901 ae 76y 1m 11d

CHALLIS, Dorothy A. b 30 Jul 1833 Hawke, NH d/o CHALLIS, Jos & BLAKE, Dorothy

CHALLIS, Elbridge G. b Danville, NH s/o CHALLIS, Jos H. & QUIMBY, Rhoda; md JOHNSON, Mary; d 22 Jan 1911 Danville, NH; d ae 66y 7m 7d

CHALLIS, Ella b 1832 Hawke, NH d/o CHALLIS, Jos & BLAKE, Dorothy

CHALLIS, Emma M. d 28 Sep 1965 ae 74y

CHALLIS, Gershom C. b 08 Dec 1824 Hawke, NH s/o CHALLIS, Jos & BLAKE, Dorothy

CHALLIS, Hannah b 12 Mar 1816 Hawke, NH d/o CHALLIS, Jos &

CHALLIS (Cont.) SHOWELL, Judith

CHALLIS, Hannah D. b 29 Mar 1817 Hawke, NH d/o CHALLIS, Jos & BLAKE, Dorothy; md 01 Dec 1841 Raymond, NH ANDERSON, Moses; d 23 Sep 1903 Danville, NH

CHALLIS, Harrison b 03 May 1813 Hawke, NH s/o CHALLIS, Jos & BLAKE, Dorothy; d 08 Feb 1890 Danville, NH ae 77y of Cardiac-dropsy

CHALLIS, Henry Everett b 30 Oct 1870 E. Hampstead, NH s/o CHALLIS, Elbridge G. & JOHNSON, Mary; md SARGENT, Junietta; d 23 Nov 1939 Danville, NH

CHALLIS, Irene C. b 17 Nov 1829 Hawke, NH d/o CHALLIS, Jos & BLAKE, Dorothy; md COLLINS, Jos

CHALLIS, John md 26 Apr 1770 Hawke, NH SLEEPER, Dolly; md by Rev John Page

CHALLIS, Jos b c1792 Amesbury, MA; md 01 Dec 1810 Hawke, NH BLAKE, Dorothy; d 22 Jan 1862 Danville, NH ae 72y

CHALLIS, Jos H. b 26 Jan 1819 Hawke, NH s/o CHALLIS, Jos & BLAKE, Dorothy; md 30 Dec 1841 Danville, NH QUIMBY, Sarah H.; d 04 May 1877 Danville, NH ae 58y

CHALLIS, Lucinda b 29 Nov 1826 Hawke, NH d/o CHALLIS, Jos & BLAKE, Dorothy; d 04 Dec 1849 Danville, NH

CHALLIS, Mary C. b 12 Aug 1820 Hawke, NH d/o CHALLIS, Jos & BLAKE, Dorothy; d 03 Jul 1883 Danville, NH

CHALLIS, Mary D b c1854 Hampstead, NH; md 08 Nov 1874 Danville, NH HAM, Henry

CHALLIS, Olive S. b c1910; d 23 Sep 1973 Danville, NH ae 63y

CHALLIS, Oren b 22 Mar 1815 Hawke, NH s/o CHALLIS, Jos & BLAKE, Dorothy

CHALLIS, Sarah b 1822 Hawke, NH d/o CHALLIS, Jos & BLAKE, Dorothy

CHALLIS, Sarah b 1849 Danville, NH d/o CHALLIS, Clark D. & LADD, Tammary H.

CHALLIS, Sarah A. b 30 Nov 1830 Hawke, NH d/o CHALLIS, Jos &

CHALLIS (Cont.) BLAKE, Dorothy

CHALLIS, Sarah A. b Dec 1852 Danville, NH d/o CHALLIS, Clark D. & LADD, Tammary H.; md LADD, ---- ; d 29 Sep 1898 Danville, NH

CHALLIS, Thos md 05 Nov 1771 Hawke, NH FRENCH, Molly; md by Rev John Page

CHALLIS, ---- b 23 May 1899 d/o CHALLIS, Henry Everett & SARGENT, Junietta

CHAMBERLIN, Kelly Annet b 20 Jul 1964 Danville, NH d/o CHAMBERLIN, Wayne D. & GALLANT, Diane M.

CHAMBERLIN, Lisa L. md 09 Apr 1988 Danville, NH ATWOOD, James E.; md by Rich J. Rondeau (JP)

CHAMBERS, Arlene Frances md 12 Dec 1989 Danville, NH SUTER, David Wayne; md by Rich J. Robdeau (JP)

CHAMBERS, Mary A. md 11 Nov 1972 Danville, NH BUCHIKOS, Louis A.; md by Leona A. Sciaudone (JP)

CHAMPIGNY, Paul M. md 12 May 1984 Danville, NH CUMMINGS, Sue D.; md by Rev James A. Magnusson

CHAMPION, John s/o CHAMPION, James & McNEIL, Nancy; d 17 Sep 1924 Danville, NH ae 78y 11m 27d

CHANEY, Joan md 01 Jan 1980 Danville, NH NYBERG, Forrest W.; md by Rev Wendall J. Irvine

CHAPUT, Kyle Stuart b 31 Oct 1974 Haverhill, MA s/o CHAPUT, Francis W. & COOKE, Janet E.

CHARNLEY, Kenneth b 1944 Haverhill, MA; md 26 May 1967 Danville, NH DUCHEMIN, Brenda Mae; md by Leona A. Sciaudone (JP)

CHASE, Adele Blanche b d/o CHASE, Wm & EATON, Bessie; md COLLINS, ---- ; d 07 Nov 1988 Danville, NH ae 84y

CHASE, Annie F. b c1841 Kingston, NH; md 13 Feb 1864 Danville, NH BROWN, Nathaniel C.

CHASE, Beverley A. b 1945 Merrimac, MA; md 26 Apr 1963 Danville, NH WOODSUM, Leon E.; md by Edward Lamb (JP)

CHASE, Blossom Ruth b d/o CHASE, Henry A. & BATCHELDOR, Daisey; d 19 May 1960 Danville, NH ae 78y

CHASE, Chas Ed b 1863 Haverhill, MA s/o CHASE, Chas F. & WORKS, Sarah; md 08 Dec 1932 Danville, NH MERRICK, Etta M.; d 17 Aug 1939 Danville, NH; md by Rev Harold C. Ross

CHASE, Florence L. b Marblehead, MA d/o CHASE, Lewbertien & FAYE, Emma H.; d 23 Nov 1965 Danville, NH ae 85y

CHASE, Francis b of Newton, NH md 23 Nov 1769 Hawke, NH HUBBARD, Sarah; md by Rev John Page

CHASE, Jane E. md 20 Dec 1986 Danville, NH CALHOUN, Bradley J.; md by Rev Everett E. Palmer

CHASE, John b c1846; d 01 Sep 1865 Danville, NH ae 19y

CHASE, Julia A. b Bridgton, ME d/o CHASE, Rufus & LITTLEFIELD, Sarah; d 17 Jan 1899 ae 75y 5m 16d

CHASE, Mary b 15 Jun 1783 d/o CHASE, Simon & GEORGE, Mary

CHASE, Mary b 03 Oct 1784 d/o CHASE, Simon & GEORGE, Mary

CHASE, Rich I. md 11 Oct 1986 Danville, NH CLERK, Katherine; md by Rev Marcia A. Dorey

CHASE, Robert I. 2nd b 25 Feb 1970 Methuen, MA s/o CHASE, Robert I. & HUTCHINSON, Lorraine H.

CHASE, Sally b 09 Mar 1787 d/o CHASE, Simon & GEORGE, Mary

CHASSE, Jennifer Rose b 26 Sep 1989 Exeter, NH d/o CHASSE, Wm E. & BAKIOS, Paula J.

CHAVERS, David A. md 28 Sep 1985 Danville, NH RICHER, Victoria L.; md by Daniel J. Messier (P)

CHENEY, Bertha b d/o CHENEY, Laburton & HAYNES, Harriet; md RIVERS, ---- ; d 14 Sep 1985 Danville, NH ae 81y

CHENEY, Edna J. b 1901 Kingston, NH d/o CHENEY, Laburton H. & HAYNES, Hattie M.; md FULLER, James R. d 12 Aug 1924 Danville, NH

CHENEY, Florence H. b NH; d/o HARTSONE, Benj & MITCHELL, Delia; d 07 Jul 1958 Danville, NH ae 81y

CHENEY, Forest A. b 14 Aug 1881 Danville, NH s/o CHENEY, George H. & ANDERSON, Rhoda J.; d 17 Apr 1969 Danville, NH

CHENEY, George H. b 1838 Kingston, NH s/o CHENEY, Nathaniel & HOYT, Mary E.; md ANDERSON, Rhoda J.; d 07 Oct 1925 Danville, NH

CHENEY, Laburton H. b 26 Jun 1872 Danville, NH s/o CHENEY, George H. & ANDERSON, Rhoda J. md HAYNES, Lois E.; d 08 May 1944 Danville, NH

CHENEY, Mary C. b c1846 Kingston, NH; md 16 Jun 1880 Danville, NH ADAMS, George G.

CHENEY, Sarah E. b c1842 Kingston, NH; md 01 Jul 1860 Danville, NH TUCKER, Otis

CHENEY, Wilbur A. b 1874 Danville, NH s/o CHENEY, George H. & ANDERSON, Rhoda J.; d 29 Nov 1877 Danville, NH ae 3y

CHENEY, Wilbur B b 27 Dec 1905 Danville, NH s/o CHENEY, Laburton H. & HAYNES, Hattie M.

CHENEY, ---- b 20 Nov 1921 Danville, NH ?/o CHENEY, Hayden & OSBORNE, Freda; d Nov 1921 Danville, NH

CHENG, Minnie md 25 Sep 1981 Danville, NH NAGI, Victor M.; md by Eleanor B. Barron (JP)

CHENNIE, Delphine C. b d/o CHENNIE, Pierre & DUYREE, Adelaide; md PELON, ---- ; d 03 Feb 1915 Danville, NH

CHESLEY, MALE b 14 Apr 1855 Danville, NH s/o CHESLEY, John G. & W ----, C.

CHICKERING, Anelous b Barre, VT; md CUMMINGS, Minnie C.

CHICKERING, Herbert Wes b 04 Dec 1910 Danville, NH s/o CHICKERING, Wm H. & BOWLEY, Annie E.

CHICKERING, Kenneth Saw b 05 Dec 1910 Danville, NH s/o CHICKERING, Anelous O. & CUMMINGS, Minnie C.

CHICKERING, Wm H. b Barre, VT; md BOWLEY, Annie E.

CHILDS, Stephen Andrew b 22 Jun 1982 Lawrence, MA s/o CHILDS, Edward H. & WARRINER, Cathy M.

CHILDS, Thos Edward b 30 Mar 1981 Lawrence, MA s/o CHILDS, Edward H. & WARRINER, Cathy M.

CHIVERS, Charlotte b England d/o CHIVERS, Thos & FLEMING, Olivia; d 10 Jul 1858 Danville, NH ae 81y

CHIVERS, Mary Jane b d/o CURIVEN, Thos & MARTIN, Margaret; d 29 Mar 1957 Danville, NH

CHOUINARD, Brian R. md 15 Jun 1980 Danville, NH WICKER, Varerie

CHOUINARD, Robert Ryan b 20 May 1987 Exeter, NH s/o CHOUINARD, Brian R. & WICKER, Valerie J.

CHRISTENSEN, Walter Rudolph b s/o CHRISTENSEN, Hans & GANSMOA, Lena; d 27 Nov 1989 Danville, NH ae 77y

CHRISTMANN, Ruth M. b Bergen Norway; s/o OEN, Sigvold; md 06 Sep 1947 Danville, NH FANNING, Frank; md by Rev W. C. Chappell

CHURCH, Emily I. b1926; md 17 May 1968 Danville, NH NOLAN, Rich F.; md by Rev Douglas Abbott

CHURCH, Frederick L. b 1932 VT s/o CHURCH, Frederick L.; md 17 Nov 1956 Danville, NH OTTATI, Marguerite E.; md by Rev Albion Bulgar (P)

CHURCH, Lorraine Florence b 1934 VT d/o CHURCH, Frederick L.; md 03 Jul 1954 Danville, NH DESILETS, Norman Carroll; md by Agnes H. Collins (JP)

CHURCH, Raymond Harold of Haverhill, MA md 26 Jun 1992 GRACIALE, Audrey Marie

CILLEY, Benj b 14 Oct 1765 Hawke, NH s/o CILLEY, John & CLARK, Abigail

CILLEY, Benj Ensign b c1713; md DARLING, Judith; d 23 Sep 1765 Hawke, NH ae 52y

CILLEY, Daniel b 01 Mar 1762 Hawke, NH s/o CILLEY, John & RING, Abigail

CILLEY, Ebenezer b 28 Nov 1767 Hawke, NH s /o CILLEY, John & CLARK, Abigail

CILLEY, Jacob b 14 Oct 1774 Hawke, NH s/o CILLEY, John & CLARK, Abigail

CILLEY, John md 15 Jul 1761 HAWKE, NH CLARK, Abigail

CILLEY, John b 02 Apr 1772 Hawke, NH s/o CILLEY, John & CLARK, Abigail

CILLEY, Judith b 06 Dec 1763 Hawke NH d/o CILLEY, John & CLARK, Abigail d 07 Jun 1773 Hawke NH

CILLEY, Mary md 05 Dec 1762 Hawke, NH THORN, John Jr.

CILLEY, Mildred b c1878 d/o CILLEY, Oscar & BURNHAM, Inez md BROWNSEY, ---- ; d 21 Jun 1968 Danville, NH

CILLEY, Moses b 25 Jan 1779 Hawke, NH s/o CILLEY, John & CLARK, Abigail; or b 1777 ?

CILLEY, Wm b 24 Oct 1769 Hawke, NH s/o CILLEY, John & CLARK, Abigail

CLARK, Abigail md 15 Jul 1761 HAWKE, NH CILLEY, John

CLARK, Ann-Marie md 21 Jul 1990 Danville, NH LONG, Francis D.; md by Rich J. Rondeau (JP)

CLARK, Calvin T. b Kingston, NH; md 30 Apr 1842 Danville, NH SEAVER, Martha

CLARK, Elmer Howard b 1927 Haverhill, MA s/o CLARK, John U.; md 25 Jul 1953 Danville, NH FILES, Phyllis Evelyn

CLARK, Helen b Dorchester, MA d/o CLARK, Wm & McNEIL, Jessie; d 19 Jun 1928 ae 17y 23d

CLARK, Janice Ruth md 20 Nov 1971 Danville, NH McCLARY, Kenneth Alan; md by Rev Cathleen R. Narowitz

CLARK, Jessie M. b c1898 Stonington, ME s/o CLARK, Lyman; md 10 Jul 1915 Dover, NH AVERY, Ernest C.; md by Rev Earle B. Cross

CLARK, Jonathan md 03 Jun 1773 Hawke, NH BUSWELL, Jane

CLARK, Kenneth Alden b 15 Oct 1957 Danville, NH s/o CLARK, Lambert Wesley & HULL, Virginia Bickford

CLARK, Lawrence Clyde b 19 Jul 1952 Danville, NH s/o CLARK, Lambert Wesley & HALL, Virginia Bickford; md 1st 29 Jan 1972 Danville, NH THIBEAULT, Martha J. by Rev Henry Sawatzky 2nd 10 Sep 1983 Danville, NH DRISCOLL, Nancy E. by Rev Edward J. Charest

CLARK, Mary Virginia b 1943; md 19 Sep 1961 Danville, NH HUNT, Ernest Raymond

CLARK, Mellisa Lyn b 23 Aug 1976 Manchester, NH d/o CLARK, Lawrence C. & THEIBEAULT, Martha J.;

CLARK, Nancy Ellen b 1948 Beverley, MA; md 31 Aug 1966 Danville, NH COOLEN, Scott Leslie; md by Leona A. Sciaudone (JP)

CLARK, Nancy Virginia b 12 May 1955 Danville, NH d/o CLARK, Lambert Wesley & HULL, Virginia Bickford; md 18 May 1974 Danville, NH JENDRICK, David Phillip; md by Rev Cathleen R. Narowitz

CLARK, Nathaniel md 20 Jan 1813 Hawke, NH FRENCH, Polly

CLARK, Philip Michael b 15 Jul 1975 Manchester, NH s/o CLARK, Lawrence C. & THIBEAULT, Martha J.

CLARK, Robert Anthony of Billercia, MA md FLAHERTY, Deborah Anne by Rich J. Rondeau JP

CLARK, Sarah md HOOK, Elisha; d 11 Mar 1808 Hawke, NH

CLARKE, Hazel H. b d/o CLARKE, Roland H. & HENDERSON, Anne; md WYATT, ---- ; d 11 Nov 1947 Danville, NH ae 66y

CLAYTON, Bruce Kendall of Haverhill MA md 10 Oct 1992 LINDROTH, Jacqeline Gale by Rich J. Rondeau JP

CLAYTON, Sarah M b E Hampstead, NH; md FOGG, George F.

CLEAVES, Orville L. b c1849 Peru, NY s/o CLEAVES, John & WHITE, Mary; md 24 Oct 1882 Danville, NH GRIFFIN, Martha I.; d 21 Jun 1917 Danville, NH

CLEMENT, Chas A. b c1880 Fremont, NH s/o CLEMENT, George A.; md 27 Nov 1907 Danville, NH QUIMBY, Alice A.; md by Rev W. C. Chappell

CLEMENT, Ethel M. b 03 May 1922 Danville, NH d/o CLEMENT, Jos D. & CARSON, Christie

CLEMENT, Jos D. b Lowell, MA; md CARSON, Christie

CLEMENTS, Dorothy b of Hawke, NH; md 20 Feb 1803 Kingston, NH BARTLETT, Samuel

CLEMENTS, Ebenezer md 14 Nov 1805 Hawke, NH BROWN, Sally

CLERK, Katherine md 11 Oct 1986 Danville, NH CHASE, Rich I.; md by Rev

CLERK (Cont.) Marcia A. Dorey

CLIFFORD, Caroline M. b 1835 Hawke, NH d/o CLIFFORD, Daniel & BARTLETT, Clarissa; d 11 Apr 1888 Danville, NH; Not Married

CLIFFORD, Chas C. b 08 Aug 1865 Danville, NH s/o CLIFFORD, Eliphalet B. & DEARBORN, Lizzie

CLIFFORD, Chas S. b 29 May 1857 Danville, NH s/o CLIFFORD, Daniel & CHAFFE-LANE, Mary

CLIFFORD, Clara E. b 15 Nov 1850 Danville, NH d/o CLIFFORD, Daniel & BARTLETT, Clarissa; md 20 Apr 1876 Danville, NH ENGLAND, John L.

CLIFFORD, Clarence b 1863 Danville, NH s/o CLIFFORD, Eliphalet B. & DEARBORN, Lizzie

CLIFFORD, Daniel b c1806 Brentwood, NH s/o CLIFFORD, Samuel & BROWN, Nancy; md 29 Dec 1832 Hawke, NH BARTLETT, Clarissa; d 25 Aug 1897 Danville, NH ae 90y 11m

CLIFFORD, Daniel A. b 02 Apr 1844 N Danville, NH s/o CLIFFORD, Daniel & BARTLETT, Clarissa; d 30 Sep 1916 Danville, NH

CLIFFORD, Dorothy Ann b 25 Mar 1833 Hawke, NH s/o CLIFFORD, Daniel & BARTLETT, Clarissa; md 20 Jun 1850 Danville, NH GORDON, Levi Sanborn; d 24 Oct 1907 Danville, NH

CLIFFORD, Eliphalet B. b 1836 Danville, NH s/o CLIFFORD, Daniel & BARTLETT, Clarissa

CLIFFORD, George A. b 07 Apr 1837 Danville, NH s/o CLIFFORD, Daniel & BARTLETT, Clarissa; d 03 May 1842 Danville, NH

CLIFFORD, George W. b 1873 Walden, VT s/o CLIFFORD, Wm & LANE, Celia; md 01 Apr 1896 Fremont, NH DEZAND, Emeline; md by Chas W. Follett (JP); Occupation Farmer

CLIFFORD, Hannah b 28 Sep 1761 Hawke, NH d/o CLIFFORD, Jos & WADLEIGH, Eleanor

CLIFFORD, Isaac b Rumney, NH; md 29 Dec 1768 Hawke, NH Young, Ruth; md by Rev John Page

CLIFFORD, Issac md 24 Nov 1774 Hawke, NH FOLLINSBY, Alice; md by Rev John Page

CLIFFORD, Jos Lt. md FRENCH, Eliz & FIFIELD, Meriam; d 13 Apr 1810 Hawke, NH ae 72y

CLIFFORD, Mary md 17 Nov 1771 Hawke, NH BROWN, Nathaniel

CLIFFORD, Mary S. b 15 Jan 1853 Danville, NH d/o CLIFFORD, Daniel & BARTLETT, Clarissa; d 21 Sep 1930 Danville, NH

CLIFFORD, Michael Robert b 07 Feb 1984 Haverhill, MA s/o CLIFFORD, Stephen P. & DAY, Roberta A.

CLIFFORD, Samuel b Brentwood, NH; md BROWN, Nancy

CLIFFORD, Sarah B. b 02 Jun 1848 Danville, NH d/o CLIFFORD, Daniel & BARTLETT, Clarissa

CLIFTON, Alfred Rich b Dunham Quebec s/o CLIFTON, Thos & TAR-RANT, Emma; d 19 Jan 1949 Danville, NH ae 72y

CLOUGH, Abigail b of Brentwood, NH; md 30 May 1764 SMITH, John; md by Rev John Page

CLOUGH, Arthur Buswell b 10 Dec 1885 Danville, NH s/o CLOUGH, Edward B. & BUSWELL, Etta L.

CLOUGH, Bessie M. b 08 Jul 1885 Danville, NH d/o CLOUGH, Isaac H. & PERLEY, Mary L.

CLOUGH, Eliz b of Sandown, NH; md 22 Oct 1765 Danville, NH

CLOUGH, Hannah b of Poplin, NH; md 09 Oct 1766 MORRILL, Jabez; md by Rev John Page

CLOUGH, Issac H. b Plaistow, NH; md ----, Mary L.

CLOUGH, Josie M. b 10 Apr 1887 Danville, NH d/o CLOUGH, Issac H. & ----, Mary L.; d May 1887 ae 22d

CLOUGH, Judith b Hawke, NH; md 22 Nov 1769 Hawke, NH SLEEPER, Benj; md by Rev John Page

CLOUGH, Moses b of Nottingham, NH; md 08 Nov 1764 CRAM, Mary; md by Rev John Page

CLOUGH, Nancy b d/o CLOUGH, Zaccheus; d 18 May 1777 Hawke, NH

CLOUGH, Norman Everett md 11 Jun 1977 Danville, NH FISHER, Christine Marie; md by Rob't D. Rousseau (JP)

CLOUGH, Sarah b md 19 Nov 1767 Hawke, NH DOLLIFFE, Nicholas

CLOUGH, Sarah md 04 Mar 1772 Hawke, NH BLAISDELL, Henry; also md to ---- DOLLIFFE

CLOUGH, Susanna b c1795 Hawke, NH; md 10 Jul 1820 Kingston, NH ELKINS, Henry; d 09 May 1834 Hawke, NH ae 39y

CLOUGH, Tabetha b 29 Mar 1760 Hawke, NH d /o CLOUGH, Elisha & WELCH, Mary

CLOUGH, Theodate b of Sandown, NH; md 22 Oct 1765 WELLS, Sargent; md by Rev John Page

CLOUGH, Timothy Norman b 10 Nov 1977 Exeter, NH s/o CLOUGH, Norman C. & FALL, Christine Marie

CLOUTIER, Emma b Lawrence, MA; md 17 Jul 1887 Exeter, NH SANBORN, J. Fred; md by Rev W. Canning

CLUKER, Mary A. b c1871 3 Rivers, Canada d/o CLUKER, Maddle; md 17 May 1919 E Hampstead, NH GLOVER, Henry A.; md by Rev F. W. Farrell; 1st md to ---- SANBORN

CLYNTON, Bella b c1854 Cuba; md 02 Nov 1870 Danville NH SILLOWAY, Elmer R.

COBB, Richard Arthur b Newbury-port, MA s/o COBB, Harrison & LAMBERT, Florence Agnes; d 06 Mar 1949 Danville, NH ae 9y

COBURN, Lisa B. md 15 Sep 1984 Danville, NH KIELINEN, Jeffery V.; md by Richard C. L. Webb (EP)

COBURN, Robert P. b s/o COBURN, Henry L. & FERLONG, Marie J.; d 30 May 1987 Danville, NH ae 27y

CODY, Mary Fae b 1913 Lawrence, MA d/o CODY, Frank W.; md 03 Mar 1935 Danville, NH WEBBER, Robert E.; md by Clarence M. Collins (JP)

COLBY, Abig'l b 19 Dec 1749 Chester, NH d/o COLBY, Enoch & SARGENT, Sarah; md 13 Sep 1768 Hawke NH TOWLE, Jas d 12 Feb 1820 Hawke NH bu Danville NH Old Mtg Hse Cem

COLBY, Albert F. b 02 Oct 1826 Hawke, NH s/o COLBY, Ebenezer & PHILBRICK, Sarah

COLBY, Alden Downs b 1905 Danville, NH s/o COLBY, Herbert E.; md 10 Aug 1932 Danville, NH WHITE, Frances D.; md by Rev C. L. Carter

COLBY, Alden Downs b 1905 Danville, NH s/o COLBY, Herbert E. & DOWNS, Annie H. md 25 Dec 1945 Danville, NH BLAKE, Frances Louise; md by Rev W. C. Chappell

COLBY, Alden E. b 04 Jan 1830 Hawke, NH s/o COLBY, Thos & FRENCH, Miriam; md 05 Dec 1853 Newmarket, NH SPOFFORD, Lucy Ann; d 30 Aug 1876 Danville, NH

COLBY, Anna b Hawke, NH; md 18 Mar 1779 Hawke, NH MORRILL, Henry; md by Rev John Page

COLBY, Benj P. b 21 Jul 1801 Hawke, NH s/o COLBY, Moses & PILLSBURY, Jane

COLBY, Charlotte M. b 22 Nov 1868 Danville, NH d/o COLBY, Alden E. & SPOFFORD, Lucy A.; md 23 Oct 1902 Danville, NH PEABODY, Lorenzo J.; md by Rev A. B. Howard

COLBY, Dorothy b 06 Apr 1784 Hawke, NH d/o COLBY, Enos & PAGE, Hannah

COLBY, Dorothy b c1759 d/o COLBY, Moses & TUXBURY, Anna; d 18 Sep 1777 Hawke, NH ae 18y

COLBY, Emily Tilton b 07 Mar 1817 Hawke, NH d/o COLBY, Thos & FRENCH, Miriam; md 16 Feb 1837 Danville, NH INGALLS, John C. F.

COLBY, Enos b 13 May 1761 Hawke, NH s/o COLBY, Moses & TUXBURY, Anna; md 08 May 1783 PAGE, Hannah; d 30 May 1827 Hawke, NH bu Hawke, NH Center Cem 1st peron to be bu Center Cem

COLBY, Enos b 20 Aug 1802 Hawke, NH s/o COLBY, Enos & PAGE, Hannah

COLBY, Faoline Hope b 21 Jan 1909 Danville, NH, d/o COLBY, Herbert E. & DOWNS, Annie H.; md 30 Jun 1932 Danville, NH RYLANDER, Merton L.; 03 Jan 1985 Danville, NH; md by Rev Harold C. ROSS

COLBY, Herbert E. b 22 Nov 1864 Danville, NH s/o COLBY, Alden E. & SPOFFORD, Lucy A.; md 18 Jun 1902 Danville, NH DOWNS, Annie H.; md by

COLBY (Cont.) Rev W. P. Merrill; d 26 Mar 1928 ae 63y 4m 4d

COLBY, Jane b 04 Dec 1798 Danville, NH d/o COLBY, Moses & PILLSBURY, Jane

COLBY, Jethro b of Chester, NH; md 21 Sep 1779 Hawke, NH BRADLEY, Nanny; md by Rev John Page

COLBY, John b 26 May 1824 Hawke, NH s/o COLBY, Thos & FRENCH, Miriam

COLBY, Joia b 19 Jan 1795 Hawke, NH d/o COLBY, Moses & PULLSBURY, Jane

COLBY, Lester A. b 02 Oct 1860 Danville, NH s/o COLBY, Alden E. & SPOFFORD, Lucy A.; d 10 Jul 1947 Danville, NH

COLBY, Mary b 23 Aug 1787 Hawke, NH; d/o COLBY, Enos & PAGE, Hannah

COLBY, Miriam Gertrude b 02 May 1903 Danville, NH; d/o COLBY, Herbert E. & DOWNS, Annie H.; md 21 Jun 1929 Danville, NH SUNDERLAND, Jesse E.; md by Rev W. C. Chappell

COLBY, Moses b 25 Jun 1769 Hawke, NH s/o COLBY, Moses & TUXBURY, Anna

COLBY, Moses b 25 May 1799 Hawke, NH s/o COLBY, Enos & PAGE, Hannah

COLBY, Moses b 20 Mar 1793 Hawke, NH s/o COLBY, Enos & PAGE, Hannah; d 04 Sep 1794 Hawke, NH ae 1 1/2 m

COLBY, Moses b 07 Sep 1803 Hawke, NH s/o COLBY, Moses & PILLSBURY, Jane

COLBY, Moses b c1731 Amesbury, MA; md TUXBURY, Anna; d 07 Apr 1777 Hawke, NH bu Danville, NH Old Mtg Hse Cem.; d ae 46y

COLBY, Nancy b 27 Jan 1791 Hawke, NH d/o COLBY, Enos & PAGE, Hannah; md by PAGE, John; d 02 May 1816 Hawke, NH

COLBY, Osmund Spofford b 06 Apr 1857 Danville, NH s/o COLBY, Alden E. & SPOFFORD, Lucy A.; d 24 Apr 1875 Danville, NH ae 18y

COLBY, Rebecca Ann b 23 Jan 1968 Danville, NH d/o COLBY, John Nelson & THORNTON, Marcia Grace

COLBY, Rhoda b Feb 1768 Hawke, NH d/o COLBY, Moses & TUXBURY, Anna; d 03 Mar 1768 Hawke, NH ae 20d

COLBY, Sarah md 30 Jun 1830 Hawke, NH THORN, Abram

COLBY, Selley b 18 Nov 1796 Hawke, NH d/o COLBY, Moses & PILLSBURY, Jane

COLBY, Thos Elliot b md RING, Susanna; d 04 Oct 1760 Crown Point ae 26y

COLBY, Thos Page b 23 Apr 1786 Hawke, NH s/o COLBY, Thos & PAGE, Hannah; md 01 Oct 1814 Hawke, NH FRENCH, Miriam; d 20 Dec 1858 Danville, NH ae 73y

COLCORD, Dorothy md 28 Jun 1790 Kingston, NH PHILBRICK, Jedediah

COLCORD, Susanna b c1758; md 1793 Hawke, NH EATON, Jabez; d 31 Oct 1823 Hawke, NH ae 65yr

COLE, Alice b 10 Feb 1857 Danville, NH d/o COLE, Moores (Rev) & ---- , Eliz L. d 1859 Danville, NH;

COLE, Bessie M. b Prince Edward Is. d/o COLE, Daniel; d 30 Aug 1966 Danville, NH

COLE, Frank W. b Bondville, VT; md COLLINS, Vivian F.

COLE, Loula b 1895 Putnam, CT d/o COLE, Jos H. & AMES, Minnie; md 25 Dec 1937 Danville, NH GEORGE, Richard Howard; d 25 Jun 1984 Danville, NH; md by Clarence M. Collins (JP)

COLE, Margaret (Peggy) b c1755; md SPOFFORD, Benj; d 26 Dec 1825 Hawke, NH; bu Hawke, NH Old Mtg Hse Cem.; d ae 70y

COLE, Morres Rev. b Lowell, MA; d 05 Dec 1888 Danville, NH ae 73 3m

COLE, Willard b 10 Feb 1857 Danville, NH s/o COLE, M. & ---- , E.

COLE, ---- , b 07 Mar 1964 Exeter, NH d/o COLE, Frank W. & COLLINS, Vivian F.; d 07 Mar 1964 Exeter, NH

COLEMAN, Carolyn Marie md 10 Oct 1991 Danville, NH BURKE, Kevin Michael; md by Rev Gordon S. Bates

COLES, Gail Anne b md 11 Nov 1978 Danville, NH TRUE, Richard Pillsbury; md by Rev Diane J. Augspurger

COLETTA, Eliz A. b md 01 Jun 1990 Danville, NH FICHERA, Rich J.; md by Philip D. Fichera (JP)

COLL, Kevin Wm b 09 Sep 1987 Exeter, NH s/o COLL, Mark V. & THERESA, Diane T.

COLL, Matthew Vincent b 14 Jul 1989 Exeter, NH s/o COLL, Mark V. & BECOTTE, Diana T.

COLLINS, Vivian F.; d 07 Mar 1964 Exeter, NH

COLEMAN, Carolyn Marie md 10 Oct 1991 Danville, NH BURKE, Kevin Michael; md by Rev Gordon S. Bates

COLES, Gail Anne b md 11 Nov 1978 Danville, NH TRUE, Richard PIllsbury; md by Rev Diane J. Augspurger

COLETTA, Eliz A. b md 01 Jun 1990 Danville, NH FICHERA, Richard J.; md by Philip D. Fichera (JP)

COLL, Kevin Wm b 09 Sep 1987 Exeter, NH s/o COLL, Mark V. & THERESA, Diane T.

COLL, Matthew Vincent b 14 Jul 1989 Exeter, NH s/o COLL, Mark V. & BECOTTE, Diana T.

COLLINS, Ada Frances b 29 May 1859 Danville, NH d/o COLLINS, Alva Blake & ALLEN, Mary Ann; md 27 Dec 1883 Saugas, MA

COLLINS, Clarence Morton d 01 Jan 1944 Danville, NH; bu Danville, NH Center Cem

COLLINS, Adelaide A. b 1854 Danville, NH d/o COLLINS, Jos & CHALLIS, Irene C.; d 26 Nov 1864 Danville, NH ae 10y

COLLINS, Agnes Hermione b 28 Nov 1872 Danville, NH d/o COLLINS, Leonard Washington & COLLINS, Althea J.; d 21 May 1959 Derry, NH; bu Danville, NH Center Cem; Not Married

COLLINS, Alfred Asbury b 15 Oct 1848 Danville, NH s/o COLLINS, John Hazen & COLLINS, Amy; md 1st 01 Dec 1870 Norton, MA LINCOLN, Elvira R.; d 11 Oct 1916 Danville, NH; md 2nd 14 Nov 1885 Danville, NH LOWELL, Kate Colinda; d 11 Oct 1916

COLLINS, Alice Lincoln b 04 Jan 1880 Danville, NH d/o COLLINS, Alfred Asbury & LINCOLN, Elvira R.; md 28

COLLINS (Cont.) Sep 1901 Danville, NH HUNTINGTON, Allan L.; d 11 Jun 1966 Danville, NH; d ae 85y; md by Rev A. B. Howard

COLLINS, Allen Gordon b 10 Mar 1889 s/o COLLINS, Leonard Waldo & GORDON, Elvira Clara; d 09 Jul 1963; bu Kingston, NH Plains Cem; SS 002-01-1618

COLLINS, Almira B. b 1833 Hampstead, NH d/o COLLINS, Hezekiah & MORSE, Sarah md 1860 Danville, NH DIMOND, Josiah T.; d 11 Mar 1899 Danville, NH ae 66y 8m 11d

COLLINS, Aletha J. b 28 Dec 1835 Hawke, NH d/o COLLINS, John & TOWLE, Orinda; md 16 May 1857 Danville, NH COLLINS, Leonard Washington; d 17 Sep 1923 Danville, NH; bu Danville, NH

COLLINS, Alva Blake b 27 Sep 1826 Hampstead, NH s/o COLLINS, Jonathan & DANIELS, Betsey; md 15 Nov 1849 Danville, NH ALLEN, Mary Ann; d 06 Apr 1907 Danville, NH; bu Danville, NH

COLLINS, Amos b 08 Oct 1831 Hawke, NH s/o COLLINS, Jonathan & BURNEL, Sarah

COLLINS, Amy b 14 Dec 1825 Danville, NH d/o COLLINS, John & TOWLE, Orinda; md 26 Nov 1908 Danville, NH COLLINS, John Hazen; d 16 Feb 1899 Danville, NH; bu Danville, NH Center Cem.

COLLINS, Anna May b Apr 1867 Danville, NH d/o COLLINS, Jos & CHALLIS, Irene C.; d 10 Feb 1877 Danville, NH ae 10y of Diptheria

COLLINS, Anne b 11 Jan 1783 Hawke, NH d/o COLLINS, Richard & BUSWELL, Sarah COLLINS, Arthur Allen b 09 Apr 1908 Danville, NH s/o COLLINS, Edson T. & SEAVER, Susan F.; md 14 Oct 1937 Danville, NH BOOKER, Eliz B.; md by Rev W. C. Chappell

COLLINS, Arthur S. b1828 Danville, NH; md 11 Nov 1856 Exeter, NH GEORGE, Caroline; d 28 Oct 1886 Danville, NH ae 58y

COLLINS, Austin D. b 02 Nov 1846 Danville, NH s/o COLLINS, Levi & TOWLE, Aramintha

COLLINS, Barbara Anne b 12 Dec 1932 d/o COLLINS, Herbert Morgan Sr.& HONISH, Mildre; md EMBERLEY, Edward Randolph

COLLINS, Barbara Jean b 07 Apr 1930 Danville, NH d/o COLLINS, Herbert Levi & HASKINEN, Hilja; md 24 Jul 1948 Danville, NH GROTON, George; md by Rev W. C. Chappell

COLLINS, Barbara Wayne b d/o COLLINS, Robert Hazen & SARGENT, Helen; md MIKELSEN, Carl M. Sr.

COLLINS, Bernard Ira Jr b 14 Oct 1922 Haverhill, MA s/o COLLINS, Bernard Ira Sr & McPHEARSON, Louise Eleanor; d 11 Apr 1925

COLLINS, Bernard Ira Sr b 17 May 1885 Danville, NH s/o COLLINS, Herbert Sumner & SPAULDING, Lillian Etta; md 16 Dec 1915 Ontario Canada McPHEARSON, Louise Eleanor; d 13 Feb 1967 New Westminster CN; bu Haverhill, MA

COLLINS, Bertha Malvina b 19 Jul 1871 Danville, NH d/o COLLINS, Alva Blake & ALLEN, Mary Ann; md 28 Apr 1892 Danville, NH MACE, Wm James; d 11 May 1960 Danville, NH; bu Danville, NH Center Cem; md by Rev J. A. Lowell

COLLINS, Bertie b Apr 1868 s/o COLLINS, Lorenzo B. & GRIFFIN, Mary Luella; d 29 Dec 1874 Danville, NH d ae 6y

COLLINS, Berton E. b Nov 1881 Danville, NH s/o COLLINS, Fred E. & HOYT, Mary O.; d Feb 1895

COLLINS, Beverley Joyce b 1932 Hampstead, NH d/o COLLINS, Blinn S.; md 14 Aug 1953 Danville, NH COONEY, Robert

COLLINS, Brenda Eileen b 18 Apr 1944 Danville, NH d/o COLLINS, Howard Cecil & GOLDWTHWAITE, Grace Pauline; md 22 Oct 1960 Danville, NH PERROW, John Ross md by Rev John F. Griffin

COLLINS, Brian Kieth b 26 Jul 1959 Danville, NH s/o COLLINS, Merville Sidney & HERRICK, Gloria Louise; md 15 Aug 1981 Danville, NH SHEPPARD, Tracey A.; md by Lawrence G. Brann (JP)

COLLINS, Brian Travis b 05 Jan

COLLINS (Cont.) 1988 Exeter, NH s/o COLLINS, David P. & PALMER, Rebecca D.

COLLINS, Bruce Edward b 23 Mar 1958 Danville, NH s/o COLLINS, Roy H. & HARRIS, Evelyn

COLLINS, Bruce Ian b 13 Jul 1949 Picton, Ontario Canada s/o COLLINS, Kenneth Fawcett & ROBLIN, Evalyn; d 29 Nov 1972

COLLINS, Burton D. b 1865 Danville, NH s/o COLLINS, Jos & CHALLIS, Irene C. d 14 Sep 1865 Danville, NH ae 4 1/2 m

COLLINS, Byron Edward b 1926 ----, MA s/o COLLINS, Byron E.; md 18 Nov 1950 Danville, NH ELARIO, Thelma Constance; md by Rev James W. Gilrain

COLLINS, Caleb b Jan 1837 Kingston, NH s/o COLLINS, Laban & HUNT, Rachel C.

COLLINS, Candice Joyce b 25 Oct 1946 d/o COLLINS, Cecil Spaulding & SHARPE, Joyce md 26 Jun 1965 BEST, Tony

COLLINS, Carla Marie b 11 Apr 1977 Methuen, MA d/o COLLINS, Norman H. & MARQUIS, Diane A.

COLLINS, Carlene Marie b 13 Mar 1957 Danville, NH d/o COLLINS, Merville Sidney & HERRICK, Gloria Louise; md 13 Nov 1976 Danville, NH COLLINS John; md by Robert S. Dejadon (JP)

COLLINS, Carol Ann b 06 Jan 1940 Exeter, NH d/o COLLINS, Howard Cecil & GOLDTHWAITE, Grace Pauline; md 05 Oct 1957 Danville, NH MARTIN, Donald Melvin

COLLINS, Carol Ann b d/o COLLINS, Herbert Morgan & NIGGER-MEYER, Patricia

COLLINS, Carol Lynn b 24 Sep 1962 d/o COLLINS, Cecil Spaulding & CANUEL, Marguerite

COLLINS, Carrie E. b 1861 Danville, NH d/o COLLINS, Jos & CHALLIS, Irene C.; d 17 Dec 1870 Danville, NH ae 9y

COLLINS, Cecil Spaulding b 06 Jul 1920 Haverhill, MA s/o COLLINS, Bernard Ira Sr & McPHEARSON, Louise Elean; md 20 Jul 1942 SHARPE, Joyce; 2nd md CANUEL, Margurite

COLLINS, Charles b 24 Oct 1806 Hawke, NH s/o COLLINS, Jos Jr & DEARBORN, Mary (Polly); md 29 Nov 1827 Kingston, NH SANBORN, Jane

COLLINS, Charles b 05 Oct 1764 Kingston, NH s/o COLLINS, John Dea. & CHALLIS, Sarah

COLLINS, Charles Page b Apr 1886 Danville, NH s/o COLLINS, Oren Eugene & WEBSTER, Flora M.; md 28 Jun 1919 Amesbury, MA BARNARD, Alice M.; d 16 Mar 1971 Danville, NH; md by Rev F. G. Merrill; d ae 84y

COLLINS, Chester S. b Danville, NH s/o COLLINS, Edson T. & SEAVER, Susan F. d 26 Aug 1897 Danville, NH

COLLINS, Clara Webster b 24 Aug 1885 Danville, NH d/o COLLINS, Oren Eugene & WEBSTER, Flora M.; md 14 Apr 1904 Boxford, MA WATSON, Wilmont Ansley md by Rev L. W. Snell

COLLINS, Clarence Morton b 13 Aug 1850 Danville, NH s/o COLLINS, Leonard Washington & COLLINS, Althea J.; md 27 Dec 1883 Saugus, MA COLLINS, Ada Frances; d 09 May 1942 Danville, NH; bu Danville, NH Center Cem.

COLLINS, Clarissa b 18 Mar 1826 Hawke, NH d/o COLLINS, Moses & PAGE, Hannah md 05 Jun 1849 Danville, NH ELKINS, Abel; d 08 Feb 1917 Danville, NH

COLLINS, Clement Spaulding b 17 Feb 1884 Danville, NH s/o COLLINS, Herbert Sumner & SPAULDING, Lillian Etta; md 23 Sep 1910 McCOLLISTER. Lottie; d 15 Oct 1918

COLLINS, Clifton Eveleth b 23 Nov 1887 Kingston, NH s/o COLLINS, Leslie Ashton & DAVIS, Olive Frances; md 15 Dec 1913 Plaistow, NH SULTAIRE, Anna Josephine; d 25 Feb 1966 Renton, WA; bu Renton, WA Olivet Cem; Father of the compiler of this record Elbert (Gus) Collins

COLLINS, Cora Mabel b 24 Jan 1861 Danville, NH d/o COLLINS, John Hazen & COLLINS, Amy; md 31 Dec 1885 Danville, NH WITHERELL, Edward A.

COLLINS, Dana Richard b 11 Sep 1981 Exeter, NH s/o COLLINS, Gary Robert & SKILLINGS, Pamnela J.

COLLINS, Dane Allen b 05 Nov 1961 Danville, NH s/o COLLINS, Merville Sidney & HERRICK, Gloria Louise

COLLINS, David P. md 07 Jul 1984 Danville, NH PALMER, Rebecca D.; md by Rev Everett E. Palmer

COLLINS, Diana b 28 Jun 1822 Hawke, NH d/o COLLINS, Moses & PAGE, Hannah d 1827 Hawke, NH; bu Danville, NH Old Mtg Hse Cem.; d ae 5y

COLLINS, Dorothy b d/o COLLINS, Jonathan & WEBSTER, Dorothy; md 13 Feb 1794 Hampstead, NH CORNER, Nathan

COLLINS, Dorothy b 11 Mar 1901 Danville, NH d/o COLLINS, Wilbur H. & PITTS, Hattie L.; 3rd child in family

COLLINS, Dorothy Grace b 1928 ----, OR d/o COLLINS, Herbert Levi & HOSKINEN, Hilja; md 23 Oct 1949 Danville, NH RICHMOND, Walter Rowe; md by Rev W. C. Chappell

COLLINS, Edith R. b Apr 1893 Danville, NH d/o COLLINS, Oren Eugene & WEBSTER, Flora M.; 1st md 28 Jun 1914 Danville, NH NEVERS, Cecil by Rev Allen Keith; 2nd md GERRIER, Harold

COLLINS, Edna Arlene b 1925 Kingston, NH d/o COLLINS, Oral Walter; md 08 Jun 1946 Danville, NH WEST, Chandler Bruce; md by Rev W. C. Chappell

COLLINS, Edna Blanche b 11 Jul 1880 Danville, NH d/o COLLINS, Edson T. & SEAVER, Susan F.; md 30 Dec 1899 Danville, NH AVERY, Wm P. Jr; d 22 Nov 1965 Danville, NH ae 85y

COLLINS, Edson F. b 11 Sep 1859 Danville, NH s/o COLLINS, Jos & CHALLIS, Irene C.; md SEAVER, Susan F.; d 03 Jul 1929 Danville, NH

COLLINS, Elbert Augustus b 07 Jan 1920 Plaistow, NH s/o COLLINS, Clifton Eveleth & SULTAIRE, Anna Josephine; 1st md 20 Apr 1941 Haverhill, MA FREDETTE, Marie Eva Cecile (div); 2nd md 01 Nov 1947 Tacoma, WA WYATT, Esther Louise

COLLINS, Eliz b 11 Jan 1957 Ottawa Ontario Canada d/o COLLINS, Kenneth Fawcett & ROBLIN, Evalyn; md WAYNE-JONES, Philip

COLLINS, Eliz b 17 Jan 1781 Hawke, NH d/o COLLINS, Richard & BUSWELL, Sarah

COLLINS, Eliz b 18 Jan 1919 Haverhill, MA d/o COLLINS, Bernard Ira Sr & McPHEARSON, Louise Eleanor; d 14 Apr 1920

COLLINS, Eliz b 20 Jul 1773 Hawke, NH d/o COLLINS, Jos Sr & BAGLEY, Sarah; md 11 Apr 1796 Kingston, NH DEARBORN, Josiah

COLLINS, Emily L. b 16 Jul 1823 Hawke, NH d/o COLLINS, John & TOWLE, Orinda; bu Old Mtg Hse Cem; d as infant

COLLINS, Emma Susan b 06 Feb 1851 Danville, NH d/o COLLINS, John Hazen & COLLINS, Amy; md 19 Dec 1872 Danville, NH HEATH, John F.; d 15 Oct 1887 Danville, NH

COLLINS, Enoch b 22 Jan 1773 Salisbury, MA s/o COLLINS, John & CHALLIS, Sarah

COLLINS, Erdine b 18 Sep 1874 Kingston, NH d/o COLLINS, Leon P. & ROGERS, Ellen A.

COLLINS, Eugene F. b 07 Feb 1886 Danville, NH s/o COLLINS, Edson F. & SEAVER, Susan F.; md 15 Jul 1908 Sandown, NH LeCLARE, Lydia M. md by Rev F. G. Deshies

COLLINS, Evelyn Alice b 1921 Kingston, NH d/o COLLINS, Clarence Edwin; md 07 Jun 1941 Danville, NH TROTT, Kenneth Elmer; md by Rev W. C. Chappell

COLLINS, Florence R. b 05 Dec 1889 Danville, NH d/o COLLINS, Oren Eugene & WEBSTER, Flora M.; md 11 Oct 1924 Danville, NH LANE, Harold M.; md by Rev John L. Clark

COLLINS, Floyd b 03 Aug 1889 Danville, NH s/o COLLINS, Herbert Sumner & SPAULDING, Lillian Etta

COLLINS, Francis A. b 30 Jan 1940 Danville, NH d/o COLLINS, Arthur A. & BOOKER, Eliz B.

COLLINS, Frank P. b 1852 Danville, NH s/o COLLINS, Jos & CHALLIS, Irene C.; d 25 Jan 1860 Danville, NH ae 7y

COLLINS, Frank Perley b 15 Dec 1861 Danville, NH s/o COLLINS, Perley

COLLINS (Cont.) S. & ANDERSON, Rhoda J.; md 22 Nov 1884 Danville, NH WINSLOW, Sarah H. d 20 Aug 1942 Danville, NH

COLLINS, Fred E. b 03 Sep 1859 Danville, NH s/o COLLINS, Lorenzo B. & GRIFFIN, Mary Luella; md HOYT, Mary O.; d 11 Nov 1936 Danville, NH

COLLINS, Gary Richard b 21 Sep 1952 Danville, NH s/o COLLINS, Roy H. & HARRIS, Evelyn; md SKILLINGS, Pamela J.

COLLINS, Gilman b 21 Jul 1806 Hawke, NH; md 24 Dec 1829 Kingston, NH WEBSTER, Hannah; d 21 Mar 1853 Danville, NH ae 46y

COLLINS, Gladys Lydia b 25 Jan 1909 Danville, NH d/o COLLINS, Eugene F. & LeCLARE, Lydia M.

COLLINS, Hannah b 05 Oct 1841 Kingston, NH d/o COLLINS, Laban & HUNT, Rachel C.

COLLINS, Hannah b Apr 1810; d 20 May 1863 Danville, NH ae 53y

COLLINS, Hannah b 24 Sep 1773 Hawke, NH d/o COLLINS, Tristram & HUNT, Rachel

COLLINS, Hannah b 25 May 1785 Hawke, NH d/o COLLINS, Richard & BUSWELL, Sarah

COLLINS, Hannah E. b 1849 Rumney, NH; md 23 Oct 1877 Danville, NH GEORGE, Frank W.

COLLINS, Hannah Page b 15 Dec 1833 Hawke, NH d/o COLLINS, Moses & PAGE, Hannah; md FRENCH, James

COLLINS, Harry Elwyn b 10 Mar 1882 Danville, NH s/o COLLINS, Herbert Sumner & SPAULDING, Lillian Etta; d 09 Aug 1882

COLLINS, Heather b 29 Jun 1976 Exeter, NH d/o COLLINS, John & COLLINS, Carlene M.

COLLINS, Henry b s/o COLLINS, Jos Jr & DEARBORN, Mary (Polly); md 24 Feb 1820 Kingston, NH SANBORN, Rachel

COLLINS, Herbert L. md 21 Sep 1973 Danville, NH TWOMBLEY, Emma M.; md by Rev Peter W. Lovejoy

COLLINS, Herbert Levi b 07 Jul 1888 Danville, NH s/o COLLINS, Woodbury D. & CRAM, Julia S.; 1st md

COLLINS (Cont.) 08 Nov 1912 Groveland, MA TABER, Mabel C.;2nd md KOSKINEN, Hilja; 3rd md CHASE, Blossom Ruth; 4th md WALKER, Stella; 5th md WILSON, Emma M.; d 27 Jul 1975 Danville, NH

COLLINS, Herbert Morgan Jr b 27 Dec 1936 s/o COLLINS, Herbert Morgan Sr & HONISH, Mildred; md NIGGER-MEYER, Patricia; d 21 Apr 1984 Florida

COLLINS, Herbert Morgan Sr b 26 Apr 1902 Haverhill, MA s/o COLLINS, Herbert Sumner & SPAULDING, Lillian Etta; 1st md 05 Dec 1931 HONISH, Mildred; 2nd md STEVENS, Marion; d 21 Apr 1984 Haverhill, MA; bu Haverhill, MA

COLLINS, Herbert Sumner b 25 Jun 1857 Danville, NH s/o COLLINS, John Hazen & COLLINS, Amy; md 16 Jun 1881 Danville, NH SPAULDING, Lillian Etta; d 08 Sep 1934 N Danville, NH; bu Danville, NH Center Cem

COLLINS, Hezekiah b 21 Dec 1797 Hampstead, NH s/o COLLINS, Samuel & BLAKE, Mary (Polly); md 24 Dec 1820 Hampstead, NH MORSE, Sarah; d 20 Oct 1845 Danville, NH; bu Danville, NH Center Cem

COLLINS, Howard Cecil b 11 Apr 1915 Danville, NH s/o COLLINS, Roy Cram & DAY, Mary Ethel; md 14 Oct 1937 Danville, NH GOLDTHWAITE, Grace Pauline; md by Rev W. C. Chappell

COLLINS, Howard Jos b MA; md 05 Apr 1969 Danville, NH BUTREOCCIO, Carol Anne md by Leona A. Sciaudone (JP)

COLLINS, Howard Stuart b 24 Dec 1927 Montreal Canada s/o COLLINS, Bernard Ira Sr & McPHEARSON, Louise Eleanor

COLLINS, Irene Dolly b 09 Apr 1908 Danville, NH d/o COLLINS, Edson T. & SEAVER, Susan F.; md 09 Jun 1928 Danville, NH RUMERY, Bernard E.; md by Rev Howard A. Reyman

COLLINS, Irving Mahlon b 30 Nov 1884 Danville, NH s/o COLLINS, Clarence Morton & COLLINS, Ada Frances; md 06 Jun 1907 Danville, NH DIMOND, Carrie Mabel; d 24 Sep 1983 Brentwood,

COLLINS (Cont.) NH; md by Rev W.
C. Chappell bu Danville, NH Center
Cem

COLLINS, Isa M. b N. Danville, NH
s/o COLLINS, Oren Eugene & WEB-
STER, Flora M. md LESSARD, Dana; d
08 Feb 1963 ae 71y

COLLINS, Israel b 20 Jun 1786
Hawke, NH s/o COLLINS, Benj & ----,
Sarah md Apr 1804 POLLARD, Polly

COLLINS, Jabez b 09 Aug 1781
Hampstead, NH s/o COLLINS, Jonathan
& WEBSTER, Dorothy; md 22 Dec 1802
Hampstead, NH EASTMAN, Olive; d 11
Oct 1863 Danville, NH ae 83y

COLLINS, Jacob b 06 Mar 1808
Hampstead, NH s/o COLLINS, Jabez &
EASTMAN, Olive; md 24 Nov 1831
Hawke, NH Straw, Sally H.; d 25 Dec
1882 Danville, NH ae 74y maybe m 1836

COLLINS, Jacob b 02 Jun 1790
Hawke, NH s/o COLLINS, Benj & ----,
Sarah

COLLINS, Jacob b 04 May 1821
Hampstead, NH s/o COLLINS, Hezekiah
& MORSE, Sarah md 30 Oct 1862
Danville, NH COLLINS, Susan Jane; d
14 Jan 1896 Danville, NH; bu Danville,
NH Center Cem

COLLINS, Jeanne Marie b 15 Jan
1964 d/o COLLINS, Herbert Morgan Jr
& NIGGERMEYER, Patricia

COLLINS, Jeffery Scott b 10 Sep
1965 Danville, NH s/o COLLINS, Merville Sidney & HERRICK, Gloria Louise;
md 10 May 1987 Danville, NH CALA-
BRIA, Nicole A.; md by Richard J.
Rondeau (JP)

COLLINS, Jenette Irene b 30 Sep
1926 Danville, NH d/o COLLINS, Roy
Cram & DAY, Mary Ethel; md EATON,
George B.

COLLINS, Jennie b Apr 1841 d/o
COLLINS, Edward & ----, Alice

COLLINS, Jennie Eliz b 02 Nov 1967
Danville, NH d/o COLLINS, Larry Morse
Sr & SIMANO, Elibabeth Ann

COLLINS, Jennie V. b 15 May 1931
Danville, NH d/o COLLINS, Perley
Forrest & SPITZER, Emily L.

COLLINS, Jennie W. b 11 Dec 1877
Danville, NH d/o COLLINS, Woodbury
D. & CRAM, Julia L.; md 14 Oct 1902

COLLINS, (Cont.) Danville, NH
HILL, Geo A.; md by Rev A. B. Howard

COLLINS, Jeremy Scott b 22 Jan
1987 Exeter, NH s/o COLLINS, Norman
H. & BIZEUR, Patricia

COLLINS, Jessica Lynn b 29 Jul
1982 Manchester, NH d/o COLLINS,
Brian K. & SHEPPARD, Tracy A.

COLLINS, Joel M.; md 09 Mar 1985
Danville, NH CARON, Tammy A.; md by
Francis J. McKone (P)

COLLINS, John b 13 Sep 1798
Danville, NH s/o COLLINS, Jos Jr &
DEARBORN, Mary (Polly); md 12 Mar
1823 Plaistow, NH TOWLE, Orinda; d
13 Nov 1889 Danville, NH

COLLINS, John b 23 Mar 1779
Goffstown, NH s/o COLLINS, Richard &
BUSWELL, Sarah

COLLINS, John md 19 Nov 1975
Danville, NH COLLINS, Carlene Marie;
md by Robert S. Dejadon (JP)

COLLINS, John Hazen b 31 May
1824 Hampstead, NH s/o COLLINS,
Jonathan & DANIELS, Betsey; md 26
Nov 1846 Danville, NH COLLINS, Amy;
d 23 Oct 1908 Danville, NH; bu Danville,
NH Center Cem

COLLINS, Jonathan b 16 May 1796
Hampstead, NH s/o COLLINS, Samuel
& BLAKE, Mary (Polly); md 19 Dec 1822
Hampstead, NH DANIELS, Betsy; d 15
Oct 1886 Danville, NH; bu Danville, NH

COLLINS, Jonathan b 26 Feb 1768
Kingston, NH s/o COLLINS, Jonathan &
WEBSTER, Dorothy; md PLUMER,
Alice

COLLINS, Jonathan b 16 Apr 1797
Hawke, NH s/o COLLINS, Laban &
JONES, Dorothy md ----, Sarah; d 25 Jul
1862; bu Danville, NH Center Cem

COLLINS, Jonathan b 22 Mar 1739
Hampton Falls, NH s/o COLLINS, Benj
& JONES, Mary; md 29 Apr 1761
Hampstead, NH WEBSTER, Dorothy; d
02 Mar 1818 Hampstead, NH; bu
Hampstead, NH; md by Rev John Page

COLLINS, Jos b 20 Feb 1784 Hawke,
NH s/o COLLINS, Benj & ----, Sarah

COLLINS, Jos b Apr 1828 Danville,
NH s/o COLLINS, Jonathan & DAN-
IELS, Betsy md CHALLIS, Irene C.; d 20
Mar 1897 Danville, NH ae 69y 7m 3d

COLLINS, Jos b 03 Dec 1773 Goffstown, NH s/o COLLINS, Richard &
BUSWELL, Sarah

COLLINS, Jos Jr b 17 Mar 1764
Hawke, NH s/o COLLINS, Jos Sr &
BAGLEY, Sarah; md 26 Jan 1792
Kingston, NH DEARBORN, Mary
(Polly); d 13 Mar 1847 Danville, NH; bu
Danville, NH Old Mtg Hse Cem

COLLINS, Jos Sr b Danville, NH s/o
COLLINS, Benj & JONES, Mary; md 17
Jan 1760 Danville, NH BAGLEY, Sarah;
d 13 Mar 1847 Danville, NH

COLLINS, Joshua Roy b 12 Jan 1982
Exeter, NH s/o COLLINS, Roy W. &
WILLIAMS, Holly J.

COLLINS, Julia Wilhelmina b 1920
Walla Walla, WA d/o COLLINS, Herbert
Levi & HOSKINEN, Hilja; md 26 Apr
1947 Danville, NH GIGILOTTI, Louis
Jos; md by W. C. Chappell

COLLINS, Kenneth Fawcett b 23
Nov 1916 Haverhill, MA s/o COLLINS,
Bernard Ira Sr. & McPHEARSON,
Louise Eleanor; md 19 May 1941 King-
ston, Ontario Canada ROBLYN, Evalyn

COLLINS, Kenneth Herbert b 15
May 1891 Danville, NH s/o COLLINS,
Herbert Sumner & SPAULDING, Lillian
Etta; d 08 May 1893 Danville, NH ae 1y
11m 24d

COLLINS, Laban b 27 Apr 1775
Hawke, NH s/o COLLINS, Jonathan &
WEBSTER, Dorothy md 28 Apr 1795
Kingston, NH JONES, Dorothy; d 4 Feb
1838; bu Danville, NH Family Cem on
Pleasant St

COLLINS, Laban b 03 Oct 1810
Hampstead, NH s/o COLLINS, Jabez &
EASTMAN, Olive md HUNT, Rachel C.

COLLINS, Larry Morse Jr b 26 Mar
1966 Danville, NH s/o COLLINS, Larry
Morse Sr & SIMANO, Eliz Ann

COLLINS, Larry Morse Sr b Exeter,
NH; md SIMANO, Eliz Ann

COLLINS, Laura F. b 27 Oct 1859
Danville, NH d/o COLLINS, Levi &
TOWLE, Aramintha; md 29 Nov 1877
Danville, NH WOOD, Franklin F.

COLLINS, Laura J. b 27 Oct 1849
Danville, NH d/o COLLINS, Levi &
TOWLE, Aramintha; d 12 Dec 1854
Danville, NH ae 5y

COLLINS, Lena b 23 Jul 1898
Danville, NH s/o COLLINS, Wilbur H. &
FITTS, Hattie L.; md Hewett, Robert H.;
d 1968; 2nd child in family

COLLINS, Leon P. b Apr 1852 s/o
COLLINS, Laban & HUNT, Rachel C.;
1st md 4 Feb 1868 ROGERS, Ellen A.;
2nd md 15 Mar 1874 WINSLOW, Ellen
F. 3rd md 14 Jan 1883 BLAISDELL,
Mary E.

COLLINS, Leonard Dimond b 12 Jan
1908 Danville, NH s/o COLLINS, Irving
Mahlon & DIMOND, Carrie Mabel; md
06 Jun NORMAN, Kathryn; d 14 Oct
1972 Danville, NH

COLLINS, Leonard Waldo b 26 Dec
1851 Danville, NH; s/o COLLINS, Alva
Blake & ALLEN, Mary Ann; md 11 Dec
1881 GORDON, Elvira Clara; d 17 Dec
1921; bu Kingston, NH Plains Cem; or
md 11 Apr 1883 Danville

COLLINS, Leonard Washington b
09 Nov 1829 Hampstead, NH s/o
COLLINS, Jon & DANIELS, Betsey; md
16 May 1857 Danville, NH COLLINS,
Althea J.; d 25 Jan 1907 Danville, NH

COLLINS, Leslie Ashton b 05 Jun
1857 Danville, NH s/o COLLINS, Alva
Blake & ALLEN, Mary Ann; md 15 Nov
1882 NH DAVIS, OLive Frances; d 01
Aug 1911 Plaistow, NH; bu Kingston,
NH Plains Cem

COLLINS, Levi b 1824 Hampstead,
NH s/o COLLINS, Hezekiah & MOWE,
Sarah; md 07 Jun 1846 Exeter, NH
TOWLE, Aramintha; d 06 Apr 1896 bu
Danville, NH Center Cem

COLLINS, Levi Barstow b 25 Apr
1799 Hampstead, NH s/o COLLINS,
Samuel & BLAKE, Mary (Polly); md 03
Aug 1826 BARSTOW, Almira; d 08 Jun
1884 Danville, NH

COLLINS, Lilla S. b Sandown, NH; d
12 Oct 1848 Danville, NH ae 87y 7m 5d

COLLINS, Lillian Francene b 07 Jan
1855 Danville, NH d/o COLLINS, Alva
Blake & ALLEN, Mary Ann; md 15 Apr
1873 Danville, NH GEORGE, James W.;
d 30 Dec 1918 Danville, NH

COLLINS, Lorenzo B. b 12 Aug 1836
Danville, NH s/o COLLINS, Jonathan &
DANIELS, Betsey; md GRIFFIN, Mary
Luella; d 14 Aug 1886 Danville, NH

COLLINS, Louise E. b 26 Jun 1892 Danville, NH d/o COLLINS, Clarence Morton & COLLINS, Ada Frances; d 19 Mar 1893 Danville, NH 8m 21d; 2nd Child

COLLINS, Lucille Mary b 1923 Walla Walla, WA d/o COLLINS, Herbert Levi & KOSKINEN, Hilja; md 28 Feb 1947 Danville, NH FERNALD, Ralph Alvin; md by Rev W. C. Chappell

COLLINS, Lucinda b Hawke, NH d/o COLLINS, Jos Jr & DEARBORN, Mary (Polly) md 02 Mar 1820 Kingston, NH SANBORN, Peter

COLLINS, Mahlon S. b 22 Nov 1859 Danville, NH s/o COLLINS, Leonard Washington & COLLINS, Althea J.; d 10 Jun 1870 Danville, NH Diabetes

COLLINS, Marion b 17 Apr 1888 Danville, NH d/o COLLINS, Alfred Asbury & LOWELL, Kate Colinda; md 16 Dec 1914 Danville, NH McPHERSON, Robert H.; d 03 May 1947 Danville, NH; md by Rev Allen C. Kieth

COLLINS, Martha b 24 Mar 1745 Hampton, NH d/o COLLINS, Benj & JONES, Mary; md 19 Apr 1770 Hawke, NH FOLLINSBY, Thos; md by Rev John Page

COLLINS, Mary b Kingston, NH; md 21 Nov 1771 Hawke, NH JONES, Nathan; md by Rev John Page

COLLINS, Mary b 09 Sep 1770 Hawke, NH d/o COLLINS, Jos & BAGLEY, Sarah

COLLINS, Mary b 17 Feb 1820 Hawke, NH d/o COLLINS, Moses & PAGE, Hannah; md 07 Nov 1841 Danville, NH SARGENT, Thos; d 24 Apr 1900 Danville, NH

COLLINS, Mary b 05 Sep 1757 Kingston, NH d/o COLLINS, Benj & JONES, Mary md 15 Oct 1781 Hawke, NH PEASLEE, Isaac; md by Rev John Page

COLLINS, Mary b Apr 1792 d/o COLLINS, Jos Jr & DEARBORN, Mary (Polly); md 14 Nov 1816 PAGE, John; d 20 Sep 1874 Danville, NH ae 82y

COLLINS, Mary J. b Sandown, NH d/o COLLINS, John & SAWYER, Sarah; md TEWKSBURY, ---- ; d 17 Mar 1927 Danville, NH ae 89y 3m 13d

COLLINS, Mary J. (or P. b 1829 Hawke, NH d/o COLLINS, Nathaniel & GREEN, Hannah d 05 Aug 1862 Danville, NH; bu Danville, NH Old Mtg Hse Cem; d ae 33y

COLLINS, Mary L. b Oct 1838 Kingston, NH d/o COLLINS, Laban & HUNT, Rachael C. md DAVIS, Moses Kimball; d 30 Jan 1894 Kingston, NH; bu West Kingston, NH

COLLINS, Mary S. b 11 Jun 1794 d/o COLLINS, Benj & ----, Sarah; d 08 May 1862 Danville, NH ae 67y

COLLINS, Melvin A. b 20 Mar 1857 Danville, NH s/o COLLINS, Levi & TOWLE, Aramintha

COLLINS, Melvin Russell b 22 Apr 1958 Danville, NH s/o COLLINS, Merville Sidney & HERRICK, Gloria Louise; md 14 Oct 1978 Danville, NH GOULD, Candy Ann; md by Rev Wm Ryans

COLLINS, Merville Sidney b 1939 W Kingston, NH s/o COLLINS, Leon E. Sr. md 01 Dec 1956 Danville, NH HERRICK, Gloria Louise; md by Agnes H. Collins (JP)

COLLINS, Michael Roy; md 23 Jun 1990 Danville, NH CARTER, Debra A.; md by Rev Everett E. Palmer

COLLINS, Mildred Gertrude b 16 Mar 1895 Danville, NH d/o COLLINS, Clarence Morton & COLLINS, Ada Frances; 1st md 25 May 1920 Danville, NH TAYLOR, Ralph George; 2nd md Rev Luke Monroe Bleakney; d Farmington, CT; bu Lowell, MA

COLLINS, Miriam b 1775 Hawke, NH d/o COLLINS, Tristram & HUNT, Rachel

COLLINS, Miriam (Miss) b Apr 1792 d 16 Oct 1870 Hawke, NH bu Danville, NH Old Mtg Hse Cem ae 86yr 3m

COLLINS, Molly b 03 Jul 1787 Hawke, NH d/o COLLINS, Richard & BUSWELL, Sarah

COLLINS, Moses b 05 Aug 1761 Hawke, NH s/o COLLINS, Jos & BAGLEY, Ann

COLLINS, Moses b 14 Apr 1796 Hawke, NH s/o COLLINS, Jos Jr. & DEARBORN, Mary (Polly); md 17 Aug 1820 Kingston, NH PAGE, Hannah; d 25 Apr 1845 Danville, NH; bu Danville, NH

COLLINS (Cont.) Old Mtg Hse Cem
COLLINS, Moses Newell b 21 Jul
1840 Danville, NH s/o COLLINS, Moses
& PAGE, Hannah; d 22 Mar 1927 Danville, NH

COLLINS, Muriel Eliz b 18 Apr 1912
Danville, NH d/o COLLINS, Irving
Mahlon & DIMOND, Carrie Mabel; md
TEBBETTS, Harvey Burton; d 07 Jul
1966 Danville, NH;

COLLINS, Nathaniel b Apr 1803 s/o
COLLINS, Jos Jr. & DEARBORN,
Mary (Polly) md 23 Aug 1827 GREEN,
Hannah d 05 Jun 1830 Hawke, NH ; bu
Danville, NH Old Mtg Hse Cem; d ae 27y

COLLINS, Nelson b 04 Apr 1828
Hawke, NH s/o COLLINS, Moses &
PAGE, Hannah md 24 Mar 1853 Danville, NH DUNN, Mary Ella

COLLINS, Nicholas Scott b 26 Sep
1987 Exeter, NH s/o COLLINS, Brian K.
& SHEPPARD, Tracy A.

COLLINS, Norman Day b 04 Apr
1917 Danville, NH s/o COLLINS, Roy
Cram & DAY, Mary Ethel; d 25 Feb 1918
Danville, NH

COLLINS, Norman Howard b 05
May 1951 Danville, NH s/o COLLINS,
Howard Cecil & GOLDTHWAITE, Grace
Pauli; md 14 Aug 1971 Danville, NH
MARQUIS, Diane A.; md by Romeo J.
Valliere (P)

COLLINS, Norman Howard b 05
May 1951 Danville, NH s/o COLLINS,
Howard Cecil & GOLDTHWAITE, Grace
Pauli; md 17 Sep 1982 Danville, NH
WATJEN, Patricia A. md by Ralph
Carkin (JP)

COLLINS, Obadiah S. b Kingston,
NH; md 07 Apr 1870 Danville, NH
SWEATT, Lucretia P.

COLLINS, Ola B. b 1880 Danville,
NH d/o COLLINS, Jos & CHALLIS,
Irene C. d 12 Feb 1877 Danville, NH ae
7y of Diptheria

COLLINS, Olla B. b 1871 Danville,
NH d/o COLLINS, Jos & CHALLIS,
Irene C.

COLLINS, Olla M. b 13 Dec 1884
Danville, NH d/o COLLINS, Edson F. &
SEAVER, Susan F.; md 15 Jun 1904
Danville, NH BROWN, Arthur P.; md by
Rev A. B. Howard

COLLINS, Oren Eugene b 07 Feb
1857 Danville, NH s/o COLLINS, Page
& PAGE, Iantha; md 11 Nov 1882 Danville, NH WEBSTER, Flora M.; d 05 May
1922 Danville, NH; bu Danville, NH Old
Mtg Hse Cem.

COLLINS, Orense b 1786 d 04 Aug
1866; bu Danville, NH

COLLINS, Page b 30 Apr 1830
Hawke, NH s/o COLLINS, Moses &
PAGE, Hannah md PAGE, Iantha; d 31
Mar 1857 Danville, NH

COLLINS, Pamela Lee b 25 Jun
1956 Danville, NH d/o COLLINS, Paul
David Sr. & WHITE, Patricia Elizabet;
md 19 Mar 1983 Danville, NH BRONK,
Kerry S. md by Rev Everett E. Palmer

COLLINS, David Paul b 05 Jan 1959
Danville, NH s/o COLLINS, Paul David
& WHITE, Patricia Eliz

COLLINS, Paul David b Portsmouth,
NH s/o COLLINS, Herbert Levi &
KOSKINEN, Hilja; md 23 Apr 1955
Danville, NH WHITE, Patricia Eliz; md
by Rev Theodore B. Hadley

COLLINS, Perletta b 1863 Danville,
NH d/o COLLINS, Jos & CHALLIS,
Irene C. d 21 Oct 1870 Danville, NH ae
7y

COLLINS, Perley Forrest b 13 Jun
1874 Danville, NH s/o COLLINS,
Woodbury D. & CRAM, Julia L.; md 07
May 1908 Kingston, NH MILNE, Minnie; d 18 Feb 1935 Danville, NH; md by
Rev C. A. Reed

COLLINS, Perley Lorenzo b Nov
1887 Danville, NH s/o COLLINS, Fred
E. & HOYT, Mary Olive; md ---- , Adele
B.; d 30 Oct 1973 Danville, NH ae 85y

COLLINS, Perley S. b 1839 Danville,
NH s/o COLLINS, Jonathan & ---- ,
Sarah md 04 Feb 1860 Exeter, NH
ANDERSON, Rhoda J.; d 02 Sep 1863
Morris Is. SC

COLLINS, Peter David b 18 Sep
1989 Exeter, NH s/o COLLINS, David P.
& PALMER, Rebecca D.

COLLINS, Philena b 29 Dec 1809
Hawke, NH d/o COLLINS, Laban &
JONES, Dorothy md FELLOWS, George
W.

COLLINS, Quinton Roy md Le-
CLAIR, Ernstine Althea

COLLINS, Rachel Allyssa b 03 Sep 1991 Exeter, NH d/o COLLINS, David P. & PALMER, Rebecca D.

COLLINS, Ralph Lorenzo b 22 Aug 1875 Danville, NH s/o COLLINS, Lorenzo B. & GRIFFIN, Mary Luella; md 23 Apr 1898 Danville, NH SEAVER, Carrie Bell d 16 Mar 1953 Danville, NH; md by Rev A. B. Howard

COLLINS, Ralph Waldo b 1884 East Saugus, MA s/o COLLINS, Leonard Waldo & GORDON, Elvira Clara; d 23 Oct 1909

COLLINS, Reubin Milo b 10 Sep 1896 Danville, NH s /o COLLINS, Herbert Sumner & SPAULDING, Lillian Etta; md HILLARD, Sarah Jane; d 16 Feb 1959 Danville, NH

COLLINS, Richard b Goffstown, NH; md 25 Jul 1776 Hawke, NH BUSWELL, Sarah; md by Rev John Page

COLLINS, Richard Ira b s/o COLLINS, Cecil Spaulding & SHARPE, Joyce

COLLINS, Rita L. b Baltimore, MD; d 06 Jul 1945 Danville, NH ae 36y 3m 5d

COLLINS, Robert Cecil b 28 Apr 1943 s/o COLLINS, Cecil Spaulding & SHARPE, Joyce; md 28 May 1968 OTOBON, Evelyne Marie

COLLINS, Robert Hazen b 26 Apr 1902 Haverhill, MA s/o COLLINS, Herbert Sumner & SPAULDING, Lillian Etta; md 07 Aug 1934 Danville, NH SARGENT, Helen; d 16 Jan 1975 Salem, NH; md by Rev John D. Kettelle; 2nd md ROBINSON, Evelyn Hulford

COLLINS, Robin J. md 09 Aug 1986 Danville, NH HEAD, David R.; md by Thos D. Welch Jr. (JP)

COLLINS, Roy Cram b 1892 Danville, NH s/o COLLINS, Woodbury D. & CRAM, Julia S.; md 02 May 1914 Danville, NH DAY, Mary Ethel; d 08 Jun 1962 Danville, NH md by Rev Allen C. Keith

COLLINS, Roy Wm b 21 Feb 1950 Danville, NH s/o COLLINS, Roy H. & HARRIS, Evelyn; md 24 May 1972 Danville, NH WILLIAMS, Holly J.; md by Rev Cathleen R. Narowitz

COLLINS, Ruth Gertrude b 05 Oct 1909 Danville, NH d/o COLLINS, Wilbur H. & FITTS, Hattie L.

COLLINS, Ruth Miriam b 1915 Boston, MA d/o COLLINS, Herbert Levi & KOSKINEN, Hilja; md 30 Jun 1936 Danville, NH MITCHELL, Fred Carlton; md by Rev W. C. Chappell; Maybe adopted by Herbert Levi Collins

COLLINS, Samantha Michelle b 22 Feb 1989 Exeter, NH d/o COLLINS, Wayne A. & GAGNON, Audrey A.

COLLINS, Samuel b Feb 1772 Kingston, NH s/o COLLINS, Jonathan & WEBSTER, Dorothy; md 24 Dec 1795 Kingston, NH BLAKE, Mary (Polly); d 04 Feb 1853 Danville, NH; bu Danville, NH Center Cem; d ae 81y (or b Hampstead)

COLLINS, Sandra Lyette b 04 Jun 1963 Danville, NH d/o COLLINS, Merville Sidney & HERRICK, Gloria Louise; md 07 Jun 1980 Danville, NH MAYO, Robert E. III

COLLINS, Sarah b 19 Sep 1767 Hawke, NH d/o COLLINS, Jos Sr. & BAGLEY, Sarah

COLLINS, Sarah b 13 Apr 1777 Goffstown, NH d/o COLLINS, Richard & BUSWELL, Sarah

COLLINS, Sarah M. b Apr 1832; md 1848 Danville, NH WITHERELL, Oren M. d 09 Dec 1885 Raymond, NH ae 29y

COLLINS, Sarah P. b 1849 Kingston, NH; md 08 Jan 1863 Danville, NH AUSTIN, Luther J.

COLLINS, Scott Kevin b 24 Jul 1963 Danville, NH s/o COLLINS, Paul David Sr. & WHITE, Patricia Eliz; md 30 May 1992 WICKER, Holly Gay

COLLINS, Shayna Evelyn b 26 Oct 1980 Exeter, NH d/o COLLINS, Gary Robert & SKILLINGS, Pamela J.

COLLINS, Sheryl Lynne b 26 Jan 1961 Danville, NH d/o COLLINS, Paul David Sr. & WHITE, Patricia Elizabet; md 22 Aug 1981 Danville, NH JOHNSON, Steven D. md by Rev Wm Ryans

COLLINS, Susan Jane b 02 Oct 1834 Hawke, NH d/o COLLINS, Jonathan & DANIELS, Betsey; md 30 Oct 1862 Danville, NH COLLINS, Jacob; d 26 May

COLLINS (Cont.) 1902 Danville, NH; bu Danville, NH Center Cem

COLLINS, Tabitha b 30 Sep 1776 Kingston, NH d/o COLLINS, Jonathan & WEBSTER, Dorothy; md 31 Aug 1802 Hawke, NH BROWN, Jacob

COLLINS, Tabitha b d/o COLLINS, Jonathan; d 16 Oct 1778 Hawke, NH

COLLINS, Tammi Marie b 21 Feb 1971 Haverhill, MA d/o COLLINS, Gary Robert & SKILLINGS, Pamela J.; md 07 Jan 1989 Danville, NH AMATO, David R.; md by Wm Beane (JP)

COLLINS, Theresa J. b 22 Feb 1970 Haverhill, NH d/o COLLINS, Gary Robert & SKILLINGS, Pamela J.

COLLINS, Theron Jos b 1899 Danville, NH s/o COLLINS, Edson T. & SEAVER, Susan F.; md 23 Jun 1923 Hampstead, NH PLEAU, Loretta; md by Rev Howard Collins

COLLINS, Thos Allan b 13 Apr 1962 Danville, NH s/o COLLINS, Quinton Roy & LeCLAIR, Ernestine Althe

COLLINS, Viola b Kingston, NH; md LaBELLE, Samuel

COLLINS, Violet J. b 1926 Portland. OR d/o COLLINS, Herbert Levi & KOSKINEN, Hilja; md 19 Jul 1952 Danville, NH CULLIGAN, Raymond F. d 19 Mar 1990 Danville, NH; md by Rev W. C. Chappell

COLLINS, Vivian b Kingston, NH; md COLE, Frank W.

COLLINS, Walter A. b Jun 1875 Danville, NH s/o COLLINS, Jos & CHALLIS, Irene C.; d 08 Feb 1876 Danville, NH ae 8m

COLLINS, Walter A. b 25 May 1882 Danville, NH s/o COLLINS, Edson F. & SEAVER, Susan F.

COLLINS, Wayne Alan b 28 Jan 1957 Danville, NH s/o COLLINS, Roy H. & HARRIS, Evelyn; 1st md 11 Aug 1979 Danville, NH INGERSON, Joyce Catherine; 2nd md 17 Sep 1988 Danville NH GAGNON, Audrey by Rev Everett E. Palmer

COLLINS, Wilber H. b 05 Oct 1868 Danville, NH s/o COLLINS, Jos & CHALLIS, Irene C.; md 27 Oct 1894 Danville, NH FITTS, Hattie L.; md by

COLLINS (Cont.) Rev John A. Wiggin

COLLINS, Wm b of Hawke, NH; md 24 Apr 1806 Kingston, NH GRIFFIN, Sally

COLLINS, Woodbury David b 26 Oct 1848 Danville, NH s/o COLLINS, Levi & TOWLE, Aramintha; md 23 Nov 1872 Danville, NH CRAM, Julia S.; d 29 May 1917 Danville, NH

COLLINS, MALE b 01 May 1912 Danville, NH s/o COLLINS, Perley Forrest & MILNE, Minnie; d 08 May 1912 Danville, NH

COLLINS, Michael Scott b 31 Aug 1960 s/o COLLINS, Cecil Spaulding & CANUEL, Marguerite

COLSON, Alan Carl b 1944 Bound Brook, NJ md 10 Sep 1965 Danville, NH SEARL, Alice Jean; md by Leona A. Sciaudone (JP)

COMBE, Kimberly Ann md 27 Aug 1978 Danville, NH DEJADON, Robert Wm; md by Rev P. Daniel Bakker

COMEAU, Brian M. md 31 Dec 1991 Danville, NH INGRAHAM, Christine Lyne; md by Richard J. Rondeau (JP)

COMEAU, Michael John md 27 Aug 1977 Danville, NH FOWLER, Robin Elsa;

COMETTA, Catrina Marie b 14 Aug 1992 Derry, NH d/o COMETTA, Anthony T. & CANNING, Darlene E.

COMMENDATORE, Marcia; md 12 Oct 1991 Danville, NH VALLIER, Barry Rich; md by Marjorie Maroux Fails (JP)

COMPPEN, Nicole Eliz b 17 Nov 1990 Stoneham, MA d/o COMPPEN, Chas J. & PICA, Karen L.

COMTOIS, Ronald Geo b 24 Mar 1962 Danville, NH s/o COMTOIS, Geo Arthur & BARNES, Martha Bell

COMTOIS, Ronald L. b 1937 Haverhill, MA; md 1st 29 Sep 1962 Danville, NH NOWICHI, Lorraine V. by Edward R. Lamb (JP) 2nd md 29 May 1966 Danville, NH MANSUR, Florence E.; md by Edward R. Lamb (JP)

CONANT, Glen A. md 25 May 1986 Danville, NH GAGNON, Rosemarie; md by Rev Everett E. Palmer

CONANT, Marcia Clark b 1911 Buckfield, ME; md 09 Sep 1934 Danville,

CONANT (Cont.) NH SANBORN, Melton Roland md by Rev Homer F. Carr

CONNELLY, Derek Jos b 20 Nov 1980 Exeter, NH s/o CONNELLY, Jos 3rd & OAK, Judith E.

CONNER, Benj Lee b 20 Feb 1986 Derry, NH s/o CONNER, Jesse W. & BORDERS, Susan T.

CONNER, Jesse Woodrow Jr. b s/o CONNER, Jessee Woodrow Sr. & HALE, Betty; d 18 Nov 1989 Danville, NH ae 33y

CONNERS, June Ann md 31 Dec 1991 Danville, NH BLAIR, Thos Leo; md by Richard J. Rondeau (JP)

CONWAY, Daniel A. b 1916 Haverhill, MA s/o CONWAY, Michael H.; md 21 May 1938 Danville, NH GAVIOLI, Lillian; md by Clarence N. Collins (JP)

CONWAY, Debra Jean md 11 Oct 1978 Danville, NH BRACKETT, David Bruce; md by Clara B. Shaw (JP)

COOK, A. Isabel b 16 Jul 1851 Danville, NH d/o COOK, Jos S. & DEARBORN, Almira P.; md 11 May 1971 Danville, NH HOYT, Warren; d 16 Feb 1914 Danville, NH

COOK, Addie M. b 1853 Danville, NH d/o COOK, Jos S. & DEARBORN, Almira P.; d 21 Dec 1871 Danville, NH d ae 18y

COOK, Dorothy Nellie b 1916 Revere, MA d/o COOK, James T.; md 06 May 1934 Danville, NH PASQUALE, Frederick; md by Rev Harold C. Ross; prev md to STONE, ----

COOK, Flora A. b 1848 Danville, NH d/o COOK, Jos S. & DEARBORN, Almira P.; md 24 Aug 1863 Danville, NH GRIFFIN, Harlan B.; d 09 May 1879 Danville, NH ae 31y

COOK, Helen Florence b Haverhill, MA d/o COOK, Geo A. & MOCK, Kate; d 28 Jul 1896 Danville, NH ae 3m 11d

COOK, Jos S. md 16 Sep 1846 Danville, NH DEARBORN, Almira P.

COOK, Melvin T. b 1854 Danville, NH s/o COOK, Jos S. & DEARBORN, Almira P.; md 29 May 1877 Danville, NH MARTIN, Nellie F.

COOK, Rebecca Ann b 14 Jul 1965 Danville, NH d/o COOK, Walter E. & RYAN, Elaine J.

COOK, Thos M. b 1856 Danville, NH s/o COOK, Jos S. & DEARBORN, Almira P.; md 13 Feb 1881 Danville, NH ROBERTS, Jennie W.

COOK, Walter E. b Haverhill, MA; md RYAN, Elaine J.

COOLEN, Scott Leslie b 1946 Melrose, MA; md 31 Aug 1966 Danville, NH CLARK, Nancy Ellen; md by Leona A. Sciaudone (JP)

COOLEY, ----; md; DULMAGE, Charlotte C.

COONEY, Helen b 1916 Somerville, MA d/o COONEY, Wm S.; md 10 Sep 1938 Danville, NH DAVENPORT, Aaron M

COONEY, Robert b 08 Apr 1923 Danville, NH s/o COONEY, Wm S. & HINES, Agnes; md 14 Aug 1953 Danville, NH COLLINS, Beverly Joyce

COONEY, Robert Paul b 17 Aug 1959 Exeter, NH s/o COONEY, Robert & COLLINS, Beverly Joyce; d 19 Aug 1959 Exeter, NH

COONEY, Wm b E Weymouth, MA; md HINES, Agnes

COONEY, Wm Phillip b 1913 Somerville, MA s/o COONEY, Wm Smith; md 17 Dec 1946 Danville, NH WEINS, Ruth Eleanor; md by Rev Leverett B. Davis

COONEY, William Smith b s/o COONEY, Bernard & GIVENEY, Katherine; d 17 Jan 1960 Danville, NH ae 88y

COPP, Wm b c1831 Chester, NH; md 1861 Danville, NH BROWN, Mary N.

COPPETA, Arthur Russell md 01 Aug 1989 Danville, NH COPPETA, Claire Elaine; md by Richard J. Rondeau (JP)

COPPETA, Claire Elaine md 01 Jul 1989 Danville, NH COPPETA , Arthur Russell; md by Richard J. Rondeau (JP)

CORDINGLY, Kristen Ruth md 01 Oct 1991 Danville, NH PRADO, Jorge; md by Leslie A. Alphen (JP)

COREY, Mabel H. b 1915 Melrose, MA d/o COREY, John; md 02 Apr 1938 Danville, NH PICKARD, Herbert O. Jr; md by Rev W. C. Chappell

CORMACK, James Kenneth b 1906 Everett, MA; s/o CORMACK, Alexander

CORMACK (Cont.) R.; md 20 Jul 1940 Danville, NH WELCH, Louise Rosamond; md by Rev John A. McSweeney

CORTON, Deborah Ann b 15 Dec 1964 Danville, NH d/o CORTON, Edward W. Jr. & PERROW, Sandra R.

CORTON, Edward W. Jr. b 1944 Pittsfield, MA; md 08 Feb 1964 Danville, NH PERROW, Sandra R.; md by Herbert C. Shelly (P)

CORTON, Nancy B. b 1949 MA; md 16 Nov 1968 Danville, NH MURPHY, Robert D. Jr.; md by Rev Douglas Abbott

COSGROVE, Ella M. b 1882 Hampstead, NH d/o COSGROVE, James; md 02 Jul 1924 Danville, NH KEITH, Burton L.; md by Rev T.R. Bundy; prev md GEORGE, ----

COSGROVE, Ella M. b 1882 Hampstead, NH; md HAYDEN, Frank; also md KEITH, Burton L.

COSSABOOM, Eliz A b 06 Jul 1960 Danville, NH d/o COSSABLOOM, Harvey L. & EMERY, Dorothy E.

COSSABOOM, Phil. Edwrd b 16 Mar 1958 Danville, NH s/o COSSABOOM, Harvey L. & EMERY, Dorothy E.

COTE, Alfred Francis b 03 Feb 1958 Danville, NH s/o COTE, Alfred J. & ROBIDOU, Patricia L.

COTE, Alfred J. b Lowell, MA; md ROBIDOU, Patricia L.

COTE, Brandon Chas b 29 Apr 1989 Derry, NH s/o COTE, Chas H. & FORD, Wanda

COTE, Chas Howard b 29 Oct 1964 Danville, NH s/o COTE, Alfred J. & ROBIDOU, Patricia L.; md 30 Aug 1987 Danville, NH FORD, Wanda S.; md by Rev Wendall J. Irvine

COTE, Dorothy Ann b NH; md 05 Mar 1969 Danville, NH WILSON, Robert Donald; md by Rev Geo R. Shook

COTE, Heather Margaret b 02 Jun 1992 Manchester, NH d/o COTE, Chas Howard & FORD, Wanda S.

COTE, Kathleen C. b 1942 MA; md 09 Sep 1961 Danville, NH MALO, Ronald R.; md by Rev Robert F. Griffin

COTE, Lillian C. md 17 Aug 1986 Danville, NH DORAN, Gerald R.; md by Richard J. Rondeau (JP)

COTE, Pamela J. md 12 May 1973 Danville, NH MITCHELL, Mark C.; md by Rev Peter N. Knost

COTE, Patricia Jane b 27 Nov 1952 Danville, NH d/o COTE, Alfred F. & ROBIDOU, Patricia L.; md 12 May 1973 Danville, NH MITCHELL, Mark C.

COTE, Veronica Ivy b 31 Aug 1984 Derry, NH d/o COTE, Alfred F. & RUSSO, Eliz M.

COTE, Yvonne Lucille b 1936 NH d/o COTE, Jos O.; md 20 Oct 1956 Danville, NH DUSTON, Richarl Earl; md by Rev Albian Bulger (P)

COTTON, Geo A. b c1848 Hallowell. ?; md 24 Mar 1872 Danville, NH PLUMMER, Mary W.

COTTON, Josiah Rev. d 27 May 1780 Hawke, NH

COTTON, May L. b c1837 Sandown, NH md 09 Sep 1865 Danville, NH QUIMBY, James M.

COTTON, Thos Lt. md 20 Feb 1812 Hawke, NH WILLIAMS, Sally Mrs.

COTTREAU, Leona b d/o COTTREAU, Michel & DOUCETTE, Pauline A.; md MONROE, ---- ; d 02 Dec 1991 Danville, NH

COTTREAU, Pauline Ann b Nova Scotia d/o DOUCETTE, Michael & ROBBISHEAU, Ann; d 18 Aug 1963 Danville, NH ae 101y

COURCHINE, Albert Chas b 1909 MA s/o COURCHAINE, Albert C.; md 22 Sep 1950 Danville, NH ZUJEWSKI, Alice Adele; md by Rev W. C. Chappell

COX, Mary b 1903 Ireland d/o COX, Thos; md 21 Sep 1924 Kingston, NH TAATJES, John; md by Daniel J. Bakie (JP)

CRAGGY, Byron b Wilmont, NH md CARY, Catherine; Occupation Shoemaker

CRAGGY, Byron S. b 1867 Wilmont, NH s/o CRAGGY, Thos & BROWN, Ruana; md 08 Jan 1891 Newton, NH TEWKSBURY, Mary A.; d 05 Apr 1934 Danville, NH; md by Rev James P. Nowland; Occupation - Shoemaker

CRAGGY, Edward Burton b 01 May 1906 Danville, NH s/o CRAGGY, Byron S, & TEWKSBURY, Mary A.; d 03 May 1908 Danville, NH ae 2y 2d

CRAGGY, Elberta b 06 Sep 1902 Danville, NH d/o CRAGGY, Byron S. & TEWKSBURY, Mary A.; d 29 Oct 1902 Danville, NH ae 1m 23d

CRAGGY, Elsie May b 08 Dec 1918 Danville, NH d/o CRAGGY, Byron & CARY, Catherine

CRAGGY, Lena M. b Danville, NH d/o CRAGGY, Byron S. & TEWKSBURY, Mary A.; d 25 May 1910 Danville, NH ae 19y 1m 9d

CRAGGY, Leola E. b c1882 Lowell, MA d/o CRAGGY, Chas P. & HUNTOON, Eldora; md 08 Mar 1919 Plaistow, NH TAYLOR, Perley B.; md by Rev Asa A. Morrison; d 24 Feb 1920 ae 38y 28d

CRAGGY, Ruth b d/o CRAGGY, Byron S. & TEWKSBURY, Mary A.; d 31 Mar 1988 Danville, NH ae 87y

CRAGGY, ---- b 09 May 1900 Danville, NH d/o CRAGGY, Byron S. & TEWKSBURY, Mary A.; 2nd child in family

CRAINE, Glenna Mae b 1902 Hillsboro, NH d/o CRAINE, Bert L.; md 27 Dec 1924 Westville, NH ALLARD, Frank A.; 07 May 1946 Danville, NH; md by Rev M.J. Moher; d ae 43y 7m 13d

CRAM, Julia L. b c1850 Hampton Falls, NH d/o CRAM, Benj & SMITH, Eliz; md COLLINS, Woodbury D.; d 12 Mar 1915 Danville, NH ae 64y 4m 11d

CRAM, Mary b c1844 Sandown, NH; md 22 Jun 1867 Danville, NH BEAN, John E.

CRAM, Mary b of Nottingham, NH md 08 Nov 1764 CLOUGH, Moses; md by Rev John Page

CRANDALL, ---- b 03 Sep 1953 Danville, NH ?/o CRANDALL, Horace W. & RENNARD, Marion I.; d 05 Sep 1953 Danville, NH ae 2d

CRANE, Thos P. b c1844 Plaistow, NH; md 26 Feb 1865 Danville, NH WHITE, Jane S.

CRAWFORD, Lillian b Ontario Canada; md DAY, Alfred Theo

CRITCHET, Geo E. b c1833 Sandown, NH; md 1853 Danville, NH SARGENT, Louisa M.

CRITCHET, Mary b Poplin, NH; md 15 Jul 1787 Kingston, NH QUIMBY,

CRITCHET (Cont.) Benj; d 31 Oct 1814; bu Danville NH Old Mtg Hse Cem.

CROCKER, John McKinley b 1900 Barnstable, MA s/o CROCKER, Henry; md 20 Aug 1933 Danville, NH KEEFE, Dorothy Mary; md by Clarence M. Collins (JP)

CROCKER, Veronica Louis md 16 Jul 1977 Danville, NH WHITE, Lewis Hester; md by Rev Wm Ryans

CROCKETT, Sally J. md 22 Oct 1972 Danville, NH ROBERTSON, Chas S.; md by Clara B. Snow (JP)

CROSBY, Isaiah 3rd b 1923 Melrose, MA s/o CROSBY, Isaiah Jr.; md 30 Jun 1945 Haverhill, MA TOTTEN, Jean Margaret; md by Rev James M. Cuble

CROSBY, Virginia Phyllis b 1925 Melrose, MA d/o CROSBY, Isaiah Jr.; md 28 Dec 1945 Danville NH MAIR, Jack Gordon md by Agnes H Collins (JP)

CROWELL, Donna Marie b 28 May 1948 Danville, NH d/o CROWELL, Francis Archibald & MARTIN, Alberta Irene

CROWELL, Geo Everett Sr. b 1923 MA s/o CROWELL, Chas; md 17 Jul 1949 Danville, NH MISTOWSKI, Pauline; md by Rev Harry L. Lesure

CROWELL, Geo Everett Jr. b 27 May 1952 Danville, NH s/o CROWELL, Geo Everett Sr. & MISTKOWSKI, Pauline; md 23 Sep 1978 Danville, NH CALANTONIO, Eliz Louise; md by Rev Wm Ryans

CROWELL, June E. b 1928 MA d/o CROWELL, Sylvanis; md 25 Feb 1951 Danville, NH DUNN, Wm F.; md by Agnes H. Collins (JP)

CROZIER, James C. b 1944 MA; md 21 Sep 1968 Danville, NH HAYMAN, Susan E.; md by Rev Douglas Abbott

CROZIER, Mary Eliz b 1939 d/o CROZIER, Russell; md 16 Mar 1957 Danville, NH ARNOLD, Edward Stanley

CULLIGAN, Jos Raymon b 06 Jan 1961 Danville, NH s/o CULLIGAN, Raymond F. & COLLINS, Violet Joyce

CULLIGAN, Kevin Jon b 27 Jul 1964 Danville, NH s/o CULLIGAN, Raymond F. & COLLINS, Violet Joyce

CULLIGAN, Kurt Alan b 10 Oct 1962 Danville, NH s/o CULLIGAN, Raymond F. & COLLINS, Violet Joyce

CULLIGAN, Raymond F. b 1928 Haverhill, MA s/o CULLIGAN, Jos H. &; md 19 Jul 1952 Danville, NH COLLINS, Violet Joyce; md by Rev W. C. Chappell

CUMMINGS, Ann Jeanette b d/o CUMMINGS, Chas Everett & ORDWAY, Evelyn P.; d 17 Feb 1939 Danville, NH ae 2d

CUMMINGS, Chas Everett b 1902 Amesbury, MA s/o CUMMINGS, Chas L. & WHITTIER, Grace; md 1st 29 Apr 1934 ORDWAY, Evelyn P. by Rev Donald H. Baldwin, 2nd 10 May 1978 Danville, NH LEONARD, Myra Helen; d 08 Feb 1983 Danville, NH; md by Rev Wm Ryans; d ae 80y

CUMMINGS, Harvey b s/o CUMMINGS, Chas Everett & ORDWAY, Evelyn; d 19 Nov 1970 Danville, NH ae 35y

CUMMINGS, Janet Lea b 27 Feb 1958 Danville, NH d/o CUMMINGS, Chas H. & REYNOLDS, Phyllis Anne

CUMMINGS, Lisa Ann b 05 Sep 1967 Danville, NH d/o CUNMMINGS, Steven E. & CORREY, Carol A.

CUMMINGS, Minnie C. b New Braintree, MA; md CHICKERING, Anelous O.

CUMMINGS, Paul Everett b 01 Jul 1963 Danville, NH s/o CUMMINGS, Chas H. & REYNOLDS, Phyllis Anne

CUMMINGS, Steven Scott b 19 Apr 1969 Danville, NH s/o CUMMINGS, Steven E. & TORREY, Carol A.

CUMMINGS, Sue D. md 12 May 1984 Danville, NH CHAMPIGNY, Paul M.; md by Rev James A, Magnusson

CUMMINGS, Thos Scott b 13 Oct 1949 Danville, NH s/o CUMMINGS, Chas Everett & ORDWAY, Evelyn Pearl

CUMMINGS, Vicki Lynne b 24 Nov 1956 Danville, NH d/o CUMMINGS, Chas H. & REYNOLDS, Phylliss Anne

CUNEO, Jos F. b s/o CUNEO, Guisseppi & SANGUINETTI, Angelina; d 11 Sep 1974 Danville, NH ae 81y

CUNNINGHAM, Edward Alexander b 16 May 1950 Danville, NH s/o CUNNINGHAM, Edward James & KIRWIN, Catherine Eliz; md 07 Apr 1972 Danville, NH JENSEN, Gwendolyn A. md by Rev Herbert J. Moore

CUNNINGHAM, Edward James b 1900 Lynn, MA s/o CUNNINGHAM, John & PEEDEN, Sara; md 31 Aug 1946 Exeter, NH KIRWAN, Catherine Eliz; d 05 Jun 1974 Danville, NH; md by Willard K. Tozier (JP)

CUNNINGHAM, Eileen b 27 Dec 1951 Danville, NH d/o CUNNINGHAM, Edward James & KIRWAN, Catherine Eliz

CUNNINGHAM, Harrison b Amesbury, MA s/o CUNNINGHAM, Arthur R. & DICKENS, Nellie; d 14 Jan 1964 Danville, NH ae 82y

CUNNINGHAM, Jeannie M. b 10 Jan 1947 Exeter,NH d/o CUNNINGHAM, Edward James & KIRWIN, Catherine Eliz; md 13 Apr 1963 Danville, NH SMITH, James Carlton Sr.; md by Jos H. Southwick (JP)

CURRIER, Abigail b 04 May 1815 Hawke, NH d/o CURRIER, Bernard Jr. & QUIMBY, Rhoda; d 24 Mar 1887 Danville, NH

CURRIER, Adeline M. b 1903 Haverhill, MA d/o CURRIER, Edwin E.; md 1st BURRILL, ---- , 2nd 01 Sep 1948 Danville, NH JOHNSON,John A.; md by Rev W. C. Chappell

CURRIER, Almina b c1831 Newton, NH; md 26 Jun 1883 Danville, NH DIMOND, Almon; d 12 Mar 1884 Danville, NH ae 52y

CURRIER, Bernard b c1783 S Hampton, NH; md QUIMBY, Rhoda; d 27 Jul 1854 Danville, NH ae 71y

CURRIER, Brenda Lee md 15 Jul 1989 Danville, NH HARVEYWOOD, Timothy Terrence; md by Richard J. Rondeau (JP)

CURRIER, Calvin b 26 Aug 1809 Hawke, NH s/o CURRIER, Barnard Jr & QUIMBY, Rhoda; d 01 Sep 1856 Danville, NH ae 45y

CURRIER, Carlene Mildred b 1917 Haverhill, MA d/o CURRIER, Freeman D.; md 24 Aug 1940 Danville, NH TIBBETTS, Harlan Ward; md by Rev Will C. Chappell

CURRIER, Caroline b 17 Aug 1811 Hawke, NH d/o CURRIER, Barnard Jr. & QUIMBY, Rhoda; d 23 Sep 1815 Hawke, NH ae 4y

CURRIER, Caroline b 06 Apr 1818 Hawke, NH d/o CURRIER, Barnard & BUSWELL, Rhoda

CURRIER, Catherine b Danville, NH; md 20 Nov 1838 Danville, NH BRADLEY, Issac

CURRIER, Chas b 06 Oct 1859 s/o CURRIER, Ebenezer & McCLANE, Betsy

CURRIER, Cloude b 30 Jul 1887 Danville, NH s/o CURRIER, Horance E. & ----, A. Adele; 2nd child in family

CURRIER, David Barnard b 23 Jun 1823 Hawke, NH s/o CURRIER, Bernard Jr. & QUIMBY, Rhoda; md 1st 22 Nov 1885 Danville, NH HEATH, Mary P. W., 2nd 01 Jan 1911 Danville, NH HUNKINS, Juliann

CURRIER, Dorothy May b 19 Mar 1914 Danville, NH d/o CURRIER, Mahlon C. & QUIMBY, Lena L.; md MONROE, ---- ; d 05 May 1968 Danville, NH

CURRIER, Eleanor Mae b 1927 Haverhill, NH, d/o CURRIER, Lloyd Mears & COOK, Beatrice; md 06 Oct 1945 Danville, NH GOLDTHWAITE, Clyde Ernest; d 06 Mar 1985 Danville, NH; md by W. C. Chappell

CURRIER, Eliza M. b 30 May 1853 Danville, NH d/o CURRIER, Ebenezer & ----, Betsey; d 31 Oct 1856 Danville, NH

CURRIER, Eleanora S. b 30 Oct 1853 d/o CURRIER, Ephriam C. & CURRIER, Martha Jane; d 27 Nov 1934 Danville, NH

CURRIER, Elvira A. b 09 Aug 1856 Danville, NH d/o CURRIER, David B. & HUNKINS, Juliann

CURRIER, Ephriam C. b 14 Apr 1834 Hawke, NH s/o CURRIER, Barnard & BUSWELL, Rhoda; d 12 Aug 1862 Civil War Rcds

CURRIER, Everett Albert b 03 Jun 1860 s/o CURRIER, Ebenezer & McLANE, Betsy

CURRIER, Ezra b Poplin, NH; md 29 Nov 1841 Danville, NH SPOFFORD, Mary

CURRIER, Ezra Capt b E Kingston, NH; md 09 Jun 1800 Hawke, NH SANBORN, Mary; spouse wid of Jed PHILBRICK

CURRIER, Florence M. b 28 Dec 1861 Danville, NH d/o CURRIER, David B & HUNKINS, Juliann

CURRIER, Freeman D. b 16 Mar 1857 Danville, NH s/o CURRIER, David B. & HUNKINS, Juliann; md 08 Dec 1888 Danville, NH BRICKELL, Florence N.; d 27 May 1935 Danville, NH

CURRIER, Garirecia A. b 19 Mar 1850 Danville, NH s/o CURRIER, Ebenezer & McLANE, Maria Betsey

CURRIER, Horace E. b 17 May 1862 Danville, NH s/o CURRIER, John F. & GORDON-CASS, Emily F.; md 24 Feb 1886 Danville, NH GRIFFIN, A. Adelle; d 08 Feb 1936 Danville, NH

CURRIER, Horace Wilmont b 27 Aug 1911 Danville, NH s/o CURRIER, Mahlon C. & QUIMBY, Lena L.

CURRIER, John Frank b 19 Jan 1825 Hawke, NH s/o CURRIER, Bernard Jr. & QUIMBY, Rhoda; md 1861 Danville, NH GORDON, Emily F.; d 01 Dec 1887 Danville, NH

CURRIER, Laura Ann md 29 Jun 1991 Danville, NH FISHER, Peter Raymond; md by Rich J. Rondeau (JP)

CURRIER, Lilla B. b 02 FRB 1860 Danville, NH d/o CURRIER, David B. & HUNKINS, Juliann

CURRIER, Linda J. md 15 Aug 1981 Danville, NH JENDRICK, Wayne M.; md by Rev Paul W. Daneault (P)

CURRIER, Luella b Newton, NH; md 02 Jul 1873 Newton, NH PAGE David Frank

CURRIER, Mahlon C. b c1887 Danville, NH s/o CURRIER, Horace F. & GRIFFIN, Adele; md 19 Oct 1910 Amesbury, MA QUIMBY, Lena L.; d 26 May 1961 Danville, NH; md by Rev James D. Dinwgell; d ae 73y

CURRIER, Margaret md 08 Dec 1780 Hawke, NH THAYER, Elihu Rev.; md by Rev John Page

CURRIER, Mary A. b 02 Mar 1854 Danville, NH d/o CURRIER, David B. & HUNKINS, Juliann

CURRIER, Maurice G. b 20 Aug 1886 Danville, NH s/o CURRIER, Horace E. & GRIFFIN, A. Adele; md 29 Jun 1910 Merrimac, MA KELLY, Linda H.; d 25 Apr 1949 Danville, NH; md by Rev

CURRIER (Cont.) Edward P. Kelly
CURRIER, Osmund b c1847 Fremont, NH; md 14 Feb 1870 Danville, NH DIMOND, Sabra M.
CURRIER, Ralph B. b 24 Aug 1872 s/o CURRIER, Osmund F. & DIMOND, Sabra
CURRIER, Rhoda P. b 13 Aug 1826 Hawke, NH d/o CURRIER, Barnard Jr. & BUSWELL, Rhoda; d 13 Apr 1837 Danville, NH; Mother QUIMBY?
CURRIER, Rich Edgar b 30 Jun 1924 Danville, NH s/o CURRIER, Mahlon C. & QUIMBY, Lena; md 14 Aug 1848 Newton, NH MARDEN, Marie; md by Rev John S. Viall
CURRIER, Stephen H. b 23 Aug 1810 Danville, NH s/o CURRIER, Wm & HAYNES, Sally
CURRIER, Thos Jr. b Newton NH; md 10 Mar 1827 Hawke, NH BLAKE, Irene
CURTIS, Mary md CHALLIS, Clark D.; d 06 Aug 1878 Danville, NH
CURTIS, Scott Nelson md 05 Oct 1974 Danville, NH Howard, Marion Joyce; md by Rev Thos C. Roden
CUSTEAU, Claire A. b md 14 Dec 1979 Danville, NH Van GUILDER, Bruce D.; md by John H. Lamprey (JP)
CUSTER, John Edward b s/o CUSTER, Edward & DONALSON, Eliz Jun 1982 Danville, NH d ae 70y
CUTSHALL, Nicole Danielle b 23 Mar 1985 Exeter, NH d/o CUTSHALL, Michael E. & COLLINS, Karen E.
CUTSHELL, Michael E. md 21 May 1983 Danville, NH BUTLER, Karen E.; md by Rev Everett E. Palmer
DACEY, Patrick H. b 1860 Boston, MA s/o DACEY, Timothy; md 04 Oct 1925 Kingston, NH YOUNG, Hattie E.; md by Daniel J. Bakie (JP)
DALLON, Chester Jos Jr. md 04 May 1991 Danville, NH DESMOND, Pamela Ann; md by Rich J. Rondeau (JP)
DALTON, Martha D. b Brentwood, NH d/o DALTON, Jos & PARSONS, Mary; md WEBSTER, ---- ; d 05 Dec 1911 Danville, NH ae 79y 9m 25d
DANAHY, Jaime Heather b 27 Nov 1991 Nashua, NH d/o DANAHY, John T.

DANAHY (Cont.) & EICHHORN, Beverly A.
DANIELS, Betsey b 27 Aug 1794 Lee, NH; md 19 Mar 1822 Hampstead, NH COLLINS, Jonath; d 17 May 1873 Danville, NH bu Danville, NH Center Cem.
DANIELS, Jamie Lynn b 02 Jan 1987 Exeter, NH d/o DANIELS, David S. & POWERS, Nancy L.
DANLEY, Jeremy Michael b 21 Aug 1978 Exeter, NH s/o DANLEY, Lee M. & PHILBRICK, Diane J.
DAOUST, Rich G. b Boston, MA; md FARLEY, Margaret E.
DARBE, Arletta C. d 11 May 1943 Danville, NH ae 70y 8m 27d
DARBE, Caviss W. b 15 Aug 1894 Danville, NH s/o DARBE, Elmer C. & CAVISS, Arlett
DARBE, Charles A. b c1859 Danville, NH s/o DARBE, James M. & CHALLIS, Dorothy Augusta; md 28 May 1887 Danville, NH FITTS, Annie L.; md by Rev John A. Lowell
DARBE, Charles A. b 26 Mar 1859 Danville, NH s/o DARBE, James M. & CHALLIS, Dorothy Augusta; md 05 Aug 1896 E Hampstad, NH WITHERELL, Mattie S.; md by Rev R. E. Bartlett
DARBE, Clara Augusta b Danville, NH d/o DARBE, Jas M & CHALLIS, Dorothy Augusta; md 1st DEMAINE, ----, 2nd 06 Nov 1901 McGRAPH, Sam by Rev A. B. Howard; d 29 Sep 1932 Danville, NH
DARBE, Clarissa A. b 15 Aug 1875 Danville, NH d/o DARBE, James M. & CHALLIS, Dorothy Augusta; md 24 Mar 1896 Danville, NH DEMAINE, Frank; md by Rev J. A. Wiggin;
DARBE, Elmer C. b 02 Jul 1864 Danville, NH s/o DARBE, James M. & CHALLIS, Dorothy Augusta md CAVISS, Arlett; d 06 Oct 1945 Danville NH
DARBE, Ernest James b 30 Nov 1869 Danville, NH s/o DARBE, James M. & CHALLIS, Dorothy Augusta; d 23 Feb 1935 Danville, NH ae 66y 2m 24d
DARBE, James M. b Canada s/o DARBE, Benani & CLARK, Clarisey; md CHALLIS, Dorothy Augusta; d 10 Dec

DARBE (Cont.) 1911 Danville, NH ae 79y 9m 25d

DARBE, Lucius M. b 04 Mar 1857 Danville, NH s/o DARBE, James M. & CHALLIS, Dorothy Augusta; md 03 Dec 1890 S Hampton, NH MORSE, Mary B.; md by John K. Chase VDM

DARBE, Mahlon Benoni b 26 May 1866 Danville, NH s/o DARBE, James M. & CHALLIS, Dorothy Augusta; md 22 Nov 1888 Danville, NH HEATH, Etta F.; d 01 Mar 1960 Danville, NH

DARBE, Sadie E. d 20 Aug 1972 Danville, NH d ae 83y

DARBE, Sarah V. b 21 May 1862 Danville, NH d/o DARBE, James M. & CHALLIS, Dorothy Augusta; md 27 Sep 1883 Danville, NH AVERY, Oren S.; d 23 Sep 1914 Danville, NH

DARBE, ---- b 16 Feb 1903 Danville, NH s/o DARBE, Mahlon B. & HEATH, Etta F.

DARIES, Leslie Darrill b 03 Jan 1945 Danville, NH s/o DARIES, Walter H. & BURRILL, Nathalie

DARLING, Abraham Jr. b 15 Apr 1775 Hawke, NH s/o DARLING, Abraham & RUSSELL, Molly

DARLING, Abraham Sr. md 30 Jun 1772 Hawke, NH RUSSELL, Molly; md by Rev John Page

DARLING, Daniel b 28 Mar 1767 Hawke, NH s/o DARLING, Benj & CLARK, Hannah

DARLING, Ebenezer b 11 Jan 1764 Hawke, NH s/o DARLING, Benj & CLARK, Hannah

DARLING, Judith md CILLEY, Benj Ensign

DARLING, Molly b 06 Apr 1773 Hawke, NH d/o DARLING, Abraham & RUSSELL, Molly

DARLING, Reuben b 08 Mar 1762 Hawke, NH d/o DARLING, Benj & CLARK, Hannah

DARLING, Susanna b Hawke, NH; md 21 May 1776 Hawke, NH HOLLAND, John; md by Rev John Page

DARVILLE, Mary Lou b 15 Nov 1949 Danville NH d/o DARVILLE, Leroy Lawrence & SMITH, Mary Madoline

DAUST, Ellen Marie b 22 Sep 1965 Danville, NH d/o DAUST, Rich G. &

DAUST (Cont.) FARLEY, Margaret E

DAVARICH, Hilary md 20 Sep 1986 Danville, NH McCARTHY, Thos E.; md by Glen E. French (JP)

DAVENPORT, Aaron M. b 1907 Boston, MA s/o DAVENPORT, Aaron; md 10 Sep 1938 Danville, NH COONEY, Helen; md by Clarence M. Collins (JP)

DAVENPORT, Robert Wm b 1935 ME s/o DAVENPORT, Aaron M.; md 03 Aug 1958 Danville, NH WILLIAMSON, Carol Ann; md by Rev Terry Thompson

DAVID, Brian Edmind of Danville, NH md 07 Jun 1992 BYRON, Adrienne Marie of Kingston, NH md by Rev Florent R. Bilodeau

DAVID, Mary Ann md 16 Jun 1979 Danville, NH FOURNIER, John Allan; md by Clara B. Shaw (JP)

DAVIES, Geoffrey Bruce b 21 Nov 1957 Exeter, NH; md 04 Jun 1977 Danville, NH PRINCE, Cheryl Ann (div); md by Rev Wm Ryans

DAVIES, Ronald Bruce b 1931 MA s/o DAVIES, Frank Hubert & CLARKE, Hazel Anderson; 2nd md 18 Dec 1955 Exeter, NH TEBBETTS, Joyce Collins; md by Rev W. C. Chappell

DAVIS, Addie M. b c1859 Kingston, NH; md 02 Dec 1875 Danville, NH AVERY, Frank

DAVIS, Andrew J. b c1833 Kingston, NH; md 09 May 1859 Danville, NH MANN, Sarah M.

DAVIS, Brittany Michele b 25 Feb 1985 Haverhill, MA d/o DAVIS, Scott E. & PERIN, Carla J.

DAVIS, Daniel b c1876 s/o DAVIS, Hiram & CHENEY, Georgiana; d 21 Jul 1880 Danville, NH ae 4y of Scalding

DAVIS, Edgar A. b c1892 Haverhill, MA s/o DAVIS, Frank; md 16 Sep 1914 Danville, NH KEEZER, Bernice H.; md by Rev Chellis V. Smith

DAVIS, Eliz b 1865 d/o DAVIS, John P. & ----, Mary Ann; d 03 Sep 1865 Danville, NH age 6 mo

DAVIS, Eliz Margaret b d/o DAVIS, Jos O. & DALTON, Annie; md DONAHUE, ---- ; d 28 Jun 1975 Danville, NH ae 67y

DAVIS, Emma M. b Kingston, NH d/o DAVIS, Amos K. & COLLINS, Mary

DAVIS (Cont.) L.; md 09 Sep 1880 Danville, NH DIMOND, Melburne J.; d 23 Apr 1905 Danville, NH ae 43y 9m 13d

DAVIS, Franklin b Kingston, NH; md 23 May 1833 Kingston, NH DEARBORN, Hannah

DAVIS, Hannah md 25 Dec 1798 Hawke, NH QUIMBY, John

DAVIS, Harriet b c1874 d/o DAVIS, Hiram & CHENEY, Georgiana; d 21 Jul 1880 Danville, NH age 6 yr scalding

DAVIS, Henry b Kingston, NH; md 20 May 1828 Hawke, NH FROCHOCK, Jane

DAVIS, Hiram b c1847; md CHENEY, Georgiana; d 21 Jul 1880 Danville, NH age 33 yr

DAVIS, Hugh H. md 13 Dec 1985 Danville, NH JUNICKE, Diane C.; md by Rev Ronald Gehrinann,

DAVIS, Isa Mae b 01 Oct 1893 Kingston, NH d/o DAVIS, Lavada J. & HUSE, Isella; md 17 Jan 1912 Danville, NH WITHERELL, Waldo Currier; d 03 Dec 1932 Danville, NH; md by Rev A. C. Keith

DAVIS, John O. md BROWN, Lucy S.

DAVIS, Jonathan md 01 Jul 1812 Hawke, NH PAGE, Lois

DAVIS, Jonathan F. md 20 May 18?? Danville, NH GEORGE, Catherine; md 1832 or 1838 ?

DAVIS, Lawrence Wayne b 19 Mar 1949 Danville, NH s/o DAVIS, Ralph Francis & McHarg, Gladys Lydia

DAVIS, Lillie M. b c1865 Chester, NH; md 26 Dec 1885 Danville, NH VIGNEAULT, Ulric;

DAVIS, Mahala L. b Hopkinton, NH d/o DAVIS, John O. & BROWN, Lucy S.; md GRIFFIN, John H.; d 03 May 1905 Danville, NH 74y 10m 17d

DAVIS, Scott E. md 19 Oct 1983 Danville, NH PERIN, Carla J.; md by Rich J. Rondeau (JP)

DAVIS, Scott Patrick b 28 Apr 1977 Haverhill, MA s/o DAVIS, Thos P. 3rd & BLATCHLEY, Margaret E.

DAVIS, Susan B. md 17 Apr 1982 Danville, NH MOORE, Shawn Michael; md by Rev Everett E. Palmer

DAVIS, Tryphena b Kingston, NH; md 15 Dec 1810 Kingston, NH GEORGE, Ebenezer

DAVIS, Wendy L. b md 19 Oct 1990 Danville, NH LANCIANI, Kevin P.; md by Rich J. Rondeau (JP)

DAVIS, Wm A. b Lawrence, MA; md TIBBITTS, Lillian M.

DAVIS, Wm David b09 Jan 1909 s/o DAVIS, Wm A. & TIBBITTS, Lillian M.; md 01 Apr 1934 Danville, NH WELCH, Ida; md by Rev Irving J. Enslin

DAY, Alfred Theo b 13 Feb 1929 Danville, NH s/o DAY, Theodore & WEST, Mary A.; md CRAWFORD, Lillian

DAY, Barbara Lois b 25 May 1952 Danville, NH d/o DAY, Alfred T. & CRAWFORD, Lillian

DAY, Charles b Bedaque, P. E. I. Canada s/o DAY, Kerridge & McQuery, Isabelle; d 08 Jun 1926 Danville, NH ae 82y 1m 10d

DAY, Dana Charles b 25 Feb 1962 Danville, NH s/o DAY, Daniel Charles & MILES, Phyllis A.

DAY, Etta Blanche b 08 May 1897 Danville, NH d/o DAY, Charles A. & DIMOND, Jennie S.; md 23 Jul 1919 Westville, NH BABINE, Clarence W. d 02 Feb 1926 Danville, NH; md by M. J. Moher (P)

DAY, Harold b s/o DAY, Fred & THOMPSON, Viva; d 02 Oct 1957 Danville, NH

DAY, Hazel b E Kingston, NH; md SWEET, Donald

DAY, Jane Lillian b 12 Mar 1963 Danville, NH d/o DAY, Alfred F. & CRAWFORD, Lillian

DAY, John L. Roland b c1896 Danville, NH s/o DAY, Charles A. & DIAMOND, Sophia; md 19 Feb 1915 Danville, NH WADSWORTH, Irma M.; d 24 Sep 1988 Danville, NH; md by Rev Allen C. Keith

DAY, Joy Ann b 11 Oct 1960 Danville, NH d/o DAY, Alfred Theo & CRAWFORD, Lillian

DAY, Judith Lee b 08 Sep 1959 Danville, NH d/o DAY, Alfred Theo & CRAWFORD, Lillian; md 21 Aug 1982

DAY (Cont.) Danville, NH WOLF, Eric P.; md by Rev Everett E. Palmer

DAY, Kenneth Roland b Danville, NH s/o DAY, Roland & WADSWORTH, Irma; d 15 Jun 1944 Danville, NH ae 23y 2m 28d

DAY, Lois b 01 Sep 1923 Danville, NH d/o DAY, Theodore C. & WEST, Mary A.

DAY, Mary Ethel b c1892 MT Pleasant, P.E.I d/o DAY, Charles A. & DIAMOND, Sophia; md 02 May 1914 Danville, NH COLLINS, Roy Cram; d 15 May 1984; md by Rev Allen C. Kieth; d ae 92y

DAY, Mildred E. b E Kingston, NH; md BATTIS, Albert W.

DAY, Roland Alfred b 25 Oct 1953 Danville, NH s /o DAY, Alfred T. & CRAWFORD, Lillian

DAY, Theodore C. b c1891 Bradford, MA s/o DAY, Charles A. & DYMENT, Jennie; md 01 Feb 1913 Danville, NH WEST, Mary A.; d 21 Aug 1952 Danville, NH; md by Rev Allen C. Keith; d ae 66y

DAY, Vernon Elbert b 29 Jun 1915 Danville, NH s/o DAY, Roland & WADSWORTH, Irma

DEARBORN, Almira P. b Aug 1828 Hawke, NH d/o DEARBORN, David & SHORT, Hannah; md 20 Feb 1812 Hawke, NH COOK, Jos S.; d 07 Dec 1888 Danville, NH ae 60y 4m

DEARBORN, David b 20 Apr 1801 Hawke, NH s/o DEARBORN, Josiah & COLLINS, Eliz; md SHORT, Hannah; d 28 Aug 1879 Danville, NH ae 78y

DEARBORN, Eliz R. b 18 Oct 1808 Hawke, NH d/o DEARBORN, Josiah & COLLINS, Eliz; md HUNT, John; d 07 Jul 1869 Danville, NH ae 60y

DEARBORN, Emeline M. b 31 May 1835 Hawke, NH d/o DEARBORN, James & HUNT, Miriam; md 1848 Danville, NH HOOK, Addison W.; d 05 Aug 1863 Danville, NH ae 18y

DEARBORN, Hannah b 12 Jul 1814 Hawke, NH d/o DEARBORN, Josiah & ----, Judith; md 23 May 1833 Kingston, NH DAVIS, Franklin

DEARBORN, Henry Jr. b 12 Feb 1767 Hawke, NH s/o DEARBORN, Henry Sr. & HUTCHINSON, Theodate

DEARBORN, Henry Sr. md 11 Aug 1762 Hawke, NH HUTCHINSON, Theodate

DEARBORN, James b 07 Mar 1803 Hawke, NH s/o DEARBORN, Josiah & COLLINS, Eliz; md HUNT, Meriam

DEARBORN, James P. b 1812 Hawke, NH s/o DEARBORN, James & HUNT, Miriam

DEARBORN, John b 15 Oct 1782 Hawke, NH s/o DEARBORN, Henry Sr. & HUTCHINSON, Theodate

DEARBORN, John Pollard b 1827 Hawke, NH s/o DEARBORN, Jos & HUNT, Polly; d 13 Mar 1848 Danville, NH

DEARBORN, Jonathan b 28 Sep 1784 Hawke, NH s/o DEARBORN, Henry Sr. & HUTCHINSON, Theodate; md 01 Jan 1811 Kingston, NH HILL, Sally

DEARBORN, Jonathan b 12 Jun 1779 Hawke, NH s/o DEARBORN, Henry Sr. & HUTCHINSON, Theodate

DEARBORN, Jos b 09 Feb 1799 Hawke, NH s/o DEARBORN, Josiah & COLLINS, Eliz; md HUNT, Polly; d 05 Aug 1865 Danville, NH ae 66y

DEARBORN, Josiah b 12 May 1775 Hawke, NH s/o DEARBORN, Henry Sr. & HUTCHINSON, Theodate; md 11 Apr 1796 Kingston, NH COLLINS, Eliz; d 12 Jul 1848 Danville, NH

DEARBORN, Lucy Ann b 28 Jun 1830 Hawke, NH d/o DEARBORN, James & HUNT, Miriam; md 19 Aug 1849 Danville, NH SANBORN, Moses; d 25 Jun 1856 Danville, NH

DEARBORN, Mary b 06 Jul 1766 Hawke, NH d/o DEARBORN, Henry Sr. & HUTCHINSON, Theodate; md 26 Jan 1792 Kingston, NH COLLINS, Jos Jr.; d 05 Jan 1829 Hawke, NH; bu Danville, NH Old Mtg Hse Cem.

DEARBORN, Mary A. b 24 Jun 1850 Danville, NH d/o DEARBORN, James & HUNT, Miriam

DEARBORN, Molly French b 06 Jul 1765 Hawke, NH d/o DEARBORN, Henry Sr. & HUTCHINSON, Theodate

DEARBORN, Nancy b 18 Aug 1805 Hawke, NH d/o DEARBORN, Josiah & COLLINS, Eliz

DEARBORN, Nathaniel b 23 Sep 1763 Hawke, NH s/o DEARBORN, Henry Sr. & HUTCHINSON, Theodate

DEARBORN, Sally md Sep 1809 Hawke, NH WEBSTER, Benj; spouse 2nd marr

DEARBORN, Samuel b Hawke, NH; md 25 Nov 1830 KINGSTON, NH HUNT, Betsey

DEARBORN, Sarah b 18 Feb 1771 Hawke, NH d/o DEARBORN, Henry Sr. & HUTCHINSON, Theodate;

DEARBORN, Sarah b 08 Aug 1796 Hawke, NH d/o DEARBORN, Josiah & COLLINS, Eliz

DeBLOIS, Jason Martin b 11 Oct 1986 Derry, NH s/o DeBLOIS, Martin G. & POLEY, Deborah A.

DEBOIS, Hebry F. Jr. b 1945; md 08 Jun 1968 Danville, NH EPPICH, Carolyn A.

DECKER, Jennifer L. md 19 Oct 1985 Danville, NH LYLE, Robert A.; md by Rev Leslie L. Leavitt Jr.

DECKER, Taryn Stephanie b 26 Apr 1985 Lawrence, MA d/o DECKER, Timothy C. & RAYMOND, Donna

DeCOTTO, Darlene b 21 Jan 1967 Danville, NH d/o DeCOTTO, Rich & LUSTENBERGER, Claire A

DEFRESNE, Monica Lynda b 06 Feb 1990 Exeter, NH d/o DEFRESNE, Kark J. & WAIN, Sandra

DeGRYSE, Marcelle Lynn md 26 Nov 1989 Danville, NH DEVLIN, Scott Michael; md by Rich J. Rondeau (JP)

DEJADON, Robert Wm md 27 Aug 1978 Danville, NH COMBE, Kimberly Ann; md by Rev P. Daniel Baker

DeLaHAYE, Patricia A. md 24 Aug 1983 Danville, NH LaCHANCE, Rich F.; md by Renee Houle Carkin (JP)

DELAHUNTY, Jos Lawrence b s/o DELAHUNTY, Jos Lawrence Sr.; md 29 Apr 1989 Danville, NH DeSERRES, Jeannine Yvone; md by Rev George W. Hickey

DELAY, Dennis M. md 11 Nov 1972 Danville, NH MACE, Claudia-Ann; md by Roger A. Vachon (P)

DELAY, Maura Grace b 06 Sep 1973 Lawrence, MA d/o DELAY, Dennis M. & MACE, Claudia A.

DELOREY, Alice Ann b Winchester, MA d/o DELOREY, Everett Simeo; md 05 Apr 1952 Danville, NH DUSTON, Norman Paul Sr.; md by Rev Herbert C. Mathews

DELOREY, April b 02 May 1959 Danville, NH d/o DELOREY, Edward Simon & THORSEN, Dorothy Ruth

DELOREY, Edward Scott b 16 Nov 1952 Danville, NH s/o DELOREY, Ed Simeon & THORSEN, Dorothy Ruth

DELOREY, Edward Simon b 1932 MA s/o DELOREY, Everett S. & FINCH, Helen; md 16 Jun 1952 Danville, NH THORSEN, Dorothy Ruth; d 24 Nov 1979 Danville, NH; md by Rev Stanley Dahlman

DELOREY, Neil Martin b 25 Mar 1955 Danville, NH s/o DELOREY, Edward Simon & THORSEN, Dorothy Ruth; md 21 Dec 1973 Danville, NH LEATHE, Ramona J.; md by Charles E. Estee (P)

DEMAINE, Bruce Wm b 17 May 1950 Danville, NH s/o DEMAINE, Randolph L. & GRAY, Ethel Ann

DEMAINE, Carie Ann b 11 May 1977 Exeter, NH d/o DEMAINE, Stanley K. & HUGHES, Shelly Ann

DEMAINE, David Kent b 20 Nov 1962 Danville, NH s/o DEAMAINE, Rich F. & NEWCOMB, Natalie Eleanor

DEMAINE, Deborah md 01 Oct 1983 Danville, NH GUSOSKI, Wm C.; md by Rev Wayne Hardy

DEMAINE, Douglas James b 04 Sep 1951 Danville, NH s/o DEMAINE, Rich Frank & Newcomb, Natalie Eleanor; md 1st Oct 1970 Danville, NH ZALACE, Linda, 2nd 19 Feb 1977 DUBOIS, Debra Ann; md by Rev Wm Lyons

DEMAINE, Frank b 1869 Haverhill, MA s/o DEMAINE, Daniel & KING, Julia; md 24 Mar 1896 Danville, NH DARBE, Clarrisa A.; d 03 Apr 1899; md by Rev J. A. Wiggin; d ae 30y 3m 13d; Occupation Shoemaker

DEMAINE, Gertrude Eliz b 15 Dec 1917 Danville, NH d/o DEMAINE, Merritt & RUMERY, Ethel; md 04 Oct 1933 Danville, NH HERRICK, Melvin Russell; d 16 Feb 1960 Danville, NH; md by Rev Harold C. Ross

DEMAINE, Harland Ellsworth b 20 Feb 1932 Danville, NH s/o DEMAINE, Merritt & RUMERY, Ethel; md 19 Sep 1983 Danville, NH SPOFFORD, Carolyn R.; md by Rev Franklin W. Hobbs

DEMAINE, Janet Lee b 05 Apr 1954 Danville, NH d/o DEMAINE, Rich F. & NEWCOMB, Natalie Eleanor

DEMAINE, Jason Daniel D. b 22 Jul 1971 Exeter, NH s/o DEMAINE, Douglas J. & ZALACE, Linda

DEMAINE, Mahlon Oscar b 13 Jul 1926 Plaistow, NH s/o DEMAINE, Wendall C. & MACE, Amy Lydia; md 06 Feb 1948 Danville, NH MELKONIAN, Jane Josephine; md by Rev W. C. Chappell

DEMAINE, Marion Clarissa b 22 Apr 1924 Danville, NH d/o DEMAINE, Merritt Frank & RUMERY, Ethel; md 24 Jan 1942 Danville, NH SANBORN, Robert Elkins; md by Rev W. C. Chappell

DEMAINE, Marla Jean b 15 Oct 1954 Danville, NH d/o DEMAINE, Mahlon Oscar & MELKONIAN, Jane Josephine; md 01 Mar 1977 Danville, NH KNAPP, Stephen George; md by Phillip D. Fichera (JP)

DEMAINE, Merritt Frank b 31 Oct 1898 Danville, NH s/o DEMAINE, Frank & DARBE, Clara A.; md 23 Apr 1917 Danville, NH RUMMERY, Ethel L.; d 06 Sep 1983 Danville, NH; md by Allen C. Keith

DEMAINE, Paulette Ann b 01 May 1949 Exeter, NH d/o DEMAINE, Mahlon Oscar & MELKONIAN, Jane Josephine; md 12 Aug 1967 Danville, NH DONAHUE, Edward T.; md by Roger A. Vachon (P)

DEMAINE, Philip Dean b 13 Sep 1956 Danville, NH s/o DEMAINE, Rich F. & NEWCOMB, Natalie Eleanor

DEMAINE, Randolph L. b 04 Dec 1898 Danville, NH s/o DEMAINE, Wendall Oscar & MACE, Amy Lydia

DEMAINE, Rich Dana b 11 Jul 1948 Danville, NH s/o DEMAINE, Frank Rich & NEWCOMB, Natalie Eleanor; md 21 Aug 1971 Danville, NH GRIFFIN, Nancy A.; md by Rev Peter W. Lovejoy

DEMAINE, Rich Frank b 1925 Danville, NH s/o DEMAINE, Merritt

DEMAINE (Cont.) Frank &; md 30 Mar 1944 Danville, NH NEWCOMB, Natalie Eleanor; md by Rev W. C. Chappell

DEMAINE, Rodney Frank md 05 Aug 1978 Danville SPOFFORD, Amy Grace; md by Rev Rich Grannell

DEMAINE, Stanley Kevin b 20 Jul 1951 Danville, NH s/o DEMAINE, Mahlon Oscar & MELKONIAN, Jane Josephine

DEMAINE, Terry Lynn b 26 Jul 1956 Brunswick, ME

DEMAINE, Wendall Oscar b 23 Jul 1896 Danville, NH s/o DEMAINE, Frank; md 31 Aug 1921 Danville, NH MACE, Amy Lydia; d Feb 1987; md by Rev Arnaldo Natino

DeMARCO, Angela Marie b 20 Oct 1982 Portsmouth, NH d/o DeMARCO, Jos Gordon Sr. & ARNOLD, Helen B.

DeMARCO, Jos Gordon Jr. b 12 Apr 1980 Exeter, NH s/o DeMARCO, Jos Gordon Sr. & ARNOLD, Helen B.

DeMARCO, Jos Gorden Sr. md 29 Sep 1979 Danville, NH ARNOLD, Helen B.; md by Rev Wm Ryans

DEMERITT, Clarence G. b 1901 Nottingham, NH s/o Demeritt, Lewis T.; md 02 Mar 1929 Nottingham, NH TRAFTON, Julia M.; md by Rev Ira D. Morrison

DEMERS, Harold Gary b 1932 Manchester, NH s/o DEMERS, Charles A.; md 04 Apr 1953 Danville, NH TEWKSBURY, Evelyn Louise

DEMERS, Jonathan David b 21 Sep 1986 Danville, NH s/o DEMERS, Roger A. & DAROIS, Carol A.

DEMERS, Roger A. md 01 Jul 1981 Danville, NH LeFEBURE, Carl A.; md by Bettie C. Ouellette (JP)

DEMING, Edna M. b Cambridge, MA d/o DEMING, George H.; md 07 Mar 1942 Danville, NH HUSEBY, ----; md by Rev W. C. Chappell

DEMING, George b 1881 Waterbury, CT s/o DEMING, Levings; md 27 Oct 1936 Danville, NH ARCHIBALD, Viola; md by Rev W. C. Chappell

DEMING, Viola Pauline b Haverhill, MA d/o ARCHIBALD, Gerry M. & DOLE, Pauline; d 09

DEMING (Cont.) Jun 1966 Danville, NH ae 67y

DENNETT, Lancer Francis b 1916 Amesbury, MA; md 12 Dec 1953 Danville, NH LESSARD, Flora Helen

DENNIS, Joshua Robert b 15 Sep 1992 Exeter, NH s/o DENNIS, Robert B. & CHASE, Kathleen M.

DENNIS, Michael James b 08 Feb 1989 Exeter, NH s/o DENNIS, Robert B. & CHASE, Kathleen M.

DENNIS, Wm C. md 17 Oct 1987 Danville, NH O'NIEL, Michele E.; md by Rev George F. Moore

DENNY, Margaret A. md 09 Nov 1990 Danville, NH FAWCETT, John J.; md by Rich J. Rondeau (JP)

DENTON, Bruce Dean Jr. b 25 Jul 1978 Methuen, MA s/o DENTON, Bruce Dean Sr. & COTE, Patricia M.

DENTON, Dean Michael md 14 Apr 1990 Danville, NH SARGENT, Rebecca Joy; md by Rev Everett E. Palmer

DeROCHMONT, Mary Vernon b c1864 Kingston, NH d/o DeROCHMONT, Daniel & GALE, Eliz; md 05 May 1887 Kingston, NH MERRICK, Merrill Bagley; d 18 Nov 1949 Danville, NH; md by Rev J. M. Bean

DERUSHA, Michele G. md 06 Jul 1984 Danville, NH MORGAN, Robert S.; md by Rev Robert L. Dobson

DESCHAMPS, Anne Marie b 1940 NH d/o DESCHAMPS, Leo; md 17 Oct 1959 Danville, NH DUSTON, Gerald John; md by Rev Henri Blanchard

DesCHATELETS, Jean R. b Danville, NH; md 14 Nov 1970 Danville, NH BACHOVZEFF, Olga H.

DESCHENE, Steven Edward b 01 Aug 1973 Haverhill, NH s/o DESCHENE, Dennis A. & WILLARD, Patricia A.

DeSERRES, Barbara Louise md 15 Aug 1980 Danville, NH HOWARD, Raymond James; md by Rev Wm Ryans

DeSERRES, Jeannine Yvonne md 29 Apr 1989 Danville, NH DELAHUNTY, Jos Lawrence Jr.; md by Rev George W. Hickey

DeSERRES, Norman P. md 23 Jun 1979 Danville, NH MARSHMAN, Debra T.; md by Rev Pierre Baker (P)

DeSERRES, Norman Phillip Jr. md 20 Oct 1990 Danville, NH SMART, Yvette Marie; md by Rev Everett E. Palmer

DeSERRES, Theresa Marie md 15 Jan 1977 Danville, NH STOREY, Arthur Ellis 3rd; md by Rich L. Provencher (P)

DESILETS, Norman Carrol b 1930 Epping, NH s/o DESILETS, Arthur; md 03 Jul 1954 Danville, NH CHURCH, Lorraine Florence; md by Agnes H. Collins (JP)

DESJARDINS, Steven Kieth b 28 Aug 1972 Haverhill, MA s/o DESJARDINS, Ernest J. & McINTOSH, Winnifred A.

DESMARALS, Leo V. b 1909 Salem, MA s/o DESMARALS, Louis; md 30 Jul 1929 Danville, NH SHELDON, Isabel; md by Clarence M. Collins (JP)

DESMOND, Pamela Ann md 04 May 1991 Danville, NH DALLON, Chester Jos Jr.; md by Rich J. Rondeau (JP)

DESROCHERS, Sandra F. md 29 Dec 1972 Danville, NH MITCHELL, Michael W.; md by Robert S. Dejadon (JP)

DESROSTERS, Ann Louise md 19 Aug 1989 Danville, NH MARKOVICH, Thos David; md by Rev Leslie L. Leavitt

DeVEAU, Simone R. md 05 Apr 1991 Danville, NH THAINI, Said; md by Rich J. Rondeau (JP)

DEVENY, ---- md SCICSE, Margaret

DEVLIN, Scott Michael b md 26 Nov 1989 Danville, NH DeGRYSE, Marcelle Lynn; md by Rich J. Rondeau (JP)

DEZAND, Emeline b 1872 d/o DEZAND, Lezam & HAMMEL, Betsey; md 01 Apr 1896 Fremont, NH CLIFFORD, George W.

DIAMOND, Lori Ann md 25 May 1991 Danville, NH BONCZLIEWICZ, Ron S.; md by Rev Robert F. Dobson

DIFEO, Rich P. md 05 Dec 1984 Danville, NH GALAZKA, Barbara D.; md by David T; Ingerson (JP)

DIGGINS, Ellen Veronica md 17 Sep 1988 Danville, NH KENT, Robert J.; md by Rev Everett E. Palmer

DIGIOVANNI, Sandra Lee d/o DIGIOVANNI, Keith & URBSHO, Bertha d 17 Nov 1992 ae 53y

DIMES, Douglas Rich b 1941 MA; md 25 Aug 1961 Danville, NH PARTRIDGE, Florence E.; md by Oscar W. Swenson

DIMES, Leslie A. b s/o DIMES, Bertram & SMITH, Jessie; d 25 Nov 1971 Danville, NH ae 63y

DIMOND, Abigail b 1789 Hawke, NH d/o DIMOND, Israel Jr. & EASTMAN, Abigail; md SHORT, Aaron; d 25 Dec 1846 Danville, NH d ae 57yr

DIMOND, Alice Margarette b 1929 Plaistow, NH d/o DIMOND, James Thompson; md 29 Dec 1945 Danville, NH FOWLER, Jos Edward; md by Rev W. C. Chappell

DIMOND, Almon b 08 Sep 1828 Hawke, NH s/o DIMOND, Obediah & BLAKE, Sophia D.; md 26 Jun 1883 Danville, NH CURRIER, Almina; d 30 Sep 1896 Danville, NH

DIMOND, Carrie Mabel b c1888 Danville, NH d/o DIMOND, Melburne J. & DAVIS, Emma M.; md 06 Jun 1907 Danville, NH COLLINS, Irving Mahlon; d 23 Dec 1975 Danville, NH; md by Rev W. C. Chappell

DIMOND, Cora Belle b 27 Jun 1862 Danville, NH d/o DIMOND, Josiah T. & COLLINS, Almira; md CARTER, Walter P. d Jan 1908 Danville, NH ae 45y 6m 28d

DIMOND, Dorothy b 21 Feb 1765 Hawke, NH d/o DIMOND, Israel & STEVENS, Mary; md PHILLIPS, ----

DIMOND, Eliz b 28 Dec 1785 Hawke, NH d/o DIMOND, Israel Jr. & EASTMAN, Abigail; md 21 Jul 1805 Hawke, NH QUIMBY, Aaron; d 10 Feb 1881 Danville, NH ae 95y

DIMOND, Francis F. b 16 Jan 1840 Danville, NH s/o DIMOND, Orin & BRADLEY, Mehitable; d 30 Jan 1896 Danville, NH

DIMOND, Frinkie I. b 1882 Danville NH s/o DIMOND, Melburne J. & DAVIS Emma M. md d 28 Apr 1887 Danville NH

DIMOND, Grace May b 29 Mar 1886 Danville, NH d/o DIMOND, Melburne J. & DAVIS, Emma M.; md 06 Apr 1906 Danville, NH ANDERSON, Marcus M.; d 22 Jul 1949 Danville NH; md by Rev A.

DIMOND (Cont.) B. Hyde

DIMOND, Hannah b 03 Mar 1760 Hawke, NH d/o DIMOND, Israel Capt. & STEVENS-PHILBRICK,MARY; md 31 Oct 1776 Danville, NH BLAKE, Hezekiah; d 27 Jan 1822

DIMOND, Israel b 09 Nov 1819 Hawke, NH s/o DIMOND, John & CARTER, Abigail; d 08 Mar 1897 Danville, NH

DIMOND, Israel Capt. b c1723 S Hampton, NH s/o DIMOND, Reuben & WORTHEN, Dorothy; md 1st CHANDLER, Mary & 2nd STEVENS, Mary; d 13 Apr 1800 Hawke, NH

DIMOND, Israel Jr. b 08 May 1757 Kingston, NH s/o DIMOND, Israel Capt. & STEVENS, Mary; md 27 Jan 1778 Hawke, NH EASTMAN, Abigail; d 16 Dec 1819 Hawke, NH ae 62y

DIMOND, James T. b c1897 N Sidney, C. Bret. s/o DIMOND, Melburne J. & DAVIS, Emma K.; md 06 Jul 1919 Danville, NH CARLSON, Ida T.; d 06 Apr 1952 Danville, NH; md by Rev L. M. Bleakney; Mother THOMPSON, Winnifred ?

DIMOND, John b 05 Mar 1792 Hawke, NH s/o DIMOND, Israel Jr. & EASTMAN, Abigail; md CARTER, Abigail; d 23 Jan 1845 Danville, NH

DIMOND, John b 18 Sep 1762 Hawke, NH s/o DIMOND, Israel Capt. & STEVENS-PHILBRICK, Mary

DIMOND, John T. b 09 Sep 1855 Danville, NH s/o DIMOND, Josiah T. & PEASLEE, Catherine

DIMOND, Josiah T. b 15 Apr 1827 Hawke, NH s/o DIMOND, Reuben & TEWKSBURY, Anna; md 1860 Danville, NH COLLINS, Almira B.; d 12 Jun 1862 Danville, NH; 1st Wife - PEASLEE, Catherine

DIMOND, Kate E. b 28 Jul 1857 Danville, NH d/o DIMOND, Josiah T. & PEASLEE, Catherine; 24 May 1881 Danville, NH ae 23y

DIMOND, Lavina Miss b 23 Nov 1826 Hawke, NH d/o DIMOND, Obediah & BLAKE, Sophia D.; d 06 Apr 1873 Danville, NH; d ae 46y

DIMOND, Leonard b Nov 1834 Hawke, NH s/o DIMOND, Obediah &

DIMOND (Cont.) BLAKE, Sophia D.; d 13 Mar 1835 Hawke, NH

DIMOND, Louise Winifred b Danville, NH d/o DIMOND, James T. & CARLSON, Ida; d 05 Apr 1935 Danville, NH; d ae 15y; 1st child in family

DIMOND, Maria b 10 Mar 1829 Hawke NH d/o DIMOND, John & CARTER, Abigail; md WHITTIER, ---- ; d 04 Jan 1902 Danville, NH ae 74y 9m 26d

DIMOND, Mary b c1729 d/o DIMOND, Israel Capt. & CHANDLER, Mary; d 02 Oct 1791 Hawke, NH

DIMOND, Mary B. b 23 Jul 1843 Hawke, NH d/o DIMOND, Orin & BRADLEY, Mehitable F.; d 20 Dec 1901

DIMOND, Melburne J. b 25 Jan 1858 Danville, NH s/o DIMOND, Israel & GARLAND, Hannah S.; md 09 Sep 1880 Danville, NH DAVIS, Emma M.; d 29 Nov 1922 Danville, NH

DIMOND, Molly b 24 Jan 1780 Hawke, NH d/o DIMOND, Israel Jr. & EASTMAN, Abigail

DIMOND, Naomi Tewksbury b 1820 Hawke, NH d/o DIMOND, Reuben & TEWKSBURY, Anna; md TOWLE, Jarius; d 06 May 1866 Danville, NH; bu Danville, NH Old Mtg Hse Cem.

DIMOND, Obadiah (Capt) b 26 Feb 1801 Hawke, NH s/o DIMOND, Israel Jr. & EASTMAN, Abigail; md 24 Nov 1825 Hawke, NH BLAKE, Sophia D.; d 14 Dec 1882 Danville, NH

DIMOND, Oren b c1812 s/o DIMOND, Reuben & TEWKSBURY, Anna; md 06 Dec 1837 Raymond, NH BRADLEY, Mehitable

DIMOND, Polly md 21 Jun 1804 Kingston, NH FLANDERS, James

DIMOND, Reuben Jr. b 1818 Hawke, NH s/o DIMOND, Reuben & TEWKSBURY, Anna; md 12 Oct 1843 Danville, NH CARTER, Luella; d 19 Sep 1847 Danville, NH

DIMOND, Reuben Sr. b 01 Mar 1782 Hawke, NH s/o DIMOND, Israel Jr. & EASTMAN, Abigail; md   Jun 1808 Kingston, NH TEWKSBURY, Anna Nancy; d 29 Aug 1856 Danville, NH

DIMOND, S. Francena b 12 Oct 1846 Danville, NH d/o DIMOND, Israel &

DIMOND (Cont.) GARLAND, Hannah S.

DIMOND, Sabra M. b 17 Jan 1850 Danville, NH d/o DIMOND, Orin & BRADLEY, Mehitable; md 14 Feb 1870 Danville, NH CURRIER, Osmund

DIMOND, Sarah b 06 Jan 1821 Hawke, NH d/o DIMOND, John & CARTER, Abigail; md GALE, Amos; d 09 Dec 1846 Danville, NH

DIMOND, Sarah b 02 Aug 1778 Hawke, NH d/o DIMOND, Israel Jr. & EASTMAN, Abigail

DIMOND, Sarah A. b 29 Jul 1852 Danville, NH d/o DIMOND, Orin & BRADLEY, Mehitable S.; md 27 Nov 1873 Danville, NH JUDKINS, John H. d 01 Jan 1931 Danville, NH

DIMOND, Thos b 02 Oct 1784 Hawke, NH; s/o DIMOND, Israel Jr. & EASTMAN, Abigail

DIMOND, ---- b 1831 Hawke, NH d/o DIMOND, Obediah & BLAKE, Sophia D.; d 19 Sep 1831 Hawke, NH

DIPIRRO, Aristide Dominic b 1924 MA s/o DIPIRRO, Graziano; md 01 Oct 1950 Danville, NH Longland, Alice Aldred; md by Rev W. C. Chappell

DISTEFANO, Ann Marie b md 24 Feb 1990 Danville, NH RUTLEDGE, John Chas; md by Rich J. Robdeau (JP)

DIXON, Hannah b SW Prince Edwd Is.; md 29 Aug 1887 Wilmington, DE MORRILL, John W.; md by Rev L. W. Adams

DOANE, Marion D. b d/o DOANE, Lester & ----, Margaret; md WITHER, ---- ; d 29 Aug 1981 Danville, NH ae 71y

DOCKHAM, Susan J. d 14 Apr 1938 Danville, NH ae 80

DOLCE, Nicholas Rich b 16 Nov 1987 Lawrence, MA s/o DOLCE, Floyd R. & SARCIONE, Debra L.

DOLE, Chas Edwin b 1865 Newbury, MA s/o DOLE, John H. & HUNTINGTON, Emeline B.; md 22 Jun 1894 Danville, NH ANDREWS, Luella Gray; d 13 Sep 1947 Danville, NH; md by Rev John A. Wiggin; ae 82y 4m 5d

DOLE, Doris Carmen b 1902 Georgetown, MA d/o DOLE, Chas E.; md 05 Nov 1924 Danville, NH HARPER,

DOLE (Cont.) Chas M.; md by Rev Edw L. Noble; d 04 Jun 1992 ae 89y

DOLE, Ina E. b Groveland, MA d/o DOLE, Chas E. & ANDREWS, Luella G.; d 12 Dec 1949 Danville, NH ae 51y

DOLE, John H. md HUNTINGTON, Emeline B.

DOLLIFFE, Nicholas md 19 Nov 1767 Hawke, NH CLOUGH, Sarah; d 14 Aug 1769 Hawke, NH

DOLLOFFE, Abraham b 26 Aug 1768 Hawke, NH s/o DOLLOFFE, Nicholas & CLOUGH, Sarah

DONAHUE, Alicia Lyn b 26 Apr 1976 Haverhill, MA d/o DONAHUE, Gary D. & RILEY, Deborah J.

DONAHUE, Edward T. b 1943 Malden, MA s/o DONAHUE, John J. & DAVIS, Eliz M.; md 12 Aug 1967 Danville, NH

DEMAINE, Paulette A. d 24 Dec 1980 Danville, NH; md by Roger A. Vachon (P)

DONAHUE, Joanne W. b Malden, MA; md O'BRIEN, Robert J. Sr.

DONAHUE, Joshua Jason b 21 Sep 1977 Exeter, NH s/o DONAHUE, Edward T. & DEMAINE, Paulette Ann

DONAHUE, Shawn Thos b 05 Aug 1975 Exeter, NH s/o DONAHUE, Edward T. & DEMAINE, Paulette Ann

DONAHUE, Susan L. md 28 May 1989 Danville, NH BAILEY, Jos P.; md by Rich J. Rondeau (JP)

DONOHOE, Shawn W. md 07 Sep 1985 Danville, NH MITCHELL, Kimberly J.; md by Retenah V. Pietrowski (JP)

DORAN, Gerald R. md 17 Aug 1986 Danville, NH COTE, Lillian C.; md by Rich J. Rondeau (JP)

DORSEY, Rhonda Lynne b md 25 Feb 1989 Danville, NH PAOLINO, Rich M.; md by Rev John C. Lombard

DOUCETTE, Joel David b 29 Jan 1987 Exeter, NH s/o DOUCETTE, David A. & PAGE, Deborah A.

DOUCETTE, Jos Rich md 26 Jul 1974 Danville, NH LEISHMAN, Rita Catherine; md by Leona A. Sciaudone (JP)

DOUCETTE, Laura Yvonne b 14 Sep 1984 Derry, NH d/o DOUCHETTE, Rejean J. & ROCHETTE, Susan M.

DOUGLAS, Barbara b d/o DOUGLAS, Fred S. & MAXSON, Eva M.; md STUBBS, ---- ; d 08 Oct 1972 Danville, NH ae 56y

DOW, Abbie W. b c1844 Atkinson, NH; md 06 Nov 1862 Danville, NH EMERSON, Wm E.

DOW, Diane md 26 Sep 1987 Danville, NH ATWOOD, Frank W. Jr.; md by Rich J. Rondeau (JP)

DOW, Georgianna B. b 30 Sep 1845 Danville, NH d/o DOW, Moses H. & PHILBRICK, Almira P.

DOW, Lydia b Hampton Falls, NH; md 09 Apr 1816 Hampton, NH BLAISDELL, John Jr.

DOW, Rich Stanley b 1932 MA s/o DOW, Stanley J.; md 14 Nov 1952 Danville, NH GRIFFIN, Patricia Mary; md by Rev Robert S. Walker

DOWLING, Norna Anne md 14 Jun 1975 Danville, NH ALBRECHT, Allan Peter; md by Robert S. Dejadon (JP)

DOWNES, Matthew Gardner b 30 Mar 1978 Exeter, NH s/o DOWNES, Peter W. & GRANGER, Mary Eliz

DOWNES, Wm Granger b 27 Aug 1976 Exeter, NH s/o DOWNES, Peter W. & GRANGER, Mary Eliz

DOWNEY, Cheryl A. md 25 Jul 1987 Danville, NH TRACEY, Patrick J.; md by Rich J. Rondeau (JP)

DOWNING, Alison md 22 May 1988 Danville, NH BAKER, James Roy; md by Rich J. Rondeau (JP)

DOWNS, Annie H. b Berwick, ME d/o DOWNS, Aaron K. & COOPER, Mary J.; md 18 Jun 1902 Danville, NH COLBY, Herbert E.; d 07 Mar 1968 Danville, NH; md by Rev W. P. Merrill

DOWNS, Violette L. md 13 Jun 1980 Danville, NH GAYNOR, Chas J. Jr.; md by Bettie C. Ouellette (JP)

DOWNS, ---- b 04 Feb 1853 Danville, NH s/o DOWNS, Lyman & DOWNS, Mary M.

DOYLE, Kelly Beth b 16 Aug 1982 Lawrence, MA d/o DOYLE, Thos F. Jr. & GAFFNEY, Bethann

DOYLE, Kerry Kathleen b 30 Oct 1983 Danville, NH d/o DOYLE, Thos F. Jr. & GAFFNY, Bethann

DOYLE, Maureen Denise b 1947

DOYLE (Cont.) Bronxville, NY; md 27 Dec 1967 Danville, NH ARNOLD, Gary Wayne

DRAGON, Lillian M. md 08 Jul 1977 Danville, NH LAJEUNESSE, Lucian M. Jr.; md by Clara B. Shaw (JP)

DRAGON, Rich Jos b 16 Apr 1968 Danville, NH s/o DRAGON, Rich & St Paul, Lillian M.

DRAZYK, Jan Tomas md 30 Aug 1978 Danville, NH WEST, Helen Armeda; md by June C. Loud (JP)

DREW, Thos C. d 13 Sep 1888 Danville, NH 84y 2m

DRISCOLL, Nancy E. md 10 Sep 1983 Danville, NH CLARK, Lawrence C.; md by Rev Edward J. Charest

DROUIN, Edna D. b 1903 Salmon Falls, NH d/o DROUIN, Geo; md 16 May 1937 Danville, NH BATTEN, Robert B.; md by Clarence M. Collins (JP)

DRUKER, Jessa Ann b 08 Oct 1989 Haverhill, MA d/o DRUKER, Lawrence H. & FESSENDEN, Karen L.

DUBOIS, Debra Ann md 19 Feb 1977 Danville, NH DEMAINE, Douglas James; md by Rev Wm Lyons

DUBOIS, Henry F. b 1945 NY; md 08 Jun 1968 Danville, NH EPPICH, Carolyn A.; md by Martin J. Mager (P)

DUBOIS, Kristine, M. md 02 Oct 1982 Danville, NH ERDMANN, David G.; md by Marjorie D. Moisan (JP)

DUCHEMIN, Brenda Mae b 1943 Danville, NH; md 26 May 1967 Danville, NH CHARNLEY, Kenneth; md by Leona A. Sciaudone (JP)

DUCHEMIN, Bruce L. b 1945 NH; md 21 Oct 1962 Danville, NH MUDGE, Brenda M.; md by Arthur M. Comeau

DUDLEY, Abigail b Hawke, NH; md 04 Mar 1779 Hawke, NH DUDLEY, John; md by Rev John Page

DUDLEY, Ethel b 1899 Somerville, MA d/o DUDLEY, Clifford G.; md 30 Jun 1940 Danville, NH WARD, Edwin Henry; md by Rev W. C. Chappell

DUDLEY, John b Brentwood, NH; md 04 Mar 1779 Hawke, NH DUDLEY, Abigail; md by Rev John Page

DUFFINE, Jos O. b s /o DUFFINE, John & SMITH, Mary; d 07 Nov 1977 Danville, NH ae 61y

DUFFUS, Eliza D. b Dundee Scotland d/o DUFFUS, James J. & TAYLOR, Charlotte; md 30 May 1890 Danville, NH HEATH, John F.; d 27 Dec 1934d ae 70y 1m 9d; md by Rev J. A. Lowell

DUFFUS, Nellie D. b Dundee Scotland d/o DUFFUS, James J. & TAYLOR, Charlotte; md 26 Nov 1890 Danville, NH SANBORN, John N. d 14 May 1960 Danville, NH ae 93y

DULEY, George E. b s/o DULEY, Willard H. & GOLDER, Martha M.; d 17 Apr 1952 Danville, NH; d ae 67y

DULEY, Martha F. b 1918 Boston, MA d/o DULEY, George E.; md 12 Jun 1937 Danville, NH SHATTACK, George W.; md by Rev W. C. Chappell

DULMAGE, Charlotte C. b Ontario Canada d/o DULMAGE, Jacob & DAINARD, Ellen J.; md COOLEY, ----; d 25 Oct 1963 Danville, NH ae 99y

DULONG, John Mark 4th b 06 Mar 1986 Derry, NH s/o DULONG, John Mark 3rd & DALRYMPLE, Susan T.

DUNBAR, Emma b Halifax Nova Scoti; md ELKINS, John H.

DUNHAM, Agnes Wilson d 28 Apr 1927 Danville, NH ae 67y 2m 23d

DUNHAM, Tammy b c1789 Chelsea, MA; md LADD, Caleb; d 16 Dec 1863 Danville, NH age 83 yr

DUNN, Lisa Ann md 01 Jul 1990 Danville, NH CARPENTER, Brian Keith; md by Linda S. Jette (JP)

DUNN, Mary Ella b 20 Apr 1834 Hawke, NH d/o DUNN, Samuel & QUIMBY, Sally; md 24 Mar 1853 Danville, NH COLLINS, Nelson

DUNN, Wm F. b 1930 Danville, NH s/o DUNN, Donald G.; md 25 Feb 1951 Danville, NH CROWELL, June E.; md by Agnes H. Collins (JP)

DUPRIEST, Rilla Evon b d/o DuPRIEST, Chas Everett; md CLEMENT, ----; d 04 Nov 1970 Danville, NH ae 63y

DURGIN, Patricia A. b d/o DURGIN, Edwin & RANDALL, Flora; md JOHNSON, ---- ; d 24 Mar 1987 Danville, NHd ae 49y

DUSTON, Albert Henry b 17 Aug 1936 Danville, NH s/o DUSTON, Oscar Simeon & BONAH, Blanche; md 18

DUSTON (Cont.) Sep 1971 Danville, NH FLYNN, Evelyn Loretta; md by Rich Vickery (P)

DUSTON, Bertha A. md 25 Jul 1987 Danville, NH LAVELLE, Rich Robert; md by Rev Everett E. Palmer

DUSTON, Charlene Althea b 31 Mar 1934 Danville, NH d/o DUSTON, Charles D. & MASON, Mary

DUSTON, Charles D. b 1882 Salem, NH s/o DUSTON, Edwin; md 27 Aug 1932 Danville, NH MASON, Mary; md by Mary E. Dirsa (JP)

DUSTON, Donald Roy b 19 Jan 1930 Danville, NH s/o DUSTON, Oscar & BROWN, Blanche

DUSTON, Dorothy May b 1925 Nashua, NH d/o DUSTON, Oscar Simeon; md 28 Jun 1947 Danville, NH TAYLOR, Leonidas Ellsworth Jr.; md by Rev W. C. Chappell

DUSTON, Enid Arline b 22 Feb 1933 Danville, NH d/o DUSTON, Charles D. & MASON, Mary Duston

DUSTON, Ernest Bonnah b 08 Mar 1931 Danville, NH s /o DUSTON, Oscar Simeon & BONAH, Blanche; md WILSON, Evelyn Mae

DUSTON, Ernest Scott b 07 Jul 1957 s/o DUSTON, Ernest Bonnah & Wilson, Evelyn Mae

DUSTON, Gerald John b 17 Oct 1933 Danville, NH s/o DUSTON, Oscar Simeon & BONAH, Blanche; md 17 Oct 1959 Danville, NH DESCHAMPS, Anne Marie; md by Rev Henri Blanchard

DUSTON, Joyce Jean b 01 Dec 1937 Danville, NH d/o DUSTON, Oscar Simeon & BONAH, Blanche; md 10 Nov 1956 Danville, NH POOLE, Rich Reed; md by Rev Albian Bulger (P)

DUSTON, Mary Jane b 29 May 1959 Danville, NH d/o DUSTON, Norman Paul & DELOREY, Alice A.

DUSTON, Norman Paul Sr. b 29 Mar 1932 Danville NH s/o DUSTON, Oscar Simeon & BONAH, Blanche; md 05 Apr 1952 Danville NH DELOREY, Alice Ann; md by Rev Herbert C. Mathews

DUSTON, Oscar Simeon b Salem, NH s/o DUSTON, Edwin & ---, Clara; md BONAH, Blanche d 15 Jun 1991 ae 94y

DUSTON, Penny Marie b 01 Mar 1964 Danville, NH d/o DUSTON, Norman P. Sr. & DeLOREY, Alice A.

DUSTON, Rich Earl b 10 Feb 1935 Danville, NH s/o DUSTON, Oscar Simeon & BONAH, Blanche; md 20 Oct 1956 Danville, NH COTE, Yvonne Lucille; md by Rev Albian Bulger (P)

DUSTON, Rich Lee b Mar 1953 s/o DUSTON, Ernest Bonnah & Wilson, Evelyn Mae

DUSTON, Robert James b 05 Sep 1954 Danville, NH s/o DUSTON, Norman & DELOREY, Alice; md Sep 1973 Danville, NH GRAY, Jane A.; md by Eliz G. Waitt (JP)

DUSTON, Robert Oscar b 1928 NH s/o DUSTON, Oscar; md 24 Dec 1959 Danville, NH MESSER, Marjorie Ruth; md by Rev John Wood Jr.

DUSTON, Robert Oscar md 22 Dec 1978 Danville, NH HUCKINS, Mary Louise; md by Rev Wm Ryans

DUSTON, Shirley Rae b 17 Apr 1939 Danville, NH d/o DUSTON, Oscar Simeon & BONAH, Blanche; md 24 Aug 1968 Danville, NH MAEDER, Donald Bruce; md by Peter Damian (P)

DUSTON, Steven b s/o DUSTON, Ernest Bonnah & Wilson, Evelyn Mae;

DUSTON, Sylvia Lee b 23 Feb 1961 Danville, NH d/o DUSTON, Norman Paul Sr. & DELOREY, Alice A. md 20 Jun 1992 MAXWELL, Anthony James

DUSTON, Terry Ann b 18 Aug 1957 Danville, NH d/o DUSTON, Norman Paul Sr. & DELOREY, Alice A.

DUTTON, Albert Jr. b 1937 Merrimac, MA s/o DUTTON, Albert Sr.; md 27 Jul 1958 Danville, NH BOWLEY, Juanita Gladys; md by Agnes H. Collins (JP)

DUTTON, Mildred L. b c1902 Merrimac, MA d/o DUTTON, Ben L.; md 12 Mar 1919 Milford, NH WELCH, Thos P.; md by Rev Charles A. Reese

DWYER, Mary Blanche b 1942 MA; md 02 Jul 1960 Danville, NH CARTER, Austin Robert; md by Rev Thos J. Hannigar

DYER, Jennie b Portland, ME d/o DYER, Wm & MILBAY, Phineas; md 03 Apr 1889 Danville, NH

DYKE, Flora B. md PRINCE, ---- ; d

DYKE (Cont.) 09 Apr 1977 Danville, NH ae 73y

DYMENT, Jennie b New Brunswick Canada d/o DYMENT, Moses & BRYANT, Maria; md DAY, ---- ; d 27 Apr 1945 Danville, NH ae 93y

EADES, Betsey A. b c1808 Allenstown, NH; md 1848 Danville, NH HUNTINGTON, Wm H.

EASTMAN, Abigail b 26 Apr 1757 d/o EASTMAN, Edward & WADLEIGH, Sarah; md 27 Jan 1778 Hawke DIMOND, Israel Jr.; d 22 Aug 1847 Danville; bu Danville Center Cem.; d ae 90y

EASTMAN, Abigail b c1808 d/o EASTMAN, Samuel & ---- , Polly; d 23 Dec 1810 Hawke

EASTMAN, Abigail H. b 28 MAY 1827 Hawke, NH d/o EASTMAN, Sewell & TUCKER, Abigail; md 05 MAY 1844 Kingston, NH VINCENT, Geo

EASTMAN, Ai Freeman b 19 Apr 1833 Hawke, NH s/o EASTMAN, Samuel B. & EASTMAN, Sarah

EASTMAN, Albert D. b 01 Aug 1828 Hawke, NH s/o EASTMAN, Samuel B. & EASTMAN, Sarah

EASTMAN, Alvin B. b 08 Oct 1832 Hawke, NH s/o EASTMAN, Sewell & TUCKER, Abigail

EASTMAN, Amantha b 1831 Hawke, NH d/o EASTMAN, Calvin & SAWYER, Melinda; d 1843 Danville, NH; d ae 12y

EASTMAN, Betsey b Hawke, NH; md 21 Feb 1799 Kingston, NH FELLOWS, John

EASTMAN, Betsey Mrs. b c1797; md EASTMAN, Samuel; d 06 Feb 1841 Danville, NH d ae 44y

EASTMAN, Calvin b 30 Jun 1804 Hawke, NH s/o EASTMAN, Samuel & ---- , Polly; md SAWYER, Melinda; d 04 Jun 1871 Danville, NH

EASTMAN, Chas M. b Danville, NH s/o EASTMAN, Chas H. & ROBINSON, Sarah; d 02 Sep 1935 Danville, NH; d ae 55y 23d

EASTMAN, Chas S. b 1857 Danville, NH s/o EASTMAN, Sewell Jr.

EASTMAN (Cont.) & LIBBEY, Betsey J.; md 03 Jul 1878 Danville, NH ROBINSON, Sarah J.

EASTMAN, Daniel b 05 Dec 1785 Hawke, NH s/o EASTMAN, Thos & BROWN, Sally

EASTMAN, Dorothy b 16 Apr 1765 Danville, NH d/o EASTMAN, Edward Sr. & WADLEIGH-CLOUGH, Sarah

EASTMAN, Edward 3rd b 04 Feb 1810 Hawke, NH s/o EASTMAN, Samuel B. & EASTMAN, Sarah

EASTMAN, Edward Ens. b 02 Feb 1732 s/o EASTMAN, Thos & FRENCH, Abigail; md WADLEIGH, Sarah; d 07 Nov 1815 Hawke, NH; bu: Danville, NH Old Mtg Hse Cem.; d ae 82y

EASTMAN, Edward Jr. b 28 Apr 1771 Hawke, NH s/o EASTMAN, Edward Sr. & WADLEIGH-CLOUGH, Sarah; md BEAN, Hepzibah; d 29 Sep 1848 Danville, NH ae 77y

EASTMAN, Eliz b 17 Dec 1761 Hawke, NH d/o EASTMAN, Edward Sr. & WADLEIGH-CLOUGH, Sarah

EASTMAN, Emma A. b Kingston, NH d/o EASTMAN, James & ROBINSON, Sarah J. md AVERY, Chas; d 25 Apr 1947 Danville, NH

EASTMAN, Francis Wm b 1867 Danville, NH s/o EASTMAN, Sewell Jr. & LIBBEY, Betsey J.; d 20 Nov 1935 Danville, NH

EASTMAN, Geo E. b 04 Jul 1854 Danville, NH s/o EASTMAN, Sewell Jr. & LIBBEY, Betsey J.

EASTMAN, Geo F. b 1834 Hawke, NH s/o EASTMAN, Sewell & TUCKER, Abigail

EASTMAN, Harlan B. b 13 Aug 1854 Danville, NH s/o EASTMAN, Alvin B. & ---- , Marilla

EASTMAN, Hepzibah b 15 Jun 1802 Hawke, NH d/o EASTMAN, Edward Jr. & BEAN, Hepzibah; md PAGE, Amos (Capt); d 30 Oct 1884 Danville, NH

EASTMAN, Hepzibah b 07 Jul 1815 Hawke, NH d/o EASTMAN, Samuel B. & EASTMAN, Sarah

EASTMAN, Huldah b 15 Sep 1795

EASTMAN (Cont.) Hawke, NH d/o EASTMAN, Edward Jr. & BEAN, Hepzibah

EASTMAN, Huldah Ann b c1835 Hawke, NH; md SHERBURNE, Lewis O. d 18 Mar 1862 New York, NY ae 37y

EASTMAN, Huldah Ann b 03 Nov 1825 Hawke, NH d/o EASTMAN, Samuel B. & EASTMAN, Sarah

EASTMAN, Jacob b Hawke, NH; md 16 Nov 1797 Kingston, NH CAMPBELL, Hannah

EASTMAN, James b 28 Apr 1780 Hawke, NH s/o EASTMAN, Stephen & QUIMBY, Miriam

EASTMAN, James G. b 1841 Danville, NH s/o EASTMAN, Sewell & TUCKER, Abigail; md 04 Feb 1879 Danville, NH MACK, Harriet N.

EASTMAN, John b Kingston, NH; md 17 Feb 1774 Hawke, NH FRENCH, Joanna

EASTMAN, Josiah C. b c1811 Louden, NH; md 1859 Danville, NH HARRIS, Mary H.

EASTMAN, LaRoy b 29 Nov 1843 Hawke, NH s/o EASTMAN, Calvin & SAWYER, Melinda

EASTMAN, Lydia b 1835 Hawke, NH d/o EASTMAN, Sewell & TUCKER, Abigail

EASTMAN, Mary b 13 Jan 1770 d/o EATMAN, Stephen & Miriam QUIMBY

EASTMAN, Mary b 1825 Hawke, NH d/o EASTMAN, Sewell & TUCKER, Abigail

EASTMAN, Mary d 10 Feb 1941 Danville, NH ae 68y 9m 2d

EASTMAN, Mary md 13 Jan 1788 Kingston, NH MORSE, Daniel

EASTMAN, Mary b 18 Dec 1811 Hawke, NH d/o EASTMAN, Samuel B. & EASTMAN, Sarah; md 16 Jan 1841 Raymond, NH EATON, Samuel; d 08 Aug 1872 Danville, NH ae 60y

EASTMAN, Mary A. b 10 Jul 1846 Danville, NH d/o EASTMAN, Calvin & SAWYER, Melinda

EASTMAN, Mary E. b Lowell, MA d/o EASTMAN, Nelson I. & WRIGHT, Tabitha; md AVERY, Chas H.; d 13 Nov 1911 Danville, NH

EASTMAN, Mary E. b 23 Mar 1856 Danville, NH d/o EASTMAN, Nelson I. & WRIGHT, Tabitha

EASTMAN, Mary F. b 14 MAY 1856 Danville, NH d/o EASTMAN, Alvin B. & ----, Marilla

EASTMAN, Mehitable b 30 Mar 1767 Hawke, NH d/o EASTMAN, Edward Sr. & WADLEIGH-CLOUGH, Sarah; also known as Hitter

EASTMAN, Melissa d 1782 Hawke, NH

EASTMAN, Nancy b 05 Aug 1808 Hawke, NH d/o EASTMAN, Edward Jr. & BEAN, Hepzibah; md GEORGE, Thos; d 02 Sep 1836 Danville, NH ae 28y

EASTMAN, Nelson Q. b 06 Jan 1829 Hawke, NH s/o EASTMAN, Sewell & TUCKER, Abigail; d 30 Aug 1897 Danville, NH d ae 68y 8m 21d

EASTMAN, Newell b c1800 Hawke, NH; md TUCKER, Abigail; d 11 Aug 1873 Danville, NH

EASTMAN, Obediah b 28 Nov 1768 Hawke, NH s/o EASTMAN, Edward Sr. & WADLEIGH-CLOUGH, Sarah; md EASTMAN, Jemima

EASTMAN, Olive b c1781 Hawke, NH; md 12 Nov 1803 Hampstead, NH COLLINS, Jabez; d 08 Dec 1855 Danville, NH ae abt 82

EASTMAN, Phebe b 09 Apr 1763 Hawke, NH d/o EASTMAN, Edward Sr. & WADLEIGH-CLOUGH, Sarah

EASTMAN, Prudence b 14 Oct 1805 Hawke, NH d/o EASTMAN, Edward Jr. & BEAN, Hepzibah; md PAGE, Joel; d 03 Sep 1838 Danville, NH ae 32y

EASTMAN, Rhoda b 02 Jun 1777 Hawke, NH d/o EASTMAN, Edward Sr. & WADLEIGH-CLOUGH, Sarah; md 28 Feb 1799 Kingston, NH GEORGE, Joshua

EASTMAN, Sally b 23 Mar 1792 Hawke, NH d/o EASTMAN, Edward Jr. & BEAN, Hepzibah

EASTMAN, Samuel b c1799; md EASTMAN, BETSEY; d 01 Jun 1839 Sandown, NH ae 40y

EASTMAN, Samuel b c1749; md 23 Nov 1769 Hawke, NH BLAKE, Mary; d

EASTMAN (Cont.) 26 Nov 1815 Hawke, NH; bu Hawke, NH Private Cem.; md by Rev John Page

EASTMAN, Samuel md 15 Jul 1821 PAGE, Mrs Betty

EASTMAN, Samuel 3rd Hawke, NH s/o EASTMAN, Samuel; md 27 Nov 1808 Hawke, NH ----, Sarah

EASTMAN, Samuel W. b 17 Sep 1821 Hawke, NH s/o EASTMAN, Samuel B. & EASTMAN, Sarah

EASTMAN, Sarah b Hawke, NH; md 27 Nov 1808 Hawke, NH EASTMAN, Samuel B.; d 29 Dec 1853 Danville, NH

EASTMAN, Sarah b 07 Jul 1818 Hawke, NH s/o EASTMAN, Samuel B. & EASTMAN, Sarah

EASTMAN, Sewell md 22 Jun 1822 Amesbury, MA HOYT, Abigail

EASTMAN, Sewell b 20 Mar 1800 Hawke, NH s/o EASTMAN, Sewell & TUCKER, Abigail

EASTMAN, Sewell b 25 Nov 1831 Hawke, NH s/o EASTMAN, Sam & TUCKER, Abigail; d 13 Jul 1913 Danville, NH ae 82y 9m 17d

EASTMAN, Stephen md 01 Mar 1769 Hawke, NH QUIMBY, Miriam; md by Rev John Page

EASTMAN, Thos md Jan 1729 FRENCH, Abigail

EASTMAN, Thos b 15 Sep 1760 Hawke, NH s/o EASTMAN, Edward Sr & WADLEIGH-CLOUGH, Sarah

EASTMAN, Timothy md 06 Mar 1802 Kingston, NH FELLOWS, Eliz

EASTON, Cherryl Dottie b 24 Mar 1945 Danville, NH d/o EASTON, Geo Wm & COLLINS, Jeanette Irene

EATON, Benj md PEARSON, Hannah; spouse md 2nd Moses Woodman

EATON, Edith Marilyn b Jamica Plains, MA; md WARD, Stanley Luke

EATON, Emery C. b c1846 Wakefield, NH; md 01 Jan 1874 Danville, NH MORSE, Martha E.

EATON, Geo B. md COLLINS, Jennette Irene

EATON, Jabez b c1752; md 1792 Hawke, NH COLCORD, Susanna; d 01 Jul 1837 Danville, NH ae 85y

EATON, Jane b 24 MAY 1793 Hawke, NH d/o EATON, Jabez & COLCORD, Susanna; md FRENCH, Phineas; d 01 MAY 1826 Hawke, NH

EATON, Joanne Lee b 28 Jan 1953 Danville, NH d/o EATON, Alfred W. & ANDERSON, Marlene G.

EATON, Joseph b 01 Sep 1801 s/o EASTMAN, Jabez & COLCORD, Susanna

EATON, Joseph b c1711 Salisbury, MA; md TRUE, Jane; d 15 Jan 1776 Hawke, NH ae 65y

EATON, Kenneth Roy b 09 Aug 1949 Danville, NH s/o EATON, Geo B. & COLLINS, Jeannette Irene

EATON, Marlene G. b 1932 NH; md 07 Dec 1968 Danville, NH HANNAGAN, Paul W.; md by Rev Alton Mark

EATON, Maud J. b Derry, NH d/o EATON, C. H.; md 09 Apr 1891 Danville, NH GRIFFIN, Luman B.; md by Rev J. A. Lowell

EATON, Samuel b 30 Dec 1796 Hawke, NH s/o EATON, Jabez & COLCORD, Susanna; md 16 Jan 1841 Raymond, NH EASTMAN, Mary; d 26 Nov 1871 Danville, NH ae 74y

EATON, Sukey b 19 Jul 1799 Hawke, NH d/o EATON, Jabez & COLCORD, Susanna

EBBETT, Gretchen Hannah b 18 Sep 1987 Derry, NH d/o EBBERTT, Donald M. Jr. & MURPHY, Mary E.

EDDY, Harold R. md 01 Jul 1983 Danville, NH GOLDTHWAITE, Beverley J.; md by Bette C. Ouellette (JP)

EDMONDS, Norma Alberta b d/o EDMONDS, Wm O. & LEACH, Monica M.; md LEE, ----; d 06 Oct 1976 Danville, NH ae 74y

EDWARDS, Douglas Earle md 19 Nov 1988 Danville, NH WALSH, Karen Marie; md by Richard J. Rondeau (JP)

EDWARDS, James C. b 1901 So Poland, ME s/o EDWARDS, Geo; md 29 Nov 1925 Kingston, NH STEVENSON, Gladys; md by Rev Frank Whippen

EDWINSON, Carl Gustav b 1927 Wilmington, MA; md 20 Jun 1964 Danville, NH EDWINSON, Harriet W.; md by Rev Wm B. Wylie

EDWINSON, Harriet W. b 1931 Medford, MA; md 20 Jun 1964 Danville, NH EDWINSON, Carl Gustav; md by Rev Wm B. Wylie

EDWINSON, John Edward b 03 MAY 1961 Danville, NH s/o EDWINSON, Merlin & MENOTT, Harriet Winona

EDWINSON, Merlin b Wilmington, MA s/o EDWINSON, John E. & ROBBISHEAU, Ann; d 24 Apr 1963 Danville, NH ae 39y

EDWINSON, Vera May b 22 Oct 1958 Danville, NH d/o EDWINSON, Merlin & MINOTT, Harriet W.; md 28 Oct 1978 Danville, NH KNIGHT, Kenneth Joseph; md by Rev Steven Kucharski (P)

EGGERT, Linda Dorothy md 31 Dec 1989 Danville NH TURCOTTE, Rob't Albert md by Rich J. Rondeau (JP)

ELARO, Thelma Constance b 1928 MA d/o ELARO, Leo; md 18 Nov 1950 Danville, NH COLLINS, Byron Edward; md by Rev James W. Gilrain

ELDRIDGE, Linda Mae b NH; md 22 Feb 1969 Danville, NH POSSON, Wayne Foster; md by Rev James Fitzimmons

ELKINS, Abby Clara b 24 Aug 1853 Danville, NH d/o ELKINS, Abel & COLLINS, Clarissa

ELKINS, Abel b 05 Jun 1822 Hawke, NH s/o ELKINS, Henry & CLOUGH, Susanna; md 08 Jun 1774 Hawke, NH BROWN, Sarah by Rev John Page, 2nd 05 Jun 1848 COLLINS, Clarissa; d 08 Feb 1903 Danville, NH

ELKINS, Abigail md 27 Sep 1763 Kingston, NH SANBORN, Jethro

ELKINS, Chas H. b 1836 Danville, NH s/o ELKINS, Henry & SWEATT, Mary

ELKINS, Chas H. b 22 MAY 1846 Danville, NH s/o SANBORN, John Stark & PHILBRICK, Luella B.; d 24 Mar 1867 Danville, NH

ELKINS, Dorothy b 28 MAY 1768 Hawke, NH d/o ELKINS, Peter & BUSWELL, Huldah

ELKINS, Eleanor b 18 Nov 1823 Hawke, NH d/o ELKINS, Henry &

ELKINS (Cont.)CLOUGH, Susanna; md 1840 Danville, NH KIMBALL, Lewis

ELKINS, Eliza Ann b d/o ELKINS, Henry & CLOUGH, Susanna; d Sep 1830 Hawke, NH ae 15m

ELKINS, Eliza Ann b 1836 Danville, NH d/o ELKINS, Henry & SWEATT, Mary;

ELKINS, Eliz b 13 Apr 1776 Hawke, NH d/o ELKINS, Peter & BUSWELL, Huldah

ELKINS, Ephraim b md BLAKE, Sarah; d 16 Apr 1772 Hawke, NH

ELKINS, Henry b C1796 Kingston, NH; md 1st 10 Jul 1820 Kindton, NH CLOUGH, Susanna, 2nd SWEATT, Mary; d 01 Sep 1850 Danville, NH ae 54y

ELKINS, Herman F. b 29 Jan 1860 Danville, NH s/o SANBORN, John Stark & PHILBRICK, Luella B.; d 1868 Danville, NH

ELKINS, Hulda b 17 Mar 1772 Hawke, NH d/o ELKINS, Peter & BUSWELL, Huldah

ELKINS, Jeremiah b c1759; md TOWLE, Eliz; d 30 MAY 1837 Danville, NH; bu: Danville, NH Private Cem; d ae 78yr

ELKINS, Jeremy A. b 03 Jan 1858 Danville, NH s/o ELKINS, Abel & COLLINS, Clarissa; d 02 Nov 1924 Danville, NH

ELKINS, Joanna b c1716 md FRENCH, Jonathan Lt.; d 04 Jan 1801 Hawke, NH; bu Hawke, NH; Old Mtg Hse Cem.; d ae 86y

ELKINS, John b 01 Jan 1821 Hawke, NH s/o ELKINS, Henry & CLOUGH, Susanna; md PHILBRICK, Luella B.; d 03 Aug 1879 Danville, NH ae 58y

ELKINS, John H. b Kingston, NH s/o ELKINS, Chas & TOWLE, Almira; md 12 Nov 1908 Danville, NH DUNBAR, Emma L. 1st m AKER; md Rev W. C. Chappell

ELKINS, Joseph md 18 Jan 1780 Hawke, NH WEBSTER, Hannah; md by Rev John Page

ELKINS, Laura Ella b 10 Aug 1857 Danville, NH d/o ELKINS, Chas &

ELKINS (Cont.) TOWLE, Almira; d 24 Dec 1857 Danville, NH ae 4m

ELKINS, Lillie Mary b 07 Sep 1863 Danville, NH d/o ELKINS, Abel & COLLINS, Clarissa; d 04 Jul 1951 Danville, NH ae 87y

ELKINS, Lizzie E. b Kingston, NH; md GEORGE, Archie S.

ELKINS, Martha Jane b 23 Apr 1856 Danville, NH d/o ELKINS, Abel & COLLINS, Clarissa R.; md WEBSTER, ---- ; d 15 Sep 1920 ae 63y 4m 23d

ELKINS, Mary b c1744; md 11 Jul 1763 Kingston, NH PAGE, Thos; d 19 Dec 1816 Hawke, NH; bu: Hawke, NH Old Mtg Hse Cem. ; d ae 72y

ELKINS, Mary b 05 Jun 1770 Hawke, NH d/o ELKINS, Peter & BUSWELL, Huldah

ELKINS, Mary b NH: md 27 Aug 1772 Hawke, NH WOODMAN, Jonathan

ELKINS, Mary Ellen b 07 Jul 1849 Danville, NH d/o SANBORN, John Stark & PHILBRICK, Luella B.; md 24 Apr 1878 Danville, NH; SPOFFORD, Alden E.; d 25 Jun 1898 Danville, NH

ELKINS, Obadiah b c1715; md FRENCH, Abigail; d 10 Sep 1766 Hawke, NH; bu Danville, NH Old Mtg Hse Cem.; d ae 50y

ELKINS, Obediah b 18 Feb 1774 Hawke, NH s/o ELKINS, Peter & BUSWELL, Huldah

ELKINS, Peter md 11 Jun 1767 Hawke, NH BUSWELL, Huldah; md by Rev John Page

ELKINS, Rachel md 22 Nov 1768 Hawke, NH HOOK, Abraham; md by Rev John Page

ELKINS, Sarah b 16 Jan 1844 Danville, NH d/o SANBORN, John Stark & PHILBRICK, Luella B.

ELKINS, Sarah b md 17 Jan 1760 Kingston, NH SANBORN, John

ELKINS, Susan E. b 26 Feb 1852 Danville, NH d/o SANBORN, John Stark & PHILBRICK, Luella B.; d 15 Jun 1853 Danville, NH

Elkins, Thos Capt. md BROWN, Ann; d 10 Sep 1790 Hampton Falls, NH

ELKINS, ---- b 23 MAY 1910 Danville, NH d/o ELKINS, John H. & DUNBAR, Emma

ELLINGBOE, Matthew Jeffery b 22 Jun 1988 Derry, NH s/o ELLINGBOE, Mark J. & LIVINGSTON, Jo Dee

ELLIOT, Jonathan b of Rumford, NH; md 18 Sep 1764 SWEAT, Naomi; md by Rev John Page

ELLIOTT, Edna b 1923 Pittsfield, ME d/o ELLIOTT, James; md 14 Nov 1931 Danville, NH BRENNAN, Theodore; md by Rev Harold C. Ross

ELLIS, Ronald Gene b of Salem, NH; md 26 Jul 1992 PISANELLI, Kristen Gene

ELLYSON, Alfred b md 02 Oct 1987 Danville, NH ELLYSON, Phillis I.; md by Edward A. Gagne (JP)

ELY, Roy N. md 04 Aug 1984 Danville, NH MENZIE, Donna M.; md by David T. Ingerson (JP)

EMERSON, Daniel R. b Haverhill, MA; md 01 Mar 1810 Kingston, NH TEWKSBURY, Abigail

EMERSON, Dorothy b d/o EMERSON, Albert H. & STIMSON, Susie H.; md SARGENT, ---- ; d 22 Sep 1979 Danville, NH d ae 85y

EMERSON, Mark md 16 MAY 1781 Hawke, NH HUTCHINGS, Molly; md by Rev John Page

EMERSON, Mary b 07 Jun 1786 Hawke, NH d/o EMERSON, Peter & ----, Molly md BRADLEY, John C.; d 07 Sep 1886 Danville, NH

EMERSON, Polly A. b c1783; md 08 Nov 1804 Haverhill, NH TEWKSBURY, Josiah Jr.; d 24 Jul 1859 Danville, NH ae 76y

EMERSON, Rebecca b 29 MAY 1784 Hawke, NH d/o EMERSON, Peter & ----, Molly

EMERSON, Susanna b 10 Dec 1781 Hawke, NH d/o EMERSON, Peter & ---- , Molly

EMERSON, Wm A. b c1842 Hampstead, NH; md 06 Nov 1862 Danville, NH DOW, Abbie H.

EMERSON, Moses md 21 Aug 1780 Hawke, NH JONES, Abigail; md by Rev John Page

EMERY, Elias J. b Newcastle, NH s/o EMERY, John & HUBLY, Hannah; md 03 Apr 1889 Danville, NH DYER, Jennie T.; md by Rev J. A. Lowell

EMERY, John W. b c1854 Bartlett, NH s/o EMERY, Thos R.; md 26 Mar 1914 Danville, NH MOREY, Sarah Etta; md by Rev Allen C. Kieth

EMERY, Mabel H. b c1896 Newton, NH d/o EMERY, Wm S. & Young, Eliz; md 10 Mar 1918 E. Hampstead, NH WELCH, Geo N. d 13 Feb 1987 Danville, NH md by Rev J. W. Farrell

EMERY, Mary Eliz b 13 Jun 1913 Danville, NH d/o EMERY, John & MOREY, Sarah Etta

EMILIO, Philip Lindsey Jr. b s/o EMILIO, Philip Lindsey Sr.; md 19 Jul 1975 Danville, NH SANBORN, Dorothy; md by Rev Wendell Irvine

EMILIO, Philip Lindsey Sr. b 16 Apr 1980 Exeter, NH s/o EMILLIO, Philip L. Jr

EMILIO, Gary V. md 18 Sep 1971 Danville, NH BATCHELDER, Susan Jane; md by Rev Peter Noel Knost

ENDES, Erika Veronica md 24 Oct 1986 Danville, NH BATTIS, Ronald J.; md by Rev Everett E. Palmer

ENGLAND, Celia b d/o ENGLAND, John & CLIFFORD, Clara; md MOSKOWITZ, ---- ; d 04 Jul 1949 Danville, NH ae 73

ENGLAND, John L. b c1851 W Newbury, MA; md 20 Apr 1876 Danville, NH CLIFFORD, Clara E.

ENGLISH, Diana M. md 19 Jul 1985 Danville, NH KIMBALL, Norman E.

ENGLISH, Everett Arthur b Everett, MA s/o ENGLISH, Wm Arthur J.; md 12 Aug 1942 Danville, NH EMERY, Leona Gertrude; md by Rev W. C. Chappell

ENOS, David B.md 14 Sep 1985 Danville, NH; FRIES, Jennifer M. T.; md by Rev Wendall J. Irvine

ENOS, Leo J. md 23 Aug 1986 Danville, NH LUNDSTROM, Rosemary; md by Marion E. Snell (JP)

ENSELL, Dolores J. md 07 Nov 1986 Danville, NH ENSELL, Eugene

ENSELL (Cont.) R.; md by Rev Everett E. Palmer

ENSELL, Eugene R. md 07 Nov 1986 Danville, NH ENSELL, Dolores J.; md by Rev Everett E. Palmer

EPPICH, Carl F. b s/o EPPICH, John & SCHAVER, Magdelina; d 04 Jul 1969 Danville, NH

EPPICH, Carolyn A. b 1946; md 08 Jun 1968 Danville, NH DUBOIS, Henry F. Jr. md by Martin J. Magar (P)

EPPICH, Frederick Stephen md 11 Sep 1971 Danville, NH INGALLS, Weslie Ann; md by Rev Henry K. Mack

EPPICH, Jacqueline b 18 Jul 1961 Danville, NH d/o EPPICH, Carl F. & DEMPSEY, Beryle R.

ERDMANN, David G. md 02 Oct 1982 Danville, NH DUBOIS, Kristine M.; md by Marjorie D. Moisan (JP)

ERIKSEN, Cheryl Charlene md 25 Jun 1977 Danville, NH THOMPSON, Robert Sheldon Jr.; md by Rev Wm Ryans

EUDMORE, John B. b 1941; md 28 Apr 1962 Danville, NH WEARE, Lynn Patricia; md by Arthur M. Comeau

FAIRWEATHER, John David md 24 Jun 1989 Danville, NH May, Lorraine; md by Richard J. Rondeau (JP)

FALES, Douglas Tex Jr of Danville, NH; md 13 Sep 1992 Danville, NH HAMMER, Leanne Jean

FANARAS, Wm Michael b 11 Jun 1967 Danville, NH s/o FANARAS, Cornelius Paul & DOUCETTE, Barbara Mae

FANDREY, Leo b 1906 Boston, MA s/o FANDREY, Leo C.; md 29 Aug 1936 Danville, NH BURNS, Grace; md by Clarence M. Collins (JP)

FANNING, Frank b 1915 Norwood, MA s/o FANNING, Chas W.; md 06 Sep 1947 Danville, NH CHRISTMANN, Ruth M.; md by Rev W. C. Chappell

FARLEY, Chandler R. md 17 Jun 1988 Danville, NH THIVERGE, Sandra L.; md by Rev Jas M. Delany

FARLEY, Craig A. md 24 Dec 1973 Danville, NH MERRICK, Laura A.; md by Rev Cathleen R. Narowitz

FARLEY, Margaret E. b Haverhill, MA; md DAOUST, Richard G.

FARRELL, Britney Nicole b 13 Feb 1989 Haverhill, MA d/o FARRELL, Andrew & TERBURGH, Jill J.

FARREN, Jos Gerard md 04 Jun 1977 Danville, NH HADLEY, Marie Ellen; md by Michael J. Griffin (P)

FAWCETT, John J. md 09 Nov 1990 Danville, NH DENNEY, Margaret A.; md by Richard J. Rondeau (JP)

FEATHER, Gary Michael b of Danville, NH; md 04 Sep 1992 Danville, NH FISICHELLI

FEINBERG, Patricia A. md 14 Oct 1989 Danville, NH SANFORD, Alden W.; md by Rev Wendall J. Irvine

FELCH, Phineas b c1768 Seabrook, NH; d 08 Apr 1840 Danville, NH; bu Danville, NH Center Cem. d ae 72y

FELDMAN, Carol Ann b 1948 d/o FELDMAN, Geo Wm & GRIFFIN, Louise Eleanor

FELDMAN, Geo Wm b 1915 Wilkes-Barre, PA s/o FELDMAN, John T. md 30 Jul 1944 Danville, NH GRIFFIN, Louise Eleanor; md by Rev W. C. Chappell

FELDMAN, Jill Louise b 1946 d/o FELDMAN, Geo Wm & GRIFFIN, Louise Eleanor

FELDMAN, Joel Towle b 1951 s/o FELDMAN, Geo Wm & GRIFFIN, Louise Eleanor

FELDMAN, John Griffin b 1954 s/o FELDMAN, Geo Wm & GRIFFIN, Louise Eleanor

FELLOWS, Eliz md 06 Mar 1802 Kingston, NH EASTMAN, Timothy

FELLOWS, Esther b Hawke, NH; md 17 Nov 1796 Kingston, NH JONES, Josiah

FELLOWS, Hannah b 11 Jun 1799 Hawke, NH d/o FELLOWS, Simeon & BARTLETT, Dorothy

FELLOWS, John b Hawke, NH; md 21 Feb 1799 Kingston, NH EASTMAN, Betsey

FELLOWS, John b New Chester, NH; md Oct 1785 Kingston, NH TILTON, Lois

FELLOWS, Jonathan b 18 Oct 1764 Hawke, NH s/o FELLOWS,

FELLOWS (Cont.) Samuel & RING, Mary

FELLOWS, Jos md 10 Sep 1783 Hampstead, NH QUIMBY, Sarah also rcd in 1787

FELLOWS, Molly b 10 May 1770 Hawke, NH d/o FELLOWS, Samuel & RING, Mary

FELLOWS, Patience b Kingston, NH; md 24 Nov 1796 Kingston, NH SANBORN, Phineas

FELLOWS, Russell N. b c1841 Brentwood, NH; md 29 Nov 1866 Danville, NH SANBORN, Susan

FELLOWS, Samuel md RING, Mary; d 15 Dec 1777 Hawke, NH

FELLOWS, Samuel b 30 Dec 1766 Hawke, NH s/o FELLOWS, Samuel & RING, Mary

FELLOWS, Simon b Brentwood, NH; md 12 Jun 1798 Kingston, NH BARTLETT, Dorothy

FELLOWS, Thos b of Hawke, NH; md 14 Apr 1804 Kingston, NH QUIMBY, Sally

FEOLE, Richard E. md 20 Dec 1991 Danville, NH BECHWITH, Yvette M.; md by Rich J. Rondeau (JP)

FERNALD, Marilyn Jean b 08 Oct 1951 Danville, NH d/o FERNALD, Ralph Alvin & COLLINS, Lucille Mary

FERNALD, Ralph Alvin b 1917 Haverhill, MA s/o FERNALD, Geo Alonzo; md 28 Feb 1947 Danville, NH COLLINS, Lucille Mary; md by Rev W. C. Chappell

FERNALD, Sharlyn Joyce b 17 Feb 1950 Danville, NH d/o FERNALD, Ralph A. & COLLINS, Lucille Mary

FERREN, Betsy b 31 Oct 1796 Hawke, NH d/o FERREN, Aaron & GEORGE, Dolly

FERRIERO, Louis C. md 17 Oct 1983 Danville, NH BILODEAU, Carole A.; md by Humbert M. Oliviera (P)

FICHERA, Richard J. md 01 Jun 1990 Danville, NH COLETTA, Eliz A.; md by Philip D. Fichera (JP)

FIELD, Bernard Martin b 10 Dec 1945 Danville, NH s/o FIELD, Robert H. & HUTCHINS, Helen

FIELD, Katrina Lynn b 17 Jan 1987 Exeter, NH d/o FIELD, Randy W.

FIELD (Cont.) & MARTIN, Tamara A.

FIELD, Kenneth Donald b 23 Nov 1984 Exeter, NH s/o FIELD, Randy W. & MARTIN, Tamara A.

FIELD, Kenneth Ray b 08 Jul 1951 Danville, NH s/o FIELD, Robert Harris & HUTCHINS, Lois K.

FIELD, Priscilla Helen b 26 Jul 1947 Danville, NH d/o FIELD, Robert & HUTCHINS, Helen

FIELD, Randy Wilder md 25 Jun 1979 Danville, NH MARTIN, Tamara Ann; md by Rev Wm Ryans

FIELD, Robert Harris b 1915 Waltham, MA s/o FIELD, Asa Lee; md 30 Sep 1941 Danville, NH HUTCHINS, Helen; md by Rev W. C. Chappell

FIELDER, Martha Louise b 1919 Lawrence, MA d/o FIELDER, Wm F.; md 17 Oct 1940 Danville, NH KARABULA, Emil; md by Clarence M. Collins (JP)

FIELDS, Harry Leroy b s/o FIELDS, Harrison & STEARNS, Annie; d 09 Apr 1984 Danville, NH ae 67y

FIFIELD, Diana b c1827; md WEBSTER, Stephen; d 1855 Danville, NH ae 28y

FIFIELD, Miriam b c1740; md 1st BACHELOR, Reuben, 2nd 26 Feb 1777 Sanborn, Jos Clifford; d 1838 Danville, NH ae 98y about

FIFIELD, Peter b c1793; md PAGE, Sarah; d 03 Nov 1858 Danville, NH; d ae 65y

FIFIELD, Sandra L. md 02 Aug 1986 Danville, NH SKRIBISKI, John S.; md by Rev David L. Clarke

FIFIELD, Sherborn b SAlisbury, MA; md 13 Nov 1785 Kingston, NH BARNARD, Alice

FILES, Phyllis Evelyn b 1934 Haverhill, MA d/o FILES, Francis H.; md 25 Jul 1953 Danville, NH CLARK, Elmer Howard

FINK, Christine md 18 Nov 1990 Danville, NH GREELEY, Jurgen; md by Richard J. Rondeau (JP)

FISHER, Cary L. md 21 Sep 1985 Danville, NH GAGNE, Jos P.; md by Richard J. Rondeau (JP)

FISHER, Christine Marie md 11 Jun 1977 Danville, NH CLOUGH, Norman Everett; md by Robert D. Rousseau (JP)

FISHER, Kathleen Susan md 03 Jun 1989 Danville, NH FRENCH, Rolfe Eric; md by Rev John C. Lombard

FISHER, Peter Raymond md 29 Jun 1991 Danville, NH CURRIER, Laura Ann md by Rich J. Rondeau (JP)

Fisher, Wendy Jean md 16 Jul 1988 Danville, NH GROVER, Jack Douglas; md by Rev Everett E. Palmer

FITTON, David A. md 20 Oct 1984 Danville, NH ARNOLD, Susan Elaine; md by Richard J. Rondeau (JP)

FITTON, Samantha Jo b 14 May 1987 Exeter, NH d/o FITTON, David A. & ARNOLD, Susan Elaine

FITTON, Sarah Ann b 22 Apr 1985 Manchester, NH d/o FITTON, David A. & ARNOLD, Susan Elaine

FITTS, Annie L. b c1871 Danville, NH d/o FITTS, Franklin & TABOE. Sarah J.; md 28 May 1887 Danville, NH DARBE, Chas A.; md by Rev John A. Lowell

FITTS, Bessie B. b d 14 May 1959 Danville, NH; ae 71y

FITTS, Daniel H. b 19 Mar 1882 Danville, NH s/o FITTS, Franklin & TABOR, Sarah J.; d 10 Mar 1948 Danville, NH

FITTS, Earl Otto b 30 Jun 1869 Danville, NH s/o FITTS, Franklin & TABOR, Sarah J.; md 24 Dec 1900 Hampstead, NH LITTLE, Grace M.; d 27 Jul 1946 Danville, NH

FITTS, Franklin b Sandown, NH s/o PITTS, Nathaniel & PURINGTON, Rhoda; md TABOR, Sarah J.; d 12 May 1914 Danville, NH

FITTS, Hattie L. b 14 Sep 1877 Danville, NH d/o FITTS, Franklin & TABOR, Sarah J.; md 27 Oct 1894 Danville, NH COLLINS, Wilbur H.; d 29 Mar 1939 Danville, NH; md by Rev John A. Wiggin

FITTS, Josephine C. b 1874 Danville, NH d/o FITTS, Franklin & TABOR, Sarah J.

FITTS, Norris Leon b 17 Jun 1902 Danville, NH s/o FITTS, Earl Otto &

FITTS (Cont.) LITTLE, Grace M.

FITTS, Ruby b 01 Oct 1929 Danville, NH d/o FITTS, Norris Leon & ARNOLD, Vida

FITZPATRICK, Molly McGee b 08 Feb 1977 Exeter, NH d/o FITZPATRICK, Jos F. & SAWYER, Joanne

FITZGERALD, ----, md BONNING, Gertrude F.

FLAMMIA, Katherine F. md 24 Dec 1972 Danville, NH LAPHAM, Leland C. 3rd; md by Philip D. Fichers (JP)

FLANDERS, Abigail b c1721 Salisbury, MA; md PAGE, Jabez; d 15 Oct 1791 Hawke, NH; bu Hawke, NH Old Mtg Hse Cem.; d ae 70y

FLANDERS, Daniel b S Hampton, NH; md 12 Jan 1804 Kingston, NH BARTLETT, Priscilla

FLANDERS, Issac -d 15 Jul 1776 Hawke, NH by drowning

FLANDERS, James md 21 Jun 1804 Kingston, NH DIMOND, Polly

FLANDERS, Jane E. b Salisbury, MA; md 09 Nov 1820 Hampton, NH BEAN, Gilman

FLANDERS, John -d 05 Aug 1932 Danville, NH ae 76y 7m 12d

FLANDERS, Judith b Hawke, NH; md 21 Sep 1779 Hawke, NH HARRIMAN, Jos; md by Rev John Page

FLANDERS, Laura Adele md 26 Jun 1976 Danville, NH SHEA, Michael Patrick; md by Robert S. Dejadon (JP)

FLANDERS, Miriam b of Epping, NH; md 30 Oct 1765 CASS, Jos; md by Rev John Page

FLANDERS, Simon md 29 Sep 1772 Hawke, NH LEAVITT, Hannah

FLANDERS, Stephen b Plaistow, NH; md 11 Mar 1779 Hawke, NH RING, Sarah; md by Rev John Page

FLANNERY, Samantha A. md 15 Oct 1983 Danville, NH RUSSELL, Ron E.; md by Bettie C. Oullette (JP)

FLATTERY, Wayne P. md 21 Sep 1985 Danville, NH NIHAN, Diana M.; md by Rev Everett E. Palmer

FLEISCHMAN, Rachel Beth b 02 Sep 1983 Exeter, NH d/o FLEISCHMAN, Stephen & THOMPSON, Melinda

FLEMING, Thos J. b 1944 Danvers, MA; md 11 Jun 1965 Danville, NH NYGREN, Jean Ann; md by Leona A. Schiaudone (JP)

FLETCHER, Caroline b c1837 Kennebec, ME; md 1861 Danville, NH BLAKE, Edmind R.

FLIGER, Michael L. md 17 Aug 1985 Danville, NH STALLINGS, Pamela H.; md by Rev Everett E. Palmer

FLOURDE, Deborah L. md 14 Dec 1986 Danville, NH MARCOTTE, David M.; md by Richard J. Rondeau (JP)

FLOURDE, Kevin Mark b 10 Jan 1971 Exeter, NH s/o FLOURDE, Jos J. & PELLETIER, Evelyn P.

FLYNN, Evelyn Loretta md 18 Sep 1971 Danville, NH DUSTON, Al Henry; md by Rich Vickery (P)

FOGG, Geo F. md CLAYTON, Sarah

FOGG, Mary Alice b E Hampstead, NH d/o FOGG, Geo F. & CLAYTON, Sarah M.; md 05 Jun 1901 FOSTER, Hollis D.; d 08 Mar 1903 Danville, NH ae 21y 4m 13d; md by Rev A. B. Howard

FOGG, Molly b of Raymond, NH; md 19 Jun 1779 Hawke, NH OSGOOD, Enoch; md by Rev John Page

FOGG, Willard F. b 13 Oct 1883 Danville, NH s/o FOGG, Geo F. & CLAYTON, Sarah M.

FOLEY, Edward Patrick Jr. md 30 Mar 1988 Danville, NH MURRAY, Kenyon Lee md by Rich J. Rondeau (JP)

FOLEY, Wm J. H. b Newton Junction NH s/o FOLEY, Wm & KENNEDY,; d Ellen 22 Apr 1967 Danville, NH

FOLLAND, Nancy Jean md 10 Sep 1983 Danville, NH RINES, David Freeman; md by Nancy E. Crawford (JP)

FOLLETT, Alice F. b Haverhill, MA d/o FOLLETT, Huge & DAVIS, Esther; d 08 Dec 1916 Danville, NH ae 32y 2m 17d

FOLLINSBY, Alice md 24 Nov 1774 Hawke, NH CLIFFORD, Isaac; md by Rev John Page

FOLLINSBY, James b 01 Jan 1762

FOLLINSBY (Cont.) Hawke, NH s/o FOLLINSBY, Wm & GEORGE, Sarah

FOLLINSBY, Thos b Sandown, NH; md 10 Apr 1770 Hawke, NH COLLINS, Martha; md by Rev John Page

FOLLINSBY, Wm b d 20 Feb 1769 Hawke, NH

FOLLINSBY, Wm md GEORGE, Sarah

FOLSOM, Abigail b Brentwood, NH; md 25 Jan 1821 Brentwood, NH FRENCH, Jonathan 3rd; d 27 Apr 1851 Danville, NH ae 56y

FOLSOM, Susanna b c1721 Brentwwod, NH; md MORRILL, Henry Dea.; d 17 Nov 1778 Hawke, NH d ae 57y

FOOTE, Eliz b c1900 Groveland, MA d/o FOOTE, Geo E.; md 04 Nov 1922 Bradford, MA JACKSON, Ralph R.; md by Rev Theo R. Bundy

FORD, Solome W. b c1827 Burlington, VT d/o FORD, John; md GEORGE, Albert A.; d 20 Mar 1893 Danville, NH

FORD, Wanda md 30 AOG 1987 Danville, NH COTE, Chaeles H.; md by Rev Wendall J. Irvine

FORSYTHE, Chas A. md 27 Sep 1980 Danville, NH ROGERS, Linda S.; md by Robert R. Cushing Jr (JP)

FORTIER, Roger T. md 21 Sep 1985 Danville, NH MITCHELL, Kathryn M.; md by Joyce L. Cann (JP)

FOSS, Francis M. b Dover, NH s/o FOSS, Daniel; md EMERY, ----; d 24 Aug 1906 Danville, NH ae 60y 4m 20d

FOSTER, Hollis D. b E. Machias, ME; md 05 Jun 1901 Danville, NH FOGG, Mary Alice; md by Rev A. B. Howard

FOUCHER, Randi Lynn b 24 Sep 1987 Exeter, NH d/o DAVIES, Geoffry & FOUCHER, Lauri

FOURNIER, Catherine P. md 17 Aug 1991 Danville, NH ROY, Michael James; md by Florent R. Bilodeau (P)

FOURNIER, John Allen md 16 Jun 1979 Danville, NH DAVID, Mary Ann; md by Clara B. Shaw (JP)

FOWLER, Chris Jos b 18 Apr 1967 Danville, NH s/o FOWLER, Jos E. & DIMOND, Alice M.

FOWLER, Jos Edward b 1925 Seabrook, NH s/o FOWLER, Percy Newell; md 29 Dec 1945 Danville, NH DIMOND, Alice Margarette; md by Rev W. C. Chappell

FOWLER, Josiah d 16 Feb 1781 Hawke, NH

FOWLER, Linnae Audrey b 05 Oct 1949 Danville, NH d/o FOWLER, Jos E. & DIMOND, Alice M.; md 13 Sep 1969 Danville, NH HOPEWELL, James Kennard; md by Rev Randolph K. Dales (EP)

FOWLER, Noreen Louise b 01 Oct 1946 Danville, NH d/o FOWLER, Jos E. & DIMOND, Alice M.

FOWLER, Robert b Hampton Falls, NH md 04 Jul 1776 Hawke, NH LOWELL, Mary; md by Rev John Page

FOWLER, Robin Elsa b 12 Aug 1958 Danville NH d/o FOWLER, Jos E. & DIMOND, Alice M.; md 27 Aug 1977 Danville NH COMEAU, Michael John

FRANCIS, Michael J. md 29 May 1973 Danville, NH SANBORN, Cathleen M. md by Leona A. Sciaudone (JP)

FRANCOEUR, Carol b Amesbury, MA; md McCRUSKER, Thos L.

FRANKLYN, Eleanor b Belmont, NH d/o FRANKLYN, Percival & NEWELL, Margarete; md KIMBALL. Richard Chester; d 04 Apr 1937 Danville, NH ae 19y 6m 16d

FRAUGHTON, Mabel Lucinda b d/o FRAUGHTON, Laurie J. & HARDY, Laura; md SWAIN, ---- ; d 10 Jan 1983 Danville, NH ae 79y

FRAZIER, Jake Andrew b 06 Sep 1983 Haverhill, MA s/o FRAZIER, Donald & SULLIVAN, Jo Ann

FREDERICK, Lorraine L. b 1947 Revere, MA; md 04 Feb 1967 Danville, NH MARTILLA, Leonard J.; md by Roger A. Vachon (P)

FREDRICKSON, Lillian b 1914 Lawrence, MA d/o FREDRICKSON, Carl; md 17 Jan 1935 Danville, NH MISSERVILLE, HUGO; md by Clarence M. Collins (JP)

FRENCH, Abigail b Kingston, NH; md 30 Dec 1807 Kingston, NH BACHELOR, Nathan; 3rd marr of Nathan BACHELOR

FRENCH, Abigail b c1715 Kingston, NH; md ELKINS, Obediah; d 07 Dec 1778 Hawke, NH ae 63y

FRENCH, Abram S. Dr. md 1st 29 Nov 1809 Hawke, NH STEVENS, Hannah, 2nd 06 Aug 1824 Hawke, NH LANE, Abigail

FRENCH, Anne b 11 Jan 1783 Hawke, NH d/o FRENCH, Jonathan 4th & ----, Hannah

FRENCH, Arthur C. b Oct 1827 Hawke, NH s/o FRENCH, Phineas & WORTHEN, Eliza; d 31 Aug 1863 Danville, NH

FRENCH, Arthur P. b 12 Nov 1864 Danville, NH s/o FRENCH, Robert Smith & PEASLEE, Mary C.; d 11 Nov 1934 Danville, NH

FRENCH, Barbara Louise b 28 Nov 1926 Danville, NH d/o FRENCH, Earl & SHANNON, Hattie

FRENCH, Betsey b c1783 S Hampton, NH; md HOYT, Wm Howard; d 20 Jan 1871 Danville, NH ae 88y - maybe d 1870 ?

FRENCH, David b 10 Apr 1786 Hawke, NH s/o FRENCH, Jonathan 4th & ----, Hannah

FRENCH, David b Danville, NH; md 1848 Danville, NH LITTLEFIELD, E.Frances

FRENCH, Earl b Kingston, NH; md SHANNON, Hattie

FRENCH, Eliz b c1740; md 24 Dec 1761 Hawke, NH SANBORN, Jos C. Lt.; d 08 Jun 1776 Hawke, NH ae 36y

FRENCH, Fannie E. b 29 Sep 1864 Danville, NH d/o FRENCH, James H. & COLLINS, Hannah P.

FRENCH, Henry b Hawke, NH; md 21 Dec 1769 Hawke, NH SANBORN, Judith; md by Rev John Page

FRENCH, Henry Elkins b Jul 1788 Hawke, NH s/o FRENCH, Jonathan 4th & ----, Hannah

FRENCH, Herbert Cleveland b 1889 Kingston, NH s/o FRENCH, John S.; md 28 Feb 1948 Newton, NH GRAVELLE, Gertrude May; md by Rev Thurber Weller

FRENCH, Jabez b 1824 Hawke, NH s/o FRENCH, Phineas & EATON, Jane; d 12 Feb 1830 Hawke, NH

FRENCH, James H. md COLLINS, Hannah P.

FRENCH, James M. b 1831 Hawke, NH s/o FRENCH, Phineas & WORTHEN, Eliza; md COLLINS, Hannah J.; d 24 Oct 1877 Danville, NH ae 46y

FRENCH, John S. b s/o FRENCH, Geo O. & HUBBARD, Annie s.; d 28 Nov 1975 Danville, NH ae 78y

FRENCH, John Wesley b 28 Aug 1826 Hawke, NH s/o FRENCH, Abraham & LANE, Abigail

FRENCH, Jonathan md 09 Jun 1782 Hawke, NH ----, Hannah

FRENCH, Jonathan b 27 Aug 1787 Hawke, NH s/o FRENCH, Jonath. Jr. & BACHELOR, Mary

FRENCH, Jonathan b 01 Oct 1818 Hawke, NH s/o FRENCH, Phineas & EATON, Jane; d 25 Nov 1906 Danville, NH ae 88y 1m 24d

FRENCH, Jonathan b 25 May 1799 Hawke, NH s/o FRENCH, Jonathan 4th & ----, Hannah;

FRENCH, Jonathan b 07 Aug 1761 Hawke, NH s/o FRENCH, Jonathan Jr. & BAGLEY, Ann

FRENCH, Jonathan 3rd b c1789; md 25 Jan 1821 Brentwood, NH FOLSOM, Abigail; d 05 Sep 1856 Danville, NH ae 69y

FRENCH, Jonathan 3rd b c1757; md 27 Feb 1783 Kingston, NH BATCHELDER, Mary; d 30 Aug 1828 Hawke, NH; bu Hawke, NH Private Cem.; d ae 71y

FRENCH, Jonathan Jr. b s/o FRENCH, Jon. Sr. md BAGLEY, Ann

FRENCH, Jonathan Lt. -d c1713 Salisbury, MA; md ELKINS, Joanna; d 13 Sep 1785 Hawke, NH; bu Danville, NH Old Mtg Hse Cem.; d ae 72y

FRENCH, Jos b 1822 Hawke, NH s/o FRENCH, Phineas & EATON, Jane; d 21 Feb 1865 Danville, NH ae 43y

FRENCH, Jos B. b c1832 Nottingham, NH; md 1860 Danville, NH SEVERENCE, Mary L.

FRENCH, Jos Benson b 20 May 1829 Hawke, NH s/o FRENCH, Abraham & LANE, Abigail

FRENCH, Josiah b 18 Sep 1795 Hawke, NH s/o FRENCH, Jonathan & ----, Hannah;

FRENCH, Lucy b 29 Jan 1794 Hawke, NH d/o FRENCH, Jonathan & BACHELOR, Mary; md 03 Feb 1818 Hawke, NH SPOFFORD, Osmund; d 16 Apr 1866 Danville; bu Danville, NH d ae 72yr

FRENCH, Lydia b d/o FRENCH, Jonath. Jr. & BAGLEY, Ann; d 07 Jun 1773 Hawke, NH

FRENCH, Mary b 05 Mar 1749 Kingston, NH d/o FRENCH, Jonathan & ELKINS, Joanna; md 25 Apr 1776 Hawke, NH JUDKINS, Henry; d 22 Dec 1778; Mary & Henry 1st & 2nd Cousin

FRENCH, Mary b 25 Jan 1784 Hawke, NH d/o FRENCH, Jonathan 3rd & BACHELOR, Mary

FRENCH, Mary A. b c1835 Danville, NH; md 1857 Danville, NH HOOK, Daniel C.

FRENCH, Mary E. b 31 Jul 1823 Hawke, NH d/o FRENCH, Jonathan 3rd & ----, Dorothy

FRENCH, Miriam b c1790 Hampstead, NH; md 01 Oct 1813 Hawke, NH COLBY, Thos Page; d 25 Oct 1872 Danville. NH; bu Danville, NH

FRENCH, Molly md 05 Nov 1771 Hawke, NH CHALLIS, Thos; md by Rev John Page

FRENCH, Nane b 28 Mar 1793 Hawke, NH d/o FRENCH, Jonathan 4th & ----, Hannah

FRENCH, Peter md 11 Nov 1813 Hawke, NH STEVENS, Mary

FRENCH, Phineas b 29 Nov 1790 Hawke, NH s/o FRENCH, Jonathan Jr. & BACHELOR, Mary; md 1st EATON, Jane, 2nd WORTHEN, Eliza: d 26 Sep 1857 Danville, NH

FRENCH, Polly b Hawke, NH; md 20 Jan 1813 Hawke, NH CLARK, Nathaniel

FRENCH, Robert S. b 27 Oct 1831 Hawke, NH s/o FRENCH, Jonathan & FOLSOM, Abigail; d 06 Mar 1903 Danville, NH

FRENCH, Robert Smith b 16 Mar 1801 Hawke, NH s/o FRENCH, Jona-

FRENCH (Cont.) than 3rd & BACHELOR, Mary

FRENCH, Rolfe Eric md 03 Jun 1989 Danville, NH FISHER, Kathleen Susan; md by Rev John C. Lombard

FRENCH, Sally b 01 Jul 1784 Hawke, NH d/o FRENCH, Jonathan 4th & ----, Hannah

FRENCH, Samuel Thos b 07 Dec 1991 Portsmouth, NH s'o FRENCH, Rolfe E. & FISHER, Kathleen S.

FRENCH, Sarah M. J. C. b c1832 Hampstead, NH; md 1848 Danville, NH JOHNSON, Wm

FRENCH, Shirley Louise b 27 Oct 1936 Danville, NH d/o FRENCH, Melvin Waldo & BAILEY, Katherine

FRENCH, Sophronia A. b 1839 Danville, NH d/o FRENCH, Phineas & WORTHEN, Eliza; d 24 Sep 1869 Danville, NH ae 30y

FRENCH, Susan b 1817 Hawke, NH d/o FRENCH, Phineas & EATON, Jane

FRENCH, Wm b 03 Mar 1790 Hawke, NH s/o FRENCH, Jonathan & ----, Hannah;

FRENCH, Wm Russell b 08 Jul 1924 Danville, NH s/o FRENCH, Earl & SHANNON, Hattie

FRENCH, Willis b 08 Dec 1898 Danville, NH s/o FRENCH, Earl & SHANNON, Hattie

FREY, Wm b 18 Aug 1982 Exeter, NH s/o FREY, Jos E. & BABCOCK, Carol E.

FRIES, Eliz A. md 27 May 1984 Danville, NH MASTON, Gregory A.; md by Rev Roger C. B. Daly

FRIES, Jennifer M. T. md 14 Sep 1985 Danville, NH ENOS, David B.; md by Rev Wendall J. Irvine

FROHOCK, Jane b Kingston, NH; md 20 May 1828 Hawke, NH DAVIS, Henry

FROTTEN, Mareta Hardy b Melrose, MA md BERNABY Frank Alfred Sr.

FULLER, Albert G. b Oct 1846 Danville, NH s/o FULLER, Worthen & ----, Mary

FULLER, Chas A. b 1845 Danville, NH s/o FULLER, Worthen & ---- , Mary;

FULLER (Cont.) d 12 Jan 1862 Danville, NH

FULLER, Chase b c1798 Bridgewater, MA; md BARTLETT, Nancy; d 21 Aug 1879 Danville, NH d ae 81y

FULLER, Eliza b c1824 Bridgwater, MA d/o FULLER, Chase & WORTHEN, Theodate; md SARGENT, ---- ; d 29 Mar 1896 Danville, NH

FULLER, Harriet A. b c1834; md MESERVE, Winfield S.; d 07 Nov 1859 Danville, NH d ae 24y

FULLER, James R. b Medford, MA; md CHENEY, Edna J.

FULLER, Joanna b of Chester, NH; md 11 Sep 1764 Hawke, NH ABBOTT, Joshua; md by Rev John Page

FULLER, Mary b c1825; md FULLER, Worthen; d 30 Jan 1855 Danville, NH ae abt 30y

FULLER, Mary J. b c1835; md 1857 Danville, NH WHITTIER, Geo W.

FULLER, Minerva Harriet b 22 Jul 1924 Haverhill, MA d/o FULLER, James Russell & CHENEY, Edna; md 12 Sep 1945 Danville, NH RIVERS, Marland Leroy; md by rev W. C. Chappell

FULLER, Paul E. md 20 Jun 1986 Danville, NH GREENE, Debra M. md by Richard J. Rondeau (JP)

FULLER, Paul Eliot b 16 Sep 1989 Exeter, NH s/o FULLER, Paul E. & GREENE, Debra M.

FULLER, Russell D. b 16 Jun 1922 Danville, NH s/o FULLER, James R. & CHENEY, Edna J.

FULLER, Worthen md ---- , Mary

FULLMORE, Eliz b Five Island, ? d/o FULMORE, John md HARRIS, ----; d 21 Jan 1946 Danville, NH ae 80y 5m 9d

FULLONTON, Mary D. b c1820 Raymond, NH d/o FULLONTON, Jeremiah & DUDLEY, Hannah; md KIMBALL, Geo F.; d 07 Sep 1893 Danville, NH ae 73y 6m

FUSCHETTI, Carman Genna md 07 Jul 1974 Danville, NH ARSENAULT, Marilyn Ann; md by Clara B. Shaw (JP)

GABLASKY, Velma b c1895 So Boston, MA d/o GABLASKY, Paul J.; md 12 Sep 1921 Danville, NH RANDALL, Leonard M.; md by Rev L.M. Bleakney

GABRY, Mark A. md 20 Jul 1985 Danville, NH REED, Shelia A.; md by Rev Everett E. Palmer

GAFF, Kerri Ann b 19 Nov 1971 Haverhill, MA d/o GAFF, Thos F. & MARAZZI, Mary J.

GAFF, Kristi Marie b 02 Jan 1970 Haverhill, MA d/o GAFF, Thos F. & MARAZZI, Mary J.

GAGE, Albert J. 3rd md 13 Mar 1971 Danville, NH JEWELL, Jeanine Y.; md by Rev Cathleen R. Narowitz

GAGE, Annie Noel b 25 Dec 1972 Exeter, NH d/o GAGE, Donald R. & WACKER, Lola G.

GAGE, Laura Jean b 24 Sep 1971 Exeter, NH d/o GAGE, Albert J. & JEWELL, Jeanine Y.

GAGE, Michael Palmer md 31 May 1975 Danville, NH SKINNER, Kathleen Mary; md by Richard L. Provencher (P)

GAGE, Steven J. md 27 Sep 1975 Danville, NH HUGHES, Jane R.; md by Clara B. Shaw (JP)

GAGNE, Joseph P. md 21 Sep 1985 Danville, NH FISHER, Cary L.; md by Richard J. Rondeau (JP)

GAGNE, Lindsay Anna b 10 Nov 1987 Exeter, NH d/o GAGNE, Joseph P. & FISHER, Cary L.

GAGNON, Alfe W. b Epping, NH s/o GAGNON, Eugene & LeCHAND, Eliza; d 04 Jan 1904 Danville, NH ae 1y 2m 29d

GAGNON, Alfred D. Jr. 1932 MA s/o GAGNON, Alfred D. Sr.; md 04 Mar 1955 Danville, NH GRIFFIN, Barbara M.; md by Agnes H. Collins (JP)

GAGNON, Audrey A. md 04 Sep 1982 Danville, NH ARNOLD, Russell W.; md by Michael J. Griffin (P)

GAGNON, Audrey A. md 17 Sep 1988; COLLINS, Wayne A.; md by Rev Everett E. Palmer

GAGNON, Hal Edward md 17 Mar 1879 Danville, NH GOUTIER, Cynthia Louis; md by Rev Steven Kucharski (P)

GAGNON, Rosemarie md 25 May 1986 Danville, NH CONANT, Glen A.; md by Rev Everett E. Palmer

GALANTE, Graziano b 1936 Italy; md 17 Dec 1966 Danville, NH SAN-

GALANTE (Cont.) SERVERO, Susan P.; md by Leona A. Sciaudone (JP)

GALASKA, Barb D. md 05 Dec 1984 Danville, NH DIFEO, Rich D.; md by David T; Ingerson (JP)

GALE, Amos b Newton, NH; md DIMOND, Sarah C.

GALLAGHER, Hector E. b s/o GALLAHER, Owen E.; d 05 Mar 1957 Danville, NH ae 71y

GALLANT, Joseph Christopher b 11 Aug 1983 Stoneham, MA s/o GALLANT, Stephen & ALDRO, Pamelo

GAMBLE, Allison Lee b 22 Jan 1989 Exeter, NH d/o GAMBLE, Raymond A. & CAMMETT, Michelle A.

GAMBLE, Dominick Raymond b 01 Mar 1992 Exeter, NH s/o GAMBLE, Raymond A. & CAMMETT, Michelle M.

GANSENBERG, Jon Joseph md 24 Jun 1989 Danville, NH ARMSTRONG, Caroline Ellisa; md by Richard J. Rondeau (JP)

GARDELLA, Dorothy F. b 1910 Haverhill, MA d/o GARDELLA, Antonio F.; md 12 Oct 1929 Northwood, NH GEORGE, Walter S.; md by Rev A. Herbert Armes

GARDELLA, Gerald R. b 1914 Haverhill, MA s/o GARDELLA, Antonio; md 19 May 1932 Danville, NH CAMP-BELL, Theresa R.; md by Geo A. Gilmore (JP)

GARDNER, Arthur E. b Williamstown, MA s/o GARDNER, Herbert L. & WERE, Clara; d 17 Jun 1959 Danville, NH ae 66y

GAREY, Lillian I. b 1889 Lynn, MA d/o CAREY, Arthur F.; md 23 Oct 1937 Danville, NH WITHERELL, Waldo C.; md by Rev W. C. Chappell

GARON, Stephen Robert md 28 Oct 1990 Danville, NH CARVER, Wendy Jane; md by Richard J. Rondeau (JP)

GATES, Emma M. b Nova Scotia d/o GATES, John & HARRIS, Hattie M.; md BLISS, ----; d 07 Feb 1955 Danville, NH

GATES, James b Nova Scotia s/o GATES, H. John & HARRIS, Harriet; d 04 Jan 1908 Danville, NH ae 33y 8m 4d

GATES, Mary E. md 21 Jan 1888 Danville, NH McClure, Geo S.

GATES, Percy M. b Endfield, MA s/o GATES, John H. & HARRIS, Harriet; d 05 Jun 1901 ae 20y 6m; both parents from Nova Scotia

GATES, ---- b 13 Jul 1900 Danville, NH s/o GATES, James K. & WOODARD, Agnes L.; 2nd child in family

GAUDETTE, Richard R. md 26 Sep 1987 Danville, NH TRAVERS, Rachel M.; md by Renee Houle Carkin (JP)

GAUDINO, Marion Eliz md 09 Nov 1975 Danville NH LAUBENSTEIN, Chas Edmund md by Robt S Dejadon (JP)

GAUNTT, Charlotte M. md 21 Nov 1979 Danville, NH JENDRICK, Dennis S.; md by John H. Lamprey (JP)

GAUVIN, Albert R. b Haverhill, MA; md KENNEY, Barbara J.

GAUVIN, David Joseph b 07 Nov 1966 Danville, NH s/o GAUVIN, Albert R. & KENNEY, Barbara J.

GAVIOLI, Lillian b 1919 Haverhill, MA d/o GAVIOLI, Louis; md 21 May 1938 Danville, NH CONWAY, Daniel A.; md by Clarence N. Collins (JP)

GAYNOR, Chas J. Jr. md 13 Jun 1980 Danville, NH DOWNS, Violette L.; md by Bettie C. Ouellette (JP)

GAZETTE, Anthony Harold b 1911 PA s/o SHHENCK, John; md 11 Nov 1949 Danville, NH STETSON, Kathleen Louise; md by Rev W. C. Chappell

GEISLER, Shelia J. md 19 Jul 1986 Danville, NH LEMOINE, Mark A.; md by Philip D. Fichera (JP)

GELIN, Stanley Glenn md 01 Oct 1977 Danville, NH NICHAUD, Gail Ann; md by Clara B. Shaw (JP)

GEORGE, Ada Lillian b 14 Jun 1877 Danville, NH d/o GEORGE, James W. & COLLINS, Lillian Francene; md 04 Dec 1897 Danville NH HUNTINGTON, Sidney W.; d 27 Jun 1965 Salisbury, MA bu Danville, NH Center Cem.; d Greenleaf Nursing Home

GEORGE, Albert A. b 01 May 1852 Danville, NH s/o GEORGE, James M. & FORD, Salome W.

GEORGE, Albert Freeman b Sandown, NH s/o GEORGE, Purley H. & PURINGTON, Clara A.; d 19 Aug 1945

GEORGE (Cont.) Danville, NH
GEORGE, Alice M. b 26 Feb 1861
Danville, NH d/o GEORGE, Harrison &
PRATT, Harriet M.; md 24 Mar 1887
Danville, NH BAGLEY, Samie E.; d 03
May 1934 Danville, NH; md by Rev J.
Eastwood

GEORGE, Allen P. b Kingston, NH;
md ANDERSON, Charlotte L.

GEORGE, Anna b 06 Mar 1816
Hawke, NH d/o GEORGE, Nathaniel &
SHOWELL, Lydia; md MARCH, ---- ; d
29 Dec 1892 Danville, NH

GEORGE, Anthony b 11 Feb 1992
Exeter, NH s/o GEORGE, Roland G. &
TUCCO, Mary A.

GEORGE, Archie S. b 03 Jan 1853
Danville, NH s/o GEORGE, Harrison &
PRATT, Harriet M.; d 15 Aug 1934
Danville, NH

GEORGE, Benj b 24 Mar 1810
Hawke, NH s/o GEORGE, Nathaniel &
SHOWELL, Judith

GEORGE, Betsy b 12 Aug 1786
Kingston, NH d/o GEORGE, Gideon &
STEVENS, Deborah; d 1789 Kingston,
NH

GEORGE, Betsy b 23 Mar 1812
Hawke, NH d/o GEORGE, Nathaniel &
SHOWELL, Judith

GEORGE, Caroline P. b 27 Mar 1826
Hawke, NH d/o GEORGE, Nathaniel &
SHOWELL, Judith; md 11 Nov 1856
Exeter, NH COLLINS, Arthur S.; d 25
Aug 1900 Danville, NH

GEORGE, Carrie Gertrude b 23 Dec
1917 Danville, NH d/o GEORGE, Daniel
G. & ARNOLD, Gertrude B.; d 08 Jan
1918 Danville, NH d ae 16d

GEORGE, Carrie Iola b d/o
GEORGE, James M. & FORD, Salome
W.; d 20 Sep 1863 Danville, NH ae 5y

GEORGE, Catherine md 20 May ????
Danville, NH DAVIS, Jonathan F.; md
1832 or 1838 ?

GEORGE, Clarence W. b c1885
Sandown, NH s/o GEORGE, Joseph W.;
md 29 Apr 1904 Sandown, NH LADD,
Ida B.; md by John J. Goodwin (JP)

GEORGE, Currier b c1841 Hawke,
NH; md 28 Apr 1830 Fremont, NH
SPOFFORD, Sophronia; d 17 Aug 1863
Danville, NH ae 59y

GEORGE, Daniel G. b Derry, NH;
md ARNOLD, Gertrude D.

GEORGE, Darius b 07 Oct 1807
Hawke, NH s/o GEORGE, Nathaniel &
SHOWELL, Judith; md BRACKETT,
Abigail; d 24 Nov 1868 Danville, NH

GEORGE, David Quimby b 01 Feb
1793 s/o GEORGE, Wm & JOHNSON,
Hannah

GEORGE, Deborah b 08 Aug 1962
Kingston, NH d/o GEORGE, Gideon &
STEVENS, Deborah; md FLANDERS,

GEORGE, Dolly b 02 Sep 1769
Kingston, NH d/o GEORGE, Gideon &
STEVENS, Deborah; Not Married

GEORGE, Ebenezer b 06 Feb 1790
s/o GEORGE, Wm & JOHNSON,
Hannah

GEORGE, Ebenezer b md 15 Dec
1810 Kingston, NH DAVIS, Tryphena

GEORGE, Elbertine F. b ABT 1849
d/o GEORGE, Harrison & PRATT,
Harriet M.; d 30 Nov 1856 Danville, NH
ae 7y

GEORGE, Elmer R. b Kingston, NH
s/o GEORGE, Ora P. & SILLOWAY,
Abby; d 25 Jan 1932 Danville, NH ae 65y
1m 9d

GEORGE, Elmer S. b c1894 Dan-
ville, NH s/o GEORGE, Albert F.; md 15
Sep 1915 Newton, NH PAGE, Florence
A.; md by Rev Wm P. Richards

GEORGE, Ephraium b 09 May 1782
Kingston, NH s/o GEORGE, Gideon &
STEVENS, Deborah; md CLOUGH,
Sally

GEORGE, Erastus b Jan 1838
Danville, NH s/o GEORGE, Currier &
SPOFFORD, Sophronia; d 18 Feb 1838
Danville, NH ae 21d

GEORGE, Erving Erastus b 20 Jun
1882 Danville, NH s/o GEORGE, Albert
M. & HALL, Hattie B.

GEORGE, Evaline b 1849 Danville,
NH d/o GEORGE, Harrison & PRATT,
Harriet M.

GEORGE, Frank md 23 Oct 1877
Danville, NH COLLINS, Hannah E.

GEORGE, Frank B. b 22 Mar 1886
Danville, NH s/o GEORGE, James W. &
COLLINS, Lillian Francene

GEORGE, Frank B. b 26 Mar 1859

GEORGE (Cont.) s/o GEORGE, James M. * FORD, Salome W.

GEORGE, Frank P. b c1858 s/o GEORGE, Currier & SPOFFORD, Sophronia; d 26 Aug 1876 Danville, NH ae 18y

GEORGE, Fred L. b 03 Jun 1883 Danville, NH s/o GEORGE, James W. & COLLINS, Lillian Francene; md PAYNE, Josephine M.

GEORGE, Fred Rufus b 1885 Kingston, NH s/o GEORGE, Ora & SILLOWAY, Abbie; md SPOFFORD, Mabel Edith; d 19 Aug 1943 Danville, NH ae 58y 5m 6d

GEORGE, Frank Wm b May 1849 s/o GEORGE, Wm & ADES, Sarah

GEORGE, Gideon md 24 May 1810 Kingston, NH WOODWARD, Sarah; d 1822 Hawke, NH ae 85y

GEORGE, Gideon b 08 Nov 1760 Kingston, NH s/o GEORGE, Gideon & STEVENS, Deborah; md CHASE, Susan

GEORGE, Gideon md STEVENS, Deborah; d 1822 Hawke, NH d ae 85y md 2nd Sarah

GEORGE, Hannah b 09 May 1779 Kingston, NH d/o GEORGE, Gideon & STEVENS, Deborah; md BLAKE, Stevens

GEORGE, Hannah b c1778 Hawke, NH; md 21 Apr 1800 Kingston, NH BLAKE, Stevens; d 04 Oct 1844 Danville, NH ae 66y

GEORGE, Hannah md JOHNSON, Daniel

GEORGE, Harold b 1893 Derry, NH s/o GEORGE, James H. & FITTS, Josephine; d 12 Apr 1893 Danville, NH ae 20d

GEORGE, Harold W. b 20 Mar 1893 Danville, NH s/o GEORGE, James H. & FITTS, Josephine

GEORGE, Harriet b 1840 Danville, NH d/o GEORGE, Harrison & PRATT, Harriet M.

GEORGE, Harrison b c1814 Sandown, NH; md PRATT, Harriett M.; d 04 Feb 1887 Danville, NH

GEORGE, Helen F. b c1845; md 05 May 1861 Danville, NH BULLARD, Henry N.

GEORGE, Hepzabah b 06 Dec 1829 d/o GEORGE, Thos & EASTMEN, Nancy; d 03 Jun 1831

GEORGE, Hershel W. b 20 Mar 1893 Danville, NH s/o GEORGE, James H. & FITTS, Josephine; d 01 Jul 1893 Danville, NH ae 3m 8d

GEORGE, Ida b Sandown, NH d/o GEORGE, Perley & PURINGTON, Clara; md SHUFELT, David Leon; d 14 Dec 1935 Danville, NH ae 74y 1m 13d

GEORGE, James b 21 NAR 1769 Kingston, NH s/o GEORGE, Gideon & STEVENS, Deborah; Not Married

GEORGE, James M. b 1824 Hawke, NH s/o GEORGE, Nathaniel & SHOWELL, Judith; d 21 Apr 1899 ae 75y

GEORGE, James W. b s/o REMICK, John & BRACKETT, Hannah; d 29 Feb 1936 Danville, NH; adoped by GEORGE d 90y 4m 12d

GEORGE, John b 07 Nov 1764 Kingston, NH s/o GEORGE, Gideon & STEVENS, Deborah

GEORGE, Joseph C. b 02 Mar 1847 Danville, NH s/o GEORGE, Harrison & PRATT, Harriet M.; d 21 Aug 1865 Savannah, GA Civil War Rcds

GEORGE, Joshua b Sandown, NH; md 28 Feb 1799 Kingston, NH EASTMAN, Rhoda

GEORGE, Keith Allen b 02 Nov 1957 Danville, NH s/o GEORGE, Allen P. & ANDERSON, Charlotte M.

GEORGE, Kenneth W. b 06 May 1906 Danville, NH s/o GEORGE, Clarence S. & LADD, Ida A.

GEORGE, Kevin Wayne b 27 Oct 1959 Danville, NH s/o GEORGE, Allen P. & ANDERSON, Charlotte M.

GEORGE, Laura Annette b 22 Jun 1828 Danville, NH d/o GEORGE, Thos & EASTMAN, Nancy; md 1859 Danville, NH BLAISDELL, Samuel A.

GEORGE, Lewis H. b 14 Jan 1859 Danville, NH s/o GEORGE, Harrison & PRATT, Harriet M.; md 03 Apr 1890 Danville, NH SARGENT, Augusta T.; d 24 Aug 1919 Danville, NH; md by Rev J. A. Lowell

GEORGE, Lillian G. b 24 Oct 1884

GEORGE (Cont.) Danville, NH d/o
GEORGE, Albert M. & HALL, Hattie B.

GEORGE, Lyman b 14 Apr 1814
Hawke, NH s/o GEORGE, Nathaniel &
SHOWELL, Judith

GEORGE, Mary B. b 1831 Hawke,
NH d/o GEORGE, Nathaniel &
SHOWELL, Judith; d 09 Sep 1851
Danville, NH

GEORGE, Mary E. b 10 Sep 1873
Danville, NH d/o GEORGE, James W. &
COLLINS, Lillian Francene; md 1st 16
Jun 1892 Danville, NH RUEE, Henry A.
by Rev J. A. Lowell, 2nd 16 Jan 1909
Danville, NH PATTEN, Herbert by Rev
W. C. Chappell; d 04 Jul 1951 Danville,
NH

GEORGE, Maurice C. b 23 Jun 1894
Danville, NH s/o GEORGE, Lewis H. &
SARGENT, Augusta T.; md 25 Dec 1922
Plymouth, NH SPENCER, Marion E.;
md by Rev J. R. Copplestone

GEORGE, Melvin Arnold b 28 May
1911 Danville, NH s/o GEORGE, Daniel
G. & ARNOLD, Gertrude B.

GEORGE, Merrill S. b 18 Dec 1855
Danville, NH s/o GEORGE, Harrison &
PRATT, Harriet M.; d 22 Sep 1887
Danville, NH

GEORGE, Molly b 08 Jul 1759
Kingston, NH d/o GEORGE, Gideon &
STEVENS, Deborah; md CHASE, Simon

GEORGE, Nathaniel b c1786; md
SHOWELL, Judith; d 28 Jan 1845
Danville, NH ae 59y

GEORGE, Nathaniel b 06 Sep 1783
Kingston, NH s/o GEORGE, Gideon &
STEVENS, Deborah; md SHOWELL,
Judith

GEORGE, Nellie F. b 26 Jul 1875
Danville, NH d/o GEORGE, James W. &
COLLINS, Lillian Francene; md 04 Nov
1893 Danville, NH KIMBALL, Laburton;
d 06 Feb 1924 Danville, NH; md by Rev
J. A. Wiggin

GEORGE, Richard Howard b 1890
Keene, NH s/o GEORGE, Frank; md 25
Dec 1937 Danville, NH COLE, Loula; md
by Clarence M. Collins (JP)

GEORGE, Sally b 08 Jul 1774 Kingston, NH d/o GEORGE, Gideon &
STEVENS, Deborah; md STEVENS, ----

GEORGE, Samuel b 25 Oct 1776
Kingston, NH s/o GEORGE, Gideon &
STEVENS, Deborah; md HEATH,
Rachel

GEORGE, Sarah S. b 19 Jun 1821
Hawke, NH d/o GEORGE, Nathaniel &
SHOWELL, Judith; md 30 Nov 1841
Raymond, NH JAMES, Jonathan L.; d
25 Mar 1898 Danville, NH

GEORGE, Stephen b 17 Dec 1771
Kingston, NH s/o GEORGE, Gideon &
STEVENS, Deborah; md 27 Jul 1797
Kingston, NH TOWLE, Sally

GEORGE, Thelma P. b 12 Dec 1902
Danville, NH d/o GEORGE, Fred L. &
PAYNE, Josephine M.

GEORGE, Thos md 12 Mar 1828
Hampstead, NH EASTMAN, Nancy

GEORGE, Thos b Hawke, NH; md 01
Feb 1838 Raymond, NH JONES, Waitley
A.

GEORGE, Walter S. b 14 Aug 1905
Danville, NH s/o GEORGE, Fred R. &
SPOFFORD, Mabel; md 12 Oct 1929
Northwood, NH GARDELLA, Dorothy
F.; md by Rev A. Herbert Armes

GEORGE, Wm b 19 Jun 1818
Hawke, NH s/o GEORGE, Nathaniel &
SHOWELL, Judith

GEORGE, Wm md 15 Oct 1789
Kingston, NH JOHNSON, Hannah

GEORGE, ---- b 16 Dec 1883 Danville, NH s/o GEORGE, Archie S. &
ELKINS, Lizzie E.

GERMAN, Priscilla S. md 14 Feb
1984 Danville, NH BRAULT, Rex J.; md
by Rich J. Rondeau (JP)

GERRISH, Eliss b ?/o GERRISH,
Nat & JONES, Charlotte; md COOMBS,
---- ; d 06 Apr 1977 Danville, NH ae 75y

GERRISH, Richard Earl md 11 Sep
1977 Danville, NH INGALLS, Joy
Lenore; md by Rev Robert E. Aspinwall

GERRY, Evelyn M. b Malden, MA
d/o GERRY, Eldridge D. & ----, Maude;
md CARBONE, ---- ; d 25 Dec 1965
Danville, NH ae 55y

GERRY, Maude Gertrude b d/o
TILTEN, Samuel & DALTON, Millicent;
d 27 Mar 1953 Danville, NH ae 79y

GERRY, Otis P. b c1834; d 27 Jun
1894 Danville, NH

GERRY, RUTH G. b d/o GERRY, Eldridge & TILDEN, Maude; md THORSEN, ---- ; d 13 Nov 1992

GIANATTASIO, Jeffery Francis b 07 May 1990 Exeter, NH s/o GIANATTASIO, Richard & HOOKER, Lynn A.

GIANATTASIO, Jessilyn Anne b 22 Jun 1992 Exeter, NH d/o GIANATTASIO, Richard & HOOKER, Lynne A.

GIBBS, Hannah - d 30 Dec 1879 Danville, NH ae 69y; also rcd 1876

GIBEL, Scott Ryan b 18 May 1985 Beverly, MA s/o GIBEL, John R. & LeMERE, Christine J.

GIGLIOTTi, Craig L. b s/o GIGLIOTTI, Louies Jos & COLLINS, Wilhelmin Julia; d 24 Jul 1978 Danville, NH

GIGLIOTTI, James Frank b 16 Aug 1948 Danville, NH s/o GIGLIOTTI, Louis Joseph & COLLINS, Wilhelmina Julia

GIGLIOTTi, Louis Joseph b 1925 Boonton, NJ s/o GIGIOTTI, Frank & DONATO, Angela; md 26 AOR 1947 Danville, NH COLLINS, Wilhelmina Julia; d 03 Jun 1974 Danville, NH; md by W. C. Chappell

GILBERT, Harry Joseph Jr. b 1930 NY s/o GILBERT, Harry Joseph Sr.; md 22 Nov 1952 Danville, NH OTTATI, Antoinette E.; md by Agnes H. Collins (JP)

GILBERT, Joseph Henry b s/o GILBERT, Wm C. & CALAN, Ella Mae; d 12 May 1979 Danville ae 89y

GILES, Norman Fletcher b 1938 MA s/o GILES, Paul T.; md 03 Jun 1958 Danville, NH SMITH, Sandra Lee; md by Agnes H. Collins (JP)

GILES, Shirley C. b 1916 Halifax, Nova Scotia d/o GILES, James H.; md 12 Aug 1937 Danville, NH BATTLES, James H.; md by Rev W. C. Chappell

GILLEN, Barbara Louise b 1937 MA d/o GILLEN, Robert L.; md 24 May 1956 Danville, NH KIMBALL, Merle David; md by Rev W. C. Chappell

GILMAN, Clara M. b c1852 W Newbury, MA; md 19 Jun 1870 Danville, NH TUCKER, Jeremiah

GILMAN, John Moody b of Kingston, NH; md 02 Apr 1765 RANOUGH, Eliz; md by Rev John Page

GILMAN, Jos. H. b c1844 Fremont, NH; md 25 Feb 1864 Danville, NH NORRIS, Meria J.

GILMAN, Robert b Hawke, NH; md 02 Mar 1797 Kingston, NH SANBORN, Abigail

GLAUDE, Jessica Lyn md 24 Aug 1991 Danville, NH MITCHELL, Michael James; md by Rev Robert E. Aspinwall

GLIDDEN, Simeon md 19 Oct 1767 Hawke, NH SMITH, Rebecca; md by Rev John Page

GLIONNA, Bruce Michael b 18 Oct 1983 Exeter, NH s/o GLIONNA, Bruce & STEAD, Cheryl

GLONET, Robert Michael md 26 Jan 1974 Danville, NH STOREY, Cynthia Nancy; md by James L. Sullivan (P)

GLOVER, Henry A. b c1879 Nottingham, NH s/o GLOVER, Sam; md 17 May 1919 E Hampstead, NH CLUKER, Maddie; md by Rev J. W. Ferrell

GOLDSMITH, Dorcus Alice b 1927 Fremont, NH d/o GOLDSMITH, Nelson W.; md 04 Aug 1944 Danville, NH WELCH, John Benj; md by Rev W. T. Shannon

GOLDSMITH, Gordon L. b 10 Oct 1938 Danville, NH s/o GOLDSMITH, Howard S. & GEORGE, Eliz P.

GOLDSMITH, Hiland Dexter b Beverly, MA s/o GOLDSMITH, Nathan B. & CLARK, Rebekah F.; d 12 Dec 1949 Danville, NH ae 81y

GOLDTHWAITE, Beth Lynn b 02 Apr 1958 Danville, NH d/o GOLDTHWAITE, Clyde E. & CURRIER, Eleanor M.; md 27 Feb 1982 Danville, NH CALLOUETTE, Bruce E.; md by Rev Everett E. Palmer

GOLDTHWAITE, Beverly J. md 01 Jul 1983 Danville, NH EDDY, Harold R.; md by Bettie C. Ouellette (P)

GOLDTHWAITE, Clyde Ernest b 1923 Kingston, NH s/o GOLDTHWAITE, Ernest; md 06 Oct 1945 Danville, NH CURRIER, Eleanor Mae; md by Rev W. C. Chappell

GOLDTHWAITE, Ernest N. b c1794 s/o GOLDTHWAITE, Evereard & SARGENT, Grace; d 21 Jan 1968 Danville, NH

GOLDTHWAITE, Ethelyn Louise b 1926 Epping, NH d/o GOLDTHWAITE, Ernest; md 05 Oct 1945 Danville, NH SWAIN, Albert Elmer; md by Rev W. C. Chappell

GOLDTHWAITE, Evelyn Frances b 1925 Epping, NH d/o GOLDTHWAITE, Ernest; md 26 Dec 1945 Danville, NH ARNOLD, Gayle Phillip; md by Rev W. C. Chappell

GOLDTHWAITE, Everard E. b Kingston, NH; md ROBINSON, Janice Marion

GOLDTHWAITE, Grace Paul b 1919 Kingston, NH d/o GOLDTHWAITE, Ernest N.; md 14 Oct 1937 Danville, NH COLLINS, Howard Cecil; md by Rev W. C. Chappell

GOLDTHWAITE, Heather Ann b 26 Feb 1964 Danville, NH d/o GOLDTH-WAITE, Rich E. & BEEDE, Christine Elaine; md 06 May 1983 Danville NH WALL, Michael R.; md by Rev Everett E. Palmer

GOLDTHWAITE, Joyce Eva b 17 Sep 1940 Danville, NH d/o GOLDTH-WAITE, Everard & ROBINSON, Janice M.; md SPERO, Richard

GOLDTHWAITE, Richard Ernest b 1934 NH; s/o GOLDTHWAITE, Everard E. & ROBINSON, Janice Marion; md 29 Jan 1954 Danville, NH BEEDE, Chris Elaine; md by Rev Rob S. Walker

GOLDTHWAITE, Richard Ernest b 03 Feb 1961 Exeter, NH s/o GOLDTH-WAITE, Richard Ernest & BEEDE, Christine Elaine; md 10 Jun 1983 Danville, NH CARON, Diane P.; md by Rev Florent R. Bilodeau (P)

GOLDTHWAITE, Suzanne Lynn b 16 Feb 1957 Danville, NH d/o GOLDTHWAITE, Rich Ernest & BEEDE, Christine Elaine; md 1st 15 Nov 1976 Danville, NH TODD, Mason Rhodes md by Rev Robert Aspinwall, 2nd 16 Mar 1991 Danville, NH LANE, John J. Jr. by Rev Everett E. Palmer

GOLDTHWAITE, Thos Lee b 18 Oct 1945 Danville, NH s/o GOLDTHWAITE, Everard & ROBINSON, Janice Marion

GOLDTHWAITE, Clyde Ernest b Kingston, NH s/o GOLDTHWAITE, Ernest N.; md 06 Oct 1945 Danville, NH

GOLDTHWAITE (Cont.) CURRIER, Eleanor Mae

GOLDTHWAITE, Evelyn Frances b 1926 Epping, NH d/o GOLDTHWAITE, Ernest N.; md 26 Dec 1945 Danville, NH ARNOLD, Gayle Phillip

GONYER, Julie Ann b 13 Jan 1961 Danville, NH d/o GONYER, Ralph Sr. & SCIMONE, Arline S.

GOOD, Marjorie B. b 1935 Miami, FL; md 22 Feb 1964 Danville, NH SMITH, Clifford B. Jr.; md by Edward R. Lamb (JP)

GOODRICH, Abbie L. b c1871 Danville, NH; md 13 Aug 1887 Haverhill, MA SMITH, Daniel C.; md by Rev C. N. Taylor

GOODRICH, Grafton M. b 1872 Danville, NH s/o GOODRICH, Lewis M. md 12 Apr 1893 Kingston, NH GOODWIN, Mattie E.; md by Rev Wm A. Patten

GOODRICH, Helen b New York; d/o GOODRICH, Barak & St JONE, Perlatta; md MARCH, ----; d 12 Nov 1920 Danville, NH

GOODRICH, Lewis N. b c1845 Newton, NH; md 07 Jan 1865 Danville, NH MARCH, Abbie L.

GOODWIN, Ada F. b 1875 Kingston, NH d/o GOODWIN, Hazen O. & SHORES, Mary E.; md 11 Nov 1890 Danville, NH TEWKSBURY, Aliston E. by Rev J. A. Lowell; d 09 Dec 1901 ae 26y 8m 16d

GOODWIN, Alice M. b 27 Sep 1872 Lawrence, MA d/o GOODWIN, Hazen O. & SHORES, Mary E.; md 18 Feb 1911 Plaistow, NH JOHNSON, Mahlon E.; md by Rev Chas A. Towle

GOODWIN, Benj md 21 Dec 1769 Hawke, NH WORTH, Lydia; md by Rev John Page

GOODWIN, Dorothy b c1779; md BRACKETT, Hanover D.; d 24 Dec 1867 Danville, NH ae 90y

GOODWIN, Emma A. b c1884 Kingston, NH d/o GOODWIN, Hazen O. & SHERES, Mary; md 23 Nov 1904 Danville, NH WEST, Nathan A.; d 06 Apr 1965 Danville, NH; md by Rev A. B. Hyde

GOODWIN, Hazen O. b Kingston,

GOODWIN (Cont.) NH s/o GOODWIN, Frank & WHITE, Sarah; md; SHORES, Mary E.; d 16 Jan 1936 Danville, NH ae 83y

GOODWIN, Henry K. b c1848 Lawrence, MA; md 18 Mar 1870 Danville, NH BRAGG, Martha A.

GOODWIN, John H. md GRIFFIN, Emma

GOODWIN, Mattie E. b Kingston, NH d/o GOODWIN, Daniel N.; md GOODRICH, Grafton M.; md by Rev Wm A. Patten

GOODWIN, Wm md ---- Ruth C

GORDON, Clyde M. Jr. b s/o GORDON, Clyde M. Sr. & WILLEY, Helen; d 07 Dec 1983 Danville, NH ae 58y

GORDON, Dan md 30 Oct 1766 Hawke, NH BRAZEAL, Eliz; md by Rev John Page

GORDON, Dudley b c1799 Brentwood, NH; md 04 Sep 1824 SANBORN, Dorothy; d 10 Sep 1838 Danville, NH ae 39y

GORDON, Elma Lavina b 13 Sep 1850 Danville, NH d/o GORDON, Levi Sanborn & CLIFFORD, Dorothy Ann; md TOWLE, Ransom Forest; d 26 Oct 1931 Danville, NH

GORDON, Elvira Clara b 17 May 1854 Danville, NH d/o GORDON, Levi Sanborn & CLIFFORD, Dorothy Ann; md 11 Apr 1883 Danville, NH COLLINS, Leonard Waldo; d 1935 Kingston, NH; bu Kingston, NH PLains Cem.

GORDON, Emily Frances b 29 Dec 1834 Hawke, NH d/o GORDON, Dudley & SANBORN, Dorothy; md 1st 1859 Danville, NH CASS, Warren, 2nd 25 Apr 1861 Danville, NH CURRIER, John Frank

GORDON, Flora b 01 Aug 1858 Danville, NH d/o GORDON, Levi Sanborn & CLIFFORD, Dorothy Ann; md

GORDON, Levi Sanborn b 25 Dec 1825 Hawke, NH s/o GORDON, Dudley & SANBORN, Dorothy; md 20 Jun 1850 Danville, NH CLIFFORD, Dorothy Ann; d 10 Jan 1894 Danville, NH

GORDON, Sarah E. b c1838 Brentwood, NH; md 1959 Danville, NH TUCK, John L.

GORDON, Vera G. b 1899 Haverhill, MA d/o GORDON, F. G. R.; md 03 Jul 1930 Danville, NH SANBORN, Sherburne J.; md by Rev O.L. Broensey; prev md GARDELLA, ----?

GORTON, Geo b 1927 Hampstead, NH s/o GORTON, Geo A.; md 24 Jul 1948 Danville, NH COLLINS, Barbara Jean; md by Rev W. C. Chappell

GORTON, Jacqueline Barb b 17 Sep 1952 Danville, NH d/o GORTON, Geo & COLLINS, Barbara Jean

GORTON, James Geo b 28 Aug 1974 Exeter, NH s/o GORTON, Peter Alfred & SCIACCA, Mary Ellen

GORTON, Jeffery Wayne b 08 Dec 1954 Danville, NH s/o GORTON, Geo & COLLINS, Barbara Jean

GORTON, Kimberlee Sue b 15 Apr 1977 Exeter, NH d/o GORTON, Peter Alfred & SCIACCA, Mary Ellen

GORTON, Linda Sue b 04 Apr 1965 Danville, NH d/o GORTON, Geo & COLLINS, Barbara Jean; md 28 Oct 1989 Danville, NH McGAUNN, Kevin D.; md by Rev Everett E. Palmer

GORTON, Lisa Jean b 12 Mar 1959 Danville, NH d/o GORTON, Geo & COLLINS, Barbara Jean

GORTON, Lori A. md 26 Jan 1982 Danville, NH BASSETT, Fred K.; md by Rev Everett E. Palmer

GORTON, Peter Alfred b 30 Sep 1951 Danville, NH s/o GORTON, Geo & COLLINS, Barbara Jean

GOSS, Judy E. b Laconia, NH; md OTTATI, Louis Jr.

GOULD, Candy Ann md 14 Oct 1978 Danville, NH COLLINS, Melvin Russel; md by Rev Wm Ryans

GOULD, Daniel (Major) b Lineboro, ??; md 1st Appleton, ---- 2nd 15 Nov 1798 Kingston, NH HOOK, Mary

GOULD, Eliz C. md BLAKE, Jos Wm d 21 Oct 1882 Danville, NH ae 77y

GOULDING, Rachel Eliz b 23 Aug 1992 Derry, NH d/o GOULDING, James M. & KLING, Colleen K.

GOULET, Lisa Joy md 12 Oct 1991 Danville, NH QUEEN, John Edward; md by Rev Robert F. Dobson

GOUTIER, Cynthia Louise md 17 Mar 1879 Danville, NH GAGNON, Hal

GOUTIER (Cont.) Edward; md by Rev Steven Kucharski (P)

GOVE, Arline Priscilla b Lynn, MA; md INGALLS, Norman Robert

GOVE, Kirk b Wilmont, NH s/o GOVE, Wm; md 17 Aug 1890 Newton Juc, NH SILLOWAY, Mirtie B.; md by Rev J. P. Nowlan

GOVE, Lucile A. b Fremont, NH d/o GOVE, Cyrus A.; md 12 Jun 1920 Derry, NH HOBBS, Edwin Howard; md by Rev W. B. Morrison

GOVE, Mary L. b c1827 Newburyport, MA; md 1848 Danville, NH HALE, Issac Jr.

GOVE, Stella M. b d/o GOVE, Kirk & SILLOWAY, Myrtle; md LEMAN, ---- ; d 30 Dec 1958 Danville, NH ae 64y

GOVE, Susanna md 04 Sep 1766 Hawke, NH WORTH, Timothy

GRAHAM, John F. b Nova Scotia; s/o GRAHAM, Andrew & WADE, ---- ; d 09 Jan 1930 Danville, NH ae 76y 10m 26d

GRANA, Pilar md 25 Oct 1975 Danville, NH BONCZKIEWICZ, Ron S.; md by Rev Ron E. Fortin

GRANEY, Wm Peter b 1941 MA; md 25 Aug 1961 Danville, NH THIBEAULT, Katherine June; md by Rev Wendall J. Irvine

GRANT, Douglas James md 01 Oct 1988 Danville, NH SIPPEL, Deanna Marie; md by Maurice D. Lavque (P)

GRAVELLE, Gertrude May b 1901 Grensville, Ontario d/o GRAVELLE, Chas; md 28 Feb 1948 Newton, NH FRENCH, Herbert Cleveland; md by Rev Thurber Weller

GRAVES, Marshall E. b Vienna, ME; d 16 Jan 1920 ae 74y

GRAY, Dennis Patrick b 23 Jul 1986 Derry, NH s /o GRAY, Erbest L. & KAHN, Leslie P.

GRAY, Donald Kenneth b 1938 MA; md 16 Jul 1960 Danville, NH HAM, Joan Frances; md by Rev Wendall J. Irvine

GRAY, James Henry b 1931 Tewksbury, MA s/o GRAY, Victor H.; md 18 Dec 1954 Danville, NH OTTATI, Lucy Mary; md by Rev J. T. Sullivan (P)

GRAY, Jane A. md Sep 1973 Danville, NH DUSTON, Robert James; md by Eliz G. Waitt (JP)

GRAY, Robin D. md 23 Aug 1986 Danville, NH SPICER, Chas A.; md by Rich J. Rondeau (JP)

GRAY, Warren Otis b 1921 Waterboro, MA s /o GRAY, Emery; md 15 Dec 1946 Danville, NH McPHERSON, Marion Eliz; md by Rev W. C. Chappell

GREELEY, Daniel Edward b 29 Jul 1967 Danville, NH s/o GREELEY, Francis B. & La FOUNTAIN, Maureen

GREELEY, Jurgen md 18 Nov 1990 Danville, NH FINK, Christine; md by Rich J. Rondeau (JP)

GREELEY, Michael Patrick b 23 Oct 1968 Danville, NH s/o GREELEY, Francis B. & La FOUNTAIN, Maureen; md 16 Jun 1990 Danville, NH PACKARD, Kristi Lynn; md by Robert J. Kemmery (P)

GREELY, Nancy A. b Cannan, NH d/o GREELY, Shubeil & WHITNEY, Lydia; md MARCH, ----; d 09 Jan 1904 Danville, NH ae 91y 6m 27d

GREEN, Abigail (Miss) b ABT 1797; d 01 Oct 1885 Danville, NH ae 88y

GREEN, Hannah b 1806 Hamptonz, NH d/o GREEN, John & REDMOND, Eliz; md 1st PEASLEE, Caleb, 2nd 23 Aug 1827 COLLINS, Nathaniel; d 19 Jan 1899; bu Danville NH Old Mtg Hse Cem.

GREEN, John b Hampton, NH; md REDMOND, Eliz

GREEN, Melanie Ann md 11 Mar 1978 Danville, NH WARD, Andrew Wm; md by Rev Robert E. Crabtree

GREEN, Rebecca md TILTON, David

GREENE, Debra M. md 20 Jun 1986 Danville, NH FULLER, Paul E.; md by Rich J. Rondeau (JP)

GREENWOOD, Maureen M. md 27 May 1989 Danville, NH NUTTER, Robert C.; md by Rich J. Rondeau (JP)

GREER, Roland L. d 21 Feb 1978 Danville, NH ae 88y

GREGG, Wm b of Derry, NH; md 23 Nov 1799 Hawke, NH ABBOT, Eliz; md by Rev John Page

GREGOR, Emily Frances b d/o & ----, Emily; md ORNER, ----; d 28 Dec 1981 Danville, NH d ae 87y

GRENDEL, Daniel b of Savilla, ? md 20 Feb 1780 Hawke NH TANDY, Eliz

GRIFFIN, Abigail b 07 Jul 1822 Hawke, NH d/o GRIFFIN, Daniel & BLAKE, Sarah

GRIFFIN, Abigail b 31 Mar 1810 Hawke, NH d/o GRIFFIN, Daniel & BLAKE, Sarah; d 03 May 1820 Hawke, NH

GRIFFIN, Addie Adele b 21 Sep 1867 Danville, NH d/o GRIFFIN, Harlan Boyden & COOK, Flora A.; md 24 Feb 1886 Danville, NH CURRIER, Horace E.; d 05 Jan 1948 Danville, NH

GRIFFIN, Allan Louis b 1946 s/o GRIFFIN, Forest Boyden & KANTEN-WEIN, Ruth

GRIFFIN, Arletta b 07 Sep 1873 Danville, NH d/o GRIFFIN, John F. & CAVISS, Belinda A.

GRIFFIN, Barbara M. b 1933 MA; d/o GRIFFIN, Patrick; md 04 Mar 1955 Danville, NH GAGNON, Alfred D. Jr.; md by Agnes H. Collins (JP)

GRIFFIN, Benj b 1876 Danville, NH s/o GRIFFIN, John F. & CAVISS, Belinda A.

GRIFFIN, Calvin Benj b Danville, NH s/o GRIFFIN, John F. & McINTIRE, Belinda R.; md 06 Nov 1897 Danville, NH HUNTINGTON, Dora B.; d 04 Jun 1947 Danville, NH; md by A. B. Howard (JP); d ae 72y 0om 3d

GRIFFIN, Calvin B. b c1843 Chelsea, MA; md Mar 1863 Danville, NH HOYT, Mary A.

GRIFFIN, Camilla Christine b 13 Sep 1974 Exeter, NH d/o GRIFFIN, Robert Christo & CHENEY, Nancy Jane

GRIFFIN, Chas O. P. b 25 Jul 1853 Danville, NH; s/o GRIFFIN, John H. & DAVIS, Mahala L.; d 15 Jan 1897 Danville, NH

GRIFFIN, Chas W. b 30 Mar 1835 Hawke, NH s/o GRIFFIN, Daniel & BLAKE, Sarah; md 26 Mar 1864 Danville, NH BLAKE, Sarah E.

GRIFFIN, Clara B. b c1858 Sandown, NH d/o GRIFFIN, James & KENNY, Abigail; md 05 Jun 1881 Danville, NH KIMBALL, Everett W.; d 05 Apr 1907 Danville, NH

GRIFFIN, Daniel b 22 Oct 1832 Hawke, NH s/o GRIFFIN, Daniel & BLAKE, Sarah

GRIFFIN, Daniel b c1779 Sandown, NH md 24 Sep 1808 Hawke NH BLAKE, Sarah d 12 Aug 1840 Danville NH

GRIFFIN, David b 07 Feb 1812 Hawke, NH s/o GRIFFIN, Daniel & BLAKE, Sarah; md 1st LADD, Salina, 2nd 03 Jan 1881 Danville, NH BRACK-ETT, Abby, 3rd 15 Dec 1883 Danville, NH QUIMBY, Sarah H.; d 07 Oct 1892 Danville, NH

GRIFFIN, Dororthy Adele b 1915 d/o GRIFFIN, Louis & TOWLE, Mable E.; md PRYOR, Chas

GRIFFIN, Dorothy b c1754; md 12 Jan 1780 Hawke, NH HOOK, Israel; d 30 Nov 1836 Danville, NH; bu Danville, NH Old Mtg Hse Cem. md by Rev John Page

GRIFFIN, Elinor Ann b 1955 d/o GRIFFIN, Forest Boyden & KANTEN-WEIN, Ruth

GRIFFIN, Eliz b c1858 d/o GRIFFIN, Harlan P. & ----, Tamar N.; d 24 Dec 1862 Danville, NH ae 4y - Diptheria

GRIFFIN, Emily Louise b 19 Mar 1978 Exeter, NH d/o GRIFFIN Robt C. & CHENEY, Nancy J.

GRIFFIN, Emma b 1850 Danville, NH d/o GRIFFIN, Harlan P. & ----, Tamar N.; md GOODWIN, John H.; d 28 Feb 1872 Danville, NH ae 21y

GRIFFIN, Eva J. b 04 Feb 1856 Danville, NH d/o GRIFFIN, Samuel C. & PEASLEE, Dolly; d 06 Sep 1863 Danville, NH

GRIFFIN, Flora L. S. d 21 May 1940 Danville, NH d ae 85y 2m 5 d

GRIFFIN, Floyd Thorton b 22 Mar 1898 Danville, NH s/o GRIFFIN, Calvin B. & HUNTINGTON, Dora B.

GRIFFIN, Forrest Boyden b 07 Aug 1919 Danville, NH s/o GRIFFIN, Lewis M. & TOWLE, Mabel E. md KAN-TENNWEIN, Ruth

GRIFFIN, Fred L. b 16 Mar 1874 Danville, NH; s/o GRIFFIN, Harlan Boyden & COOK, Flora A.

GRIFFIN, Geo md 31 May 1781 Hawke, NH RING, Esther; md by Rev John Page

GRIFFIN, Hannah D. b 26 Mar 1820 Hawke, NH d/o GRIFFIN, Daniel & BLAKE, Sarah; md 22 Dec 1841 Dan-

GRIFFIN (Cont.) ville, NH ALLEN, Josep H.; d 06 Aug 1865 Danville, NH ae 45y

GRIFFIN, Harlan Boyden b 06 Apr 1846 Danville, NH s/o GRIFFIN, Harlan P. & ----, Tamar N.; md 24 Aug 1863 Danville, NH COOK, Flora A.; d 10 Sep 1926 Danville, NH

GRIFFIN, Harlan P. b 22 Feb 1814 Hawke, NH s/o GRIFFIN, Daniel & BLAKE, Sarah

GRIFFIN, Harriet b c1854 d/o GRIFFIN, Harlan P. & ----, Tamar N.; d 18 Dec 1862 Danville, NH ae 8y - Diptheria

GRIFFIN, Hezekiah b 10 Mar 1827 Hawke, NH s/o GRIFFIN, Daniel & BLAKE, Sarah

GRIFFIN, Horace M. b 1852 Danville, NH s/o GRIFFIN, Samuel C. & PEASLEE, Dolly; d 1854 Danville, NH

GRIFFIN, Ida M. b c1846 Milton, NH d/o GRIFFIN, Samuel C. & PEASLEE, Dolly; md CLEAVES, ----; d 27 Jan 1893 Danville, NH

GRIFFIN, Iva E. b 21 Sep 1869 Danville, NH d/o GRIFFIN, Harlan Boyden & COOK, Flora A.; md 22 Aug 1888 Danville, NH MARTIN, Wm; d 15 Sep 1894 Danville, NH

GRIFFIN, John F. b 10 Oct 1844 Danville, NH s/o GRIFFIN, David & LADD, Salina; d; 17 Jun 1911 Danville, NH

GRIFFIN, John H. Rev. b 28 Feb 1816 Hawke, NH s/o GRIFFIN, Daniel & BLAKE, Sarah; md DAVIS, Mahala; d 23 Dec 1874 Danville, NH

GRIFFIN, Louis Melvin b 30 May 1872 Danville, NH s/o GRIFFIN, Harlan Boyden & COOK, Flora A. md 24 Nov 1910 Danville, NH TOWLE, Mabel E.; d 02 Mar 1943 Danville, NH; md by Rev Allen C. Keith

GRIFFIN, Louise Elinor b 02 Mar 1921 Danville, NH d/o GRIFFIN, Louis M. & TOWLE, Mabel E.; md 30 Jul 1944 Danville, NH FELDMAN, Geo Wm; md by Rev W. C. Chappell

GRIFFIN, Luman Boyd b 30 May 1864 Danville, NH s/o GRIFFIN, Harlan Boyden & COOK, Flora A.; md 09 Apr 1891 Danville, NH EATON, Maude J.; d

GRIFFIN (Cont.) 23 Dec 1945 Danville, NH; md by Rev J. A. Lowell

GRIFFIN, Martha I. b c1845 Milton, NH; md 24 Oct 1882 Danville, NH CLEAVES Orville L.

GRIFFIN, Mary Alice b Boston, MA d/o GRIFFIN, Thos & O'DEA, Beatrice; md McKENNA, ---- ; d 03 Mar 1931 Danville, NH ae 30y 6m 16d

GRIFFIN, Mary L. b 1839 Sandown, NH d/o GRIFFIN, James & KENNEY, Abigail; md 13 Oct 1887 Hampton Falls, NH PURINGTON, Chas C.; d 09 Jun 1921 Danville, NH d ae 82y 2m 1d; md by Rev R. F. Gardner

GRIFFIN, Minnie B. b 1874 Danville, NH d/o GRIFFIN, John F. & CAVISS, Belinda A.

GRIFFIN, Moses b 20 Sep 1825 Hawke, NH s/o GRIFFIN, Danie & BLAKE, Sarah; d 19 Aug 1863 Danville, NH - Civil War Rcds

GRIFFIN, Nancy A. md 21 Aug 1971 Danville, NH DEMAINE, Rich D.; md by Rev Peter W. Lovejoy

GRIFFIN, Patricia Mary b 1934 MA d/o GRIFFIN, Patrick Gordon; md 14 Nov 1952 Danville, NH DOW, Richard Stanley; md by Rev Robert S. Walker

GRIFFIN, Robert L. b 1948 s/o GRIFFIN, Forest Boyden & KANTENWEIN, Ruth; md CHENEY, Nancy J.

GRIFFIN, Robert Raymond b 1928 MA s/o GRIFFIN, Patrick Gordon; md 01 Oct 1949 Danville, NH SMITH, Lorraine Frances; md by Rev Harry L. Lesure

GRIFFIN, Sally md 24 Apr 1805 Hawke, NH COLLINS, Wm

GRIFFIN, Sally md 20 Sep 1806 Hawke, NH SARGENT, Sam; d 13 Jan 1853 Danville, NH   bu

GRIFFIN, Samuel C. b 12 May 1818 Hawke, NH s/o GRIFFIN, Daniel & BLAKE, Sarah; md PEASLEE, Dolly; d 29 Sep 1881 Danville, NH d ae 23y

GRIFFIN, Sarah Ann b 03 Nov 1835 Hawke, NH d/o GRIFFIN, David & LADD, Salina; md 09 Nov 1852 Danville, NH SHUFELT, Samuel; d 04 Nov 1914 Danville, NH; Also md to HUNT ?

GRIFFIN, Susan H. b 06 Nov 1829 Hawke, NH d/o GRIFFIN, Daniel & BLAKE, Sarah; md 1858 Danville, NH

GRIFFIN (Cont.) BAILEY, Jos G.; d 06 Jul 1915 Danville, NH

GRIFFIN, Thos F. b S Boston, MA s/o GRIFFIN, Patrick & FLARETY, Sarah; d 07 Mar 1930 Danville, NH

GRIFFITH, Jeffery Chas b of Lowell, MA; md 26 Sep 1991 ALLICON, Pamelyn Marie; md by Rev Laurence J. Strtondak

GROVER, Dylan Ashworth b 21 Nov 1989 Haverhill, MA s/o GROVER, Jack D. & FISHER, Wendy S.

GROVER, Jack Douglas md 16 Jul 1988 Danville, NH FISHER, Wendy Jean; md by Rev Everett E. Palmer

GRUBBS, Melissa Ashley b 18 Dec 1986 Derry, NH d/o GRUBBS, Robert M. & BRAGAN, Lisa M.

GUGGAN, Cornelia S. b 1948 MA; md 14 Feb 1968 Danville, NH JONES, Ronald Barry; md by Leona A. Sciaudone (JP)

GUSCHETTI, Marilyn Dian b 27 Nov 1974 Haverhill, NH d/o GUSCHETTI, Paul Frederi & STULTZ, Marilyn A.

GUSCORA, Anthony b 1915 Haverhill, MA s/o GUSCORA, Jos; md 15 Aug 1936 Danville, NH STEVENS, Maxine; md by Rev O. L. Brownsey

GUSOSKI, Wm Chas Jr. b 17 Feb 1984 Haverhill, MA s/o GUSOSKI, Wm Chas & DEMAINE, Deborah S.

GUSOSKI, Wm Chas Sr. md 01 Oct 1983 Danville, NH DEMAINE, Deborah S.; md by Rev Wayne Hardy

GUSTAVSON, Jonathan Paul b 10 Dec 1974 Exeter, NH s/o GUSTAVSON, Paul Frederick & BUSTARD, Eliz May

HADLEY, Derek Jos b 19 Sep 1982 Exeter, NH s/o HADLEY, Jos A. & LeBLANC, Sandra M.

HADLEY, Marie Ellen md 04 Jun 1977 Danville, NH FARREN, Jos Gerard; md by Micheal J. Griffin (P)

HADLEY, Rae b Hampstead, NH

HADLEY, Robert Arthur b 23 Oct 1935 Danville, NH s/o HADLEY, Rae

HADLEY, Wm Frank b 30 Nov 1971 Exete, NH s/o HADLEY, Lewis F. & HUNT, Nancy B.

HADLOCK, Elsie b d/o HADLOCK, Sidney & GRAGDON, Eliz B.; md

HADLOCK (Cont.) NICKETT, ---- ; d 06 Feb 1979 Danville, NH ae 98y

HAGGETT, Ewell Donald Jr. b 08 Jan 1959 Danville, NH s/o HAGGETT, Ewell Don Sr. & WHITNEY, Hazel M.

HAGGETT, John W. b 1911 Hooksett, NH s/o HAGGETT, Lorenzo W.; md 02 May 1936 Danville, NH SMITH, Evangeline S.; md by Rev Jas W. Bixler

HAGGETT, Martha Jean b 09 Feb 1944 Danville, NH d/o HAGGETT, John Wm & SMITH, Evageline Sylvia

HAGGETT, Rodney Forrest b 27 Jun 1940 Danville, NH s/o HAGGETT, John W. & SMITH, Evangeline S.

HAGGETT, Steven Craig b 15 Aug 1960 Danville, NH s/o HAGGETT, Ewell R. & WHITNEY, Hazel

HALE, Issac Jr. b c1825 Newburyport, MA; md 1848 Danville, NH GOVE, Mary L.

HALFHILL, Amanda Jeanne b 29 Dec 1984 Manchester, NH d/o HALFHILL, David F. Jr. & PERVERLEY, Cynthia J.

HALFHILL, David F. Jr. md 29 May 1984 Danville, NH PEVERLEY, Cynthia J.; md by Rev WEndall J. Irvine

HALFHILL, Kieth David b 15 Aug 1986 Exeter, NH s/o HALFHILL, David F. & PEVERLEY, Cynthia J.

HALFHILL, Kyle Ronald b 25 Jun 1990 Exeter, NH s/o HALFHILL, David F. Jr. & PEVERLEY, Cynthia J.

HALL, Allen E. b c 1894 Danville, NH s/o HALL, Frank A.; md 01 Dec 1914 Danville, NH WEST, Cora; md by Rev Lyman D. Bragg

HALL, Anson b 1845 s/o HALL, Henry A. & BARTLETT, Palomy; d 13 Apr 1903 Danville, NH

HALL, Austin E. b c1901 Danville, NH s/o HALL, Frank A. & METERIER, Mary A.; d 25 Sep 1916 Danville, NH ae 15y 6m 15d

HALL, Carroll Frank b 07 Feb 1897 Danville, NH s/o HALL, Frank A. & METEVIER, Mary A. d 22 Aug 1980

HALL, Clarence Metivier b 02 Mar 1908 Danville, NH s/o HALL, Frank A. & METERIER, Mary A.; d 17 Apr 1908 Danville, NH

HALL, Flossie M. b Aug 1892 Nashua, NH d/o HALL, Frank A. & METIVIER, Mary A.; d 05 Sep 1908 Danville, NH ae 16y 11d

HALL, Frank A. b 1861 Salem, NH s/o HALL, John & MARSHALL, Sarah; md METIEVER, Mary A.; d 19 Mar 1933 Danville, NH ae 72y 1m 10d

HALL, Helen Louise b 02 Mar 1908 Danville, NH d/o HALL, Frank A. & METIVIER, Mary A. d 18 Apr 1908 Danville, NH ae 1m 21d

HALL, Henry A. b 1817 Nottingham, NH; d 04 Feb 1890 Danville, NH ae 73y Gastric fever-pneumonia

HALL, Levi M. b c1850 Fremont, NH; md 26 Jan 1871 Danville, NH LUNT, Julia A. Mrs.

HALL, Mabel Cora b 30 Oct 1902 Danville, NH d/o HALL, Frank A. & METIVIER, Mary A.

HALL, Polana B. b Danville, NH; d 26 Jul 1898 Danville, NH ae 81y 10d

HALL, Wilbur J. b 1889 Winthrop, ME s/o HALL, Jos & PAYHEUR, Helen; md 31 Oct 1937 Danville, NH SAN- BORN, Grace S.; d 21 Jul 1948 Danville, NH; md by Rev W. C. Chappell; d ae 59y 2m 22d

HALLIMAN, Richard Wm b 19 Dec 1934 Danville, NH s/o HALLIMAN, Richard & COONEY, Helen

HAM, Anna D. b 1864; d 15 Feb 1926 Danville, NH

HAM, Henry b c1854 Portsmouth, NH; md 08 Nov 1874 Danville, NH CHALLIS, Mary D.

HAM, Herbert D. d 03 Jan 1927 Danville, NH ae 62y 5m

HAM, Joan Frances b 1940 MA; md 16 Jul 1960 Danville, NH GRAY, Donald Kenneth; md by Rev Wendall J. Irvine

HAMEL, Justin Andrew b 24 Jan 1984 Lawrence, MA s/o HAMEL, Andrew S. & LARRABEE, Joan D.

HAMILTON, David Theron b 27 Apr 1936 Danville, NH s/o HAMILTON, Chas G. & NEWCOMB, Viola

HAMILTON, Gertrude E. b Malden, MA; md YOUNG, Theron G.

HANKERSON, Mary b d/o HAN- KERSON, James; md HARMON, ---- ; d 08 Apr 1954 Danville, NH ae 83y

HANLEY, Mary A. b Salem, NH; md RUMERY, Bernard E.

HANLON, Claudia A. b d/o HANLON, Albert A. & NOLAN, Mary C.; d 10 Jul 1981 Danville, NH ae 68y

HANNAGAN, Kathleen A. b 23 Jan 1970 Haverhill, MA d/o HANNAGAN, Paul & ANDERSON, Marlene G.

HANNAGAN, Paul W. b 1928 MA; md 07 Dec 1968 Danville, NH EATON, Marlene G.; md by Rev Alton Mark

HANNAGEN, Kathleen A. b md 31 May 1987 Danville, NH SCHAFFER, Jeffery W.; md by Rev Wm L. Shafer

HANSCOM, Eva M. b 07 Jul 1903 Danville, NH d/o HANSCOM, G. Edward & SARGENT, Anne May; d 15 Dec 1903 Danville, NH ae 5m 15d

HANSON, Daniel Benj b 19 Sep 1989 Exeter, NH s/o HANSON, Douglas A. & KIMBALL, Loralyn

HANSON, Douglas A. md 23 Oct 1982 Danville, NH KIMBALL, Loralyn; md by Rev Everett E. Palmer

HANSON, Joshua Ryan b 29 Jul 1984 Exeter, NH s/o HANSON, Douglas A. & KIMBALL, Loralyn

HANSON, Karen L. md 24 Dec 1989 Danville, NH LAWRENCE, David M; md by Geo M. DePace (JP)

HANSON, Mindy Leigh b 30 Aug 1986 Exeter, NH d/o HANSON, Douglas A. & KIMBALL, Loralyn

HANSON, Patricia M. b 1948 Amesbury, MA; md 10 Jul 1965 Danville, NH CARROLL, Chas E.; md by Roger A. Vachon (P)

HANSON, Richard Stephen b 11 Apr 1978 Haverhill, NH s/o HANSON, Richard S. Sr. & BRIDGES, Carole S.

HARMON, Robert W. Jr. md 23 Jun 1973 Danville, NH SLETTEN, Joyce M.; md by Rev Justin J. Hartman

HARMS, Kevin Scott md 18 Feb 1978 Danville, NH MAXWELL, Carol- Jean; md by Michael Griffin (P)

HARPER, Chas M. b 1906 Manches- ter, NH s/o HARPER, Herbert & JOHNSON, Maude; md 05 Nov 1924 Danville, NH DOLE, Doris C.; d 01 Oct 1976 Danville, NH; md by Rev Edw L. Noble; d ae 70y

HARPER, Diane Marie b 1943 NH;

HARPER (Cont.) md 12 Aug 1961 Danville, NH BOWLEY, Leonard Paul; md by Rev Wendall J. Irvine

HARPER, George Thos md COHEN, Annie D.

HARPER, Mary Mabel b Fremont, NH d/o HARPER, Geo. Thos & COHEN, Annie D.; md PASCOE, ---- ; d 12 Mar 1944 Danville, NH ae 75y 0m 8d

HARRIGAN, Richard M. d 07 Jun 1975 Danville, NH ae 19y

HARRIMAN, Herbert Wm b 1934 ME s/o HARRIMAN, Paul; md 19 Sep 1958 Danville, NH TEBBETTS, Janice Dimond; md by Rev Karl J. Hislop

HARRIMAN, Jos b Plaistow, NH; md 21 Sep 1779 Hawke, NH FLANDERS, Judith; md by Rev John Page

HARRIMAN, Wallace b s/o HARRI-MAN, Elliott & BISHOP, Vivian; d 10 Dec 1988 Danville, NH ae 56y

HARRIS, Dennis G. md 27 Apr 1986 Danville, NH NIHAN, Linda S.; md by Rev Everett E. Palmer

HARRIS, Hannah S. b c1861 Plaistow, NH d/o HARRIS, Gilman & KIMBALL, Susan; md 02 Jul 1884 Danville, NH KIMBALL, Walter A.; d 01 May 1916 Danville, NH

HARRIS, Jerome Dr. b Hampstead, NH; md 19 Dec 1833 Kingston, NH TEWKSBURY, Mary

HARRIS, John b s/o HARRIS, Thos & RICHARDSON, Annie; d 17 May 1978 Danville, NH ae 17y

HARRIS, Mary H. b c1836 Amesbury, MA; md 1859 Danville, NH EASTMAN, Josiah C.

HARRIS, Roy Franklin b s/o HARRIS, Horance & DAVIS, Louisa; d 05 Jun 1953 Danville, NH ae 77y

HARRISON, Don Everett b 1925 MA s/o HARRISON, Herbert; md 01 Oct 1949 Danville, NH STANCIMBE, Marion Bertha; md by Rev Harry L. Lesure

HARRISON, Tammy L. md 19 Mar 1982 Danville, NH KIMBALL, Steven L.; md by Rev Everett E. Palmer

HART, Tracey Lee b 27 Dec 1969 Danville, NH d/o HART, Bennett E. & HEALEY, Linda J.

HARTFORD, Bertha L. b Stratham, NH; md THIBEAULT, Wilfred J.

HARTFORD, Daniel Franklin Sr b s/o HARTFORD, Wm H. & BEAUDRY, Marie A.; d 20 Aug 1992 ae 50y

HARTFORD, Ernest b Deerfield, NH; md CONNERS, Georgia

HARTFORD, Ida Frances b 17 Nov 1937 Danville, NH d/o HARTFORD, Richard Jennes & HILL, Florence Eliz

HARTFORD, John Tyler b 27 Nov 1934 Danville, NH s/o HARTFORD, Frederick F. & DOWE, Lillian

HARTFORD, Mitchell E. b 12 Mar 1935 Danville, NH s/o HARTFORD, Richard Jennes & HILL, florence Eliz

HARTFORD, Pearl b Deerfield, NH; SHEYS, Harry

HARTFORD, ---- b 07 Nov 1928 Danville, NH ?/o HARTFORD, Ernest & CONNERS, Georgia

HARTSONE, Florence H. -B; NH D/o HARSTSONE, Benj & MITCHELL, Delia; d 07 Jul 1958 Danville, NH ae 81y

HARVEL, Robert b 07 Dec 1948 Danville, NH s/o HARVEL, John Herbert & KIRWAN, Alice Virginia

HARVEY, Frederick W. md 31 Dec 1983 Danville, NH MILLER, Kathleen A.; md by Linda L. Meader (JP)

HARVEY, Frederick Wilfred 4 b 14 Jul 1984 Exeter, NH s/o HARVEY, Fred. Wilfred & MILLER, Kathleen A.

HARVEYWOOD, Timothy Terrance md 15 Jul 1989 Danville, NH CURRIER, Brenda Lee; md by Rich J. Rondeau (JP)

HASKELL, Benj b c1889 Westbrook, ME s/o HASKELL, Edwin J.; md 26 Aug 1914 Danville, NH; YORK, Eva M.; md by Rev Dorr A. Hudson

HASKINEN, Hilia b Finland; md COLLINS, Herbert L.

HASKINS, Gail P. md 20 Oct 1985 Danville, NH ROESSLER, Paul W.; md by Leo E. Beaulieu (JP)

HASSETT, Catherine M. b Nova Scotia d/o HASSETT, Wm & McALPIN, Margaret; md SMITH, ---- ; d; 22 Dec 1899 ae 61y

HASSETT, Grace E. b 1888 Weymouth, Nova Scotia d/o HASSETT, Wm & McALPIN, Margaret; md 03 Jul 1903

HASSETT (Cont.) Portsmouth, NH
YEATON, Everett H.; md by Rev Geo. E.
Leighton

HATCH, Etta b c1856 Fairfield, ME
d/o HATCH, Benj F.; md 25 Jun 1910
Danville, NH JOHNSON, George H. M.;
md by Clarence M. Collins (JP); 3rd mar

HAYDEN, Leslie Jean md 24 Aug
1991 Danville, NH WEBB, Leslie Jean;
md by Rev Robert W, Karman

HAYDEN, Walter b 14 Feb 1908
Danville, NH s/o HAYDEN, Frank &
COSGROVE, Ella; d 20 Aug 1908 Dan-
ville, NH ae 6m 19d

HAYES, Doris M. md 12 Oct 1984
Danville, NH MITCHELL, Robert C.; md
by Steven W. Lewis (JP)

HAYES, Judith A. md 11 Apr 1987
Danville, NH MacDONALD, Jos J.; md
by Rev Everett E. Palmer

HAYFORD, Sarah Etta b c1889
Haverhill, MA d/o HAYFORD, Henry H.;
md 26 Mar 1914 Danville, NH EMERY,
John W.; md by Rev Allen C. Keith; Also
md to MOREY, ----

HAYMAN, Susan E. b 1949 MA; md
21 Sep 1968 Danville, NH CROZIER,
James E.; md by Rev Douglas Abbott

HAYNES, Harriet May b Newton,
NH d/o HAYNES, Bradley M. &
BARKER, Sarah A.; md CHENEY, ---- ;
d 23 Oct 1949 Danville, NH

HAYNES, Sylvester b c1789 Sud-
bury, MA; md 1859 Danville, NH
PIERCE, Nancy

HEAD, Adah b Salem, NH s/o
HEAD, Chas & HUMPREY, Barbara;
md MOREY, ---- ; d 30 Dec 1908 Danville, NH ae 44y 2m 27d

HEAD, David R. md 09 Aug 1986
Danville, NH COLLINS, Robin J.; md by
Thos D. Welch Jr. (JP)

HEALEY, Brian K. md 22 Jun 1985
Danville, NH BROWN, Lori A.; md by
Rev Everett E. Palmer

HEALEY, Lillian b 1925 Chester,
NH d/o HEALEY, Everett F.; md 03 Feb
1934 Danville, NH SEAVER, Gerald; md
by Rev James A. Sawyer

HEANEY, Donald M. Jr. b 13 Aug
1936 Danville, NH s/o HEANEY, Donald
M. Sr. & BRYANT, Marion Eloizabeth

HEANEY, Judith b 01 Nov 1937
Danville, NH d/o HEANEY, Donald M.
Sr. & BRYANT, Marion Eliz

HEATH, Carroll Richard b Danville,
NH; s/o HEATH, John F. & DUFFUS,
Eliza; d 20 Nov 1942 Danville, NH ae
51y 3m 19d

HEATH, David James b 1927
Cambridge, MA s/o HEATH, Carroll
Rich; md 03 Jul 1949 Danville NH
BROWN, Doris Eliz; md by Rev Harry L.
Lesure

HEATH, David Wayne b 18 Sep 1951
Danville, NH s/o HEATH, David James
& BROWN, Doris Eliz

HEATH, Edgar Andrew b 19 Aug
1941 Danville, NH s/o HEATH, Edgar
Ernest & KENNY, Annamae

HEATH, Edgar Ernest b Kingston,
NH; md KENNY, Annamae

HEATH, Enoch b Hampstead, NH;
md 23 Apr 1803 Hampstead, NH
PLUMMER, Hannah

HEATH, Ethel Louise b 26 Jun 1879
Danville, NH d/o HEATH, John F. &
BEATTIE, Mary; d 03 Oct 1951 Danville,
NH; or mother COLLINS, Emma S.

HEATH, Etta A. b c1870 E Hamp-
stead, NH d/o HEATH, Waldo &
COLLINS, Philura; md 22 Nov 1888
Danville, NH DARBE, Mahlon B.; d 09
Mar 1937 Danville, NH ae 72y 6m 26d

HEATH, Fred Andrew b 02 Mar
1883 S Kingston, NH s/o HEATH,
Franklin G. A. & KIMBALL, Ellen; d 23
May 1958 Danville, NH

HEATH, George E. b c1856 s/o
HEATH, Wm S. L. & WEBSTER, Dorothy; d 25 Aug 1858 Danville, NH ae 2y

HEATH, Howard C. b 19 Dec 1883
Danville, NH s/o HEATH, John F. &
COLLINS, Emma Susan

HEATH, John F. b c1846 Haverhill,
MA s/o HEATH, John Peaslee &
SOUTHER, Eliza Ann; md 30 May 1890
Danville, NH DUFFUS, Eliza; d 28 Sep
1931 Danville, NH; 2nd m of John F.; md
by Rev J. A. Lowell

HEATH, John W. b c1840 Kingston,
NH; md 27 Nov 1864 Danville, NH
WHITE, Alice A.

HEATH, Mary b c1860; d 19 Jan

HEATH (Cont.) 1860 Danville, NH ae 1y

HEATH, Mary McKinney d 08 Feb 1972 Danville, NH ae 85y

HEATH, Mary P. W. b c1830 Kingston, NH d/o HEATH, Neld & WINSLOW, Eliza; md 22 Nov 1885 Danville, NH CURRIER, David B.; d 07 Jun 1913 Danville, NH ae 83y; 2nd m Mary & 2nd David

HEATH, Rhoda b Hawke, NH; md 21 Nov 1794 Kingston, NH PLUMMER, Nathan

HEATH, Waldo md COLLINS, Philura

HEATH, Wm Folsom b 1854 Kingston, NH s/o HEATH, Wm S. L. & WEBSTER, Dorothy; md 31 Dec 1896 Danville, NH WILSON, Agnes; d 05 Nov 1929 Danville, NH; md by Rev Rufus P. Gardner; also md to TUTTLE, ----

HEATH, Wm S. L. b c1834 Kingston, NH s/o HEATH, Weld & WINSLOW, Eliza; md WEBSTER, Dorothy; d 29 Apr 1919 Danville, NH ae 85y 1m 29d

HEATH, Wm T. b Salisbury, MA; md 02 Feb 1842 Raymond, NH SARGENT, Sarah

HECKMAN, Erik Banks b 17 Jun 1967 Danville, NH s/o HECKMAN, Robert Tracey & TRACEY, Martha Gay

HECKMAN, Kenneth C. b 13 Apr 1970 Exeter, NH s/o HECKMAN, Robert T. & TRACEY, Martha Gay

HENDERSON, Edward K. b 30 Jan 1896 Danville s/o HENDERSON, Fred & DAVIS, May

HENDERSON, Fred md DAVIS, May

HENDERSON, Wm McCR b Watertown, MA s/o HENDERSON, James R. & McCREARY, Celestine; d 26 Jan 1947 Danville ae 67y 5m 26d

HENRY, Sara C. md 01 Nov 1986 Danville, NH O'NEIL, Michael J.; md by Richard J. Rondeau (JP)

HERRICK, Gloria Louise b 07 Jul 1942 Haverhill, MA d/o HERRICK, Melvin R. & DEMAINE, Gertrude E.; md 01 Dec 1956 Danville, NH COLLINS, Merville Sidney; md by Agnes H. Collins (JP)

HERRICK, Margaret Verna b 02 May 1934 Danville, NH d/o HERRICK, Melvin R. & DEMAINE, Gertrude E.; md 07 Nov 1959 Danville, NH WAGNER, Andrew Jos; md by L. Evelyn Bake (JP)

HERRICK, Melvin Russell b 1912 Hampton Falls, NH s/o HERRICK, Robert F.; md 04 Oct 1933 Danville, NH DEMAINE, Gertrude Eliz; md by Rev Harold C. Ross

HERRICK, Monika Erika b 20 Oct 1967 Danville d/o HERRICK, Wayne R. & KRAUSCH, Christa H.

HERRICK, Richard Wesley b Plaistow, NH; md 05 Dec 1970 Danville, NH BARBEAU, Betty Jane

HERRICK, Wayne Russell b 23 Jan 1939 Danville, NH s/o HERRICK, Melvin Russell & DEMAINE, Gertrude E.; md 02 Sep 1961 Danville, NH KRAUSCH, Christa H.; md by Rev John Wood Jr.

HERSEY, Clifford Leroy b 1903 MA s/o HERSEY, Frederick J. & BROWN, Hattie L.; md 08 Oct 1950 Danville, NH YOUNG, Ruth Sarah; d 25 May 1974 Danville, NH; md by Rev W. C. Chappell; d ae 71y

HEWEY, Cora M. b 1923 Milo, Me d/o HEWEY, Ellery B.; md 07 Nov 1942 Danville, NH BOOTHBY, Robert C.; md by Rev W. C. Chappell

HEWINS, Walter E. b s/o HEWINS, Walter B. & BANCROFT, Emma; d 03 Nov 1971 Danville, NH ae 89y

HEWITT, Robert d 22 Feb 1946 Danville, NH ae 54

HICKOX, Williame Bisban b Litchfield, MA s/o HICKOX, George & BRISBANE, Mary; d 23 Dec 1941 Danville, NH ae 78y 9m 5d

HICKS, Robert Arthur b s/o HICKS, Chas & NESTER, Sarah; d 11 May 1957 Danville, NH

HICKS, Ronald A. b 1938 Newburyport, MA; md 03 Apr 1965 Danville, NH SWEET, Shelia Ann; md by Rev Douglas W. Abbott

HILBERG, Herbert J. b 1896 Salem, NH s/o HILBERG, Julius; md 12 Dec 1935 Danville, NH LAWRENCE, Evelyn M.; md by Rev W. C. Chappell

HILDRETH, Teri Lynn md 21 Jun 1975 Danville, NH BORGES, Frank Michael; md by Joan M. Pichowicz (JP)

HILL, Doris Collins b 25 Oct 1906 Danville, NH d/o HILL, George & COLLINS, Jennie W.

HILL, Ella F. b c1868 Kittery, ME; md 17 Jun 1884 Danville, NH BROWN, Harry D.

HILL, George b c1875 Haverhill, MA s/o HILL, G. J.; md 14 Oct 1902 Danville, NH COLLINS, Jennie W.; md by Rev A. B. Howard

HILL, Louise b 1906 Laconia, NH d/o HILL, A. E.; md 30 Oct 1925 Exeter, NH JACKSON, Wilfred L.; md by Frank A. Batchelder (JP)

HILL, Newell F. b c1843 S Hampton, NH; md 28 Feb 1864 Danville, NH TUCKER, Emma

HILL, Priscilla J. b 1949 NH; md 12 Oct 1968 Danville, NH MUDGE, David T.; md by Rev John Wood

HILL, Sally b c1792 Hawke, NH; md 01 Jan 1811 Kingston, NH DEARBORN, Jonathan; d 21 May 1885 Danville, NH

HILLARD, Sarah J. md COLLINS, Reubin Milo

HILLNER, Adam John b 02 Oct 1976 Lawrence, MA s/o HILLNER, John R. & HOVANASIAN, Ann E.

HILLNER, Benj Wm b 14 Apr 1979 Lawrence, MA s/o HILLNER, John R. & HOVANASIAN, Ann E.

HIMOT, David Nathan b 02 Aug 1972 Haverhill, MA s/o HIMOT, Peter & BOWDEN, Jain

HINCHCLIFFE, Patricia H. md 17 Aug 1991 Danville, NH BEAN, David Wm; md by Richard J. Rondeau (JP)

HINES, Agnes Leath b Boston, MA d/o HINES, John & ROBINSON, Ann; md COONEY, Wm; d 16 Aug 1947 Danville, NH

HINES, Edward W. b Haverhill, MA; md 03 Sep 1881 Danville, NH MERRICK, Annie C.

HOBBS, Edwin Howard b; Manchester, NH s/o HOBBS, Thos; md 12 Jun 1920 Derry, NH by Rev W. H. Morrison

HOBBS, Eliz b of Brentwood, NH; md 02 Sep 1781 KINESTON, Job; md by Rev John Page

HOBBS, Sarah b c1702 d/o HOBBS, Morris; md TOWLE, Anthony

HOCH, Sandra Marie md 29 Sep 1990 Danville, NH MANGINE, John O'Donnell; md by Wallace J. Anctil (JP)

HODGKINS, F. A. E. b 1871 Newburyport, MA s/o HODGKINS, B. G.; md 20 Sep 1890 Danville, NH SARGENT, Edith E.; md by Rev J. A. Lowell

HOEFFLIN, Debra A. md 09 Jun 1991 Danville, NH BROCKELBANK, Richard L.; md by Richard J. Rondeau (JP)

HOIT, Eliz b of Poplin, NH; md 28 Feb 1769 Hawke, NH SLEEPER, Gideon; md by Rev John Page

HOLBROOK, Arthur L. b s/o HOLBROOK, Amos M. & STOCKER, Emma; d 13 Jul 1975 Danville ae 69y

HOLDER, Jason Daniels md 26 Jun 1976 Danville, NH BOYLE, Anne Eliz; md by Robert J. Boyle (P)

HOLDER, Jason John b 06 Dec 1978 Exeter, NH s/o HOLDER, Jason Daniels & BOYLE, Anne Eliz

HOLLAND, Geo D. b 1887 Concord, NH s/o HOLLAND, James & DERBY, Agnes; d 03 Aug 1955 Danville, NH

HOLLAND, Ida May b Boston, MA d/o PERKINS, Chas & MAIN, Prudence; d 21 Nov 1963 Danville, NH ae 74y

HOLLAND, John b Brentwood, NH; md 21 May 1776 Hawke, NH DARLING, Susanna; md by Rev John Page

HOLLORAN, Timothy A. md 10 Aug 1985 Danville, NH MULCHAHEY, Pamela H.; md by John H. Lamprey (JP)

HOLMAN, Arthur J. Francis b 1930 MA s/o BRENT, Willoughby A. & md 01 Nov 1958 Danville, NH KENT, Joanne Perley; md by Edward Brunault (JP)

HOLMAN, Jos Allen b 12 Jul 1954 Danville, NH s/o HOLMAN, Arthur J. & CANIDA, Hattie M.

HOLT, Harvey C. b 26 Apr 1893 Danville NH s/o HOLT, Henry & LADD, Etta A.

HOLT, Henry M. C. md LADD, Etta A.; d 16 Nov 1940 Danville, NH ae 77y 9m 28d

HOLT, Louisa b 1889 Sandown, NH d/o HOLT, Henry & LADD, Etta A. d 26 Aug 1891 Danville, NH ae 2y

HOLT, Newell B. b s/o HOLT, Alfred & CHALLIS, Sarah; d 22 Feb 1932 Danville, NH ae 77y 10m 20d

HOLT, Roscoe b 15 Feb 1869 Danville, NH s/o HOLT, Alfred & CHALLIS, Irene C.; d 14 Aug 1943 Danville, NH

HOLT, Roswel b Plaistow, NH d/o HOLT, Alfred & CHALLIS, Sarah; d 27 Sep 1959 Danville, NH ae 86y

HOLT, Victor C. b c1865; d 13 Sep 1865 Danville, NH ae 9m

HONISH, Mildred md 05 Dec 1931 COLLINS, Herbert Morgan

HONSINGER, Lee Vincent b s/o HONSINGER, Jackson E. & SCHILLING, Mildred; d 13 Oct 1975 Danville, NH ae 78y

HOOK, Abigail b 01 Aug 1761 Hawke, NH d/o HOOK, Jacob & BACHELOR, Mary; d 18 Nov 1764 Hawke, NH ae 3y

HOOK, Abraham md 22 Nov 1768 Hawke, NH ELKINS, Rachel; md by Rev John Page

HOOK, Addison W. b Poplin, NH; md 1848 Danville, NH DEARBORN, Emaline M.

HOOK, Andrew Jackson b 16 Dec 1814 Hawke, NH s/o HOOK, Reuben & HOOK, Sarah; d 30 Jul 1817 Hawke, NH ae 2y 7m

HOOK, Anna b 09 Jan 1777 Hawke, NH d/o HOOK, Humphrey & KIMBALL-REDDINGTON, Sara

HOOK, Chas b 21 Jan 1813 Hawke, NH s/o HOOK, James T. & SPOFFORD, Permelia; d 28 Jul 1860 Danville, NH ae 47y

HOOK, Daniel C. b c1831 Fremont, NH; md 1857 Danville, NH FRENCH, Mary A.

HOOK, Dorothy b 03 Jun 1817 Hawke, NH d/o HOOK, James T. & SPOFFORD, Permelia; d 13 Dec 1820 HAWKE, NH ae 3y

HOOK, Dyer Jr. b s/o HOOK, Dyer Sr.; md 01 Dec 1774 Hawke, NH SLEEPER, Sarah

HOOK, Dyer Sr. Lt. b c1720 Salisbury, MA; md BROWN, Hannah; d 11 Mar 1776 Hawke, NH; bu Hawke, NH Old Mtg Hse Cem; d ae 56y

HOOK, Elisha Capt. b c1748; md 1st CLARK, Sarah, 2nd 06 Apr 1809 JONES-LOVERING, Miriam; d 22 Feb 1831 Hawke, NH

HOOK, Eliz b 30 Mar 1760 Hawke, NH d/o HOOK, Humprey & PHILBRICK, Hannah; md 16 Jan 1771 Hawke, NH SANBORN, John; md by Rev John Page

HOOK, Hannah b 15 Apr 1762 Hawke, NH d/o HOOK, Humphrey & PHILBRICK, Hannah

HOOK, Harriet b 05 Apr 1809 Hawke, NH d/o HOOK, Reuben & HOOK, Sarah; md HOYT, Wm

HOOK, Helen M. b c1840 Fremont, NH; md 01 Aug 1863 Danville, NH SARGENT, Bailey

HOOK, Humphrey Jr. b 28 May 1765 Hawke, NH s/o HOOK, Humphrey & PHILBRICK, Hannah; md KIMBALL, Sarah

HOOK, Humphrey Sr. b c1722 Salisbury, MA; md 1st PHILBRICK, Hannah, 2nd KIMBALL, Sarah; d 08 Jan 1801 Hawke ae 79y NH; bu Hawke, NH Old Mtg Hse Cem.

HOOK, Israel b c1754; md 12 Jan 1780 Hawke, NH GRIFFIN, Dorothy; d 23 Mar 1813 bu Danville, NH Old Mtg Hse Cen; d ae 59y Revolution

HOOK, Issac b c1781 s/o HOOK, Israel & GRIFFIN, Dorothy; d 20 Feb 1865 Danville, NH ae 84y

HOOK, Jacob b 10 Jul 1764 Hawke, NH s/o HOOK, Humphrey & PHILBRICK, Hannah; d 10 Jul 1764 Hawke, NH - Infant

HOOK, Jacob Jr. b s/o HOOK, Jacob Sr.; md BACHELOR, Mary; d Dec 1804 Hawke, NH ae 80y

HOOK, James b 05 Apr 1809 Hawke, NH s/o HOOK, James T. & SPOFFORD, Permelia; md 10 Sep 1837 Raymond, NH; SANBORN, Lavina

HOOK, James True b c1798 Hawke, NH; md 27 Sep 1807 Kingston, NH SPOFFORD, Permelia; d 03 Aug 1851 Danville, NH ae 63y

HOOK, Lucy b 15 Oct 1817 Hawke, NH d/o HOOK, Reuben & HOOK, Sarah; d 22 May 1834 Hawke, NH

HOOK, Luella A. b c1775 d/o HOOK, Humphrey & KIMBALL, Sarah; d 21 Sep 1778 Hawke, NH ae 3y

HOOK, Martha b Hawke, NH; md 16 Nov 1769 Hawke, NH SMITH, Jabez; md by Rev John Page

HOOK, Mary md 04 Jan 1769 Hawke, NH QUIMBY, Jeremiah; md by Rev John Page

HOOK, Mary b Hawke, NH; md 1st APPLETON, ---- , 2nd 15 Nov 1798 Kingston, NH GOULD, Daniel (Major)

HOOK, Mary md Aug 1807 Kingston BROWN, Jeremiah

HOOK, Mary b c1794; md 1st SANBORN, Levi, 2nd 18 May 1841 Raymond, NH KIMBALL, Caleb; d 16 Oct 1874 Danville, NH

HOOK, Matilda b 03 Oct 1801 Hawke, NH d/o HOOK, Samuel (of Sandown) & WILLIAMS, Judith

HOOK, Moody A. b 1824 Hawke, NH s/o HOOK, Moody M. & SAWYER, Sarah; d 1839 Danville, NH

HOOK, Moody M. b 1794 Hawke, NH s/o HOOK, Israel & GRIFFIN, Dorothy; md 29 Oct 1818 Kingston, NH SAWYER, Sarah; d 21 Jul 1864 Danville, NH ae 70y

HOOK, Moses b 16 Feb 1823 Hawke, NH s/o HOOK, James T. & SPOFFORD, Permelia; md 09 Jul 1846

HOOK, Oren Spofford b 01 Jun 1825 Hawke, NH s/o HOOK, James T. & SPOFFORD, Permelia; d 27 Feb 1862

Hook, Permelia A. b 1827 Hawke, NH d/o HOOK, James T. & SPOFFORD, Permelia; md 1848 Danville, NH BARTLETT, Hosea B.

HOOK, Peter b 15 Dec 1763 Hawke, NH s/o HOOK, Dyer & BROWN, Hannah

HOOK, Phineas b 07 Jul 1820 Hawke, NH s/o HOOK, James T. & SPOFFORD, Permelia

HOOK, Phineas md 14 Feb 1822 Hampton, NH SAWYER, Betsey

HOOK, Phineas b 26 Feb 1811 Hawke, NH s/o HOOK, James T. & SPOFFORD, Permelia; d 30 Mar 1813 Hawke, NH ae 2y

HOOK, Rebecca b 15 Oct 1801 Hawke, NH s/o HOOK, Reuben &

HOOK (Cont.) HOOK, Sarah; d 07 Jan 1886 Danville, NH

HOOK, Reuben b 22 Jul 1768 Hawke, NH s/o HOOK, Humphrey & PHILBRICK, Hannah; d 24 Dec 1768 Hawke, NH ae 5m

HOOK, Reuben (Capt) b 16 Nov 1778 Hawke, NH s/o HOOK, Humphrey & KIMBALL-REDINGTON,Sara; md 16 Apr 1801 Hawke, NH HOOK, Sarah; d 07 May 1819 Hawke, NH ae 40y

HOOK, Sally b 28 Mar 1815 Hawke, NH d/o HOOK, James T. & SPOFFORD, Permelia; md 10 Mar 1836

HOOK, Sally N. b 24 Dec 1819 Hawke, NH d/o HOOK, Moody M. & SAWYER, Sarah; md 27 Feb 1840 Raymond, NH HOYT, Nathan; d 25 Jul 1879 Danville, NH ae 59y

HOOK, Samuel b Sandown, NH; md 30 Aug 1798 Kingston, NH WILLIAMS, Judith

HOOK, Sarah b 22 Dec 1765 Hawke, NH d/o HOOK, Jacob & BACHELOR, Mary

HOOK, Sarah b Hawke, NH; md 16 Apr 1801 Hawke, NH HOOK, Reuben (Capt) d 23 Jan 1865 Danville, NH ae 85y

HOOK, Sarah Ann b 15 Apr 1812 Hawke, NH d/o HOOK, Reuben & HOOK, Sarah

HOOKE, Helen M. b 1840 Fremont, NH d/o HOOKE, Moses & DIMOND, Nancy; md SARGENT, ---- ; d 13 Mar 1926 Danville, NH

HOPEWELL, James Kennard b Germany; md 13 Sep 1969 Danville, NH FOWLER, Linnnea Audrey; md by Rev Randolph K. Dales (EP)

HORNE, Joanne Glass md 15 Aug 1989 Danville, NH PERREAULT, Frank J.; md by Richard J. Rondeau (JP)

HOSMAN, Kevin D. md 14 Oct 1988 Danville, NH SHEEHAN, Marianne; md by Richard J, Rondeau (JP)

HOULE, Donna Lee b Haverhill, MA; md 02 Jan 1965 Danville, NH HUNT, Harold Alan; md by Rev Douglas W. Abbott

HOWARD, Catherine Nora b 18 Jul 1961 Danville, NH d/o HOWARD, Martin I. & BURKE, Doris L.

HOWARD, Donna M. b Haverhill, MA; md MACKIE, James L.

HOWARD, Ethelyn A. b d/o HOWARD, Wm & COBURN, Carrie; d 19 Feb 1976 Danville, NH ae 84y

HOWARD, Fannie M. b c1851 Haverhill, MA; md 21 Oct 1876 Danville, NH WEBBER, Leonard E.

HOWARD, Frances b 1919 Laconia, NH; d/o HOWARD, George; md 16 Apr 1937 Danville, NH KUTSUMAKIS, Michael; md by Rev O. L. Brownsey

HOWARD, Jennifer Yvonne b 10 Sep 1982 Exeter, NH d/o HOWARD, Raymond, J. Jr. & DeSERRES, Barbara L.

HOWARD, Mariah b c1820; md WOOD, Albert G. Sr; d 30 Sep 1867 Danville, NH ae 47y

HOWARD, Marion Joyce md 05 Oct 1974 Danville, NH CURTIS, Scott Nelson; md by Rev Thos C. Roden

HOWARD, Raymond James Jr. md 15 Aug 1980 Danville, NH DeSERRES, Barbara Louise; md by Rev Wm Ryans

HOWARD, Rebecca Mehgan b 09 Apr 1984 Exeter, NH d/o HOWARD, Raymond J. Jr. & DeSERRES, Barbara Louise

HOWARD, Richard b s/o GEORGE, Frank & HOWE, Manelta; d 17 Nov 1981 Danville, NH ae 91y

HOWE, Celestia E. b Ipswich, MA d/o HOWE, Nathaniel & CHAPMAN, Susan; md BROWN, ---- ; d 31 May 1932 Danville, NH ae 85y 0m 21d

HOWE, Jeffery Marshall b 31 Jul 1977 Haverhill, MA s/o HOWE, Herbert R. & DAYS, Patricia A.

HOWE, Joshua Patrick b 06 Sep 1979 Haverhill, MA s/o HOWE, H. Ronald & DAYS, Patricia A.

HOYT, Abigail b c1798 Amesbury, MA; md 22 Jun 1822 Amesbury, MA EASTMAN, Sewell; d 12 Jul 1823 Hawke, NH ae 25y

HOYT, Andrew Jackson b 02 Sep 1830 Hawke, NH s/o HOYT, Wm & HOOK, Harriet

HOYT, Anne Belle b 14 Aug 1859 Danville, NH d/o HOYT, Nathan & HOOK, Sarah N. md JOHNSON, ---- ; d 04 Oct 1913 Danville, NH

HOYT, Bernard b Haverhill, MA s/o HOYT, Warren & COOK, Isabell; d 13 Feb 1966 Danville, NH ae 67y

HOYT, Betty b 14 Feb 1775 Hawke, NH d/o HOYT, Moses & NELSON, Mary

HOYT, Carrie I. b 11 Aug 1858 Danville, NH d/o HOYT, Nathan & HOOK, Sarah N.

HOYT, Charlotte E. S. b 14 Aug 1849 Danville, NH d/o HOYT, Nathan & HOOK, Sarah N.

HOYT, Ebenezer b 15 Dec 1766 Hawke, NH s/o HOYT, Moses & NELSON, Mary

HOYT, Emma S. b 31 Mar 1840 Danville, NH d/o HOYT, Willaim & HOOK, Harriet; d 19 Dec 1922 Danville, NH

HOYT, Eva b d/o HOYT, Francis M. & MESERVE, Eliza; d Jul 1869 Danville, NH

HOYT, Francis M. b 29 Mar 1842 Danville, NH s/o HOYT, Nathan & HOOK, Sarah N.

HOYT, Hazel Marie b c1886 Valpariso, IN d/o HOYT, Will I.; md 28 Aug 1907 Haverhill, NH WITHERELL, Clem. W.; md by Rev Arthur G. Lyon

HOYT, Huldah b c1839 Sandown, NH; md MESERVE, Winifield S. d 04 Aug 1872 Danville, NH; ae 33y

HOYT, Ida b d/o HOYT, Francis M. & MESERVE, Eliza; d Jul 1869 Danville, NH

HOYT, Jos (Capt) md 06 Mar 1820 Hawke, NH ----, BROWN, Ruth

HOYT, Laura A. b 14 Oct 1847 Danville, NH d/o HOYT, Nathan & HOOK, Sarah N.

HOYT, Levi b 1836 Chester, NH s/o HOYT, Batchelder & TILTON, Sarah; d 30 Apr 1891 Danville, NH ae 55y; Occupation Merchant

HOYT, Lewis C. b 26 Jan 1833 Hawke, NH s/o HOYT, Wm & HOOK, Harriet; d 12 Nov 1860 Danville, NH ae 28y

HOYT, Lois b 08 Dec 1768 Hawke, NH d/o HOYT, Moses & NELSON, Mary

HOYT, Lucy Ann b 07 Jan 1837 Danville, NH d/o HOYT, Wm & HOOK, Harriet

HOYT, Luella b c1850 Hampstead, NH; md 24 Jul 1870 Danville, NH SARGENT, Moses H.

HOYT, Mary A. b c1844 Hampstead, NH; md Mar 1863 Danville, NH GRIFFIN, Calvin B.

HOYT, Mary O. b Danville, NH d/o HOYT, Stephen; md COLLINS, ---- ; d 31 Dec 1933 Danville, NH ae 74y 6m 12d

HOYT, Molly b 14 Feb 1775 Hawke, NH d/o HOYT, Moses & NELSON, Mary

HOYT, Moses b 11 Apr 1773 Hawke, NH s/o HOYT, Moses & NELSON, Mary

HOYT, Nathan b Hawke, NH; md 27 Feb 1840 Raymond, NH HOOK, Sally N.

HOYT, Nathan b 1821 Sandown, NH s/o HOYT, Wm Howard & FRENCH, Betsy; md 30 Nov 1893 Manchester, NH OSGOOD, Mary A.; d 22 Feb 1903 Danville, NH; md by Rev Nath'l L. Colby

HOYT, Otis A. b c1820; d 07 Sep 1887 Danville, NH

HOYT, Sarah A. b 19 Apr 1845 Danville, NH d/o HOYT, Wm & HOOK, Harriet; d 18 Apr 1925 Danville, NH

HOYT, Simeon md 23 Dec 1777 Hawke, NH MORRILL, Miriam

HOYT, Warren b 04 Jan 1843 Hawke, NH s/o HOYT, Wm & HOOK, Harriet; md COOK, Isabel; d 26 Apr 1918 Danville, NH ae 75y 3m 22d

HOYT, Wm b 1806 Sandown, NH; s/o HOYT, Wm Howard & FRENCH, Betsy; md HOOK, Harriet; d 01 Jun 1892 ae 85y 6m; Occupation - Farmer

HOYT, Wm Howard b 05 Jul 1782 Hawke, NH s/o HOYT, Ebenezer & NICHOLS, Sarah; md FRENCH, Betsy

HOYT, Wm Jr b of Chester, NH; md 07 Sep 1802 Hawke, NH BASFORD, Betsey

HOYT, Wilton Harland b 1896 s/o HOYT, WArren & COOK, Isabell; d 11 Jun 1956 Danville, NH

HUBBARD, Mercy md 1st PRESSY, Paul, 2nd James Nichols

HUBBARD, Sarah b of KIngston, NH; md 23 Nov 1769 Hawke, NH CHASE, Francis; md by Rev John Page

HUCKINS, Edmond James b 1926 MA s/o HUCKINS, Everett P.; md 31 Mar 1951 Sandown, NH THIBEAULT, Mary Louise; md by Rev Wm B. Wylie

HUCKINS, Mary Louise md 22 Dec 1978 Danville, NH DUSTON, Robert Oscar; md by Rev Wm Ryans

HUDSON, Rebekah Susan b 16 Jul 1981 Manchester, NH d/o HUDSON, David W. & CONEFREY, Shirley A.

HUGHES, Jane R. md 27 Sep 1975 Danville, NH GAGE, Steven Lindsay

HUGHES, John Kenneth md 22 Jun 1991 Danville, NH MULCAHEV, Barbara Hope; md by Rev Kent W. Johnson

HUGHES, Mary E. b c1834 Hampstead, NH; md 1857 Danville, NH WOOD, Orville

HUGHES, Wm Lawrence Jr. md 12 Aug 1990 Danville, NH MURPHY, Elanor; md by Richard J. Rondeau (JP)

HUNDLEY, Rachael Eliz b 07 Apr 1987 Lawrence, MA d/o HUNDLEY, Roy A. Sr. & MARR, Roblyn P.

HUNKINS, E. L. b c1841 Haverhill, MA; md 09 Feb 1866 Danville, NH BLAKE, Hannah R.

HUNKINS, Juliann b c1831 Haverhill, MA; md CURRIER, David Barnard; d 15 Jun 1871 Danville, NH ae 40y

HUNKINS, Nellie L. b 1875 Haverhill, MA; d/o HUNKINS, Daniel & HAMMETT, Mary A.; md 01 Nov 1896 Haverhill, MA MERRILL, Lewis S.

HUNT, Albert b s/o HUNT, Mansfield & QUINN, Maria; d 14 Jan 1982 Danville, NH ae 87y

HUNT, Arlene Beatrice b 18 Apr 1943 Danville, NH d/o HUNT, John Hollowell & ARNOLD, Beatrice Helen; md 27 Aug 1959 Danville, NH POND, Edward Emerson; md by John O. Perkins (JP)

HUNT, Barbara Elaine b 1938 d/o HUNT, John H.; md 29 Dec 1957 Danville, NH KING, Jos Austin

HUNT, Betsey b Hawke, NH; md 25 Nov 1830 Kingston, NH DEARBORN, Samuel

HUNT, Betsey b Sandown, NH; md 08 Oct 1809 Hawke, NH ANDERSON, Moses

HUNT, Betsy b 31 Dec 1811 Hawke, NH d/o HUNT, Henry & POLLARD, Mercy

HUNT, Chas Pollard. b 1861 Danville, NH s/o HUNT, Oliver & BROWN,

HUNT (Cont.) Sarah; d 20 Jun 1876 Danville, NH ae 15y

HUNT, Dororthy P. b 14 Jul 1815 Hawke, NH d/o HUNT, Henry & POLLARD, Mercy; md 24 Nov 1831 Kingston, NH WEBSTER, Elihu T.; d 08 Mar 1833 Hawke, NH ae 17y 8m

HUNT, E. Woodbury b Danville, NH s/o HUNT, Oliver & PAGE, Lydia; d 02 Apr 1911 Danville, NH ae 64y 3m 26d

HUNT, Eben Woodward b 25 Dec 1846 Danville, NH; md 1861 Danville, NH BATCHELDER, Hannah W.

HUNT, Ernest Raymond b 20 Mar 1940 Danville, NH s/o HUNT, John H. & ARNOLD, Beatrice H.; md 19 Sep 1961 Danville, NH CLARK, Mary Virginia; md by Rev Wendall J. Irvine

HUNT, Hannah b 1821 Hawke, NH d/o HUNT, Henry & POLLARD, Mercy; d 24 Dec 1825 Hawke, NH

HUNT, Harold Allen b 02 Jul 1945 Derry, NH s/o HUNT, John Hallowell & ARNOLD, Beatrice Helen; md 02 Jan 1965 Danville, NH HOULE, Donna Lee; md by Rev Douglas W. Abbott

HUNT, Henry b c1797; d 29 Jul 1870 Danville, NH ae 73y 9m

HUNT, Henry b 10 Nov 1782 Hawke, NH s/o HUNT, Moses & PEASLEE, Mary;md POLLARD. Mercy; d 01 Sep 1862 Danville, NH ae 80y

HUNT, Henry md 22 Mar 1770 Hawke, NH SEVER, Eliz; md by Rev John Page

HUNT, Hilda b Hudson, NH; md ARNOLD, Theodore F.

HUNT, Hilda May b d/o HUNT, John & BALL, Lucy md TOWNE, ---- ; d 18 Jul 1971 Danville, NH ae 55y

HUNT, John b 08 Oct 1807 Hawke, NH s/o HUNT, Henry & POLLARD, Mercy; md DEARBORN, Eliz R.; d 02 May 1885 Danville, NH ae 77y

HUNT, John Hallowell b Haverhill, MA; md ARNOLD, Beatrice Helen

HUNT, John P. b 03 Sep 1838 Danville, NH s/o HUNT, John & DEARBORN, Eliz R.; md 1st 1859 Danville, NH WITHERELL, Sarah L., 2nd 16 Apr 1864 Danville, NH GRIFFIN, Sarah A.; d 1889 Danville, NH

HUNT, Leon Ernest b 13 Aug 1972 Exeter, NH s/o HUNT, Ernest R. & GRABIEC, Susan L.

HUNT, Lucy b 22 Apr 1817 Hawke, NH d/o HUNT, Henry & POLLARD, Mercy; md Jul 1834 Hawke, NH WEBSTER, Elihu T.; d 12 Jul 1840 Danville, NH ae 23y

HUNT, Lucy Alcina b 10 Feb 1841 Danville, NH d/o HUNT, John & DEARBORN, Eliz R.; md 09 Jan 1862 Danville, NH TOWLE, Frederick A.

HUNT, Mabel b S Hampton, NH; md McNEIL, Stanley

HUNT, Malcolm Hallowwell b 28 Sep 1937 Danville, NH s/o HUNT, John H. & ARNOLD, Beatrice H.; md 18 Oct 1962 Danville, NH WEIZANSKI, Janice Kershaw; md by Arthur M. Comeau

HUNT, Miriam b 20 Dec 1809 Hawke, NH; d/o HUNT, Henry & POLLARD, Marcy; md DEARBORN, James; d 13 Mar 1853 Danville, NH

HUNT, Miriam b Kingston, NH; md 03 Feb 1789 Kingston NH QUIMBY, Paul

HUNT, Miriam md May 1809 Kingston, NH BLAKE, Israel

HUNT, Nancy W. b Kingston, NH; md c1855 Danville, NH BASSETT, Amos

HUNT, Nathan B. b 1835 Hawke, NH s/o HUNT, John & DEARBORN, Eliz R.; d 18 Oct 1838 Danville NH ae 3y

HUNT, Oliver b; Kingston, NH s/o HUNT, Steven & WOODMAN, Polly; d 21 Mar 1901 ae 82y 2m 19d

HUNT, Page A. b 1845 Danville, NH s/o HUNT, Oliver & PAGE, Lydia; md BRADLEY, Mary; d 01 Oct 1876 Danville, NH ae 31y

HUNT, Polly b 03 Jul 1806 Hawke, NH d/o HUNT, Henry & POLLARD, Mercy; md DEARBORN, Jos; d 19 Jul 1892 Danville, NH

HUNT, Ruth S. b Kingston, NH; md 06 Apr 1841 Raymond, NH WEBSTER, Elihu T.

HUNT, Sally b 17 Oct 1813 Hawke, NH d/o HUNT, Henry & POLLARD, Mercy

HUNT, Sarah J. b c1837 Kingston, NH; md c1855 Danville, NH JOHNSON,

HUNT (Cont.) Nathaniel K.

HUNT, Sherry Lee b 03 May 1971 Exeter, NH d/o HUNT, Ernest R. & GRABLEC, Susan L.

HUNT, Stephen b Kingston, NH; md 2nd Feb 1796 Kingston, NH WOOD-MAN, Polly

HUNT, ---- b: 05 Sep 1941 Danville, NH ?/o HUNT, John H. & ARNOLD, Beatrice H.

HUNTINGTON, AlLan L. b Danville, NH s/o HUNTINGTON, Chas P.; md 28 Sep 1901 COLLINS, Alice Lincoln

HUNTINGTON, Allen A. b 01 Feb 1881 Danville, NH s/o HUNTINGTON, Chas H. & SIMMONDS, Nellie B.; d 24 Sep 1965 Danville, NH

HUNTINGTON, Chas B. b 1849 Danville, NH s/o HUNTINGTON, Wm & BLAISDELL, Eliz; d 10 Oct 1890 Danville, NH d ae 41y 7m 2d of Consumption

HUNTINGTON, Clara b 21 Dec 1873 Danville, NH d/o HUNTINGTON, Chas H. & SIMMONDS, Nellie B.

HUNTINGTON, Dana C. b 29 Nov 1898 Danville, NH s/o HUNTINGTON, Sidney W. & GEORGE, Ada L.;

HUNTINGTON, Donald Remick -b; 20 May 1901 s/o HUNTINGTON, Sidney W. & GEORGE, Ada L.; 2nd child in family

HUNTINGTON, Dora B. b 26 Apr 1876 Danville, NH d/o HUNTINGTON, Chas H. & SIMMONDS, Nellie B.; md 06 Nov 1897 Danville, NH GRIFFIN, Calvin B.; d 03 Apr 1958 Danville, NH; md by A. B. Howard (JP)

HUNTINGTON, Grace C. b 1874 Danville, NH d/o HUNTINGTON, Chas H. & SIMMONDS, Nellie B.; md 02 May 1896 Danville, NH MARTIN, Wm; d 05 Mar 1951 Danville, NH; md by Rev J. A. Wiggin; also md SMITH, ----

HUNTINGTON, Hannah b Amesbury, MA; md 18 Mar 1824 Amesbury, MA PLUMMER, Samuel

HUNTINGTON, Harry b c1882 Danville, NH s/o HUNTINGTON, Chas H. & SIMMONDS, Nellie B.; d 10 Jan 1906 Danville, NH

HUNTINGTON, John H. b 08 Jun 1883 Danville, NH; s/o HUNTINGTON, Chas H. & SIMMONDS, Nellie B.

HUNTINGTON, Mary E. b 25 Feb 1836 Hawke, NH d/o HUNTINGTON, Wm & BLAISDELL, Mary E.; md SHORES, ----; d 15 Apr 1912 Danville, NH

HUNTINGTON, Mary E. b 08 Dec 1879 Danville, NH d/o HUNTINGTON, Chas H. & SIMMONDS, Nellie B.

HUNTINGTON, Sidney Wm b 24 Sep 1878 Danville, NH s/o HUNTING-TON, Chas H. & SIMMONDS, Nellie B.; md 04 Dec 1897 Danville, NH GEORGE, Ada Lillian; d 11 May 1944 Danville, NH; md by A. B. Howard (JP)

HUNTINGTON, Wm b Amesbury, MA; md BLAISDELL, Eliz

HUNTINGTON, Wm H. b c1808 Danville, NH; md 1848 Danville, NH EADES, Betsey A.

HUNTLEY, Delbert M. b s/o HUNTLEY, Irvin & GALLISON, Ina L.; d 23 Mar 1975 Danville, NH ae 57y

HUNTLEY, Ina b d/o GALLISON, Wm & BUZZELL, Eliz; d 22 Feb 1967 Danville, NH ae 73y

HUNTOON, Diane B. md 12 Oct 1985 Danville, NH POST, Mark R.; md by Rev Donald F. Jennings

HUNTOON, John b Jan 1838 s/o HUNTOON, Wm & ----, Mary; d 07 Feb 1838 Danville, NH age 21 days

HURD, Cherie A. md 22 Apr 1990 Danville, NH LAMB, Edward Reeves; md by Rev Allen W. Cook

HURD, Harry Elmore b 1889 Goshen, NH s/o HURD, Henry; md 03 Sep 1934 Danville, NH MAGISON, Eleanor R.; md by Clarence M. Collins (JP)

HUSEBY, George A. b Boston, MA s/o HUSEBY, Adolph L. &; md 07 Mar 1942 Danville, NH DEMING, Edna M.; md by Rev W. C. Chappell

HUSSEY, Cora Belle b Newburyport, MA d/o HUSSEY, Benj & TEEL, Louise; md GRIFFIN, ---- ; d 16 Apr 1944 Danville, NH ae 69y 11m 16d

HUTCHINGS, Molly md 16 May 1781 Hawke, NH EMERSON, Mark; md by Rev John Page

HUTCHINS, Helen b 1916 Dennisport, MA d/o HUTCHINS, Wm; md 30 Sep 1941 Danville, NH FIELD, Robert Harris; md by Rev W. C. Chappell

HUTCHINS, Neil Francis b 04 Apr 1937 Danville, NH s/o HUTCHINS, Orville R. & HUSTON, Ida

HUTCHINSON, Heather Ann b 05 Jun 1977 Beverly, MA d/o HUTCHINSON, Robert L. & GRAY, Bonnie Lee

HUTCHINSON, Matthew Garrett b 05 Jul 1981 Exeter, NH s/o HUTCHINSON, Robert L. Jr. & GRAY, Bonnie Lee

HUTCHINSON, Theodate md 11 Aug 1762 Hawke, NH DEARBORN, Henry

HYDE, Emma M. b Danville, NH d/o HYDE, Alban B. & MARROW, Edith B.; d 12 Mar 1905 Danville, NH ae 3m 22d

INGALLS, John C. F. md 16 Feb 1837 Danville, NH COLBY, Emily Tilton

INGALLS, Joy Lenore md 11 Sep 1977 Danville, NH GERRISH, Richard Earl; md by Rev Robert E. Aspinwall

INGALLS, Norman Robert b Eppimg, NH; md: GOVE, Arline Priscilla

INGALLS, Wendall Norman b 08 Jan 1955 Danville, NH s/o INGALLS, Norman Rob't & GOVE, Arline Priscilla

INGALLS, Weslie Ann md 11 Sep 1971 Danville, NH EPPICH, Frederick Stephen; md by Rev Henry K. Mack

INGERSON, Joyce Catherine md 08 Sep 1979 Danville NH COLLINS, Wayne Allan; md by Steven Kucharski (P)

INGLES, Frank b Tupperville Nova Scotia md DANIELS, Dora

INGLES, Dorothy Tryphenia b 28 Aug 1933 Danville, NH d/o INGLIS, Frank & DANIELS, Dora

INGRAHAM, Christine Lyne md 31 Dec 1991 Danville, NH COMEAU, Brian M.; md by Rich J. Rondeau (JP)

INGRAM, Michael Ernest md 08 Apr 1978 Danville, NH SMITH, Deborah Lynn; md by Roy Daubenspeck (JP)

INGRAM, Robert E. b s/o INGRAM, Edward & ARSENAULT, Mary J.; d 25 Sep 1979 Danville, NH; d ae 56y

IRVING, Orphia L. b 1868 d/o IRVING, Chas & BOODAY, Lazetta md EASTMAN, ----; d 10 Mar 1924 Danville, NH ae 55y 5m 5d

JACKMAN, Lance Earl b 09 May 1950 Danville, NH s/o JACKMAN, Leon Wesley & HARGRAVES, Florence Evelyn

JACKMAN, Lee Hargraves b 22 Apr 1944 Danville, NH s/o JACKMAN, Leon Wesley & HARGRAVES, Florence Evelyn

JACKMAN, Leon Ernest b Windsor, ?; md HARGRAVES, Florence Evelyn

JACKMAN, Linda b 19 Aug 1941 Danville, NH d/o JACKMAN, Leon Wesley & HARGRAVES, Florence Evelyn

JACKSON, Arthur b 09 Jun 1908 Danville, NH s/o JACKSON, Lester & AVERY, Viola

JACKSON, Barbara L. md 13 Oct 1985 Danville, NH BRIGGS, Walter H.; md by Bette C. Ouellette (JP)

JACKSON, Donna Mae b 1936 MA; md 22 Sep 1956 Danville, NH StONGE, Leo F.; md by Rev C. F. Cahill (P)

JACKSON, Edith b 12 Dec 1913 Danville, NH s/o JACKSON, Raymond & Anderson, Marcia; md BURBANK, ---- ; 6th child in family

JACKSON, Eleanor Annie b 23 Dec 1907 Danville, NH d/o JACKSON, Raymond & ANDERSON, Marcia

JACKSON, Guy d 23 Dec 1941 Danville, NH ae 72y 2m 17d

JACKSON, Louise H. d 07 Mar 1977 Danville, NH ae 71y

JACKSON, Ralph R. b 1902 Kenabunkport, ME s/o JACKSON, Raymonbd W.; md 04 Nov 1922 Bradford, MA FOOTE, Eliz V.; md by Rev Theo R. Bundy

JACKSON, Raymond b Kenabunkport, ME; md ANDERSON, Marcia

JACKSON, Raymond W. b Portsmouth, NH s/o JACKSON, Wesley & LORD, Addie; md 30 Nov 1901 by Rev A. B. Howard; d 21 Feb 1920 ae 37y 6m 12d Danville, NH

JACKSON, Richard W. b s/o JACKSON, Wilfred Lester Sr. & HILL, Louise; d 24 Mar 1939 Danville, NH

JACKSON, Thelma May b 21 Mar 1912 Danville, NH d/o JACKSON, Raymond & ANDERSON, Marcia

JACKSON, Wilfred Lester Jr. b 10 May 1927 Danville, NH s/o JACKSON, Wilfred Lester Sr. & HILL, Louise; d 14 Feb 1953 Danville, NH

JACKSON, Wilfred Lester Sr. b 1904 Danville, NH s/o JACKSON, Raymond & ANDERSON, Marcia; md 30 Oct 1925 Exeter, NH HILL, Louise; md by Frank A. Batchelder (JP)

JACKSON, ---- b 10 Aug 1903 Danville, NH s/o JACKSON, Raymond & ANDERSON, Marcia; d 10 Aug 1903 Danville, NH

JACKSON, ---- b 08 Apr 1926 Danville, NH ?/o JACKSON, Wilfred Lester Sr. & HILL, Louise

JAMES, Annie A. b 12 Aug 1852 Danville, NH d/o JAMES, Jonathan & GEORGE, Sarah; md ARNOLD, James M. d 20 Mar 1902 Danville, NH

JAMES, Jonathan L. md 30 Nov 1841 Raymond, NH GEORGE, Sarah; d 27 Oct 1884 Danville, NH; age 66

JAMES, Mary Frances b 1846 Danville, NH d/o JAMES, Jonathan L. & GEORGE, Sarah; md 18 Jan 1847

JAMES, Mary Teresa b Jan 1849 Danville, NH d/o JAMES, Jonathan L. & GEORGE, Sarah d 09 Jun 1849 Danville, NH

JANOTTA, Ashley Lee b 25 Jul 1988 Haverhill, MA d/o JANOTTA, Kim R. & DUNN, Dorothy J.

JASPER, Dorothy E. b Kingston, NH; md WEST, Chandler B.

JEANS, Kathleen Ann b 1945 MA d/o JEANS, Arthur W.; md 20 Mar 1959 Danville, NH ANDERSON, Harold Curtis; md by Rev John Wood Jr.

JEANS, Marilyn Sandra b 1936 Winchester d/o JEANS, Arthur W.; md 22 Nov 1957 Danville, NH BATTIS, Edward Theodore

JEDRICK, James Thos md 16 May 1978 Danville, NH SILVA, Bonnie Jean; md by Clara B. Snow (JP)

JEFFERSON, Wm Dean b 24 Jan 1976 Manchester, NH s/o JRFFERSON, Norman R. & BURKE, Cynthia R.

JENDRICK, David Phillip md 18 May 1974 Danville, NH CLARK, Nancy Virginia; md by Rev Cathleen R. Narowitz

JENDRICK, Dennis S. md 21 Nov 1979 Danville, NH GAUNTT, Charlotte M.; md by John H. Lamprey (JP)

JENDRICK, James T. md 08 Dec 1979 Danville, NH NICOLO, Jacqueline T.; md by Rev Kenneth A. Dunn

JENDRICK, Lois b Danville, NH; md 14 Nov 1970 Danville, NH KNIGHT, Joseph

JENDRICK, Veronica Lynn b 07 Nov 1980 Haverhill, MA d/o JENDRICK, Frederick P. & WEDGE, Connie B.

JENDRICK, Wayne M. md 15 Aug 1981 Danville, NH CURRIE, Linda J.; md by Rev Paul W. Daneault (P)

JENKINS, Stephen Michael b of Danville, NH; md COMTOIS, Viddle Jean

JENNINGS, John C. md 04 Aug 1984 Danville, NH BYRON, Marie Yvonne; md by Everett E. Palmer

JENSEN, Gwendolyn A. md 07 Apr 1972 Danville, NH CUNNINGHAM, Edward A.; md by Rev Herbert J. Moore

JEWELL, John Putnam b 1929 VT s/o JEWELL, George L.; md 22 Oct 1954 Danville, NH THIBEAULT, Emily BerthA; md by Rev Robert S. Walker

JEWELL, Timothy b Newton, NH; md 12 Jul 1764 Hawke, NH WADLEIGH, Ruth; md by Rev John Page

JILLSON, Travis Keith b 04 Feb 1987 Derry, NH s/o JILLSON, Mark S. & FRAIZE, Cathy M.;

JOHNSON, Alden M. b 19 Feb 1858 Danville, NH s/o JOHNSON, Chas K. & MERRILL, Martha L.; md HOYT, Annie Belle; d 11 Apr 1921 Danville, NH

JOHNSON, Chas H. b 15 Oct 1881 Danville, NH s/o JOHNSON, Alden M. & HOYT, Annie B.; md 21

JOHNSON (Cont.) Sep 1904 Danville, NH KIMBALL, Susie M. by Rev A. B. Howard; d 03 Aug 1928 ae 46y 9m 18d

JOHNSON, Chas K. b 29 Aug 1834 Hawke, NH s/o JOHNSON, Daniel & GEORGE, Hannah; md 01 Sep 1854 Danville, NH; MERRILL, Martha L.; d 07 Jul 1865 Danville, NH; or d age 34, 13 Jul 1868

JOHNSON, Daniel b 1809; md GEORGE, Hannah; d 10 Apr 1885 Danville, NH; d age 76 yr

JOHNSON, Daniel S. b 1863 Danville, NH; md 07 Jan 1863 Danville, NH MARCH, Adeline B. d 02 Dec 1871 age 40 yr - Civil War

JOHNSON, Derek Scot b 16 Sep 1989 Exeter, NH s/o JOHNSON, Gardner A. Jr. & MAYO, Tamela A.

JOHNSON, Donald Wm Jr. b 16 Mar 1990 Exeter, NH s/o JOHNSON, Donald Wm Sr. & SOUTHWICK, Deanna J.

JOHNSON, George H. M. b 1863 Hampstead, NH s/o JOHNSON, Moses H. & md 25 Jun 1910 Danville, NH HATCH, Etta; md by Clarence A, Collins (JP)

JOHNSON, Hannah md 15 Oct 1789 Kingston, NH GEORGE, Wm

JOHNSON, Hannah F. md 03 Jan 1847 Danville, NH; JONES, Ezekiel

JOHNSON, Hattie M. b 20 Sep 1867 Danville, NH d/o JOHNSON, Chas K. & MERRILL, Martha L.; md WITHERELL, Wm A.; also rcd in 1869

JOHNSON, Helen Louise b 11 Aug 1907 Danville, NH d/o JOHNSON, Chas & KIMBALL, Susie

JOHNSON, James b 1822 Hampstead, NH; md 1848 Danville, NH FRENCH, Sarah M. J. C.

JOHNSON, James b 1822 Sandown, NH; md 1848 Danville, NH CANNEY, Angeline

JOHNSON, Jennie L. b Danville, NH; md 09 Sep 1879 Danville, NH WOOD, James R.

JOHNSON, John A. b 1903 Australia s/o JOHNSON, James; md 01 Sep 1948 Danville, NH CURRIER, Adeline M.; md by Rev W. C. Chappell; sp 1st

JOHNSON (Cont.) m BURRILL, ----

JOHNSON, John A. b AL; md 18 Oct 1969 Danville, NH BERNABY, Carol Ann; md by Carleton Eldridge (JP)

JOHNSON, John H. b 1838 Newfields, NH; md 01 May 1876 Danville, NH WELCH, Sarah J. M.

JOHNSON, Joni L. md 04 Oct 1986 Danville, NH TAMMANY, Christopher C.; md by Rev Everett E. Palmer

JOHNSON, Judy Elaine md 19 Apr 1974 Danville, NH MOORE, Barry Bernard; md by Rev George S. Fisher

JOHNSON, Kimberly A. md 31 Aug 1984 Danville, NH KIMBALL, Dana S.; md by Rev Everett E. Palmer

JOHNSON, Leona Gertrude b 1918 Portland, ME d/o JOHNSON, Forrest Wheeler; md 12 Aug 1942 Danville, NH ENGLISH, Everett Arthur; md by Rev W. C. Chappell

JOHNSON, Lois Kimball b 18 Mar 1919 Danville, NH d/o JOHNSON, Chas Hoyt & KIMBALL, Susie; md 09 Aug 1946 Kingston, NH MEANEY, Edward F.; md by Gardner H. Conant (JP)

JOHNSON, Louisa B. M. b 1864 Danville, NH d/o JOHNSON, Chas K. & MERRILL, Martha L.; d Oct 1865 Danville, NH

JOHNSON, Mahlon Elgin b 1884 Kingston, NH s/o JOHNSON, Henry S. & WOOD, Lydia A.; md Feb 1911 Plaistow, NH GOODWIN, Alice M. d 20 Aug 1927 Danville, NH; md by Rev Charle A. Towle; d ae 42y 11m 2d

JOHNSON, Moses H. b Kingston, NH s/o JOHNSON, Jeremiah & KELLEY, Sarah; d 20 Jan 1905 Danville, NH; d ae 63y 9m 22d

JOHNSON, Nathaniel K. b 1836 Kingston, NH; md 1855 Danville, NH HUNT, Sarah J.

JOHNSON, Obidiah Q. b 1812 Hawke, NH s/o JOHNSON, Daniel & GEORGE, Hannah; d 29 May 1871 Danville, NH

JOHNSON, Paul Sherman md 21 Apr 1990 Danville, NH O'BRIEN, Colleen Carolyn; md by Rev Everett E. Palmer

JOHNSON, Richard b s/o JOHN-SON, Harold & RUSE, Myrtis; d 16 Jul 1929 Danville, NH; d ae 2y 4m 12d

JOHNSON, Roxy b 1891 Deerfield, NH d/o JOHNSON, Thos A.; md 26 Dec 1933 Danville, NH McDONALD, James J. md by Rev David J. Caron

JOHNSON, Ruth b Hampstead, NH; md 25 Sep 1800 Hampstead, NH TEWKSBURY, David

JOHNSON, Ruth b Hampstead, NH; md 07 Jan 1778 Hampstead, NH CAMPBELL, Alexander

JOHNSON, Sally b 1810; d 13 Jul 1880 Danville, NH; d age 70 yr

JOHNSON, Sally b Hampstead, NH; md 12 Sep 1797 Hampstead, NH PAGE, John; spouse son of Rev John PAGE

JOHNSON, Samuel d 31 Dec 1888 Danville, NH; d ae 54y Pneumonia

JOHNSON, Steven D. md 22 Aug 1981 Danville, NH COLLINS, Sheryl Lynne; md by Rev Wm Ryans

JOHNSON, Steven R. md 13 Jul 1985 Danville, NH ALLICON, Rose-mary A.; md by Rev James C. Blough

JOHNSON, Winifred L. d 06 Jan 1959 Danville, NH; d ae 87y

JOLIN, Delvina b s/o JOLIN, Francis & SIMONEAU, Leonore; md BOISVERT, ---- d 11 Feb 1933

JONE, Ronald Barry b 1946; md 14 Feb 1968 ---- , DUGGAN, Comelia S.

JONES, Abbot L. md ----, Sarah A.

JONES, Abigail md 21 Aug 1780 Hawke, NH EMERSON, Moses; md by Rev John Page

JONES, Alice b 06 Jun 1794 Hawke, NH d/o JONES, Jonathan & ----, Hanney

JONES, Amos b 18 Mar 1773 Hawke, NH s/o JONES, Nathan Jr & COLLINS, Mary

JONES, Ardis Susan b 12 Oct 1904 Haverhill, MA d/o JONES, Edward Warren & JACKSON, Ida Frances; md 31 Aug 1931 Danville, NH MACE, Lowell Clinton; md by Rev Henry O. Martin

JONES, Betty b 02 Nov 1797 Hawke, NH d/o JONES, Jonathan & ----, Hanney

JONES, Charlotte b 09 Jul 1791 Hawke, NH d/o JONES, Jonathan & ----, Hanney

JONES, Dorothea b 12 Jul 1777 Hawke, NH d/o JONES, Jonathan & ---- , Judith; md 28 May 1795 Kingston, NH COLLINS, Laban

JONES, Enoch b 19 Jul 1781 Hawke, NH d/o JONES, Jonathan & ----, Hanney

JONES, Ezekial b 19 Jan 1796 Hawke, NH s/o JONES, Jonathan & ---- , Hanneymd:

Jones, Ezekiel md 03 Jan 1847 Danville, NH JOHNSON, Hannah F.

JONES, Ezra Jr. b 11 Feb 1771 Hawke, NH S/0 JONES, Ezra Sr. & BEAN, Mehitable

JONES, Ezra Sr. b Hawke, NH; md 08 Nov 1764 Hawke, NH BEAN, Mehitable; md by Rev John Page

JONES, Francis Merle b s /o JONES, John W. & GOULD, Eva; d 28 Aug 1991 Danville, NH ae 74y

JONES, Hanney b 30 Sep 1784 Hawke, NH s/o JONES, Jonathan & ---- , Hanney

JONES, Joanna b Hawke, NH; md 27 Sep 1770 Hawke, NH PLUMMER, Henry; md by Rev John Page

JONES, John b md 06 Dec 1770 Hawke, NH BARNARD, Abigail; md by Rev John Page

JONES, Jonathan b 04 Jun 1818 Hawke, NH s/o JONES, Jonathan & PIERCE-SAWYER, Lydia; d 09 Nov 1904 Danville, NH;

JONES, Josiah b 09 Feb 1775 Hawke, NH s /o JONES, Jonathan & ----, Hanney; md 17 Nov 1796 Kingston, NH FELLOWS, Esther

JONES, Mary b 25 Oct 1768 Hawke, NH d/o JONES, Ezra & BEAN, Mehitable

JONES, Miriam b 23 May 1770 Hawke, NH d/o JONES, Ephriam; md HOOK, Elisha; d 26 Dec 1846 Danville, NH; also md to ---- , Lovering

JONES, Miriam b 10 Feb 1787 Hawke, NH d/o JONES, Jonathan & ---- , Hanney;

JONES, Miriam md 04 Apr 1767 Hawke, NH PLUMMER, Samuel

JONES, Miriam b 23 May 1770 Hawke, NH d/o JONES, Ephriam & md LOVERING, ---- ; d 26 Dec 1846 Danville, NH also md to Elisha HOOK

JONES, Molly b 08 Apr 1773 Hawke, NH d/o JONES, Jonathan & ----, Hanney

JONES, Nathan b Hawke, NH; md 21 Nov 1771 Hawke, NH COLLINS, Mary; md by Rev John Page

JONES, Nellie A. b 03 Sep 1874 Danville, NH d/o JONES, Abbot L. & ----, Sarah A.

JONES, Paula N. md 14 Jun 1986 Danville, NH WILSON, George H.; md by Rev Edward J. Charest

JONES, Ronald Barry b 1946 RI; md 14 Feb 1968 Danville, NH DUGGAN, Cornelia S.; md by Leona A. Sciaudone (JP)

JONES, Rose L. b Hampstead, NH d/o JONES, Chas; md WEBBER, ----

JONES, Timothy b 05 Mar 1766 Hawke, NH; s/o JONES, Ezra & BEAN, Mehitable

JONES, Waitley A. b Hawke, NH; md 01 Feb 1838 Raymond, NH GEORGE, Thos

JONES, Wm H. b New York, NY s/o JONES, Jesse & DODGE, Clara; d 23 Dec 1927 Danville, NH

JONES, FEMALE b 17 Feb 1876 Danville, NH d/o JONES, Abbott L. & ----, Sarah A.; d 14 Mar 1876 Danville, NH; d infant

JOSEPH, Melamie Alexandra b 28 Jun 1989 Derry, NH d/o JOSEPH, Rich S. & DONADIO, Maria N.

JOY, Annie L. b d/o JOY, Melien S.; d ae 63y

JOY, Pearl A. b 1869 Ellsworth, ME d/o JOY, Jos & ROYAL, Lucy M.; md 15 Aug 1936 Danville NH SARGENT, Sarah J.; d 17 Mar 1939 Danville NH; md by Rev W. C. Chappell

JUDKINS, Francis A. b Haverhill, MA s/o JUDKINS, John A. & DIMOND Sarah A. d 14 Oct 1966 Danville NH

JUDKINS, Hannah b 09 Sep 1777 Kingston, NH d/o JUDKINS, Henry & FRENCH, Mary; d 08 Sep 1800 Kingston, NH

JUDKINS, Henry b 05 Dec 1750 Kingston, NH s/o JUDKINS, Joel & ELKINS, Mehitable; md 25 Apr 1776 Hawke, NH FRENCH, Mary d 25 Sep 1825 Kingston, NH; 2nd md 09 Nov 1780 to BARNARD, Mary d 25 Sep 1825 Kingston, NH; md by Rev John Page

JUDKINS, John A. b 1848 Kingston, NH; md 27 Nov 1873 Danville, NH DIMOND, Sarah H.

JUDKINS, Mary b 12 Dec 1778 Kingston, NH d/o JUDKINS, Henry & FRENCH, Mary; md 21 Jul 1802 Kingston, NH SANBORN, Reuben

JUDKINS, Rebecca b Brentwood, NH d/o JUDKINS, Zechariah & ----, Rachel md 22 Jul 1771 Hawke, NH SANBORN, Lowell; d 21 Jul 1848 Guilford, NH; bu Guilford, NH McCoy Cem; md by Rev John Page

JUDKINS, Rosella b 1828 Palmyra, NH; md LUREY, James Sr.; d 03 Jul 1873 Danville, NH

JUDSON, Thos b England; md ----, Carrie

JUDSON, ---- b 05 Dec 1887 Danville, NH ?/o JUDSON, Thos & ---- , Carrie; 1st Child in Family

JUNICKE, Diane C. md 13 Dec 1985 Danville, NH DAVIS, Hugh H.; md by Rev Ronald Gehrinann

KAFKA, Rosemary E. md 01 Dec 1986 Danville, NH RENMARK, Ford; md by Rich J. Rondeau (JP)

KARABULA, Emil b 1919 Lawrence, MA s/o KARABULA, Stanley; md 17 Oct 1940 Danville, NH FIELDER, Martha Louise; md by Clarence M. Collins (JP)

KAUFMAN, Kelly B. md 04 Jun 1988 Danville, NH NUTE, Robert Allen; md by Rev Robert F. Dobson

KAWA, Amanda Sue b 06 May 1987 Lawrence, MA d/o KAWA, Edward S. Jr. & MIDGLEY, Susan G.

KAWA, Ed Stanly 3rd b 10 Jan 1989 Exeter, NH s/o KAWA, Edward Stanley Jr. & MIDGLEY, Susan G.

KEAY, Warren S. b 04 Jun 1868 Danville, NH s/o KEAY, Orestes & PAGE, Mary

KEDDY, Louise Gertrude b 1934 MA d/o KEDDY, Frederick D.; md 27 Apr 1951 Danville, NH SARGENT, Wm Roy; md by Rev W. C. Chappell

KEEFE, Dorothy Mary b 1901 Newburyport, MA d/o KEEFE, Joseph; md 20 Aug 1933 Danville, NH CROCKER, John McKinley; md by Clarence M. Collins (JP)

KEEHAN, Kelly Jean b 06 Feb 1982 Exeter, NH d/o KEEHAN, Edward K. & WOLFE, Cathy F.

KEEZER, Bernice H. b c1892 Plaistow, NH d/o KEEZER, Wallace; md 16 Sep 1914 Danville NH DAVIS, Edgar A.

KEEZER, Carter Dimond b 02 Jan 1909 Danville, NH s/o KEEZER, George Burton & CARTER, Sadie

KEEZER, Elvira Iona b 17 Mar 1879 Danville, NH; d/o KEEZER, Mary

KEEZER, George Burton b 1890 E Hampstead, NH s/o KEEZER, Wallace; md 30 May 1908 Danville, NH CARTER, Sadie A.; md by Rev W. C. Chappell

KEEZER, George W. b c1842 Plaistow, NH; md 17 Jun 1865 Danville, NH KIMBALL, Nellie

KEEZER, Mary Susan b Hampstead, NH d/o KEEZER, Wm J. & WILLIAMS, Mary J. md 20 Nov 1886 Danville, NH WELCH, George W.; d 09 Mar 1938 Danville, NH ae 82y 11m 9d

KEEZER, Pauline Hope b 30 Mar 1911 Danville, NH s/o KEEZER, Wallace & PAGE, Clara

KEEZER, Wallace b Hampstead, NH; PAGE, Clara

KEEZER, Wm J. b c1858 Hampstead, NH; md 03 Apr 1881 Danville, NH AUSTIN, Inez S.

KEIR, Florence d 26 Dec 1990 Danville, NH ae 84y

KEITH, Burton L. b 1852 VT s/o KEITH, James & HOYT, Adaline; md 02 Jul 1924 Danville, NH COSGROVE, Ella M.; : 18 Aug 1924 Danville, NH; md by Rev T. R. Bundy

KEITH, Douglas b 1938 Scotland; md 07 Oct 1963 Danville, NH VILLA-CARO, Sharon L.; md by Rev John Wood Jr.

KELLENBACK, Etta F. b d/o KELLENBACK, Christophe & LORD, Hannah E.; md McNABB, ----; d 04 Sep 1973 Danville, NH ae 94y

KELLEY, Mary C. b c1831; md 1853 Danville, NH BLAISDELL, Josiah T.;

KELLY, Alfred J. b Plaistow, NH; md 09 Jul 1881 Danville, NH MARCO, Mary

KELLY, Linda H. b c185 Merrimac, MA d/o KELLY, Willard B. & THORNE, Harriet; md 29 Jun 1910 Merrimac, MA CURRIER, Maurice G.; 01 Feb 1958 Danville, NH; md by Rev Edward P. Kelly; d ae 73y

KELLY, Martha M b 04 Feb 1905 Danville, NH d/o KELLY, Robert H.& STEWART, Florence E.

KELLY, Patricia I. b Salt Lake City, UT; md WALKER, Robert S.

KENDRICK, Rebecca B. md 10 Feb 1990 Danville, NH SWEENY, Patrick J.; md by Robert J. Kemmery (P)

KENNERSON, Frank Burroughs J b 25 Feb 1966 Danville, NH s/o KENNERSON, Frank B. Sr. & COLLINS, Brenda E.

KENNEY, Barbara J. b Melrose, MA; md GAUVIN, Albert R.

KENT, Joanne Perley b 1938 Haverhill, MA d/o KENT, Gerald D.; md 01 Nov 1958 Danville, NH HOLMAN, Arthur J. Francis; md by Edward Brunault (JP)

KENT, Mary E. b 1857 Lynn, MA d/o KENT, Samuel & O'NEIL, ---- ; md KELLEY, ---- ; d 27 Nov 1933 Danville, NH ae 76y 1m 14d

KENT, Robert J. md 17 Sep 1988 Danville, NH DIGGINS, Ellen Veronica; md by Rev Everett E. Palmer

KERR, Robert John b 1932 PA s/o KERR, Paul E.; md 31 Mar 1956 Danville, NH SANBORN, Jean; md by Rev Arthur Webster

KERRY, Carol M. md 26 Nov 1982 Danville, NH PUTNEY, Gary W.; md by Wm E. Beane (JP)

KERSHAW, Barbara Ann b 1942 Danville, NH; md 18 Feb 1962 Danville, NH ARNOLD, Nelson Bruce;; md by Arthur M. Comeau

KERSHAW, Wm A. b s/o KER-
SHAW, Arthur & BROWN, Eileen; d
29 Mar 1962 Danville, NH ae 11y

KERWAN, Catherine Eliz b 1920
Melrose, MA d/o KERWAN, Wm
Andrew;; md 31 Aug 1946 Exeter, NH
CUNNINGHAM, Edward James

KETCHEN, Marion Gertrude b
Belchertown, MA; md BURT, Herschel
Bacon

KETCHEN, Michael A. Sr. b md 03
Nov 1990 Danville, NH LANGLOIS,
Hedi Janice; md by Rich J. Rondeau
(JP)

KEZER, James Chamberlin b 1936
MA s/o KEZER, Fayette; md 22 Aug
1959 Danville, NH THIBEAULT,
Norma Irene; md by Rev Albert
Cornwell

KIELINEN, Jeffrey V. md 15 Sep
1984 Danville, NH COBURN, Lisa B.;
md by Rich C. L. Webb (EP)

KIMBALL, Adria Dawne b 14 Jun
1990 Exeter, NH d/o KIMBALL,
Steven L. & SCHIER, Dawn L.

KIMBALL, Albert Chester b 08 Jul
1933 Danville, NH s/o KIMBALL,
Howard Lovering & LANGLEY, Eliz J.;
d 23 Jan 1934 Danville, NH;

KIMBALL, Albert G. b 12 Oct 1859
Danville, NH s/o KIMBALL, George F.
& FULLONTON, Mary D.

KIMBALL, Alfred Spencer b 08 Jul
1933 Danville, NH s/o KIMBALL,
Howard Lovering & LANGLEY, Eliz J.

KIMBALL, Anson B. b 20 Mar 1855
Danville, NH s/o KIMBALL, George F.
& FULLONTON, Mary D.

KIMBALL, Benj b 08 Mar 1792
Hawke, NH s/o KIMBALL, Moses &
PAGE, Mary

KIMBALL, Bernice L. b 30 Mar
1894 Danville, NH d/o KIMBALL,
Laburton & GEORGE, Nellie E.

KIMBALL, Caleb md HOOK,
Mary; Spouse md 1st Levi Sanborn

KIMBALL, Caleb b Poplin, NH; md
18 May 1841 Raymond, NH SAN-
BORN, Mary Mrs.

KIMBALL, Carolyn Rosalie b 25
Mar 1937 Danville, NH d/o KIMBALL,
Rich C. & FRANKLYN, Eleanor; md
AL-EGAILY, Salah Salman

KIMBALL, Carroll M. b s/o
KIMBALL, Chas H. & MORSE, Neva
L.; d 02 Nov 1987 Danville, NH ae 76y

KIMBALL, Chas E. b Bath, NH s/o
KIMBALL, Wm L. & FRENCH, Mary
S.; d 12 Oct 1966 Danville, NH

KIMBALL, Chas H. b 03 May 1885
Danville, NH s/o KIMBALL, Elmer
Ellsworth & RUEE, Florence S.; md
MORSE, Neva: Jd: 15 Jun 1937 Dan-
ville, NH ae 52y 1m 12d

KIMBALL, Chester Arthur b 1883
Danville, NH s/o KIMBALL, Elmer
Ellsworth & RUEE, Florence S.; md 01
Sep 1902 Danville, NH LOVERING,
Cora B.; d 04 Mar 1957 Danville, NH;
md by Rev A. B. Howard

KIMBALL, Clifton E. b 1892
Danville, NH s/o KIMBALL, Eugene F.
& PAGE, Dora S.; d 28 Dec 1893
Danville, NH ae 1y 4m 2d

KIMBALL, Corinne Janice b 27
Jun 1950 Danville, NH d/o KIMBALL,
Merle David & BATTLES, Elva Jan-
nette; md by Rev John Wood

KIMBALL, Cortinne J. b 1950; md
30 May 1968 Danville, NH REES,
Harry R.

KIMBALL, Dana Scott b 19 Aug
1958 Danville, NH s/o KIMBALL,
Merle David & GILLEN, Barbara
Louise; md 31 Aug 1984 Danville, NH
JOHNSON, Kimberly A.; md by Rev
Everett E. Palmer

KIMBALL, David Brian b 25 Jan
1957 Danville, NH s/o KIMBALL,
Merle David & GILLEN, Barbara
Louise; md 12 Jun 1992 LANCASTER,
Cheryl Ann

KIMBALL, Dean Edward b 04 Mar
1958 Danville, NH s/o KIMBALL,
Norman & WHITE, Sylvia

KIMBALL, Donald Morse b 16 Jul
1941 Exeter, NH s/o KIMBALL, Merle
Donald & BATTLES, Elva Jeannette;
md 26 Feb 1965 Danville, NH SWEET,
Mary Lou; md by Rev Wendall J. Irvine

KIMBALL, Douglas Nolan b 14 Sep
1954 Danville, NH s/o KIMBALL,
Leonard H. & ARNOLD, Susie B.

KIMBALL, Edwin James b 11 Oct
1897 Danville, NH s/o KIMBALL,
Elmer Ellsworth & RUEE, Florence S.

Kimball, Ellen C. b 1860 Danville, NH d/o KIMBALL, Gardner & ---- , Charlotte; md HEATH, Franklin Gilbert

KIMBALL, Elmer A. b 16 Dec 1883 Danville, NH s/o KIMBALL, Elmer Ellsworth & RUEE, Florence S.; md 04 Oct 1904 Fremont, NH TUTTLE, Gertrude O.; md by Rev A. B. Hyde

KIMBALL, Elmer Ellsworth b 27 Feb 1861 Danville, NH s/o KIMBALL, James M. & QUIMBY, Eliz Ann; md 06 Jul 1881 Danville, NH RUEE, Florence S.; d 22 Nov 1943 Danville, NH

KIMBALL, Eugene F. b 15 Aug 1866 Danville, NH s/o KIMBALL, George F. & FULLENTON, Mary D.; md 31 Dec 1887 Plaistow, NH PAGE, Dora S.; d 30 Apr 1935 Danville, NH; md by Rev W. M. Weeks

KIMBALL, Eva Mira b 15 May 1873 Danville, NH d/o KIMBALL, James M. & QUIMBY, Eliz Ann; md 11 Sep 1894 Manchester, NH BASSETT, Joseph P.; md by Rev W. H. Morrison

KIMBALL, Everett W. b c1858 Kingston, NH; md 05 Jun 1881 Danville, NH GRIFFIN, Clara B.

KIMBALL, Fannie May b 10 Oct 1868 Danville, NH d/o KIMBALL, James M. & QUIMBY, Eliz Ann; md 1st 08 Oct 1891 Danville, NH SARGENT, Walter H., 2nd 29 Jun 1907 Danville, NH TUCKER, ---- ; d 23 Jun 1952; md by Rev W. C. Chappell

KIMBALL, ---- b d/o KIMBALL, Edwin C. & FLANAGAN, Patricia A.; d 07 Jun 1971 Danville, NH

KIMBALL, Freddie L. b 25 Jan 1864 Danville, NH s/o KIMBALL, James M. & QUIMBY, Eliz Ann; d 21 Aug 1867 Danville, NH

KIMBALL, George A. b s/o KIMBALL, Eugene & PAGE, Dora S.; d 04 Mar 1950 Danville, NH ae 61y

KIMBALL, George W. b s/o KIMBALL, George W. & HEATH, Mary P.; d Jun 1954 Danville, NH ae 101y

KIMBALL, Harold W. b 1889 Danville, NH s/o KIMBALL, Walter A. & HARRIS, Hannah S.; d 20 Nov 1889 Danville, NH d ae 8m

KIMBALL, Howard Lovering Jr. b 17 Jul 1932 Danville, NH s/o KIMBALL, Howard Lovering Sr. & LANGLEY, Eliz; md 13 Jul 1957 Danville, NH MOULTON, Jacquelyn

KIMBALL, Howard Lovering Sr. b 02 Oct 1908 Danville, NH s/o KIMBALL, Chester Arthur & LOVERING, Cora B.; md 24 Jun 1931 Danville, NH LANGLEY, Eliz J.; d 22 Jan 1957 Danville, N; md by Rev Harold C. Ross

KIMBALL, James A. b 18 Sep 1865 Danville, NH s/o KIMBALL, James M. & QUIMBY, Eliz Ann; d 15 Apr 1866 Danville, NH ae 7m

KIMBALL, James M. b c1838 Raymond, NH s/o KIMBALL, John & PAGE, Fanny; md 1st 30 Sep 1859 Danville, NH QUIMBY, Eliz Ann, 2nd 15 Nov 1891 WOLKERSON, Merinda: d 14 Feb 1914 Danville, NH; Occupation - Carpenter

KIMBALL, John md 12 May 1831 Kingston, NH PAGE, Fanny

KIMBALL, John md 31 Oct 1765 TAYLOR, Dorothy; md by Rev John Page

KIMBALL, John C. d 02 Sep 1863 Danville, NH

KIMBALL, John E. b 23 Apr 1859 Danville, NH s/o KIMBALL, George F. & FULLONTON, Mary D.

KIMBALL, Kathleen Gwenn b 20 Jan 1957 Danville, NH d/o KIMBALL, Norman & WHITE, Sylvia

KIMBALL, Kayla Nicole b 27 Aug 1990 Exeter, NH d/o KIMBALL, Dana S. & MOORE, Kimberly A.

KIMBALL, Laburton b 1867 Kingston, NH s/o KIMBALL, Geo W. & HEATH, Mary P.; md GEORGE, Nellie F.; d 19 Apr 1934 Danville, NH; md by J. A. Wiggin

KIMBALL, Laurel Lee b 29 Aug 1953 Danville, NH d/o KIMBALL, Leonard Hazen & ARNOLD, Susie B.

KIMBALL, Leonard Hazen b 13 Jan 1935 Danville, NH s/o KIMBALL, Merle Donald & BATTLES, Elva Jeannette; md 10 Jan 1953 Danville, NH ARNOLD, Susie Blanche

KIMBALL, Lesa Gaye b 10 Apr 1963 Danville, NH d/o KIMBALL,

KIMBALL (Cont.) Merle David & GILLEN, Barbara Louise
KIMBALL, Lewis b Vienna; md 1840 Danville, NH ELKINS, Eleanor
KIMBALL, Lewis H. b 23 Oct 1841 Danville, NH s/o KIMBALL, Lewis & ELKINS, Eleanor
KIMBALL, Loralyn b md 23 Oct 1982 Danville, NH HANSON, Douglas A.; md by Rev Everett E. Palmer
KIMBALL, Martha J. b Hampstead, NH d/o KIMBALL, Jonathan & GEORGE, Betsy; d 01 Mar 1905 Danville, NH ae 62y
KIMBALL, Maurice K. b 1909 Hampstead, NH s/o KIMBALL, Chas H.; md 14 Jun 1929 Fremont, NH MARCOTTE, Pauline H.; md by Rev S. B. Enman
KIMBALL, Merle David b 09 Jul 1932 Danville, NH s/o KIMBALL, Merle Donald & BATTTLES, Elva Jannette; md 24 May 1956 Danville, NH GILLEN, Barbara Louise; md by Rev W. C. Chappell
KIMBALL, Merle Donald b 1909 Hampstead, NH s/o Kimball, Chas H. & MORSE, Neva L.; md 01 Aug 1931 Danville, NH BATTLES, Elva Jeannette; d 01 Dec 1976 Danville, NH; md by Rev Samuel B. Enman
KIMBALL, Moses md 01 Feb 1792 PAGE, Polly
KIMBALL, Nellie b c1847 Plaistow, NH; md 17 Jun 1865 Danville, NH KEEZER, George W.
KIMBALL, Norman Edward b 21 Sep 1936 Danville, NH s/o KIMBALL, Merle Donald & BATTLES, Elva Jeannette; md 19 Jul 1985 Danville, NH ENGLISH, Diana M.
KIMBALL, Rich Chester b 01 May 1915 Danville, NH s/o KIMBALL, Chester Arthur & LOVERING, Cora B.; md 1st FRANKLYN, Eleanor, 2nd 30 Jul 1942 Danville, NH SHANAMAN, Amy Ruth by; md by Rev W. C. Chappell
KIMBALL, Rich Leslie b 28 Jul 1943 Danville, NH s/o KIMBALL, Frank Alfred & SHUNAMAN, Amy Ruth

KIMBALL, Robert Carroll b 28 Nov 1932 Danville, NH s/o KIMBALL, Carroll M. & SARGENT, Marjorie A.
KIMBALL, Sally md Aug 1799 Hawke, NH PAGE, Jabez
KIMBALL, Sally Elaine b 30 Jan 1940 Danville, NH d/o KIMBALL, Howard Lovering & LANGLEY, Eliz J.; md 15 Mar 1958 Danville, NH LONGLAND, Herbert Newton; md by Rev Wendall J. Irvive
KIMBALL, Sarah b c1743; md 1st REDDINGTON, Abraham, 2nd HOOK, Humphrey; d 28 Sep 1823 Newburyprt, MA
KIMBALL, Sarina Meghan b 19 Aug 1986 Exeter, NH d/o KIMBALL, Dana S. & JOHNSON, Kimberly A.
KIMBALL, Shirley Joanne b 14 Jul 1936 Danville, NH d/o KIMBALL, Carroll M. & SARGENT, Marjorie
KIMBALL, Steven Lee Sr. b 07 Feb 1962 Danville, NH s/o KIMBALL, Merle David & GILLEN, Barbara Louise; md 1st 19 Mar 1982 Danville, NH HARRISON, Tammy L.by Rev Everett E. Palmer, 2nd 03 Aug 1985 Danville, NH SCHIER, Dawn L. by Linda S. Jette (JP)
KIMBALL, Steven Lee Jr. b 28 Jul 1982 Exeter, NH s/o KIMBALL, Steven Lee Sr. & WATERMAN, Tammy L.
KIMBALL, Susie M. b 26 Feb 1885 Danville, NH d/o KIMBALL, Walter A. & HARRIS, Hannah S.; md 21 Sep 1904 Danville, NH JOHNSON, Chas H.; d 26 Jun 1946 Danville, NH; md by Rev A. B. Howard
KIMBALL, Walter A. b c1862 Kingston, NH s/o KIMBALL, George W. & HEATH, Mary P.; md 02 Jul 1884 Danville, NH HARRIS, Hannah S.; d 05 May 1921 Danville, NH ae 59y 4m 20d
KIMBALL, Wm Porter b Hampstead, NH s/o KIMBALL, Jonathan & GEORGE, Betsey; d 16 Mar 1932 Danville, NH
KIMBALL, ---- b 12 Nov 1852 Danville, NH s/o KIMBALL, John G.; d 12 Nov 1852 Danville, NH; Stillborn
KIMBALL, ---- b 12 Jun 1907

KIMBALL (Cont.) Danville, NH s/o KIMBALL, Chester Arthur & LOVERING, Cora B.; d 12 Jun 1907 Danville, NH

KINESTON, Job b of Exeter, NH; md 02 Sep 1781 HOBBS, Eliz; md by Rev John Page

KING, Joseph Austin b 1922 s/o KING, Wm; md 29 Dec 1957 Danville, NH HUNT, Barbara Elaine

KINHART, Brittany Ann b 15 Feb 1990 Exeter, NH d/o KINHART, Russell G. & CACCIOLA, Anne M.

KINHART, Joshua Glenn b 28 Feb 1988 Exeter, NH s/o KINHART, Russell G. & CACCIOLA, Ann M.

KINNEAR, Lindsey Roland -b 1920 Dundee Scotland s/o KINNEAR, Lindsay; md 26 Sep 1940 Danville, NH WELCH, Madeline; md by Clarence M. Collins (JP)

KIRWAIN, Catherine E. b d/o KIRWAIN, Wm & McCARTHY, Mary; md CUNNINGHAM, ---- d 19 Sep 1981 Danville, NH ae 61y

KIRWAN, Catherine Eliz b 1920 Medford, MA d/o KIRWAN, Wm Andrew &; md 31 Aug 1946 Exeter, NH CUNNINGHAM, Edward James; md by Willard K. Tozier (JP)

KIRWAN, Helen Ann b 1930 MEDFORD, MA d/o KIRWIN, Wm Andrew; md 18 Feb 1947 Plaistow, NH BOTHWICK, Harold Martin; md by Rev James W. Gilrain

KIRWAN, John Rich b 05 Aug 1945 Exeter, NH s/o KIRWAN, Wm Andrew & SPEAR, Lorraine Gertrude; md BRADLEY, Mary Ann R.

KIRWAN, Lorraine Gertrude b 1942 MA d/o KIRWAN, Wm; md 05 Apr 1959 Danville, NH ROCK, Leonard Joseph; md by Ferne Prescott (JP)

KIRWAN, Maureen Kathryn b 09 Oct 1966 Danville, NH s/o KIRWAN, John R. & BRADLEY, Mary Ann R.

KIRWAN, Wm A. b Medford, MA s/o KIRWAN, Pat H. & MORRISSEY, Eliz; d 17 Jan 1966 Danville NH ae 76y

KIRWIN, Alice Virginia b 1925 d/o KIRWIN, Wm A.; md 01 Jun 1950 Danville, NH MOODY, Maurice Martin

KNAPP, Derek Steven b 18 Jul 1990 Derry, NH s/o KNAPP, Steven J. & DUPLIS, Cinthia J.

KNAPP, Stephen Geo b md 01 Mar 1977 Danville, NH DEMAINE, Marla Jean; md by Phillip D. Fichera (JP)

KNIGHT, Joseph b Danville, NH; md 14 Nov 1970 Danville, NH JENDRICK, Lois

KNIGHT, Kenneth Jos md 28 Oct 1978 Danville, NH EDWINSON, Vera May; md by Rev Steven Kucharski (P)

KNOTT, Sharon Ann md 31 Dec 1991 Danville, NH THYLANDER, Harold Jos Jr. md by Leo Beaulieu (JP)

KOMUSIN, Nancy J. md 19 Sep 1987 Danville, NH LEE, Gary G.; md by Rev Everett E. Palmer

KOMUSIN, Robert John Sr. b s/o KOMUSIN, Robert John Sr. & SCHIRMER, Emily; d 10 Mar 1990 Danville, NH ae 52y

KOONS, Kandi-Sue md 11 Oct 1989 Danville, NH PHILIPP, Lawrence Hamilton; md by Rich J. Rondeau (JP)

KOSAK, Matthew David b 07 Feb 1986 Malden, MA s/o KOSAK, Rich S. & KIBBY, Deborah L.

KOSKINER, Hilja b 1891 Finland; md COLLINS, ---- ; d 06 Feb 1956 Danville, NH

KRAMER, John Mark Jr. b 1947 Beverley, MA; md 01 Jul 1967 Danville, NH WARD, Gloria Jean; md by Leona A. Sciaudone (JP)

KRAUSCH, Christa H. b 1942 Germany; md 02 Sep 1961 Danville, NH HERRICK, Wayne Russell; md by Rev John Wood Jr.

KRULEVICH, John b s/o KRULEVICH, Domenick & ---- , Lillian; d 07 Dec 1962 Danville, NH

KUTSUMAKIS, Michael b 1915 Greece s/o KUTSUMAKIS, George; md 16 Apr 1937 Danville, NH HOWARD, Frances; md by Rev O. L. Brownsey

KUZMICKI, Edward M. md 17 Mar 1991 Danville, NH WOODARD, Kathy A.; md by Rich J. Rondeau (JP)

LaBELLE, Hazel Louise b 02 Aug 1917 Danville, NH d/o LaBELLE, Samuel & COLLINS, Viola

LaBRANCHE, Karen b 22 Jan 1954 Danville, NH d/o LaBRANCHE, Roland J. & NELSON, Wilma Christine

LACASSE, June D. md 02 Aug 1973 Danville, NH RONDEAU, Rich J. Jr; md by Phyllis A. Raynowska (JP)

LaCHANCE, Rich F. md 24 Aug 1983 Danville, NH DeLaHAYE, Patricia A.; md by Renee Houle Carkin (JP)

LADD, Alice L. b 19 Nov 1886 Danville, NH d/o LADD, Josiah S. & CHALLIS, Sarah A.; md 12 Oct 1909 Danville, NH TUCK, Wm C; md by Rev W. C. Chappell. 2nd 26 Nov 1915 ROSS, Alonzo W.

LADD, Alta M. b 1889 Franklin Falls, NH d/o LADD, Wm J.; md 09 Jun 1909 Danville, NH TUCKER, Ernest G.; md by Rev W. C. Chappell

LADD, Bernard b 25 Mar 1905 Danville, NH s/o LADD, Ottero & PAGE, Gertrude M.; d 22 Oct 1905 Danville, NH ae 6m 27d

LADD, Caleb b c1781 Chelsea, MA; md DUNHAM, Tammy; d 14 May 1865 Danville, NH ae 84y

LADD, Elijah d 27 Aug 1890 Danville, NH

LADD, Esther F. b 14 Feb 1881 Danville, NH d/o LADD, Josiah S. & CHALLIS, Sarah A.; md 01 Sep 1902 Danville, NH WINSLOW, John C.; d 03 Feb 1956 Danville, NH; md by Rev A. B. Howard

LADD, Etta A. b 1861 Hampstead, NH d/o LADD, Josiah & CHALLIS, Sarah; md McHOLT, Henry; d 10 Apr 1936 Danville, NH

LADD, Harry W. b 1891 Fremont, NH s/o LADD, Wm J.; md 15 Jun 1912 Danville, NH BURBANK, Emma J.; md by Rev A. C. Keith

LADD, Ida B. b c1889 Danville, NH d/o LADD, Josiah S. & CHALLIS, Sarah A.; md 29 Apr 1904 Sandown, NH GEORGE, Clarence W.; md by John J. Goodwin (JP)

LADD, Isaac b c1808; md ---- , Lucy A.; d 12 Dec 1854 Danville, NH

LADD, James M. b c1841 Worcester, MA; md 20 Jun 1861 Danville, NH QUIMBY, Amy L.

LADD, John b c1812 Hampstead, NH; md 28 Aug 1862 Danville, NH WALES, Mary Mrs.

LADD, Josiah S. b 1843 s/o LADD, Elijah; md CHALLIS, Sarah A.; d 23 Jan 1929 Danville, NH

LADD, Marcia E. b c1897 Kingston, NH d/o LADD, Ottero & PAGE, Gertrude M.; md 16 Aug 1915 Plaistow, NH REYNOLDS, Adelbert W.; md by Rev Challis V. Smith

LADD, Martha C. b c1838 Worcester, MA; md 1857 Danville, NH TEWKSBURY, Martin Van Buren

LADD, Mary E. d 17 Nov 1938 Danville, NH ae 75y8m 5d

LADD, Mary Etta b 11 Apr 1869 Danville, NH d/o LADD, Josiah S. & CHALLIS, Sarah A.

LADD, Olla M. b 01 Apr 1879 Danville, NH d/o LADD, Joseph S. & CHALLIS, Sarah A.; md ARNOLD, Warren M.; d 23 May 1924 Danville, NH

LADD, Ollard b 1875 Danville, NH s/o LADD, Josiah S. & CHALLIS, Sarah A.; d 20 Jun 1876 Danville, NH; d age 1 yr

LADD, Orlando b 1873 Danville, NH s/o LADD, Josiah S. & CHALLIS, Sarah A.; d 13 Jun 1876 Danville, NH ge 3y

LADD, Oscar b 1871 Danville, NH s/o LADD, Josiah S. & CHALLIS, Sarah A.; d 26 Jun 1876 Danville, NH ae 5y

LADD, Ottero A. b 11 Mar 1872 Plaistow, NH s/o LADD, Josiah S. & CHALLIS, Sarah A.; md 1st 28 Aug 1896 Kingston, NH PAGE, Gertrude M. 2nd 22 Nov 1930, 3rd WATSON. Ellen, 3rd 01 Nov 1938 VANDERFORD, Florence; d 19 Apr 1947

LADD, Salina b Chelsea, MA; md GRIFFIN, David; d 25 Jan 1880 Danville, NH ae 68y

LADD, Tammary b c1828 Chelsea, MA; md CHALLIS, Clark D.; d 02 Mar 1873 Danville, NH ae 45y

LADD, Wm J. b 14 Apr 1865 Danville, NH s/o LADD, James & QUIMBY, Amy L.; md:d 24 Nov 1937 Danville, NH

LaFOND, Viola L. b 1923 NH; md 18 Aug 1967 Danville, NH PRETTY, Harold J.; md by Edward R. Lamb (JP)

LaFRENIERE, Kenneth C. b 1932 Chicago, IL; md 20 Jun 1964 Danville, NH LYNCH, Maron F.; md by Leona A, Sciandone (JP)

LAIDLAW, Bruce H.b of East Hampstead, NH; md 16 Oct 1992 LEE, Linda R.; md by Mark R. Murabito (JP)

LAJEUNESSE, Lucian M. Sr. md 08 Jul 1977 Danville, NH DRAGON, Lillian M.; md by Clara B. Shaw (JP)

LAMB, Edward Reeves b 06 Dec 1955 Danville, NH s/o LAMB, Edward Ridgeway & SNELL, Charlotte Marie; md 22 Apr 1990 Danville, NH HURD, Cherie A.; md by Rev Allen W. Cook

LAMB, Edward Ridgwauy b 1909 Addison, NY s/o LAMB, Walter; md 20 Mar 1955 Danville, NH SNELL, Charlotte Marie; md by Rev W. C. Chappell

LAMB, Gertrude b Newfoundland d/o MEWS, Geo & KELSON, Frances; d 31 Jan 1957 Danville, NH ae 82y

LAMB, Wm Ridgway b13 Dec 1956 Danville, NH s/o LAMB, Edward R. & SNELL, Charlotte M.; d 29 Oct 1976 Danville, NH

LAMB. Edward Ridgway b s/o LAMB, Walter & MEWS, Gertrude; md 20 Mar 1955 Danville, NH SNELL, Charlotte Marie; d 01 Jan 1969 Danville, NH ae 60y

LAMBERT, Florence Agnes b Newburyport, MA d/o LAMBERT, Arthur & TOBIN, Florence; md COBB, Harrison; d 06 Mar 1949 Danville, NH

LAMBERT, Robert J. b s/o LAMBERT, Frank H. & VERBIEST, Meinsje M.; d 10 Mar 1978 Danville, NH ae 17y

LAMBERTSEN, Kristen Sue md 17 May 1988 Danville, NH TILL, Robert EDward; md by Rich J. Rondeau (JP)

LANCASTER, Cheryl Ann b of Danville, NH; md 12 Jun 1992 KIMBALL, David Brian; md by Cathy A Drff (JP)

LANCIANI, Kevin P. md 19 Oct 1990 Danville, NH DAVIS, Wendy L.; md by Rich J. Rondeau (JP)

LANDERS, Bonny Fay b 11 Mar 1955 Danville, NH d/o LANDERS, Robert Victor & PLUMB, Marion Gertrude

LANDMAN, Elbert A. Dr. b Londonderry, NH; md BARNARD, Pearl

LANDMAN, Kelsie Howard b 15 Sep 1901 s/o LANDMAN, Elbert A. & BARNARD, Pearl S.

LANDMAN, Vivian Ione b 24 Apr 1903 Danville, NH d/o LANDMAN, Elbert A. Dr & BARNARD, Pearl

LANDRY, Frank Joseph b 1931 Shirley, MA; md 28 Mar 1963 Danville, NH MOREAU, Marjorie Cummings; md by Rev John Wood Jr.

LANE, Abigail b Hawke, NH; md 06 Aug 1824 Hawke, NH FRENCH, Abraham S. Dr.

LANE, Hannah md SANBORN, Reuben

LANE, Harold M. b 1896 Exeter, NH s/o LANE, Chas A.; md 11 Oct 1924 Exeter, NH COLLINS, Florence R.; md by Rev John L. Clark

LANE, John L. Jr. md 16 Mar 1991 Danville, NH GOLDTHWAITE, Suzanne L.; md by Rev Everett E. Palmer

LANE, Preston Leroy b 1913 MA s/o LANE, Chester Leroy; md 1st KUMIS, ---- , 2nd 30 Dec 1951 Danville, NH WILCOX, Elizabeth; md by Rev Robert S. Walker

LANGLEY, Elizabeth J. b Halifax, Nova Scot d/o LANGLEY, Spencer H.; md 24 Jun 1931 Danville, NH KIMBALL, Howard Lovering; md by Rev Harold C. Ross

LANGLOIS, Heidi Janice md 03 Nov 1990 Danville, NH KETCHEN, Michael A. Sr.; md by Rich J. Rondeau (JP)

LANGLOIS, John Peter md 25 May 1991 Danville, NH RUBINO, Patricia E.; md by Rev Elliot N. Howard

LAPHAM, Leland C. 3rd; md 24 Dec 1972 Danville, NH FLAMMIA, Kathleen F.; md by Phil D. Fichers (JP)

LAPHAM, Leland Chandous b: 25 Apr 1973 Haverhill, MA s/o LAPHAM, Leland C. 3rd & FLAMMIA, KATHLEEN F.

LAPIERRE, Thos U. Jr. md 21 Aug 1982 Danville, NH WATERS, Michelle D.; md by Everett E. Palmer

LARATONDA, Francis A. md 27 Apr 1986 Danville, NH PIMENTEL, Denise; md by Wm E. Beane (JP)

LARKIN, Dwight D. md 19 Feb 1983 Danville, NH WOOD, Kathleen L.; md by Rev Everett E. Palmer

LARKIN, Dwight David md 07 Jan 1989 Danville, NH WILLIAMS, Anita Michelle; md by Wm Beane (JP)

LARKIN, Erik M. md 14 Sep 1985 Danville, NH VALLEY, Lori R.; md by Rev Everett E. Palmer

LARKIN, Lilly Elfreda md 21 May 1988 Danville, NH MARTIN, Donald Wm; md by Rev Byran E. Moore

LASATER, Donna Marie md 14 Feb 1991 Danville, NH BARCLAY, Geo Ingram; md by Rich E. Rondeau (JP)

LAUBENSTEIN, Chas ED md 09 Nov 1975 Danville, NH GAUDINO, Marion Elizabeth; md by Robert S. Dejadon (JP)

LAUGHTON, Bruce A. md 04 Mar 1972 Danville, NH NOYES, Brenda L.; md by James Gilmore (JP)

LaVALLEE, Paul Joseph b 15 May 1972 Haverhill, MA s/o LaVALLEE, Arthur P. & NICOLORO, Michele A.

LAVALLEE, Rich Robert md 25 Jul 1987 Danville, NH DUSTON, Bertha A.; md by Rev Everett E. Palmer

LAVALLEE, David J. md 12 Apr 1980 Danville, NH NEWTON, Rebecca R.; md by Rev John Rea Chapman

LAVELLEE, Amber Jean b 04 Jan 1988 Haverhill, MA d/o LAVRLLEE, Rich A. & DUSTON, Bertha A.

LAVELLEE, Leo S. b s/o LAVEL-LEE, Napoleon & BRUNNELL, Chatta; d 12 Dec 1988 Danville, NH ae 80y

LAVERY, Michael Jas md 19 Oct 1991 Danville, NH BARTLETT, Ellen Marie; md by Rich J. Rondeau (JP)

LAWRENCE, David M. md 24 Dec 1989 Danville, NH HANSON, Karen L.; md by George M. DePace (JP)

LAWRENCE, Evelyn M. b 1914 Salem, NH d/o PENNY, Frank; md 12 Dec 1935 Danville, NH HILBERG, Herbert J.; md by Rev W. C. Chappell

LAY, Crystal L. md 22 Sep 1973 Danville, NH LORENZ, Eric R.; md by Retenah V. Pietrowski (JP)

LAY, Julie Ann b 11 Mar 1972 Exeter, NH d/o LAY, Chas D. & ADAMS, Crystal L.

LEACH, Maslcolm F. b s/o LEACH, Philip & BENNETT, Margaret; d 11 Feb 1990 Danville, NH d ae 64y

LEATHE, Ramona J. md 21 Dec 1973 Danville, NH DELOREY, Neil M.; md by Chas E. Estee (P)

LEAVITT, Chas L. md BROWN, Isabel

LEAVITT, Ella M. b 07 Aug 1882 Danville, NH d/o LEAVITT, Chas L. & BROWN, Isabel

LEAVITT, Hannah b Epping, NH; md 29 Sep 1772 Hawke, NH FLAN-DERS, Simon

LeBEL, Robbin Edith b 22 Jun 1971 Exeter, NH d/o LeBEL, Euclide, J. & HULL, Donna R.

LeBLANC, Barbara Ann md 07 Dec 1991 Danville, NH LYNCH, Robery Frazier; md by Rich J. Rondeau (JP)

LeCLARE, Delia 1887; d 12 Oct 1890 Danville, NH

LeCLARE, Ernestine Althea md COLLINS, Quinton Roy

LeCLARE, Lydia M. b Ashburn-ham, MA d/o LeCLAIRE, Isaac; md 15 Jul 1908 Danville, NH COLLINS, Eugene F.; md by Rev F. G. Deshies

LeCLERE, Lena J. b 25 Jul 1894 Danville, NH d/o LeCLERE, Leon & McLENCON, Sophie

LeCLERE, Leon b Canada; md McLENEON, Sophie

LEE, Gary G. md 19 Sep 1987 Danville, NH KOMUSIN, Nancy J.; md by Rev Everett E. Palmer

LEE, Linda R. b of Danville, NH; md 16 Oct 1992 LAIDLAW, Bruce H.

LEE, Wm b 1869 England; d 17 Dec 1956 Danville, NH

LeFEBURE, Carol A. md 01 Jul 1981 Danville, NH DEMNERS, Roger A.; md by Bettie C. Ouellette (JP)

LEGASSE, Raymond J. b 1913 Haverhill, MA d/o LEGASSE, Ernest A.; md 11 Aug 1934 Danville, NH SWEETSIR, Hazel Beatrice; md by

LEGASSE (Cont.) Clarence M. Collins (JP)

LEGERS, Wm R. md 05 Feb 1983 Danville, NH AMAZEEN, Judith A.; md by Rev Wendell J. Irvine

LEGG, Nicole Ashley b 22 Sep 1987 Haverhill, MA d/o LEGG, David M. & McLARNON, Karen L.

LEGRO, E. Albert b c1856; d 29 Nov 1958 Danville, NH ae 14m

LEISHMAN, Rita Catherine md 26 Jul 1974 Danville, NH DOUCETTE, Joseph Richad; md by Leona A. Sciaudone (JP)

LeMOINE, Arthur Peter b 1921 Amesbury, MA s/o LeMOINE, Joseph; md 29 Mar 1946 Danville, NH GAMLIN, Charlotte May; md by Rev W. C. Chappell

LEMOINE, Derek Lee b 17 Aug 1987 Haverhill, MA s/o LEMOINE, Mark A. & GEISLER, Sheiler J.

LEMOINE, Mark A. md 19 Jul 1986 Danville, NH GEISLER, Shella J.; md by Philip D. Fichera (JP)

LEONARD, Myra Helen md 10 May 1978 Danville, NH CUMMINGS, Chas Ever; md by Rev Wm Ryans

LeROY, Jennifer Nicole b 07 Jun 1982 Exeter, NH d/o LeROY, Gregory V. & SHAMBERG, Nancy M.

LESLIE, David Brian b 1941 MA; md 23 Mar 1968 Danville, NH MUZRALL, Mary Ellen; md by Edward R. Lamb (JP)

LESSARD, Arthur Eugene b 09 Jan 1917 Danville, NH s/o LESSARD, Dana & COLLINS, Isa May; md 23 Dec 1943 Danville, NH WALKER, Ernestine Lucille; md by Rev W. C. Chappell

LESSARD, Barbara May b 31 Jul 1944 Danville, NH d/o LESSARD, Arthur Eugene & WALKER, Ernestine Lucile

LESSARD, Beth Ellen b 17 Feb 1952 Danville, NH d/o LESSARD, Lloyd A. & FOLLANSBEE, Virginia L

LESSARD, Dana b Auburn, NH s/o LESSARD, Onesime & RIVARD, Leonie M.; md COLLINS, Isa M.; d 14 Jun 1971 Danville, NH ae 78y

LESSARD, Diane Elaine b 29 Mar 1950 Danville, NH d/o LESSARD,

LESSARD (Cont.) Lloyd Allen & FOLLENSBE, Virginia Lorraine

LESSARD, Flora Helen b 02 Nov 1915 Danville, NH d/o LESSARD, Dona & COLLINS, Isa M.; md 12 Dec 1953 Danville, NH DENNETT, Lancer Francis

LESSARD, Isa Collins b N Danville, NH s/o LESSARD, Aren E. & WEBSTER, Flora; d 08 Feb 1963 Danville, NH; d ae 71Y

LESSARD, Lloyd Allen b 29 Apr 1921 Danville, NH s/o LESSARD, Dona & COLLINS, ISA M.; md FOLLANS-BEE, Florence Evelyn

LESSARD, Marian P. b 05 Aug 1922 Danville, NH d/o LESSARD, Dona & COLLINS, Isa M.

LESSARD, Oliver Wendall b 03 Apr 1919 Danville, NH s/o LESSARD, Dona & COLLINS, Isa M.; md 26 Jun 1945 Danville, NH BRAINARD, Ruth Ellen md by Rev Norman R. Farnum Jr.

LESSARD, Pauline Gertrude b 26 Mar 1924 Danville, NH d/o LESSARD, Dona & COLLINS, Isa M.; md 01 Nov 1952 Danville, NH SIMES, Merle Kenneth; d 20 Feb 1975 Danville, NH; md by rev W. C. Chappell

LESSARD, Rebecca Louise b 27 Feb 1918 Danville, NH d/o LESSARD, Dona & COLLINS, Isa M.

LESSARD, Rich Allen b 27 Dec 1947 Danville NH s/o LESSARD, Lloyd Allen & FOLLANSBEE, Virginia Lor

LESSARD, Ruth Barbara b 08 Jul 1926 Danville, NH d/o LESSARD, Dona & COLLINS. Isa M.

LESTER, Robyn Jean md 19 Nov 1988 Danville, NH SKINNER, John Wm; md by Rich J. Rondeau (JP)

LEWIS, Ethel Wilson b d/o LEWIS, Wm M. & DELANO, Martha; md WATERMAN, ---- ; d 10 Jan 1973 Danville, NH; d ae 90y

LEWIS, George d 04 Aug 1927 Danville, NH d ae 68y 7m 5d

LEWIS, Ida A. d 28 Oct 1934 Danville, NH ae 74y 7m 13d

LEWIS, WIlliam Percival b s/o LEWIS, Marshall & DELANO, Martha; d 30 Jun 1971 Danville NH; ae 86y

LIBBY, Daniel Ernest b s/o LIBBY, Albert E. & CUMMINGS, Margaret; d 01 Aug 1960 Danville, NH ae 2m

LIBBY, Thos Irving b 06 Jun 1907 Danville, NH s/o LIBBY, Thos & BOWLEY, Lottie

LIBBY, Thos J. b Portland. ME; md BOWLEY, Lottie M.

LINCOLN, Elvira R. b Sep 1844 Norton, MA d/o LINCOLN, Elkaah; md 01 Dec 1870 Norton, MA COLLINS, Alfred Asbury; d 14 May 1881 Danville, NH; 1st wife of Alfred Collins

LINEHAM, Erin Elizabeth b 14 Mar 1979 Exeter, NH d/o LINEHAM, James D. & BABCOCK, Carol A.

LIPKA, Barbara A. md 22 Jun 1991 Danville, NH SANBORN, Alden M.; md by Rev Rich H. Freeman

LISTO, Christopher md 25 Oct 1991 Danville, NH LISTO, Emanuel; md by Gerard W. Timmerman (P)

LISTO, Emanual md 25 Oct 1991 Danville, NH LISTO, Christopher; md by Gerard W. Timmerman (P)

LITTLE, Grace b Hampstead, NH d/o LITTLE, John W.; 24 Dec 1900 HAMPSTEAD, NH FITTS, Earl O.; d 11 Mar 1973 Danville, NH ae 92y

LITTLE, John W. d 30 May 1918 Danville, NH ae 82y

LITTLEFIELD, E. Frances b Danville, NH; md 1848 Danville, NH FRENCH, David

LOBLEY, Katrina Marie b 01 Jan 1978 Exeter, NH d/o LOBLEY, John G. & OVERLOCK, Sharon A.

LOCK, Horance b c1815 Franklin, NH; md 1848 Danville, NH SPOF-FORD, Elizabeth M.

LOCKHART, Jacqueline A. b d/o LOCKHART, James C. & LATOUR, Corinne M.; md TWASKA, ---- ; d 10 Sep 1989 Danville, NH

LOFARO, Jill Angelica md 21 Feb 1988 Danville, NH WHITEMAN, George Gilbert Jr.; md by Rich J. Rondeau (JP)

LONG, Francis D. md 21 Jul 1990 Danville, NH CLARK, Ann-Marie; md by Rich J. Rondeau (JP)

LONGLAND, Alice Aldred b 1926 MA d/o LONGLAND, Herbert; md 01

LONGLAND (Cont.) Oct 1950 Danville, NH DiPIRRO, Aristide Dominic; md by Rev W. C. Chappell

LONGLAND, Evelyn Amy b 1930 MA d/o LOMGLAND, Herbert Newton & KIMBALL, Sally Elaine; md 17 Oct 1958 Danville, NH PRESCOTT, Stanley Warren; md by Rev Karl J. Hislop

LONGLAND, Herbert M. b 1934 Boston, MA; md 12 Oct 1963 Danville, NH SHACKLES, Sharon P.; md by Elizabeth H. Bragg (JP)

LONGLAND, Herbert Newton b 1934 MA s/o LONGLAND, Herbert M.; md 15 Mar 1958 Danville, NH KIMBALL, Sally Elaine; md by Rev Wendell J. Irvine

LONGLAND, SAlly K. b 1940 Exeter, NH; md 14 Jul 1963 Danville, NH McCARTHY, Robert F.; md by Rev Wendall J. Devine

LOPEZ, Paul md 07 Sep 1985 Danville, NH TRKULJA, Dancia; md by Philip D. Fichera (JP)

LORD, Jared Boyle b 25 May 1982 Exeter, NH s/o LORD, Wm N. & BOYLE, Diana M.

LORENZ, Eric R. md 22 Sep 1973 Danville, NH LAY, Crystal L.; md by Retenah V. Pietrowski (JP)

LOSH, Darrel K. b MA; md 27 Dec 1969 Danville, NH RICH, Laura Ellen; md by Rich D. Boner (P)

LOVERING, Cora Bell b c1876 Chester, NH d/o LOVERING, Ivory J. & MARDEN, Sarah Josephine;; md 01 Sep 1902 Danville, NH KIMBALL, Chester A.; d 06 Oct 1947 Danville, NH; md by Rev A. B. Howard

LOVERING, Etta Abbie b 1873 Chester, NH d/o LOVERING, Ivory J. & MARDEN, Sarah Josephine; md HERSOM, ---- , d 07 Aug 1955 Danville, NH

LOVERING, Oscar Marden b 1878 s/o LOVERING, Ivory J. & MARDEN, Sarah Josephine

LOVERING, Sarah b -c1809 Hawke, NH; md 02 Feb 1821 Hawke, NH WEBSTER, Nathaniel; d 18 Mar 1885 Danville, NH ae 76y

LOVLIEN, Lyman Wm b 1934 Eau Claire, WI s/o LOVLIEN, Ludwig M.;

LOVLIEN (Cont.) md 26 Feb 1955 Danville, NH BICKFORD, Helen Delores; md by Rev J. T. Sullivan

LOWELL, Kate Colinda b c1861 d/o LOWELL, John A. Rev. & CHASE, Julia; md 14 Nov 1885 Danville, NH COLLINS, Alfred; d 26 Mar 1939 Danville, NH

LOWELL, Mary b Hawke, NH; md 04 Jul 1776 Hawke, NH FOWLER, Robert; md by Rev John Page

LUCY, Mary M. b c1839 Hampstead, NH; md 08 May 1865 Danville, NH STEVENS, Daniel

LUNDIN, Gary F. md 21 Sep 1987 Danville, NH SEMPLE, Victoria A.; md by Marjorie Marcoux Faiia (JP)

LUNDSTROM, Rosemary md 23 Aug 1986 Danville, NH ENOS, Leo J.; md by Marion E. Snell (JP)

LUNNIN, Alice E. b 14 Nov 1886 Danville, NH d/o LUNNIN, Wm & WELCH, Evie T.

LUNNIN, Chas T. md 23 Apr 1886 Danville, NH WELCH, Evis S.

LURVEY, James M. Jr. b c1848 Palmyra, ME s/o LURVEY, James M. Sr. & JUDKINS, Rosella; md 13 Jun 1874 Cannan, NH McCONNELL, Sarah M.

LUSCHER, Louis John md 26 Sep 1976 Danville, NH PIRZ, Patricia Eliz; md by Robert S. Dejadon (JP)

LYLE, Robert R. md 19 Oct 1985 Danville, NH DECKER, Jennifer L.; md by Rev Leslie L. Leavitt Jr.

LYMAN, Patricia Frances b 1924 d/o LYMAN, Joseph N.; md 14 Oct 1950 Plaistow, NH BELYEA, Wm Francis

LYNCH, Maron F. b 1942 Boston, MA; md 11 Jul 1964 Danville, NH LaFRENIERE, Kenneth C.; md by Leona A. Sciandone (JP)

LYNCH, Robery Frazier md 07 Dec 1991 Danville, NH LeBLANC, Barbara Ann; md by Rich J. Rondeau (JP)

MacCOLMAN, Natalie Anne b 03 Feb 1987 Winchester, MA; d/o MacCOLMAN, Jack K. & KATZ, Lauretta J.

MACE, Amy Lydia b 21 Jan 1899 Danville, NH d/o MACE, Wm James & COLLINS, Bertha Malvina; md 31 Aug 1921 Hampstead, NH DEMAINE, Wendall Oscar; d Dec 1972 Danville, NH; bu Danville, NH; md by Rev Arnaldo Natino

MACE, Carlton Alva b 12 Jun 1897 Danville, NH s/o MACE, Wm James & COLLINS, Bertha Malvina; md 27 Aug 1960 W. Fremont, NH WEST, Bernice Mae; d 11 Sep 1981; md by Rev Wm Wylie

MACE, Carlton Alva b 12 Jun 1897 Danville, NH s/o MACE, Wm James & COLLINS, Bertha Malvina; md 25 Dec 1918 Danville, NH BROWN, Evelyn Lucrecia; d 11 Sep 1981; md by Rev Luke M. Bleakney

MACE, Claudia-Ann md 11 Nov 1972 Danville, NH DELAY, Dennis M; md by Roger A. Vachon (P)

MACE, Donald Carlton b 21 Dec 1921 Danville, NH s/o MACE, Carlton Alva & BROWN, Violet Lucrecia; md 03 Sep 1945 Danville, NH RYDER, Elna Verna; md by rev W. C. Chappell

MACE, Donna Evelyn b 22 Sep 1949 Hartford, CT d/o MACE, Donald Carlton & RYDER, Elena Verna

MACE, Douglas Cameron b 24 Mar 1956 Hartford, CT s/o MACE, Donald Carlton & RYDER, Elena Verna

MACE, Evelyn Lucille b 28 Dec 1919 Danville, NH d/o MACE, Carlton Alva & BROWN, Violet Lucrecia; md 10 Jun 1939 MURRAY, Wm Francis

MACE, Janis Elaine b 11 Aug 1948 Hartford, CT d/o MACE, Donald Carlton & RYDER, Elena Verna

MACE, Kimberly Ann b 03 Mar 1977 Exeter, NH d/o MACE, Wm J. Jr. & MORRISON, Deborah E.

MACE, Lowell Clinton b 18 Jan 1893 Danville, NH d/o MACE, Wm James & COLLINS, Bertha Malvina; md 31 Aug 1931 Danville, NH JONES, Ardis Susan; d Jan 1987 Haverhill, MA; md by Rev Henry O. Martin

MACE, Mark Wayne b 06 Jul 1946 Hartford, CT; s/o MACE, Donald Carlton & RYDER, Elna Verna

MACE, Priscilla Frances b 09 Oct 1933 Haverhill, MA d/o MACE, Lowell Clinton & JONES, Ardis Susan; md 21 Jan 1953 BAYRD, Leon Earl

MACE, Reginald Collins b 07 Oct 1923 Danville s/o MACE, Carlton Alva & BROWN, Violet Lucrecia; d 25 Sep 1928 ae 4y 11m 18d

MACE, Stephen Justin b 23 Oct 1962 Danville s/o MACE, Wm J. & HANLON, Clarie E.; md 29 Nov 1990 Danville, NH SCARAFONE, Kelly Ann; md by Richard J. Rondeau (JP)

MACE, Wm James b 10 Jan 1868 Fremont, NH s/o MACE, Daniel W. & WILKERSON, Marinda Lydia; md 28 Apr 1892 Danville, NH COLLINS, Bertha Malvina; d 21 Mar 1957 Danville, NH; bu Danville, NH Center Cem.; md by Rev J. A. Lowell; Occupation Shoemaker

MacGILLIVRAY, Robert A. md 04 May 1971 Danville, NH HILTZ, Lorraine M.; md by Rev Cathleen R. Narowitz

MACHADO, James E. md 14 Feb 1987 Danville, NH SNOW, Judith A.; md by Joan Maria Pichowicz (JP)

MACK, Harriet N. b c1830 Canterbery, NH; md 04 Feb 1879 Danville, NH EASTMAN, James

MACKIE, James b 1851 England; d 27 May 1935 Danville, NH

MACKIE, James L. b Londonderry, NH; md HOWARD, Donna M.

MACKIE, Johanna C. d 31 Jul 1943 Danville, NH ae 72y 6m 27d

MACKIE, Joseph H. Jr. md 22 Apr 1972 Danville, NH WAIN, Donna L.; md by Rev Peter W. Lovejoy

MACKIE, Michael Lee b 03 Mar 1968 Danville, NH s/o MACKIE, James L. & HOWARD, Donna M.

MACKIE, Victoria Lee b 09 Feb 1966 Danville, NH d/o MACKIE, James L. & HOWARD, Donna M.; md 28 May 1983 Danville, NH ARNOLD, Wm M.; md by Florent R. Bilodeau (P)

MaCLEAN, Christina d/o MaCLEAN, Donald & HILL, Jane; md BUTTERS, ----; d 09 May 1976 Danville, NH ae 93y

MaCLEAN, James Calvin b Nova Scotia s/o MacLEAN, Wm & LOGAN, Eliza; d 01 Jun 1962 Danville, NH

MacLEAN, Tammy Ann b 27 Aug 1958 Danville, NH d/o MacLEAN, John F. & COMEAU, Janice A.

MacNEFF, Eliz b c1892 Boston, MA d/o MacNEFF, Philip; md 21 Jun 1913 Danville, NH SANBORN, Herman E.; md by Allen C. Keith

MacNEIL, Carol Ann b 21 Sep 1956 Danville, NH d/o MacNEIL, John O. & McPHEARSON, Patricia; md 22 Jun 1974 Danville, NH SIMPSON, Robert Edward; md by Rev Richard L. Provencher

MacNEILL, Mae M. b d/o MacNEILL, Neil & McDONALD, Christine; md TUCK, ---- ; d 07 Sep 1970 Danville, NH ae 72y

MAEDER, Donald Bruce b 1940 SD; md 24 Aug 1968 Danville, NH DUSTON, Shirley Rae; md by Peter Damian (P)

MAGLIO, Robert S. Sr. md 29 Mar 1986 Danville, NH STURK, Barbara J.; md by David T. Ingerson (JP)

MAIONE, Lorraine A. md 15 Sep 1985 Danville, NH NICI, Eugene A; md by Rochelle Lafontaine (JP)

MAIR, Jack Gordon b 1921 Stockton, CA s/o MAIR, James Gordon; md 28 Dec 1945 Danville, NH CROSBY, Virginia Phyillis; md by Agnes H. Collins (JP)

MALCOLM, Mary E. b 1878 Lee, ME; md 08 May 1928 Hampstead, NH WHITCHER, Elmer; md by Irving Leighton, (JP)

MALEY, Margaret Jane b Gleasonville, MA d/o MALEY, Daniel & BIRMINGHAM, Katherine; md MERRICK, ----; d 20 Dec 1951 Danville, NH

MALO, Ronald R. b 1940 MA; md 09 Sep 1961 Danville, NH COTE, Kathleen C.; md by Rev Rob F. Griffin

MANCHESTER, Esther b c1897 Lawrence, MA s/o MANCHESTER, Fred; md 15 Dec 1920 Methuen, MA WELCH, John B. by Rev John Ward Moore

MANGANARO, Jos Jas b 1923 MA s/o MANGANARO, Salvatore; md 24 Dec 1950 Danville, NH BEACH, Marj. Ann md by Agnes H. Collins (JP)

MANGENE, Louise M. b Malden, MA; md TAATJES, Gerard

MANGINE, John O'Donald md 29 Sep 1990 Danville, NH HOCH, Sandra Marie; md by Wallace J. Anctil (JP)

MANIKIAN, Carl R. md 25 May 1980 Danville, NH STEPHENSON, Jamie; md by Rev Wm Ryans

MANN, Florence E. b Lawrence, MA; md 06 May 1886 Danville BUSWELL, Edwin A.

MANN, Sarah M. b c1837 Barton, VT; md 09 May 1859 Danville, NH DAVIS, Andrew J.

MANNING, Esther Cadwell b d/o MANNING, Frank Milton & CAD-WELL, Esther; md WILSON, ----; d 30 Jul 1990 Danville, NH ae 75y

MANSUR, Florence E. b 1942 Haverhill, MA; md 29 May 1966 Danville, NH COMTOIS, Ronald L.

MANUEL, Florence N. b 1895 Provincetown, MA d/o MANUEL, Wm O.; md 30 Sep 1916 Cummaquid, MA ROCK, Rodney; md by Rev Edward P. Fuller

MARCELAIS, Irene Theresa b 1921 Haverhill, NH d/o MARCELAIS, Alphonse; md 19 Apr 1947 Danville, NH MEANEY, James Leo; md by Rev W. C. Chappell

MARCELLO, Jacob Allen b 25 Jul 1983 Lawrence, MA s/o MARCELLO, Kenneth & FODERARO, Lisa

MARCH, Abbie L. b 1844 Danville, NH d/o MARCH, Geo W. & GEORGE, Annie; md 07 Jan 1865 Danville, NH GOODRICH, Lewis N.

MARCH, Adeline B. b c1844 Danville, NH; md 07 Mar 1863 Danville, NH JOHNSON, Daniel S.

MARCH, Annie Hainsworth b 1890 MA d/o MARCH, Chas W.; md 14 Mar 1956 Danville, NH TOWLE, Herbert Jarius; md by Agnes H. Collins (JP)

MARCH, Arvilla Anna b Sandown, NH d/o MARCH, Geo H. & GEORGE, Anna; md TUCKER, ---- ; d 13 Apr 1911 Danville, NH ae 73 2m 4d

MARCH, Augusta A. b c1845 d/o MARCH, Isaac & GREELEY, Nancy; d 1847 Danville, NH ae 2y

MARCH, Etta Ann b Jan 1874 Danville, NH d/o MARCH, Geo W. & GOODRICH, Helen M.; md 1st 29 Aug 1892 Danville, NH RUEE, Charles F., 2nd 10 Aug 1927 Danville, NH TALBEE, Frank Edward by Rev Howard Reyman; d 26 Mar 1973 Danville, NH

MARCH, Geo W. b c1841 Lowell, MA; md 14 Jun 1870 Danville, NH Morrill, Helen M. Mrs.; d 01 Mar 1905 Danville, NH ae 64y 9m

MARCH, Isaac W. b Newburyport, MA s/o MARCH, Nathaniel & JE-WETT, Hannah; d 16 May 1898 Danville, NH

MARCH, John d 15 Jan 1776 Hawke, NH

MARCH, Nathaniel b Ipswich, MA; md JEWETT, Hannah

MARCH, Nathaniel O. b Lowell, MA s/o MARCH, Isaac & GREELEY, Nancy A.; d 05 Aug 1923 Danville, NH

MARCHAND, Gerard Emile md 01 Dec 1990 Danville, NH BEAM, Juanita Audrey; md by Rich J. Rondeau (JP)

MARCO, Mary b Plaistow, NH; md 09 Jul 1881 Danville, NH KELLY, Alfred Jr.

MARCOTTE, David M. md 14 Dec 1986 Danville, NH FLOURDE, Deborah L.; md by Richard J. Rondeau (JP)

MARCOTTE, Pauline H. b 1911 Fremont, NH d /o MARCOTE, Geo E.; md 14 Jun 1929 Fremont, NH KIMBALL, Maurice K.; md by Rev S.B. Enman

MARDEN, Marie b 1924 Newton, NH d/o MARDEN, Ralph Wilson; md 14 Aug 1948 Newton, NH CURRIER, Richard Edgar; md by Rev John S. Viall

MARDEN, Sarah Josephine b c1849 Chester, NH d/o MARDEN, Ebenezer & BOSFORD, Abigail; md LOVERING, Ivory J.; d 15 Jan 1910 Danville, NH ae 60y 11m 14d

MARENA, Robert Clark md 18 May 1991 Danville, NH SMITH, Tara Beth Ann; md by Everett E. Palmer

MARGGRAF, Charles b 1912 Methuen, MA s/o MARGGRAF, Fred; md 30 Jan 1936 Danville, NH MILLER, Frances; md by Rev W. C. Chappell

MARINO, John Charles b 1920 Swampscott, MA s/o MARINO, Orazio; md 21 May 1953 Danville, NH DeCILLO, Jean Graves

MARKOVICH, Thomas David md 19 Aug 1989 Danville, NH DESROSIERS, Ann Louise; md by Rev Leslie L. Leavitt

MARNARD, Esther b Hawke, NH; md 14 Jul 1768 Hawke, NH RING, Issacher

MARQUIS, Diane A. md 14 Aug 1971 Danville, NH COLLINS, Norman Howard; md by Romeo J. Valliere (P)

MARSAN, Dennis J. md 01 Jun 1990 Danville, NH MARTIN, Diane E.; md by Richard J. Rondeau (JP)

MARSH, Walter b E Kingston, NH s/o MARSH, Charles; d 16 Jul 1948 Danville, NH ae 86y 10m 4d

MARSHALL, Anna M. b 1893 Redstone, NH d/o MARSHALL, John B.; md 29 Apr 1944 Danville, NH NEWTON, Freeman Geo; md by Rev Byron O. Waterman; Prev md BESSETTE, ----

MARSHALL, Clifford A. b s/o MARSHALL, Joseph & BLYNN, Mary; d 23 Nov 1987 Danville, NH ae 77y

MARSHMAN, Debra T. md 23 Jun 1979 Danville, NH DeSERRES, Norman P.; md by Rev Pierre Baker (P)

MARTEL, Louis b Lawrence, MA s/o MARTEL, Wilfred & LeMAY, Marie L.; d 31 Dec 1965 Danville, NH ae 61y

MARTILLA, Leonard J. b 1942 Peabody, MA; md 04 Feb 1967 Danville, NH FREDERICK, Lorraine L.; md by Roger A. Vachon (P)

MARTIN, Abbie L. d 11 Feb 1939 Danville, NH ae 69y 11m 20d

MARTIN, Dawn Lynn b 22 Oct 1966 Danville, NH d/o MARTIN, Donald Melvin & COLLINS, Carol Ann; md 01 Aug 1987 Danville, NH VIENS, Mark W.; md by Rev Everett E. Palmer

MARTIN, Diane E. md 01 Jun 1990 Danville, NH MARSAN, Dennis J.; md by Richard J. Rondeau (JP)

MARTIN, Donald Melvin b 1937 Kingston, NH s/o MARTIN, Melvin; md 05 Oct 1957 Danville, NH COLLINS, Carol Ann

MARTIN, Donald Wm md 21 May 1988 Danville, NH LARKIN, Lilly Elfreda; md by Rev Byran E. Moore

MARTIN, Everett Geo b 02 Aug 1934 Danville, NH s/o MARTIN, Melvin & EMERY, Ruth

MARTIN, Hannah b Kingston, NH; md 11 Apr 1830 Hawke, NH TUCKER, Moses

MARTIN, Jeffery C. md 25 Nov 1989 Danville, NH MARTIN, Joleen Marie; md by Richard J. Rondeau (JP)

MARTIN, Joleen Marie b 27 Aug 1960 Danville, NH d/o MARTIN, Donald Melvin & COLLINS, Carol Ann; md 25 Nov 1989 Danville, NH EATON, Jeffery C.; md by Richard J. Rondeau (JP)

MARTIN, Jonathan b Atkinson, NH; md 01 May 1806 Kingston, NH BLAKE, Mehitable

MARTIN, Laura J. md 20 Sep 1986 Danville, NH STANDING, Wm H. 3rd; md by Rev Everett E. Palmer

MARTIN, Michele md 07 May 1983 Danville, NH MUDGE, David T.; md by Rev Everett E. Palmer

MARTIN, Nellie F. b c1857 Hampstead, NH; md 29 May 1877 Danville, NH COOK, Melvin T.

MARTIN, Patricia Jean b 06 Mar 1964 Danville, NH d/o MARTIN Donald Melvin & COLLINS, Carol Ann; md 11 Jun 1988 Danville, NH THOMPSON, Roger Michael; md by Rev Everett E. Palmer

MARTIN, Tamera Ann b 01 Feb 1958 Danville, NH d/o MARTIN, Donald Melvin & COLLINS, Carol Ann; md 25 Jun 1978 Danville, NH FIELD, Randy Wilder; md by Rev Wm Ryans

MARTIN, Wm b c1867 Salisbury, VT s/o MARTIN, John; md 22 Aug 1888 Danville, NH GRIFFIN, Iva A.

MARTIN, Wm b 1864 Salisbury, MA s/o MARTIN, John & REED, Matilda; md 02 May 1896 Danville, NH HUNTINGTON, Grace C.; md by Rev J. A. Wiggin; Ocupationc Shoe Cutter

MASCHETTO, Nellie b 1918 Methuen, MA d/o MASCHETTO, Joseph; md 15 May 1936 Danville, NH BOILS, Vincent; md by Clarence M. Collins (JP)

MASKELL, ALBERT Alton b 1933 Fremont, NH s/o MASKELL, Alton R.; md 14 Aug 1954 Danville, NH CARBONE, Shirley Elaine; md by Rev Stanley Dahlman

MASKELL, Kevin Douglas b 14 Jul 1955 Danville, NH s/o MASKELL, Albert Alton & CARBONE, Shirley Elain

MASON, Mary b 1910 Atkinson, NH d/o MASON, Geo; md 27 Aug 1923 Danville, NH DUSTON, Charles D.; md by Mary E. Dirsa (JP)

MASON, Shayla Jean b 14 Nov 1986 Manchester, NH d/o MASON, Martin W. & JEAN, Sherry A.

MASSEY, Phyllis b s/o MASSEY, Silas Torrey & KEISER, Edith; md STAFFORD, ----; d 18 Jul 1990 Danville, NH ae 68y

MASTIOLILLO, Scott Andrew b 16 Apr 1964 Danville, NH s/o MASTIO-LILLO, Pat A. & SCIAUDONE, Fay K.

MASTON, Gregory A. md 27 May 1984 Danville, NH FRIES, Eliz; md by Rev Roger C. B. Daly

MATHESON, Mary b d/o MATHE-SON, Malcolm & MacKENZIE, Mary; md PLUMMER, ---- ; d 31 May 1976 Danville, NH ae 83y

MAXWELL, Carol Jean md 18 Feb 1978 Danville, NH HARMS, Kevin Scott; md by Michael Griffin (P)

MAXWELL, Chris md 23 Oct 1982 Danville, NH NIKOLAUS, Barbara L.; md by John H. Lamprey (JP)

MAXWELL, Jas W. b s/o MAX-WELL, Thos H. & DONAHUE, Nora A.; d28 Dec 1990 Danville, NH ae 68y

MAXWELL, Nicholas John b 15 Jan 1990 Exeter, NH s/o MAXWELL, Christopher & NICHOLAUS, Barbara L.

MAXWELL, Wm James b 23 Nov 1986 Exeter, NH s/o MAXWELL, Christopher & NICHOLAUS, Barb. L.

May, Lorraine; md 24 Jun 1989 Danville, NH FAIRWEATHER, John David; md by Richard J. Rondeau (JP)

May, Timothy Mark b 01 Feb 1990 Nashua, NH s/o May, Mark R. & GAUVIN, Dianne M.

MAYO, Andrew Joseph b 05 Sep 1984 Exeter, NH s/o MAYO, Robert E. 3rd & COLLINS, Sandra L.

MAYO, Angela Marie b 25 Jul 1989 Exeter, NH d/o MAYO, James D. & McGILVRAY, Corinne M.

MAYO, Robert E. b 07 Jun 1980 Danville, NH; md COLLINS, Sandra L.; md by Rev Wm Ryans

MAYO, Zachery Reed b 06 Jul 1988 Exeter, NH s/o MAYO, James D. & McGILVERAY, Corrine M.

MAZUR, Michael Paul b 10 Feb 1983 Exeter, NH s/o MAZUR, Richard & PHILLIPS, Nancy

MAZZOTTA, Michael Keenan md 24 Dec 1990 Danville, NH St PIERRE, Laura May; md by Rich J Rondeau (JP)

McBRIDE, Carol Sue md 17 Dec 1988 Danville, NH BREWER, David Thos; md by Everett J. Rondeau (JP)

McCALLUM, Richard David b s/o McCALLUM, Francis H. & CLARK, Leona M.; d 24 Dec 1980 Danville, NH ae 36y

McCARRON, Jeanne M. md 28 Mar 1987 Danville, NH STEELE, Michael J.; md by Rev Robert F. Dobson

McCARTHY, Robert F. b 1938 Haverhill, MA; md 14 Jul 1963 Danville, NH LONGLAND, Sally K.; md by Rev Wendall J. Devine

McCARTHY, Thomas E. md 20 Sep 1986 Danville, NH DAVARICH, Hilary; md by Glen E. French (JP)

McCLARY, Kenneth Alan b md 20 Nov 1971 Danville, NH CLARK, Janice Ruth; md by Rev Cathleen R. Narowitz

McCLURE, Alexander G. b Salem, MA; d 23 Dec 1910 Danville, NH ae 77y 11m 26d

McCLURE, Austin W. b 1889 Danville, NH s/o McCLURE, Geo S. & GATES, Emma May; d 05 May 1905

McClure (Cont.) Danville, NH ae 16y 3m 2d

McCLURE, Doris Emma b 02 Apr 1901 d/po McCLURE, Geo S. & GATES, E. May; 6th child in family

McCLURE, Geo S. b c1860 Attleboro, MA; md 21 Jan 1888 Danville, NH GATES, Emma Mary

McCLURE, Hilda A. b Danville, NH d/o McCLURE, Geo S. & GATES, Emma May; md FOOTE, ----; d 20 Sep 1951 Danville, NH; bu Danville, NH; d ae 72y

McCLURE, Lydia M. d/o REICH, Adam; d 26 May 1953 Danville, NH ae 62y

McCLURE, Sidney Allan b s/o McCLURE, Geo S. & GATES, Emma May; d 23 Apr 1974 Danville, NH ae 74y

McCLUSKY, Bernard Vincet b 1914 Lynn, MA s/o McCLUSKY, Bernard Vincent Sr. md 16 Nov 1947 Danville, NH SOVULIS, Eleanor A.; md by Rev W. C. Chappell

McCOLLISTER, Lottie md 23 Sep 1910 COLLINS, Clement S.

McConnell, Sarah M. b c1854 Warren, NH; md 13 Jun 1874 Cannan, NH LUREY, James M.

McCRUSKER, Timothy Patrick b 11 Aug 1964 Danville, NH s/o McCRUSKER, Thos L. & FRANCOEUR, Carol

McCUSHER, Thomas Leo b 22 Dec 1961 Danville, NH s/o McCRUSHER, Thomas L. & FRANCOEUR, Carol J.

McCUSKER, Theresa Ann b 17 Mar 1963 Danville, NH d/o McCRUSKER, Thomas L. & FRANCOEUR, Carol J.

McCUSKER, Thomas L. b Malden, MA; md FRANCOEUR, Carol

McDONALD, Eliz A. b 1868 Westville, NH d/o McDONALD, James & KENNEDY, Mary; md BATCHELDER, ----; d 25 Jul 1938 Danville, NH

McDONALD, James J. b 1896 Manchester, NH s/o McDONALD, James P.; md 26 Dec 1933 Danville, NH JOHNSON, Roxy; md by Rev David J. Caron

McDONALD, Joseph J. md 11 Apr

McDonald (Cont.) 1987 Danville, NH HAYES, Judith A.; md by Rev Everett E. Palmer

McDONALD, Wm A. b 1946; md 09 Nov 1968 Danville, NH O'BRIAN, Joanne W.; md by Leona A. Sciaudone (JP)

McFARLAND, Marcia Ann b d/o McFARLAND, Earl & ASHE, Flora M.; md HARTFORD, ----; d 01 Aug 1981 Danville, NH ae 32y

McFARLAND, Tammy May md 07 Jul 1979 Danville, NH WELCH, Tomothy W. G.; md by Robert J. Dejdon (JP)

MCGAUNN, Kevin D. md 28 Oct 1989 Danville, NH GORTON, Linda Sue; md by Rev Everett E. Palmer

McGRATH, Ashley B. b 06 Sep 1905 Danville, NH s/o McGRATH, Samuel & DARBE, Clara A.; d 28 Feb 1941 Danville, NH

McGRATH, Cedric b 09 May 1908 Danville, NH s/o McGRATH, Samuel & DARBE, Clara; md 22 Nov 1926 Derry, NH CAMERON, Charlotte A.; md by Rev Arthur D. Woodworth

McGRATH, Doris E. b 29 Aug 1923 Danville, NH d/o McGRAPH, Rodney J. & BRUCE, Annie B.

McGRATH, Madelyne Shirley b 09 Jun 1927 Danville, NH d/o McGRATH, Cedric D. & CAMERON, Charlotte A

McGRATH, Maralyn Lucie b 30 May 1926 Danville, NH d/o McGRATH, Ashley & JOHNSON, Helen J.

McGRATH, Marshall Conrad b 08 Dec 1928 Danville, NH s/o McGRATH, Cedric & CAMERON, Charlotte; 2nd child in family

McGRATH, Mavis Elaine b 11 Apr 1927 Danville, NH d/o McGRATH, Rodney J. & BRUSE, Annie B.

McGRATH, Rodney James b 18 Mar 1902 Danville, NH s/o McGRATH, Samuel & DARBE, Clara; md 03 Oct 1920 BRUCE, Annie B.; md by Rev Arnaldo Natina; md BRUCE, Annie B.; d 21 Jan 1955 Danville, NH

McGRATH, Samuel b 1858 New Brunswick, Canada s/o McGRATH, Euzbe & LeBLANT, Susan; md 1st 11 Aug 1894 Danville, NH MALY, Jennie

McGrath (Cont.) by Rev John A. Wiggin, 2nd DARBE, Clara A.

McGRATH, Samuel b Buctouche, NB CANADA; d 15 Nov 1907 Danville, NH ae 50y 10m 13d

McGRATH, Therza Augusta b 04 Aug 1921 Danville, NH d/o McGRATH, Rodney J. & BRUCE, Annie B.

McGUIRE, Patricia A. md 26 Aug 1989 Danville, NH ROSS, Scott A.; md by Richard J. Rondeau (JP)

McGUNNIGLE, Chas R. b c1862 E Boston, MA s/o McGUNNIGLE, Jas; md 29 Dec 1906 Haverhill, MA SANBORN, Mary E.; md by Rev Arthur G. Lyon

McGUNNIGLE, James Dewitt b 22 Jun 1909 Danville, NH s/o McGUNNIGLE, Chas R. & CLOUCHER, Mary E.

McHOLT, Gladys A. b 20 Dec 1900 Danville, NH d/o McHOLT, Henry & LADD, Etta A.; 6th Child in Family

McINTIRE, Ruby E. b Woodland d/o McINTIRE, Jas & WILSON, Martha d 11 Jan 1966 Danville, NH ae 68y

McINTOSH, Pamela Jean md 03 Sep 1988 Danville, NH MILLS, Samuel Henry; md by Rev Peter W. Mercer

McINTYRE, Franklin J. md 15 Dec 1973 Danville, NH O'NEIL, Margaret J.; md by Rev Henry Sawatzky

McINTYRE, Scott Allan b 07 Aug 1971 Methuen, MA s/o MCINTYRE, Franklin J. & ROBIN, Elaine L.

McKAY, Daniel W. md 23 Nov 1984 Danville, NH BEATON, Patricia I.; md by Richard J. Rondeau (JP)

McKENNA, Philip J. b Hyde Park, MA s/o McKenna, Patrick; md 19 Aug 1933 Danville, NH Moore, Ethlyn M.; md by Rev Edmond T. Quirk

McKEON, Eliz C. b 1914 West Chester, PA d/o McKEON, Matthew; md 15 Mar 1936 Danville, NH SMITH, Lawrence S.; md by Clarence M. Collins (JP)

McKINNEY, Mary Jo md 14 Feb 1988 Danville, NH SHURTLEFF, Scott Leslie; md by Rev Robert E. Aspinwall

McLANE, Hannah M. b 1848 d/o McLANE, Samuel & ROBERTS, Betsy B.

McLANE, Maria Betsy b 26 Feb 1832 d/o McLANE, Samuel & ROBERTS, Betsy B.

McLANE, Sally B. b 06 Feb 1830 Hawke, NH d/o McLANE, Samuel & ROBERTS, Betsey; d 17 Feb 1843 Danville, NH; or d 27 Jul 1838 ?

McLANE, Samuel b 11 Dec 1807 Plymouth, NH s/o McLANE, Obediah & ----, Hannah; md 04 Apr 1829 Hawke, NH ROBERTS, Betsey

McLANE, Sylvester b 15 Jul 1810 Plymouth, NH s/o McLANE, Obediah & ----, Hannah

McLANE, ---- b 1848 Danville, NH d/o McLANE, Samuel & ROBERTS, Betsey; d 21 Sep 1848 Danville, NH

McLEAN, Colin Francis Jr. md 25 May 1991 Danville, NH TILLSON, Karen Eliz; md by Francis T. Christian (P)

McLURE, Hilda A. b 16 Jul 1897 Danville, NH d/o McLURE, Geo S. & GATES, Emma M.

McLYNCH, Bryan F. md 07 Oct 1989 Danville, NH RAYMOND, Marilyn A.; md by Rev Everett E. Palmer

McMANUS, Margaret b d/o McMANUS, Cormic & REID, Margaret; md SAYRE, ----; d 14 Sep 1979 Danville, NH ae 76y

McMillian, Anna-Jane b d/o McMILLIAN, Francis B. & MERRITT, Geraldine; md SANFORD, ----; d 02 Aug 1987 Danville, NH ae 65y

McNEFF, Eliz b Boston, NH; md SANBORN, Herman

McNEIL, Ernest b Danville, NH s/o McNEIL, Stanley & HUNT, Edith M.; d 20 May 1901

McNEIL, John M. s/o McNEIL, Hector & McNEIL, Sarah; d 03 Aug 1928 ae 68y 3m 2d

McNEIL, Marion R. b 01 Jan 1905 Danville, NH d/o McNEIL, Stanley & HUNT, Mabel; 4 Child in family

McNEIL, Stanley b Nova Scotia; md HUNT, Mabel

McNEIL, ---- b 03 Jun 1900 Danville, NH s/o McNEIL, Stanley & HUNT, Mabel; 2nd Child in Family

McPHERSEON, Alan Bruce b 27 Apr 1948 Danville, NH s/o McPHER-

McPherson (Cont.) SON, Robert Collins & WESTON, Marion Priscilla

McPHERSON, Brian Douglas b 06 Apr 1952 Danville, NH s/o McPHERSON, Robert Collins & WESTON, Marion Priscilla

McPHERSON, Ellen b 08 Sep 1950 Danville, NH d/o McPHERSON, Robert Collins & WESTON, Marion Priscilla

McPHERSON, Louise Eleanor b 07 Apr 1893 Grand Valley, OT d/o McPHEARSON, Wm James & FAWCETT, Eliz; md 16 Dec 1910 Grand Valley, OT COLLINS, Bernard Ira Sr.; d 24 Jun 1957 Haverhill, MA bu Haverhill, MA

McPHERSON, Marion Eliz b 1926 Dodsland, Sask CN d/o McPHERSON, Rob't Harvel & COLLINS, Marion; md 15 Dec 1946 Danville, NH GREY, Warren Otis; md by Rev W. C. Chappell

McPHERSON, Robert Collins b 11 Feb 1916 Danville, NH s/o McPHERSON, Robert Harvel & COLLINS, Marion; md 15 Jun 1946 Laconia, NH WESTON, Marion Priscilla; d 17 May 1964 Danville, NH; md by Rev Robert Henry Holn

McPHERSON, Robert Harvel b c1881 E Luther, Ontario, Canada s/o McPHERSON, Wm J. & FAWCETT, Eliz; md 16 Dec 1914 Danville, NH COLLINS, Marion; d 17 Sep 1973 Danville, NH; md by Rev Allen C. Kieth

McRAE, Shella Ann b 22 Nov 1968 Danville, NH d/o McRAE, David Joseph & SILVER, Shirley Ruth

MEANEY, Claire Irene b 23 Feb 1983 Lawrence, MA d/o MEANEY, James & DUBE, Donna

MEANEY, Edward F. b 1917 New York, NY d/o MEANEY, Matthew;md 09 Aug 1946 Kingston, NH Johnson, Lois Kimball; md by Gardner H. Conant (JP)

MEANEY, Edward Francis b 23 Dec 1946 Haverhill, MA s/o MEANEY, Edward James & KIRWAN, Catherine Eliz; md 22 Jul 1967 Danville, NH TURNER, Sharon Elaine; md by Rev Wm. B. Whyle

MEANEY, Ellen M. d 01 Jan 1990 Danville, NH ae 98y

MEANEY, James Leo b 1921 New York, NY s/o MEANEY, Matthew; md 19 Apr 1947 Danville, NH MARCELAIS, Irene Theresa; md by Rev W. C. Chappell

MEANEY, Karen Sue b 02 Jul 1949 Danville, NH d/o MEANEY, Edward F. & JOHNSON, Lois K.

MEANEY, Patrick b 16 Mar 1948 Danville, NH s/o MEANEY, Edward F. & JOHNSON, Lois K. d 16 Mar 1948 Danville, NH

MEANEY, Robert Charles b 17 Jul 1951 Danville, NH s/o MEANEY, Edward F. & JOHNSON, Lois K.

MEESE, Lillian E. b 1939 FL; md 13 Apr 1968 Danville, NH CARR, Rich F.; md by Edward R. Lamb (JP)

MEIGS, Eliz Sutton b 26 Nov 1959 Exeter, NH d/o MEIGS, Peter S. & SMITH, Deb d 26 Nov 1959 Exeter, NH

MEIGS, Ellen Jo b 21 Dec 1966 Exeter, NH d/o MEIGS, Peter S. & SMITH, Deborah

MEIGS, Guy Remington b 18 Jun 1964 Exeter, NH s/o MEIGS, Peter & SMITH, Deborah

MEIGS, Peter b Lynn, MA; md SMITH, Deborah

MEIGS, Warren Sanford b 27 Mar 1963 Danville, NH s/o MEIGS, Peter S. & SMITH, Deborah

MELKONIAN, Aram Richard b 1919 Boston, MA s/o MELKONIAN, Geo Herbert; md 05 Oct 1946 Danville, NH YOUNG, Dorothy Agnetta; md by Rev W. C. Chappell

MELKONIAN, Geo Herbert b Constantinople, Turkey s/o MELKONIAN, Henry & KRIKONIAN, Mary; d 19 Mar 1948 Danville, NH ae 56y 4m 18d

MELKONIAN, Jane Josephine b 1930 New York, NY d/o MELKONIAN, Geo H.; md 06 Feb 1048 Danville, NH DEMAINE, Mahlon Oscar; md by Rev W. C. Chappell

MELKONIAN, Jon Herbert b 18 Feb 1954 Danville, NH s/o MELKONIAN, Herbert G. & McGRAPTH, Maralyn Lucile

MELKONIAN, Lana Joyce b 16 Aug 1948 Danville, NH d/o MELKONIAN, Aram Richard & YOUNG, Dorothy Agnetta; md 01 Jun 1968 Danville, NH BROWN, Dennis C.; md by Rev Douglas Abbott

MELKONIAN, Mark Alan b 21 Oct 1950 Danville, NH s/o MELKONIAN, Herbert T. & McGRATH, Maralyn L.

MELKONIAN, Michael McGrath b 25 Jun 1948 Danville, NH s/o MELKONIAN, Herbert T. & MCGRATH, Maralyn L.

MELKONIAN, Nancy Gail b 25 Aug 1949 Danville, NH d/o MELKONIAN, Aram Richard & YOUNG, Dorothy Agnetta; md 07 Aug 1971 Danville, NH SUE, Stephen Louis; md by Richard Vickery (P)

MELKONIAN, Randall Aaram b 27 Feb 1951 Danville, NH s/o MELKONIAN, Aaram Rich & YOUNG, Dorothy Agnetta

MENCKE, Keith Wm md 09 Jul 1988 Danville, NH PEDERSEN, Cheri Lynn; md by Rev David M. Midwood

MENZIE, Donna M. b md 04 Aug 1984 Danville, NH ELY, Roy N.; md by David T. Ingerson (JP)

MERCER, Kenneth Bartley b 17 Jan 1989 Exeter, NH s/o MERCER, Mathew H. & SULLIVAN, Alicia P.

MERRICK, Annie C. b Hampstead, NH; md 03 Sep 1881 Danville, NH HINES, Edward W.

MERRICK, Edith b Hampsted, NH; md REYNOLDS, Byron

MERRICK, Edith M. b Hampstead, NH d/o MERRICK, Frank; md SHELDON, ---- ; d 07 Aug 1959 Danville, NH ae 85y

MERRICK, Edward d 18 Sep 1934 Danville, NH ae 90y 2m 1d

MERRICK, Ernest D. b 1897 Danville, NH s/o MERRICK, Merrill B. md 02 Oct 1927 Kingston, NH PATTEN, Lena md by Rev Asa Bradley

MERRICK, Ernest E. b 1865; d 19 Jan 1866 Danville, NH ae 3m

MERRICK, Esther b Danville, NH; md SEWARD, Wm

MERRICK, Etta M. b 06 Feb 1880 Danville, NH d/o MERRICK, Henry W.

MERRICK (Cont.) & MALEY, Jennie; md 1st 01 Sep 1909 Danville, NH WINSLOW, Wm W.; d 12 Aug 1978 Danville NH by Rev W. C. Chappell, 2nd 08 Dec 1932 Danville, NH CHASE, Charles E.

MERRICK, Florence W. b 01 Jan 1894 Danville, NH d/o MERRICK, Merrill B. & De ROCHMOND, Mary V.

MERRICK, Jos G. b c1826 Hampstead, NH; md 03 Dec 1873 Danville NH SAWYER, Roseann; d 31 Oct 1886 Danville NH Roseann prev md to BROWN

MERRICK, Laura Ann b 23 May 1954 Danville, NH d/o MERRICK, Ray. S. & MCCALLUM, Shirley Ann; md 24 Dec 1973 Danville, NH FARLEY, Craig A.; md by Rev Cathleen R. Narowitz

MERRICK, Leona M. md 12 Jun 1971 Danville, NH BEZANSON, Daniel S. md by Rev Cathleen R. Narowitz

MERRICK, Mary A. d Danville, NH ae 78y 11m 23d

MERRICK, Merrill Bagley b Hampstead, NH s/o MERRICK, Stephen & GEORGE, Harriet; md 05 May 1887 Kingston, NH DeROCHMOND, Mary V.; d 26 Sep 1945 Danville, NH ae 89y 2m 20d; md by Rev J. M. Bean

MERRICK, Raymond S. md McCALLUM, Shirley Ann

MERRICK, Sidney Corliss b 1893 Danville, NH s/o MERRICK, Merrill B. & DEROCHEMONT, Mary V.; md 10 Feb 1923 Chester, NH WEST, Bernice M.; d 24 Jan 1957 Danville, NH; md by Rev Silas N. Adams; d ae 64y

MERRICK, Stephen b c1817 Hampstead, NH; md BAGLEY, Harriet; d 02 Apr 1883 Danville, NH ae 66y

MERRICK, Wm E. b 10 Mar 1872 Danville, NH s/o MERRICK, Edward & DEARBORN, Mary A.; d 31 Dec 1943 Danville, NH

MERRICK, ---- b 07 Jan 1890 Danville, NH s/o MERRICK, Merrill B. & DeROCHEMONT, Mary V.

MERRICK, ---- b 11 Feb 1899 Danville, NH D/o MERRICK, Merrill B. & DeROCHEMONT; 7th child in family

MERRICK, ---- b 12 Jan 1903 Danville, NH s/o MERRICK, Merrill B. & DeROCHEMONT, Mary V.

MERRIFIELD, Gail Sandra b 1939 Haverhill, MA d/o MERRIFIELD, Kenneth L.; md 16 Aug 1957 Danville, NH POND, Henry Herbert

MERRILL, Bruce Ed Sr. md 07 Apr 1974 Danville, NH MOORE, Kristina Marie; md by Clara B. Snow (JP)

MERRILL, Bruce Edward Jr. b 17 Nov 1974 Exeter, NH s/o MERRILL, Bruce Edward Sr. & MOORE, Kristina Marie

MERRILL, Enoch b Andover, MA; md 02 Dec 1839 Raymond, NH Mrs Susan Plummer

MERRILL, Hattie M. b c1871 West Rumney, NH d/o MERRILL, Charles; md 14 Jun 1913 Franklin, NH SHELDON, Geo H.; md by Rev Rufus P. Gardner; 1st md WELCH, ----

MERRILL, James b 1911 Boston, MA s/o MERRILL, Thomas; md 07 Oct 1937 Danville, NH RANDALL, Eliz P.; md by Clarence M. Collins (JP)

MERRILL, Jennifer Leigh b 02 Nov 1986 Haverhill, MA d/o MERRILL, Richard W. & GORDON, Sandra A.

MERRILL, Karen Lee md 16 Nov 1990 Danville, NH SPENCER, WAlter Edward Jr.; md by Rich J Rondeau (JP)

MERRILL, Martha b c1838 d/o MERRILL; md c1845 Danville, NH JOHNSON, Charles K.; d 20 Mar 1874 Danville, NH ae 36y

MERRILL, Sarah b Amesbury, MA d/o MERRILL, B. & EASTMAN, Sarah; md 16 Mar 1820 Hawke, NH BAGLEY, Wm; d 19 Dec 1891 Danville, NH

MERRILL, Wm W. md 02 Mar 1837 Danville, NH TEWKSBURY, Louisa B.

MESERVE, Horace b c1827; d 07 Feb 1860 Danville, NH ae 33y

MESERVE, Horance C.b 30 Apr 1858 Danville, NH s/o MESERVE, Winfield S. & FULLER, Harriet A.

MESERVE, James D. d 18 Jul 1863 Fort Wagner ae 21y - Civil War Rcds

MESERVE, Lura Jane b d/o MESERVE, Winfield S. & FULLER, Harriet A.; d 1856 Danville, NH

MESERVE, Mary b 25 Mar 1849 Danville, NH d/o MESERVE, Winfield S. & FULLER, Harriet A.

MESERVE, Mary H. S. b 1870 Danville, NH d/o MESERVE, S. & HOYT, Huldah; d 22 Aug 1964 Danville, NH

MESERVE, Melissa b c1822 Jackson; md 1848 Danville, NH TEWKSBURY, Enos F.

MESERVE, Winifield S. md 1st FULLER, Harrieta 2nd HOYT, Huldah

MESSER, Marjorie Ruth b 1922 Brentwood, NH d/o MASSER, Daniel & EVANS, Bertha A.; md 24 Dec 1959 Danville, NH DUSTON, Robert Oscar; d 17 May 1978 Danville, NH; md by Rev John Wood Jr.; d ae 55y

METCALF, Ronald Alton md 24 Jun 1989 Danville, NH WATERS, Constance Ann; md by Rev Everett E. Palmer

METEVIER, Henry b 28 Feb 1881 Danville, NH s/o METEVIER, Peter & RAINVILLE, Clara

METEVIER, Mary b 3 Rivers Canada d/o METEVIER, Peter; d 09 Sep 1964 Danville, NH ae 91y

METEVIER, Mary S. b d 03 Feb 1940 Danville, NH ae 87y 6m 4d

METEVIER, Peter b 1848 Canada; md RAINVILLE, Clara; d 14 Dec 1926 Danville, NH

METEVIER, Lorrane Frances b 15 Dec 1939 Danville, NH d/o METEVIER, Urban & ANDERSON, Beatrice L.

MEUNO, Joseph A. b Danville, NH s/o MEUNO, Jos & SEARS, Josephine; d Mar 1894 Danville, NH ae 8m 6d

MEUSE, Jacqueline b 17 Apr 1975 Derry, NH d/o MEUSE, Clarence J. & MARTENSEN, Christine A.

MEUSE, John b 06 Dec 1973 Derry, NH s/o MEUSE, Clarence J. & MORTENSEN, Christine A; d 06 Dec 1973 Derry, NH

MEUSE, Shawn Edward b 19 Aug 1977 Derry, NH s/o MEUSE, Clarence J. & MARTINSEN, Christine A.

MEUSE, Stacey Ann b 12 May 1970 Derry, NH d/o MEUSE, Clarence J. & MARTINSON, Christine A.

MICHAUD, Gail Ann md 01 Oct

MICHAUD (Cont.) 1977 Danville, NH GALIN, Stanley Glenn

MICHAUD, Susan Galager b 26 Apr 1991 Stoneham, MA d/o MICHAUD, Rich G. & GALLAGHER, Kristine

MIDDLEMAN, Lena M. b Germany d/o MIDDLEMAN, Clarence & BENNETT, Cecelia; md YOUNG, John Angus; d 31 Dec 1952 Danville, NH ae 63y

MIDGREN, Cindy R. md 22 May 1983 Danville, NH MITCHELL, Ronald S.; md by Wm Dearman (EP)

MIEROP, Daniel T. md 14 Jul 1984 Danville, NH REYNOLDS, Pamela D.; md by Rev Wm A. Mierop

MIEROP, Timothy David b 21 Jun 1988 Exeter, NH s/o MIEROP, Daniel T. & REYNOLDS, Pamela D.

MIGGINS, Christine M. b d/o HOGGINS, Patrick & MALLOY, Catherine; md MURTAGH, ----; d 13 Nov 1977 Danville, NH ae 66y

MILES, Shannon M. b md 16 Jul 1988 Danville, NH TELLIER, Raymond E.; md by Wm A. Ining (JP)

MILLER, Charles d 12 Dec 1975 Danville, NH ae 73y

MILLER, Doreen D. md 23 Jan 1988 Danville, NH ATWOOD, Bruce D.; md by Richard J. Rondeau (JP)

MILLER, Frances b 1912 Lawrence, MA d/o MILLER, James; md 30 Jan 1936 Danville, NH MARGGRAF, Charles; md by Rev W. C. Chappell

MILLER, Kathleen A. md 31 Dec 1983 Danville, NH HARVEY, Frederick W.; md by Linda L. Meader (JP)

MILLS, Jeannette M. md 10 Mar 1973 Danville, NH BORGES, Michael F.; md by John H. Roby (P)

MILLS, Rob d 19 Jun 1863 Danville, NH ae 82y - Occupation Cooper

MILLS, Sam'l Henry md 03 Sep 1988 Danville, NH McINTOSH, Pamela Jean; md by Rev Peter W. Mercer

MILNE, Minnie b Dundee Scotland d/o MILNE, Wm; md 07 May 1908 Danville, NH COLLINS, Perley Forrest; d 04 May 1912 Danville, NH; md by Rev C. A. Reed

MILONE, Rosemary Joy md 30 Dec 1989 Danville, NH BURTON, Glenn Scott; md by Barbara A. LaPointe (JP)

MISSERVILLE, Hugo b 1914 Lawrence, MA s/o MISSERVILLE, Vincent; md 17 Jan 1935 Danville, NH FREDRICKSON, Lillian; md by Clarence M. Collins (JP)

MISTOWKI, Pauline b 1922 MA d/o MISTOWKI, Joseph; md 17 Jul 1949 Danville, NH CROWELL, Geo Everett; md by Rev Harry L. Lesure

MITCHELL, Arthur Edward b 18 Sep 1960 Danville, NH s/o MITCHELL, James A. Sr. & CHASE, Licile

MITCHELL, Fred Carlton b 1916 Haverhill, MA s/o MITCHELL, Wesley H. & GARRISH, Blanche; md 30 Jun 1936 Danville, NH COLLINS, Ruth Miriam; d 23 Jan 1988; md by Rev W. C. Chappell; d a ae 72y

MITCHELL, Geoffrey Nathaniel b 02 Sep 1983 Derry, NH s/o MITCHELL, Mark C. & COTE, Pamela J.

MITCHELL, Jamie Dean b 30 Apr 1983 Exeter, NH s/o MITCHELL, Robert & BOULANGER, Laurie

MITCHELL, Judith A. b Haverhill, MA; md CAILLOUETTE, Joseph J.

MITCHELL, Kathryn M. md 21 Sep 1985 Danville, NH FORTIER, Roger T.; md by Joyce L. Cann (JP)

MITCHELL, Kim J. md 07 Sep 1985 Danville, NH DONOHOE, Shawn W.; md by Retenah V. Pietrowski (JP)

MITCHELL, Mark C. md 12 May 1973 Danville, NH COTE, Pamela J.; md by Rev Peter N. Knost

MITCHELL, Matthew Charles b 14 Aug 1982 Derry, NH s/o MITCHELL, Mark C. & COTE, Pamela J.

MITCHELL, Michael James md 24 Aug 1991 Danville, NH GLAUDE, Jessica Lyn; md by Rev Robt E. Aspinwall

MITCHELL, Michael W. md 29 Dec 1972 Danville, NH DESROCHERS, Susan F.; md by Robert S. Dejadon (JP)

MITCHELL, Patricia Jean b 21 Jun 1950 Danville, NH d/o MITCHELL, Fred Carlton & COLLINS, Ruth Miriam; md 26 Jul 1968 Danville, NH MURPHY, Jas Francis; md by Rev

MITCHELL (Cont.) Henry Sawatsky

MITCHELL, Randy Dean b 07 Aug 1983 Manchester, NH s/o MITCHELL, Christopher & NANARTONIS, Linda

MITCHELL, Randy Jay b 17 Jan 1967 Haverhill, MA s/o MITCHELL, Rob Carlton & BARLOW, Gail Frances; d 27 Feb 1967 Danville, NH ae 1m

MITCHELL, Richard John b 02 Sep 1961 Danville, NH s/o MITCHELL, Robert Carlton & BARLOW, Gail Frances; d 10 Nov 1961 Danville, NH

MITCHELL, Robert C. md 12 Oct 1984 Danville, NH HAYES, Doris M.; md by Steven W. Lewis (JP)

MITCHELL, Robert Carlton b 1937 MA s/o MITCHELL, Fred Carlton; md 24 Oct 1958 Danville, NH BARLOW, Gail Frances; md by Rev Wendall J. Irvine

MITCHELL, Robert Dean md 03 Nov 1978 Danville, NH BOULANGER, Laurie Ann; md by Rev Wm Ryans

MITCHELL, Ronald Scott b 10 Mar 1963 Danville, NH s/o MITCHELL, Robert C. & BARLOW, Gail F.; md 22 May 1983 Danville, NH WIDGREN, Cindy R.; md by Wm Dearman (EP)

MITCHELL, Sean Henry b 13 Nov 1986 Manchester, NH s/o MITCHELL, Chris A. & NANARTONIS, Linda M.

MOBERG, Jason Edward b 25 Jul 1975 Exeter, NH s/o MOBERG, Clifton E. & O'BRIEN, Nancy M.

MODIGLIANI, David S. md 24 Nov 1990 Danville, NH VALCOURT, Julianne Patricia; md by Rich J. Rondeau (JP)

MOLSON, Arthur F. b c1884 Canada s/o MOLSON, Pierre & FERBAIND, Obline; d 02 Sep 1914 Danville, NH

MONROE, Bruce Alan b 14 Dec 1947 Danville, NH s/o MONROE, Donald W. & RAYMOND, Shirley I.

MONROE, Don Wilson b Haverhill, MA; md RAYMOND, Shirley Irene

MONROE, Geo b s/o MONROE, Lawrence C. & WARD, Lillian; d 06 May 1975 Danville, NH ae 72y

MONROE, Gordon Freeman b 22 Dec 1948 Danville, NH s/o MONROE,

MONROE (Cont.) Donald W. & RAYMOND, Shirley I.

MONROE, John b c1873 Danielson, CT s/o MONROE, Onisim; md 31 Aug 1921 Kingston, NH SARGENT, Mary B.; md by Rev Edvilla A. Roys; md ae 48

MONROE, John B. b Canada s/o MONROE, Onesime & BERNIER, Aglass; d 16 Apr 1944 Danville, NH ae 71y 1m 12d

MONTGOMERY, Richard Lov b 1922 Portsmouth, NH s/o MONTGOMERY, Fred E.; md 21 Mar 1953 Danville, NH ALLARD, Christine May

MOODY, Maurice Martin b 1928 NH s/o MOODY, Benj F. md 01 Jun 1950 Manchester, NH HARVELL, Alice Virginia; md by Rob C. Laing (JP)

MOONEY, Rhonda L. md 22 Jun 1985 Danville, NH RAGONESE, John A.; md by Robert J. Kemmery (P)

MOORE, Barry Bernard md 19 Apr 1974 Danville, NH JOHNSON, Judy Elaine; md by Rev Geo S. Fisher

MOORE, Eric Matthew b 08 Feb 1974 Haverhill, MA s/o MOORE, Robert S. & STILLGOE, Doreen M.

MOORE, Ethlyn M. b 1893 Wellensberg, VA d/o MOORE, Thomas; md 19 Aug 1933 Danville, NH McKENNA, Philip J.; md by Rev Edmund T. Quirk; also md to BARRY, ----

MOORE, Kristina Marie md 07 Apr 1974 Danville, NH MERRILL, Bruce Edward; md by Clara B. Snow (JP)

MOORE, Lorraine M. md 24 Mar 1985 Danville, NH BERUBE, Michael A.; md by Rev Dennis G. Campbell

MOORE, Shawn Michael md 17 Apr 1982 Danville, NH DAVIS, Susan B.; md by Rev Everett E. Palmer

MORAN, Napoleon b c1860 Canada s/o MORAN, Peter; d 14 Jul 1893 Danville, NH

MOREAU, Marjorie Cummings b 1937 Brentwood, NH; md 28 Mar 1963 Danville, NH LANDRY, Frank Joseph; md by Rev John Wood Jr.

MOREAU, Ovide S. b c1892 Haverhill, MA s/o MOREAU, Oliver; md 27 Sep 1920 Plaistow, NH by M. J. Moher (P)

MOREY, Angie M. b c1898 Groveland, MA d/o MOREY, Geo; md 28 Jul 1917 Kingston, NH YORK, Wm J.; md by Rev H. McCarthy

MOREY, Daisy Ann d 04 Dec 1951 Danville, NH ae 71y

MOREY, Geo N. b 1866 Haverhill, MA s/o MOREY, Nelson & WILLIAMS, Susan; d 23 Jan 1934 Danville, NH ae 67y 1m 21d

MORGAN, Kevin L. md 03 May 1987 Danville, NH SPEARS, Melissa A.; md by Rev Everett E. Palmer

MORGAN, Mary b 1912 E Boston, MA d/o MORGAN, Alexander; d 23 Aug 1926 Danville, NH

MORGAN, Robert S. md 06 Jul 1984 Danville, NH DERUSHA, Michele G.; md by Rev Robert L. Dobson

MORIARTY, Conner Patrick b 01 Mar 1988 Exeter, NH s/o MORIARTY, Jonathan F. & GRAFTON, Gail E.

MORIN, Mary b 1891 Haverhill, MA d/o MORIN, Napoleon & NEWRY, Rosa; d 23 Jul 1891 Danville, NH ae 3m 16d

MORRILL, Appia md 06 Dec 1770 Hawke, NH SLEEPER, Nehemiah; md Rev John Page

MORRILL, Betty b of Raymond, NH; md 01 Sep 1779 Hawke, NH WHITTIER, Reuben; md by Rev John Page

MORRILL, Edward 1 b 08 Jun 1790 Hawke, NH s/o MORRILL, Nathaniel & EASTMAN, Eliz; Recorded in Eastman Gen.

MORRILL, Edward 2 b 21 Jun 1791 Hawke, NH s/o MORRILL, Nathaniel & EASTMAN, Eliz; Recorded in Eastman Gen.

MORRILL, Folsom b 09 Dec 1798 Hawke, NH s/o MORRILL, Nathaniel & EASTMAN, Eliz

MORRILL, Henry b 05 May 1784 Hawke, NH s /o MORRILL, Nathaniel & EASTMAN, Eliz

MORRILL, Henry md 18 Mar 1779 Hawke, NH COLBY, Anna; md by Rev John Page

MORRILL, Henry Dea. b c1716 Salisbury, MA; md 1st FOLSOM, Susanna, 2nd 18 Mar 1779 Hawke, NH

MORRILL (Cont.) TUXBURY, Anna; d 19 Oct 1799 Hawke, NH

MORRILL, Henry Jr. b 13 Mar 1768 Hawke, NH s/o MORRILL, Henry Dea. & FOLSOM, Susanna

MORRILL, Israel b 05 Jul 1786 Hawke, NH s/o MORRILL, Nathaniel & EASTMAN, Eliz

MORRILL, Jabez md 09 Oct 1766 CLOUGH, Hannah; md by Rev John Page

MORRILL, John W. b Nashua, NH; md OSGOOD, Mary A.

MORRILL, John W. b Nashua, NH; md 29 Aug 1887 Wilmington, DE DIXON, Hannah; md by Rev L. W. Adams

MORRILL, Lewis S. b 09 Jun 1867 Danville, NH s/o MORRILL, John Wm & OSGOOD, Mary Anna; md 04 Nov 1896 Haverhill, MA HUNKINS, Nellie L.; md by Rev L. B. Twitchell; Occupation - Mechanic

MORRILL, Lola Maude b 13 Jul 1871 d/o MORRILL, John Wm & OSGOOD, Mary Anna

MORRILL, Martha Jane b 24 Jul 1868 Danville, NH d/o MORRILL, John Wm & OSGOOD, Mary Anna; md ROBINSON, ----; d 25 May 1970 Danville, NH

MORRILL, Maude L. b c1872 Brentwood, NH d/o MORRILL, John W. & ----, Mary; md 12 Mar 1887 Danville, NH BAKER. Willie A.; md by Rev John A. Lowell

MORRILL, Miriam md 23 Dec 1777 Hawke, NH HOYT, Simeon

MORRILL, Nancy b 09 May 1793 Hawke, NH d/o MORRILL, Nathaniel & EASTMAN, Eliz

MORRILL, Nathaniel b 01 Oct 1762 Hawke, NH s/o MORRILL, Henry Dea. & FOLSOM, Susanna; md 19 Jun 1783 EASTMAN, Eliz

MORRILL, Obadiah Eastmam b 21 Mar 1796 Hawke, NH s/o MORRILL, Nathaniel & EASTMAN, Eliz

MORRILL, Susanna md 22 Dec 1763 Hawke, NH BLAKE, Timothy

MORRILL, Susanna md 01 Dec 1784 Hawke, NH STANYAN, Levi

MORRILL, Susannah b 14 Oct

MORRILL (Cont.) 1788 Hawke NH d/o MORRILL Nath. & EASTMAN Eliz MORRILL, ---- b 07 Jul 1885 Danville, NH d/o MORRILL, John W. & ----, Nancy J.; d 07 Jul 1885 Danville, NH stillborn

MORRISON, Steven J. md 08 Oct 1983 Danville, NH PERIN, Laurie B.; md by Rev Rich Russell (Jehovah Witness)

MORRISON, Vincent Joseph b s/o MORRISON, Michael J. & McMENI-MON, Katherine; d 13 Aug 1984 Danville, NH ae 59y

MORROW, Albert R. md 02 Dec 1983 Danville, NH CASTANHERIA, Lydia S.; md by Rich J. Rindeau (JP)

MORROW, John Francis b s/o MORROW, John Francis III & SAI-DEL, Goldie A.; d 20 Feb 1985 Danville, NH ae 26y

MORROW, Wm C. Jr. b 1934 MA s/o MORROW, Wm C. Sr.; md 07 Sep 1956 Danville, NH CERASUOLO, Elaine; md by Agnes H. Collins (JP)

MORSE, Alice Pomeroy b 1912 Haverhill, MA d/o MORSE, Harold R.; md 01 Dec 1946 Danville, NH PEDER-SEN, Elmer A.; md by Rev Kendig B. Culley

MORSE, Christopher Keith b 29 Jun 1987 Exeter, NH s/o MORSE, Keith R. & FRANCIS, Linda A.

MORSE, Daniel b Hampstead, NH; md 13 Jan 1788 Kingston, NH EASTMAN, Mary

MORSE, Florence b c1845 Hampstead, NH; md Mar 1865 Danville, NH BUSWELL, Albee C.

MORSE, Geo b 1865 Hampstead, NH s/o MORSE, Samuel & SHANNON, Sarah H.; d 19 Oct 1938 Danville, NH ae 73y 3m 16d

MORSE, John Page b 19 Jan 1798 Hawke, NH s/o MORSE, Sam & PAGE, Sarah; d 31 Dec 1798 Hawke, NH ae 11m

MORSE, Leigh Anne b 01 Jun 1981 Haverhill, MA d/o MORSE, Larry B. & CASE, Catherine E.

MORSE, Martha E. b c1853 Hampstead, NH; md 01 Jan 1874 Danville, NH EATON, Emery C.

MORSE, Mary B. b 1861 E Hampstead, NH d/o MORSE, Samuel; md 03 Dec 1890 S Hampton, NH DARBE, Lucius M.; md by John K. Chase VDM

MORSE, Melissa Amy b 18 Jun 1978 Lawrence, NH d/o MORSE, Wm C.& TRACY, Susan J.

MORSE, Randolph P. Jr. md 06 Apr 1974 Danville, NH STRATOS, Anne E.; md by Bettie Quellette (JP)

MORSE, Samuel b Hampstead, NH; md 1st 11 Aug 1797 Hawke, NH PAGE, Sarah, end 27 Apr 1806 Hampstead, NH PAGE, Anna (Nancy)

MORSE, Sarah b Jan 1797 Hill, NH; md 24 Dec 1820 Hampstead, NH COLLINS, Hezekiah; d 29 Jul 1869 Danville, NH; bu Danville, NH Center Cem; d age 72 yr MOORE or MORSE ?

MORSE, Tyler Richard b 17 Oct 1990 Exeter, NH s/o MORSE, Keith R. & FRANCIS, Linda A.

MOSES, Audrey A. md 05 Oct 1986 Danville, NH WATJEN, Glenn L.; md by Rev Philip M. Polhemis

MOSES, Brett E. md 05 Aug 1980 Danville, NH ARSENNAULT, Jeanne M.; md by Edward C. Garvey (JP)

MOSES, Eric Jason b 15 Feb 1981 Exeter, NH s/o MOSES, Brett E. & ARSENAULT, Jeanne M.

MOTTRAM, Jillian Beth b 30 Aug 1985 Haverhill, MA d/o MOTTRAM, David B. & GERMAN, Priscilla A.

MOULTON, Jacquelyn b 1937 d/o MOULTON, Lee B.; md 13 Jul 1957 Danville NH KIMBALL, Howard L. Jr.

MOULTON, Mary J. b Hampstead, NH d/o MOULTON, Caleb; md JONES, ----; d 09 Sep 1912 Danville, NH

MOYER, Herbert Stewart b 05 Feb 1946 Danville, NH s/o MOYER, Wm J. G. & CROWELL, Amy V.

MUDGE, Brenda M. b 1943 MA; md 21 Oct 1962 Danville, NH DUCHEMIN, Bruce L.; md by Arthur M. Comeau

MUDGE, David T. b 1946 NH; md 1st 12 Oct 1968 Danville, NH HILL, Priscilla J.; md by Rev John Wood; md 2nd 07 May 1983 Danville, NH MARTIN, Michele D.; md by Rev Everett E. Palmer

MUKCHANEY, Pamela L. md 10 Aug 1985 Danville, NH HOLLORAN, Tim. A.; md by John H. Lamprey (JP)

MULCAHEV, Barbara Hope md 22 Jun 1991 Danville, NH HUGHES, John Kenneth; md by Rev Kent W. Johnson

MULDOWNEY, Nancy J. md 23 Aug 1973 Danville NH WRIGLEY, Rich J. md by Rev Kathleen R. Narowitz

MUNNIS, Carol Ann b of Danville, NH; md 22 Jan 1974 SIMES, Marvin Edward; md by Rev Ivan Smith Jr.

MUNROE, Barry Wayne b 13 Apr 1952 Danville, NH s/o MINROE, Don Wilson & RAYMOND, Shirley Irene

MUNROE, David Raymond b 04 Apr 1955 Danville, NH s/o MUNROE, Damald Wilson & RAYMOND, Shirley Irene

MUNROE, Donald Wilson b 20 Mar 1950 Danville, NH s/o MUNROE, Don Wilson & RAYMOND, Shirley Irene

MURPHY, Elanor md 12 Aug 1990 Danville, NH HUGHES, Wm Lawrence Jr.; md by Richard J. Rondeau (JP)

MURPHY, James Francis b 1950 MA; md 26 Jul 1968 Danville, NH MITCHELL, Patricia Jean; md by Rev Henry Sawatsky

MURPHY, Joel Steven b 28 Sep 1971 Haverhill, NH s/o MURPHY, James F. & MITCHELL, Patricia

MURPHY, Margaret M. b Springfield, NH; md BARCH, Jos Henry

MURPHY, Robert D. b 1944; md 16 Nov 1968 Danville, NH CORTON, Nancy B.; md by Rev Douglas Abbott

MURPHY, Robert Daniel b 17 Dec 1971 Exeter, NH s/o MURPHY, Roberet D. Jr. & CORTON, Nancy B.

MURRAY, Kenyon Lee md 30 Mar 1988 Danville, NH FOLEY, Ed Patrick Jr.; md by Rich J. Rondeau (JP)

MURRAY, Wm Francis Jr. b 07 Jul 1941 Boston, MA s/o Murray, Wm Frances Sr. & MACE, Evelyn Lucille

MURRAY, Wm Francis Sr. md 10 Jun 1939 MACE, Evelyn Lucille

MURTAGH, Margaret C. b of Bronx, NY; md 10 Nov 1973 Danville,

MURTAGH (Cont.) NH STUBBS, Gerald S.; md by Rev Chas P Calcagni

MURTAGH, Susan M. md 29 Aug 1987 Danville, NH CABRAL, Jos D.; md by Deborah R. McCaffery (JP)

MUSSO, Ashley May b 29 Aug 1985 Nashua, NH d/o MUSSO, Jos M. & NORWOOD, Linda L.

MUSSO, Laura Lee b 29 Aug 1985 Nashua, NH d/o MUSSO, Jos M. & NORWOOD, Linda L.

MUSSO, Linda Lee md 19 May 1990 Danville, NH AREL, Peter John; md by Phillippe A. Arel (JP)

MUZRALL, Mary Ellen b 1925; md 23 Mar 1968 Danville, NH LESLIE, David Brian; md by Ed R. Lamb (JP)

MYERS, Allison Karen b 12 Jul 1988 Exeter, NH d/o MYERS, James T. & COBURN, Jane L.

MYERS, Ashley Jane b 23 May 1987 Exeter, NH d/o MYERS, James T. Jr. & COBURN, Jane L.

NASH, Sally md 06 Jun 1799 Kingston, NH TOWLE, James

NASON, Albert Leonard b 06 May 1934 Danville, NH s/o NASON, Lester F. & PECK, Anna C.

NASON, Frances L. b 1916 d/o Nason, Harold & STONE, Annie; md WHITE, ---- ; d 08 Feb 1977 Danville, NH ae 61y

NASON, Lester Farnsworth b 15 Apr 1927 Danville, NH s/o NASON, Lester F. & PECK, Anna C.

NASON, Mildred b Kingston, NH; md TEWKSBURY, Fred

NASON, Nathan Jr. b 1834 Kingston, NH s/o NASON, Nathan Sr.; md 13 Sep 1852 Danville, NH PAGE, Sarah K.

NASON, Wealthea b 24 Nov 1928 d/o NASON, Lester F. & PECK, Anna C.; 2nd child in family

NELSON, Phil. b Perrystown, NH; md 30 Nov 1779 Hawke, NH QUIMBY, Hannah; md by Rev John Page

NEURY, Edward b Canada; md RINVILLE, Mary

NEURY, Jos b 18 Jan 1892 Danville NH s/o NEURY, Edward & RINVILLE, Mary

NEVERS, Cecil E. b c1892 Harrison, ME s/o NEVERS, Frank A.; md 28 Jun 1914 Danville, NH COLLINS, Edith R.; md by Rev Allen C. Keith

NEVERS, Rachel Jane b 18 Jun 1914 Danville, NH d/o NEVERS, Cecil E. & COLLINS, Edith R.

NEWCOMB, Natalie Eleanor b 1921 Quincy, MA d/o NEWCOMB, Roland Downer & MOULSASON, Katherine; d 28 Nov 1988; md 30 Mar 1944 Danville, NH DEMAINE, Richard Frank; md by Rev W. C. Chappell

NEWELL, Alice E. M. b 1913 Manchester, NH d/o NEWELL, Arthur H.; md 23 Nov 1935 Danville, NH BEEDE, Arnold H.; md by Rev Frank Dunn

NEWTON, Freeman Geo b 1893 Lempster, NH s/o NEWTON, Frank; md 29 Apr 1944 Danville, NH BESSETTE, Anna M.; md by Rev Byron O. Waterman

NEWTON, Rebecca R. md 12 Apr 1980 Danville, NH LAVELLE, David J.; md by Rev John Rea Chapman

NEWTON, Wm md 28 Jan 1766 Hawke, NH RANOUGH, Mary; md by Rev John Page

NGAI, Victor M. md 25 Sep 1981 Danville, NH CHENG, Minnie; md by Eleanor B. Barron (JP)

NICHOLS, Hannah Mrs. b c1802; d 29 Jun 1838 Hawke, NH ae 36y

NICHOLS, Jas md 15 Dec 1761 Hawke, NH HUBBARD-PRESSEY, Mercy

NICHOLS, Marie E. md 28 Sep 1991 Danville, NH O'CONNOR, Walter J.; md by Rev Edward J. Charest

NICHOLS, Martha b 23 Oct 1762 Hawke, NH d/o NICHOLS, James & HUBBARD-PRESSEY, Mercy

NICHOLS, Moses b 1871 Danville, NH s/o NICHOLS, Moses & POST, Ann C.; d 24 Sep 1872 Danville, NH ae 1y

NICHOLS, Ruth Ann b 14 Feb 1873 Danville, NH d/o NICHOLS, Moses & POST, Ann C.

NICHOLS, Tricia Marle b 15 Apr 1968 Danville, NH d/o NICHOLS, Tucker J. & THURLO, Janice Marie

NICHOLSON, Peter Richard b 1943 Lynn, MA; md 20 Nov 1964 Danville, NH WALTERS, Maryann; md by Leona A. Sciandone (JP)

NICI, Eugene A. md 15 Sep 1985 Danville, NH MAIONE, Lorraine A; md by Rochelle Lafontaine (JP)

NICI, Eugene Arthur b 24 Nov 1975 Haverhill, MA s/o NICI, Eugene A. & BLACKADAR, Linda G.

NICI, Jos Jay b 11 Jan 1978 Haverhill, MA s/o NICI, Eugene A. & BLACKADAR, Linda G.

NICKERSON, Alice Gertrude b 1909 Arlington Height d/o NICKERSON, Wallace F.; md 08 May 1927 Danville, NH STAMATELLO, Milton; md by Rev Howard A. Reyman

NICKERSON, Geo W. b c1878 Gloucester, MA s/o NICKERSON, Wm J.; md 07 Sep 1902 Kingston, NH SHERMAN, Gertrude M.; md by Rev J. W. Strout

NICKERSON, ---- b 16 Aug 1902 Danville, NH d/o NICKERSON, Geo & SHERMAN, Gertrude

NICKETT, Ed T. b Newington, NH s/o NICKETT, Edward & MURPHY, Bridget; d 24 Apr 1928 ae 67y 23d

NICOLAISEN, Hans M. md 10 Sep 1983 Danville, NH O'NEIL, Dawn Marie; md by Priscilla R. Schumm (JP)

NICOLI, Jerry J. md 27 May 1989 Danville, NH SPARKS, Linda; md by Rev Carlos F. Paz

NICOLO, Jacqueline T. md 08 Dec 1979 Danville, NH JENDRICK, James T.; md by Rev Kenneth A. Dunn

NIHAN, Diana M. md 21 Sep 1985 Danville, NH FLATTERY, Wayne P.; md by Rev Everett E. Palmer

NIHAN, Linda S. md 27 Apr 1986 Danville, NH HARRIS, Dennis G.; md by Rev Everett E. Palmer

NIKOLAUS, Barbara L. md 23 Oct 1982 Danville, NH MAXWELL, Chrostopher; md by John H. Lamprey (JP)

NIKOLAUS, Christina md 12 Jan 1985 Danville, NH CALDWELL, James Rowe Sr.

NIKOLAUS, Erick Michael b 03 Aug 1978 Exeter, NH s/o NIKOLAUS, Ronald J. & COSTELLO, Catherine M.

NOLAN, Mary C. b d/o NOLAN, Patrick & MacDONALD, Mary; md HANLON, ---- ; d 01 Mar 1979 Danville, NH ae 90y

NOLAN, Richard F. b 1930 MA; md 17 May 1968 Danville, NH CHURCH, Emily L.; md by Rev Douglas Abbott

NORRIS, Meria J. b c1841 Kingston, NH; md 25 Feb 1864 Danville, NH GILMAN, Jos H.

NORTH, Timothy md 04 Sep 1766 Hawke, NH GOVE, Susanna

NORTON, Emma 1870; d 10 Jul 1938 Danville, NH ae 68y 3m 11d

NORTON, Helena b 06 Nov 1972 Manchester, NH d/o NORTON, Everett L. & LEWIS, Marina E.

NORY, Johnny b 15 Apr 1900 Danville, NH; s/o NORY, Emede & RANVEIL, Mary; 10th child in family

NOURY, Emidie b c1861 Canada d/o NOURY, Louis & METEVIER, Odelia; md 02 Feb 1884 Danville, NH RAINVILLE, Mary; d 05 Nov 1949 Danville, NH; or spelled Amedee

NOURY, Georgie May b 21 Jun 1887 Danville, NH d/o NOURY, Meade & ----, Mary R.

NOURY, ---- b 11 Nov 1884 Danville, NH s/o NOURY, Emedie & RAINVILLE, Mary & KEEZER Harriet

NOWICHI, Lorraine V. b 1942 Haverhill, MA; md 29 Sep 1962 Danville, NH COMTOIS, Ron L.; md by Ed R. Lamb

NOYER, Ashley Ann b 13 Dec 1986 Lawrence, MA d/o NOYER, David A. Jr. & DeMARS, Darlene A.

NOYES, Brenda L. md 04 Mar 1972 Danville, NH LAUGHTON, Bruce A.; md by James Gilmore (JP)

NOYES, Jeffrey Chas b 08 May 1967 Danville, NH s /o NOYES, Joshua C. & HOUSTON, Nancy A.

NOYES, Joshua C. Jr. b Atkinson, NH s/o NOYES, Joshua C. Sr. & FARRINGTON, Hazel; d 05 Jul 1966 Danville, NH

NOYES, Nancy Ellen md 31 Dec 1990 Danville, NH NUGENT, Francis Anthony; md by Florent Bilodeau (P)

NUGENT, Francis Anthony md 31 Dec 1990 Danville, NH NOYES, Nancy Ellen; md by Florent Bilodeau (P)

NUTE, Lauren Brook b 19 Feb 1991 Derry, NH d/o NUTE, Robert A. & KAUFMANN, Kelly B.

NUTE, Robert Allen md 04 Jun 1988 Danville, NH KAUFMAN, Kelly B.; md by Rev Robert F. Dobson

NUTTER, Rob C. md 27 May 1989 Danville, NH GREENWOOD, Maureen M. md by Rich J Rondeau (JP)

NYBERG, Forrest W. md 01 Jan 1980 Danville, NH CHANEY, Joan; md by Rev Wendall J. Irvine

NYGREN, Jean Ann b 1947 Peabody, MA; md 11 Jun 1965 Danville, NH; FLEMING, Thos J.; md by Leona A. Schiaudone (JP)

O'BRIEN, Colleen Carolyn md 21 Apr 1990 Danville, NH JOHNSON, Paul Sherman; md by Rev Everett E. Palmer

O'BRIEN, Courtney Eliz b 21 Feb 1989 Derry, NH d/o O'Brien, Wm E. III & MATICIC, Odessa M.

O'BRIEN, Isabelle b d/o O'BRIEN, John & HIGGINS, Elvie; md MacLEAN, ---- ; d 12 Jul 1952 Danville, NH ae 69y

O'BRIEN, Janet D. md 28 Nov 1985 Danville, NH BRODIE, Edward C.; md by Richard J. Rondeau (JP)

O'BRIEN, Joanne W. b 1947 MA; md 09 Nov 1968 Danville, NH McDONALD, Wm A.; md by Leona A. Sciaudone (JP)

O'BRIEN, Katie b Ireland; md ROONEY, Harry

O'BRIEN, Kelly Kathleen b 17 Jul 1972 Methuen, MA d/o O'BRIEN, Richard H. & BIZEUR, Carolyn C.

O'BRIEN, Mary A. b Lynn, MA d/o O'BRIEN, John & HIGGINS, Elsie; md SANBORN, ----; d 18 Oct 1966 Danville, NH

O'BRIEN, Robert Joseph b 28 Mar 1964 Danville, NH s/o O'BRIEN, Robert Jos & DONAHUE, Joanne W.

O'BRIEN, Robert Joseph b Somerville, MA; md DONAHUE, Joanne W.

O'BRIEN, Sarah Beth b 04 Feb 1987 Derry, NH d/o O'BRIEN, Wm E. III & MATICIC, Odessa M.

O'CONNER, Walter J. b md 28 Sep 1991 Danville, NH NICHOLS, Marie E.; md by Rev Edward J. Charest

O'NEIL, Dawn Marie b 10 Jul 1962 Danville, NH d/o O'NEIL, Daniel J. & KERSHAW, Margaret; md 10 Sep 1983 Danville, NH NICOLAISEN, Hans M.; md by Priscilla R. Schumm (JP)

O'NEIL, Margaret J. b md 15 Dec 1973 Danville, NH McINTYRE, Franklin J.; md by Rev Henry Sawatzky

O'NEIL, Michael J. md 01 Nov 1986 Danville, NH HENRY, Sara C.; md by Richard J. Rondeau (JP)

O'NEIL. Julie A. md 19 May 1990 Danville, NH RENNIE, Mark M.; md by Rev Robert F. Dobson

O'SHAUGHNESSY, Scott Jonathan b 09 May 1983 Exeter, NH s/o O'SCHAUGHNESSY, Kevin & GODDARD, Linda

O'SHEA, Katherine Jean b 29 Sep 1964 Danville, NH d/o O'SHEA, Seth S. & ROUTHIER, Jean M.

O'SHEA, Seth S. b Plymouth, MA; md ROUTHIER, Jean M.

O'SHEA, Wm Kevin b 25 Mar 1961 Danville, NH s/o O'SHEA, Seth S. & ROUTHIER, Jean M.

OAK, Catherine Marie b md 28 Sep 1974 Danville, NH BORGES, Sidney Francis; md by Rev Cathleen R. Harowitz

OAK, Judith Evan b 25 Jul 1961 Danville, NH d/o OAK, Ivan Ray & DIXON, Evelyn D.

OAK, Richard Dixon 1st md 11 Jan 1975 Danville, NH WEEKS, Joanne by Robert S. Dejadon (JP); 2nd md 17 Oct 1992 ANTHONY, Row

OAK, Russell Allan b 91 Jun 1960 Danville, NH s/o OAK, Ivan R. & DIXON, Evelyn D.; d 01 Sep 1981 Danville, NH

OERIN, Carla J. md 19 Oct 1983 Danville, NH DAVIS, Scott E.; md by Richard J. Rindeau (JP)

OLCOTT, Wm Thomas Jr. md 10 Feb 1990 Danville, NH BERRY, Debra Jean; md by Rev Everett E. Palmer

OLIVER, Angie b Carroll, NH d/o OLIVER, Henry; md LEE, ---- ; d 17 Mar 1931 Danville, NH   bu

OLIVER, Eric Daniel b 10 Feb 1978 Exeter, NH s/o OLIVER, John H. & HAMILTON, Priscilla A.

OLSON, Roy E. md 21 Jun 1987 Danville, NH CATTO, Nancy J.; md by Rev Everett E. Palmer

ORDWAY, Eveleyn P. b 1913 Sandown, NH d/o ORDWAY, David; md 29 Apr 1934 Danville, NH CUMMINGS, C. Everett; md by Rev Donald H. Baldwin

ORDWAY, Evelyn b d/o ORDWAY, James & HOYT, Ora; md CUMMINGS, ---- ; d 12 Dec 1975 Danville, NH ae 58y

ORDWAY, Jacob Lieut. b 1741 E. Kingston, NH; md 03 Jun 1772 Hawke, NH TILTON;; d 04 Sep 1811 bu E. Kingston, NH Union Cem.; md by Rev John Page

ORDWAY, Jessica Eliz b 04 Feb 1987 Exeter, NH d/o ORDWAY, Michael J. & HALL, Cathy L.

ORDWAY, Linwood C. b c1904 Hampstead, NH s/o ORDWAY, Rich; md 21 Oct 1922 Kingston, NH ARNOLD, Mildred; md by Rev A. M. Morrison

ORDWAY, Ruth b 27 Jun 1773 Hawke, NH d/o ORDWAY, Nehemiah & ---- , Ruth

OSBORNE, Andrew Lasky Taylor b 15 Sep 1992 Exeter, NH s/o OSBORNE, Jos P. & TAYLOR, Mary E.

OSBORNE, David H. b Hammonvale, New Brunswick, Canada; s/o OSBORNE, Samuel & SHERWOOD, Matilda; md SHERWOOD, Emma A.; d 12 Mar 1932 Danville, NH d ae 64y 9m 21d Occupation - Boxmaker

OSBORNE, Freda Amelia b 15 Aug 1901 Danville, NH d/o OSBORNE, David H. & SHERWOOD, Emma A.; 3rd child in family

OSBORNE, Herbert S. b c1895 Danville, NH /o OSBORNE, David H.& SHERWOOD, Emma A.; md 04 May 1917 Kingston, NH SILLOWAY, Grace B.; md by Rev F. W. Whippen

OSBORNE, Mabel Irene b 15 Sep 1892 Danville, NH d/o OSBORN, David

OSBORNE (Cont.) H. & SHER-
WOOD, Emma A.; 1st Child in Family
   OSBORNE, Robert Vincent b 05 May
1918 Danville, NH s/o OSBORNE,
Herbert & SILLOWAY, Grace
   OSBORNE, Wilton Leslie b 02 Jul
1920 Danville, NH s/o OSBORNE,
Herbert S. & SILLOWAY, Grace; 2nd
child in family
   OSGOOD, Enoch b of Epping, NH;
md 19 Jun 1779 Hawke, NH FOGG,
Molly; md by Rev John Page
   OSGOOD, Jonathan b Amesbury,
MA s/o OSGOOD, Rich & RUSSELL,
Mary; d 07 Apr 1897 Danville, NH
   OSGOOD, Mary A. b 24 Mar 1844
Danville, NH d/o OSGOOD, Jonathan &
PAGE-WORTHEN, Hannah; md
MORRILL, John W.; 2nd m to HOYT,
Nathan 30 Nov 1893
   OSGOOD, Mary A. b 24 Mar 1844
Danville, NH d/o OSGOOD, Jonathan &
PAGE-WORTHEN, Hannah; md 30 Nov
1893 Manchester, NH HOYT, Nathan;
md by Rev Nathaniel L. Colby; 2nd M for
Mary & Nathan
   OTATTI, Gertrude E. d 11 Sep 1970
Danville, NH d ae 56y
   OTTARI, Phylis Marie b 01 Jul 1956
Danville, NH d /o OTTARI, Louis &
WALTERS, Gertrude Eliz
   OTTATI, Antoinette F. b 1933 MA
d/o OTTATI, Louis & WALTERS, Ger-
trude Eliz; md 22 Nov 1952 Danville, NH
GILBERT, Harry Joseph Jr.; md by
Agnes H. Collins (JP)
   OTTATI, Francis Peter b 09 Feb
1949 Danville, NH s/o OTTATI, Louis &
WALTERS, Gertrude Eliz
   OTTATI, Louis 3rd b 17 Apr 1965
Danville, NH s/o OTTATI, Louis Jr. &
GOSS, Judy E.
   OTTATI, Louis Michael Jr. b 13 Feb
1952 Danville, NH s/o OTTATI, Louis M.
Sr. & WALTERS, Gertrude Eliz; md
GOSS, Judy E.
   OTTATI, Lucy Mary b 1936 NH d/o
OTTATI, Louis Sr. & WALTERS, Ger-
trude Eliz; md 18 Dec 1954 Danville, NH
GRAY, Jas Henry; md by Rev J. T. Sulli-
van (P)

   OTTATI, Marguerite E. b 1938 MA
d/o OTTATI, Louis Sr. & WALTERS,
Gertrude Eliz; md 17 Nov 1956 Dan-
ville, NH CHURCH, Fred. L.; md by
Rev Albion Bulgar (P)
   OUELLETTE, David A. b 1940
Newburyport, MA; md 07 Oct 1966
Danville, NH SWEET, Mary Lou; md
by Rev Douglas Abbott
   OUELLETTE, Dawn Marie md 20
Aug 1988 Danville NH BENNETT, Rob
Clay IV; md by Rev Everett E. Palmer
   OUELLETTE, Luke David b 30
Nov 1992 Derry, NH s/o OUELLETTE,
David J. & HEFFERMAN, Lynne M.
   OUELLETTE, Michelle Ann b 01
Aug 1966 Danville, NH d/o OUEL-
LETTE, David A. & SWEET, Mary
Lou
   OWEN, Kennet H. Jr. md 13 Jun
1987 Danville, NH PERALTA, Ann R.;
md by Renee Houle Carkin (JP)
   OWLES, Marjorie b Wakefield, MA
d/o Owles, Thomas D. & TAATYES,
Theckler; d 05 Dec 1920 ae 4m 14d
   PAGE, Aaron b 1800 Hawke, NH
s/o PAGE, Benj & QUIMBY, Rebecca;
md 1st ALLEN, Nancy, 2nd ALLEN,
Valeria Keay; d 19 Sep 1975 Danville,
NH ae 75y
   PAGE, Abigail b 23 Mar 1761
Hawke, NH d/o PAGE, Ephraim &
CURRIER, Hannah
   PAGE, Abigail b 11 Jun 1768
Hawke, NH d/o PAGE, John (Rev) &
STEVENS, Mary
   PAGE, Abner Dr. b New Durham,
NH; md 10 Feb 1803 Kingston, NH
TEWKSBURY, Hannah
   PAGE, Alice M. b 13 Jan 1880
Danville, NH d/o PAGE, Herbert A. &
GRIFFIN, Florence; d 27 Jun 1883
Danville, NH of Typhoid Fever
   PAGE, Amos b 07 Aug 1797
Hawke, NH s/o PAGE, Simon &
SANBORN, Phebe; md EASTMAN,
Hephzibah; d 24 Nov 1880 Danville,
NH ae 83y
   PAGE, Andrew b 27 Oct 1812
Hawke, NH s/o PAGE, Amos &
EASTMAN, Hepzibah

PAGE, Anna b 08 Mar 1781 Hawke, NH d/o PAGE, John (Rev) & STEVENS, Mary; md 27 Apr 1806 Hampstead, NH MORSE, Samuel spouse 2nd marr

PAGE, Anna b 25 Aug 1790 Hawke, NH d/o PAGE, Simon & SANBORN, Phebe

PAGE, Anna b 30 Apr 1763 Hawke, NH d/o PAGE, Ephriam & CURRIER, Hannah

PAGE, Benj b c1798 s/o PAGE, Benj & QUIMBY, Rebecca; d 30 Oct 1817 Hawke, NH ae 19y

PAGE, Benj b 10 Mar 1762 Hawke, NH s/o PAGE, John & WEBSTER, Anne

PAGE, Benj b 18 Apr 1814 Hawke, NH s/o PAGE, John & COLBY, Nancy

PAGE, Benj b 1834 Hawke, NH s/o PAGE, Aaron & ----, Nancy; d 26 Mar 1836 Hawke, NH

PAGE, Benj b Hawke, NH; md 05 Feb 1788 Kingston, NH QUIMBY, Rebecca; d 17 Feb 1828 Hawke, NH ae 66y

PAGE, Betty b 22 Apr 1802 Hawke, NH d/o PAGE, Simon & SANBORN, Phebe; md 11 Apr 1823 Hawke, NH BUSWELL, David

PAGE, Betty b 26 Sep 1770 Hawke, NH d/o PAGE, John (Rev) & STEVENS, Mary

PAGE, Chas B. b 1864 Danville, NH s/o PAGE, John Burton & WOOD, Lydia A.; d 06 Mar 1869 Danville, NH age 5 yr

PAGE, Chas C. b 1841 Danville, NH s/o PAGE, Oren & TOWLE, Clarinda; d 03 Mar 1860 Danville, NHd age 19 yr

PAGE, Clara b Danville, NH; md KEEZER, Wallace

PAGE, Clarence b 22 Sep 1876 Danville, NH s/o PAGE, Herbert A. & GRIFFIN, Florence

PAGE, Clarinda b 27 Feb 1868 Danville, NH d/o PAGE, John Burton & WOOD, Lydia A.

PAGE, Daniel b 01 Jan 1769 Hawke, NH; s/o PAGE, Thos & ELKINS, Mary; md 31 Dec 1789 Hawke, NH TOWLE, Mary (Polly); d

PAGE (Cont.) 13 Mar 1853 Danville, NH age 84 yr

PAGE, David Frank b 1844 Danville, NH s/o PAGE, Oren & TOWLE, Clarinda; md 02 Jul 1873 Newton, NH CURRIER, Luella

PAGE, Dora S. b 27 Oct 1869 Danville, NH d/o PAGE, John Burton & WOOD, Lydia A. (Johnson); md 31 Dec 1887 Plaistow, NH KIMBALL, Eugene F. d 19 Dec 1938 Danville, NH; md by Rev W. M. Weeks

PAGE, Dorothy b 07 Jun 1767 Hawke, NH d/o PAGE, Ephriam & CURRIER, Hannah

PAGE, Eleanor b 27 Sep 1776 Hawke, NH d/o PAGE, Thos & ELKINS, Mary; md YOUNG, Aaron; d 25 Aug 1858 Danville, NHd age 82 yr

PAGE, Eleanor b 07 Jun 1771 Hawke, NH d/o PAGE, Ephriam & CURRIER, Hannah

PAGE, Emily Jane b c1831 d/o PAGE, Joel & EASTMAN, Prudence; d 24 Mar 1850 Danville, NH ae 19y

PAGE, Ephriam md CURRIER, Hannah

PAGE, Fanny md 12 May 1831 Kingston, NH KIMBALL, John;

PAGE, Florence A. b c1898 Kingston, NH d/o PAGE, Clarence; md 15 Sep 1915 Newton, NH GEORGE, Elmer S.; md by Rev Wm P. Richards

PAGE, Freddie A. b 01 Aug 1873 Danville, NH s/o PAGE, Herbert A. & GRIFFIN, Florence; d 27 Sep 1876 Danville, NH ae 2y of Typhoid Fever

PAGE, Gertrude M. b 1869 Kingston, NH d/o PAGE, Ezra & SHAW, Augusta; md 28 Aug 1896 Kingston, NH LADD, Ottero; d 01 Jan 1930 Danville, NH ae 62y 2m 24d

Page, Hannah b 23 Jul 1801 Hawke, NH d/o PAGE, Daniel & TOWLE, Mary; md 17 Aug 1820 Hawke, NH COLLINS, Moses; d 18 Sep 1892 Danville, NH; bu Danville, NH Old Mtg Hse Cem.

PAGE, Hannah b 11 Mar 1809 Hawke, NH d/o PAGE, Simon & SHAW, Abigail; md OSGOOD, Jonathan; d 17 Nov 1902 Danville, NH

PAGE, Hannah b 11 Feb 1777

PAGE (Cont.) Hawke, NH d/o PAGE, John (Rev) & STEVENS, Mary

PAGE, Hannah b Salem, NH; md 22 Feb 1802 Hampstead, NH WEBSTER, Jos Jr.

PAGE, Hannah b 24 Sep 1775 Hawke, NH d/o PAGE, Ephriam & CURRIER, Hannah

PAGE, Hannah b 24 Feb 1765 Hawke, NH d/o PAGE, Thos & ELKINS, Mary

PAGE, Hannah b Hawke, NH; md 30 Apr 1829 Kingston, NH WORTHEN, Walter

PAGE, Hannah b 1821 Hawke, NH d/o PAGE, Aaron & ----, Nancy

PAGE, Hannah b c1821 Hawke, NH; md 03 Oct 1839 Danville, NH QUIMBY, Elisha; d 16 Jun 1890 Danville, NH

PAGE, Henry b Sandown, NH; md 21 May 1778 Hawke, NH PAGE, Sarah

PAGE, Henry b 1887 NH s/o PAGE, Ernest; md 08 Oct 1949 Plaistow, NH PIDGEON, Hazel Ida; md by Wallace E. Card (JP)

PAGE, Hepzibah b 12 Nov 1827 Hawke, NH d/o PAGE, Amos & EASTMAN, Hepzibah; d 01 Oct 1913 Danville, NH

PAGE, Herbert A. b 03 Jul 1851 Danville, NH s/o PAGE, Aaron & ALLEN-KEAY, Valeria

PAGE, Huldah b d/o PAGE, Joel & EASTMAN, Prudence; d 30 Jan 1828 Hawke, NH age 2 yr

PAGE, Iantha b 1836 Danville, NH d/o PAGE, Oren & TOWLE, Clarinda; md COLLINS, Page; d 13 Jul 1858 Danville, NH ae 22y

PAGE, Jabez b 14 Jul 1771 Hawke, NH s/o PAGE, Thos & ELKINS, Mary; md Aug 1799 Hawke, NH KIMBALL, Sally

PAGE, Jabez b c1711 Salisbury, MA; md FLANDERS, Abigail; d 04 May 1782 Hawke, NH; bu Hawke, NH Old Mtg Hse Cem.; d ae 71y

PAGE, Joanna b c1801 d/o PAGE, Benj & QUIMBY, Rebecca; d 12 Sep 1803 Hawke, NH ae 2 + y

PAGE, Joel b 27 Sep 1795 Hawke, NH s/o PAGE, Simon & SANBORN,

PAGE (Cont.) Phebe; md EASTMAN, Prudence; d 1880 Sandown, NH ae 85y

PAGE, John b 24 May 1769 Hawke, NH s/o PAGE, Ephriam & CURRIER, Hannah

PAGE, John b 23 Nov 1788 Hawke, NH s/o PAGE, Benj & QUIMBY, Rebecca

PAGE, John md COLBY, Nancy

PAGE, John b Hawke, NH; md 20 Feb 1811 Kingston, NH SANBORN, Dorothy

PAGE, John b 20 Mar 1785 Hawke, NH s/o PAGE, Thos & ELKINS, Mary; md SANBORN, Dorothy; d 04 Sep 1823 Hawke, NH age 38 yr

PAGE, John b 16 Jul 1772 Hawke, NH s/o PAGE, John (Rev) & STEVENS, Mary; md 12 Sep 1797 Hampstead, NH JOHNSON, Sally

PAGE, John b c1728 Salisbury, MA; md WEBSTER, Anne; d 08 Jul 1767 Hawke, NH ae 39y; bu Hawke, NH Old Mtg Hse Cem.

PAGE, John b c1790 md COLLINS, Mary; d 20 Dec 1858 Danville, NH ae 68y

PAGE, John b 03 Jun 1790 Hawke, NH s/o PAGE, Daniel & TOWLE, Mary

PAGE, John (Rev) b c1739 Salem, NH; md 12 Jan 1764 Hawke, NH STEVENS, Mary; d 20 Jan 1782 Hawke, NH; bu Hawke, NH Old Mtg Hse Cem.; d smallpox; spouse of Salem

PAGE, John Burton b 1838 Danville, NH s/o PAGE, Oren & TOWLE, Clarinda; md 1860 Danville, NH WOOD, Lydia A.; d 06 Aug 1872 Danville, NH

PAGE, John Emery b Mar 1837 Danville, NH s/o PAGE, Aaron & ----, Nancy E.; 30 Aug 1837 Danville, NH

PAGE, Jos Wright b 02 Feb 1765 Hawke, NH s/o PAGE, John (Rev) & STEVENS, Mary

PAGE, Jos Wright b 19 Aug 1798 Hawke, NH s/o PAGE, John Jr. & JOHNSON, Sarah

PAGE, Juliette b 01 Sep 1821 Hawke, NH d/o PAGE, John & COLLINS, Mary; md PEASLEE, ---- ; d 04 Dec 1911 Danville, NH ae 90y 3m 17d

PAGE, Laura E. md CLEMENT, ---- ; d 1884 Manchester, NH; also m to SPAULDING & PLUMMER

PAGE, Lois b 05 Jun 1787 Hawke, NH d/o PAGE, Thos & ELKINS, Mary; md 01 Jul 1812 Hawke, NH DAVIS, Jonathan

PAGE, Lois b 09 May 1814 Hawke, NH d/o PAGE, Daniel & TOWLE, Mary; md 17 Jun 1833 Hawke, NH SARGENT, Samuel, d 26 Feb 1897 Danville, NH

PAGE, Lydia b c1829; md HUNT, Oliver; d 13 May 1855 Danville, NH ae 26y

PAGE, Mary b 27 Jun 1773 Hawke, NH d/o PAGE, Thos & ELKINS, Mary

PAGE, Mary b 03 Jan 1800 Hawke, NH d/o PAGE, John Jr. & JOHNSON, Sarah

PAGE, Mary b 14 Sep 1793 Hawke, NH d/o PAGE, Simon & SANBORN, Phebe

PAGE, Mary b 04 May 1764 Hawke, NH d/o PAGE, John & WEBSTER, Anne

PAGE, Mary b Kingston, NH; md 30 Sep 1839 Raymond, NH YOUNG, Daniel

PAGE, Mary (Polly) b Hawke, NH; md 30 Sep 1810 Kingston, NH SPOFFORD, Benaiah

PAGE, Mary A. b c1835 Danville, NH; md 02 Mar 1863 Danville, NH KEAY, Orestes H.

PAGE, Mary Ann b 05 Dec 1830 Hawke, NH d/o PAGE, Amos & EASTMAN, Hepzibah

PAGE, Molley b 07 Jul 1766 Hawke, NH d/o PAGE, John (Rev) & STEVENS, Mary

PAGE, Moses b Hawke, NH; md 21 Jul 1828 Kingston, NH TUCKER, Angeline

PAGE, Oren b c1822 s/o PAGE, John;; md TOWLE, Clarinda Y.; d 29 Oct 1879 Danville, NH ae 64y

PAGE, Oren Freeman b 04 Apr 1840 Danville, NH s/o PAGE, Oren & TOWLE, Clarinda; md 1864 Danville, NH WASON, Chastina

PAGE, Phineas b 17 Feb 1779 Hawke, NH s/o PAGE, John (Rev) &

PAGE (Cont.) STEVENS, Mary

PAGE, Polly md THORN, Abraham; d 27 Sep 1829 Danville, NH ae 26y

PAGE, Polly b 1806 Danville, NH d/o PAGE, Daniel & YOUNG, Mary; md DEARBORN, ---- ; d 19 Jul 1891 Danville, NH

PAGE, Polly b 09 Aug 1792 Hawke, NH d/o PAGE, Daniel & TOWLE, Mary

PAGE, Prudence d d/o PAGE, Joel & EASTMAN, Prudence; d 11 Jul 1826 Hawke, NH ae 2y

PAGE, Purley R. b 1825 Hawke, NH s/o PAGE, John & COLLINS, Mary; d 06 Nov 1825 Hawke, NH d ae 2 mo

PAGE, Rebecca b 14 Nov 1807 Hawke, NH d/o PAGE, Simon & SHAW, Abigail

PAGE, Ruth b d/o PAGE, Jabez; md 13 Dec 1759 Kingston, NH TOWLE, Caleb

PAGE, Sally b 28 Nov 1795 Hawke, NH d/o PAGE, Daniel & TOWLE, Mary

PAGE, Sarah b Hawke, NH; md 21 May 1778 Hawke, NH PAGE, Henry

PAGE, Sarah b 17 Nov 1766 Hawke, NH s/o PAGE, Thos & ELKINS, Mary

PAGE, Sarah b Hawke, NH; md FIFIELD, Peter; d 1868 Danville, NH ae 73y

PAGE, Sarah b 11 May 1774 Hawke, NH d/o PAGE, John (Rev) & STEVENS, Mary; md 11 Aug 1797 Hawke, NH MORSE, Samuel; or b Salem ?

PAGE, Sarah b c1767; md 28 Apr 1785 Hawke, NH WEBSTER, Benj; d 03 Jun 1809 Hawke, NH d ae 42y

PAGE, Sarah Hannah b 08 Oct 1805 Hawke, NH d/o PAGE, John Jr. & JOHNSON, Sarah

PAGE, Sarah K. b 1834 Kingston, NH; md 13 Sep 1852 Danville, NH NASON, Nathan Jr.

PAGE, Simon b 25 Nov 1763 Hawke, NH s/o PAGE, Thos & ELKINS, Mary; md 1st 23 Dec 1788 Kingston, NH SANBORN, Phebe, 2nd 05 Mar 1806 Hawke, NH; SHAW, Abigail. 3rd 11 May 1815 Hawke, NH

PAGE (Cont.) Winlow, Sarah; d 06 Nov 1819 Hawke, NH bu Hawke, NH Old Mtg Hse Cem.

PAGE, Sushannah b 16 Mar 1765 Hawke, NH d/o PAGE, Ephraim & CURRIER, Hannah

PAGE, Thos b c1733 Hawke, NH; md 11 Jul 1763 Kingston, NH EL-KINS, Mary; d 26 Jun 1829 Hawke, NH; bu Hawke, NH Old Mtg Hse Cem. d ae 86y

PAGE, Thos b Kingston, NH; md 15 Oct 1832 Hawke, NH BICKFORD, Eliza

PAGE, ---- b 25 Jul 1775 Hawke, NH s/o PAGE, Thos & ELKINS, Mary; d 27 Jul 1775 Hawke, NH Twin Sons

PAGE, ---- b 30 Nov 1818 Hawke, NH ?/o PAGE, Simon & WINSLOW, Sarah; d 30 Nov 1818 Hawke, NH d same day

PAGE. Mariah b Sandown, NH d/o PAGE, James & EASTMAN, Prudence; d 12 Jun 1851 Danville, NH d ae 14y

PAGLIARULO, Donna Jean md 12 Aug 1989 Danville, NH WARD, Jos Hogkins; md by Rev Harold E. Small

PAIGE, Alberta Ellen b 1925 NH d/o PAIGE, Walter E.; md 1st CURRI-ER, ---- , 2nd 16 Jun 1951 Exeter, NH ARNOLD, Karl James; md by Rev Paul T. Martion

PAJEK, Allen b of Danville, NH; md 30 Jun 1992 TUTTLE, Margaret A.

PALMER, Muriel D. md 21 Jul 1990 Danville, NH BASILE, David S.; md by Richard J. Rondeau (JP)

PALMER, Rebecca D. md 07 Jul 1984 Danville, NH COLLINS, David P.; md by Rev Everett E. Palmer

PAOLINO, Richard M. md 25 Feb 1989 Danville, NH DORSEY, Rhonda Lynne; md by Rev John C. Lombard

PAOLUCCI, Louis 3rd b 28 Aug 1954 Danville, NH s/o PAOLUCCI, Louis Jr. & CAPOPOSTOS, Anna

PAPPALARDO, Robyn Jeanne md 22 Apr 1990 Danville, NH PERIN, Timothy Jeanne; md by Richard J. Rondeau (JP)

PARKER, Nellie b 1864 Kingston, NH d/o PARKER, Henry & ---- , Fanny; d 17 Apr 1864 Danville, NH ae 4m

PARKER, Wilfred b Haverhill, NH s/o PARKER, Francis & SARGENT, Esther; d 30 Sep 1966 Danville, NH ae 60y

PARLEE, Ronald b 1944 Ayer, MA; md 01 Jan 1964 Danville, NH; ROWEN, Diane; md by Edward R. Lamb (JP)

PARSONS, Lauren Eliz b 15 Jun 1984 Exeter, NH d/o PARSONS, Wade H. & TODD, Margaret E.

PARSONS, Lindsay Ellen b 03 May 1982 Exeter, NH d/o PARSONS, Wade H. & TODD, Margaret E.

PARTRIDGE, Florence E. b 1945 MA; md 25 Aug 1961 Danville, NH DIMES, Douglas Richard; md by Oscar W. Swenson

PASCOE, James b England s/o PASCOE, Francis & SPARGO, Prudence; d 13 Jun 1949 Danville, NH

PASQUALE, Frederick b 1904 Boston, MA s/o PASQUALE, Francisco; md 06 May 1934 Danville, NH COOK, Dorothy Nellie md by Rev Harold C. Ross

PATTEE, Annie S. b Haverhill, MA; d/o JONES, Harry E. & MARLIN, Clara B.; d 17 Mar 1967 Danville, NH d ae 70y

PATTEN, Herbert b c1867 Amesbury, MA s/o PATTEN, Jos W.; md 16 Jan 1909 Danville, NH GEORGE, Mary E.; md by Rev W. C. Chappell; 2nd m for both

PATTEN, Lena F. b 1907 Raymond, NH d/o PATTEN, Jenness W.; md 02 Oct 1927 Danville, NH MER-RICK, Ernest D.; md by Rev Asa M. Bradley

PAUL, Derek Kent b 23 Sep 1984 Lawrence, MA; s/o PAUL, Geo H. & KENT, Debra

PAYNE, Josephine M. b Londonderry, NH; md GEORGE, Fred L.

PEABODY, Lorenzo J. b c1867 Levant, ME s/o PEABODY, Wm B; md 23 Oct 1902 Danville, NH COLBY, Charlotte M.; md by Rev A. B. Howard

PEARSON, Hannah b md 1st EATON, Benj 2nd WOODMAN, Moses; d Aug 1850 Danville, NH

PEARSON, Hannah A. b 1847

PEARSON (CONT.) Danville, NH d/o PEARSON, Henry N & LADD, Mary G.; md BLAKE, ---- ; d 21 Jul 1963 Danville, NH

PEARSON, Karl M. b 1905 Salem, MA; md 03 Jul 1965 Danville, NH CARLSON, Mary O.; md by Rev F. Kieths

PEASE, Ernest Linwood Jr. b NH; md 08 Aug 1969 Danville, NH PERROW, Sandra Renaye; md by Marian T. Brewster (JP)

PEASLEE, Caleb Jr. b c1825 s/o PEASLEE, Caleb Sr. & GREEN, Hannah; d 03 Dec 1843 Danville, NH ae 18y

PEASLEE, Caleb Sr. b c1783 Newton, NH; md GREEN, Hannah R.; d 31 Jan 1870 Danville, NH; sp. md 2nd Nathaniel COLLINS

PEASLEE, Catherine M. b c1832; md DIMOND, Josiah T.; d 15 Sep 1858 Danville, NH ae 26y

PEASLEE, Dolly b c1823; md GRIFFIN, Samuel C.; d 16 Jul 1867 Danville, NH ae 44y

PEASLEE, Henrietta M. b Kingston, NH d/o PEASLEE, Jacob C. & PAGE, Julietta; d ae 85y 0m 22d

PEASLEE, Isaac b Perrystown, ?; md 15 Oct 1781 Hawke COLLINS, Mary; md by Rev John Page

PEASLEE, Jacob C. b Kingston, NH s/o PEASLEE, Daniel & SECOMB, Eliz; d 29 Nov 1894 Danville, NH ae 86y 1m 26d

PEASLEE, Mary C. b 23 Dec 1840 Danville, NH d/o PEASLEE, Caleb Sr. & GREEN, Hannah; md FRENCH, ----; d 17 Sep 1897 Danville, NH

PEASLEE, Wm b Newton, NH; md 04 Jul 1805 Kingston, NH CAMP-BELL, Dorothy

PEAVEY, Hannah b c1869 Alton, NH d/o PEAVEY, Jos; md WIGGIN, ---- 03 Feb 1896 Danville, NH

PEDERSEN, Cheri Lynn md 09 Jul 1988 Danville, NH MENCKE, Keith Wm; md by Rev David M. Midwood

PEDERSEN, Elmer A. b 1898 Oslo Norway s/o PEDERSEN, Anders; md 01 Dec 1946 Danville, NH MORSE, Alice Pomeroy; md by Rev Kendig B.

PENDERSON (Cont.) Culley

PEDERSEN, Eric James b 23 Apr 1975 Haverhill, MA s/o PEDERSEN, Robert A. & BOYNTON, Linda L.

PEDERSEN, Jessica Lee b 24 Mar 1973 Haverhill, NH d/o PEDERSEN, Robert A. & BOYNTON, Linda I.

PELCZAR, Antonia b 1914 Newmarket, NH d/o PELCZAR, Michael & SMITH, V. Catherine; md 14 Aug 1948 Windham, NH TEWKS-BURY, Fred Herbert; d 14 Apr 1980 Danville, NH; md by Carolyn B. Cochran (JP)

PELON, Sandra J. b 1937 Boston, MA; md 28 Oct 1966 Danville, NH WARE, John; md by Leona A. Sciaudone (JP)

PENTON, Anna M b Fago N Fou; md AVERY, Lucius O.

PERACCHI, Louis C. md 28 Jul 1979 Danville, NH SHEPPARD, Diane N.; md by Anita L. Gallien (JP)

PERALTA, Ann R. md 13 Jun 1987 Danville, NH OWEN, Kenneth H. Jr.; md by Renee Houle Carkin (JP)

PERIN, Laurie B. md 08 Oct 1983 Danville, NH MORRISON, Steven J.; md by Rev Richard Russell (Jehovah Witness)

PERIN, Timothy Alan md 22 Apr 1990 Danville, NH PAPPALARDO, Robyn Jeanne; md by Rich J. Rondeau (JP)

PERIN, Tyler Alan b 28 Oct 1992 Exeter, NH s/o PERIN, Timothy A. & PAPPALARDO, Robyn J.

PERKINS, Moses b Sandown, NH; md 02 Feb 1843 Danville, NH BROWN, Sarah

PERREAULT, Frank J. b md 15 Aug 1989 Danville, NH HORNE, Joanne Glass; md by Rich J. Rondeau (JP)

PERROU, Jodi Lee b 11 Jan 1960 Danville, NH d/o PERROU, John Ross & COLLINS, Brenda Eileen

PERROU, John Ross b KS; md 22 Oct 1960 Danville, NH COLLINS, Brenda Eileen; md by Rev Robert F. Griffin

PERROW, Sandra R. b 1945 Carthage, MO; md 08 Feb 1964 Dan-

PERROW (Cont.) ville, NH COR-TON, Edward W. Jr.; md by Herbert C. Shelly (P)

PERROW, Sandra Renaye b 1945 Carthage, MO; md 08 Aug 1969 Danville, NH PEASE, Ernest Linwood Jr.; md by Marian T. Brewster (JP)

PERRY, Anthony b Portugal; d 07 Nov 1921 Danville, NH ae 54y

PETERSON, Laura Ann b 13 Dec 1979 Lawrence, MA d/o PETERSON, Paul C. & TARBOX, Kathleen L.

PETTENGILL, Benj b of Salisbury, MA; md 09 Dec 1799 Hawke, NH SLEEPER, Lydia md by Rev John Page

PEVEARE, Ella M. b 1851 Sandown, NH d/o PEVEARE, Hazen & BURRILL, Harriet; md RICHARDSON ---- ; d 21 Mar 1924 Danville, NH

PEVERLEY, Cynthia J. md 29 May 1984 Danville, NH HALFHILL, David F. Jr.; md by Rev WEndall J. Irvine

PEVERLEY, Lisa A. md 14 Sep 1985 Danville, NH SHURTLEFF, Eric C.; md by Rev Wendall J. Irvine

PHERIN, Alphesus b md 08 Dec 1780 Hawke, NH CURRIER, Margaret; md by Rev John Page

PHILBRICK, Almira b 09 Jan 1827 Hawke, NH d/o PHILBRICK, Josiah & QUIMBY, Sarah

PHILBRICK, Almon Quimby b 27 Jul 1822 Hawke, NH s/o PHILBRICK, Josiah & QUIMBY, Sarah; d 26 Sep 1853 Danville, NH

PHILBRICK, Andrew J. b 26 May 1837 Danville, NH s/o PHILBRICK, Josiah & DIMOND, Sarah; d 19 Dec 1853 Danville, NH ae 85y 7m 19d

PHILBRICK, Andrew J. b 04 Sep 1829 Hawke, NH s/o PHILBRICK, Jedediah & BARTLETT, Susanna; d 17 Jul 1830 Hawke, NH

PHILBRICK, Betsy b Hawke, NH; md 02 Mar 1798 Kingston, NH SMITH, Jacob

PHILBRICK, Dolly b 18 Jan 1786 Hawke, NH d/o PHILBRICK, Jedediah & SANBORN, Mary

PHILBRICK, Elbridge G. b 09 Sep 1833 Hawke, NH s/o PHILBRICK, Jedediah & BARTLETT, Susanna; d 03 Nov 1881 Danville, NH

PHILBRICK, Eliz b 15 Aug 1777 Hawke, NH d/o PHILBRICK, Jedediah & SANBORN, Mary

PHILBRICK, Geo W. b 30 Jul 1827 Hawke, NH s/o PHILBRICK, Jedediah & BARTLETT, Susanna; d 19 Apr 1901 ae 71y 8m 19d

PHILBRICK, Hannah b 27 Jun 1783 Hawke, NH d/o PHILBRICK, Jedediah & SANBORN, Mary

PHILBRICK, Hannah b c1723; md HOOK, Humphrey; d 28 Aug 1771 Hawke, NH; bu Hawke, NH Old Mtg Hse Cem.; d ae 48y

PHILBRICK, Harriet P. 1 b 02 Dec 1819 Hawke, NH d/o PHILBRICK, Jedediah & BARTLETT, Susanna; d 30 Nov 1820 Hawke, NH ae 1y

PHILBRICK, Harriet P. 2 b 07 May 1822 Hawke, NH d/o PHILBRICK, Jedediah & BARTLETT, Susanna d 06 Dec 1825 Hawke, NH

PHILBRICK, Jedediah b 31 Jan 1797 Hawke, NH s/o PHILBRICK, Josiah & TEWKSBURY, Sarah; md 15 Jul 1819 Hawke, NH BARTLETT, Susanna; d 27 Jul 1864 Danville, NH ae 67y

PHILBRICK, Jedediah md 28 Jun 1790 Kingston, NH COLCORD, Dorothy

PHILBRICK, Jedediah b c1745; md 07 Dec 1769 Hawke, NH SANBORN, Mary; d 17 May 1790 Hawke, NH ae 45y

PHILBRICK, Joanna B. b 14 Nov 1824 Hawke, NH d/o PHILBRICK, Jedediah & BARTLETT, Susanna; md 12 Feb 1843 Danville, NH SANBORN, John Stark

PHILBRICK, John b 31 Jul 1788 Hawke, NH s/o PHILBRICK, Jedediah & SANBORN, Mary; md WEBSTER, Paulina

PHILBRICK, Josiah b 26 Jan 1800 Hawke, NH s/o PHILBRICK, Josiah & TEWKSBURY, Sarah; md 2nd TILTON, Sarah; d 09 Nov 1863 Danville, NH

PHILBRICK, Josiah b 26 Jan 1800 Hawke, NH s/o PHILBRICK, Josiah & TEWKSBURY, Sarah; md QUIMBY, Sarah; d 09 Nov 1863 Danville, NH

PHILBRICK, Josiah 1 b 20 Mar 1770 Hawke, NH s/o PHILBRICK, Jedediah & SANBORN, Mary

PHILBRICK, Josiah 2 b 02 Mar 1771 Hawke, NH s/o PHILBRICK, Jedediah & SANBORN, Mary

PHILBRICK, Josiah 3 b 23 Sep 1772 Hawke, NH s/o PHILBRICK, Jedediah & SANBORN, Mary; md 27 Oct 1796 Kingston, NH TEWKSBURY, Sally; d 25 Dec 1827 Hawke, NH ae 55y

PHILBRICK, Josiah M. b 13 Jan 1830 Hawke, NH s/o PHILBRICK, Josiah & QUIMBY, Sarah; d Feb 1848 Danville, NH

PHILBRICK, Leroy B. b 31 Dec 1845 Danville, NH s/o PHILBRICK, Almon Q. & WILCOM, Susan E.

PHILBRICK, Luella B. b 10 Mar 1824 Hawke, NH d/o PHILBRICK, Josiah & QUIMBY, Sarah; md ELKINS, John; d 15 Oct 1899 ae 75y 6m 28d

PHILBRICK, Mary Sanborn b 08 Apr 1775 Hawke, NH d/o PHILBRICK, Jedediah & SANBORN, Mary

PHILBRICK, Matilda S. b 05 Mar 1845 Danville, NH d/o PHILBRICK, Josiah & HOYT, Sarah; md 1865 Danville, NH TRUE, Horance E.;

PHILBRICK, Nancy b 18 Oct 1803 Hawke, NH d/o PHILBRICK, Josiah & TEWKSBURY, Sarah

PHILBRICK, Rosina E. b 01 Dec 1841 Danville, NH d/o PHILBRICK, Josiah & DIMOND, Sarah

PHILBRICK, Sally b 11 Aug 1831 Hawke, NH d/o PHILBRICK, Jedediah & BARTLETT, Susanna; d 16 Jul 1833 Hawke, NH

PHILBRICK, Samuel Major d 04 Apr 1799 Danville, NH

PHILBRICK, Sarah b 12 Jul 1808 Hawke, NH d/o PHILBRICK, Josiah & TEWKSBURY, Sarah

PHILBRICK, Sarah b 18 Dec 1779 Hawke, NH d/o PHILBRICK, Jedediah & SANBORN, Mary

PHILBRICK, Sarah b 15 Dec 1781 Hawke, NH d/o PHILBRICK, Jedediah & SANBORN, Mary

PHILBRICK, Sarah A. b 15 Jul 1839 Danville, NH d/o PHILBRICK, Josiah & DIMOND, Sarah

PHILBRICK, Sarah Quimby b 06 Aug 1832 Hawke, NH d/o PHILBRICK, Josiah & QUIMBY, Sarah; d 21 Nov 1832 Hawke, NH ae 3m

PHILIPP, Lawrence Hamilton md 11 Oct 1989 Danville, NH KOONS, Kandi-Sue; md by Rich J. Rondeau (JP)

PHILLIPS, Eliz Ann md 12 Feb 1991 Danville, NH BOSSIO, Donald; md by Richard E. Rondeau (JP)

PHILLIPS, Jos Dewey b 1901 Sandown, NH s/o PHILLIPS, Joshua & REIBER, Pauline; md 11 Jan 1964 Danville, NH ANDERSON, Gertrude K.; d 29 Jun 1987 Danville, NH; md by Rev Theodore B. Hadley

PICKARD, Herbert O. Jr. b 1913 Rowley, MA s/o PICKARD, Herbert O. Sr.; md 02 Apr 1938 Danville, NH COREY, Mabel H.; md by Rev W. C. Chappell

PIDGEON, Hazel Ida b 1892 MA d/o PIDGEON, Chas Henry; md 08 Oct 1949 Plaistow, NH PAGE, Henry; md by Wallace E. Card (JP); prev md McHarg, ----

PIERCE, Arthur E. Jr. md 29 Sep 1973 Danville, NH WARD, Susan E.; md by Rev Henry K. Mook

PIERCE, Charlotte May b 1923 Amesbury, MA d/o PIERCE, Eugene Leonard; md 29 May 1946 Danville, NH LeMOINE, Arthur Peter; md by W. C. Chappell

PIERCE, Eleanor G. b Danville, NH; md 26 Dec 1970 Danville, NH SMITH, Herbert R.

PIERCE, Louise b 1918 d/o PIERCE, Walter & HARRIMAN, Mary; md PARKER, ---- ; d 27 Feb 1977 Danville, NH ae 59y

PIERCE, Lydia b c1784 Plaistow, NH; md JONES, Jonathan; d 04 Apr 1860 Danville, NH; d age 76 yr - also md CURRIER

PIERCE, Mary b Burlington, VT d/o PIERCE, Jason Lee & GOUYER, Mable; md DOUGLAS, ---- ; d 26 May 1964 Danville, NH

PIERCE, Nancy b c1809 S Hampton, NH; md 1859 Danville, NH HAYNES, Sylvester

PIERGENTILI, Candia Roselli b d/o PIERGENTILI, Luigi & ROSELLI, Angelia; md BERNABY, ---- d 26 Sep 1972 Danville, NH ae 84y

PIKE, Abigail md CAMPBELL, Annas; spouse from Ireland

PIKE, Mary b c1744; md Williams, Jos Capt.; d 01 Jan 1804 Hawke, NH; bu Hawke, NH Old Mtg Hse Cem.; d ae 60y

PILLSBURY, Jane md 20 Nov 1793 Hampstead, NH COLBY, Moses

PILON, Calice b 08 May 1900 Danville, NH d/o PILON, Calice & CHENEY, Delphine; 4th child in family

PILON, Marie Joe Eugenie b 29 Aug 1901 d/o PILON, Calice & CHENEY, Delphine; 6th child in family

PIMENTAL, Denise md 27 Apr 1986 Danville, NH LARATONDA, Francis A.; md by Wm E. Beane (JP)

PIMENTAL, Gilbert Jos b s/o PIMENTAL, Jos & MARSHALL, Sylvia; d 17 Nov 1992

PINCENCE, Jacqueline Paige b 27 Jun 1991 Exeter, NH d/o PINCENCE Wayne E. & BIJEOL, Robin D.

PINGREY, Sarah b 06 Jun 1782 Hawke, NH d/o PINGREY, Samuel & ----, Sarah

PIRZ, Patricia Eliz md 26 Sep 1976 Danville, NH LUSCHER, Louis John; md by Robert S. Dejadon (JP); or spelled PIRS?

PITMAN, Bonnie Elaine b 1944 Presque Is, ME; md 01 May 1964 Danville, NH BATTIS, Paul Wm; md by Rev Wm Sleamaker

PLAISTED, David C. md 24 Jun 1990 Danville, NH PYNN, Kristine R.; md by Rev Chas D. H. Barton

PLAISTED, Hunter Scott b 14 Sep 1990 Manchester, NH s/o PLAISTED, David C. & PYNN, Kristine R.

PLEAU, Loretta b 1897 Haverhill, MA d/o PLEAU, Louis; md 23 Jun 1923 Hampstead, NH COLLINS, Theron J.; md by Rev Howard Collins

PLIMPTON, Henry Clay Jr. b 1925 Gilsom, NH s/o PLIMPTON, Henry-Clay Sr.;md 15 Jun 1947 Danville, NH SWAIN, Medora Fraughten; md by Rev W. C. Chappell

PLUMMER, Hannah b 07 Jul 1783 Hawke, NH d/o PLUMMER, Samuel & JONES, Miriam; md 23 Apr 1803 Hampstead, NH HEATH, Enoch

PLUMMER, Henry b Hampstead, NH; md 27 Sep 1770 Hawke, NH JONES, Joanna; md by Rev John Page

PLUMMER, Henry b 03 Apr 1787 Hawke, NH s/o PLUMMER, Samuel & JONES, Miriam

PLUMMER, Mary W. b c1843 Sandown, NH; md 24 Mar 1872 Danville, NH COTTON, Geo A.

PLUMMER, Moses b 13 Jun 1791 Hawke, NH s/o PLUMMER, Samuel & JONES, Miriam

PLUMMER, Nathan md 21 Nov 1794 Kingston, NH NEATH, Rhoda

PLUMMER, Samuel b Hawke, NH; md 18 Mar 1824 Amesbury, MA HUNTINGTON, Hannah

PLUMMER, Samuel b Hawke, NH; md 20 Dec 1800 Hampstead, NH VANCE, Anna

PLUMMER, Samuel md 04 Apr 1767 Hawke, NH JONES, Miriam

PLUMMER, Susan Mrs. md 02 Dec 1839 Raymond, NH MERRILL, Enoch

PODLASKI, Mary M. md 09 Feb 1985 Danville, NH PODINSKI, Valentine P.; md by Rochelle LaFontaine (JP)

PODLASKI, Valentine P. md 09 Feb 1985 Danville, NH PODINSKI, Mary M.; md by Rochelle LaFontaine (JP)

POLK, Earle F. md 14 Jun 1986 Danville, NH SHATTUCK, Barbara;; md by Richard J. Rondeau (JP)

POLK, Earle F. b s/o POLK, James & MUISE, Mary E.; d 17 Dec 1986 Danville, NH ae 54y

POLK, Barbara Jean md 22 May 1992 TRUSSELL, Thos C.

POLLARD, Ella M. b Barre, MA d/o POLLARD, David N.; md 27 Jun 1906 Exeter, NH SARGENT, Chas H.; md by Rev W. L. Anderson

POLLARD, Mercy b c1786; md HUNT, Henry; d 24 Jun 1867 Danville, NH ae 81y

POLY, Stephen Gregory b 11 Jan 1970 Haverhill, MA s/o POLY, Geo F. & CORTHELL, Janet C.

POND, Edward Emerson b 1939 NH s/o POND, Geo; md 27 Aug 1959 Danville, NH HUNT, Arlene Beatrice; md by John O. Perkins (JP)

POND, Henry Herbert b 1935 Derry, NH s/o POND, Geo; md 16 Aug 1957 Danville, NH MERRIFIELD, Gail Sandra

POND, Sandra Gail b 09 Feb 1959 Danville, NH d/o POND, Henry & MERRIFIELD, Gail SAndr

POOLE, Richard Reed b 1932 MA s/o POOLE, Harold N.; md 10 Nov 1956 Danville, NH DUSTON, Joyce Jean; md by Rev Albian Bulger (P)

POOR, Susan d 22 May 1863 Danville, NH ae 77y

POPE, Alan Richard b 15 Jul 1961 Danville, NH s/o POPE, Richard Allen & THIBEAULT, Priscilla Lorraine

POPE, Richard Allan b 1941 MA; md 30 Jan 1961 Danville, NH THIBEAULT, Priscilla Lorraine; md by Rev Harvey Cossaboom

PORTERFIELD, Claudia M b 25 Jan 1944 Danville, NH d/o PORTERFIELD, Claude Edward & COLLINS, Ruth Wilhelmina

POSSON, Wayne Foster b NY; md 22 Feb 1969 Danville, NH ELDRIDGE, Linda Mae; md by Rev James Fitzimmons

POST, Mark R. md 12 Oct 1985 Danville, NH HUNTOON, Diane B.; md by Rev Donald F. Jennings

POST, Sherry Ann b 30 Jul 1972 Methuen, MA d/o POST, Russell H. Jr. & POTVIN, Constance S.; md 29 Feb 1992 RILEY, Paul Dennis Jr

POTTER, Conway Lincoln b 1925 MA d/o POTTER, Wm P.; md 20 Dec 1952 Danville, NH BUCKNAM, Doris Geraldine; md by Rev W. C. Chappell

POTTS, Florence Irene b 1927 Lynn, MA d/o POTTS, Harry L.; md 10 Nov 1950 Danville, NH WEEDEN, John Haley; md by Rev W. C. Chappell

POWERS, Paul Michael Jr. b 24 May 1984 Exeter, NH s/o POWERS, Paul Michael Sr. & SULLIVAN, Debra A.

PRADO, Jorge md 01 Oct 1991 Danville, NH CORDINGLY, Kristen Ruth; md by Leslie A. Alphen (JP)

PRATT, Harriet M. b Boston, MA; d/o PRATT, Obed & MILLET, Harriet; md:GEORGE, Harrison; d 12 Mar 1908 Danville, NH ae 80y 5m 16d

PRATT, Kimberly Ann b 05 Jun 1977 Haverhill, MA d/o PRATT, Robert J. & MAILLOUX, Carol A.

PRATT, Sarah I. b Springfield, MA d/o PRATT, Arthur H. & WHITE, Nellie; md Shattuck, ---- ; d 10 Dec 1950 Danville, NH ae 78y

PRATT, Tomothy Robert b 12 Mar 1980 Haverhill, MA s/o PRATT, Robert J. & MAILLOUX, Carol A.

PRESCOTT, Nellie Frances b d/o PRESCOTT, Edgar & WEBSTER, Carrie; md HATCH, ---- ; d 04 Dec 1972 Danville, NH ae 80y

PRESCOTT, Rebecca b 27 Sep 1711 Hampton, NH d/o PRESCOTT, James; md Jan 1729 TOWLE, Caleb; d 01 Feb 1795 Hawke, NH; bu Danville, NH Old Mtg Hse Cem.; d age 84 yr

PRESCOTT, Ruth b Hawke, NH; md 15 Oct 1820 Kingston, NH BATCHELDER, Elisha

PRESCOTT, Stanley Warren b 1933 NH s/o PRESCOTT, Geo; md 27 Aug 1959 Danville, NH LONGLAND, Evelyn Amy; md by Rev Karl J. Hislop

PRESSEY, Geo b c1826 Sandown, NH; md 05 Feb 1862 Danville, NH SWASEY, Rebecca E.

PRESSEY, Paul md HUBBARD, Mercy; d 1760 Hawke, NH ae 31y; Occupation - Blacksmith

PRETTY, Harold J. b 1924 Nova Scotia; md 18 Aug 1967 Danville, NH LaFOND, Viola L.; md by Edward R. Lamb (JP)

PRIES, Jean b d/o PRIES, Henry; 24 Jan 1972 Danville, NH ae 37y

PRINCE, Sheryl Ann md 04 Jun 1977 Danville, NH DAVIES, Geoffrey Bruce; md by Rev Wm Ryans

PROCTOR, Linda K. md 09 Sep

PROCTOR (Cont.) 1991 Danville, NH BOLDUC, Bruce L.; md by John H. Lampray (JP)

PROSSEE, Pauline b Haverholl, MA d/o PROSSEE, Wm T. & BECKETT, Annie B.; d 21 Jul 1901 d ae 11y 1m 14d

PRUNIER, Bernard W. Jr. b s/o PRUNIER, Bernard W. S. & KRAMER, Katherine; d 23 Feb 1972 Danville, NH

PRUNIER, Bernard Warren b 30 Sep 1971 Haverhill, MA; d/o PRUNIER, Bernard W. & KRAMER, Katherine M.

PRYOR, Arthur b 1948 s/o PROYER, Chas & GRIFFIN, Dorothy Adele

PRYOR, Don b 1952 s/o PROYER, Chas & GRIFFIN, Dorothy Adele

PRYOR, Ralph b 1947 s/o PROYER, Chas & GRIFFIN, Dorothy Adele

PUCHTLER, Christine Den b 17 May 1971 Haverhill, MA d/o PUCH-TLER, Dennis R. & DYLESKI, Aline D.

PURINGTON, Clara b c1843 Epping, NH d/o PURINGTON, Joshua & DOW, Sarah; md GEORGE, ----, d 15 May 1914 Danville, NH

PURRINGTON, Chas C. b Fremont, NH s/o PURINGTON, Geo & ----, Fannie; md 13 Oct 1887 Hampton Falls, NH GRIFFIN, Mary L.; md by Rev R. F. Gardner

PURRINGTON, Geo F. b Fremont, NH s/o KIMBALL, Caleb & SCRIBNER, Lou; md ---- , Mary D.; d 09 Nov 1902 Danville, NH

PURRINGTON, Gregory W. md 11 Feb 1972 Danville, NH BOWLEY, Shela M.; md by Rev Robert W. Lewis

PUTNAM, Ashleigfh Eliz b 27 Feb 1981 Exeter, NH d/o PUTNAM, John C. & McLAUGHLIN, Colleen E.

PUTNAM, Marisa Mary b 16 Dec 1988 Exeter, NH d/o PUTNAM, John C. & McLAUGHLIN, Coleen E.

PUTNEY, Gary W. md 26 Nov 1982 Danville, NH KERRY, Carol M.; md by Wm E. Beane (JP)

PYNN, Kristine R. md 24 Jun 1990 Danville, NH PLAISTED, David C.; md by Rev Chas D. H. Barton

QUEEN, John Edward md 12 Oct 1991 Danville, NH GOULET, Lisa Joy; md by Rev Robert F. Dobson

QUIGLEY, Grace M. b 1944 Peabody, MA; md 25 Mar 1966 Danville, NH BULLERWELL, Harry A.; md by Leona A. Sciaudone (JP)

QUIMBY, Aaron b 02 Oct 1817 Hawke, NH s/o QUIMBY, Aaron & DIMOND, Eliz; d 15 Jul 1823 Hawke, NH age 5 yr

QUIMBY, Aaron b c1784; md DIMOND, Eliz; d 02 Apr 1822 Hawke, NH ae 38y

QUIMBY, Aaron md 02 Aug 1760 Hawke, NH TOWLE, Mary; 2nd mar of Aaron Quimby

QUIMBY, Aaron Col b 06 Jun 1799 Hawke, NH s/o QUIMBY, Elisha & BADGER, Hannah; md 26 Feb 1833 Hawke, NH BLAKE, Mary S.; d 09 Sep 1886 Danville, NH

QUIMBY, Aaron Page b 19 Dec 1846 Danville, NH s/o QUIMBY, Elisha & PAGE, Hannah; md 21 Jul 1805 Hawke, NH DIMOND, Eliz; d 10 Apr 1873 Danville, NH ae 26y Btsy

QUIMBY, Abigail b 07 Feb 1773 Hawke, NH d/o QUIMBY, Samuel & YOUNG, Ann

QUIMBY, Alfred b 31 Jul 1806 Hawke, NH s/o QUIMBY, Aaron & DIMOND, Eliz; d 07 Aug 1826 Hawke, NH

QUIMBY, Alice b 17 Jun 1886 Danville, NH; s/o QUIMBY, Charles E. & RUEE, Lizzie B.; md 27 Nov 1907 Danville, NH CLEMENT, Charles A.; md by Rev W. C. Chappell

QUIMBY, Almira P. 1 b 16 Jun 1825 Hawke, NH d/o QUIMBY, Nicholas & ----, Sarah; d 12 Sep 1825 Hawke, NH

QUIMBY, Almira P. 2 b 27 Sep 1831 Hawke, NH d/o QUIMBY, Nicholas & ----, Sarah

QUIMBY, Amy Lucinda b 13 Dec 1843 Danville, NH d/o QUIMBY, Elisha & PAGE, Hannah; md 20 Jun 1861 Danville, NH LADD, James M.; d 31 Mar 1873 Danville, NH age 29 yr

QUIMBY, Anna b 22 Sep 1760 Hawke, NH d/o QUIMBY, Samuel & YOUNG, Ann

QUIMBY, Benj b 07 Jul 1763 Hawke, NH s/o QUIMBY, Samuel &

QUIMBY (Cont.) YOUNG, Ann; md 15 Jul 1787 Kingston, NH CRITCHET, Mary; d 31 Aug 1811; bu Danville, NH Old Mtg Hse Cem.; d in war / spouse of Poplin

QUIMBY, Betsy b d/o QUIMBY, Aaron & DIMOND, Eliz; d 06 Aug 1829 Danville, NH

QUIMBY, Charles E. b Oct 1867 Danville, NH s/o QUIMBY, Alden Brown & LADD, Amy; md 04 Jul 1885 Danville, NH RUEE, Lizzie B.

QUIMBY, Charlotte E. b c1888 Danville, NH d/o QUIMBY, Chas E. & RUEE, Lizzie B.; md 19 Apr 1916 Danville, NH WEBSTER, Leon C.; d 18 Feb 1921 Danville, NH; md by Rev Allen C. Keith; d ae 33y 2m 4d

QUIMBY, Currier b 02 Aug 1805 Hawke, NH s/o QUIMBY, Thos & FITTS, Anne

QUIMBY, Daniel b 02 Nov 1767 Hawke, NH s/o QUIMBY, Samuel & YOUNG, Ann

QUIMBY, David b 24 Apr 1795 Hawke, NH s/o QUIMBY, Thomas & FITTS, Anne

QUIMBY, David b 02 Mar 1771 Hawke, NH s/o QUIMBY, Samuel & YOUNG, Ann; md 17 Nov 1796 Kingston, NH CAMPBELL, Polly

QUIMBY, David Col. b c1732 Hawke, NH; md WADLEIGH, Mary; d 19 Dec 1794 Hawke, NH bu Hawke, NH Old Mtg Hse Cem. d ae 63y

QUIMBY, David Jr b 13 Mar 1762 Hawke, NH s/o QUIMBY, David Col. & WADLEIGH, Mary; d 09 Jun 1781 age 19 yr - drowned

QUIMBY, DeForest b 27 Jan 1842 Hawke, NH s/o QUIMBY, Elisha & PAGE, Hannah; d 20 Jun 1842 Danville, NH

QUIMBY, Dorothy b 10 Jan 1771 Hawke, NH d/o QUIMBY, Moses & BEAN, Judith

QUIMBY, Elihu Thayer b 17 Jul 1826 Hawke, NH s/o QUIMBY, Nicholas & ----, Sarah

QUIMBY, Elisha b 19 Apr 1819 Hawke NH s/o QUIMBY, Aaron & DIMOND, Eliz; md 03 Oct 1839 Danville NH PAGE, Hannah d 06 Jan 1881

QUIMBY (Cont.) Danville, NH ae 61y

QUIMBY, Elisha b Danville, NH s/o QUIMBY, Charles F. & RUEE, Lizzie B.; d 08 Sep 1910 Danville, NH

QUIMBY, Elisha b 01 May 1767 Hawke, NH s/o QUIMBY, Aaron & TOWLE, Mary; md 16 Aug 1794 Kingston, NH BADGER, Hannah; d 21 Jun 1844 Danville, NH ae 77y

QUIMBY, Eliz b 02 Apr 1765 Hawke, NH d/o QUIMBY, Samuel & YOUNG, Ann

QUIMBY, Eliz Ann b 13 Apr 1840 Danville, NH d/o QUIMBY, Elisha & PAGE, Hannah; md 20 Sep 1859 Danville, NH KIMBALL, James M.; d 11 Dec 1880 Danville, NH; d ae 39y; also rcd 1 Dec 79

QUIMBY, Elvira Stevens b 19 Jul 1828 Hawke, NH d/o QUIMBY, Nicholas & ----, Sarah

QUIMBY, Erminie Lavern b 18 Aug 1901 s/o Quimby, Fred C. & AVERY, Sadie E.; 2nd child in family

QUIMBY, Eunice md 16 Dec 1777 Hawke, NH TILTON, David; md by Rev John Page

QUIMBY, Fred C. b Haverhill, MA s/o QUIMBY, Enoch R.; md 10 May 1899 AVERY, Sadie E.

QUIMBY, George W. b 20 Oct 1820 Hawke, NH s/o QUIMBY, Nicholas & ----, Sarah; d 06 Aug 1823 Hawke, NH

QUIMBY, Hannah b 28 Feb 1804 Hawke, NH d/o QUIMBY, John & DAVIS, Hannah

QUIMBY, Hannah b 17 Feb 1779 Hawke, NH d/o QUIMBY, Samuel & YOUNG, Ann

QUIMBY, Hannah b Hawke, NH; md 30 Nov 1779 Hawke, NH NELSON, Philip; md by Rev John Page

QUIMBY, James M. b c1832 Kingston, NH; md 09 Sep 1865 Danville, NH COTTON, May L.

QUIMBY, Jeremiah md 04 Jan 1769 Hawke, NH HOOK, Mary; md by Rev John Page

QUIMBY, Joanna b 22 Mar 1809 Hawke, NH d/o QUIMBY, Aaron & DIMOND, Eliz; d 28 Apr 1833 Hawke, NH

QUIMBY, John b 25 Dec 1774 Hawke, NH s/o QUIMBY, Samuel & YOUNG, Ann; md 25 Dec 1798 Hawke, NH DAVIS, Hannah

QUIMBY, John Emery b 18 Nov 1849 Danville, NH s/o QUIMBY, Elisha & PAGE, Hannah; d 29 Apr 1867 Danville, NH

QUIMBY, Joseph Badger b 15 Nov 1817 Hawke, NH s/o QUIMBY, Nicholas & BADGER, Sarah

QUIMBY, Judith b 25 Dec 1768 Hawke, NH d/o QUIMBY, Moses & BEAN, Judith

QUIMBY, Lena L. b 1887 Amesbury, MA d/o QUIMBY, Wilmont B. & TITCOMB, Mary O.; md 19 Oct 1910 Amesbury, MA CURRIER, Mahlon C.; d 16 Jul 1926 Danville, NH; md by Rev James D. Dinwgell

QUIMBY, Lucy b 31 Mar 1814 Hawke, NH d/o QUIMBY, Aaron & DIMOND, Eliz; d 13 Jul 1830 Hawke, NH

QUIMBY, Lucy b 28 Jan 1766 Hawke, NH d/o QUIMBY, David & WADLEIGH, Mary; md 1st QUIMBY, Elisaha, 2nd 09 May 1794 Kingston, NH BUSWELL, Joseph; d 1824 Hawke, NH; Will Probate 14 Oct 1824

QUIMBY, Mary b 15 Dec 1864 Danville, NH d/o QUIMBY, Elisha & PAGE, Hannah; d 05 Mar 1867 Danville, NH

QUIMBY, Mary b 17 Sep 1761 Hawke, NH d/o QUIMBY, Moses & BEAN, Judith

QUIMBY, Mary b 06 Nov 1760 Hawke, NH d/o QUIMBY, David & WADLEIGH, Mary; md 14 Feb 1790 Kingston, NH BROWN, Benjamin; spouse of Corinth, VT

QUIMBY, Mary Miss -d 19 Sep 1829 Danville, NH ae 58y

QUIMBY, Mary Mrs? -d 21 Mar 1834 Hawke, NH

QUIMBY, Miriam b Hampstead, NH; md 01 Mar 1769 Hawke, NH EASTMAN, Stephen; md by Rev John Page

QUIMBY, Miriam b Hawke, NH; md 06 Nov 1810 Kingston, NH BROWN, Elijah

QUIMBY, Moses b Hampstead, NH; md 1849 Danville, NH SWEATT, Marrianda

QUIMBY, Nelson French b 13 Nov 1818 Hawke, NH s/o QUIMBY, Nicholas & ----, Sarah; d 09 Aug 1823 Hawke, NH

QUIMBY, Nicholes b 23 May 1796 Hawke, NH s/o QUIMBY, Elisha & BADGER, Hannah

QUIMBY, Obediah Dimond b 01 JUB 1821 Hawke, NH s/o QUIMBY, Aaron & DIMOND, Eliz; d 05 Nov 1841 Danville, NH

QUIMBY, Paul b 29 Jun 1764 Hawke, NH s/o QUIMBY, David & WADLEIGH, Mary; md HUNT, Meriam; d 15 Jul 1807 Hawke, NH ae 43y

QUIMBY, Polly b 1770 Hawke, NH d/o QUIMBY, Moses & BEAN, Judith

QUIMBY, Rebecca b 02 Oct 1765 Hawke, NH d/o QUIMBY, Aaron & TOWLE, Mary; md 05 Feb 1788 Kingston, NH PAGE, Benjamin; d 13 Mar 1836 Danville, NH ae 71y

QUIMBY, Rhoda b 01 Jan 1770 Hawke, NH d/o QUIMBY, David & WADLEIGH, Mary; d 03 Aug 1772 Hawke, NH ae 2y

QUIMBY, Rhoda b 31 May 1789 Hawke, NH d/o QUIMBY, Elisha & QUIMBY, Lucy; md CURRIER, Bernard

QUIMBY, Sally b 03 Jun 1802 Hawke, NH d/o QUIMBY, John & DAVIS, Hannah

QUIMBY, Sally b Hampstead, NH; md 14 Apr 1804 Kingston, NH FELLOWS, Thomas

QUIMBY, Sally b 18 Jan 1808 Hawke, NH d/o QUIMBY, Aaron & DIMOND, Sally; d 15 Nov 1826 Hawke, NH ae 18y

QUIMBY, Samuel md YOUNG, Ann

QUIMBY, Samuel b 12 Sep 1800 Hawke, NH s/o QUIMBY, John & DAVIS, Hannah

QUIMBY, Sarah b 07 Oct 1848 Danville, NH d/o QUIMBY, Elisha & PAGE, Hannah; d 07 Mar 1851 Danville, NH

QUIMBY, Sarah b 31 May 1765 Hawke, NH d/o QUIMBY, Moses & BEAN, Juduth

QUIMBY, Sarah b 10 Aug 1769 Hawke, NH d/o QUIMBY, Samuel & YOUNG, Ann

QUIMBY, Sarah b 30 May 1803 Hawke, NH d/o QUIMBY, Elisha & BADGER, Hannah; md PHILBRICK, Josiah; d 18 Aug 1832 Hawke, NH ae 29y

QUIMBY, Sarah b of Hampstead, NH; md 16 Sep 1783 Hampstead, NH FELLOWS, Jos

QUIMBY, Sarah H. b Hampstead, NH; md 30 Dec 1841 Danville, NH CHALLIS, Jos H.

QUIMBY, Serena C. b 03 Jun 1833 Hawke, NH d/o QUIMBY, Nicholas & ----, Sarah

QUIMBY, Stephen b 20 Jul 1801 Hawke, NH s/o QUIMBY, Elisha & BADGER, Hannah

QUIMBY, Thos b 27 Oct 1771 Hawke, NH s/o QUIMBY, David & WADLEIGH, Mary

QUIMBY, Titcomb b 15 Jan 1806 Hawke, NH s/o QUIMBY, John & DAVIS, Hannah

QUIMBY, Woodbury D. b 13 Mar 1835 Hawke, NH s/o QUIMBY, Aaron Col. & BLAKE, Mary S.; d 02 Oct 1843 Danville, NH ae 8y

QUIMBY, Zipporah b 08 Mar 1763 Hawke, NH d/o QUIMBY, Aaron & TOWLE, Mary; d 21 Dec 1792 Hawke, NH ae 29y

QUIMBY, ---- b 27 Dec 1887 Danville, NH d/o QUIMBY, Chas E. & RUEE, Lizzie R.; 2nd child in family

QUIMBY, ---- b 28 May 1808 Hawke, NH d/o QUIMBY, John & DAVIS, Hannah

QUIMBY, ---- b 23 Jan 1900 Danville, NH d/o QUIMBY, Fred C. & AVERY, Sadie E.; 1st child in family

QUINTEL, Ida M. b Haverhill, MA d/o QUINTEL, Euclid & NOURY, Orella; d 11 Oct 1898 Danville, NH

QUINTO, Scott Michael md 11 May 1991 Danville, NH TAYLOR, Christina Lynn; md by Rich J. Rondeau (JP)

RADULSKI, Lindsay Marie b 01 Jan 1989 Haverhill, MA d/o RADULSKI, Keith A. & SARGENT, Laurie

RAGONESE, Eric Samuel b 16 Mar 1990 Derry, NH s/o RAGONESE, John A. J. & COONEY, Rhonda L.

RAGONESE, John A. md 22 Jun 1985 Danville, NH COONEY, Rhonda L.; md by Robert J. Kemmery (P)

RAGONESE, Mark Robert b 04 Dec 1987 Haverhill, MA s/o RAGONESE, John A. & COONEY, Rhonda L.

RAGONESE, Michael Nicholas b 12 Apr 1991 Derry, NH s/o RAGONESE, John A. & COONEY, Rhonda L.

RAINVILLE, Mary R. b c1861 Canada; md 02 Feb 1884 Danville, NH NOURY, Emedie; d 21 Dec 1943 Danville, NH

RAMBO, Muriel L. b d/o RAMBO, Alexis & BRYANT, Sarah; md SAVARESE, ---- ; d 09 Dec 1990 Danville, NH ae 82y

RAMSDELL, Reginald b 10 May 1911 Danville, NH s/o RAMSDELL, Howard & SEAVER, Maud; d 04 Dec 1911 Danville, NH

RANCK, Rita A. b 1917 Dorchester, MA d/o RANCK, Carl Otto; md 20 Aug 1938 Danville, NH DIDGWAY, Lincoln; md by Clarence M. Collins (JP)

RANCOURT, Katelyn Marjorie b 18 Dec 1987 Derry, NH d/o RANCOURT, Jules V. & STRAW, Judy L.

RAND, Alla b Hawke, NH; md 19 Feb 1789 Hawke, NH SAWYER, James Sr.; d 21 Jul 1833 Hawke, NH; bu Hawke, NH Private Cem.

RAND, Betty b Hawke, NH; md 28 Jul 1798 Kingston, NH SANBORN, Benj

RAND, Shirley Frances b 1925 d/o RAND, Forrest N.; md 22 Nov 1952 Danville, NH BURLEIGH, Don Francis

RANDALL, Daniel md 07 Nov 1794 Kingston, NH BARNARD, Sarah

RANDALL, Eliz P. b 1917 Lynn, MA d/o RANDALL, Arthur; md 07 Oct 1937 Danville, NH MERRILL, James; md by Clarence M. Collins (JP)

RANDALL, Leonard M. b c1895 Seabrook, NH s/o RANDALL, Geo W.;

RANDALL (Cont.) md 12 Sep 1921 Danville, NH GABLASKY, Velma; md by Rev L.M. Bleakney

RANDALL, Wm P. md 22 Jun 1980 Danville, NH BARHANYS, Jeannine M.; md by Rev Steven Kucharski (P)

RANOUGH, Eliz b of Kingston, NH; md 02 Apr 1765 GILMAN, John Moody; md by Rev John Page

RANOUGH, Mary md 28 Jan 1766 Hawke, NH NEWTON, Wm; md by Rev John Page

RATNER, Andrew Mark md 19 May 1991 Danville, NH SIWIK, Barb. Lorraine; md by Rich J. Rondeau (JP)

RATTE, Stephen W. Jr. b 30 Jun 1992 Derry, NH s/o RATTE, Stephen Sr. & ARSENAULT, Joanne

RAUMIKAITIS, Mark A. md 17 Apr 1982 Danville, NH NAULT, Margaret A.; md by Donald C. Burgeson (JP)

RAYMOND, Geo Curtis b 15 Sep 1952 Danville, NH s/o RAYMOND, Geo C. & BOOTH, Evelyn R.

RAYMOND, Kathleen Louise b 1915 NH d/o RAYMOND, John; md 11 Nov 1949 Danville, NH GAZETTE, Anthony Harold; md by Rev W. C. Chappell

RAYMOND, Marilyn A. md 07 Oct 1989 Danville, NH McLYNCH, Bryan F.; md by Rev Everett E. Palmer

RAYMOND, Shirley I. b Raymond, NH; md MUNROE, Donald W.

REARDON, Bryan Wm b 01 Mar 1992 Exeter, NH s/o REARDON, Michael P. & CUNNINGHAM, Lorraine M.

REARDON, Kellie Lee md 10 Nov 1991 Danville, NH VanRAVERSTYN, Michael Paul; md by Rich J. Rondeau (JP)

RECTOR, Rob Roy b Boston, MA s/o RECTOR, Jos & SMITH, Isabelle; d 28 Feb 1945 Danville, NH ae 81y 1m 22d

REDDAM, Robert P. b s/o REDDAM, Timothy M. & MAHONEY, Mary F. d 10 Apr 1987 Danville, NH ae 61y

REED, Mary A d 02 Oct 1905 Danville, NH ae 55y

REED, Matthew John md 08 Jan 1977 Danville, NH SKINNER, Mary Ellen; md by Michael J. Griffin (P)

REED, Shelia A. md 20 Jul 1985 Danville, NH GABRY, Mark A.; md by Rev Everett E. Palmer

REES, Harry A. b 1948; md 30 Jun 1968 Danville, NH KIMBALL, Corinne J.; md by Rev John Wood

REID, Alice Mabel b Stoneham, MA d/o REID, Geo & HYDE, Jane; d ae 72y 6m 18d

REMICK, Ham b Hawke, NH; md 18 Sep 1832 Kingston, NH TODD, Sarah

REMICK, Hannah J. b 15 Jan 1847 Danville, NH d/o REMICK, John & BRACKETT, Hannah

REMICK, John F. b 20 Feb 1852 Danville, NH s/o REMICK, John & BRACKETT, Hannah

REMICK, Mary b 23 Jul 1848 Danville, NH d/o REMICK, John & BRACKETT, Hannah

REMICK, Sophronia b 18 May 1850 Danville, NH d/o REMICK, John & BRACKETT, Hannah

RENMARK, Ford md 01 Dec 1986 Danville, NH KAFKA, Rosemary E.; md by Rich J. Rondeau (JP)

REYMAN, Barbara Jean b 27 Jul 1927 Danville, NH d/o REYMAN, Howard A. & ROCKHILL, Rozetta

REYNOLDS, Adelbert b c1888 s/o REYNOLDS, Byron; md 16 Aug 1915 Plaistow, NH LADD, Marcia E.; md by Rev Challis V. Smith

REYNOLDS, Albert M. b 11 Apr 1908 Danville, NH s/o REYNOLDS, Byron & MERRICK, Edith

REYNOLDS, Cary Abbott b 1914 Haverhill, MA s/o REYNOLDS, Homer H.; md 01 Sep 1935 Danville, NH CARROLL, Cary Lida; md by Clarence M. Collins (JP)

REYNOLDS, Cecille Adelbert b 30 Mar 1916 Danville, NH s/o REYNOLDS, Adelbert Wm & LADD, Marcia; md 01 Jun 1946 Danville, NH TODD, Loree; md by Rev W. C. Chappell

REYNOLDS, Kenneth Ladd b 16 Mar 1917 Danville, NH s/o REYNOLDS, Adelbert Willard & LADD,

REYNOLDS (Cont.) Marcia; md 31 Jul 1947 Danville, NH KING, Teresa Marie; md by Rev W. C. Chappell

REYNOLDS, Pamela D. md 14 Jul 1984 Danville, NH MIEROP, Daniel T.; md by Rev Wm A. Mierop

RHINERSON, Tanya Lee b 26 Apr 1987 Stoneham, MA d/o RHINERSON, Paul C. & LARSON, Kristina E.

RHODES, Mary A. b c1821; md LADD, Elijah D.; d 21 Dec 1886 Danville

RICH, James Albert b 10 Mar 1985 Nashua, NH s/o RICH, Timothy A. & HEALD, Deborah A.

RICH, Laura Ellen md 27 Dec 1969 Danville, NH LOSH, Darrell K.

RICH. Bernard Morton b 1926 Haverhill, MA s/o RICH, Samuel; md 19 Sep 1948 Danville, NH ROCHE, Catherine Mary; md by Agnes H. Collins (JP)

RICHARDSON, Cheri md 16 Jun 1990 Danville, NH CAVICCHI, David James; md by Rich J. Rondeau (JP)

RICHARDSON, Lulu May b 1877 Danville, NH d/o RICHARDSON, Newton & CASS, Sarah J.; d 22 Sep 1897 Danville, NH

RICHARDSON, Lyle H. md 24 Oct 1985 Danville, NH BROWN, Barbara J.; md by David T. Ingerson (JP)

RICHARDSON, Newton b c1844 Chester, NH s/o RICHARDSON, Elizha & ABOTT, Jane; md CASS, Sarah J.; d 14 Sep 1921 Danville, NH ae 77y 9m 8d

RICHER, Victoria L. md 28 Sep 1985 Danville, NH CHAVERS, David A.; md by Daniel J. Messier (P)

RICHER, Walter T. b Limerick, ME; md 05 Feb 1965 Danville, NH SIMONEAU, Avis I.; md by Retenah Pietrowski (JP)

RIDGWAY, Lincoln b 1907 Boston, MA s/o RIDGWAY, Herbert N.; md 20 Aug 1938 Danville, NH RANCK, Rita A.; md by Clarence M. Collins (JP)

RIED, David Neil b Murray Harbor N.P.E.I.; d 07 May 1946 Danville, NH ae 75y

RIFE, Neal Dwayne b 1928 ID s/o RIFE, Harvey Francis; md 07 Nov 1952

RIFE (Cont.) Danville, NH BICKFORD, Eileen Eliz; md by Rev W. C. Chappell

RIICHETT, Rich A. d 06 Apr 1984 Danville, NH ROACH, Twyla D.; md by Rev James C. Wideman

RILEY, Eva May b Somerville. MA d 15 Feb 1963 Danville, NH ae 67y

RILEY, Geo Allen of Haverhill, MA md 17 Oct 1992 BOUTIN, Carol Lee

Riley, Lucy E. b s/o RILEY, Geo; md MEUSE, ---- ; d 02 Sep 1985 Danville, NH ae 80y

RILEY, Michael Jos md 07 Dec 1974 Danville, NH BLANEY, Charlotte Victoria; md by Michael L. Griffin (P)

RILEY, Paul Dennis Jr. of Danville, NH md 29 Feb 1992 POST, Sherry Ann

RILEY, Wm Francis b s/o RILEY, Chas & GRADY, Catherine; d 17 Apr 1962 Danville, NH ae 71y

RINES, David Freeman b md 10 Sep 1983 Danville, NH FOLLAND, Nancy Jean; md by Nancy E. Crawford (JP)

RING, Esther b of Chester, NH; md 31 May 1781 Hawke, NH GRIFFIN, Geo; md by Rev John Page

RING, Issachar b Salisbury, MA; md 14 Jul 1768 Hawke, NH BARNARD, Esther; md by Rev John Page

RING, Jonathan b of Poplin, NH; md 22 Nov 1764 CALF, Martha; md by Rev John Page

RING, Mary md FELLOWS, Sam

RING, Sarah b Hawke, NH; md 11 Mar 1779 Hawke, NH FLANDERS, Stephen; md by Rev John Page

RING, Susanna b c1727 Salisbury, MA; md COLBY, Thos Elliot; d 15 Jan 1778 Hawke, NH ae 51y

RINVILLE, Mary b Canada; md NEURY, Edward

RIOUX, Jos David b 02 Dec 1987 Exeter, NH s/o RIOUX, Jos P. & SIMPSON, Donna A. M.

RIVELA, Cathy Ann md 05 Aug 1989 Danville, NH RUBINO, Jos Rosario; md by Leo Beaulieu (JP)

RIVERS, Anita Darlene b 11 Nov 1952 Danville, NH d/o RIVERS, Marland L. & FULLER, Minerva H.

RIVERS, Eric Lee b 05 Nov 1954 Danville, NH s/o RIVERS, Marland L. & FULLER, Minerva H.; d 21 Aug 1973 Danville, NH

RIVERS, Marland Leroy b 1920 Hampstead, NH s/o RIVERS, Arnold Leonard; md 12 Sep 1945 Danville, NH FULLER, Minerva Harriet; md by rev W. C. Chappell

ROACH, Twya D. md 06 Apr 1984 Danville, NH RICHETT, Rich A.; md by Rev James C. Wideman

ROBERTS, Betsey b Hawke, NH; md 04 Apr 1829 Hawke, NH McLANE, Samuel

ROBERTS, Eliza d/o ROBERTS, Wm & TAYLOR, Harriot d 09 Mar 1992 ae 87y

ROBERTS, Florence S. b d/o ROBERTS, Wm & TAYLOR, Harriet; md PETERSON, ----; d 24 Oct 1900 Danville, NH; d ae 78y

ROBERTS, Jennie b c1857 Hampstead, NH; md 13 Feb 1881 Danville, NH COOK, Thos M.

ROBERTS, Polly D. b 21 Jun 1828 Hawke, NH; d/o ROBERTS, Betsey

ROBERTSON, Annie L. b New Bedford, MA d/o ROBERTSON, Wm & ----, Annie; md HINES, ---- ; d 11 Jan 1928 ae 70y 7m 6d

ROBERTSON, Chas S. md 22 Oct 1972 Danville, NH CROCKETT, Sally J.; md by Clara B. Snow (JP)

ROBEY, Ichabod b 15 Apr 1762 Hawke, NH s/o ROBEY, Samuel & MERRILL, Hannah

ROBEY, James b 25 Oct 1767 Hawke, NH s/o ROBEY, Samuel & MERRILL, Hannah

ROBEY, Lucy b 06 Mar 1760 Hawke, NH s/o ROBEY, Samuel & MERRILL, Hannah

ROBEY, Samuel b 25 Mar 1765 Hawke, NH s/o ROBEY, Samuel & MERRILL, Hannah

ROBIDAU, Priscilla Jane b 1933 MA d/o CUMMINGS, Howard; md 02 Jul 1954 Danville, NH SMITH, Wm Russell; md by Rich Margelot (JP)

ROBINSON, Alice G. b Sandown, NH; d 25 Jul 1877 Danville, NH ae 3y

ROBINSON, Chas W. b Kingston,

ROBINSON (Cont.) NH; md SMITH, Louisa

ROBINSON, Daniel Paul b 02 Apr 1976 Manchester, NH s/o ROBINSON, Donald E. & VERSAKAS, Debra L.

ROBINSON, Ellen A. md 10 Oct 1987 Danville, NH SOUCY, Mark L.; md by Rev Everett E. Palmer

ROBINSON, Fannie A. b 1847 Brockton, MA; d 05 Jun 1891 Danville, NH

ROBINSON, Henry Willard d 23 Feb 1947 Danville, NH d ae 77y 3m 6d

ROBINSON, Janice M. b Haverhill, MA; md GOLDTHWAITE, Everard

ROBINSON, John b c1839; d 25 NON 1876 Danville, NH d ae 37y

ROBINSON, Lucy b Exeter, NH; md 18 Feb 1777 Hawke, NH BLAKE, Jonathan

ROBINSON, Mary b of Deerfield NH; md 20 Oct 1768 Hawke NH TUCKER, Henry md by Rev John Page

ROBINSON, Morris R. b 1927 Intervale, NJ s/o EATON, Wm Henry; md 27 Apr 1947 Danville, NH BOUCHARD, Pearl; md by Rev W. C. Chappell

ROBINSON, Sarah J. b c1860 Kingston, NH; md 03 Jul 1878 Danville, NH EASTMAN, Chas C.

ROBINSON, ---- b 05 May 1897 Danville, NH d/o ROBINSON, Chas W. & SMITH, Louisa

ROCHE, Catherine Mary b 1925 Pert Amboy, NJ d/o ROCHE, John E.; md 19 Sep 1948 Danville, NH RICH, Bernard Morton; md by Agnes H. Collins (JP)

ROCHE, John Michael b Manchester, NH s/o ROCHE, David; md 02 Apr 1946 Manchester NH WELCH, Mahalath md by Rev Raymond Burns (P)

ROCHLEAU, Jos A. b St Gregroir, Qebec, Canada s/o ROCHLEAU, Octave & GUILLETTE, Louise; d 03 Mar 1908 Danville, NH

ROCK, Carol Anne b 20 Nov 1958 Danville, NH d/o ROCK, Nelson E. & KIRWAN, Carilyn E.

ROCK, Deborah Lenore b 07 Jun 1959 Danville, NH d/o ROCK, Leonard Jos & KIRWAN, Lorraine Gertrude

ROCK, Jennifer Denise b 16 Jan 1986 Concord, NH d/o ROCK, Dennis T. & QUAIN, Marilyn A.

ROCK, Leonard Jos b 1935 NH s/o ROCK, Jos L.; md 05 Apr 1959 Danville, NH KIRWAN, Lorraine Gertrude; md by Ferne Prescott (JP)

ROCK, Rodney b 1879 Brentwood, NH s/o ROCK, Jos; md 30 Sep 1916 Cummaquid, MA MANUEL, Florence N.; md by Rev Edward P. Fuller

ROCKWELL, David Scott b 23 Dec 1967 Danville, NH s/o ROCKWELL, Davod J. & HOTCHKISS, Nancy J.

ROESSLER, Paul W. md 20 Oct 1985 Danville, NH HASKINS, Gail P.; md by Leo E. Beaulieu (JP)

ROGERS, Dannielle Marie b 14 Dec 1983 Lawrence, MA d/o ROGERS, Daniel & MATTE, Sharon

ROGERS, David R. b md 03 Oct 1982 Danville, NH WHITE, Veronica L.; md by Marjorie D. Moisan (JP)

ROGERS, Frederick F. Jr. md 13 Sep 1980 Danville, NH BRIBK, Heide L.; md by Rev Peter W. Lovejoy

ROGERS, Harry C. b 12 May 1884 Danville, NH s/o ROGERS, Geo A. & PAGE, Sarah O.

ROGERS, Jo-Ann E. md 05 Jun 1982 Danville, NH THORNTON, Peter S.; md by Rev Loren R. Murray

ROGERS, Linda S. md 27 Sep 1980 Danville, NH FORSYTHE, Chas A.; md by Robert R. Cushing Jr. (JP)

ROGERS, Margaret L. md 26 Jan 1980 Danville, NH SAWYER, Guy P.; md by Rev Steven Kucharski (P)

ROKES, Susan A. md 28 Jul 1972 Danville, NH WERNER, Roy J.; md by Clara B. Snow (JP)

ROLLINS, Alan Jos b 08 Dec 1986 Winchester, MA s/o ROLLINS, Alan J. & PENTZ, Roberta T.

ROLLINS, Geo F. b Epping, NH s/o ROLLINS, Jonathan; d 07 Nov 1897 Danville, NH

ROMANO, Anthony Paul Jr. b s/o ROMANO, Anthony Paul Sr.; md 26 Jun 1988 Danville, NH BARTLETT, Debra Marie; md by Carol A. McEachern (JP)

ROMANO, Carolanne md 27 Aug 1988 Danville, NH BOTTAI, Allan Michael; md by Rich J. Rondeau (JP)

RONDEAU, Kevin James md 18 Jan 1975 Danville, NH SYKES, Joyce Marle; md by Rev Henry K. Mook

RONDEAU, Rich Jos Jr. md 1st 02 Aug 1973 Danville, NH LACASSE, June D. by Phyllis A. Raynowska (JP), 2nd 13 Aug 1988 Danville, NH RIZKALLA, June Ellen by Rich J. Rondeau (JP)

ROONEY, Ethel F. b 16 Aug 1893 Danville, NH d/o ROONEY, Harry & O'BRIEN, Katie

ROONEY, Harry b Ireland; md O'BRIEN, Katie

ROSS, Alice E. d 24 Nov 1973 Danville, NH ae 87y

ROSS, Alonza W. b Nova Scotia s/o ROSS, John E. & McDONALD, Eliz A.; md 26 Nov 1925 Danville, NH LADD, Alice L.; d 16 Jan 1966 Danville, NH; md by Rev E.A. McKenzie

ROSS, Arthur Everett b Nova Scotia s/o ROSS, John & McDONALD, Eliz d 24 Aug 1969 Danville NH ae 82y

ROSS, Scott A. md 26 Aug 1989 Danville, NH McGUIRE, Patricia A.; md by Rich J. Rondeau (JP)

ROUSSEAU, Dorothy Suzann b 08 Oct 1969 Danville, NH d/o ROUSSEAU, Paul Sherman & O'BRIEN, Frances Jean

ROUTHIER, Jean M. b Franklin, NH; md O'SHEA, Seth S.

ROWE, Geo W. b Danville, NH; md 12 Sep 1839 Raymond, NH BAGLEY, Emmeline

ROWE, Heather Jeanne b 05 Oct 1992 Exeter, NH d/o ROWE, Wilford A. & COOK, Stephanie A.

ROWE, Hannah b 15 Aug 1761 Hawke, NH d/o ROWE, John & GOSS, Hannah; d 21 Dec 1764 Hawke, NH ae 3y

ROWE, John b 30 Nov 1766 Hawke, NH s/o ROWE, John & GOSS, Hannah

ROWE, John b c1842; d 31 Oct 1865 Danville, NH ae 23y - Civil War Rcds

ROWE, John b 11 Sep 1762 Hawke, NH s/o ROWE, John & GOSS, Hannah; d 11 Dec 1764 Hawke, NH ae 2y

ROWE, Rich Walter b 1928 NH s/o ROWE, James; md 23 Oct 1949 Danville, NH COLLINS, Grace Dorothy; md by Rev W. C. Chappell

ROWE, Sarah b c1848 Danville, NH d/o ROWE, Geo & BAGLEY, Emeline; md Apr 1864 Danville, NH SARGENT, James B.; d 03 Feb 1896 Danville, NH

ROWE, Simon b c1807 Brentwood, NH; d 04 Mar 1875 Danville, NH ae 68y

ROWELL, Eleanor R. b 1890 Sandown, NH d/o ROWELL, Geo A.; md 1st MAGISON, ----, 2nd 03 Sep 1934 Danville, NH HURD, Harry Elmore; md by Clarence M. Collins (JP)

ROWEN, Diane b 1946 Jackson, MI; md 01 Jan 1964 Danville, NH PARLEE, Ronald; md by Edward R. Lamb (JP)

ROY, Andrew Paul b 19 Jul 1967 Danville, NH s/o ROY, James C. & BOLDUE, Doris A.

ROY, Camille D. b c1894 Canada d/o ROY, Razian; md 24 Feb 1914 Danville, NH WHITMORE, Alice M.; md by Rev J. H. Cote

ROY, Hermon David b 09 Jun 1913 Danville, NH s/o ROY, Camille & WHITMORE, Alice M.

ROY, Michael James md 17 Aug 1991 Danville, NH FOURNIER, Catherine P.; md by Florent R. Bilodeau (P)

RUBINO, Jos Rosario b md 05 Aug 1989 Danville, NH RIVELA, Cathy Ann; md by Leo Beaulieu (JP)

RUBINO, Patricia E. md 25 May 1991 Danville, NH LANGLOIS, John Peter; md by Rev Elliot N. Howard

RUEE, Chas F. b 1867 Newcastle, NH s/o RUEE, John H. & BAKER, Amanda; md 29 Aug 1892 Danville, NH MARCH, Etta A.; d 09 Jun 1925 Danville, NH; md by Rev J. A. Lowell

RUEE, Eliz B. b C1868 Newcastle, NH d/o RUEE, John H. & BAKER, Amanda; md 1st 04 Jul 1885 Danville, NH Quimby, Chas E., 2nd 31 May

RUEE (Cont.) 1898 CLOUCHE, Zeb; d 22 Jun 1930 Danville, NH ae 62y 3m 26d

RUEE, Elwyn F. b 23 Jul 1893 Danville, NH s/o RUEE, Henry A. & GEORGE, Mary E.; d 16 Jan 1894 Danville, NH ae 5m 21d

RUEE, Florence Salina b c1861 Newcastle, NH d/o RUEE, John & BAKER, Mandy; md 06 Jul 1881 Danville, NH KIMBALL, Elmer E.; d 29 Feb 1940 Danville, NH ae 77y 4m 23d

RUEE, Henry A. b 1865 New Castle, NH s/o RUEE, John H. & BAKER, Amanda; md 16 Jun 1892 Danville, NH GEORGE, Mary; d 09 Oct 1904 Danville, NH; md by Rev J. A. Lowell

RUEE, John H. b 1844 Eliot, ME s/o RUEE, Thos; md BAKER, Amanda; d 07 Jul 1924 Danville, NH; ae 80y 1m 20d

RUFFEN, Kyle Jos b 27 Nov 1991 Nashua, NH s/o RUFFEN, David J. & SHAMBARGER, Cheryl L.

RUMERY, Alonzo Wakefiel b 1878 Lyman, ME s/o RUMERY, Levi & WAKEFIELD, Sarah; d 09 Jan 1950 Danville, NH ae 72y

RUMERY, Benard E. b 11 Dec 1905 Danville, NH s/o RUMNEY, Horance G. & GOWEN, Lois Eliz; md 08 May 1928 Danville, NH COLLINS, Irene Dolly; md by Rev Howard A. Reyman

RUMERY, Bernard Elmore b 22 Jan 1930 Haverhill, MA s/o RUMERY, Bernard E. & COLLINS, Irene Dolly; md HANLEY, Mary A.

RUMERY, Daniel Stephen b 05 Sep 1933 Danville, NH s/o RUMERY, Bernard E. & COLLINS, Irene Dolly; d 20 Jun 1988 Danville, NH ae 54y

RUMERY, Dwight David b 14 Nov 1964 Danville, NH s/o RUMERY, Berbard E. & HANLEY, Mary A.

RUMERY, Ethel Lettie b c1899 Lawrence, MA d/o RUMERY, Horace G. & GOWEN, Eliz Lois; md 23 Apr 1917 Danville, NH DEMAINE, Merritt; d 08 Jan 1970 Danville, NH; md by Allen C. Keith

RUMERY, Harold L. b Biddeford,

RUMERY (Cont.) ME s/o RUMERY, Horance G. & GOWEN, Lois E.; d 28 Jan 1920 ae 20y 28d
RUMNEY, Horace G. b Lyman. ME s/o RUMNEY, Levi Jefferson & WAKEFIELD, Sarah Jane; md GOWEN, Lois Eliz; d 18 Jan 1935 Danville, NH ae 61y 8m 6d
RUSBY, Martha b Lawrence, MA d/o RUSBY, John & WARHURST, Martha; md BURRILL, ---- ; d 26 May 1946 Danville, NH
RUSSELL, Barnabas B. b Solon, ME s/o RUSSELL, Robert & SMYLEY, Joanna; d 10 Mar 1900 Danville, NH
RUSSELL, Molly/Mary b Hawke, NH; md 30 Jun 1772 Hawke, NH DARLING, Abraham; md by Rev John Page
RUSSELL, Ron E. md 15 Oct 1983 Danville NH FLANNERY, Samantha A.; md by Bettie C. Oullette (JP)
RUSSMAN, Joanne Winifred md 23 Sep 1989 Danville, NH VARNEY, Robert Mark md by Rev Everett E. Palmer
RUSSO, Jos Vincent b 28 Nov 1971 Haverhill, MA s/o RUSSO, Vincent M. & CAHILL, Andrea L.
RUTLEDGE, John Chas md 24 Feb 1990 Danville, NH DISTEFANO, Amm Marie; md by Rich J. Robdeau (JP)
RYAN, Elaine J. b Haverhill, NH; md COOK, Walter E.
RYAN, Helen b c1901 Lincoln, VT d/o RYAN, Michael & BROWN, Jennie; md 18 Oct 1919 Danville, NH ARNOLD, Clinton John Sr.; d 09 Jun 1959 Danville, NH; md by Rev L.M. Bleakney; d ae 57y
RYAN, Jos Francis b s/o RYAN, Patrick J. & O'CONNELL, Mary F.; d 21 Nov 1983 Danville, NH ae 43
RYDER, Elena Verna b 1920 Greenville Jct. ME d/o RYDER, Jas Fred; md 03 Sep 1945 Danville, NH MACE, Don Carlton; md by rev W. C. Chappell
RYLANDER, Merton L. b 1908 Marlboro, MA s/o RYLANDER, Leslie A.; md 30 Jun 1932 Danville, NH COLBY, Faoline Hope; md by Rev

RYLANDER (Cont.) Harold C ROSS
SAHLIN, Lucy S. b 1906 NH; md 12 Feb 1961 Danville, NH SINSKIE, Lewis J.; md by Glenn W. Douglas
SAIDEL, Wm b s/o SAIDEL, Zachery & CHATTUCK, Elsie; d 26 Jun 1984 Danville, NH ae 36y
SALIMBENE, Chas C. b 1913 Boston, MA s/o SALIMBENE, Sabastian; md 27 Jul 1935 Danville, NH SORRENTINI, Palmira A.; md by Clarence M. Collins (JP)
SALO, Theresa I. b 1948 Bondville, VT; md 27 Nov 1966 Danville, NH BATTIS, Rich Day; md by Rev Douglas W. Abbott
SANBORN, Abigail b 30 Dec 1779 Hawke, NH d/o SANBORN, John & ELKINS, Sarah; md 02 Mar 1797 Kingston, NH GILMAN, Robert
SANBORN, Abraham b 01 Oct 1787 Hawke, NH s/o SANBORN, Jos & FIFIELD-BACHELOR, Miria
SANBORN, Alden Melton b 18 Oct 1937 Danville, NH s/o SANBORN, Melton R. & CONANT, Marcia; md 22 Jun 1991 Danville, NH LIPKA, Barbara A.; md by Rev Rich H. Freeman
SANBORN, Annie b Danville, NH; md WATTERS, Walden W.
SANBORN, Barbara b 08 Jul 1941 Danville, NH d/o SANBORN, Melton Roland & CONANT, Marcia Clark; md 13 Jul 1959 Danville, NH BYRNE, Nornan Jas; md by Rev Guy Judkins
SANBORN, Benj b Hawke, NH; md 28 Jul 1798 Kingston, NH RAND, Betty
SANBORN, Caroline W. b c1898 Sandown, NH d/o SANBORN, John N. & DUFFUS, Nellie D.; md 28 Jul 1917 Danville, NH SCHROEDER, Chas F. Jr.; md by Rev C. W. Gordon
SANBORN, Catherine May md 20 Apr 1974 Danville, NH BUTEAU, Dennis M.; md by Rev Cathleen R. Narowitz
SANBORN, Cathleen Mae b 23 Sep 1953 Danville, NH d/o SANBORN, Robert Elkins & DEMAINE, Marion Claris; md 29 May 1973 Danville, NH FRANCIS, Michael J.; md by Leona A.

SANBORN (Cont.) Sciaudone (JP)
SANBORN, Clifton b 24 Aug 1885
Danville, NH s/o SANBORN, Daniel T.
& ELKINS, Abby C.

SANBORN, Dan T. b Chester, NH
s/o SANBORN, Merrill; d 10 Jan 1915
Danville, NH ae 64y 11m 29D

SANBORN, Dana E. b 10 Jun 1860
Danville, NH s/o SANBORN, Jos C &
DIMOND, Lenora E.; d 26 Oct 1880
Danville, NH ae 20y

SANBORN, David b 27 Jul 1783
Hawke, NH s/o SANBORN, Elijah &
TILTON, Eliz

SANBORN, Dorothy b Kingston,
NH; md 20 Feb 1811 Kingston, NH
PAGE, John

SANBORN, Dorothy b 09 Jan 1805
Hawke, NH d/o SANBORN, Obediah &
BACHELER, Miriam; md GORDON,
Dudley; d 01 Jan 1894 Danville, NH

SANBORN, Dorothy b 29 May 1949
Danville, NH d/o SANBORN, Melton
Roland & CONANT, Marcia Clark; md
19 Jul 1975 Danville, NH EMILLO,
Philip Lindsay Jr.; md by Rev Wendell
J. Irvine

SANBORN, Dorothy (Miss) b 16
Feb 1780 Hawke, NH d/o SANBORN,
Jos & FIFIELD-BACHELOR, Miria; d
1866 Danville, NH age 85 yr

SANBORN, Ebenezer b 12 Jan
1780 Hawke, NH s/o SANBORN,
Elijah & TILTON, Eliz; md Apr 1799
Hawke, NH BEAN, Lydia

SANBORN, Elijah b Poplin, NH;
md 07 Sep 1779 Hawke, NH TILTON,
Eliz

SANBORN, Eliz b 26 May 1769
Hawke, NH d/o SANBORN, Jos Cliford
& FRENCH, Eliz

SANBORN, Eliz b 07 Feb 1761
Hawke, NH d/o SANBORN, John &
ELKINS, Sarah; md 23 Oct 1780
Hawke, NH TOWLE, Wm

SANBORN, Eliz d 04 Mar 1957
Danville, NH ae 70y

SANBORN, Emma d 28 Nov 1863
Danville, NH ae 13y - Diptheria

SANBORN, Enoch b 23 Jan 1766
Hawke, NH s/o SANBORN, John &
ELKINS, Sarah; d 09 Apr 1792 Hawke,
NH ae 26y

SANBORN, Eugene S. b 26 Jan
1853 Danville, NH s/o SANBORN,
John Stark & PHILBRICK, Joanna B.;
d Jun 1855 Danville, NH

SANBORN, Eva C. b 26 Sep 1877
Danville, NH d/o SANBORN, Daniel T.
& ELKINS, Abby C.; md SARGENT,
---- ; d 11 Jul 1963 Danville, NH

SANBORN, Fairenne b Poplin, NH;
md 30 Jan 1823 Kingston, NH
SAWYER, James Jr.

SANBORN, Frances/Fanny b 05
Apr 1795 Hawke, NH d/o SANBORN,
Obadiah & BACHELOR, Miriam; d
1867 Danville, NH ae 72y

SANBORN, Frank L. b 21 Jun
1862 Danville, NH s /o SANBORN, Jos
C. & CARTER, Lenora E.

SANBORN, Geo A. b 15 Nov 1850
Danville, NH s/o SANBORN, Moses &
DEARBORN, Lucy A.

SANBORN, Grace S. b 1884
Newton, NH; d/o SANBORN, Frank L.
& BLAKE, Carrie; md 1st TRASK, ---- ,
2nd 31 Oct 1937 Danville, NH HALL,
Wilbur J.; d 05 Dec 1946 Danville, NH;
md by Rev W. C. Chappell

SANBORN, Harold Bailey b s/o
SANBORN, J. Fred & CLOUTIER,
Mary Emma; d 09 Dec 1974 Danville,
NH ae 79y

SANBORN, Helen d 31 Dec 1954
Danville, NH ae 91y

SANBORN, Herman E. b 11 May
1879 Danville, NH s/o SANBORN,
Daniel T. & ELKINS, Abby C.; md 21
Jun 1913 Danville, NH MacNEFF,
Eliz; d 22 Oct 1958 Danville, NH; md
by Allen C. Keith

SANBORN, Issacher b 11 Nov 1805
s/o SANBORN, Reuben & JUDKINS,
Mary; d 22 Aug 1808 Hawke, NH ae 6y

SANBORN, J. Fred b Danville, NH
s/o SANBORN, John Stark & PHIL-
BRICK, Joanna B.; md 17 Jul 1887
Exeter, NH CLOUTIE, Emma; d 26
Nov 1904 Danville, NH ae 46y 6m 26d;
md by Rev W. Canning

SANBORN, James E. b 30 Apr
1858 Danville, NH s/o SANBORN,
John Stark & PHILBRICK, Joanna B.

SANBORN, Jane b 14 Feb 1804
Hawke, NH d/o SANBORN, Phineas &

SANBORN (Cont.) FELLOWS, Patience; md 20 Nov 1827 Hawke, NH COLLINS, Chas

SANBORN, Jean b 13 Feb 1936 Danville, NH d/o SANBORN, Melton R. & CONANT, Marcia; md 31 Mar 1956 Danville, NH KERR, Robert John; md by Rev Arthur Webster

SANBORN, Jethro md 27 Sep 1763 Kingston, NH ELKINS, Abigail; d 24 Jan 1811

SANBORN, Joanna b 07 Nov 1770 Hawke, NH d/o SANBORN, Jos Cliford & FRENCH, Eliz

SANBORN, John b c1736; md 17 Jan 1760 Kingston, NH ELKINS, Sarah; d 12 Nov 1800 Hawke, NH ae 64y

SANBORN, John b Kingston, NH; md 16 Jan 1771 Hawke, NH HOOK, Eliz; 2nd Marr for John Sanborn

SANBORN, John E. b 06 Jan 1853 Danville, NH s/o SANBORN, Moses & DEARBORN, Lucy A.

SANBORN, John N. b 1849 Sandown, NH s/o SANBORN, Geo & WELLS, Caroline; md 26 Nov 1890 Danville, NH DUFFUS, Nellie D.; d 12 Mar 1934 Danville, NH; md by Rev J. A. Lowell

SANBORN, John Stark b 05 Oct 1821 Hawke, NH s/o SANBORN, Levi & HOOK, Mary; md 12 Feb 1843 Danville, NH PHILBRICK, Joanna; d 19 Apr 1873 Danville, NH ae 51y

SANBORN, Jon b c1714 Kensington, NH; md BACHELOR, Mary; d 20 May 1790 Hawke, NH ae 76y

SANBORN, Jonathan b 12 Apr 1764 Hawke, NH s/o SANBORN, Jos Cliford & FRENCH, Eliz

SANBORN, Jonathan b 04 Mar 1760 Hawke, NH s/o SANBORN, Jonathan & BACHELOR, Mary

SANBORN, Jonathan b 05 Jan 1799 Hawke, NH s/o SANBORN, Jonathan Lt & BACHELOR, Anne; d 03 Dec 1880 Danville, NH ae 81y

SANBORN, Jonathan Lt. md 05 Dec 1784 Hawke, NH Bachelor, Anne; d 30 Mar 1813 Hawke, NH; bu Hawke, NH Old Mtg Hse Cem.; d ae 53y Revolution

SANBORN, Jos b 26 Oct 1774 Hawke, NH s/o SANBORN, Jos Cliford & FRENCH, Eliz

SANBORN, Jos Clifford md 1st 24 Dec 1761 Hawke, NH FRENCH, Eliz, 2nd 26 Feb 1777 Hawke, NH FIFIELD, Miriam; d 13 Apr 1810 Hawke, NH; bu Hawke, NH Old Mtg Hse Cem.; 2nd Marr of both; md by Rev John Page

SANBORN, Josiah b 11 Jul 1769 Hawke, NH s/o SANBORN, John & ELKINS, Sarah

SANBORN, Judith b 06 Jun 1776 Hawke, NH d/o SANBORN, Jos Clifford & FRENCH, Eliz

SANBORN, Judith b Kingston, NH; md 21 Dec 1769 Hawke, NH FRENCH, Henry; md by Rev John Page

SANBORN, Lavina b 23 Sep 1812 Hawke, NH d/o SANBORN, Levi & HOOK, Mary; md 10 Sep 1837 Raymond, NH HOOK, James

SANBORN, Leslie A. b 1887 Newton, NH s/o SANBORN, Frank L. & BLAKE, Carrie; d 15 Aug 1936 Danville, NH

SANBORN, Levi b 12 Jun 1809 s/o SANBORN, Reuben & JUDKINS, Mary

SANBORN, Levi b 03 Mar 1789 Hawke, NH s/o SANBORN, Obediah & BACHELOR, Miriam; md HOOK, Mary; d 01 Feb 1825 Hawke, NH; Spouse md 2nd Caleb Kinball

SANBORN, Levi F. b 01 Jun 1843 Hawke, NH s/o SANBORN, John Stark & PHILBRICK, Joanna B.; md 1867 NORRIS, Mary E.

SANBORN, Levi Hook b 15 Apr 1824 Hawke, NH s/o SANBORN, Levi & HOOK, Mary; d 25 Mar 1873 Danville, NH ae 49y

SANBORN, Lillian L. b 19 Oct 1882 Danville, NH d/o SANBORN, Daniel T. & ELKINS, Abby C.; d 23 May 1886 Danville, NH ae 4y

SANBORN, Love b 08 Jan 1802 Hawke, NH d/o SANBORN, Phineas & FELLOWS, Patience

SANBORN, Lowell b 30 Jun 1751 Hampton Falls, NH s/o SANBORN, Abner Dea. & LOWELL, Lucy; md 22

SANBORN (Cont.) Jul 1771 Hawke, NH JUDKINS, Rebecca; d 14 Sep 1823 Guilford, NH; bu Guilford, NH McCoy Cem.

SANBORN, Mary md 07 Dec 1769 Hawke, NH PHILBRICK, Jedediah

SANBORN, Mary b 21 Apr 1765 Hawke, NH d/o SANBORN, Jos Clifford & FRENCH, Eliz

SANBORN, Mary b 05 Jun 1817 Hawke, NH d/o SANBORN, Reuben & JUDKINS, Mary; md BROWN, Nathan; d 27 Feb 1877 Danville, NH; ae 60y

SANBORN, Mary b c1720 Hampton Falls, NH d/o SANBORN, John & FIFIELD, Mehitable; md 02 Jun 1736 Hampton Falls, NH BLAKE, Jonathan; d 05 May 1808 Hawke, NH ae 89y

SANBORN, Mary b 18 Mar 1782 Hawke, NH d/o SANBORN, John & ELKINS, Sarah

SANBORN, Mary b c1754 Hawke, NH; md 09 Jun 1800 Hawke, NH CURRIER, Ezra (Capt); d 1820 Hawke, NH; also widow of Jed. PHILBRICK

SANBORN, Mary A. b Sandown, NH; md 23 Sep 1846 Danville, NH SLEEPER, David T.

SANBORN, Mary Emma b c1870 3 Rivers, Canada; md 29 Dec 1906 Haverhill, MA McGUNNIGLE, Chas R.; d 07 Jul 1951 Danville, NH ae 80y; md by Rev Arthur G. Lyon

SANBORN, Mary J. b 31 Mar 1858 Danville, NH d/o SANBORN, Oliver & SARGENT, Dorothy J.

SANBORN, Mary S. b 10 Nov 1846 Danville, NH d/o SANBORN, John Stark & PHILBRICK, Joanna B.

SANBORN, Melton Roland b 1909 Danville, NH; md 09 Sep 1934 Danville, NH CONANT, Marcia Clark; md by Rev Homer F. Carr

SANBORN, Miriam b 31 May 1794 Hawke, NH d/o SANBORN, Jonathan Lt. & BACHELOR, Anne

SANBORN, Moses b 17 Dec 1807 s/o SANBIRN, Reuben & JUDKINS, Mary

SANBORN, Moses b c1803 Danville, NH md 1st 19 Aug 1849 Danville, NH DEARBORN, Lucy Ann, 2nd 1857

SANBORN (Cont.) Danville, NH CARR, Ann; d 14 Oct 1865 Danville, NH

SANBORN, Muriel b 31 Dec 1939 Danville, NH d/o SANBORN, Melton R. & CONANT, Marcia; d 18 Jun 1956 Danville, NH

SANBORN, Nabby b 25 Dec 1762 Hawke, NH d/o SANBORN, Jos Cliford & FRENCH, Eliz; md 18 Jul 1781 Hawke, NH TRUE, Benj; md by Rev John Page

SANBORN, Nancy b 28 Apr 1789 Hawke, NH d/o SANBORN, Jonathan Lt. & BACHELOR, Anne; d 06 Nov 1825 Hawke, NH

SANBORN, Nathan 1 b 06 Feb 1771 Hawke, NH s/o SANBORN, John & ELKINS, Sarah; d 18 Mar 1776 Hawke, NH ae 5y

SANBORN, Nathan 2 b 15 Jan 1777 Hawke, NH s/o SANBORN, John & ELKINS, Sarah

SANBORN, Obediah b 25 Jan 1768 Hawke, NH s/o SANBORN, John & ELKINS, Sarah; md 24 Dec 1788 Hawke, NH BACHELOR, Miriam; d 29 Jun 1850 Danville, NH ae 82y

SANBORN, Oliver S. b 16 Nov 1803 Hawke, NH s/o SANBORN, Jonathan Lt. & BACHELOR, Anne; md 1848 Danville, NH SARGENT, Dorothy Jane; d 31 Jan 1881 Danville, NH ae 77y

SANBORN, Patricia Ann b 21 Sep 1951 Danville, NH d/o SANBORN, Robert Elkins & DEMAINE, Marion Claris; md 30 Oct 1971 Danville, NH TURNER, Dale Edwin; md by Rev Alton P. Mark

SANBORN, Peter b 17 Nov 1797 Hawke, NH s/o SANBORN, Phineas & FELLOWS, Patience

SANBORN, Peter b 17 Dec 1772 Hawke, NH s/o SANBORN, John & ELKINS, Sarah; d 18 Mar 1776 Hawke, NH ae 4y

SANBORN, Phebe b c1765; md 23 Dec 1788 Kingston, NH PAGE, Simon; d 24 Dec 1804 Hawke, NH; bu Hawke, NH Old Mtg Hse Cem.; Phebe - 1st of Sinons 3 wives

SANBORN, Phineas b 17 Sep 1774

SANBORN (Cont.) Hawke, NH s/o SANBORN, John & ELKINS, Sarah; md 24 Nov 1796 Kingston, NH FELLOWS, Patience

SANBORN, Phineas b c1753; md 02 Mar 1767 Hawke, NH ADAMS, Mary; d Jul 1773 Hawke, NH ae 20y

SANBORN, Rachel b 30 Aug 1799 Hawke, NH d/o SANBORN, Phineas & FELLOWS, Patience; md 24 Feb 1820 Hawke, NH COLLINS, Henry

SANBORN, Reuben b 15 Sep 1785 Hawke, NH s/o SANBORN, Jonathan Lt. & BACHELOR, Anne; md LANE, Hannah; d 17 Nov 1844 Danville, NH

SANBORN, Reuben b 09 Feb 1778 Hawke, NH s/o SANBORN, Jos & FIFIELD-BACHELOR, Miriam; md 21 Jul 1802 Kingston, NH JUDKINS, Mary; d 20 Dec 1855 Danville, NH

SANBORN, Robert Elkins b 20 Oct 1918 Danville, NH s/o SANBORN, Herman Elkins & McNEFF, Eliz; md 24 Jan 1942 Danville, NH DEMAINE, Marion Clarissa; d 03 Feb 1984 Danville, NH; md by Rev W. C. Chappell

SANBORN, Roseana b 09 Jun 1819 Hawke, NH d/o SANBORN, Levi & HOOK, Mary

SANBORN, Ruth b 16 Apr 1763 Hawke, NH d/o SANBORN, John & ELKINS, Sarah

SANBORN, Salina E. b 06 Mar 1854 Danville, NH d/o SANBORN, Oliver & SARGENT, Dorothy J.; d 16 Mar 1937 Danville, NH ae 83y 10d

SANBORN, Samuel Adams b 22 Nov 1769 Hawke, NH d/o SANBORN, Phineas & ADAMS, Mary

SANBORN, Sarah b 06 Jul 1790 Hawke, NH d/o SANBORN, Jonathan Lt. & BACHELOR, Anne; d 11 Nov 1862 Danville, NH ae 72y

SANBORN, Sarah b 01 Nov 1772 Hawke, NH d/o SANBORN, Jos Clifford & FRENCH, Eliz

SANBORN, Sarah b 30 Jun 1764 Hawke, NH d/o SANBORN, John & ELKINS, Sarah

SANBORN, Sherburne J. b 29 Sep 1898 Danville, NH s/o SANBORN, John N. & CURRIER, Nellie D.; md 03 Jul 1930 Danville, NH GARDELLA,

SANBORN (Cont.) Vera G.; md by Rev O.L. Brownsey

SANBORN, Susan b c1846 Danville, NH; md 29 Nov 1866 Danville, NH FELLOWS, Russell N.

SANBORN, Susan Sawyer md 15 Jul 1989 Danville, NH VAILLAN-COURT, Romeo John; md by Rev Everett E. Palmer

SANBORN, Sylvia b 17 Oct 1945 Danville, NH d/o SANBORN, Melton Roland & CONANT, Marcia Clark

SANBORN, Vivian Lee b 13 Oct 1942 Haverhill, MA d/o SANBORN, Robert Elkins & DEMAINE, Marion C.; md 18 Feb 1961 Danville, NH WICKER, Roger Benj; md by Rev John Wood Jr.

SANBORN, Wm Bradford b Cambridge, MA s/o SANBORN, Chas A. & ROYAL, Lucy M.; d 12 May 1942 Danville, NH ae 67y 3m 1d

SANBORN, ---- b 27 Jan 1890 Danville, NH s/o SANBORN, J. Fred & CLOUTIE, Emma; 2nd Child in Family

SANBORN, ---- b 30 Jan 1923 Danville, NH ?/o SANBORN, Herman; & McNeff, Eliz; d 30 Jan 1923 Danville, NH

SANDILANDS, John J. b s/o SANDILANDS, Hugh & McKENNA, Mary; d 19 May 1979 Danville, NH ae 83y

SANFORD, Alden W. md 14 Oct 1989 Danville, NH FEINBERG, Patricia A.; md by Rev Wendall J. Irvine

SANSERVERO, Susan P. b 1946 Italy; md 17 Dec 1966 Danville, NH GALANTE, Graziano; md by Leona A. Sciaudone (JP)

SANTOS, Nancy B. md 11 Aug 1979 Danville, NH WEST, Chester Stuart; md by Rev Peter W. Lovejoy

SARGENT, Adele B. b 10 Mar 1877 Danville, NH; d/o SARGENT, James B. & ROWE, Sarah E.

SARGENT, Alfred Bailey b 30 Aug 1870 Danville, NH s/o SARGENT, Bailey & HOOK, Helen M.; d 17 Sep 1944 Danville, NH

SARGENT, Alicia Marie b 16 May 1971 Haverhill, MA d/o SARGENT, Wilfred P. & MANSFIELD, Diane M.

SARGENT, Amanda T. b 14 May 1849 Danville, NH d/o SARGENT, David A. & FULLER, Eliz B.; d 24 May 1853

SARGENT, Augusta T. b 1868 Danville, NH d/o SARGENT, John Harriman & BEATTIE, Mary; md 03 Apr 1890 Danville, NH GEORGE, Lewis H.; d 01 Sep 1952 Danville, NH ae 83y; md by Rev J. A. Lowell

SARGENT, Bailey b 14 Mar 1838 Danville, NH s/o SARGENT, Samuel Jr. & PAGE, Lois; md 01 Aug 1863 Danville, NH HOOK, Helen M.; d 08 Jan 1901 ae 62y 9m 24d

SARGENT, Bessie J. b 1850 Danville, NH d/o SARGENT, Peter & BARTLETT, Lydia S.; md 1967 Danville, NH BROWN, Chas W.; d 28 Feb 1874 Danville, NH; d age 24 - Spouse of Fremont

SARGENT, Challis b 08 Jul 1800 Hawke, NH s/o SARGENT, Samuel & WOODMAN, Polly

SARGENT, Chas A. b 26 May 1846 Danville, NH s/o SARGENT, David A. & FULLER, Eliz B.; d 26 Nov 1864 Salisbury, MA ae 18y - Civil War Rcds

SARGENT, Chas H. b 22 Nov 1867 Danville, NH s/o SARGENT, Bailey & HOOK, Helen M.; md 27 Jun 1906 Exeter, NH POLLARD. Ella M.; d 10 Feb 1936 Danville, NH; md by Rev W. L. Anderson

SARGENT, Chas S. b Sandown, NH; md WELCH, Jennie S.

SARGENT, David A. b 23 Feb 1812 Hawke, NH s/o SARGENT, Samuel & GRIFFIN, Sally; d 13 Sep 1890 Danville, NH

SARGENT, David M. b Sep 1812 Hawke, NH s/o SARGENT, Peter & BARTLETT, Lydia S.; d 08 Aug 1850 Danville, NH

SARGENT, Dorothy Jane b 20 Oct 1820 Hawke, NH d/o SARGENT, Samuel & GRIFFIN, Sally; md 1848 Danville, NH SANBORN, Oliver S.; d 04 Jul 1885 Danville, NH ae 65y

SARGENT, Edith E. b 1875 Danville, NH d/o SARGENT, John Harriman & BEATTIE, Mary; md 20 Sep 1890 Danville, NH HODGKINS, F. A.

SARGENT (Cont.) E.; md by Rev J. A. Lowell

SARGENT, Eliz b 27 Oct 1796 Hawke, NH d/o SARGENT, Samuel & WOODMAN, Polly md d 25 Feb 1827 Hawke, NH

SARGENT, Ella P. d 23 Nov 1931 Danville, NH ae 57y 2m 2d

SARGENT, Ernest V. b 11 Mar 1896 Danville, NH s/o SARGENT, Walter E. & AVERY, Carrie J.

SARGENT, Fronie J. b May 1864 Danville, NH d/o SARGENT, David A. & FULLER, Eliz B.; d 09 Aug 1878 Danville, NH ae 14y

SARGENT, Grace L. d 18 May 1932 Danville, NH ae 47y 10m 6d

SARGENT, Hannah b 29 Dec 1803 Hawke, NH d/o SARGENT, Samuel & WOODMAN, Polly; d 26 Feb 1857 Danville, NH; not married

SARGENT, Hattie A. b Sep 1854 Danville, NH d/o SARGENT, David A. & FULLER, Eliz B.; d 03 Aug 1873 Danville, NH ae 18y 1m

SARGENT, Helen b 1914 Binghamton, NY d/o SARGENT, Herbert L. & OSBORN, Mary E.; md 07 Aug 1934 Danville, NH COLLINS, Robert Hazen; d 04 Jun 1949 Danville, NH; md by Rev John D. Kettelle; prev md to WAYNE, ----

SARGENT, Herbert L. b 06 May 1880 Danville, NH s/o SARGENT, Bailey & HOOK, Helen M.; md OSBORN, Mary E.; d 24 Jan 1967 Danville, NH

SARGENT, Howard b Sep 1843 Hawke, NH s/o SARGENT, Thomas & COLLINS, Mary; d 16 Aug 1871 Danville, NH ae 27y 11m

SARGENT, Howard F. b 01 Jul 1879 Danville, NH s/o SARGENT, John Harrima & BEATTIE, Mary; d 31 Oct 1966 Danville, NH

SARGENT, Infant Dau b Feb 1837 d/o SARGENT, Samuel Jr. & PAGE, Lois; d 02 Mar 1837 Danville, NH ae 3 weeks

SARGENT, Infant Son b May 1843 Danville, NH s/o SARGENT, Wm & BARTLETT, Palowna; d 10 May 1843 Danville, NH infant

SARGENT, James B. b 19 Oct 1846 Danville, NH s/o SARGENT, Peter & BARTLETT, Lydia S.; md Apr 1864 Danville, NH ROWE, Sarah E.; d 27 Feb 1923 Danville, NH

SARGENT, John H. b c1839 Danville, NH; md 28 Jun 1864 Danville, NH BEATTIE, Mary

SARGENT, John Wesley b 03 Apr 1841 Danville, NH s/o SARGENT, Samuel Jr. & PAGE, Lois

SARGENT, Jonathan b 26 Jul 1798 Hawke, NH s/o SARGENT, Samuel & WOODMAN, Polly; d 16 Jan 1861 Danville, NH ae 62y

SARGENT, Junietta b 1870 Danville, NH d/o SARGENT, John Harriman & BEATTIE, Mary

SARGENT, Lillie M. b Dec 1876 Danville, NH d/o SARGENT, John Harriman & BEATTIE, Mary; md 31 May 1898 Danville, NH STEVENSON, Frank A.; d 12 Jul 1914 Danville, NH

SARGENT, Lisa Ann md 29 Dec 1990 Danville, NH WALUKEVICH, Jos Michael; md by Rich J. Rondeau (JP)

SARGENT, Louisa M. b 1835 Hawke, NH d/o SARGENT, Samuel Jr. & PAGE, Lois; md 1852 Danville, NH CRITCHET, Geo E.

SARGENT, Marcia E. b 15 Aug 1879 Danville, NH d/o SARGENT, James B. & ROWE, Sarah E.

SARGENT, Mary b 11 May 1810 Hawke, NH d/o SARGENT, Sam & GRIFFIN, Sally; md CASS, David Jr. d 28 Apr 1902 Danville, NH ae 91y 11m 25d

SARGENT, Mary md 12 Sep 1765 Hawke, NH TOWLE, Jeremy

SARGENT, Mary B. b c1885 d/o SARGENT, James B. & ROWE, Sarah; md 31 Aug 1921 Kingston, NH MONROE, John; d 20 Apr 1955 Danville, NH; md by Rev Edville A. Roys

SARGENT, Melissa T. b Nov 1856 Danville, NH d/o SARGENT, David A. & FULLER, Eliz B.; d 06 Oct 1873 Danville, NH ae 16y 11m

SARGENT, Moses b 1834 Hawke, NH s/o SARGENT, Pete & BARTLETT, Lydia S. d 20 Mar 1836 Hawke, NH

SARGENT, Moses H. b c1842 Danville, NH; md 24 Jul 1870 Danville, NH HOYT, Luella

SARGENT, Omer B. b 1867 Danville, NH s/o SARGENT, John Harriman & BEATTIE, Mary; md 23 Jan 1906 Danville, NH SHANNON, Georgianna; md by Rev A. B. Hyde

SARGENT, Perley b 19 Oct 1899 Danville, NH s/o SARGENT, Chas S. & WELCH, Jennie S.; 1st child in family

SARGENT, Peter b c1807 Hawke, NH; md BARTLETT, Lydia S.; d 09 Mar 1867 Danville, NH ae 60y

SARGENT, Ralph WAllice b 15 Apr 1901 Danville, NH s/o SARGENT, Walter E. & AVERY, Carrie J.; 3rd child in family

SARGENT, Rebecca Joy md 14 Apr 1990 Danville, NH DENTON, Dean Michael; md by Rev. Everett E. Palmer

SARGENT, Roland R. b c1871 Danville, NH s/o SARGENT, James B. & ROWE, Sarah E.; d 14 Dec 1888 Kingston, NH ae 17y 7m drowning

SARGENT, Sally b 28 Apr 1814 Hawke, NH d/o SARGENT, Samuel & GRIFFIN, Sally

SARGENT, Samuel Sr. b 02 Mar 1774 Hawke, NH s/o SARGENT, Challis & BUSWELL, Jane; md 1st 12 Nov 1795 Hawke, NH WOODMAN, Polly, 2nd 20 Sep 1805 Hawke, NH; d 03 Jan 1849 Danville, NH

SARGENT, Samuel Jr. b 27 Feb 1808 Hawke, NH s/o SARGENT, Samuel & GRIFFIN, Sally; md 17 Jun 1833 Hawke, NH PAGE, Lois; d 02 May 1890 Danville, NH

SARGENT, Sarah b Hawke, NH; md 02 Feb 1842 Raymond, NH HEATH, Wm T.

SARGENT, Sarah J. b 1859 Syracuse, NY d/o SARGENT, Thomas D. & TENNEY, Eliz; md 15 Aug 1936 Danville, NH JOY, Pearl A.; d 05 Dec 1939 Danville, NH; md by Rev W. C. Chappell; prev md to SCHWARTZ, ----

SARGENT, Sarah T. b 1847 Danville, NH d/o SARGENT, David A. & FULLER, Eliz B.; md STEVENSON, Moses; d 25 Mar 1879 Danville, NH ae 32y

SARGENT, Sophonia md 29 Dec 1863 Danville, NH TOWLE, Wm L.

SARGENT, Susan N. b 9th Oct 1901 d/o SARGENT, Chas S. & WELCH, Jennie S.; 2nd child in family

SARGENT, Thomas b 28 Dec 1816 Hawke, NH s/o SARGENT, Samuel & GRIFFIN, Sally; md COLLINS, Mary; d 05 Jan 1882 Danville, NH

SARGENT, Tryphena b 11 Apr 1844 Danville, NH d/o SARGENT, Peter & BARTLETT, Lydia S.; md 1st 29 Dec 1863 Danville, NH TOWLE, VanBuren L., 2nd 21 Sep 1867 Danville, NH SPOFFORD, Chas A.

SARGENT, Walter E. b 1862 Concord, NH s/o SARGENT, James B. & ROWE, Sarah E.; md 06 Aug 1892 Kingston, NH AVERY, Carrie J.; d 07 Jun 1963 Danville, NH; md by Rev J. H. Knott

SARGENT, Walter F. b 26 Jul 1873 Danville, NH s/o SARGENT, Bailey & HOOK, Helen M.; md 16 Aug 1905 Danville, NH SANBORN, Eva C.; d 15 Mar 1939 Danville, NH; md by Rev Jessie G. Nichols

SARGENT, Walter Harriman b 1865 Canada s/o SARGENT, John Harriman & BEATTIE, Mary; md 08 Oct 1891 Danville, NH KIMBALL, Fannie M.; d 28 Jan 1904 Danville, NH; Occupation Shoemaker

SARGENT, Wilfred P. md MANS-FIELD, Diane M.

SARGENT, Wm b 1812 Hawke, NH s/o SARGENT, Samuel & GRIF-FIN, Sally; md BARTLETT, Palowna; d 27 Mar 1858 Danville, NH

SARGENT, Wm Roy b 1930 NH; s/o SARGENT, Lawrence D.; md 27 Apr 1951 Danville, NH KEDDY, Louise Gertrude; md bt Rev W. C. Chappell

SARGENT, Woodbury Q. b 11 Jan 1846 Danville, NH s/o SARGENT, Samuel Jr. & PAGE, Lois

SAUNDERS, Robert J. Jr. md 15 Sep 1984 Danville, NH BENNETT, Irene M.; md by Rev James C. Pirie

SAWYER, Alla b 25 Nov 1790 Hawke, NH d/o SAWYER, James Sr. & RAND, Alla

SAWYER, Betsey md 14 Feb 1822 Hampton, NH HOOK, Phineas

SAWYER, Betty b 12 Dec 1800 Hawke, NH s/o SAWYER, James

SAWYER, Charlotte b 15 Aug 1782 Hawke, NH d/o SAWYER, Joathum & ----, Mary

SAWYER, Eliz md 16 Aug 1840 Danville, NH TUCKER, FIFIELD

SAWYER, Gideon b c1729; md BARTLETT, Sarah; d 26 Dec 1806 Hawke, NH bu Hawke, NH Old Mtg Hse Cem.; d ae 87y

SAWYER, Guy P. md 26 Jan 1980 Danville, NH ROGERS, Margaret L.; md by Rev Steven Kucharski (P)

SAWYER, Hannah b c1760 d/o SAWYER, Gideon & BARTLETT, Sarah; md NOT MARRIED; d 04 May 1820 Hawke, NH ae 60y

SAWYER, James A. b s/o Sawyer, James Jr. & SANBORN, Fairenne; d 21 Sep 1845 Danville, NH ae 16y

SAWYER, James Jr. b 04 Oct 1796 Hawke, NH s/o SAWYER, James Sr. & RAND, Alla; md 30 Jan 1823 Kingston, NH SANBORN, Fairenne; d 17 Jan 1873 Danville, NH ae 76y

SAWYER, James Sr. b Hawke, NH; md 19 Feb 1789 Hawke, NH RAND, Alla; d 08 Nov 1828 Hawke, NH; bu Hawke, NH Private Cem.; d ae 74y

SAWYER, Melinda b Plaistow, NH d/o SAWYER, Nathaniel & PIERCE, Lydia; md EASTMAN, Calvin; d 18 Nov 1899 ae 91y 10m 7d

SAWYER, Monica Jean of Haverhill, MA; md 17 Oct 1992 RILEY, Geo Allen

SAWYER, Nathaniel b Plaistow, NH; md PIERCE, Lydia

SAWYER, Reuben d 18 Dec 1789 Hawke, NH

SAWYER, Rose Ann b 184? Danville, NH d/o SAWYER, James Jr. & SANBORN, Fairenne; md 1st B ROWN, Lowell Morris, 2nd 03 Dec 1873 Danville, NH MERRICK, Jos G.; d 03 Nov 1883 Danville, NH;

SAWYER, Sarah b 25 Aug 1794 Hawke, NH d/o SAWYER, James Sr. & RAND, Alla; md 29 Oct 1818 Kingston,

SAWYER (Cont.) NH HOOK, Moody M.; d 1873 Danville, NH

SAWYER, Walker Colby b 31 May 1782 Hawke, NH s/o SAWYER, Joathum & ----, Mary

SCALZO, Jeffery John md 13 Jun 1987 Danville, NH VALCOURT, Leslie S.; md by Rev Anthony Jarek Glidden

SCALZO, Jeffery John md 07 Apr 1990 Danville, NH STRATTON, Cynthia Dale; md by Rev Edward Charest

SCARAFINE, Kelly Ann md 29 Nov 1990 Danville NH MACE, Stephen Justin; md by Rich J. Rondeau (JP)

SCHAFFER, Jeffery W. md 31 May 1987 Danville, NH HANNAGEN, Kathleen A.; md by Rev Wm L. Shafer

SCHOFIELD, Wm R. b s/o SCHOFIELD, Roland & SMITH, Ida; d 27 Mar 1992 ae 65y

SCHROEDER, Chas F. Jr. b c1889 Chelsea, MA s/o SCHROEDER, Chas F. Sr. & md 27 May 1917 Hampstead, NH SANBORN, Caroline W.; md by Rev C. W. Gordon

SCHULTZE, Ehren Fred b 31 May 1980 Manchester, NH s/o SCHULTZE, Henry F IV & McQUISTON Jacqueline

SCHUMANN, Keith M. b s/o SCHUMANN, Royce L. & MAYO, Marilyn; d 04 Apr 1970 Danville, NH ae 15y

SCHURMAN, Rebecca b 22 Apr 1975 Derry, NH d/o SCHURMAN, Douglas J. & WEST, Roberta L.

SCHWARZER, Brittany Nicole b 12 Jan 1987 Exeter, NH d/o SCHWARZER, Gaylan P. & DeSALVO, Laura S.

SCIEZE, John Bernard b Ireland s/o SCEIZE, Thomas & BURKE, Mary; d 16 Jun 1965 Danville, NH ae 80y

SCIEZE, Margaret b Ireland d/o SCIEZE, Thomas & BURKE, Mary d 06 Apr 1960 Danville, NH ae 86y

SCOTT, Caroline b 1939 Providence, RI; md 19 Jun 1962 Danville, NH WHITNEY, Chas Stephen; md by Arthur M. Comeau

SCRIBNER, John md 29 Dec 1794 Kingston, NH BACHELOR, Hulda

SCYZGIAL, Maureen md 07 Sep 1991 Danville, NH TRAMMELL, Glen Albert; md by John H. Lampray (JP)

SEARL, Alice Jean b 1945 Lawrence, MA; md 10 Sep 1965 Danville, NH COLSON, Alan Carl

SEARS, Alton Trafton b 16 Jun 1949 Danville, NH s/o SEARS, Robert Alton & HATCH, Virginia

SEARS, Marianne Grace b 02 Dec 1961 Danville, NH d/o SEARS, Robert Alton & HATCH, Virginia

SEARS, Martha Eleanor b 23 Sep 1952 Danville, NH d/o SEARS, Robert Alton & HATCH, Virginia

SEARS, Robert A. b s/o SEARS, Alton E. & TRAFTON, Grace L.; d 24 Dec 1982 Danville, NH ae 66y

SEASTEDT, Lindsey Lee b 09 May 1975 Exeter, NH d/o SEASTEDT, Todd R. & PETERSON, Jacquelyn A.

SEAVER, Augustus F. b c1861 Sandown, NH s/o SEAVER, Daniel P. & GEORGE, Dolly; md 23 Jul 1885 Danville, NH BAILEY, Louie Glenn; d 05 Nov 1934 Danville, NH

SEAVER, Barbara Ann b 1935 Danville, NH s/o SEAVER, Gerald H. & HEALEY, Lillian I.; md 12 Apr 1953 Danville, NH BURLEIGH, Wm Alle

SEAVER, Bertram Albert b 13 May 1944 Danville, NH s/o SEAVER, Gerald Homber & HEALEY, Lillian Imorgine; md 26 Oct 1968 Danville, NH WALDRON, Darlene L.; md by Rev Douglas Abbott

SEAVER, Carrie b Kingston, NH d/o SEAVER, Daniel P. & GEORGE, Dolly C.; md 23 Apr 1898 Danville, NH COLLINS, Ralph Lorenzo; md by Rev A. B. Howard

SEAVER, Fred H. b 04 Aug 1907 Danville, NH s/o SEAVER, Herbert & TEWKSBURY, Addie

SEAVER, Gerald H. b 1914 Danville, NH; md 03 Feb 1934 Danville, NH HEALEY, Lillian I.; md by Rev James A. Sawyer

SEAVER, Herbert C. b c1890 Kingston, NH s/o SEAVER, John P. & HALL, Florence G.; md TEWKSBURY, Addie; d 09 Feb 1907 Danville, NH ae 17y 10m 12d

SEAVER, Mabel B. b 17 Nov 1886 Danville, NH d/o SEAVER, Augustus F. & SEAVER, Louie Glenn; md 29

SEAVER (Cont.) May 1915 Danville, NH SMITH, Forrest by Rev Allen C. Kieth; d 12 Mar 1937 Danville, NH

SEAVER, Martha b Kingston, NH; md 30 Apr 1842 Danville, NH CLARK, Calvin T.

SEAVER, Maude B. b 10 Jan 1886 Danville, NH d/o SEAVER, Augustus F. & BAILEY, Louie Glenn; md 01 May 1920 Danville, NH SNAY, Albert H.

SEAVER, Nellie Geogiana b c1891 Plaistow, NH d/o SEAVER, John P. & HULL, Florence; md 22 Jun 1911 Kingston, NH BURRILL, Harry E.; d 19 Oct 1931 Danville, NH; md by Rev Fred V. Stanley; or b Kingston?

SEAVER, Susan F. b Sandown, NH d/o SEAVER, Daniel P. & GEORGE, Dolly C.; md COLLINS, Edson T.; d 27 Feb 1927 Danville, NH; d ae 61y 11m

SEAWARD, David P. b md 14 Mar 1986 Danville, NH THOMPSON, Melinda A.; md by Kathleen E. Abbott (JP)

SEAY, Betty Lou b d/o SEAY, Aron N. & COOK, Alice V.; md DEMAINE, ---- ; d 21 Apr 1983 Danville, NH ae 44y

SEITTER, Vera A. b d/o SEITTER, Theodore & COWLEY, Clara Ellen; md NACOVSKY, ---- ; d 13 Nov 1992

SELL, Scott Allen b 28 Sep 1967 Danville, NH s/o SELL, Robert Henry & KNOWLES, Beverly Jean

SELLEY, Mary b Hawke, NH; md 22 Dec 1768 Hawke, NH TUCKER, Ebenezer Jr.; md by Rev John Page

SELPH, Bartow B. md 10 Jun 1971 Danville, NH BERNABY, Judith M.; md by Leo R. Dupuis (JP)

SEMPLE, Victoria A. b md 21 Sep 1987 Danville, NH LUNDIN, Gary F.; md by Marjorie Marcoux Faiia (JP)

SENTER, Amy Denise b 05 Oct 1969 Danville, NH d/o SENTER, Harry C. & PRAY, Beverly K.

SENTER, Deborah J. md 09 Apr 1983 Danville, NH BILO, Jos A.; md by Rev Everett E. Palmer

SENTER, John Edward b 03 Jun 1959 Danville, NH s/o SENTER, John E. & DEBBRATZ, Frances M.

SENTER, Nellie J.b Sandown, NH d/o SENTER, Samuel & HOYT, Pollie;

SENTER (Cont.) md DARBE, ---- ; d 08 May 1932 Danville, NH ae 64y 8m 1d

SENTER, Samuel b Londonderry, NH; d 20 Sep 1906 Danville, NH ae 79y 6m 29d

SENTER, Scott A. of Plaistow, NH; md 04 Oct 1992 AVERILL, Carolyn S. of Danville, NH

SERAUNIAN, Veronica Ann b 14 Jan 1962 Danville, NH d/o SERAUNIAN, Harry M. Jr. & MARTIN, Patricia A.

SEROUNIAN, Alexandria b 23 May 1972 Exeter, NH d/o SEROUNIAN, Harry M. & MARTIN, Patricia

SEVER, Eliz b of Kingston, NH; md 22 Mar 1770 Hawke, NH HUNT, Henry; md by Rev John Page

SEVERENCE, Jonathan b md 18 Jan 1781 BROWN, Abigail; md by Rev John Page

SEVERENCE, Mary L. b c1843 Kingston, NH; md 1860 Danville, NH FRENCH, Jos B.

SEVERENCE, Samuel Jr. b Kingston, NH; md 08 Jan 1802 Kingston, NH TOWLE, Judith

SEWARD, Irene Esther b 1923 Dover, NH d/o SEWARD, Wm & MERRICK, Esther; d 11 Apr 1924 Danville, NH ae 1y 3m 5d;

SEWARD, Wm b Exeter, NH; md MERRICK, Esther

SEWARD, Wm Albert b 26 Feb 1924 Danville, NH s/o SEWARD, Wm & MERRICK, Esther

SEWASKY, Josephine b 1921 Haverhill, MA d/o SEWASKY, Wm; md 05 May 1934 Danville, NH SLIPOY, Michael; md by Clarence M. Collins (JP)

SHACKLES, Sharon P. b 1941 Birmingham, AL; md 12 Oct 1963 Danville, NH LOMGLAND, Herbert M.; md by Eliz H. Bragg (JP)

SHANNON, Georgianna b EPPING, NH d/o SHANNON, Edward; md 23 Jan 1906 Danville, NH SARGENT, Omer B.; md by Rev A. B. Hyde

SHANNON, Hattie b Epping, NH; md FRENCH, Earl

SHARPE, Joyce b 27 Jan 1924; md 20 Jul 1942 COLLINS, Cecil Spaulding

SHATTACK, Geo W. b 1917 Hollis s/o SHATTACK, Geo A.; md 12 Jun 1937 Danville, NH DULEY, Martha E.

SHATTACK, Louis Elmer b Woburn, MA s/o SHATTACK, Geo F. & FOLLANSBEE, Ella; md PRATT, Sarah; d 21 Aug 1942 Danville, NH

SHATTIER, Scott Michael b 11 Apr 1974 Haverhill, MA s/o SHATTIER, Lester & OUELLETTE, Diane T.

SHATTIER, Justin Evan b 09 Jan 1976 Haverhill, MA s/o SHATTIER, Lester & OUELLETTE, Diane T.

SHATTUCK, Barbara J. md 14 Jun 1986 Danville, NH POLK, Earle F.; md by Rich J. Rondeau (JP)

SHATTUCK, Clara L. b d/o SHATTUCK, Louis Elmer. & PRATT, Sarah L.; d 29 Nov 1972 Danville, NH ae 82y

SHATTUCK, Elmer Wm b 1904 Marlborough, MA s/o SHATTUCK, Louis Elmer & PRATT, Sarah L.; md 31 Mar 1944 Danville, NH TUCKER, Nellie Ruth; d 23 May 1946 Danville, NH; md by W. C. Chappell

SHATTUCK, Geo L. b NH; md 27 Jul 1968 Danville, NH TURNER, Jane; md by Rev Alton Mark

SHATTUCK, Geo Louis b 28 Jun 1945 Danville, NH s/o SHATTUCK, Elmer Wm & TUCKER, Nellie Ruth

SHATTUCK, Geo Michael b 12 Jul 1949 Danville, NH s/o SHATTUCK, Geo Wm & DULEY, Martha Elisabeth

SHATTUCK, Geo W. b 1917 Hollis, NH s/o SHATTUCK, Geo A.; md 12 Jun 1937 Danville, NH DULEY, Martha Eliz; md by Rev W. C. Chappell

SHATTUCK, Lissa b md 17 Jun 1988 Danville, NH BROWNLEE, Kenneth David; md by Rich J. Rondeau (JP)

SHATTUCK, Wm Arthur b 13 Jul 1944 Danville, NH s/o SHATTUCK, Geo Wm & DULEY, Martha Eliz

SHAW, Abigail md 05 Mar 1806 Hawke, NH PAGE, Simon; d 15 Mar 1814 Hawke, NH 2nd wife of Simon Page

SHAW, Gertrude A. b 1900 Ames-

SHAW (Cont.) bury, MA d/o SHAW, Albert E.; md 15 May 1931 Danville, NH WEST, Elmer E.; md by Rev Geo Lee Fish

SHAW, Hattie M. b Canada; md ALLARD, Fred

SHAW, John S. Jr. md 12 Feb 1989 Danville, NH WALSH, Erie F.; md by Rich J. Rondeau (JP)

SHAW, Mary b of Haverhill, MA; md 12 Jul 1770 Hawke, NH BADGER, Enoch; md by Rev John Page

SHAY, Margaret M. b 1901 Lawrence, MA d/o SHAY, Robert; md 08 Apr 1932 Danville, NH WILLIAMS, Humphrey S.; md by Clarence M. Collins (JP)

SHEA, Devan Emily b 27 Jan 1991 Exeter, NH d/o SHEA, Kevin M. & SHEA, Cathleen A.

SHEA, Jeanne M. md 24 Apr 1987 Danville, NH ANALETTO, Benj Jr.; md by Rich J. Rondeau (JP)

SHEA, Kevin Michael md 03 Jun 1989 Danville, NH SHEA, Cathleen Ann; md by Florent R. Bilodeau (P)

SHEA, Michael Patrick md 26 Jun 1976 Danville, NH FLANDERS, Laura Adele; md by Robert S. Dejadon (JP)

SHEA, Michael Terrance b 05 Oct 1992 Exeter, NH s/o SHEA, Kevin M. & SHEA, Cathleen A.

SHEEHAN, Kathleen b d/o SHEEHAN, Patrick & CRONIN, Abugail; md HARRINGTON, ---- ; d 06 Oct 1988 Danville, NH ae 82y

SHEEHAN, Marianne md 14 Oct 1988 Danville, NH HOSMAN, Kevin D.; md by Rich J. Rondeau (JP)

SHELDON, Chas b Old Town. ME s/o SHELDON, Chas; d 06 May 1942 Danville, NH ae 92y 4m 12d

SHELDON, Geo H. b ABT 1887 Fremont, NH s/o SHELDON, Chas A.; md 14 Jun 1913 Franklin, NH MERRILL, Hattie M.; md by Rev Rufus P.Gardner

SHELDON, Isabel b 1912 Kingston, NH d/o SHELDON, Chas; md 30 Jul 1929 Danville, NH DESMARALS, Leo V.; md by Clarence M. Collins (JP)

SHELIA, Dawn L. md 03 Aug 1985 Danville, NH KIMBALL, Steven L.; md

SHEILA (Cont.) by Linda S. Jette (JP)

SHEPARD, Samuel b c1762 Brentwood, NH s/o SHEPARD, Samuel Dr. & ----, Eliz; d 20 Apr 1787 Hawke, NH ae 26y

SHEPPARD, Diane M. md 28 Jul 1979 Danville, NH PERACCHI, Louis C.; md by Anita L. Gallien (JP)

SHEPPARD, Tracey A. md 15 Aug 1981 Danville, NH COLLINS, Brian K.; md by Lawrence G. Brann (JP)

SHERBURNE, Helen C. b 1852 Jersey City, NJ d/o SHERBURNE, Lewis & EASTMAN, Annie; md ANDERSON, ----; d 04 Mar 1926 Danville, NH

SHERIDAN, Hannah Lyhne b 01 Jun 1989 Exeter, NH d/o SHERIDAN, Michael P. & LYHNE, Sandra A.

SHERMAN, Chas H. b Dover, NH; md 09 Oct 1842 Danville, NH SLEEPER, Marinda S.

SHERMAN, Gertrude M. b c1880 Lynn, MA d/o SHERMAN, Geo M.; md 07 Sep 1902 Kingston, NH NICKERSON, Geo W.; md by Rev J. W. Strout

SHERWOOD, Emma A. b New Brunswick, CN d/o SHERWOOD, Robert & ODELL, Phoebe; md OSBORNE, ----; d 23 Oct 1947 Danville, NH ae 81y 6m 22d

SHEYS, Harry b Kingston, NH; md HARTFORD, Pearl

SHEYS, Harry Colcord b 15 Dec 1918 Danville, NH s/o SHEYS, Harry & HARTFORD, Pearl

SHIRT, Aaron b Amesbury, MA; md DIMOND, Abigail

SHORES. Mary E. md GOODWIN, Hazen O.; d 1885 Danville, NH ae 28y

SHORES, Oliver b Portsmouth, NH s/o SHORES, Peter & MOORE, Statirl: d 14 Jun 1901 ae 71y 7m 22d

SHORES, Peter b; Porstmouth, NH; md MOORE, Statirl

SHORT, Hannah b Amesbury, MA; md DEARBORN, David; d 07 May 1884 Danville, NH

SHOWELL, Judith b c1788; md GEORGE, Nathaniel; d 30 Apr 1866 Danville, NH ae 78y

SHUFELT, David Leon b 21 Aug 1855 Danville, NH s/o SHUFELT, Sam & GRIFFIN, Sarah A.; md GEORGE, Ida d 12 Sep 1932 Danville NH

SHUFELT, Nellie b 18 Sep 1857 Danville, NH d/o SHUFELT, Samuel & GRIFFIN, Sarah A.;

SHUFELT, Samuel b Candia, NH; md 09 Nov 1852 Danville, NH GRIFFIN, Sarah Ann; d 22 Sep 1863 New Orleans ae 34y - Civil War Rcds

SHUNAMAN, Amy Ruth b 1916 Hudson, NH d/o SHUNAMAN, Chas Gasper; md 30 Jul 1942 Danville, NH KIMBALL, Rich Chester; md by Rev W. C. Chappell

SHURTLEFF, Eric C. md 14 Sep 1985 Danville, NH PEVERLEY, Lisa A.; md by Rev Wendall J. Irvine

SHURTLEFF, Scott Leslie md 14 Feb 1988 Danville, NH McKINEY, Mary Jo; md by Rev Robt E. Aspinwall

SILLOWAY, Agnes Lillian b d/o SILLOWAY, Frank W. & OSGOOD, Annie B.; md WHITNEY, ----; d 10 Feb 1981 Danville, NH ae 58y

SILLOWAY, Alden W. b Kingston, NH s/o SILLOWAY, Isaac & WEST, Emma; d 03 Nov 1959 Danville, NH

SILLOWAY, Elmer R. b c1849 Kingston, NH; md 02 Nov 1870 Danville, NH CLYNTON, Bella

SILLOWAY, Grace B. b 1897 Kingston, NH d/o SILLOWAY, Everett W.; md 04 May 1917 Kingston, NH OSBORNE, Herbert S.; md by Rev F. W. Whippen

SILLOWAY, James W. b Kingston, NH s/o SILLOWAY, Jos & CASS, ----; md VINCENT, Annie H.; d 02 Sep 1908 Danville, NH ae 60y 6m

SILLOWAY, Mertie B. b 16 May 1872 Danville, NH s/o SILLOWAY, James W. & VINCENT, Annie H.; md 17 Aug 1890 Newton Junction, NH GOVE, Kirk M.; d 23 Jun 1954 Danville, NH also md TUCK, ----; md by Rev J. P. Nowland

SILLOWAY, Myra A. b 20 Sep 1881 Danville, NH d/o SILLOWAY, James W. & VINCENT, Anna H.; md 31 Jan 1904 Hampstead, NH STICKNEY, Geo

SILLOWAY (Cont.) H.; md by Rev W. H. Woodsum

SILVA, Bonnie Jean md 16 May 1978 Danville, NH JEDRICK, James Thos; md by Clara B. Snow (JP)

SILVERMAN, Jerome M. md 21 Jan 1973 Danville, NH WALKER, Lesley A.; md by Leona A. Sciaudone (JP)

SIMANO, Eliz Ann b Derry, NH; md COLLINS, Larry Carlton Sr.

SIMES, Marvin Edward b md 22 Jan 1974 Danville, NH MUNNIS, Carol Ann; md by Rev Ivan Smith Jr.

SIMES, Merle Kenneth b 1913 MA s/o SIMES, Edward D.; md 01 Nov 1952 Danville, NH LESSARD, Pauline Gertrude; md by rev W. C. Chappell

SIMMONDS, Darrin J. md 07 Sep 1985 Danville, NH AVERILL, Lauren E.; md by Rev Fay L. Gemmell

SIMONEAU, Avis I. b Brentwood, NH; md 05 Feb 1965 Danville, NH RICHER, Walter T.; md by Retenah Pietrowski (JP)

SIMONS, Nellie B. b Grand River P.E.I. Canada d/o SIMONS, Edmund & BANKS, Eliz; md HUNTINGTON, Chas; d 24 Oct 1920

SIMPSON, Brandan K. md 28 Dec 1985 Danville, NH THOMPSON, Kathryn R.; md by Steven M. Kucharaski (P)

SIMPSON, Frances Lucille b 1922 MA; d/o SIMPSON, James Clarence; md 01 Aug 1949 Danville, NH TUCKER, Frank Ernest; md by Agnes H. Collins (JP)

SIMPSON, Robert Edw md 22 Jun 1974 Danville, NH MacNEIL, Carol Ann; md by Rev Rich L. Provencher

SIMUZNINK, Waldyslaw b Poland; d 19 Oct 1966 Danville, NH

SINAPIUS, Shawn Michael b 24 Oct 1985 Exeter, NH s/o SINAPIUS, Gerald E. & PELLETIER, Claire M.

SINGELAIS, Sharyn Rose b 01 May 1965 Danville, NH d/o SINGELAIS, Cliffard A. & KELLEHER, Barb

SINS, Lewis J. b 1896 NY; md 12 Feb 1061 Danville, NH SAHLIN, Lucy S.; md by Glenn W. Douglas

SIPPEL, Deanna Marie md 01 Oct 1988 Danville, NH GRANT, Douglas James; md by Maurice D. Lavque (P)

SIWIK, Barb. Lorraine md 19 May 1991 Danville, NH RATNER, Andrew Mark; md by Rich J. Rondeau (JP)

SILLOWAY, Agnes Lillian b d/o SILLOWAY, Frank W. & OSGOOD, Annie B.; md WHITNEY, ---- ; d 10 Feb 1981 Danville, NH ae 58y

SILLOWAY, Alden W. b Kingston, NH s/o SILLOWAY, Isaac & WEST, Emma; d 03 Nov 1959 Danville, NH

SILLOWAY, Elmer R. b c1849 Kingston, NH; md 02 Nov 1870 Danville, NH CLYNTON, Bella

SILLOWAY, Grace B. b 1897 Kingston, NH d/o SILLOWAY, Everett W.; md 04 May 1917 Kingston, NH OSBORNE, Herbert S.; md by Rev F. W. Whippen

SILLOWAY, James W. b Kingston, NH s/o SILLOWAY, Jos & CASS, ---- ; md VINCENT, Annie H.; d 02 Sep 1908 Danville, NH ae 60y 6m

SILLOWAY, Mertie B. b 16 May 1872 Danville, NH d/o SILLOWAY, James W. & VINCENT, Annie H.; md 17 Aug 1890 Newton Junction, NH GOVE, Kirk M.; d 23 Jun 1954 Danville, NH; also md TUCK, ---- ; md by Rev J. P. Nowland

SILLOWAY, Myra A. b 20 Sep 1881 Danville, NH d/o SILLOWAY, James W. & VINCENT, Anna H.; md 31 Jan 1904 Hampstead, NH STICKNEY, Geo H.; md by Rev W. H. Woodsum

SILVA, Bonnie Jean md 16 May 1978 Danville, NH JEDRICK, James Thos; md by Clara B. Snow (JP)

SILVERMAN, Jerome M. md 21 Jan 1973 Danville, NH WALKER, Lesley A.; md by Leona A. Sciaudone (JP)

SIMANO, Eliz Ann b Derry, NH; md COLLINS, Larry Carlton Sr.

SIMES, Marvin Edward md 22 Jan 1974 Danville, NH MUNNIS, Carol Ann; md by Rev Ivan Smith Jr.

SIMES, Merle Kenneth b 1913 MA s/o SIMES, Edward D.; md 01 Nov 1952 Danville, NH LESSARD, Pauline

SIMES (Cont.) Gertrude; md by Rev W. C. Chappell

SIMMONDS, Darrin J. md 07 Sep 1985 Danville, NH AVERILL, Lauren E.; md by Rev Fay L. Gemmell

SIMONEAU, Avis I. b Brentwood, NH; md 05 Feb 1965 Danville, NH RICHER, Walter T.; md by Retenah Pietrowski (JP)

SIMONS, Nellie md HUNTING-TON, Chas

SIMPSON, Brandan K. md 28 Dec 1985 Danville, NH THOMPSON, Kathryn R.; md by Steven M. Kucharaski (P)

SIMPSON, Frances Lucille b 1922 MA d/o SIMPSON, James Clarence; md 01 Aug 1949 Danville, NH TUCKER, Frank Ernest; md by Agnes H. Collins (JP)

SIMPSON, Robert Edward md 22 Jun 1974 Danville, NH MacNEIL, Carol Ann; md by Rev Rich L. Provencher

SIMUZNINK, Waldyslaw b Poland; d 19 Oct 1966 Danville, NH

SINAPIUS, Shawn Michael b 24 Oct 1985 Exeter, NH s/o SINAPIUS, Gerald E. & PELLETIER, Claire M.

SINGELAIS, Sharyn Rose b 01 May 1965 Danville, NH d/o SINGE-LAIS, Cliffard A. & KELLEHER, Barbara

SINSKI, Lewis J. b 1896 NY; md 12 Feb 1061 Danville, NH SAHLIN, Lucy S.; md by Glenn W. Douglas

SIPPEL, Deanna Marie md 01 Oct 1988 Danville, NH GRANT, Douglas James; md by Maurice D. Lavque (P)

SIWIK, Barbara Lorraine md 19 May 1991 Danville, NH RATNER, Andrew Mark; md by Rich J. Rondeau (JP)

SKIDMORE, Bonnie E. md 21 Feb 1981 Danville, NH AYOTTE, Mark; md by Phyllis A. Raynowski (JP)

SKIDMORE, Francis A. md 06 Sep 1986 Danville, NH BRADY, Jacqueline A.; md by David T. Ingerson (JP)

SKINNER, John Wm md 19 Nov 1988 Danville, NH LESTER, Robyn Jean; md by Rich J. Rondeau (JP)

SKINNER, Karl S. Jr. b MA; md 11 Jan 1969 Danville, NH STONSIFER, Barbara A.; md by Leona A. Sciaudone (JP)

SKINNER, Kathleen Mary md 31 May 1975 Danville, NH GAGE, Michael Palmer; md by Richard L. Provencher (P)

SKINNER, Mary Ellen md 08 Jan 1977 Danville, NH REED, Matthew John; md by Michael J. Griffin (P)

SKINNER, Michelle Rita b 03 Aug 1971 Haverhill, MA d/o SKINNER, Karl S. & KEARNEY, Barbara A.

SKRIBISKI, John S. md 02 Aug 1986 Danville, NH FIFIELD, Sandra L.; md by Rev David L. Clarke

SLAVINSKY, Agnes M. E. b d/o SLAVINSKY, John Dutra & ----, Emily; d 22 Jul 1991 Danville, NH ae 80y

SLAVINSKY, Alfred W. b s/o SLAVINSKY, Adam & WILLIAMS, Julia; d 01 Feb 1983 Danville, NH ae 71y

SLEEPER, Benj b Sandown, NH; md 22 Nov 1769 Hawke, NH CLOUGH Judith md by Rev John Page

SLEEPER, Benj md 17 May 1781 Hawke, NH BEAN, Ruth; md by Rev John Page

Sleeper, David b md 11 Jan 1770 Hawke, NH THURSTON, Mary; md by Rev John Page

SLEEPER, David T. b Sandown, NH; md 23 Sep 1846 Danville, NH SANBORN, Mary A.

SLEEPER, Dolly b of Kingston, NH; md 26 Apr 1770 Hawke, NH CHALLIS, John; md by Rev John Page

SLEEPER, Gideon md 28 Feb 1769 Hawke, NH HOIT, Eliz; md by Rev John Page

SLEEPER, Henry b 10 Oct 1773 Hawke, NH s/o SLEEPER, Nehemiah Sr. & MORRILL, Apphia; md 25 Sep 1794 Kingston, NH BEAN, Kezia

SLEEPER, Jonas b 07 Jan 1785 Hawke, NH s/o SLEEPER, Nehemiah Sr. & MORRILL, Apphia

SLEEPER, Jos b 10 Sep 1782 Hawke, NH s/o SLEEPER, Nehemiah Sr. & MORRILL, Apphia; d 13 Nov

SLEEPER (Cont.) 1788 Hawke, NH
SLEEPER, Jos Sr. b 09 Apr 1776
Hawke, NH s/o SLEEPER, Nehemiah
Sr. & MORRILL, Apphia; d 13 Nov
1778 Hawke, NH ae 1+y
SLEEPER, Lois b 17 Aug 1782
Hawke, NH d/o SLEEPER, Nehemiah
Sr. & MORRILL, Apphia
SLEEPER, Lydia b of Brentwood,
NH; md 09 Dec 1799 Hawke, NH
PETTENGILL, Benj
SLEEPER, Marinda S. b Poplin,
NH; md 09 Oct 1842 Danville, NH
SHERMAN, Chas H.
SLEEPER, Mary b Brentwood, NH;
md 29 Sep 1779 Hawke, NH BEAN,
Benj; md by Rev John Page
SLEEPER, Nehemiah Jr. b 04 Jul
1787 Hawke, NH s/o SLEEPER,
Nehemiah Sr. & MORRILL, Apphia
SLEEPER, Nehemiah Sr. md 06
Dec 1770 Hawke, NH MORRILL,
Apphia; md by Rev John Page
SLEEPER, Sarah b Kingston, NH;
md 01 Dec 1774 Hawke, NH Hook,
Dyer Jr.
SLEEPER, Susanna b 17 Aug 1771
Hawke, NH d/o SLEEPER, Nehemiah
Sr. & MORRILL, Apphia; d 07 Jun
1776 Hawke, NH ae 5y
SLETTEN, Joyce M. md 23 Jun
1973 Danville, NH HARMON, Robert
W. Jr.; md by Rev Justin J. Hartman
SLIPOY, Michael b 1904 Russia s/o
SLIPOY, John; md 05 May 1934 Dan-
ville, NH SEWASKY, Josephine; md by
Clarence M. Collins (JP)
SLYE, Christine Lynn b 28 Nov
1978 Methuen, MA d/o SLYE, Gordon
C. & CONNER, Pamela A.
SLYE, Kathryn Ann b 16 Apr 1985
Lawrence, MA d/o SLYE, Gordon C. &
CONNER, Pamela A.
SMALL, Helen b d/o SMALL,
Leslie; md DONAHUE, ---- ; d 08 Dec
1987 Danville, NH; d ae 79y
SMART, Eliz A. b 19 Oct 1866
Danville, NH; d/o SMART, John A. &
WORTHEN, Lydia; d 23 Apr 1886
Danville, NH
SMART, Joanne Etta b d/o
SMART, Cornelius & AMES, Marhu-
erite; md BOWLEY, ---- ; d 03 Jul 1991

SMART (Cont.) Danville, NH ae 55y
SMART, John d 03 Nov 1874
Danville, NH ae 49y
SMART, Yvette Marie md 20 Oct
1990 Danville, NH DeSERRES,
Norman Phillip Jr.; md by Rev Everett
E. Palmer
SMITH, Abraham md 17 Oct 1822
Kingston, NH TOWLE, Abigail
SMITH, Chas Linwood b New
Brunswick Canada s/o SMITH, James
& ATWOOD, Sarah; d 19 Jan 1969
Danville, NH ae 91y
SMITH, Charlotte H. b c1890
Marblehead, MA d/o SMITH, Daldry R.
& HARRIS, Alice; md 08 Mar 1913
Plaistow, NH AVERY, Lewis Freeman;
d 20 Apr 1976 Danville, NH; md by Rev
Charle A Towne
SMITH, Clifford B: Jr. b 1937
Beverly, MA; md 22 Feb 1964 Danville,
NH GOOD, Marjorie B.; md by Edward
R. Lamb (JP)
SMITH, Daniel C. b Ipswich, MA;
md 13 Aug 1887 Haverhill, MA
GOODRICH, Abbie L.; md by Rev C. N.
Taylor
SMITH, Deborah b Medford, MA;
md MEIGS, Peter S.
SMITH, Deborah Lynne md 08 Apr
1978 Danville, NH INGRAM, Michael
Ernest; md by Roy Daubenspeck (JP)
SMITH, Dennis W. md 10 Jun 1992
HARRIMAN, Lorraine F.; md by Rich
J. Rondeau (JP)
SMITH, Donald Edward b 19 Nov
1964 Danville, NH s/o SMITH, James
Carlton & CUNNINGHAM, Jeannie M.
SMITH, Donald P. b s/o SMITH,
Bion B. & SUTTON, Kathlyn; d 21 Feb
1989 Danville, NH ae 63y
SMITH, Eliz b c1827; md AVERY,
Jos; d 22 Mar 1872 Danville, NH ae
45y
SMITH, Ernest B. b Lynn, MA s/o
SMITH, Daniel C. md 15 Mar 1890
Danville, NH WORTHEN, Josie E.; md
by Rev C. H. Smith
SMITH, Eudora Delia b W Epping,
NH d/o SMITH, Francis; md 04 Mar
1884 Danville, NH TOWLE, Frank; d
03 Mar 1947 Danville, NH ae 84y 6m
10d

SMITH, Evangeline Sylvia b 11 Mar 1917 Danville, NH d/o SMITH, Forrest & SEAVER, Mabel; md 02 May 1936 Danville, NH HAGGETT, John W.; md by Rev James W. Bixler

SMITH, Florence b 23 Aug 1885 Danville, NH; d/o SMITH, Fred W. & ----, Margaret A.

SMITH, Forrest b c1881 Kingston, NH s/o SMITH, Frank H.; md 29 May 1915 Danville, NH SEAVER, Mabel B.; md by Rev Allen C. Keith

SMITH, Frank Wm Jr. b 02 Apr 1961 Danville, NH s/o SMITH, Frank Wm Sr. & MARTIN, Gertrude; d 02 Apr 1961 Danville, NH bu SMITH, Geo Henry b E Kingston, NH; s/o SMITH, Chas H. & CURRIER, Betsy; d 22 Jul 1948 Danville, NH

SMITH, Harry b c1873 Halifax, England s/o SMITH, Geo; md 11 Apr 1909 Danville, NH BRADLEY, Bertha E.; md by Rev W. C. Chappell

SMITH, Herbert R. b Londonderry, NH; md 26 Dec 1970 Danville, NH PIERCE, Eleanor G.

SMITH, Jabez b Brentwood, NH; md 16 Nov 1769 Hawke, NH HOOK, Martha; md by Rev John Page

SMITH, Jacob b Brentwood, NH; md 02 Mar 1798 Kingston,, NH PHILBRICK, Betsy

SMITH, Jaime Erna b 31 Jul 1976 Lawrence, MA d/o SMITH, Forrest & BEAUVAIS, Penny M.

SMITH, James Carlton Jr. b 21 Apr 1966 Danville, NH s/o SMITH, James Carlton Sr. & CUNNINGHAM, Jeanne M.;d 02 Sep 1970 Danville, NH

SMITH, James Carlton Sr. b 1944 Plaistow, NH; md 13 Apr 1963 Danville, NH CUNNINGHAM, Jeannie M.; md by Jos H. Southwick (JP)

SMITH, James Wm b 21 Mar 1960 Danville, NH s/o SMITH, Wm Russeel & ROBIDAU, Priscilla Jane; md 28 May 1983 Danville, NH BROWN, Lisa G.; md by Rev Wendall J. Irvine

SMITH, Jeffrey Brian b 15 Oct 1989 Manchester, NH s/o SMITH, James W. & BROWN, Lisa G.

SMITH, John b of Chester, NH; md 30 May 1764 CLOUGH, Abigail; md by

SMITH (Cont.) Rev John Page

SMITH, Lawrence S. b 1914 Brockton, MA s/o SMITH, Samuel F.; md 15 Mar 1936 Danville, NH McKEON, Eliz C.; md by Clarence M. Collins (JP)

SMITH, Lloyd Ernest b 1931 Haverhill, MA s/o SMITH, LLOYD G.; md 01 Feb 1953 Danville, NH YOUNG, Edythe May

SMITH, Lorraine Frances b 1928 MA d/o SMITH, John Harry; md 01 Oct 1949 Danville, NH GRIFFIN, Robert Raymond; md by Rev Harry L. Lesure

SMITH, Louisa b Epping, NH; md ROBINSON, Chas W.

SMITH, Lucinda b Kingston, NH; md WEST, Chas Will

SMITH, Martha b of Brentwood, NH; md 17 Jun 1779 Hawke, NH CAMMET, Silas; md by Rev John Page

SMITH, Martha Esther b 1927 New London, CT d/o SMITH, Max Lee; md 12 Feb 1949 Danville, NH WELCH, John Russell; md by Rev W. C. Chappell

SMITH, Mary E. d/o SMITH, Jos & SULLIVAN, Annie; md GREER, ---- ; d 13 Jul 1970 Danville, NH ae 69y

SMITH, Mary L. b Sandown, NH s/o SMITH, Henry & GEORGE, Matilda; md SPOFFORD, Frank A.; d 06 Sep 1900 Danville, NH

SMITH, Max Lee b s/o SMITH, Everett; d 07 Feb 1953 Danville, NH ae 55y

SMITH, Perry Cloudman b md 18 May 1991 Danville, NH AVERILL, Katherine M.; md by Rev Wendell J. Irvine

SMITH, Rebecca b of Deerfield, NH; md GLIDDEN, Simeon; md by Rev John Page

SMITH, Sandra Lee b 1940 MA d/o SMITH, Kenneth E.; md 03 Jun 1958 Danville, NH GILES, Norman Fletcher; md by Agnes H. Collins (JP)

SMITH, Tara Beth Ann b md 18 May 1991 Danville, NH MARENA, Robert Clark; md by Everett E. Palmer

SMITH, Theodate b c1730; md BACHELOR, Elisha Dea.; d 25 Mar 1807 Hawke, NH ae 77y

SMITH, Wm Russell b 1933

SMITH (Cont.) Amesbury, MA s/o
SMITH, Clyde E.; md 02 Jul 1945
Danville, NH ROBIDON, Priscilla
Jane; md by Rich Margelot (JP)

SMREKAR, Larry E. b md 22 Nov
1991 Danville, NH ADAMS, Christine
C.; md by Rich J. Rondeau (JP)

SNELL, Charlotte Marie b 1919
Downingtown, PA d/o SNELL, Slias;
md 20 Mar 1955 Danville, NH LAMB,
Edward Ridgeway; md by Rev W. C.
Chappell

SNOW, Doris Theresa b 30 Oct
1963 Danville, NH d/o SNOW, Raymond, F. & St CYR, Francoise D.

SNOW, Judith A. md 14 Feb 1987
Danville, NH MACHADO, James E.;
md by Joan Maria Pichowicz (JP)

SNOW, Paul Raymond b 09 Mar
1954 Danville, NH s/o SNOW, Raymond F. & ST CYR, Francoise Doris

SNOW, Wm Chas b 03 Nov 1972
Haverhill, MA s/o SNOW, Chas W. &
CASE, Doreen R.

SNYDER, Don G. md 05 Sep 1980
Danville, NH BUCHANAN, Leslie L.;
md by Rev Janet H. Bowering

SORRENTINI, Palmira A. b 1916
Boston, MA d/o SORRENTINI, Nicolo;
md 27 Jul 1935 Danville, NH SALIM-
BENE, Chas C.; md by Clarence M.
Collins (JP)

SOTT, Jacqualine Ann b d/o SOTT,
Donald & GUINEY, Mary Jane; md
MOCAL, ----; d 16 Apr 1989 Danville,
NH

SOUCY, Mark L. md 10 Oct 1987
Danville, NH ROBINSON, Ellen A.;
md by Rev Everett E. Palmer

SOVULIS, Eleanor A. b 1917 Lynn,
MA d/o PATTEN, Roberet Ardell; md
16 Nov 1947 Danville, NH
McCLUSKY, Bernard Vincent Jr.; md
by Rev W. C. Chappell

SPARKS, Linda L. md 27 May 1989
Danville, NH NICOLI, Jerry J.; md by
Rev Carlos F. Paz

SPAULDING, Chas Henry b 1927
NH s/o SPAULDING, Henry A. & md
19 Jun 1954 Danville, NH EMERSON,
Ann; md by Wendall J. Irving (JP)

SPAULDING, Lillias Etta b 07 Mar
1861 Sandown, NH d/o SPAULDING,

SPAULDING (Cont.) Chas E. &
PAGE, Laura E.; md 16 Jun 1881
Danville, NH COLLINS, Herbert
Sumner; d 12 Oct 1948 bu Danville,
NH Center Cem.

SPEARS, Geo Wm b 1907 s/o
SPEARS, Harry & WILBUR, Annie; d
04 Dec 1955 Danville, NH

SPEARS, Marie Michelle b 06 Oct
1976 Exeter, NH d/o SPEARS, Wm A.
& St LAURENT, Marilyn A.

SPEARS, Mary Ann b 26 Feb 1973
Exeter, NH d/o SPEARS, Wm A. & St
LAURENT, Marilyn A.

SPEARS, Melissa A. md 03 May
1987 Danville, NH MORGAN, Kevin
L.; md by Rev Everett E. Palmer

SPEARS, Wm A. b 1940 Medford,
MA; md 21 Jun 1965 Danville, NH St
LAURENT, Marilyn A.; md by Leona
A. Schiaudone (JP)

SPENCER, Marion E. b 1898
Plymouth, NH d/o SPENCER, Louis A.;
md 25 Dec 1922 Plymouth, NH
GEORGE, Maurice C.; md by Rev J. R.
Copplestone

SPENCER, Thos Ralph b VT; md
21 Jun 1969 Danville, NH WARD,
Louise Dianne; md by Rev Douglas W.
Abbott

SPENCER, Walter Edward Jr. b
md 16 Nov 1990 Danville, NH Merrill,
Karen Lee; md by Rich J. Rondeau (JP)

SPERO, Michael Rich b 20 Dec
1960 Danville, NH s/o SPERO, Rich A.
& GOLDTHWAITE, Joyce E.

SPICER, Chas A. md 23 Aug 1986
Danville, NH GRAY, Robin D.; md by
Rich J. Rondeau (JP)

SPITZER, Emily L. b Vennia
Austria; md COLLINS, P. Forrest

SPOFFORD, Alden E. b 28 Feb
1848 Danville, NH s/o SPOFFORD,
Moses & TEWKSBURY, Emily; md 24
Apr 1878 Danville, NH ELKINS, Mary
Ellen

SPOFFORD, Amy Grace md 05
Aug 1978 Danville NH DEMAINE,
Rodney Frank; md by Rev Rich Gran-
nell

SPOFFORD, Benaiah b 10 Sep
1786 Hawke, NH s/o SPOFFORD,
Benjamin & COLE, Margaret (Peggy);

SPOFFORD (Cont.) md 30 Sep 1810 Kingston, NH PAGE, Mary (Polly)

SPOFFORD, Benj b c1755; md COLE, Margaret (Peggy); d 25 Nov 1814 Hawke, NH; bu Hawke, NH Old Mtg Hse Cem.; d ae 59y

SPOFFORD, Carolyn R. md 19 Sep 1983 Danville, NH DEMAINE, Harland E.; md by Rev Franklin W. Hobbs

SPOFFORD, Celia May b 1892 Danville, NH; d/o SPOFFORD, Alden E. & ELKINS, Nellie; md STOCKER, ---- ; d 06 Jun 1933 Danville, NH ae 41y 3m 28d

SPOFFORD, Chas A. b 22 Jul 1842 Chester, NH s/o SPOFFORD, John P. & ---- , Bethia J.; md 21 Sep 1867 Danville, NH SARGENT-TOWLE, Tryphen; d 05 Oct 1898 Danville, NH

SPOFFORD, Charlotte T. b 29 Jun 1832 Hawke, NH d/o SPOFFORD, Osmund & FRENCH, Lucy; d 26 Oct 1873 Danville, NH ae 41y

SPOFFORD, Eliza Cole b 16 Sep 1846 Danville, NH d/o SPOFFORD, John P. & ---- , Bethia J.

SPOFFORD, Eliza E. b 06 AOG 1849 Danville, NH d/o SPOFFORD, Moses & TEWKSBURY, Emily

SPOFFORD, Eliz M. b c1822 Danville, NH; md 1848 Danville, NH LOCK, Horance

SPOFFORD, Evelina b 12 Apr 1815 Hawke, NH d/o SPOFFORD, Benaiah & PAGE, Polly

SPOFFORD, Ezra G. b 12 Aug 1852 Danville, NH s/o SPOFFORD, Moses & TEWKSBURY, Emily

SPOFFORD, Frank A. b Chester, NH; md SMITH, Mary L.

SPOFFORD, John E. b 20 Jun 1884 Danville, NH s/o SPOFFORD, Alden E. & ELKINS, Nellie E.

SPOFFORD, John P. b 17 Sep 1819 Hawke, NH; d 13 Jul 1862 Savage Station Civil War Records

SPOFFORD, Jos b 26 Jun 1817 Hawke, NH s/o SPOFFORD, Benaiah & PAGE, Polly

SPOFFORD, Lucy Ann b 12 Nov 1828 Hawke, NH s/o SPOFFORD, Osmund & FRENCH, Lucy; md 05 Dec 1853 Newmarket, NH COLBY, Alden

SPOFFORD (Cont.) E.; d 30 May 1917 Danville, NH

SPOFFORD, Mabel Edith b 11 Dec 1882 Danville, NH d/o SPOFFORD, Chas A. & SARGENT, Tryphena T.; md GEORGE, Fred; d 25 Jun 1944 Danville, NH

SPOFFORD, Mary b 02 May 1818 Hawke, NH d/o SPOFFORD, Osmund & FRENCH, Lucy

SPOFFORD, Mary b Danville, NH d/o SPOFFORD, md 29 Nov 1841 Danville, NH CURRIER, Ezra

SPOFFORD, Mary E. b 16 Mar 1846 Danville, NH d/o SPOFFORD, Moses & TEWKSBURY, Emily

SPOFFORD, Mary P. b 27 Mar 1844 Danville, NH d/o SPOFFORD, John & ----, Bethia J.

SPOFFORD, Moses b 15 May 1821 Hawke, NH s/o SPOFFORD, Osmund & FRENCH, Lucy; d 11 Apr 1892

SPOFFORD, Nabby b 16 Feb 1785 Hawke, NH d/o SPOFFORD, Benj & COLE, Margaret (Peggy)

SPOFFORD, Orlando b 07 Sep 1791 Hawke, NH s/o SPOFFORD, David & BACHELOR, Dorothy

SPOFFORD, Osmund b 02 Dec 1793 Hawke, NH s/o SPOFFORD, Benj & COLE, Margaret (Peggy); md 02 Feb 1818 Hawke, NH FRENCH, Lucy; d 07 Sep 1872 Danville, NH ae 78y

SPOFFORD, Permelia b 02 Feb 1788 Hawke, NH d/o SPOFFORD, Benj & COLE, Margaret (Peggy); md 27 Sep 1807 Kingston, NH HOOK, James T.; d 21 Apr 1853 Danville, NH

SPOFFORD, Sally b 04 Apr 1813 Hawke, NH d/o SPOFFORD, Benaiah & PAGE, Polly

SPOFFORD, Sebastien b 22 May 1797 Hawke, NH s/o SPOFFORD, Benj & COLE, Margaret (Peggy)

SPOFFORD, Sophronia b 12 Feb 1811 Hawke, NH d/o SPOFFORD, Benaiah & PAGE, Polly; md 11 Apr 1830 Kingston, NH GEORGE, Currier; d 20 Nov 1880 Sandown, NH ae 69y

SPOFFORD, Stephen b 11 Jun 1898 Danville, NH s/o SPOFFORD, Frank A. & SMITH, Mary L.

SPOFFORD, Wm A. b 13 Mar 1852

SPOFFORD (Cont.) Danville, NH s
/o SPOFFORD, John P. & ----, Bethia J.
SPOFFORD, Winthrop W. b c 1889
Danville, NH s /o SPOFFORD, Alden
E. & ELKINS, Nellie E.; d 11 Apr 1893
Danville, NH ae 3y 9m
ST PIERRE, Laura May md 24 Dec
1990 Danville NH MAZZOTTA, Michael Keenan; md by Rich J. Rondeau
(JP)
St. CYR, Francoise Doris b d/o ST.
CYR, Arthur & DUHAIME, Marie
Rose; md SNOW, ---- ; d 20 Mar 1969
Danville, NH ae 44y
St. JOHN, Brenda L. md 29 Mar
1980 Danville, NH WHEELER, Rich
C.; md by Robert S. Dejadon (JP)
St. JOHN, Don O. md 23 Jan 1971
Danville, NH EDWINSON, Brenda
Lee; md by Robt S. Dejadon (JP)
St. JOHN, Donald Oliver b 04 Aug
1971 Haverhill, MA s/o St. JOHN,
Donald O. & EDWINSON, Brenda Lee
St. LAURENT, Marilyn A. b 1947
Exeter, NH d/o St. LAURENT, Wilfred
& BUSWELL, Elsie M.; md 21 Jun
1965 SPEARS, Wm A.; d 18 Aug 1990
Danville, NH ae 43y; md by Leona A.
Sciaudone (JP)
St. OMGE, Leo F. b 1937 MA s/o St
ONGE, Henry L.; md 22 Sep 1956
Danville, NH JACKSON, Donna Mae;
md by Rev C. F. Cahill (P)
St. PIERRE, Leslye G. b 1946
Haverhill, MA; md 08 Jun 1964 Danville, NH BOUCHARD, Curtis C.; md
by Edward R. Lamb (JP)
STALLINGS, Pamela L.md 17 Aug
1985 Danville, NH FLIGER, Michael
L.; md by Rev Everett E. Palmer
STAMATELLO, Milton b 1907
Boston, MA s/o STAMATELLO,
Stamatios; md 08 May 1927 Danville,
NH NICKERSON, Alice Gertrude; md
by Rev Howard A. Reyman
STANCOMBE, Marion Bertha b
1920 MA; d/o STANCOMBE, Archie;
md 01 Oct 1949 Danville, NH HARRISON, Donald Everett; md by Rev
Harry L. Lesure
STANDING, Wm H. 3rd md 20 Sep
1986 Danville, NH MARTIN, Laura J.;
md by Rev Everett E. Palmer

STANYAN, Levi b Chichester, NH;
md MORRILL, Susanna
STARKEY, Mary Alice b 1891
Hampstead, NH md ARNOLD Karl Jas
STARTOS, Anne E. md 06 Apr
1974 Danville, NH MORSE, Randolph
P. Jr.; md by Bettie C. Ouellette (JP)
STATCOMBE, Marion Bertha b
1920 d/o STATCOMBE, Archie; md 01
Oct 1949 Danville, NH HARRISON,
Donald Harris
STEELE, Allison Paige b 02 Dec
1992 Derry, NH d/o STEELE, Wm V. &
BRESNAHAN, Kathleen A.
STEELE, Jeremy Michael b 21 Mar
1988 Exeter, NH s/o STEELE, Wm V.
& BRESNAHAN, Kathleen A.
STEELE, Michael J. md 28 Mar
1987 Danville, NH McCARRON,
Jeanne M.; md by Rev Rob F. Dobson
STEELE, Sean Ryan b 18 Jul 1991
Exeter, NH s/o STEELE, Wm V. &
BRESNAHAN, Kathleen A.
STEELE, Wm V. md 01 Aug 1987
Danville, NH BRESNAHAN, Kathleen
A.; md by Rev John M. Grace (P)
STEPHENSEN, Jamie md 25 May
1980 Danville, NH MANIKIAN, Carl
R.; md by Rev Wm Ryans
STEVENS, Alfred b 21 Jul 1806
Hawke, NH s/o STEVENS, Peter & ----,
Hannah
STEVENS, Angela b 03 Sep 1831
Hawke, NH d/o STEVENS, Samuel &
HOOK, Sarah Ann
STEVENS, Anna b 20 Jun 1804
Hawke, NH d/o STEVENS, Peter & ----,
Hannah
STEVENS, Annie B. b Hillsboro
Brdg, NH; md WIGGINS, Walter
STEVENS, Betsey b c1797; md
TEWKSBURY, Thos; d 13 Nov 1830
Hawke, NH; 2nd wife of Thos
TEWKSBURY
STEVENS, Daniel b c1835 Plaistow, NH; md 08 May 1865 Danville,
NH LUCY, Mary M.;
STEVENS, Eliz b 26 Dec 1801
Hawke, NH d/o STEVENS, Peter & ----,
Hannah
STEVENS, Geo b 11 Feb 1835
Hawke, NH s/o STEVENS, Samuel &
HOOK, Sarah Ann

STEVENS, Hannah b c1839; d 02 Jan 1863 Danville, NH ae 24y - Diptheria

STEVENS, Hannah md 29 Nov 1809 Hawke, NH FRENCH, Abraham Dr.; d 24 Mar 1824 Hawke, NH

STEVENS, Hannah b 07 Jul 1791 Hawke, NH d/o STEVENS, Peter & ----, Hannah

STEVENS, Jemima b 25 Nov 1798 Hawke, NH d/o STEVENS, Peter & ----, Hannah

STEVENS, John P. H. b 28 Jun 1846 Danville, NH s/o STEVENS, Samuel & HOOK, Sarah Ann

STEVENS, Laura F. b 19 Jul 1839 Danville, NH d/o STEVENS, Jacob & STRAW, Sally H.

STEVENS, Lydia b 01 Oct 1809 Hawke, NH d/o STEVENS, Peter & ----, Hannah

STEVENS, Mary b Salem, NH; md 12 Jan 1764 Hawke, NH PAGE, John Rev.; d 12 Sep 1820 Salem, NH bu Hawke, NH Old Mtg Hse Cem.

STEVENS, Mary b 15 Jul 1794/5 Hawke, NH d/o STEVENS, Peter & ----, Hannah; md 11 Nov 1813 Hawke, NH FRENCH, Peter

STEVENS, Mary French b 05 Jan 1842 Danville, NH d/o STEVENS, Samuel & HOOK, Sarah Ann

STEVENS, Maxine b 1918 Haverhill, MA d/o STEVENS, Harold; md 15 Aug 1936 Danville, NH GUSCORA, Anthony; md by Rev O. L. Brownsey

STEVENS, Peter b c1765; md ---- , Hannah; d 31 Mar 1835 Danville, NH bu Danville, NH Center Cem.

STEVENS, Prudence md 1st BRYANT, ----, 2nd EASTMAN, Edward Ens.; d 09 Apr 1813 Hawke, NH

STEVENS, Sarah b 05 Aug 1796 Hawke, NH d/o STEVENS, Peter & ----, Hannah

STEVENS, Sarah Ann b 24 May 1837 Danville, NH d/o STEVENS, Samuel & HOOK, Sarah Ann

STEVENS, Selyna b 08 Feb 1833 Hawke, NH d/o STEVENS, Samuel & HOOK, Sarah Ann

STEVENS, Susan Durgin b 22 Nov 1840 Danville, NH d/o STEVENS,

STEVENS (Cont.) Samuel & HOOK, Sara Ann

STEVENSON, Frank A. b 1876 Danville, NH s/o STEVENSON, Moses P. & SARGENT, Sarah J.; md 1st 31 May 1898 Danville, NH SARGENT, Lillie M. by Rev W. F; Warren 2nd md 21 Mar 1917 Danville, NH TOWLE, S. Gertrude by Rev F. W. Whippen

STEVENSON, Gladys b 25 Nov 1907 Danville, NH d/o STEVENSON, Frank A. & SARGENT, Lillie M; md 29 Nov 1925 Kingston, NH EDWARDS, James C.; md by Rev Frank Whippen

STEVENSON, Moses P. b c1839 Fremont, NH s/o STEVENSON, Peesley & BUSBY, ---- ;md SARGENT, Sarah T.; d 19 Dec 1915 Danville, NH ae 75y 1m 6d

STEWART, Phyllis b 1946 Boston, MA; md 11 Jun 1966 Danville, NH CARRINGTON, David Louis; md by Rev John Wood Jr.

STEWART, Rosanna L. b c1846 Danville, NH; md 03 Nov 1868 Danville, NH WHITTIER, Jacob

STEWART, Samuel md 28 Jun 1781 Hawke, NH BROWN, Hannah; md by Rev John Page

STICKNEY, Geo H. b c1879 Haverhill, MA s/o STICKNEY, John H.; md 31 Jan 1904 Hampstead, NH SILLOWAY, Myra A.; md by Rev W. H. Woodsum

STICKNEY, John b 19 Feb 1906 Danville, NH s/o STICKNEY, Geo & SILLOWAY, Myra A.

STONESIFER, Barbara A. b MA; md 11 Jan 1969 Danville, NH SKINNER, Karl S. Jr.; md by Leona A. Sciaudone (JP)

STOREY, Arthur Ellis 3rd md 15 Jan 1977 Danville, NH DESERRES, Theresa Marie; md by Rich L. Procencher (P)

STOREY, Arthur Ellis Jr. b s/o STOREY, Arthur Ellis Sr. & PREBLE, Eleanor L.; md d 18 Jul 1972 Danville, NH

STOREY, Cynthia Nancy md 26 Jan 1974 Danville, NH GLONET, Robert Michael; md by James L. Sullivan (P)

STRAFFORD, Henry T. Jr. b c1826 Belpee Eng; s/o STRAFFORD, Henry T. Sr. & PALMER, Susan; d 04 Feb 1902 Danville, NH

STRATOS, Anne E md 06 Apr 1974 Danville NH MORSE, Randolph Nancy

STRATTON, Cynthia Dale md 07 Apr 1990 Danville, NH SCALZO, Jeffery John; md by Rev Edward Charest

STRATZ, Timothy Christrpher b 26 Aug 1985 Exeter, NH s/o STRATZ, Stephen J. & DORA, Mary L.

STRAW, Sally H. md 24 Nov 1831 Hawke, NH COLLINS, Jacob; d 04 Oct 1886 Danville, NH ae 74y

STREETER, Jillian Renee b 29 Oct 1992 Exeter, NH d/o STREETER, Paul J. & LAVOIE, Sherry R.

STUBBS, Gerald S. md 10 Nov 1973 Danville, NH MURTAGH, Margaret C.; md by Rev Chas P. Calcagni

STUBBS, Maxine S. b d/o STUBBS, Elmer Lee & CROCKETT, Sadie; md ROSS, ---- ; d 29 Sep 1977 Danville, NH ae 72y

STURGIS, Jason Edward b 22 Aug 1973 Exeter, NH s/o STURGIS, Chas E.& HASKELL, Brenda A.

STURGIS, Caryn Beth b 21 Feb 1966 Danville, NH d o STURGIS, Rich T. & STRATTON, Mary J.

STURGIS, Chas Jr. b 1943 Newburyport, MA; md 15 Oct 1966 Danville, NH ZIMMERMAN, Marilyn M. md by Rev Theodore B. Hadley

STURGIS, Rich T. b 1942 Brentwood, NH s/o STURGIS, Chas E. & WHITE, Louise; md STRATTON, Mary J.; d 19 Jan 1977 Danville, NH; d ae 35y

STURK, Barbara J..md 29 Mar 1986 Danville, NH MAGLIO, Robert S. Sr.; md by David T. Ingerson (JP)

SUE, Stephen Louis md 07 Aug 1971 Danville, NH MELKONIAN, Nancy Gail; md by Rich Vickery (P)

SULLIVAN, Bertha J. b Deerfield, NH d/o SULLIVAN, John & GANNON, Ann; md KNOWLES, ---- ; d 19 Dec 1965 Danville, NHd ae 84y

SUNDERLAND, Jesse E. b 1900 Georgia, VT s/o SUNDERLAND, Oscar

SUNDERLAND (Cont.) F.; md 21 Jun 1929 Danville, NH COLBY, Miriam Gertrude; md by Rev W. C. Chappell

SUTER, Ravid Wayne md 12 Dec 1989 Danville, NH CHAMBERS, Arlene Frances; md by Rich J. Robdeau (JP)

SWAIN, Albert Elmer b Melrose, MA s/o SWAIN, Alfred Elmer md 05 Oct 1945 Danville, NH GOLDTHWAITE, Ethelyn L; md by rev W. C. Chappell

SWAIN, Albert Everett b s/o SWAIN, Elmer D. & MacGREGOR, Isabella; d 18 Jul 1972 Danville, NH ae 84y

SWAIN, Medora Fraughten b 1928 Melrose, NH d/o SWAIN, Alfred Elmer; md 15 Jun 1947 Danville, NH PLIMPTON, Henry Clay Jr.; md by Rev W. C. Chappell

SWAIN, Stephen Alfred b 28 Feb 1947 Danville, NH s/o SWAIN, Alfred Elmer & GOLDTHWAITE, Ethelyn L.;

SWASEY, Rebecca E. b c1832 Brentwood, NH; md 05 Feb 1862 Danville, NH PRESSEY, Geo W.

SWEAT, Naomi b of Kingston, NH; md 18 Sep 1764 ELLIOT, Jonathan; md by Rev John Page

SWEATT, Marrianda b Hampstead, NH; md 10 Jul 1949 Danville, NH QUIMBY, Moses

SWEATT, Nancy b c1805; md ELKINS, Henry; d 12 Jun 1836 Danville, NH; 2nd wife of Henry ELKINS

SWEATT, Peter b Hawke, NH; md 12 Jun 1780 Hawke, NH WADLEIGH, Molly; md by Rev John Page

SWEATT, Sarah b 17 Nov 1785 Hawke d/o SWEAT, Peter & ---- , Sarah; md ELKINS, Henry

SWEATT, ---- b 22 Aug 1853 Danville, NH s/o SWEATT, J. S. & ---- , Lucretia

SWEENEY, Elaine Lillian b 1922 Newton, MA d/o SWEENEY, Clarence Lancey; md 01 Dec 1946 Danville, NH TALBOT, Ralph Francis; md by Rev W. C. Chappell

SWEENY, Patrick J. md 10 Feb 1990 Danville, NH KENDRICK,

SWEENY (Cont.) Rebecca B.; md by Robert J. Kemmery (P)

SWEET, Donald md DAY, Hazel

SWEET, Earl D. b 1946 Hillsboro, NH; md 21 May 1966 Danville, NH BROWN, Carol A.; md by Rev Douglas Abbott

SWEET, Earl Day b 16 Jul 1967 Danville, NH s/o SWEET, Earl D. & BROWN, Carol A.

SWEET, Jason Jeremy b 20 Oct 1976 Exeter, NH s/o SWEET, Earl D. & BROWN, Carol A.

SWEET, Jeffery Phillip b 18 Feb 1971 Exeter, NH s/o SWEET, Earl D. & BROWN, Carol A.

SWEET, Laurie Lynn b 06 Aug 1974 Exeter, NH d/o SWEET, Earl Day & BROWN, Carol Ann

SWEET, Lisa Ann b 22 Apr 1969 Danville, NH d/o SWEET, Earl D. & BROWN, Carol A.

SWEET, Lorraine Frances b 23 Jul 1941 Brentwood, NH d/o SWEET, Donald & DAY, Hazel; d 23 Jul 1941 Danville, NH

SWEET, Mary Lou b Jeffersonville, VT; md 26 Feb 1965 Danville, NH KIMBALL, Donald Morse; md by Rev Wendall J. Irvine

SWEET, Mary Lou b 1947 Cambridge, VT; md 07 Oct 1966 Danville, NH OUELLETTE, David A.; md by Rev Douglas W. Abbott

SWEET, Shelia Ann b 1943 Derring, NH; md 03 Apr 1965 Danville, NH HICKS, Ronald A.; md by Rev Douglas W. Abbott

SWEETSIR, Hazel Beatrice b 1913 Haverhill, MA d/o SWEETSIR, Herbert A.; md 11 Aug 1934 Danville, NH LEGASSE, Raymond J.; md by Clarence M. Collins (JP)

SWENSEN, Erika Leslie b 15 May 1985 Danville, NH d/o SWENSEN, Kenneth L. & BURGESS, Rebecca S.

SWENSON, Aaron Jon b 14 Mar 1979 Stoneham, NH s/o SWENSON, Kenneth L. & BURGESS, Rebecca S.

SWENSON, Heather Loren b 22 Jun 1982 Danville, NH d/o SWENSON, Kenneth L. & BURGESS, Rebecca S.

SWETT, Mark md VINCENT, Amanda A.

SWIER, Karen md 10 Oct 1990 Danville, NH WILMARTH, Thos Paul; md by Rich J. Rondeau (JP)

SYKES, Joyce Marle md 18 Jan 1975 Danville, NH RONDEAU, Kevin James; md by Rev Henry K. Mook

TAATJES, Emma B. d 13 May 1952 Danville, NH ae 80y

TAATJES, Ermina Theodore b 09 Jul 1925 Danville, NH s/o TAATJES, John Sr. & COX, Mary

TAATJES, Gerard b Holland; md MANGENE, Louise M.

TAATJES, John Jr. b 25 Jun 1927 Danville, NH s/o TAATJES, John Sr. & COX, Mary

TAATJES, John Sr. b 1902 Holland s/o TAATJES, Nicholas; md 21 Sep 1924 Kingston, NH COX, Mary; md by Daniel J. Bakie (JP)

TAATJES, Nicholas E. b Holland s/o TAATJES, Gerard & OPDENBERG, Katherine; d 16 Sep 1934 Danville, NH

TAATJES, Roland b 17 Aug 1922 Danville, NH s/o TAATJES, Gerard & MANGENE, Louise M.

TABELING, Mary Ann md 04 Apr 1987 Danville, NH BOTTINO, James; md by Rich J. Rondeau (JP)

TABOR, Mabel C. b 1893 Bradford, MA d/o TABER, Herbert; md 08 Nov 1912 Groveland, MA COLLINS, Herb Levi; md by Rev Andrew Campbell

TABOR, Sarah J. b 1841 Salem, NH d/o TABOR, Eben & JACK, Sarah; md FITTS, Franklin; d 19 Jul 1891 Danville, NH

TAILLON, Bradley James b 22 Aug 1991 Exeter, NH s/o TAILLON, Mark F. & LOVELY, Carol M.

TALBEE, Frank Edward b 1870 Bristol, RI s/o TALBEE, Edward; md 10 Aug 1927 Danville, NH RUEE, Etta Ann; md by Rev Howard A. Reyman

TALBOT, Ralph Francis b 1922 Boston, MA s/o TALBOT, Ralph Francis; md 01 Dec 1946 Danville, NH SWEENEY, Elaine Lillian; md by Rev W. C. Chappell

TALBOT, Thos A. md 25 Mar 1990 Danville, NH WILSON, Linda A.; md by Rich J. Rondeau (JP)

TAMMANY, Christopher C. md 04 Oct 1986 Danville, NH JOHNSON, Joni L.; md by Rev Everett E. Palmer

TAMMANY, Eliz b Kingston, NH; md 20 Feb 1780 Hawke, NH GRENDEL, Daniel; md by Rev John Page

TAYLOR, Andrew S. b 20 Jun 1954 s/o TAYLOR, Normam Collins & STEMMLER, Adele Madeline

TAYLOR, Christina Lynn md 11 May 1991 Danville NH QUINTO, Scott Michael md by Rich J. Rondeau (JP)

TAYLOR, Daniel Collins b 26 Aug 1952 s/o TAYLOR, Norman Collins & STEMMLER, Adele Madeline

TAYLOR, Dorothy b of Poplin, NH; md 31 Oct 1765 KIMBALL, John; md by Rev John Page

TAYLOR, Harvey W. b s/o TAYLOR, Jack & VITITO, Eliza; d 19 Aug 1982 Danville, NH ae 92y

TAYLOR, John b Poplin, NH; d 14 Feb 1779 Hawke, NH

TAYLOR, Leonidas Ellsworth J b 1915 Yarmouth, MA s/o TAYLOR, Leonidas Taylor Sr.; md 28 Jun 1947 Danville, NH DUSTON, Dorothy May; md by Rev W. C. Chappell

TAYLOR, Norman Collins b 29 Oct 1923 Lowell, MA s/o TAYLOR, Ralph Geo & COLLINS, Mildred Gertrude; md 08 Jul 1950 STEMMLER, Adele Madeline

TAYLOR, Perley B. b c1881 Lisbon, NH s/o TAYLOR, Chester; md 08 Mar 1919 Plaistow, NH CRAGGY, Leola E.; md by Rev Asa A. Morrison

TAYLOR, Ralph Geo b 08 Jul 1894 Lowell, MA s/o TAYLOR, Geo H. & MORRILL, Hattie J.; md 25 May 1920 COLLINS, Mildred Gertrude.; d 25 Apr 1958 Danville, NH; bu Lowell, MA Edson Cem.

TAYLOR, Samuel Eaton b 12 Dec 1958 s/o TAYLOR, Norman Collins & STEMMLER, Adele Madeline

TAYLOR, Stanley M. b 13 May 1921 Lowell, MA

TBAINI, Sais md 05 Apr 1991 Danville, NH DeVEAU, Simone R.; md

TBAINI (Cont.) by Rich J. Rondeau (JP)

TEBBETTS, Harvey Burton Jr. b 16 Jan 1937 Danville, NH s/o TEBBETTS, Harvey Burton Sr. & COLLINS, Muriel Eliz

TEBBETTS, Harvey Burton Sr. b Haverhill, MA; md COLLINS, Muriel Eliz

TEBBETTS, Janice Dimond b 02 Jun 1938 Danville, NH d/o TEBBETTS, Harvey B. & COLLINS, Muriel Eliz; md 02 Jul 1958 Danville, NH HARRIMAN, Herbert Wm(div); md by Rev Karl J. Hislop

TEBBETTS, Joyce Collins b 21 Jul 1935 Danville, NH d/o TEBBETTS, Harvey D. & COLLINS, Muriel Eliz; md 18 Dec 1955 Danville, NH DAVIES, Ronald Bruce; md by Rev W. C. Chappell

TEBO, Craig Edward b 25 Mar 1969 Danville, NH s/o TEBO, David Allen & BEZANSON, Linda Mae

TEBO, Tracy Evelyn b 26 Apr 1973 Haverhill, MA d/o TEBO, David Allen & BEZANSON, Linda M.

TELLIER, Raymond E. md 16 Jul 1988 Danville, NH MILES, Shannon M.; md by Wm A. Ining (JP)

TEMPLE, Becky DeAnne b 13 May 1968 Danville, NH d/o TEMPLE, Clarence B. & EARLY, Mary M.

TESTA, Jos Robert b d/o TESTA, Vincenzo & PALERMO, Carmela; d 21 Jan 1987 Danville, NH d ae 63y

TETREAULT, Deborah L. md 05 Oct 1980 Danville, NH BOWLEY, Donald F.; md by Retenah V. Pietrowski (JP)

TEWKSBURY, Abigail b 14 Apr 1782 Hawke, NH d/o TEWKSBURY, Josiah Sr. & TUXBURY, Anna; md 01 Mar 1810 Kingston, NH EMERSON, Daniel R.; d 24 Jul 1850 Danville, NH ae 68y

TEWKSBURY, Addie b Danville, NH; md SEAVER, Hebert

TEWKSBURY, Alburger F. b 1871 Danville, NH s/o TEWKSBURY, Perley & COLLINS, Mary; d 04 May 1873 Danville, NH ae 2y

TEWKSBURY, Alliston E. b 11 Oct

TEWKSBURY (Cont.) 1865 Danville, NH so TEWKSBURY, Martin VanBuren & LADD, Martha C.; md 11 Nov 1890 Danville, NH GOODWIN, Ada F.; d 06 Mar 1959 Danville, NH; md by Rev J. A. Lowell

TEWKSBURY, Amos b 1824 Hawke, NH s/o TEWKSBURY, Thos & STEVENS, Betsey; d 11 Jul 1847 Danville, NH

TEWKSBURY, Amos b 05 Jun 1814 Hawke, NH s/o TEWKSBURY, Thos & ---- , Naomi; d 1816 Hawke, NH ae 2y

TEWKSBURY, Anna (Nancy) b 10 Jan 1784 Hawke, NH d/o TEWKSBURY, Josiah Sr. & TUXBURY, Anna; md Jun 1808 Kingston, NH DIMOND, Reuben; d 12 Dec 1857 ---- ,

TEWKSBURY, Anna M. b 22 Jul 1868 Danville, NH d/o TEWKSBURY, Josiah & HAYES, Lena M.

TEWKSBURY, Anne b d/o TEWKSBURY, Josiah Jr. & EMERSON, Polly A.; d ae 15y

TEWKSBURY, Bertrand H. b 01 Dec 1872 Danville, NH s/o TEWKSBURY, Josiah & HAYNES, Lena M.

TEWKSBURY, Danie b 03 Jun 1810 Hawke, NH ?/o TEWKSBURY, Moses & ---- , Sally

TEWKSBURY, David b 11 May 1776 Hawke, NH s/o TEWKSBURY, Josiah Sr. & TUXBURY, Anna; md 25 Sep 1800 Hampstead, NH JOHNSON, Ruth; d 08 Jul 1838 Danville, NH ae 62y

TEWKSBURY, Dorothy b 03 Apr 1829 Hawke, NH d/o TEWKSBURY, Enos F. & BARTLETT, Mary; d 19 Apr 1844 Danville, NH

TEWKSBURY, Eliz b Jan 1821 Hawke, NH d/o TEWKSBURY, Enos F. & BARTLETT, Mary; d 28 Jun 1828 Hawke, NH ae 7y

TEWKSBURY, Emily S. b 22 May 1825 Hawke, NH d/o TEWKSBURY, Thos & STEVENS, Betsey; md SPOFFORD, ---- ; d 09 Sep 1896 Danville, NH ae 71y 3m 18d

TEWKSBURY, Enos F. b 26 Feb 1794 Hawke, NH s/o TEWKSBURY, Josiah Sr. & TUXBURY, Anna; md 1st

TEWKSBURY (Cont.) BARTLETT, Mary, 2nd 1848 Danville, NH MESERVE, Melissa; d 03 Mar 1873 Danville, NH

TEWKSBURY, Eugene b 20 Jul 1858 Danville, NH s/o TEWKSBURY, Perley & COLLINS, Mary; d 06 Jul 1872 Danville, NH ae 14y

TEWKSBURY, Evelyn Louise b 25 Jul 1933 Danville, NH d/o TEWKSBURY, Fred H. & NASON, Mildred; md 04 Apr 1953 Danville, NH DEMERS, Harold Gary

TEWKSBURY, Fred Herbert b 1907 Danville, NH s/o TEWKSBURY, Otis & TEWKSBURY, Addie; md 14 Aug 1948 Windham, NH MYLES, Antonina; d 07 Dec 1974 Danville, NH; md by Carolyn B. Cochran (JP); md 1st NASON, Mildred

TEWKSBURY, Hannah b 21 Nov 1804 Hawke, NH d/o TEWKSBURY, Moses & ---- , Sally

TEWKSBURY, Hannah b 23 Apr 1786 Hawke, NH d/o TEWKSBURY, Josiah Sr. & TUXBURY, Anna; md 10 Feb 1803 Kingston, NH PAGE, Abner Dr

TEWKSBURY, Issac b Hampstead, NH; md 07 Jan 1808 Hawke, NH BROWN, Hannah

TEWKSBURY, Josiah b 30 Jun 1807 Hawke, NH s/o TEWKSBURY, Moses & ---- , Sally

TEWKSBURY, Josiah b 26 Apr 1835 s/o TEWKSBURY, Enos & BARTLETT, Mary

TEWKSBURY, Josiah Jr. b 25 Apr 1780 Hawke, NH s/o TEWKSBURY, Josiah Sr. & TUXBURY, Anna; md 08 Nov 1804 Haverhill, MA EMERSON, Polly A.; d 30 Dec 1861 Danville, NH ae 81y

TEWKSBURY, Josiah Sr. b c1750; md 07 Feb 1771 Hawke, NH TUXBURY, Anna; d 17 Jul 1843 Danville, NH ae 93y

TEWKSBURY, Julia A. b 15 Feb 1827 Hawke, NH d/o TEWKSBURY, Enos F. & BARTLETT, Mary; d 02 Jun 1860 Danville, NH ae 33y

TEWKSBURY, Katie H. b c1864; d/o TEWKSBURY, J. & ---- , P. A.; d 26

TEWKSBURY (Cont.) Aug 1865 Danville, NH ae 18m

TEWKSBURY, Lida O.b 26 Mar 1867 Danville, NH d/o TEWKSBURY, Josiah & HAYNES, Lena M.

TEWKSBURY, Louisa B. b 17 Apr 1818 Hawke, NH d/o TEWKSBURY, Enos F. & BARTLETT, Mary; md 02 Mar 1837 Danville, NH MERRILL, Wm W.; d 20 Mar 1842 Danville, NH ae 23y

TEWKSBURY, Marion E. b Danville, NH D/o TEWKSBURY, Alliston E. & GOODWIN, Ada F.; d 18 Dec 1901 ae 2y 7m 4d

TEWKSBURY, Martin VanBuren b 25 Jul 1833 Hawke, NH s/o TEWKSBURY, Enos F. & BARTLETT, Mary; md 1857 Danville, NH LADD, Martha C.; d 01 Mar 1900 Danville, NH

TEWKSBURY, Mary b Hawke, NH; md 19 Dec 1833 Kingston, NH HARRIS, Jerome Dr.

TEWKSBURY. Mary b 18 Feb1816 d/o Josiah Jr. & EMERSON, Polly A.

TEWKSBURY, Mary b 25 Dec 1771 Hawke, NH d/o TEWKSBURY, Josiah Sr. & TUXBURY, Anna

TEWKSBURY, Mary A. b 04 Nov 1869 Danville, NH d/o TEWKSBURY, Martin VanBuren & LADD, Martha C.; md 08 Jan 1891 Newton, NH CRAGGY, Byron; d 25 Jul 1907 Danville, NH; md by Rev James P. Nowland

TEWKSBURY, Mary Bartlett b 1865 d/o TEWKSBURY, Josiah & HAYNES, Philina; d 02 Sep 1865 Danville, NH ae 5m

TEWKSBURY, Moses b 28 Jan 1778 Hawke, NH s/o TEWKSBURY, Josiah Sr. & TUXBURY, Anna; d 02 Dec 1830 Hawke, NH ae 52y

TEWKSBURY, Nancy b c1817 Danville, NH d/o TEWKSBURY, Thos; md DAVIS, ---- ; d 12 Oct 1897 Danville, NH

TEWKSBURY, Perley R. b 1838 Danville, NH s/o TEWKSBURY, Thos & ---- , Abigail

TEWKSBURY, Sally b c1773 Hawke, NH; md 27 Oct 1796 Kingston, NH PHILBRICK, Josiah; d 03 Feb 1835 Hawke, NH ae 62y

TEWKSBURY, Sarah b 10 Aug 1818 d/o TEWKSBURY, Enos & FRENCH, Sarah

TEWKSBURY, Sarah b d/o TEWKSBURY, Josiah & EMERSON, Polly A.; d 02 Mar 1828 ae 18y

TEWKSBURY, Sarah b 19 Jan 1774 Hawke, NH d/o TEWKSBURY, Josiah Sr. & TUXBURY, Anna

TEWKSBURY, Sarah B. b c1836 Danville, NH d/o TEWKSBURY, Enos F. & BARTLETT, Mary; d 27 Sep 1845 Danville, NH

TEWKSBURY, Thos b 03 Sep 1788 Hawke, NH d/o TEWKSBURY, Josiah Sr. & TUXBURY, Anna; md 1st ----, Naomi 2nd SREVENS, Betsy ---- , 3rd ? ----, Abigail; d 25 Dec 1870 Danville, NH

TEWKSBURY, Vernon L. b 29 Nov 1869 Danville, NH s/o TEWKSBURY, Josiah & HAYNES, Lena M.

THAYER, Elihu Rev. md 28 Dec 1780 CALF, Hannah; md by Rev John Page

THERRIEN, Lynn Marie b 16 Oct 1972 Exeter, NH d/o THERRIEN, Wm J. & EDWARDSON, Merle L.

THERRIEN, Wm J. b 1948 Amesbury, MA; md 29 Apr 1967 Danville, NII BURNETT, Ruth E.; md by Roger A. Vachon (P)

THIBEAULT, Edward Tuscon b 21 Dec 1948 Haverhill, MA s/o THIBEAULT, Wilfred Jos Sr. & HARTFORD, Bertha Louise; md 23 Sep 1967 Danville, NH WALDRON, Charlene F.; md by Rev John L. Gallagher

THIBEAULT, Emily Bertha b 06 Dec 1934 Danville, NH d/o THIBEAULT, Wilfred Jos Sr. & HARTFORD, Bertha Louise; md 22 Oct 1954 Danville, NH JEWELL, John Putnam; md by Rev Robert S. Walker

THIBEAULT, Eva Jean b 09 Nov 1936 Danville, NH d/o THIBEAULT, Wilfred Jos Sr. & HARTFORD, Bertha Louise

THIBEAULT, Katherine June b 1943 NH; md 25 Aug 1961 Danville, NH GRANEY, Wm Peter; md by Rev Wendall J. Irvine

THIBEAULT, Martha J. md 29 Jan

THIBEAULT (Cont.) 1972 Danville, NH CLARK, Lawrence C.; md by Rev Henry Sawatzky

THIBEAULT, Mary Louise b 1934 MA d/o THIBEAULT, Wilfred J. & HARTFORD, Bertha Louise; md 31 Mar 1951 Sandown, NH HUCKINS, Edmund James br Rev Wm Wylie, 2nd ----, DUSTON; d 21 Jan 1988

THIBEAULT, Norma Irene b 14 Oct 1938 Danville, NH d/o THIBAULT, Wm Jos Sr. & HARTFORD, Bertha Louise; md 1st 23 Jan 1954 Danville, NH BREEN, Robert Morris by Agnes H. Collins (JP) 2nd 22 Aug 1959 KEZER, James Chamberlinby by Rev Albert Cornwall

THIBEAULT, Priscilla Lorraine b 25 Dec 1940 Danville, NH d/o THIBEAULT, Wilfred Jos Sr. & HARTFORD, Bertha Louise; md 30 Jan 1961 Danville, NH OPOE, Rich Allan; md by Rev Harvey Cossaboom

THIBEAULT, Shallon Lynn b 11 Feb 1979 Manchester, NH d/o THEIBEAULT, Raymond F. & GRAY, Barbara J.

THIBEAULT, Simon-Peter b 12 Aug 1980 Exeter, NH s/o THIBEAULT, Raymond F. & GRAY, Barbara J.

THIBEAULT, Wilfred Jos Sr. b Nottingham, NH s/o THIBEAULT, ISADORE & THERRIAN, Marie md HARTFORD, Bertha Louise; d 13 Mar 1976 Danville, NH

THIBEAULT, Wilfred Jos Jr. b 08 Mar 1947 Danville, NH s/o THEIBEAULT, Wilfred Jos Sr. & HARTFORD, Bertha Louise

THIBODEAU, Sharon Janet b 07 Jul 1953 Danville, NH d/o THIBODEAU, Ernest R. & GUADET, Agnes G.

THIVERGE, Sandra L. md 17 Jun 1988 Danville, NH FARLEY, Chandler L.; md by Rev James M. Delany

THOMPSON, Alexander G. b d/o THOMPSON, Alexander G. & FINLEY, Jessie; d 20 Jul 1979 Danville, NH ae 74y

THOMPSON, Jessica Jean b 17 Nov 1983 Exeter, NH d/o THOMPSON, Edwin & HENDERSON, Josephine

THOMPSON, Kathryn R. md 28 Dec 1985 Danville, NH SIMPSON, Brandan K.; md by Steven M. Kucharaski (P)

THOMPSON, Kathryn Rui b 04 Jul 1962 Danville, NH d/o THOMPSON, Robert S. & KATOKA, Rui (b Japan)

THOMPSON, Melinda A. md 14 Mar 1986 Danville, NH SEAWARD, David P.; md by Kathleen E. Abbott (JP)

THOMPSON, Melissa Aneil b 18 Mar 1978 Exeter, NH d/o THOMPSON, Peter J. & KROM, Florence V.

Thompson, Robert Sheldon md 25 Jun 1977 Danville, NH ERIKSEN, Cheryl Charlene md by Rev Wm Ryans

Thompson, Roger Michael md 11 Jun 1988 Danville, NH MARTIN, Patricia Jean; md by Rev Everett E. Palmer

THORN, Aaron b c1825 s/o THORN, Abraham & PAGE, Polly; d 04 Jul 1829 Danville, NH ae 4y

THORN, Abraham md PAGE, Polly

THORN, Abram md 30 Jun 1830 Hawke, NH COLBY, Sarah

THORN, Ezekiel b 02 Mar 1779 Hawke, NH s/o THORN, James & SANBORN, Abigail

THORN, Henry b 22 Oct 1770 Hawke, NH s/o THORN, John Jr. & CILLEY, Mary

THORN, Joanna b 02 Sep 1793 Hawke, NH d/o THORN, James & SANBORN, Abigail

THORN, John Jr. b s/o THORN, John Sr.; md 05 Dec 1762 Hawke, NH CILLEY, Mary

THORN, Louise b 24 May 1782 Candia, NH d/o THORN, James & SANBORN, Abigail

THORN, Marcy b 07 Nov 1766 Hawke, NH d/o THORN, John Jr. & CILLEY, Mary

THORN, Mary b 29 Nov 1768 Hawke, NH d/o THORN, John Jr. & CILLEY, Mary

THORN, Miriam b 26 Feb 1789 Hawke, NH d/o THORN, James & SANBORN, Abigail

THORN, Nabba b 18 Dec 1785 Hawke, NH d/o THORN, James &

THORN (Cont.) SANBORN, Abigail
THORN, Phineas b 27 Feb 1764
Hawke, NH s/o THORN, John Jr. &
CILLEY, Mary

THORN, Sarah b 1824 Hawke, NH
d/o THORN, Abraham & PAGE, Polly;
d 13 Oct 1825 Hawke, NH ae 18m

THORNTON, Peter S. md 05 Jun
1982 Danville, NH ROGERS, Jo-Ann
E.; md by Rev Loren R. Murray

THORSEN, Dorothy Ruth b 1934
MA d/o THORSEN, Lewis Austin; md
16 Jun 1952 Danville, NH DELOREY,
Ed. Scott; md by Rev Stanley Dahlman

THORSEN, James E. b Malden,
MA s /o THORSEN, Arthur C. &
AUSTIN, Caroline; d 18 Dec 1959
Danville, NH ae 52y

THORSEN, Lewis Austin b E
Boston, MA s/o THORSEN, Arthur C.
& AUSTIN, Caroline; d 30 Jan 1964
Danville, NH ae 65y

THURSTON, Mary b of Poplin,
NH; md 11 Jan 1770 Hawke, NH
SLEEPER David md by Rev John Page

THURSTON, Willie b Newton, NH
s/o THURSTON, Melvin; d 26 Dec 1947
Danvill, NHd ae 68y 6m 29d

THYLANDER, Harold Roger Jr.
md 31 Dec 1991 Danville, NH KNOTT,
Sharon Ann; md by Leo Beaulheu (JP)

TIBBETTS, Harlan Ward b 1912
Haverhill, MA s/o TIBBETTS, Wm D.;
md 24 Aug 1940 Danville, NH CURRI-
ER, Carlene Mildred; md by Rev Will
C. Chappell

TIBBETTS, Harvey md COLLINS,
Muriel Eliz

TIBBETTS, Lillian M. b Fall River,
MA; md DAVIS, Wm A.

Till, Rob't Edward md 17 May 1988
Danville, NH LAMBERTSEN, Kristen
Sue; md by Rich J. Rondeau (JP)

TILLSON, Karen Eliz md 25 May
1991 Danville, NH McLEAN, Colin
Francis Jr.; md by Francis T. Christian
(P)

TILLY, Brian K. md 28 Jul 1990
Danville, NH CASSELL, Deborah A.;
md by Rich J. Rondeau (JP)

TILTON, David md 16 Dec 1777
Hawke, NH QUIMBY, Eunice; md by
Rev John Page

TILTON, Deborah b 29 May 1761
Hawke, NH d/o TILTON, David &
GREEN, Rebecca

TILTON, Eliz md 07 Sep 1779
Hawke, NH SANBORN, Elijah

TILTON, Hannah b c1772 Hawke,
NH d/o TILTON, David & GREEN,
Rebecca; d 13 Jun 1776 Hawke, NH ae
4y

TILTON, Huldah b 18 Mar 1765
Hawke, NH d/o TILTON, David &
GREEN, Rebecca

TILTON, John b 08 May 1770
Danville, NH s/o TILTON, David &
GREEN, Rebecca

TILTON, Josiah b 23 Feb 1768
Hawke, NH s/o TILTON, David &
GREEN, Rebecca; d 07 Jan 1772
Hawke, NH ae 4y

TILTON, Lois - md Oct 1785
Kingston, NH FELLOWS, John

TILTON, Mary b Hawke, NH; md
03 Jun 1772 Hawke, NH ORDWAY,
Jacob; md by Rev John Page

TILTON, Rebecca b 04 Jan 1763
Hawke, NH d/o TILTON, David &
GREEN, Rebecca

TILTON, Sarah P. b c1810; md
PHILBRICK, Josiah; d 20 May 1870
Danville, NH

TOBYNE, Nellie B. b Hampstead,
NH; md 18 Mar 1880 Danville, NH
ABBOTT, Isaac D.

TODD, Loree Pearson b 1916
Whiteville, NC d/o TODD, Leo; md; 01
Jun 1946 Danville, NH REYNOLDS,
Cecil Adelbert; md by W. C. Chappell

TODD, Mason Rhodes md 15 Nov
1976 Danville, NH GOLDTHEAITE,
Suzanne Lynn; md by Rev Robert E.
Aspinwall

TODD, Sarah b Hawke, NH; md 18
Sep 1832 Danville, NH REMICK, Ham

TOTTEN, Jean Margaret b Somerville, MA d/o TOTTEN, James Mathew;
md 30 Jun 1945 Haverhill, MA
CROSBY, Isaiah (3rd); md by Rev
James M. Cuble

TOWLE, Abigail md 05 Sep 1780 S
Hampton, NH BROWN, Jos Jr.

TOWLE, Abigail b 24 Mar 1761
Hawke, NH d/o TOWLE, Caleb &
PAGE, Ruth; maybe b 1765 ?

TOWLE, Abigail b 1809 d/o TOWLE, Caleb & WEST, Esther; d 30 Jul 1827 Danville, NH age 18 yr

TOWLE, Abigail md 17 Oct 1822 Kingston, NH SMITH, Abraham

TOWLE, Almira L. b 12 Feb 1839 Danville, NH d/o TOWLE, Amos Gale & YOUNG, Mary P.; d 22 Apr 1839 Danville, NH

TOWLE, Amos Gale b 28 Dec 1853 Danville, NH s/o TOWLE, Amos C. & ----, Mary; md 04 Jun 1837 Danville, NH YOUNG, Mary P.

TOWLE, Anna b 1728 Hawke, NH d/o TOWLE, Caleb & PRESCOTT, Rebecca; md 12 Mar 1752 LONG, Ebenezer

TOWLE, Anthony b 30 Apr 1703 s/o TOWLE, Caleb & BRACKETT, Zipporah; md 07 Nov 1734 HOBBS, Sarah

TOWLE, Aramintha b 1826 Hawke, NH d/o TOWLE, Nicholas & ----, Mary; md 07 Jun 1846 Danville, NH COLLINS, Levi; d 01 Dec 1890 Danville, NH; bu Danville, NH Center Cem.; d diabetis

TOWLE, Bertha b d/o TOWLE, James Byron & WEBSTER, Ella

TOWLE, Caleb b 26 Dec 1783 Hawke NH s/o TOWLE, Jas & COLBY, Abigail; md 09 Apr 1809 WEST, Esther; d 13 Apr 1859 Danville, NH; bu Danville, NH Old Mtg Hse Cem.

TOWLE, Caleb b 05 Sep 1766 Hawke, NH s/o TOWLE, Jeremy & SARGENT, Mary

TOWLE, Caleb b 14 May 1678 s/o TOWLE, Phillip & AUSTIN, Isabelle; md 19 Apr 1698 BRACKETT, Zipporah

TOWLE, Caleb b 09 May 1701 Hampton, NH s/o TOWLE, Caleb & BRACKETT, Zipporah; md Jan 1729 PRESCOTT, Rebecca; d 03 Feb 1795 Hawke, NH; bu Hawke, NH Old Mtg Hse Cem.; d age 94 yr

TOWLE, Caleb Austin b 24 Nov 1841 s/o TOWLE, James Wm & YORK, Lucinda T.; d 30 Sep 1849 ae 8y

TOWLE, Caleb Jr. b 1737 Hawke, NH s/o TOWLE, Caleb & PRESCOTT, Rebecca; md 13 Dec 1759 Kingston, NH PAGE, Ruth; d 09 Aug 1765 Hawke,

TOWLE (Cont.) NH; bu Hawke, NH Old Mtg Hse Cem.; d ag 27y 7m 7d

TOWLE, Carroll N. b 07 May 1846 s/o TOWLE, Amos G & YOUNG Mary P.

TOWLE, Chas S. b 15 Jul 1849 s/o TOWLE, Amos G. & YOUNG, Mary

TOWLE, Charlotte b 1809 Hawke, NH d/o TOWLE, Caleb & WEST, Esther; d 30 Jul 1827 Hawke, NH; bu: Hawke, NH Old Mtg Hse Cem.; d age 18 yr

TOWLE, Charlotte b 1827 Danville, NH d/o TOWLE, Caleb & WEST, Esther; d 26 Jul 1832 Danville, NH; Old Mtg Hse Cem.; d ae 5y

TOWLE, Chester Phillip b 02 Oct 1915 s/o TOWLE, Edward Austin & MARDEN, Alice Linnie; md DUNN, Esther

TOWLE, Clarence b s/o TOWLE, James Byron & WEBSTER, Ella

TOWLE, Clarinda Y. b 1810 d/o TOWLE, Caleb & WEST, Esther; md PAGE, Oren; d 19 Nov 1890 Danville, NH

TOWLE, Cynthia A. b 31 Aug 1841 Danville, NH d/o TOWLE, Amos Gale & YOUNG, Mary P.; md

TOWLE, Daniel b 12 Oct 1740 s/o TOWLE, Caleb & PRESCOTT, Rebecca

TOWLE, Dorinda b 19 Sep 1802 Hawke, NH d/o TOWLE, Reuben & BROWN, Abigail

TOWLE, Edna Gordon b 25 Jun 1881 Danville, NH d/o TOWLE, Ransom Forrest & GORDON, Elma Lavina; d 08 Jun 1964 Exeter, NH ae 82y

TOWLE, Edward Austin b 28 May 1882 s/o TOWLE, James Wm & BROWN, Sarah Jane; md MARDEN, Alice Linnie; d 17 Aug 1955

TOWLE, Effe E. b 1898 d/o TOWLE, J. Everett; d 21 Apr 1958 Danville, NH ae 60y

TOWLE, Elisha b 1730 s/o TOWLE, Caleb & PRESCOTT, Rebecca; md 27 Dec 1753 Raymond, NH BROWN, Eliz

TOWLE, Eliz d 04 Jan 1785 Hawke, NH

TOWLE, Eliz b 06 Jan 177 Hawke, NH d/o TOWLE, James & COLBY,

TOWLE (CONT) Abigail; md ELKINS, Jeremiah; d 22 Jun 1852 Danville, NH; bu Danville, NH Private Cem

TOWLE, Eliz b 09 Dec 1699 d/o TOWLE, Caleb & BRACKETT, Zipporah; md BROWN, Josiah

TOWLE, Ella F. b 1864 Danville, NH d/o TOWLE, Frederick A. & HUNT, Lucy Alcima; d 13 Nov 1869 Danville, NH age 5 yr

TOWLE, Ellen J. b 20 Jun 1850 Danville, NH d/o TOWLE, Jarius & DIMOND, Naomi Tewksbury md

TOWLE, Elva C. b Danville, NH d/o TOWLE, Frederick A. & HUNT, Lucy Alcima; d 15 Jul 1888 Danville, NH 18y 1m

TOWLE, Elva Carrie b Jun 1870 d/o TOWLE, Ransom & GORDON, Elma L.

TOWLE, Emery C. b 1872 Danville, NH s/o TOWLE, Frederick A. & HUNT, Lucy Alcima; d 27 Sep 1936 Danville, NH

TOWLE, Eri b s/o TOWLE, Nehemiah & ----, Abigail; d 24 Mar 1845 Danville, NH

TOWLE, Esther b 1786 Kingston, NH d/o TOWLE, James & COLBY, Abigail; d 13 Nov 1853

TOWLE, Esther b 07 Aug 1772 Hawke, NH; d/o TOWLE, James & COLBY, Abigail; d 1855 Danville, NH

TOWLE, Francis b 13 Jan 1711 s/o TOWLE, Caleb & BRACKETT, Zipporah; md 04 Jun 1730 SARGENT, Judith

TOWLE, Frank b 27 May 1852 Danville, NH s/o TOWLE, Jarius & DIMOND, Naomi Tewksbury; md 04 Mar 1884 Danville, NH SMITH, Eudora D.; d 11 Jun 1909 ae 57y 14d

TOWLE, Fred A. b 1874 Danville, NH s/o TOWLE, Frederick A. & HUNT, Lucy Alcima

TOWLE, Frederick A. b 1834 Hawke, NH s/o TOWLE, Nicholas & ----, Mary; md 09 Jan 1862 Danville, NH HUNT, Lucy Alcima; d 14 Sep 1874 Danville, NH

TOWLE, Fronie Esther b 1889 d/o TOWLE, Ransom Forest & GORDON,

TOWLE (Cont.) Elma Lavina; d 22 Sep 1924 Danville, NH ae 35y 2m

TOWLE, Geo Wm b 1921 s/o TOWLE, Gerald Chas & BUZZELL, Wilma Lois

TOWLE, Gerald Chas b 22 Oct 1912 s/o TOWLE, Chas W. & WILLEY, Clara Ann; md BUZZELL, Wilma Lois

TOWLE, Hannah b 28 Mar 1714 d/o TOWLE, Caleb & BRACKETT, Zipporah

TOWLE, Henry b s/o TOWLE, James Byron & WEBSTER, Ella

TOWLE, Herbert b 1854 Danville, NH s/o TOWLE, Jarius & DIMOND, Naomi Tewksbury; d 19 Nov 1863 Danville, NH ae 9y

TOWLE, Herbert Jarius b 1888 NH s/o TOWLE, Frank & SMITH, Endora; md 14 Mar 1956 Danville, NH MARCH, Annie Hainsworth; d 03 Nov 1961 Danville, NH; md bu Agnes H. Collins (JP); d ae 73y

TOWLE, James b 1736 s/o TOWLE, Caleb & PRESCOTT, Rebecca; d young

TOWLE, James b 19 Nov 1877; md SANBORN, Ella Josaphine; d 16 Dec 1955

TOWLE, James b 07 Jul 1772 Hawke, NH s/o TOWLE, James & COLBY, Abigail; md 06 Jun 1799 Kingston, NH NASH, Sally

TOWLE, James b 31 Dec 1747 Kingston, NH s/o TOWLE, Caleb & PRESCOTT, Rebecca; md 13 Sep 1768 Hawke, NH COLBY, Abigail; d 31 Dec 1825 Hawke, NH; bu Hawke, NH Old Mtg Hse Cem.

TOWLE, James b 07 Jul 1777 Hawke, NH s/o TOWLE, Jonathan & ----, Hanney

TOWLE, James Byron b 1843 Danville, NH s/o TOWLE, Jarius & DIMOND, Naomi Tewksbury; md 27 Feb 1867 Danville, NH WEBSTER, Ella G.

TOWLE, James Wm b 18 Mar 1906 s/o TOWLE, Edward Austin & MARDEN, Alice Linnie

TOWLE, James Wm Jr. b 20 Jul 1851 s/o TOWLE, James Wm & YORK, Lucinda T.; md 14 Jun 1873 BROWN, Sarah Jane

TOWLE, James Wm Sr. b 10 Oct 1813 Hawke, NH s/o TOWLE, Caleb & WEST, Esther; md 04 Jun 1837 Brentwwod, NH YORK, Lucinda; d 18 Aug 1868 Chester, NH; Lucinda is a Penobscot Indian

TOWLE, Jarius b 1818 s/o TOWLE, Caleb & WEST, Esther md DIMOND, Naomi Tewksbury; d 21 Aug 1879 Danville, NH; bu Danville, NH Old Mtg Hse Cem.; d ae 61y

TOWLE, Jeremiah b 12 Dec 1709 s/o TOWLE, Caleb & BRACKETT, Zipporah; md 1st DEARBORN, Hannah, 2nd TUCK, Sarah

TOWLE, Jeremy b 19 Jun 1745 s/o TOWLE, Caleb & PRESCOTT, Rebecca; md 1st 19 Sep 1765 Hawke, NH SARGENT, Mary, 2nd YOUNG, Hannah

TOWLE, Joyce b c1945 d/o TOWLE, Geo Wm & ---- , Jeanette

TOWLE, Judith b 06 Jul 1783 Hawke, NH d/o TOWLE, Jeremy & SARGENT, Mary; md 08 Jan 1802 Hawke, NH SEVERENCE, Samuel Jr.

TOWLE, Laird Chas b s/o TOWLE, Gerald Chas & BUZZELL, Wilma Lois; md TOWNE, Marlene Ann

TOWLE, Lucinda b 09 Mar 1800 Hawke, NH d/o TOWLE, Reuben & BROWN, Abigail; md 17 Oct 1822 Kingston, NH SMITH, Abraham

TOWLE, Lucy b 12 Mar 1787 Hawke, NH d/o TOWLE, Jeremy & SARGENT, Mary

TOWLE, Ludevicus b 05 Nov 1795 Hawke, NH s/o TOWLE, Reuben & BROWN, Abigail

TOWLE, Mabel E. b 03 Feb 1877 Danville, NH d/o TOWLE, Ransom Forrest & GORDON, Elma Lavina; md 24 Nov 1910 Danville, NH GRIFFIN, Louis M.; d 06 Mar 1961 Danville, NH; md by Rev Allen C. Keith

TOWLE, Marcus M. b 12 Jan 1843 Hawke, NH s/o TOWLE, Amos Gale & YOUNG, Mary P.

TOWLE, Marilla b 1838 Danville, NH s/o TOWLE, Nicholas & ---- , Mary; md 06 Oct 1863 Danville, NH BREWSTER, Jonathan M.

TOWLE, Mary b c1769 Hawke, NH; md 31 Dec 1789 Kingston, NH PAGE, Daniel; d 28 Sep 1851 Danville, NH ae 82y

TOWLE, Mary b 1732 Hawke, NH d/o TOWLE, Caleb & PRESCOTT, Rebecca; md 02 Aug 1760 Hawke, NH QUIMBY, Aaron; 2nd mar of Aaron Quimby

TOWLE, Mary Eleanor b 19 Oct 1850 Danville, NH d/o TOWLE, Amos Gale & YOUNG, Mary P.

TOWLE, Matthias b 13 Aug 1707 s/o TOWLE, Caleb & BRACKETT, Zipporah; d before 16 Sep 1764

TOWLE, Molly b 06 Jan 1769 Hawke, NH d/o TOWLE, Jeremy & SARGENT, Mary

TOWLE, Nancy Ann b d/o TOWLE, Geo Wm & ---- , Jeanette

TOWLE, Nathaniel b 25 May 1716 s/o TOWLE, Caleb & BRACKETT, Zipporah; md TILTON, Lydia; d 09 Apr 1803

TOWLE, Nehemiah b 01 Mar 1781 Hawke, NH s/o TOWLE, James & COLBY, Abigail; md 04 Jan 1808 Kingston, NH BEAN, Abigail S. (Nabb; d 11 Sep 1861 Danville, NH ae 80y

TOWLE, Nicholas b 05 May 1777 Hawke, NH s/o TOWLE, Jeremy & SARGENT, Mary; d 07 Oct 1778 Hawke, NH ae 1y

TOWLE, Nicholas b 10 Aug 1797 Hawke, NH s/o TOWLE, Reuben & BROWN, Abigail; md ----- , Mary; d 23 Feb 1868 Danville, NH ae 70y

TOWLE, Olive R. b 20 Jan 1848 d/o TOWLE, Amos & YOUNG, Mary P.

TOWLE, Orinda b 20 Oct 1804 Hawke, NH d/o TOWLE, Reuben & BROWN, Abigail; md 12 Mar 1823 Danville, NH COLLINS, John; d 07 Apr 1888 Danville, NH bu Danville NH

TOWLE, Phebe b 06 Aug 1779 HAWKE, NH d/o TOWLE, Jeremy & SARGENT, Mary; md 26 Nov 1807 Kingston, NH YOUNG, Jonathan; d 29 May 1877 Danville, NH ae 98y

TOWLE, Phillip b c1616; md 19 Nov 1657 Hampton, NH AUSTIN, Isabelle; d 11 Dec 1696

TOWLE, Phillip b 18 Aug 1698 s/o TOWLE, Caleb & BRACKETT, Zipporah; md DOW, Lydia; d 15 Feb 1785

TOWLE, Porter Burbank b 22 Feb 1852 Danville, NH s/o TOWLE, Amos Gale & YOUNG, Mary P.

TOWLE, Ransom Forest b 18 Sep 1847 Danville, NH s/o TOWLE, Jarius & DIMOND, Naomi Tewksbury; md 27 Oct 1875 Danville, NH GORDON, Elma Lavina; d 05 Mar 1902 Danville, NH

TOWLE, Reuben b 14 Jun 1774 Hawke, NH s/o TOWLE, Jeremy & SARGENT, Mary; md 21 May 1795 Raymond, NH BROWN, Abigail; d 04 Jan 1853 Danville, NH; Spouse b 16 Jun 1773 Raymond

TOWLE, Rhoda b 06 Jan 1770 Hawke, NH d/o TOWLE, James & COLBY, Abigail

TOWLE, Ruth Ann b 04 Dec 1886 Danville, NH d/o TOWLE, Ransom Forrest & GORDON, Elma Lavina; d 31 Aug 1970 Danville, NH

TOWLE, S. Gertrude b 1886 Danville, NH d/o TOWLE, Frank & SMITH, Dora; md 21 Mar 1917 Kingston, NH STEVENSON, Frank A.; d 20 Mar 1950 Danville; md by Rev F. W. Whippen; d ae 64y

TOWLE, Sally b Hawke, NH; md 27 Jul 1797 Kingston, NH GEORGE, Stephen

TOWLE, Sarah b 07 Sep 1771 Hawke, NH d/o TOWLE, Josiah & SARGENT, Mary

TOWLE, Sarah Alice b 09 Nov 1874; md BEEDE, Ernest; d BEF 1939

TOWLE, Sarah G. b 10 May 1885 Danville, NH d/o TOWLE, Frank & SMITH, Eudora

TOWLE, Sarah M. b 08 Nov 1844 d/o TOWLE, Amos G. & YOUNG, Mary P.

TOWLE, Sophronia D. b 11 Mar 1841 Danville, NH d/o TOWLE, Nicholas & PAGE, Mary; md 14 Dec 1858 Danville, NH TUCK, Freeman W.; d 07 Dec 1917 Danville, NH

TOWLE, Wm b Raymond, NH; md 23 Oct 1780 Hawke, NH SANBORN, Eliz

TOWLE, Wm L. b c1837 Danville, NH; md 29 Dec 1863 Danville, NH SARGENT, Sophonia

TOWLE, Zechariah b 13 Aug 1705 s/o TOWLE, Caleb & BRACKETT, Zipporah; md GODFREY, Anne; d 05 Aug 1787

TOWNE, Travis Jeffery b 12 Oct 1989 Exeter, NH s/o TOWNE, Jeffery A. & NILSSON, Pamela S.

TOZIER, Robin E. md 23 Sep 1987 Danville, NH YOUNG, Roger S.; md by Charlton J. Swasey (JP)

TRACEY, Patrick J. md 25 Jul 1987 Danville, NH DOWNEY, Cheryl; md by Rich J. Rondeau (JP)

TRAFTON, Julia M. b 1902 Union, NH d/o TRAFTON, Ashton; md 02 Mar 1929 Nottingham, NH DEMERITT, Clarence G.; md by Rev Ira D Morrison

TRAMMELL, Glen Albert md 07 Sep 1991 Danville, NH SCYZGIAL, Maureen; md by John H. Lampray (JP)

TRAVERS, Rachel M. md 26 Sep 1987 Danville, NH GAUDETTE, Rich R.; md by Renee Houle Carkin (JP)

TRIBLAY, Mildred J. b 1915 Niskayuna, NY d/o TRIBLEY, Albert; md 01 Jan 1935 Danville, NH BROWNSEY, Bruce D.; md by Rev Overt L. Brownsey

TRIJILLO, Frank Curtis b 09 Jul 1968 Danville, NH s/o TRIJILLO, Philip John & BERNABY, Kathleen J.

TRIJILLO, Philip John b 1946 New York, NY; md 16 Sep 1967 Danville, NH BERNABY, Kathleen J.; md by Edward J. Massa (P)

TRKULJA, Danica md 07 Sep 1985 Danville, NH LOPEZ, Paul; md by Philip D. Fichera (JP)

TROMBLEY, Dorothy Mae b 1928 Derry, NH d/o TROMBLEY, Alfred; md 15 Feb 1947 Fremont, NH WELCH, Wm Edgar; md by Rev W. T. Shannon

TROTT, Kenneth Elmer b 1918 Milton, MA s/o TROTT, Geo Sidney; md 07 Jun 1941 Danville, NH COLLINS, Evelyn Alice; md by Rev W. C. Chappell

TRUE, Benj md 18 Jul 1781 Hawke, NH SANBORN, Nabby; md by Rev John Page

TRUE, Betty b 26 Mar 1782 Hawke, NH d/o TRUE, Reuben & OSGOOD, Hannah

TRUE, Hannah b 21 May 1773 Hawke, NH d/o TRUE, Reuben & OSGOOD, Hannah

TRUE, Horance E. b ABT 1843 Chester, NH; md 1865 Danville, NH PHILBRICK, Matilda S.

TRUE, Jane md EATON, Jos

TRUE, John b 10 Dec 1774 Hawke, NH s/o TRUE, Reuben & OSGOOD, Hannah; d 10 Oct 1778 ae 4y

TRUE, John b 29 Jun 1784 Hawke, NH s/o TRUE, Reuben & OSGOOD, Hannah

TRUE, Jonathan b 14 Jul 1769 Hawke, NH s/o TRUE, Reuben & OSGOOD, Hannah; d 13 Aug 1769 Hawke, NH ae 1m

TRUE, Jos b 07 May 1777 Hawke, NH s/o TRUE, Reuben & OSGOOD, Hannah

TRUE, Molly b 04 Aug 1779 Hawke, NH d/o TRUE, Reuben & OSGOOD, Hannah

TRUE, Moses b 12 Mar 1765 Hawke, NH s/o TRUE, Reuben & OSGOOD, Hannah

TRUE, Osgood b 21 Jul 1771 Hawke, NH s/o TRUE, Reuben & OSGOOD, Hannah

TRUE, Rich Pillsbury md 11 Nov 1978 Danville, NH COLES, Gail Anne; md by Rev Diane J. Augspurger

TRUE, Susannah b 16 Mar 1765 Hawke, NH d/o TRUE, Reuben & OSGOOD, Hannah

TRUE, Wm b 01 May 1767 Hawke, NH s/o TRUE, Reuben & OSGOOD, Hannah

TRUSSELL, Thos C. md 22 May 1992 POLK, Barbara Joan

TUCK, Arthur Wilfred b 01 Feb 1872 Danville, NH s/o TUCK, Freeman W. & TOWLE, Sophina; md 28 May 1908 Danville, NH WHITTIER, Grace J.; d 05 Jan 1946 Danville, NH; md by Rev W. C. Chappell; also md CUM-MINGS

TUCK, Flora M. b 23 Oct 1862 Danville, NH d/o TUCK, Freeman W. & TOWLE, Sophina; d 18 Nov 1933

TUCK (Cont.) Danville, NH ae 71y 0m 26d

TUCK, Freeman W. b c1836 Fremont, NH s/o TUCK, Israel S. & TUCK, Rachel; md 14 Dec 1858 Danville, NH TOWLE, Sophina D.; d 02 Jan 1923 Danville, NH

TUCK, Geo d 09 Dec 1959 Danville, NH ae 86y

TUCK, Grace J.(Mrs) b Merrimac, MA d/o WHITTIER, Walter; d 03 Nov 1959 Danville, NH ae 84y

TUCK, John L. b c1834 Fremont, NH; md 1859 Danville, NH GORDON, Sarah E.

TUCK, Paul B. b 10 Feb 1902 Danville, NH s/o TUCK, Willis C. & HUNTINGTON, Mary E.; d 14 Jul 1958 Danville, NH

TUCK, Willis C. b 13 May 1875 Danville, NH s/o TUCK, Freeman W. & TOWLE, Sophina; md 1st 31 Dec 1900 Danville, NH HUNTINGTON, Mary E., 2nd 12 Oct 1909 Danville, NH LADD, Alice E. by Rev W. C. Chappell; d 07 Aug 1920 ae 45y 2m 8d

TUCKER, Abigail b c1800; md EASTMAN, Sewell; d 10 Dec 1880 Danville, NH ae 80y

TUCKER, Amos b c1789; d 07 Sep 1856 Danville, NH ae c67y

TUCKER, Angeline b Sandown, NH; md 21 Jul 1828 Kingston, NH PAGE, Moses

TUCKER, Benj b Poplin, NH; md 06 Apr 1796 Kingston, NH BEAN, Huldah;

TUCKER, Betsey b d/o TUCKER, Amos; d 07 Sep 1861 Danville, NH

TUCKER, Deborah b 16 Jun 1767 Hawke, NH d/o TUCKER, Jos & ----, Susey

TUCKER, Ebenezer Jr. b Hampton Falls, NH s/o TUCKER, Ebenezer Sr. & BLAKE, Deborah; md 22 Dec 1768 Hawke, NH SELLEY, Mary; md by Rev John Page

TUCKER, Ebenezer Sr. b c1708 Salisbury, MA; md BLAKE, Deborah; d 07 May 1776 Hawke, NH ae 68y

TUCKER, Emma b c1846 Kingston, NH; md 28 Feb 1864 Danville, NH HILL, Newell F.

TUCKER, Ernest G. b c1889 Plaistow, NH s/o TUCKER, Geo H.; md 09 Jun 1909 Danville, NH LADD, Alta M.; md by Rev W. C. Chappell

TUCKER, Fifield md 16 Aug 1840 Danville, NH SAWYER, Eliz

TUCKER, Frank Ernest b 1915 MA s/o TUCKER, Everett Ernest; md 01 Aug 1949 Danville, NH SIMPSON, Frances Lucille; md by Agnes H. Collins (JP)

TUCKER, Hannah b 24 Sep 1775 Hawke, NH d/o TUCKER, Jos & ----, Susey

TUCKER, Harry Adelbert b 06 Sep 1867 Danville, NH s/o TUCKER, Mason W. & MARCH, Arvilla A. md 29 Jun 1907 Danville, NH KIMBALL, Fannie M.; d 26 Dec 1945 Danville, NH; 2nd mar; md by Rev W. C. Chappell

TUCKER, Hemrietta b c1849 Plaistow, NH; md 18 Oct 1871 Danville, NH WILLIAMS, Chas W.

TUCKER, Henry b 25 Oct 1769 Hawke, NH s/o TUCKER, Jos & ----, Susey

TUCKER, Henry md 20 Oct 1768 Hawke, NH ROBINSON, Mary; md by Rev John Page

TUCKER, ---- ?/o TUCKER, Fifield & SAWYER, Eliz; d 29 Sep 1847 Danville, NH as infant

TUCKER, Jeremiah b c1850 Kingston, NH; md 19 Jun 1870 Danville, NH GILMAN, Clara M.

TUCKER, Jonathan b 19 Mar 1763 Hawke, NH s/o TUCKER, Jos & ----, Susey

TUCKER, Jonathan b 12 Aug 1773 Hawke, NH s/o TUCKER, Ebenezer Jr. & CILLEY, Mary

TUCKER, Jonathan b 13 Nov 1769 Hawke, NH s/o TUCKER, Ebenezer Jr. & CILLEY, Mary; d 20 Feb 1770 Hawke, NH ae 2m

TUCKER, Jos b Hampton Falls, NH; md ----, Susey; d 28 Sep 1777 Hawke, NH

TUCKER, Jos b 23 Dec 1764 Hawke, NH s/o TUCKER, Jos & ----, Susey

TUCKER, Moses b 15 Feb 1771 Hawke, NH s/o TUCKER, Ebenezer Jr. & CILLEY, Mary

TUCKER, Moses Jr. b Kingston, NH s/o TUCKER, Moses Sr.; md 11 Apr 1830 Hawke, NH MARTIN, Hannah

TUCKER, Nellie Ruth b 1910 Kingston, NH d/o TUCKER, Wm Franklin & SIMES, Nellie; md 31 Mar 1944 Danville, NH SHATTUCK, Elmer Wm; d 13 Aug 1973 Danville, NH; md by W. C. Chappell

TUCKER, Otis b c1838 Kingston, NH; md 01 Jul 1860 Danville, NH CHENEY, Sarah E.

TUCKER, Samuel b 12 Mar 1772 Hawke, NH d/o TUCKER, Jos & ----, Susey

TUCKER, Susey b 27 May 1777 Hawke, NH d/o TUCKER, Jos & ----, Susey

TURCOTTE, Robert Albert md 31 Dec 1989 Danville, NH EGGERT, Linda Dorothy; md by Rich J. Rondeau (JP)

TURNER, Dale Edwin md 30 Oct 1971 Danville, NH SANBORN, Patricia Ann; md by Rev Alton P. Mark

TURNER, Isaac b Kithley England s/o TURNER, Jos & MOSLEY, ----; d 12 Mar 1903 Danville, NH ae 68y 2m 13d

TURNER, Jane b 1947 NH; md 27 Jul 1968 Danville, NH SHATTUCK, Geo L.; md by Rev Alton Mark

TURNER, Peter M. md 02 Aug 1981 Danville, NH ARNOLD, Sharon J.; md by Rev Roberet E Aspenwall

TURNER, Sharon Elaine b 1946 Jefferson, ME; md 22 Jul 1967 Danville, NH MEANEY, Edward F.; md by Rev Wm. B. Whyle

TURPIN, Elsie b Troy, ?; md BUNDY, Theodore R.

TUTTLE, Frank b Derry, NH s/o TUTTLE, Lambert & STEVENS, Harriet; d 27 Feb 1931 Danville, NH ae 71y 11m 7d

TUTTLE, Gertrude O. b c1882 W Epping, NH d/o TUTTLE, Walter; md 04 Oct 1904 Fremont, NH KIMBALL, Elmer A.; md by Rev A. B. Hyde

TUTTLE, Margaret A. md 30 Jun 1992 PAJEK, Allen

TUTTLE, Warren C. b s/o TUTTLE. Thos; d 20 Jan 1932 Danville, NH ae 49y 8m 10d

TUXBURY, Anna b c1754 S Hampton, NH; md 07 Feb 1771 Hawke, NH TEWKSBURY, Joisha; d 13 May 1842 Danville, NH; d age 88 yr

TUXBURY, Anna b c1726; md 1st 18 Mar 1779 Hawke, NH MORRILL, Henry 2nd COLBY, Moses; d 06 Apr 1804 Hawke, NH ae 88y

TUXBURY, Priscilla md 01 Jan 1762 Amesbury, MA BARTLETT, Geo

TWADDELL, Ann b 03 Jan 1963 Danville, NH d/o TWADDELL, Stephen F. & WHITNEY, Doris

TWOMBLY, Emma M. md 21 Sep 1973 Danville, NH COLLINS, Herbert L.; md by Rev Peter W. Lovejoy

TYLER, Amy b d/o TYLER, Geo C. & NEWTON, Lula; md LONGLAND, ---- ; d 24 Dec 1974 Danville, NH ae 83y

UHLMAN, Virginia L. b d/o UHLMAN, Riley & MORRISON, Annie; md WELDY, ---- ; d 02 Jun 1979 Danville, NH; d ae 52y

VACCARELLO, Michael David b 08 Jun 1986 Cambridge, MA s /o VACCARELLO, David J. & BARBUSH, Alice T.

VAILLANCOURT, Romeo John md 15 Jul 1989 Danville, NH SANBORN, Susan Sawyer; md by Rev Everett E. Palmer

VALCOURT, Julianne Patricia md 24 Nov 1990 Danville, NH MODIGLIANI, David S.; md by Richard J. Rondeau (JP)

VALCOURT, Leslie S. md 13 Jun 1987 Danville, NH SCALZO, Jeffery J.; md by Rev Anthony Jarek Glidden

VALLEY, Lori R. md 14 Sep 1985 Danville, NH LARKIN, Erik M.; md by Rev Everett E. Palmer

VALLIER, Barry Rich md 12 Oct 1991 Danville NH COMMENDATORE, Marcia; md by Marjorie Maroux Fails (JP)

VANCE, Anna b Hampstead, NH; md 20 Dec 1800 Hampstead, NH

VANCE (Cont.) PLUMMER, Samuel

VANDFORD, Florence b 1873 Salem, MA d/o VANFORD, Benj; md 1st FOSTER, ---- , 2nd 01 JUL 1938 Danville, NH LADD, Ottero A.; md by Clarence M. Collins (JP)

VanGUILDER, Amanda Sue b 12 Dec 1980 Exeter, NH d/o VaNGUILDER, Bruce D. & CUSTEAU, Claire A.

VanGUILDER, Bruce D. md 14 Dec 1979 Danville, NH CUSTEAU, Claire A.; md by John H. Lamprey (JP)

VanRAVESTYN, Michael Paul md 10 Nov 1991 Danville, NH REARDON, Kellie Lee; md by Rich J Rondeau (JP)

VARNEY, Robert Mark md 23 Sep 1989 Danville, NH RUSSMAN, Joanne Winifred; md by Rev Everett E. Palmer

VEAUDRY, Thomas b 21 Jan 1989 Derry, NH s/o VEAUDRY, Thomas A. Jr. & CYR, Kathleen D.

VEINS, Mark W. md 01 Aug 1987 Danville, NH MARTIN, Dawn Lynn; md by Rev Everett E. Palmer

VENTIRA, Cheryl Ann b 24 Apr 1969 Danville, NH d/o VENTURA, Thomas Paul & LAWTON, Patricia Arleen

VENTURA, Paul Thos b 12 Apr 1968 Danville, NH s/o VENTURA, Thos Paul & LAWTON, Patricia Arleen

VIGNEAULT, Aime b 01 Sep 1882 Danville, NH d/o VIGNEAULT, Urban & GERMAINE, Adeline

VIGNEAULT, Ulric b c1865 Canada; md 26 Dec 1885 Danville, NH DAVIS, Lillie M.

VILLACARO, Carol A. b 1947 Haverhill, MA; md 18 Aug 1846 Danville, NH WEBB, Lyle R. Jr.; md by R. V. Pletrowskie (JP)

VILLACARO, Heide Sue b 28 Dec 1962 Danville, NH d/o VILLARCARDO, James & HALLIER, Eliz

VILLACARO, Sharon L. b 1945 Haverhill, MA; md 07 Oct 1963 Danville, NH KEITH, Douglas; md by Rev John Wood Jr.

VILLETTA Teresa Marie b 1920 Haverhill, MA d/o VILLETTA, Emelio James; md 31 Jul 1947 Danville, NH

VILLETTA (Cont.) REYNOLDS, Kenneth Ladd; md by Rev W. C. Chappell; prev md KING, ----

VINCENT, Amanda A. b c1848 Kingston, NH; md SWETT, Mark; d 22 Jun 1877 Danville, NH; ae 29y

VINCENT, Anna H. b Danville, NH d/o VINCENT, Geo & EASTMAN, Abigail H.; md SILLOWAY, James W.; d 28 Aug 1944 Danville, NH

VINCENT, Frank M. b 28 Feb 1857 Danville, NH s/o VINCENT, Geo & EASTMAN, Abigail H.

VINCENT, Geo b Marblehead, MA; md 05 May 1844 Kingston, NH EASTMAN, Abigail H.; d 18 JUL 1863 Fort Wagner; From Civil War Rcds

VINCENT, Georgette b 13 Oct 1862 Danville, NH d/o VINCENT, Geo & EASTMAN, Abigail H.

VINCENT, Huldah A. b 31 Oct 1854 Danville, NH d/o VINCENT, Geo & EASTMAN, Abigail H.

VINCENT, Ida A. b 07 Mar 1860 Danville, NH d/o VINCENT, Geo & EASTMAN, Abigail H.

VOLGER, Brandon Chas b 26 Mar 1983 Derry, NH s/o VOLGER, Dwight C. & SANDS, Sandra A.

VOLGER, Brittany Lynn b 05 May 1989 Derry, NH d/o VOLGER, Dwight C. & SANDS, Sandra A.

WADLEIGH, Arvilla d 11 Jun 1870 Danville, NH ae 14y

WADLEIGH, John b c1864; d 27 Jun 1870 Danville, NH ae 6y

WADLEIGH, Jonathan b C1817 Kingston, NH; md c1855 Danville, NH WOODMAN, Louisa

WADLEIGH, Mary md QUIMBY, David Col.; d 31 Oct 1814 Hawke, NH ae 82y; bu Hawke, NH Old Mtg Hse Cem.

WADLEIGH, Molly b Kingston, NH; md 12 Jun 1780 Hawke, NH SWEATT, Peter; md by Rev John Page

WADLEIGH, Ruth b of Kingston, NH; md 12 Jul 1764 Hawke, NH JEWELL, Tim.; md by Rev John Page

WADLEIGH, Sarah b c1729 Kingston, NH; md EASTMAN, Edward; d 30 Dec 1782 Hawke bu Danville, NH

WADLEIGH (Cont.) Old Mtg Hse Cem.; d ae 55y also md CLOUGH

WADSWORTH, Irma M. b c1891 Merrimac, MA d/o WADSWORTH, Spencer; md 19 Feb 1915 Danville, NH DAY, J. L. Roland; md by Rev Allen C. Keith

WAGNER, Andrew Jos b 1924 Haverhill, MA s/o WAGNER, Leopold & GERMAINE, Antoinette; md 07 Nov 1959 Danville, NH HERRICK, Margaret Verna; d 01 Apr 1977 Danville, NH ae 52y; md by L. Evelyn Bake (JP)

WAGNER, Anita Dawn b 20 Jul 1964 Danville, NH d/o WAGNER, Andrew Jos & HERRICH, Margaret Verna

WAGNER, Craig Vincent b 29 Mar 1962 Danville, NH s/o WAGNER, Andrew Jos & HERRICK, Margaret Verna

WAGNER, Tim Greg b 25 Jun 1960 Danville, NH s/o WAGNER, Andrew Jos & HERRICK, Margaret Verna

WAHLBERG, Axel A. b Boston, MA s/o WAHLBERG, Nicholas A. & AXELQUIST, Caroline C.; d 22 Aug 1920 ae 61y 11m 3d

WAIN, Donna L. md 22 Apr 1972 Danville, NH MACKIE, Jos Jr.; md by Rev Peter W. Lovejoy

WALDRON, Charlene F. b 1950 Exeter, NH; md 22 Sep 1967 Danville, NH THIBEAULT, Edward T.; md by Rev John L. Gallagher

WALDRON, Darlene L. b 1948 NH; md 26 Sep 1968 Danville, NH SEAVER, Bertram Albert; md by Rev Douglas Abbott

WALES, Mary Mrs. b c1818 Haverhill, MA; md 28 Aug 1862 Danville, NH LADD, John

WALKER, Albert E. s/o WALKER, Henry I. & McMILLIAN, Myrtle L.; d 12 Sep 1981 Danville, NH ae 71y

WALKER, Elizabth b Ireland d/o SCHERELL, Wm; d 28 Oct 1953 Danville, NH ae 62y

WALKER, Ernesta Lucille b 1924 FREMONT, NH d/o WALKER, Allan Barry; md LESSARD, Arthur Eugene; md by Rev W. C. Chappell

WALKER, Kerry Lyn b 21 Dec 1980 Lawrence, MA d/o WALKER, Chester Jr. & LaROCHE, Kathleen

WALKER, Kristen Lee b 21 Dec 1980 Lawrence, MA d/o WALKER, Chester Jr. & LaROCHE, Kathleen

WALKER, Lesley A. md 21 Jan 1973 Danville, NH SILVERMAN, Jerome M.; md by Leona A. Sciaudone (JP)

WALKER, Martha Mitsu b 05 Oct 1951 Danville, NH d/o WALKER, Robert S. & KELLY, Patricia J.

WALKER, Mary b Sceone Scotland d/o WALKER, John & SMITH, Mary; md STEVENS, ---- ; d 04 Sep 1910 Danville, NH ae 77y 10m 27d

WALKER, Robert S. b Seattle, WA; md KELLY, Patricia J.

WALKER, Wendy Colleen b 17 Jul 1950 Danville, NH d/o WALKER, Robert S. & KELLY, Patricia I.

WALL, Austin Ernest b 10 Feb 1902 s/o WALL, Frank A. & METIVER, Mary A.; 4th child in family

WALL, Frank A, b Salem, MA; md METIVER, Mary A. of Canada

WALL, Michael R md 06 May 1983 Danville, NH GOLDTHWAITE, Heather Ann; md by Rev Everett E. Palmer

WALLACE, Clara D. b 17 Jan 1883 Danville, NH d/o WALLACE, Lewis & ALLUETER, Sophronia

WALLACE, Geraldine Estella b 1909 Lakeport, NH d/o WALLACE, Carl & md 10 Jan 1947 Laconia, NH BROWN, Roger Warren; md by Rev Frank J. Colman

WALSH, Erie F. md 12 Feb 1989 Danville, NH SHAW, John S. Jr.; md by Rich J. Rondeau (JP)

WALSH, Karen Marie md 19 Nov 1988 Danville, NH EDWARDS, Douglas Earle; md by Rich J. Rondeau (JP)

WALTERS, Maryann b 1946 Peabody, MA; md 20 Nov 1964 Danville, NH NICHOLSON, Peter Rich

WALUKEVICH, Jos Michael md 29 Dec 1990 Danville, NH SARGENT, Lisa Ann; md by Rich J. Rondeau (JP)

WARD, Andrew Wm b 16 Mar 1959 Danville, NH s/o WARD, Stanley Luke

WARD (Cont.) & EATON, Edith Marilyn; md 11 Mar 1978 Danville, NH GREEN, Melanie Ann; md by Rev Tobert E. Crabtree

WARD, Arthur Luke b 29 May 1962 Danville, NH s/o WARD, Stanley Luke & EATON, Edith Marilyn

WARD, Christopher Allen b 10 Feb 1965 Danville, NH s/o WARD, Stanley Luke & EATON, Edith Marilyn

WARD, Edwin Henry b 1898 Stroughton, MA s/o WARD, John H. R.; md 30 Jun 1940 Danville, NH DUDLEY, Ethel; md by Rev W. C. Chappell

WARD, Gloria Jean b 1949 Beverly, MA; md 01 Jul 1967 Danville, NH KRAMER, John Mark Jr.; md by Leona A. Sciaudone (JP)

WARD, Harriet b d/o WARD, James & ATWELL, Ivy; d 14 Jul 1984 Danville, NH ae 85y

WARD, Jos Hodgkins b 01 Oct 1960 Danville, NH s/o WARD, Stanley Luke & EATON, Edith Marilyn; md 12 Aug 1989 Danville, NH PAGLIARULO, Donna Jean; md by Rev Harold E. Small

WARD, Louise Diane b MA; md 21 Jun 1969 Danville, NH SPENCER, Thos Ralph md by Rev Doug W. Abbott

WARD, Max Elias b 10 Jul 1955 Danville, NH s/o WARD, Stanley Luke & EATON, Edith Marilyn

WARD, Stanley Luke b Norwood, MA; md EATON, Edith Marilyn

WARD, Susan E. md 29 Sep 1973 Danville, NH PIERCE, Arthur E. Jr.; md by Rev Henry K. Mook

WARE, John b 1912 Boston, MA; md 28 Oct 1966 Danville, NH PELON, Sandra J.; md by Leona A. Sciaudone (JP)

WARREN, Herbert C. b s/o WARREN, Chas & MARTON, Clara; d 19 Sep 1981 Danville, NH ae 66y

WASON, Chastina b c1837 Chester, NH; md 1864 Danville, NH PAGE, Oren F.

WATERS, Constance Ann md 24 Jun 1989 Danville, NH METCALFE, Ronald Alton; md by Rev Everett E. Palmer

WATERS, Francis P. Jr. b s/o
WATERS, Francis P. Sr. & PULEO,
Grace; d 21 May 1986 Danville, NH ae
41y

WATERS, Francis Patrick b 21 Feb
1972 Methuen, MA s/o WATERS,
Francis P. & STAROSCIAK, Constan-
ceA

WATERS, Michelle D. md 21 Aug
1982 Danville, NH LAPIERRE, Thos
U. Jr.; md by Everett E. Palmer

WATERS, Raplh Elmond b 1924 s/o
WATERS, Paul C.; md 16 May 1952
Danville, NH HODGES, Phyliss Ann;
md by Agnes H. Collins (JP)

WATERS, Sean Patrick b 08 Jan
1976 Methuen, MA s/o WATERS,
Francis P. Jr. & STAROSCIAK, Constance

WATJEN, Glenn L. md 05 Oct 1986
Danville, NH MOSES, Audrey A.; md
by Rev Philip M. Polhemis

WATJEN, Patricia A. md 17 Sep
1982 Danville, NH COLLINS, Norman
Howard; md by Ralph Carkin (JP)

WATSON, Ellen b 1875 Ireland d/o
WATSON, James; md 23 Nov 1930
Danville, NH LADD, Ottero; md by
Clarence M. Collins (JP)

WATSON, Judith L. b Melrose,
MA; md ABBOTT, Douglas W.

WATSON, Wilmont Ansley b c1868
New Brunswick, Canada; s/o WAT-
SON, Ansley; md 14 Apr 1904 Boxford,
MA COLLINS, Clara Webster; md by
Rev L. W. Snell

WATTERS, Merton S. b 03 May
1923 Danville, NH s/o WATTERS,
Walden W. & SANBORN, Annie

WATTERS, Walden W. b Brandon,
VT md SANBORN, Annie b Danville,
NH

WATTS, Annie M. b 1840 Cape
Breton d/o WATTS, Geo; md COL-
LINS, ---- ; d 07 Feb 1922 Danville, NH

WEARE, Lynn Patricia b 1942
Bridgewater, MA; md 28 Apr 1962
Danville, NH EUDMORE, John B.; md
by Arthur M. Comeau

WEBB, Betsy Lee b 30 Jul 1965
Danville, NH d/o WEBB, Lyle R. Jr. &
VILLACARO, Carol A. md

WEBB, Daniel b Canterbury, NH;
md 16 Jul 1801 Hawke, NH WIL-
LIAMS, Betsey G.

WEBB, Lyle R. Jr. b 1947 Exeter,
NH; md 18 Aug 1964 Danville, NH
VILLACARO, Carol A.; md by R. V.
Pletrowskie (JP)

WEBB, Wayne Dwight md 24 Aug
1991 Danville, NH HAYDEN, Leslie
Jean; md by Rev Robert W, Karman

WEBBER, Florence M. b Hampstead, NH d/o WEBBER, Frank P. &
JONES, Rose L.; d 31 Dec 1896 Danville, NH ae 18y 5m 11d

WEBBER, Leonard E. b c1858
Hampstead, NH; md 1st 03 Jul 1871
WILLIAMS, Bertha A., 2nd 21 Oct
1876 Danville, NH HOWARD, Fannie
M.

WEBBER, Robert b 1913 Methuen,
MA; s/o WEBBER, Henry; md 03 Mar
1935 Danville, NH CODY, Mary Fae;
md by Clarence M. Collins (JP)

WEBER, Bette Ann b c1948 d/o
WEBER, Henry A. & BROWN, Edith
P.; d 31 Dec 1968 Danville, NH

WEBSTER, Ada b d/o WEBSTER,
Stephen & ---- , Diana; d 1855 Danville,
NH

WEBSTER, Albert b 05 May 1825
Hawke, NH s/o WEBSTER, Nathaniel
& LOVERING, Sarah

WEBSTER, Albert b Chicago, IL; d
28 Feb 1945 Danville, NH ae 81y 1m
22d

WEBSTER, Anne b c1738; md
PAGE, John; d 29 Apr 1822 Hawke,
NH; bu Hawke, NH Old Mtg Hse Cem;
d ae 93y

WEBSTER, Benjamin md 28 Apr
1785 Hawke, NH PAGE, Sarah

WEBSTER, Benj b Kingston, NH;
md Sep 1809 Hawke, NH DEARBORN,
Sally

WEBSTER, Dolly b of Kingston,
NH; md 05 Apr 1770 Hawke NH
BADGER, Stephen; md by Rev John
Page

WEBSTER, Dorothy b 1835
Hawke, NH d/o WEBSTER, Elihu T. &
HUNT, Lucy; md HEATH, Wm S. L. d
11 Jul 1921 Danville, NH ae 86y 6m

WEBSTER (Cont.) 13d

WEBSTER, Dorothy b 10 Sep 1735 Kingston, NH d/o WEBSTER, Samuel & BURNHAM, Eliz; md 29 Apr 1761 Hawke, NH COLLINS, Jonathan; d 24 Aug 1805 Hampstead, NH bu Hampstead, NH; md by Rev John Page

WEBSTER, Elihu T. md 1st or 2nd Jul 1834 Hawke, NH HUNT, Lois, 3rd 06 Apr Raymond, NH HUNT, Ruth S.

WEBSTER, Eliz md 12 Dec 1765 Hawke, NH CAMPBELL, Annas Jr.; md by Rev John Page

WEBSTER, Ella b 28 Jun 1848 Danville, NH d/o WEBSTER, Jacob & QUIMBY, Hannah; TOWLE, James Byran; d Exeter, NH

WEBSTER, Eva L. b 27 Mar 1870 Danville, NH d/o WEBSTER, John P. & BROWN, Lavina; d 11 May 1872 Danville, NH ae 2y

WEBSTER, Flora M. b 13 Nov 1859 Kingston, NH d/o WEBSTER, Elihu T. & HUNT, Ruth S.; md 11 Nov 1882 Danville, NH COLLINS, Oren Eugene; d 02 Jul 1900 Danville, NH bu Danville, NH Old Mtg Hse Cem.

WEBSTER, Fred H. b 1877 s/o WEBSTER, John P. & BROWN, Lavina; d 16 May 1879 ae 2y

WEBSTER, Geo E. b Grafton, NH s/o WEBSTER, Geo W. md 22 Jan 1892 Danville, NH ANDERSON, Leonora M.; md by Rev J. A. Lowell; Occupation - Shoemaker

WEBSTER, Geo W. b 15 May 1832 Hawke, NH s/o WEBSTER, Elihu T. & HUNT, Dorothy P.

WEBSTER, Hannah b Kingston, NH; md 24 Dec 1829 Kingston, NH COLLINS, Gilman

WEBSTER, Hannah md 18 Jan 1780 Hawke, NH ELKINS, Jos; md by Rev John Page

WEBSTER, Honare Hook b 07 Dec 1821 Hawke, NH d/o WEBSTER, Nathaniel & LOVERING, Sarah; d 26 May 1840 Danville, NH

WEBSTER, Ina E. b 07 Oct 1877 Danville, NH d/o WEBSTER, Eastman J. & ELKINS, Martha J.

WEBSTER, John P. b c1834 Gilford, NH s/o WEBSTER, Wm W. &

WEBSTER (Cont.) SANBORN, Sally D.; md 26 Nov 1869 Danville, NH BROWN, Lavina F.; d 09 Jan 1915 Danville, NH; d ae 83y 6m 28d

WEBSTER, John W. b 05 Mar 1821 Hawke, NH s/o WEBSTER, Henry & MARTIN, Sally

WEBSTER, Jos b Hampstead, NH; md 22 Feb 1802 Hampstead, NH PAGE, Hannah

WEBSTER, Juliette b 20 Jun 1840 Danville, NH; d/o WEBSTER, Nathaniel & LOVERING, Sarah

WEBSTER, Leon C. b c1889 Danville, NH s/o WEBSTER, Eastman J.; md 19 APT 1916 Danville, NH QUIMBY, Charlotte E.; md by Rev Allen C. Keith

WEBSTER, Martha T. b 03 Jun 1833 Hawke, NH d/o WEBSTER, Nathaniel & LOVERING, Sarah

WEBSTER, Mary P. b 17 Jun 1827 Hawke, NH; d/o WEBSTER, Nathaniel & LOVERING, Sarah

WEBSTER, Nathaniel b c1794; md 02 Feb 1821 Hawke, NH LOVERING, Sarah; d 13 Apr 1871 Danville, NH ae 77y

WEBSTER, Nathaniel Rev. b of Biddeford, ME; md 01 Sep 1779 Hawke, NH BROWN, Judith; md by Rev John Page

WEBSTER, Paulina md 24 Nov 1811 Danville, NH PHILBRICK, John

WEBSTER, Perley L. b 04 Oct 1875 Danville, NH s/o WEBSTER, Eastman J. & ELKINS, Martha J.

WEBSTER, Sarah A. b 12 Feb 1840 Danville, NH d/o WEBSTER, Elihu T. & HUNT, Lucy; md 22 Nov 1861 Danville, NH BROWN, Jos B.; d 15 Mar 1886 Danville, NH ae 46y

WEBSTER, Sarah Ann b 13 Apr 1831 Hawke, NH d/o WEBSTER, Nathaniel & LOVERING, Sarah; md BROWN, Isaac B.; d 24 May 1871 Danville, NH ae 49y

WEBSTER, Stephen md FIFIELD, Diana

WEBSTER, Sylvina b c1852 d/o WEBSTER, Stephen & FIFIELD, Diana; d 20 Jan 1854 Danville, NH ae 3y

WEBSTER, Viola b 1879 Danville, NH d/o WEBSTER, Eastman J. & ELKINS, Martha J.; d 17 Oct 1886 Danville, NH ae 7y

WEED, Carl Monroe b 22 Nov 1973 Haverhill, MA s/o WEED, Donald R. & WILSON, Dorothy L.

WEED, Laura Ann b 07 Feb 1975 Haverhill, MA; d/o WEED, Donald R. & WILSON, Dorothy L.

WEEDEN, Daniel Thos b 10 Dec 1951 Danville, NH s/o WEEDEN, John Haley & POTTS, Florence Irene

WEEDEN, John Haley b 1916 Nova Scotia s/o WEEDEN, Frederick D.Dr; md 10 Nov 1950 Danville, NH POTTS, Florence Irene; md by Rev W. C. Chappell

WEEKS, Joanne md 11 Jan 1975 Danville, NH OAK, Rich Dixon; md by Robert S. Dejadon (JP)

WEIDMAN, Stephanie Lee b d/o WEIDMAN, Robert F. & BREWER, Susan

WEINHOLD, Byron W. md 14 Dec 1985 Danville, NH BOTTAI, Patti A.; md by Rich Rondeau (JP)

WEINS, Ruth Eleanor b 1913 New York, NY d/o WEINS, Jos Peter; md 17 Dec 1946 Danville, NH COONEY, Wm Phillip; md by Rev Leverett B. Davis

WEIZANSKI, Janice Kershaw b 1940 NH; md 18 Oct 1962 Danville, NH HUNT, Malcolm H.; md by Arthur M. Comeau

WELCH, Chas A. b c1886 Amesbury, MA s/o WELCH, David B. & BELL, Cora A.; d 13 JUB 1887 Danville, NH

WELCH, Chas S. b s/o WELCH, Maurice TRACEY, Mary; d 22 Sep 1952 Danville, NH ae 65y

WELCH, Constance Ann b 11 Nov 1950 Danville, NH d/o WELCH, John Benjamin & GOLDSMITH, Dorcas A.

WELCH, Cynthia Louise b 12 Dec 1951 Danville, NH d/o WELCH, John Benjamin & GOLDSMITH, Dorcas A.

WELCH, David B. b c1861 Newton, NH; md 31 Oct 1885 Danville, NH BELL, Cora A.

WELCH, Eliza b Kingston, NH d/o WELCH, Geo W. & KEEZER, Mary S.;

WELCH (Cont.) md YOUNG, ----- ; d 16 Apr 1910 Danville, NH

WELCH, Eliza C. b c 1861 Newton, NH; d 10 Jul 1870 Danville, NH ae 9y

WELCH, Evis S. b Danville, NH; md 23 Apr 1886 Danville, NH LUNNIN, Chas T.

WELCH, Frank b c1860 s/o WELCH, John & HUBBARD, Susan; d 08 Jan 1880 Danville, NH ae 20y

WELCH, Geo N. b c1896 Kingston, NH s/o WELCH, Geo W. & KEEZER. Mary S.; md 18 Mar 1918 E. Hampstead, NH EMERY, Mabel H.; d 24 Sep 1958 Danville, NH; md by Rev J. W. Farrell

WELCH, Geo W. b c1844 Wilmont, NH s/o WELCH, John & HUBBARD, Susan; md 20 Nov 1886 Danville, NH KEEZER, Mary Susan; d 07 Aug 1907 Danville, NH; d ae 63y 3m 15d

WELCH, Helen Sheehan b Newburyport, MA; d 08 May 1967 Danville, NH ae 80y

WELCH, Ida b 1915 Portland, ME d/o WELCH, John J. md 01 Apr 1934 Danville, NH DAVIE, Wm D.; md by Rev Irving J. Enslin

WELCH, Jacon W. b Amesbury, MA; md KELLEY, Rebecca A.

WELCH, Jennie Sarah b 1880 Danville, NH d/o WELCH, Jacob W. & KELLEY, Rebecca A.; md HARTFORD, ---- ; d 19 Jan 1955 Danville, NH

WELCH, John b Thornton, ? s/o WELCH, Thos; d 12 Jul 1901 ae 84y 27d

WELCH, John Benjamin b 1891 Kingston, NH s/o WELCH, Geo W. & KEEZER, Mary; md 1st 15 Dec 1920 Methuen, MA MANCHESTER, Esther by Rev John Ward Moore, 2nd 04 Aug 1944 Danville, NH GOLDSMITH, Dorcas Alice by Rev W. T. Shannon; d 06 Oct 1970 Danville, NH

WELCH, John N. b c1896 Kingston, NH s/o WELCH, Geo W.; md 10 Mar 1918 Danville, NH EMERY, Mabel H.

WELCH, John Russell b 26 Nov 1926 Plaistow, NH d/o WELCH, John Benj & MANCHESTER, Esther; md 12

WELCH (Cont.) Feb 1949 Danville, NH SMITH, Martha Esther; md by Rev W. C. Chappell

WELCH, Katherine Esther b 21 Apr 1951 Danville, NH d/o WELCH, John Russell & SMITH, Martha Esther md

WELCH, Lawrence Michael Jr. b 11 Jul 1988 Derry, NH s/o WELCH, Lawrence Michael Sr. & HOLMES, Kellie A.

WELCH, Linda Susan b 31 Dec 1947 Danville, NH d/o WELCH, John B. & GOLDSMITH, Dorcas Alice

WELCH, Louise Rosamond b 1914 Newburyport, MA d/o WELCH, Chas S.; md 20 Jul 1940 Danville, NH CORMACK, James Kenneth; md by Rev John A. McSweeney

WELCH, Madeline b 1918 Portland, ME d/o WELCH, John J.; md 26 Sep 1940 Danville, NH KINNEAR, Lindsay Roland; md by Clarence M. Collins (JP)

WELCH, Mahalah b 14 Apr 1923 Danville, NH s/o WELCH, John B.& MANCHESTER, Esther; md 02 Apr 1946 Manchester, NH ROCHE, John Michael; md by Rev Ray Burns (P)

WELCH, Martha Jane b 10 Feb 1950 Danville, NH d/o WELCH, John Russell & SMITH, Martha Esther; md 03 Jul 1971 Danville, NH WELCH, Steven Wm; md by Rob S. Dejadon (JP)

WELCH, Miriam Janette b 12 Jun 1931 Danville, NH d/o WELCH, John B. & MANCHESTER, Esther

WELCH, Ruth E. b 24 Oct 1921 Danville, NH d/o WELCH, John B. & MANCHESTER, Esther; d 26 Oct 1921 Danville, NH ae 2d

WELCH, Sarah J. M. b c1855 Hooksett, NH; md 01 May 1876 Danville, NH JOHNSON, John H.

WELCH, Steven Wm md 03 Jul 1971 Danville, NH WELCH, Martha Jane; md by Robert S. Dejadon (JP)

WELCH, Thos Nelson b 20 Oct 1945 Danville, NH s/o WELCH, John Benjamin & GOLDSMITH, Dorcas Alice

WELCH, Thos P. b c1895 Kingston, NH s/o WELCH, Geo W. & KEEZER,

WELCH (Cont.) Mary Susan; md 12 Mar 1919 Milford, NH DUTTON, Mildred L.; md by Rev Chas A. Reese

WELCH, Timothy W. G. b 16 Mar 1957 Danville, NH s/o WELCH, Wm Edgar & TROMBLEY, Dorothy Mae; md 07 Jul 1979 Danville, NH McFARLAND, Tammy May; md by Robert J. Dejdon (JP)

WELCH, Walter Milon b 1888 Kingston, NH s/o WELCH, Geo W.; md 02 May 1918 E. Hampstead, NH BULLOCK, Ethyl; d 14 Aug 1942 Danville, NH; md by Rev J. W. Farrell; d ae 54y 7m 15d

WELCH, Warner E. b Fremont, NH s/o WELCH, Jacob W. & KELLEY, Rebecca A.; d 08 Oct 1898 Danville, NH ae 2y 5m 3d

WELCH, Wm E. b s/o WELCH, Geo N. & EMERY, Mabel H.; d 17 Jul 1990 Danville, NH ae 69y

WELCH, Wm Edgar b 1922 Raymond, NH s/o WELCH, Geo Norris; md 15 Feb 1947 Fremont, NH TROMBLEY, Dorothy Mae; md by Rev W. T. Shannon

WELCH, Wm J. b Kingston, NH; s/o WELCH, Geo W. & KEEZER, Mary J.; d 08 Dec 1963 Danville, NH ae 64y

WELCH. Madeline b 1918 Portland, ME s/o WELCH, John J.; md 26 Sep 1940 Danville, NH KINNEAR, Lindsay Roland

WELLS, Dorothy b of Kingston, NH; md 12 Dec 1769 Hawke, NH BEAN, Samuel; md by Rev John Page

WELLS, Emmogene O. b d/o WELLS, Edwin O. & LITCHFIELD, Lucretia; md KIMBALL, ---- ; d 26 Sep 1916 Danville, NH ae 52y 7m 16d

WELLS, Jacob b Sandown, NH; md 29 Sep 1772 Hawke, NH WILLIAMS, Jemima

WELLS, Sargent b Sandown, NH; md 22 Oct 1765 Danville, NH CLOUGH, Theodate; md by Rev John Page

WERNER, Eric James b 18 Jan 1975 Lawrence, MA s/o WERENER, Roy J. & ROKES, Susan A.

WERNER, Roy J. md 28 Jul 1972 Danville, NH ROKES, Susan A.; md by

WERNER (Cont.) Clara B. Snow (JP)

WERT, Janus A. b s/o WERT, Lawrence & JEWELL, Jeanine; d 11 Mar 1988 Danville, NH; d ae 7y

WEST, Allen R. b 19 Nov 1922 Danville, NH s/o WEST, Chas W. & SMITH, Lucinda

WEST, Bernice Mae b 23 May 1892 Chester, NH d/o WEST, Wm & JEWELL, Jeanine; md 1st 10 Feb 1923 Chester, NH MERRICK, Sidney Corless by Rev Wm Wylie, 2nd 27 Aug 1960 W. Fremont, NH MACE, Carlton Alva; d 01 Feb 1988;

WEST, Carilyn Faye b 13 May 1940 Danville, NH d/o WEST, Chandler B. & JASPER, Dorothy E.

WEST, Carl Stuart b 06 Feb 1973 Derry, NH s/o WEST, Carl S. & DURLING, Esther E.

WEST, Chandler Bruce b 1922 Kingston, NH s/o WEST, Chester Winfred; md 08 Jun 1946 Danville, NH COLLINS, Edna Arlene; md by Rev W. C. Chappell

WEST, Chandler H. b Danville, NH; md JASPER, Dorothy E.

WEST, Chas Will b Sandown, NH; md SMITH, Lucinda

WEST, Cheryl A. b md 12 May 1990 Danville, NH BERGERON, Paul Rich; md by Arthur P. Fortin (JP)

WEST, Chester Stuart md 11 Aug 1979 Danville, NH SANTOS, Nancy B.; md by Rev Peter W. Lovejoy

WEST, Chester Winfred b Sandown, NH s/o WEST, Walter W. & NASON, Ruth Filene; md SMITH, Lucinda d 12 Nov 1953 Danville, NH ae 59y

WEST, Cora b c1887 Fremont, NH d/o WEST, Chas; md 01 Dec 1914 Danville, NH HALL, Allen E.; md by Rev Lyman D. Bragg

WEST, Elmer E. b 1906 Haverhill, MA s/o WEST, Chas W. & SMITH, Lucinda; md 15 May 1931 Danville, NH SHAW, Gertrude A.; md by Rev Geo Lee Fish

WEST, Errol F. b 1944 W Kingston, NH; md 17 Jun 1966 Danville, NH ADAMS, Cheryl Ann md by Rev Hugh

WEST (Cont.) MacLean

WEST, Erroll Francis Jr. b 08 Jul 1967 Danville, NH s/o WEST, Erroll Francis S. & ADAMS, Cheryll Ann

WEST, Esther b c1788 Chester, NH d/o WEST, Wilkes; md 09 Apr 1809 TOWLE, Caleb; d 03 Feb 1855 Danville, NH

WEST, Helen Armeda md 30 Aug 1978 Danville, NH DRAZYK, Jan Tomas; md by June C. Loud (JP)

WEST, Henry b 03 Jun 1809 Hawke, NH s/o WEST, Jonathan & DAVIS, Polly

WEST, Henry Clinton b s/o WEST, Walter & NASON, Nellie; d 26 Jun 1973 Danville, NH ae 72y

WEST, Jonathan b s/o WEST, Stuart & ---- , Helen; d 18 Mar 1991 Danville, NH ae 42y

WEST, Mary A. b c1895 Kingston, NH d/o WEST, Daniel & SEAVER, Dora; md 01 Feb 1913 Danville, NH DAY, Theodore; d 26 Aug 1978 Danville, NH; md by Rev Allen C. Keith; d ae 84y

WEST, Maurice Gilbert b 10 May 1918 Danville, NH s/o WEST, Chas & SMITH, Lucinda; d 09 Jun 1919 Danville, NH ae 1y 29d

WEST, Nathan A. b 1877 Kingston, NH s/o WEST, Walter S. & NASON, Ruth F.; md 23 Nov 1904 Danville, NH GOODWIN, Emma A.; d 15 May 1926 Danville, NH; md by Rev A. B. Hyde

WEST, Nathaniel b 11 Nov 1806 Hawke, NH s/o WEST, Jonathan & DAVIS, Polly

WEST, Nellie Mary b Kingston, NH d/o WEST, Walter S. & NASON, Ruth; md GOLDTHWAITE, ---- ; d 06 Feb 1951 Danville, NH ae 58y

WEST, Norman Ellsworth Sr. b 31 Dec 1932 Danville, NH s/o WEST, Elmer E. & SHAW, Gertrude; md 25 Jan 1980 Danville, NH LaJEUNESSE, Lillian M.; md by Marjorie D. Moisen (JP)

WEST, Rich Willis b 26 Sep 1920 s/o WEST, Willis & SMITH, Lucinda; 7th child in family

WEST, Sarah b Brentwood, NH d/o WEST, Josiah & GLOVER, Hannah;

WEST (Cont.) md SEVERENCE, ----; d 03 May 1918 Danville, NH ae 63y 29d

WEST, Scott Michael b 04 Jan 1975 Exeter, NH; s/o WEST, Errol F. & ADAMS, Cheryll A.

WEST, Susanna b 24 Nov 1798 Hawke, NH d/o WEST, Jonathan & ----, Polly

WEST, Willis b Sandown, NH; md Smith, Lucinda of Kingston, NH

WESTON, Marion Priscilla b 1924 Temple, NH d /o WESTON, Geo Washingington & md 15 Jun 1946 Laconia, NH McPHEARSON, Robert Collins; md by Rev Robert Henry Holn

WHARTON, Henry G. b c1831 of Huntington, PA; md 13 May 1867 Danville, NH BURBANK, Fannie

WHEELER, Rich C. md 29 Mar 1980 Danville, NH St. JOHN, Brenda; md by Robert S. Dejadon (JP)

WHITAKER, Moses b Weare, NH; md 30 Oct 1787 Kingston, NH CAMPBELL, Betsy

WHITCHER, Elmer F. b 1875 Nashua, NH s/o WHITCHER, Fred; md 08 May 1928 Hampstead, NH MALCOM, Mary E.; md by Irving Leighton (JP)

WHITCHER, Mary J. b 1838 Plattsburg, NY; d 17 Nov 1925 Danville, NH

WHITE, Alice A. b c1847 Kingston, NH; md 27 Nov 1864 Danville, NH HEATH, John W.

WHITE, Barbara Jean b 1940 Lawrence, MA; md 09 Jul 1967 Danville, NH AUGUSTA, Jos L. V.; md by Edward R. Lamb (JP)

WHITE, Frances D. b 1903 Haverhill, MA d/o WHITE, Wesley G. & TRAVENS, Gertrude; md 10 Aug 1932 Danville, NH COLBY, Alden D.; d 05 Mar 1953 Danville, NH; md by Rev C. L. Carter

WHITE, Helen Veda b d/o WHITE, Issac & MIDDLEMAS, Marjorie; md PAGE, ---- ; d 11 Mar 1986 Danville, NH ae 83y

WHITE, Jane S. b c1846 Brentwood, NH; md 26 Feb 1865 Danville, NH CRANE, Thos P.

WHITE, Kenneth Paul b 21 Oct 1963 Haverhill, MA s/o WHITE, Chas H. & BOYD, Beatrice R.; d 10 Dec 1963 Danville, NH

WHITE, Lewis H. b s/o WHITE, Frederick & MICHAUD, Kathleen; d 10 Dec 1980 Danville, NH ae 69y

WHITE, Lewis Hestor md 16 Jul 1977 Danville, NH CROCKER, Veronica Louise C.; md by Rev Wm Ryans

WHITE, Patricia Eliz b 1936 Haverhill, MA d/o WHITE, Forrest Edward; md 23 Apr 1955 Danville, NH COLLINS, Paul David Sr.; md by Rev Theodore B. Hadley

WHITE, Veronica md 03 Oct 1982 Danville, NH ROGERS, David R.; md by Marjorie D. Moisan (JP)

WHITEMAN, Geo Gilbert Jr. md 21 Feb 1988 Danville, NH LOFARO, Jill Angela; md by Rich J. Rondeau (JP)

WHITMORE, Alice M. b c1886 Amesbury, MA d/o WHITMORE, Anthony; md 24 Feb 1914 Danville, NH ROY, Camille; md by Rev J. H. Cote

WHITMORE, Emma b 1892 Amesbury, MA d/o WHITMORE, Anthony; md 29 Oct 1912 Newton, NH YORK, Clarence W.; md by Rev Wm P. Richardson

WHITNEY, Chas Stephen Jr. b 1944 Lawrence, MA; md 1st 19 Jun 1962 Danville, NH SCOTT, Caroline, 2nd 28 Sep 1977 Danville, NH BEALKO, Patricia Louise by ; Bernard J. Raynowska (JP)

WHITNEY, James Robert b 22 Jan 1963 Danville, NH s/o WHITNEY, Chas Stephen Jr. & SCOTT, Caroline

WHITNEY, Jos Daniel b 03 Apr 1964 Danville, NH s/o WHITNEY, Chas Stephen Jr. & SCOTT, Caroline

WHITNEY, Lesa Marie b 20 Jun 1965 Danville, NH d/o WHITNEY, Chas Stephen Jr. & SCOTT, Caroline

WHITNEY,Chas Stephen Sr. b s/o WHITNEY, Harold E. & HALE, Gertrude; d 18 Oct 1990 Danville, NHae 68y

WHITTIER, Caroline b 12 Jul 1850 Danville, NH d/o WHITTIER, David A. & ---- , Eunice

WHITTIER, David A. md ---- , Eunice

WHITTIER, Geo W. b 19 Jun 1840 Danville, NH; md 1857 Danville, NH FULLER, Mary J.; Civil War Records

WHITTIER, Grace J.b 1886 Merrimac, MA d/o WHITTIER, Walter S.; md 28 May 1908 Danville, NH TUCK, Arthur W.; md by Rev W. C. Chappell; Widow of CUMMINGS, ----

WHITTIER, Hannah b c1846; d Jun 1855 Danville, NH ae 7y

WHITTIER, Jacob b c1844 Danville, NH s/o WHITTIER, Geo W. & LOCKE, Eunice; md 22 Aug 1869 Danville, NH STEWART-MARTIN, Rosanna

WHITTIER, James md ---- , Sarah

WHITTIER, Mary F. b Derry, NH; md Jul 1885 Danville, NH CHALLIS, Clark D.; d 19 Nov 1908 Danville, NH ae 63y

WHITTIER, Miranda Ann b c1849 d/o WHITTIER, James & ---- , Sarah; d 09 Jun 1851 Danville, NH ae 1y 6m

WHITTIER, Reuben md 01 Sep 1779 Hawke, NH MORRILL, Betty; md by Rev John Page

WHITTIER, Walter Sargent b 18 Jul 1939 E Haverhill, MA s/o WHITTIER, Issac & PATTEN, Abigail; d 18 Jul 1939 Danville, NH

WICKER, Holly Gay b 28 Dec 1966 Danville, NH d/o WICKER, Roger Benjamin & SANBORN, Vivian Lee; md 18 May 1985 Danville, NH BROWN, Ronald A.

WICKER, Roger Benjamin b 1940 Manchester, NH s/o WICKER, Michael & MADDEN, Clara; md 18 Feb 1961 Danville, NH SANBORN, Vivian Lee; d 23 May 1972 Danville, NH; md by Rev John Wood Jr.

WICKER, Valerie Joi b 10 Nov 1961 Danville, NH d/o WICKER, Roger Benjamin & SANBORN, Vivian Lee; md15 Jun 1980 Danville, NH CHOUINARD, Brian R.; md by Rev Wm Ryans

WICKER, Wendy Sue b 06 Dec 1969 Danville, NH d/o WICKER, Roger B. & SANBORN, Vivian L.

WIGGIN, Frank H. b Tuftonboro; md ---- , Mariah H.

WIGGIN, Mary H. b 11 Oct 1887 Danville, NH d/o WIGGIN, Frank H & ----, Mariah H.; 2nd Child in Family

WIGGINS, Walter b Brookline, MA; md STEVENS, Annie B.

WIGGINS, Walter Howard b 09 Nov 1909 Danville, NH s/o WIGGINS, Walter & STEVENS, Annie B.

WIGGINS, ---- b 06 Nov 1908 Danville, NH d/o WIGGINS, Walter & STEVENSON, Anna

WILCOX, Eliz b 1918 MA d/o WILCOX, Andrew; md 30 Dec 1951 Danville, NH LANE, Preston Leroy; md by Rev Robert S. Walker; 1st md to KUMIS, ----

WILKERSON, Merinda Lydia b 1849 Kingston, NH d/o WILKERSON, James W. & GOODRICH, Lydia; md 1st 15 Nov 1891 Danville, NH Kimball, James M. by Rev J. A. Lowell, 2nd MACE, Daniel W.; d 04 Mar 1926 Danville, NH

WILLETT, Cecil b 24 May 1899 Danville, NH s/o WILLETT, Octave & MARTIN, Melvina;

WILLETT, Flora b 28 Apr 1901 Danville, NH d/o WILLETT, Octave & MARTIN, Melvina; 6th child in family

WILLETT, Octave b New Brunswick, Canada; md; MARTIN, Melvina of Canada

WILLIAMS, Anita Michelle md 07 Jan 1989 Danville, NH LARKIN, Dwight David; md by Wm Beane (JP)

WILLIAMS, Benjamin md ----, Jemima; d 15 Aug 1766 Hawke, NH

Williams, Bertha A. b Plaistow, NH; md 03 Jul 1871 Danville, NH WEBBER, Leonard E.

WILLIAMS, Betsey G. b Hawke, NH; md 16 Jul 1801 Hawke, NH WEBB, Daniel

WILLIAMS, Chas W. b c1847 W Newbury, MA; md 18 Oct 1871 Danville, NH TUCKER, Henrietta

WILLIAMS, Hannah b 20 May 1768 Hawke, NH d/o WILLIAMS, Jos & PIKE, Mary

WILLIAMS, Holly J. b md 24 May 1972 Danville, NH COLLINS, Roy W.; md by Rev Cathleen R. Narowitz

WILLIAMS, Humphrey S. b 1901

WILLIAMS (Cont.) Bradford, MA s/o WILLIAMS, Humphrey; md 08 Apr 1932 Danville, NH SHAY, Margaret M.; md by Clarence M. Collins (JP)

WILLIAMS, Jemima b 27 May 1770 Hawke, NH d/o WILLIAMS, Jos & PIKE, Mary

WILLIAMS, John H. F.b 19 Sep 1862 Danville, NH s/o WILLIAMS, Chas & ----, Juliette

WILLIAMS, Jos (Capt) b 13 Sep 1787 Hawke, NH s/o WILLIAMS, Jos & PIKE, Mary; md Apr 1804 Kingston, NH BLAKE, Sally

WILLIAMS, Jos Jr. b s/o WILLIAMS, Jos Sr.; md 06 Sep 1808 Kingston, NH BLAKE, Eliz

WILLIAMS, Judith b 13 Jan 1779 Hawke, NH d/o WILLIAMS, Jos & PIKE, Mary; md 30 Aug 1798 Kingston, NH HOOK, Samuel

Williams, Leah b c1903 d/o WILLIAMS, Samuel & ----, Matilda; md WILLIAMSON, ---- ; d 02 Mar 1970 Danville, NH ae 67y

WILLIAMS, Mary J. b c1833 Plaistow, NH d/o WILLIAMS, Benjamin & ROWELL, Hannah; md JOHNSON, ----; d 30 Apr 1919 Danville, NH ae 86y 11m 6 d

WILLIAMS, Molly b 28 Jul 1766 Hawke, NH d/o WILLIAMS, Jos & PIKE, Mary

WILLIAMS, Rhoda b 22 Feb 1768 Hawke, NH d/o WILLIAMS, Thos & ----, Eliz

WILLIAMS, Sally Mrs. md 20 Feb 1812 Hawke, NH COTTON, Thos Lt.

WILLIAMS, Sally/Sarah b Hawke, NH; md 05 Mar 1795 Kingston, NH BACHELOR, Nathan; d 25 Nov 1799 Hawke, NH ae 27y

WILLIAMS, Sarah b 30 Oct 1772 Hawke, NH d/o SANBORN, Jos Cliford & FRENCH, Eliz

WILLIAMS, Thos md ---- , Eliz

WILLIAMSON, Carol Ann b 1936 Danville, NH d/o WILLIAMSON, Howard K.; md 03 Aug 1958 Danville, NH DAVENPORT, Robert Wm; md by Rev Terry Thompson

WILLIAMSON, Howard King b s/o WILLIAMSON, Thos & McKNIGHT,

WILLIAMSON (Cont.) Minnie; d 29 Jul 1990 Danville, NH ae 90y

WILMARTH, Thos Paul md 10 Oct 1990 Danville, NH SWIER, Karen; md by Rich J. Rondeau (JP)

WILSON, Agnes b 1861 Nova Scotia d/o WILSON, Wm H. & SANDERSON, Eliz md 1st TUTTLE, ----, 2nd 31 Dec 1896 Danville, NH HEATH, Wm F.

Wilson, Daniel Robert b 03 Mar 1975 Exeter, NH s/o WILSON, Robert D. & CORE, Dorothy A.

WILSON, Dorothy Ann md 10 Dec 1988 Danville, NH BILLBROUGH, Thos Floyd; md by L. Paul Blais Jr. (JP)

WILSON, Evelyn Mae b 13 Aug 1932 Plaistow, NH d/o WILSON, Harold Maxwell & SHAW, Evelyn Dorothy; md DUSTON, Ernest Bonnah

WILSON, Geo H. md 14 Jun 1986 Danville, NH JONES, Paula N.; md by Rev Edwatd J. Charest

WILSON, Kelly Ann b 18 Oct 1971 Exeter, NH d/o WILSON, Robert Donald & COTE, Dorothy Ann

WILSON, Linda A. b md 25 Mar 1990 Danville, NH TALBOT, Thos A.; md by Rich J. Rondeau (JP)

WILSON, Robert Donald b MA; md 05 Mar 1969 Danville, NH COTE, Dorothy Ann; md by Rev Geo R. Shook

WINSLOW, Eliz md BUSWELL, Wm; d 21 Mar 1796 Hawke, NH

WINSLOW, John C. b c1881 Danville, NH s/o WINSLOW, Wm W. & SILLOWAY, Eliza; md 01 Sep 1902 Danville, NH LADD, Esther F.; d 24 Aug 1932 Danville, NH; md by Rev A. B. Howard

WINSLOW, Sarah md 11 May 1815 Hawke, NH PAGE, Simon; 3rd mar of Simon PAGE

WINSLOW, Sarah H. b c1867 Kingston, NH d/o WINSLOW, Wm & SILLOWAY, Eliz md 22 Nov 1884 Danville, NH COLLINS, Perley P.; d 16 Dec 1932 Danville, NH;

WINSLOW, Wm W. b 1868 Kingston, NH s/o WINSLOW, Wm; md 01 Sep 1909 Kingston, NH MERRICK, Etta M.; md by Rev W. C. Chappell

WITHAM, Jason Wade b 13 Jul 1977 Exeter, NH s/o WITHAM, Paul H. & JUDKINS, Linda Lee

WITHAM, Scott Wayne b 22 Mar 1975 Exeter, NH s/o WHITHAM, Paul H. & JUDKINS, Linda Lee

WITHERELL, Clem. W. b c1888 Lake, OH s/o WITHERELL, Orin O.; md 28 Aug 1907 Haverhill, MA HOYT, Hazel Marie; md by Rev Arthur G. Lyon

WITHERELL, Clyde Oren b 13 Dec 1903 Danville, NH s/o WITHERELL, Wm A. & JOHNSON, Hattie M.

WITHERELL, Edward A. b c1859 Fremont, NH; md 31 Dec 1885 Danville, NH COLLINS, Cora Mabel; Occupation - Shoe Manufacturer

WITHERELL, Gordon Davis b 01 Apr 1913 s/o WITHERELL, Waldo Currier & DAVIS, Isa May; d; 18 Jun 1948 Danville, NH ae 35y 2m 17d; 1st child in family

WITHERELL, Jacob Wesley b 25 Jul 1897 Danville, NH s/o WITHERELL, Wm A. & JOHNSON, Hattie M.

WITHERELL, Lloyd C. b 10 Apr 1886 Danville, NH s/o WITHERELL, Wm A. & JOHNSON, Hattie M.

WITHERELL, Mattie S. b 1870 Toledo, OH d/o WITHERELL, Orin O. & PHILBRICK, Marinna; md 05 Aug 1896 E Hampstad, NH DARBE, Chas A.; md by Rev R. E. Bartlett; Occ Teacher

WITHERELL, Morton C. b 28 Aug 1891 Danville, NH s/o WITHERELL, Edward A. & COLLINS, Cora Mabel; 1st Child in Family

WITHERELL, Sarah L. b c1842 Chesterfield, NH; md 1859 Danville, NH HUNT, John P.

WITHERELL, Waldo Currier b c1890 Danville, NH /o WITHERELL, Wm A. & JOHNSON, Hattie; md 1st 17 Jan 1912 Danville, NH DAVIS, Isa May by Rev A. C. Keith, 2nd 23 Oct 1937 Danville, NH GAREY, Lillian I. by Rev W. C. Chappell; d 23 May 1973 Danville, NH

WITHERELL, Wm A. b Deerfield, NH; md JOHNSON, Hattie M.

WOITKUM, Ashley Marie b 15 May 1984 Lawrence, MA; d/o WOITKUM, Steven J. & CUBELLI, Corinne

WOLF, Eric P. md 21 Aug 1982 Danville, NH; DAY, Judith L.; md by Rev Everett E. Palmer

WOOD, Abby Clemintine b 17 Mar 1857 Danville, NH d/o WOOD, Albert G. Sr. & HOWARD, Maria; d 30 Nov 1858 Danville, NH

WOOD, Albert G. Jr b 27 Jul 1859 Danville, NH s/o WOOD, Albert G. Sr. & HOWARD, Maria

WOOD, Albert G. Sr. md Howard, Mariah

WOOD, Frank P. b Sandown, NH s/o WOOD, Albert G. & GRIFFIN, Betsey S.; d 21 Jun 1906 Danville, NH ae 60y 4d

WOOD, Gertrude E. b S Chelmsford, MA d/o WOOD, Wm & ---- , Matilda; md SMITH, ---- ; d 26 Oct 1966 Danville, NH

WOOD, James R. b Sandown, NH s/o WOOD, Albert G.; md 09 Sep 1879 Danville, N JOHNSON, Jennie L.; d 27 Mar 1911 Danville, NH

WOOD, Kathleen L. md 19 Feb 1983 Danville, NH LARKIN, Dwight D.; md by Rev Everett E. Palmer

WOOD, Laura d 18 Feb 1902 Danville, NH ae 62y

WOOD, Lydia A. b c1838 Sandown, NH; md 1860 Danville, NH PAGE, John Burton

WOOD, Maria E. b 27 Aug 1854 Danville, NH d/o WOOD, Albert G. Sr. & HOWARD, Maria

WOOD, Orville b c1835 Sandown, NH; md 1857 Danville, NH HUGHES, Mary E.

WOODARD, Kathy A. md 17 Mar 1991 Danville, NH KUZMICKI, Edward M.; md by Rich J. Rondeau (JP)

WOODBURY, Wm H. b 1890 Georgetown, MA s/o WOODBURY, Henry; md 01 Jan 1912 Danville, NH AVERY, Christie A.; md by Rev A. C. Keith

WOODBURY, Chas Elmer b 15 Mar 1913 s/o WOODBURY, Wm H. &

WOODBURY (Cont.) AVERY, Christie A.; 1st child in family

WOODMAN, Hannah b c1750; md BAGLEY, Wm; d 10 May 1830 Danville, NH ae 80y

WOODMAN, John b 19 Jun 1792 Hawke, NH s/o WOODMAN, Moses & PEARSON-EATON, Hannah

WOODMAN, Jon b Kingston, NH; md 27 Aug 1772 Hawke, NH ELKINS, Mary

WOODMAN, Louisa b c 1837 Kingston, NH md c1855 Danville, NH WADLEIGH, Jonathan

WOODMAN, Moses b 07 Oct 1785 Hawke, NH s/o WOODMAN, Moses & PEARSON-EATON, Hannah

WOODMAN, Moses md PEARSON, Hannah; d 1824 Hawke, NH

WOODMAN, Polly md 12 Nov 1795 Hawke, NH SARGENT, Samuel; d 23 Apr 1805 Hawke, NH

WOODMAN, Polly b Hawke, NH; md Feb 1796 Kingston, NH HUNT, Stephen

WOODSUM, Leon E. b 1942 Haverhill, MA; md 26 Apr 1963 Danville, NH CHASE, Beverley A.; md by Edward Lamb (JP)

WOODWARD, Sarah md 24 May 1810 Kingston, NH GEORGE, Gideon; 2nd mar of Gideon GEORGE

WORMWOOD, Etta Amelia b d/o WORMWOOD, David W. & PENDEXTER, Sarah; md BLACKFORD, ---- ; d 20 Apr 1945 Danville, NH ae 78y

WORTH, Anna b 25 Apr 1778 Hawke, NH d/o WORTH, Timothy & GOVE, Susanna

WORTH, Jacob b 15 Mar 1773 Hawke, NH s/o WORTH, Timothy & GOVE, Susanna

WORTH, Jos b 09 Nov 1768 Hawke, NH s/o WORTH, Tim & GOVE, Susanna

WORTH, Lydia md 21 Dec 1769 Hawke, NH GOODWIN, Benj; md by Rev John Page

WORTH, Lydia b 22 Mar 1776 Hawke, NH d/o WORTH, Tim & GOVE, Susanna

WORTH, Molly b 25 Apr 1780 Hawke, NH d/o WORTH, Timothy & GOVE, Susanna

WORTH, Nathaniel b 03 Nov 1767 Hawke, NH s/o WORTH, Timothy & GOVE, Susanna

WORTH, Sarah b 16 Dec 1770 Hawke, NH d/o WORTH, Timothy & GOVE, Susanna

WORTH, Timothy md 04 Sep 1766 Hawke, NH GOVE, Susanna

WORTHEN, Josie b Sandown, NH d/o WORTHEN, Walter; md 15 Mar 1890 Danville, NH SMITH, Ernest B.; md by Rev C. H. Smith

WORTHEN, Omer A. b c1861; d 20 Sep 1865 Danville, NHd ae 4y

WORTHEN, Sarah A. b c1831 Hawke, NH d/o WORTHEN, Walter & PAGE, Hannah; d 1832 Hawke, NH ae 1y

WORTHEN, Walter Jr. b 31 Mar 1833 Hawke, NH s/o WORTHEN, Walter Sr. & PAGE, Hannah

WORTHEN, Walter Sr. b c1807; md 30 Apr 1829 Kingston, NH PAGE, Hannah; d 1833 Hawke, NH ae 26y

WORTHEN, ---- b 20 Jan 1856 Danville, NH s/o WORTHEN, Walter & ---- , Mary

WRIGHT, Chris James b 11 Jun 1991 Manchester, NH s/o WRIGHT, Chas N. & RUBINS, Rachel A.

WRIGHT, ---- b Salem. NH d/o WRIGHT, Assa & CHANDLER, Mary; md EASTMAN, Nelson

WRIGLEY, Rich J. md 23 Aug 1973 Danville, NH MULDOWNEY, Nancy J.; md by Rev Kathleen R. Narowitz

YEATON, Everett H. b New Castle, NH s/o YEATON, Sylvester; md 03 Jul 1903 Portsmouth, NH HASSETT, Grace E.; md by Rev Geo. E. Lighton

YORK, Clarence W. b 1892 Haverhill, MA s/o YORK, Joseph W.; md 29 Oct 1912 Newton, NH WHITMORE, Emma; md by Rev Wm P. Richardson

YORK, Eva M. b c1889 Lowell, MA d/o YORK, Otis W.; md 26 Aug 1914 Danville, NH HASKELL, Benj; md by Rev Dorr A. Hudson

YORK, Herbert b Merrimac, MA s/o YORK, John & CHAFF, Ada; d 20 Dec 1921 Danville, NH ae 17y 8m 14d

YORK, Lucinda T. b 10 Jan 1813 Newberry, MA d/o YORK, Ezekiel & FOLSOM, Mary; md 04 Jun 1837 Brentwood, NH TOWLE, James Wm; d 24 Jan 1894 Chester, NH; Lucinda is a Penobscot Indian

YORK, Wm J. b c1894 Haverhill, MA s/o YORK, Joseph W.; md 28 Jul 1917 Kingston, NH MAREY, Angie M.; md by Rev H. McCarthy

YOUNG, Ann md QUIMBY, Sam

YOUNG, Daniel md 30 Sep 1839 Raymond, NH PAGE, Mary

YOUNG, Daniel b 1817; d 12 Feb 1890 Danville, NH

YOUNG, Dorothy Agnetta b 17 Jul 1926 Danville, NH d/o YOUNG, John Angus & MIDDLEMAN, Lena; md 05 Oct 1946 Danville, NH MELKONIAN, Aram Richard; md by Rev W. C. Chappell

YOUNG, Edythe May b 1933 Haverhill, MA d/o YOUNG, Raymond H.; md 01 Feb 1953 Danville, NH SMITH, Lloyd Ernest

YOUNG, Eliz b 16 Sep 1936 Danville, NH d/o YOUNG, Theron G. Sr. & HAMILTON, Gertrude; md; 09 Oct 1954 Danville, NH BALKUS, Robert Arthur; md by Rev W. C. ChappeLL

YOUNG, Ezra b 28 Sep 1803 Hawke, NH s/o YOUNG, Aaron & PAGE, Eleanor

YOUNG, Gertrude Madelene b 1921 Hamilton, MA d/o YOUNG, John Angler; md 13 Jun 1941 Danville, NH BROWN, Clifton Earl; md by Rev W. C. Chappell

YOUNG, Hattie E. b 1882 Thomaston, ME d/o YOUNG, Enoch; md 04 Oct 1925 Kingston, NH DACEY, Patrick H.; md by Daniel J. Bakie (JP); 1st md PARKER, ----

YOUNG, Irene b Dracut, MA d/o YOUNG, John & MIDDLEMAN, Lena; d 06 Nov 1963 Danville, NH ae 45y

YOUNG, Joanna b Kingston, NH; md BARTLETT, Isaac

YOUNG, John Angus b Lynn, MA s/o YOUNG, Lindley & DURIAN,

YOUNG (Cont.) Sarah; md MIDDLEMAN, Lena M.; d 05 Aug 1943 Danville, NH ae 75y 6m

YOUNG, Jon b c1783; md 26 Nov 1807 Kingston, NH TOWLE, Phebe; d 18 Jul 1850 Danville, NH ae 67y

YOUNG, Lavinia b Aug 1811 Hawke, NH d/o YOUNG, Jonathan & TOWLE, Phebe

YOUNG, Lester Allen b 05 Nov 1948 Danville, NH s/o YOUNG, Oliver Alfred & SARGENT, Grace Mabel

YOUNG, Mary P. md 04 Jun 1837 Danville, NH TOWLE, Amos G.

YOUNG, Robert Scott b 25 Aug 1988 Derry, NH s/o YOUNG, David S. & WOOLARD, Deborah

YOUNG, Roger S. md 23 Sep 1987 Danville, NH TOZIER, Robin E.; md by Charlton J. Swasey (JP)

YOUNG, Ruth b Hawke, NH; md 29 Dec 1768 Hawke, NH CLIFFORD, Isaac; md by Rev John Page

YOUNG, Ruth Sarah b 1915 MA d/o YOUNG, John Angus & MIDDLEMAN, Lena M.; md 08 Oct 1950 Danville, NH HERSEY, Clifford Leroy; d 13 Jun 1980; md by Rev W. C. Chsppell; d ae 65y

YOUNG, Samuel David b 26 Apr 1990 Exeter, NH s/o YOUNG, David S. & WOOLARD, Deborah A.

YOUNG, Shepard b E. Candia, NH; md WELCH, Eliza

YOUNG, Theron G. Sr. b 21 Feb 1910 Danville, NH s/o YOUNG, Shepard & WELCH, Eliza; md HAMILTON, Gertrude E.

YOUNG, Theron G. Jr. b 30 Apr 1938 Danville, NH s/o YOUNG, Theron G. Sr. & HAMILTON, Gertrude E.

YOUNG, Sean Roger b 13 Sep 1988 Exeter, NH s/o YOUNG, Roger S. & TOZIER, Robin E.

ZACK, Robin Ellen b 16 Jun 1978 Haverhill, MA d/o ZACK, Barry A. & KEPPLER, Linda S.

ZALACE, Linda b Danville, NH; md 31 Oct 1970 Danville, NH DEMAINE, Douglas James

ZIMMERMAN, Marilyn M. b 1943 Pottsville, PA; md 15 Oct 1966 Danville, NH STURGIS, Chas E. Jr. md by

ZIMMERMAN (Cont.) Rev Theodore
B. Hadley

ZUJEWSKI, Alice Adele b 1919 MA
d/o ZUJEWSKI, Walter; md 22 Sep 1950
Danville, NH COURCHAINE, Albert
Charles; md by Rev W. C. CHAPPELL;
prev md PEACH, ----

ZWICHER, Elliot b Framingham,
MA s/o ZWICHER, George & YOUNG,
Helen; d 18 Dec 1964 Danville, NH